NO PLACE OF GRACE

# NO PLACE OF GRACE

Antimodernism
and the
Transformation of
American Culture
1880 – 1920

## T. J. Jackson Lears

The University of Chicago Press

Chicago & London

The University of Chicago Press, Chicago 60637
The University of Chicago Press, Ltd., London
© 1981 by T. J. Jackson Lears
All rights reserved. Originally published 1983
University of Chicago Press Edition 1994

Printed in the United States of America
01 00 99 98 97 96 95 94      6 5 4 3 2 1

ISBN 0-226-46970-0 (pbk.)

Library of Congress Cataloging-in-Publication Data

Lears, T. J. Jackson, 1947–
    No place of grace : antimodernism and the transformation of
American culture, 1880–1920 / T. J. Jackson Lears. — University of
Chicago Press ed.
        p.   cm.
    Previously published: New York : Pantheon Books, c1981.
    Includes bibliographical references and index.
        1. United States—Civilization—1865–1918.   2. United States—
Intellectual life—1865–1918.   I. Title.
E169.1.L48  1994
973.8—DC20                                            93-39767
                                                         CIP

*For Karen Parker Lears*
*surrealist, seer, co-conspirator*

Endowed with means that had been reserved for Divine Providence in former times, they changed the pattern of the rains, accelerated the cycle of harvest, and moved the river from where it had always been and put it with its white stones and icy currents on the other side of the town, behind the cemetery. ... For the foreigners who arrived without love they converted the street of the loving matrons from France into a more extensive village than it had been, and on one glorious Wednesday they brought in a trainload of strange whores, Babylonish women skilled in age-old methods and in possession of all manner of unguents and devices to stimulate the unaroused, to give courage to the timid, to satiate the voracious, to exalt the modest man, to teach a lesson to repeaters, and to correct solitary people. . . .

"Look at the mess we've got ourselves into," Colonel Aureliano Buendía said at that time, "just because we invited a gringo to eat some bananas."

GABRIEL GARCÍA MÁRQUEZ
*One Hundred Years of Solitude* (1967)

For of the last stage of this cultural development, it might well be truly said: "Specialists without spirit, sensualists without heart; this nullity imagines that it has attained a level of civilization never before achieved."

MAX WEBER
*The Protestant Ethic and the Spirit of Capitalism* (1904)

# Contents

*Contents*

# Preface to the
# Paperback Edition

*No Place of Grace* has provoked a fair amount of controversy, nearly all centering on the contemporary implications of my argument. Among other things, I implied that the effects of possessive individualism have been as disintegrative in the twentieth century as they were in the nineteenth—though the newer individualism has been expressed in an upbeat rhetoric of personal liberation. I also suggested that an antimodern outlook might help us to define liberation in larger than individual terms by preserving structures of meaning outside the self. But my primary purpose was that of most historians: I wanted to reconstruct and understand the experience of people under particular historical circumstances—in this case, the experience of educated Americans grappling with the spiritual and psychological turmoil around the turn of the century. It was not until long after I had begun this historical reconstruction that the theoretical and contemporary implications of the project began to assert themselves.

I do not mean to pretend that I was drawn to my subject out of mere idle curiosity. The ferment of the late Victorian period fascinated me in part because so many of its dilemmas seemed closely to resemble those of our own time. I was particularly intrigued by the undercurrents of doubt and even despair that seemed to pervade this "age of confidence." Textbooks told of an optimistic, energetic society about to reach the full vigor of industrial maturity; to me that tale failed to account for the myriads of thoughtful Americans who, by the 1880s, had begun to question the very basis of industrial capitalist society: not merely the unjust distribution of wealth and power but the modern ethic of instrumental rationality that desanctified the outer world of nature and the inner world of the self, reducing both to manipulable objects. Antimodern dissenters recoiled from this ethic and groped for alternatives in medieval, Oriental, and other "primitive" cultures. I sensed that this antimodern dissent deserved some serious attention; historians had either ignored it, dismissed it as a late-blooming flower of "the Romantic movement," or caricatured it as a cranks' crusade. The more I read the more I realized that antimodernism ran deeper than dilettantism, that it was not merely a recurrence of a timeless romantic theme (though it drew on long-standing literary conventions), and that it was intimately bound up with specific social and cultural transformations in turn-of-the-century America.

So I went to the sources, and (taking the advice of a wise mentor) tried to let the sources speak. Consulting magazines, books, and private letters, I heard loud lamentations among the people who called themselves "the leadership class"—complaints that elites were rotting from within at the precise moment they were threatened from without by working-class unrest. The problem was far more elusive and diffuse than the familiar conflict between capital and labor; it involved a kind of cultural asphyxiation among the educated and affluent, a sense that bourgeois existence had become stifling and "unreal."

Amid this atmosphere of upper-class anxiety I discovered longings for a regeneration at once physical, moral, and spiritual. Some of those longings led backward, imaginatively invoking the intense experiences of the medieval craftsman, warrior, or saint. But I soon discovered that these apparently backward-looking impulses overlapped with more up-to-date agenda for revitalization: the cult of the strenuous life preached by Theodore Roosevelt, the emergent popular therapies which promised self-regeneration through self-manipulation. Antimodern sentiment was unstable, ambivalent. Much of it preserved an eloquent edge of protest, but much of it also helped to revitalize elite cultural domination at a crucial historical juncture.

While I was discovering the ambivalence of antimodernism, I was also reading social and demographic history which demonstrated what I had long suspected: that old-stock Northeastern elites had kept an extraordinarily tenacious hold on wealth and power since the Civil War. Contrary to conventional historical wisdom, the period 1880–1920 was not marked by democratization and elite decline, but rather by the reinforcement of elite power in new corporate and bureaucratic forms. What I was exploring was the cultural side of this story. The desperate desire to flee Victorian decorum and experience "real life" in all its intensity was potentially subversive; but it arose in a culture where loyalties beyond the self were becoming diffuse and problematic. A cult of experience that was merely self-referential provided little basis for forming alternative values; instead it became assimilated—largely if not entirely—to a new idiom of domination. The new idiom was therapeutic rather than religious; it promised self-fulfillment through intense experience rather than salvation through self-denial; it expressed a new version of possessive individualism for a new corporate society. And by helping to legitimate the power of emergent managerial elites, the new idiom helped ensure that wealth, power, and expertise would remain in the hands of a few.

As I confronted more directly these issues of authority and legitimacy, I found myself more attracted to Marxian cultural theory—particularly to Antonio Gramsci's concept of cultural hegemony. Gramsci stressed the importance of shared values in maintaining class domination; this seemed a welcome alternative not only to vulgar Marxism but also to functionalist sociology, which neglected class conflict and assumed equilibrium to be the normal state of affairs in "the social system." But Gramsci's concept could easily degenerate into a mechanistic approach: one could too easily imagine a ruling-class cultural committee conspiring to impose dominant values on hapless workers; and one could hardly imagine at all how a hegemonic culture changed in symbiosis with changing historical circumstance. On the matter of change, Raymond Williams helped some, but my own sense was that cultural transformations were even messier and more complicated than his pioneering work suggested. Ultimately, the work of Freud, Erik Erikson, and the psychoanalytic sociologist Norbert Elias proved most helpful in illuminating the unconscious determinants of changes in cultural hegemony. They helped to explain how people like antimodern dissenters could half-consciously help to create a sleeker modern culture they neither understood nor desired.

I worked from history to theory, and I tried to use theory to inform but not imprison my understanding of historical experience. An antitheoretical bias is particularly strong in Anglo-American historical circles: in part it represents a healthy suspicion of fashionable (usually French) slogans and catchwords masquerading as ideas. But the hostility to theory can also be rooted in a narrow and unimaginative cast of mind: Alfred North Whitehead called it "dustbowl empiricism." To the dustbowl empiricist, words like "hegemony" or "superego" (or even "culture"!) can be dismissed as "jargon" without the effort to think what they actually mean. And any attempt to extract larger significance from historical evidence, to construct an explanatory scaffolding however tentative or provisional, can be scoffed at as "theorizing in a void." My own view is that without an occasional dose of speculative boldness, historians are doomed to the deadly antiquarianism for which they have rightly been scorned, since George Eliot gave us the archetypal pedant-historian Casaubon in *Middlemarch.*

In the end, though, it was not the cultural theory but the cultural criticism in *No Place of Grace* that provoked the most vociferous critical responses. Clearly I touched a lot of nerves, but not in predictable ways. Reviewers seemed annoyed by their inability to categorize my point of view: here was an author who presented himself as a Marxian critic of capitalist culture, whose heroes included Henry Adams and T. S. Eliot, and who actually had a good word or two for religion.

So perhaps a brief clarification is in order. I am a product and beneficiary of the liberal tradition. I think there is much worth admiring and preserving in it, but I also think it has served to legitimate irresponsible accumulations of wealth and a corrosive doctrine of possessive individualism. I have been attracted to the Marxian critique of liberal, capitalist culture for both moral and intellectual reasons; I am less attracted to the various utopian alternatives that have been proposed in the name of Marxism or socialism, primarily because of their suppression of civil liberties, their relentless secularism, and their tendency to confuse material and moral progress. In short, while I am attracted to democratic socialism as an ideal, I think that would-be democrats (or socialists) could stand a whiff of antimodernism—the antimodernism that resisted incorporation in the dominant culture by preserving some sense of commitment outside the self and some alternative to possessive individualism.

I never intended *No Place of Grace* to be a prescriptive book, still less to have any sort of political "message." I hope that this book embodies a world view resistant to simplistic political formulas of any sort. I was attracted to antimodern thinking in part because, at its most profound, it represented a chastened skepticism about humankind's power to reshape the world in its own image, an antidote to the hubris that powers our world-destroying march of progress.

This edition has only a few insignificant changes in the text. Eileen Boris pointed out several minor factual errors in the chapter on Arts and Crafts ideology; I have corrected them. Finally, I want to take this opportunity to thank some people I left out of the original acknowledgments. Jim and Gwen Somers presided over the setting where I began writing this book, in the hills of western Connecticut. Their extraordinary generosity, wit, and warmth, their keen sense of life's absurdities, helped make that year of germination óne of the best years of my life. And the following people provided thoughtful comments and advice during the writing (Freud only knows why I failed to mention them the first time): at Chapel Hill, John Kasson; at Yale, William Hamilton, Warren Goldstein, and Steven Mintz, whose forthcoming study of Victorian families will cast unprecedented light on that vexatious subject.

*Washington, D.C.*
*March 1983*

# Preface

Toward the end of the nineteenth century, many beneficiaries of modern culture began to feel they were its secret victims. Among the educated and affluent on both sides of the Atlantic, antimodern sentiments spread. This book explores the origins and effects of American antimodernism, particularly its dominant form—the recoil from an "overcivilized" modern existence to more intense forms of physical or spiritual experience supposedly embodied in medieval or Oriental cultures. In America (as in Europe), antimodern sentiments affected more than a handful of intellectuals; they pervaded the middle and upper classes. Aesthetes and reformers sought to recover the hard but satisfying life of the medieval craftsman; militarists urged the rekindling of archaic martial vigor; religious doubters yearned for the fierce convictions of the peasant and the ecstasies of the mystic. I am not concerned with how accurately these antimodernists perceived medieval or Oriental culture; I am concerned with what their perceptions revealed about tensions and transformations in American culture.

This study argues that the antimodern impulse was both more socially and more intellectually important than historians have supposed. Antimodernism was not simply escapism; it was ambivalent, often coexisting with enthusiasm for material progress. And it was part of a much broader quest for intense experience which ranged from militarism and "Progressive" social reform to popular occultism and the early fascination with depth psychology. Far from being the nostalgic flutterings of a "dying elite," as historians have claimed, antimodernism was a complex blend of accommodation and protest which tells us a great deal about the beginnings of present-day values and attitudes.

Rooted in reaction against secularizing tendencies, antimodernism helped ease accommodation to new and secular cultural modes. This was an ironic, unintended consequence of the antimodernist efforts to salvage meaning and purpose amid the crumbling Protestant culture of the late nineteenth century. Embracing premodern symbols as alternatives to the vagueness of liberal Protestantism or the sterility of nineteenth-century positivism, antimodern seekers nevertheless adapted those symbols for modern ends. Craftsmanship became less a path to satisfying communal work than a therapy for tired businessmen. The martial ideal ennobled not a quest for the Grail but a quest for foreign markets. Even Catholic mysticism, art, and ritual were adjusted to secular purposes. They became instruments for promoting intense experience, rather than paths to salvation. By exalting "authentic" experience as an end in itself, antimodern impulses reinforced the shift from a Protestant ethos of salvation through self-denial to a therapeutic ideal of self-fulfillment in *this* world through exuberant health and intense experience. The older morality embodied the "producer culture" of an industrializing, entrepreneurial society; the newer nonmorality embodied the "consumer culture" of a bureaucratic corporate state. Antimodernists were far more than escapists: their quests for authenticity eased their own and others' adjustments to a streamlined culture of consumption.

But the accommodation was never complete. When antimodernists preserved higher loyalties outside the self, they sustained a note of protest against a complacent faith in progress and a narrow positivist conception of reality. Antimodernism energized the philosophical revolt against positivism and the artistic avant-garde's recovery of primal irrationality; it led many to see that reality was more riddled with pain and conflict than the nineteenth century had imagined. The more profound antimodernists, such as Henry Adams, preserved a tragic sense of life amid a national chorus of self-congratulation.

It is not very helpful simply to describe antimodern dissent as a "reaction" against modernizing tendencies. There were many such reactions: in each case, we need to know who was reacting, in what ways, and why. Industrial workers from agrarian or craft backgrounds often resisted factory discipline; embattled farmers sometimes imagined an agrarian paradise lost; backcountry fundamentalists raged against urban vice. The antimodernism of medievalists and Orientalists, like these other forms, reflected not only a particular world view but also a particular class and power position.

My dramatis personae came primarily from among the educated strata of the Northern bourgeoisie. (I use the words "bourgeoisie" and "bourgeois" reluctantly throughout this study because they have been devalued from polemical overuse. But I have found them indispensable because there is no English equivalent to refer to the ruling groups in a developed capitalist society.) Antimodernists were not primarily powerful businessmen or politicians; they were journalists, academics, ministers, and literati whose circumstances ranged from the wealthy to the moderately comfortable. While they often did not share the world view of businessmen or politicians, they often did share kinship ties, educational background, and sources of income. Old-stock, Protestant, they were the moral and intellectual leaders of the American WASP bourgeoisie, who joined their British counterparts in shaping a transatlantic Victorian culture and who helped (sometimes unwittingly) to maintain dominant norms and values.

To be sure, it is possible to exaggerate the influence of such "opinion-makers" on the rest of society. Yet even though these custodians of culture spoke primarily to other educated Americans, and even though there was resistance or indifference to what they said among the populace as a whole, they exercised crucial cultural power. They not only helped to establish the official "common sense" of ruling groups throughout the nation (especially north of the Potomac and east of the Mississippi); they also played a subtler historical role. As some of the most educated and cosmopolitan products of an urbanizing, secularizing society, they were the "point men" of cultural change. They experienced and articulated moral and psychic dilemmas which later became common in the wider society.

Throughout this study I have tried to use a variety of interdisciplinary skills: a sensitivity to the nuance, tone, and argument of historical "texts"; an attentiveness to the family tensions behind antimodern cultural critiques; a concern for the role of my dramatis personae in the changing American social structure. I have also drawn explicitly on sociological and psychological theory. Max Weber's concept of the rationalization of Western culture—the drive for efficient control of outer and inner life—provides a theoretical framework which helps to explain antimodern longings for liberation. In exploring the psychic tensions shaping antimodernism, I have drawn on Freud's theories of ambivalence and the return of the repressed. And in an effort to illuminate the social significance of the antimodern quest for authenticity, I have turned to the Italian Marxist Antonio Gramsci, whose concept of "cultural hegemony" provides a welcome alternative to the static, mechanistic analyses of culture one ordinarily associates with the Marxist tradition. For Gramsci, dominant social groups maintain power not through force alone but through sustaining their cultural hegemony—that is, winning the "spontaneous" loyalty of subordinate groups to a common set of values and attitudes. The shift from a Protestant to a therapeutic world view, which antimodern sentiments reinforced, marked a key transformation in the cultural hegemony of the dominant classes in America.

My use of Weber, Freud, and Gramsci points to my largest methodological aim. I want to produce an historical analysis of culture that is sensitive not only to social class but also to the complexity and variety of individual human motives. Because I am studying some of the most influential cultural spokesmen of the dominant American class, I am particularly concerned with transcending a reductionist or conspiratorial analysis. I want to revise Gramsci by drawing on Freud: to show that a change in cultural hegemony stems not only from deliberate persuasion by members of a dominant class but also from half-conscious hopes and aspirations which seem to have little to do with the public realm of class relations. I want to show how the responses of certain influential Americans to personal frustration had *unintended* social results: the revitalization and transformation of their class's cultural hegemony. Yet the private struggles are not reducible to mechanisms of capitalist domination. Like any subordinate culture, a dominant culture is a continuous process, not a static "superstructure";

it contains innumerable tensions and idiosyncrasies; it can generate dissent as well as accommodation. This book will try to catch that complexity.

Following the hints of the British cultural historian Raymond Williams, I have tried to root cultural phenomena firmly in a social matrix while avoiding a problem which has plagued many social analyses of culture: a tendency to reduce the values and beliefs of a particular class to mere "reflections" of that class's material interests. For me, culture is not "determined" by class structure. The two coexist in a dialectical process: each continually reshapes the other. And I have tried to make important connections between American families and the wider culture, demonstrating that "psychohistory" need not always be reductive pathography—that in fact a psychoanalytic dimension may inform but not imprison historical analysis. I do not think it is presumptuous to claim that this book has major theoretical significance for the study of cultural history.

Historiographically, this book has two aims. The first and more modest is to correct the stale and mistaken view that antimodernism was the death rattle of old-stock Northeastern elites unable to adjust to a raw new industrial civilization. As a number of recent studies in social and demographic history have shown, the older WASP elites have neither died nor even declined significantly; they have maintained a tenacious hold on wealth, power, and influence throughout much of the twentieth century. They have not been supplanted by a "new class" of salaried managers and professionals; for the most part they have successfully adjusted to the new corporate system. The resiliency of this "old" ruling class has rested on more than brute force (though that was surely used at crucial points); it has also required the maintenance of cultural hegemony. That is why my dramatis personae were historically important: as influential shapers of the dominant American culture, their private struggles had (often unintended) public consequences. They helped both to revitalize familiar bourgeois values and ease the transition to new ones at a critical historical moment.

My second historiographical aim is more ambitious: I hope to cast new light on the complex transition from the nineteenth century to the twentieth—to suggest a new framework for understanding this crucial period of our cultural history. I want to suggest that the twentieth century's "revolution in manners and morals" was not an overnight result of post–World War I disillusionment; that it began long before the 1920s, not only in the liberationist manifestoes of bohemian literati but also in barely articulated yearnings of the respectable bourgeoisie; and that it was part of a broader shift from a Protestant to a therapeutic orientation within the dominant culture. Far from constituting a "revolution," that shift promoted new modes of accommodation to routinized work and bureaucratic "rationality."

By charting the halting, half-conscious emergence of a therapeutic world view, and by showing how it expressed and reinforced the shift from entrepreneurial to corporate capitalism, I intend to demonstrate that the much-discussed "modernization" of culture was a far more subtle process than historians have realized. (The word "modernization" is as slippery and controversial as "bourgeois," but I have found it indispensable to characterize the complex social and cultural changes experienced by my protagonists; nothing else is quite as capacious.) Modernization has never been a neutral or inevitable process; it has nearly always been furthered by particular classes at the expense of others. Nor has it been a smooth, linear development. En route to our contemporary culture of consumption, the modern values of self-control and autonomous achievement have been derailed, even as modern bureaucratic institutions have grown larger. And along with scientific and technological advances, modernizers have nearly always brought cultural strain, moral confusion, and anomie.

This study aims to illuminate many of the ambiguities surrounding notions of modernity—including the "modernism" literary critics have identified as the distinctive imaginative mode of the twentieth century. What critics call modernism and what I call antimodernism share common roots in the *fin-de-siècle* yearning for authentic experience—physical, emotional, or spiritual. The quickest way to characterize this terminological muddle is to point out that modernity has one meaning for historians, a very different one for literary critics; in large measure, literary "modernism" has been a reaction against the constraints and evasions of historical modernity—the stodgy moralism of bourgeois society. Yet the avant-garde preoccupation with authentic experience, like that of the medievalists and Orientalists, has frequently blended with a sleeker version of modern culture stressing self-fulfillment and immediate gratification. Superficially at odds, antimodernist, avant-gardist, and advertiser have often been brothers under the skin.

The reasons for this anomalous situation lie at the heart of our contemporary cultural dilemmas. Writing this book helped me to understand (at least partially) why so much twentieth-century American dissent has been so easily reassimilated to the mainstream. Preoccupied with authentic experience as a means of revitalizing a fragmented personal identity, dissenters have often been unable to sustain larger loyalties outside the self. Their criticism has frequently dissolved into therapeutic quests for self-realization, easily accommodated to the dominant culture of our bureaucratic corporate state. I hope this book will contribute to a continuing debate about the meaning of that culture. Philip Rieff, Daniel Bell, and Christopher Lasch have all made provocative efforts—from various ideological perspectives—to grapple with the self-absorbed nihilism which pervades so much of American life today. I intend this study to bring greater historical depth and theoretical sophistication to a discussion which too often has depended on polemical simplifications. My interests are more than intellectual; they are philosophical and moral. Like Rieff, Bell, and Lasch, I am disturbed by the signs of spiritual sterility which surround us in the late twentieth century. I have tried to write an historically informed critique of modern capitalist culture without succumbing either to nostalgia or the "progressive" bromides of the Left.

All scholarship is—or ought to be—a kind of intellectual autobiography. This book is no exception. I originally felt drawn to antimodernists because I shared their discontent with modern culture: its crackpot obsession with efficiency, its humanist hubris, its complacent creed of progress. Exposure to Marxist cultural criticism persuaded me that capitalist social relations had shaped modern culture in particular ways, but I remained convinced that the acids of modernity are often as corrosive under socialist as under capitalist regimes. I concluded that the most powerful critics of capitalism have often looked backward rather than forward, directing their fire at the bureaucratic "rationality" common to all corporate systems, indicting capitalist progress for its corrosive impact on family, craft, community, or faith. A few of my dramatis personae deserve inclusion among those critics; a few resisted incorporation into an absorbent culture which too often has reduced criticism to caricature. However problematic their own sense of identity, a few preserved commitments outside the self: that was their key resource for resistance. Antecedents of my own quest for an "authentic," independent point of view, the more thoughtful antimodernists remind us of what Left critics too often forget: in a society dedicated to economic development and "personal growth" at the expense of all larger loyalties, conservative values are too important to be left to pseudo-conservative apologists for capitalism. In our time, the most profound radicalism is often the most profound conservatism.

# Acknowledgments

Writing a book, George Orwell once said, is like recovering from a long and painful illness. After so many years of convalescence it is a pleasure to acknowledge all the help I have received.

First I want to thank my parents, Walter Lee Lears and Margaret Baptist Lears, for their love and generosity and for the last line of this book. And I want to thank my brother, R.E. Lee Lears, for providing me with friendship and with an example of moral courage since the early days of the Vietnam war.

I also wish to thank my wife Karen's parents, John Bell Parker and Doris Ives Parker, for their patient encouragement and warm support throughout the last ten years.

For their unfailing courtesy and competence, I should like to thank the staffs of the Yale University libraries, the Houghton Library at Harvard University, the Massachusetts Historical Society, the Wilson Library at the University of North Carolina, and the Ellis Library at the University of Missouri. The Woodrow Wilson Fellowship Foundation, the Danforth Foundation, the Roothbert Fund, the Whiting Foundation, the Porter Prize Committee at Yale, and the University of Missouri Research Council all provided financial assistance at important stages. Beverly Cedarbaum, Donna Winsor, Phyllis Dussell, and Julie Plax typed the manuscript expertly on a tight schedule.

In the early going, at the University of North Carolina (Chapel Hill), a number of people provided me with invaluable criticism and encouragement: Donald Mathews, Joel Williamson, Peter Walker, Frank Ryan—and above all Robert Moats Miller, who confirmed my suspicion that history without a moral dimension is pedantry.

The Yale University American Studies Program proved an ideal place to pursue this subject. My fellow graduate students helped to create that rarest of academic situations, a genuine community of scholars. No list can convey my gratitude for that experience, but I want to thank Michael Smith, Jane Hunter, William Breitenbach, Joel Bernard, G. Allison Stokes, Karen Halttunen, Christopher Wilson, Eddie Ayers, and particularly Gerald Burns for many thoughtful comments and discussions. J. Gregory Conti has been in a class by himself: a comrade in every sense, every step of the way. Among the American Studies faculty, I should like to thank Sydney Ahlstrom, R.W.B. Lewis, Richard Fox, and especially Alan Trachtenberg for their criticism and advice.

I am also deeply grateful to Arthur and Kathryn Messier, who sustained me with their friendship and revitalized my sense of the absurd. They transformed the "iron New England dark" to light.

Philip Pochoda, my editor at Pantheon, deserves my thanks as well. His enthusiasm rekindled mine at just the right moments; his editorial suggestions significantly improved the final version of the manuscript. I was also blessed with the assistance of Cara DeSilva, who copy-edited the manuscript with uncommon sensitivity.

My many enjoyable conversations with Steven Watts and Kenneth Plax, two of my graduate students at the University of Missouri (Columbia) helped to clarify my conceptual framework during the final revisions. And my colleague Robert Somers, together with his wife Miko, kept me from botching Japanese words in chapters five and six.

I owe a special debt of gratitude to David Brion Davis. I could not have asked for a better mentor. His criticism was invariably thoughtful, his encouragement effusive and well-timed. From the outset, he never insisted that I narrow my approach to produce another "solid monograph"; on the contrary he suggested extending my inquiry at some crucial points. And he provided, in his own work, a model of imaginative and wide-ranging scholarship.

My largest debt is inadequately acknowledged in the dedication. Karen Parker Lears has done far more than provide financial support while I was in graduate school, and far more than type the early drafts of this manuscript. Even after the birth of our daughter Rachel (who has done "important stapling" for me), Karen has taken valuable time from her own artistic work to clarify my writing and ventilate my thinking. In matters of style, she has saved me from a thousand infelicities; in matters of substance, she has persistently urged me to confront the largest philosophical and religious implications of my work. I owe much of my argument to our innumerable discussions about antimodern dissent, the therapeutic world view, and a host of related subjects. Her most valuable contributions have been the least tangible: her artist's sensibility, her sensitive insights into modern cultural history, her questioning frame of mind, her constantly regenerative influence on my work. She believed in this book when I did not; she lived it with me; it is for her.

*Columbia, Missouri*
*December, 1980*

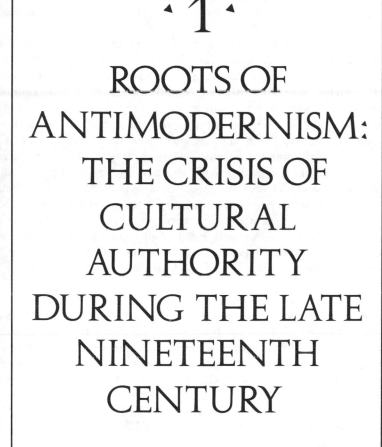

# · 1 ·

# ROOTS OF ANTIMODERNISM: THE CRISIS OF CULTURAL AUTHORITY DURING THE LATE NINETEENTH CENTURY

A CENTURY AGO, THE STOUT MIDRIFF WAS A SIGN of mature success in life. Affluent Americans devoured heavy meals at huge banquets. They accepted the congratulations of afterdinner orators. The speaker announced the marriage of material and spiritual progress. His audience nodded approval. There was no limit to American abundance. There was no impediment to the partnership of Protestantism and science. The audience applauded. They rose stiffly to leave. It was an age of confidence.

Yet one must try to imagine a kernel of doubt in the mind of the banqueter, hurrying home in the gaslit dark. Despite the Promethean optimism of the official culture, a sense of human finitude persisted among the more comfortably situated as well as those on the margins of society. Maybe doubt stemmed in part from the inescapable presence of Civil War veterans—not just heroes but hollow-eyed men who had merely survived, maimed at Antietam, gone mad at Chickamauga, reminders of the tragic limits on all human aspiration. But most families did not need reminders. They knew the arbitrariness at the heart of existence: the mother and infant dead at the moment of birth, the grandfather muddling on into hopeless senility. An entire range of human experience lay beyond the boundaries of official optimism. It was no accident that an inchoate distrust of perfectibilist schemes and technological cornucopias survived the death of Calvinist dogma. Americans, even the educated and affluent, could not remain at ease in the Zion of modern industrial society.

For some, what focused this disquiet was a long tradition of Puritan and republican moralism. For republican moralists, as for their Puritan predecessors, man was a depraved creature whose history was not a linear path of progress but a cyclical process of development and decline. The inevitable end of all human societies was not perfection but "overcivilization." In the late nineteenth century, the notion that America had become overcivilized occurred naturally to the intellectual heirs of Cotton Mather and Thomas Jefferson. Puritans and republicans alike had been haunted by fears of the urban "effeminacy" and "luxury" produced by material progress. The same idiom remained available in the industrial America of the 1880s.

But by the late nineteenth century, the feeling of overcivilization signified more than just a provincial revival of republican moralism. It was a sign of a broader transatlantic dissatisfaction with modern culture in all its dimensions: its ethic of self-control and autonomous achievement, its cult of science and technical rationality, its worship of material progress. During the 1880s, on both sides of the Atlantic, one begins to sense a restive desire for a freshening of the cultural atmosphere. Haltingly, half-consciously, Europeans and Americans alike began to recognize that the triumph of modern culture had not produced greater autonomy (which was the official claim) but rather had promoted a spreading sense of moral impotence and spiritual sterility—a feeling that life had become not only overcivilized but also curiously unreal.

For the educated bourgeoisie, authentic experience of any sort seemed ever more elusive; life seemed increasingly confined to the airless parlor of material comfort and moral complacency. Many yearned to smash the glass and breathe freely—to experience "real life" in all its intensity. Groping for alternatives to modern unreality, they sometimes clung to the shreds and patches of republican tradition, but they also turned to other cultural resources as well: the literary romantic's rejection of urban artifice in the name of a rustic or childlike "simple life"; the philosophical vitalist's rejection of all static systems in the name of the flux of "pure experience"; the avant-garde artist's rejection of bourgeois respectability in the name of primal irrationality. The very effort to categorize this *fin-de-siècle* cultural ferment oversimplifies its richness and variety.

The turmoil of the turn of the century formed the matrix of antimodernism. A common current of restiveness, a common perception of modern culture's evasions and shortcomings, linked antimodernists like Henry Adams with thinkers as diverse as Ezra Pound, Georges Sorel, and Sigmund Freud. It also joined these major figures with popularizers who addressed a wider audience: simple-lifers, militarists, mind-curists, mystics. Whether they focused on premodern character or on more recent models, all these disparate pilgrims sought "authentic" alternatives to the apparent unreality of modern existence; all have spawned descendants down to our own time. Exploring the sources of antimodernism in *fin-de-siècle* cultural ferment, one uncovers social and psychic tensions which still persist and still promote unfulfilled longings for "real life." American antimodernism, in other words, provides one illuminating angle of vision on the shaping of twentieth-century American culture.

In both Europe and America, the antimodern impulse was rooted in what can aptly be called a crisis of cultural authority, which had both public and private dimensions. Americans commonly confronted the public dimensions by turning to republican tradition. For decades republican moralists had worried that a liberal polity would be unable to contain the centrifugal tendencies in an atomized market society; the unprecedented class and ethnic conflict of the late nineteenth century intensified that worry as never before. The optimistic liberal individualism of the ruling social groups, which had only recently been reaffirmed by the Northern victory in the Civil War, seemed by the 1880s to be corrupt, evasive, illegitimate. Losing cultural authority, the leaders of the American bourgeoisie reasserted their power with rifles and bayonets. The expedient was temporarily successful but ultimately unsatisfying, because more was at stake than mere power. From the republican view, the ruling class required not only more guns but moral regeneration.

If public authority seemed to be losing legitimacy, private authority seemed on the wane as well. The internalized morality of self-control and autonomous achievement, the basis of modern culture, seemed at the end of its tether; the chief source of that morality, the bourgeois family, seemed a hothouse of suffocating repression and insoluble personal conflict. As the ethic of autonomy waned, familiar assumptions about selfhood wavered; ultimately even personal identity seemed affected by the unreality of modern existence. Worse: the religious sanction for bourgeois morality, the supernatural framework which gave life meaning and purpose, seemed to be dissolving in a haze of enlightened platitudes. As Protestantism liberalized, it accommodated itself to secular habits of mind and lost much emotional power. It was not surprising, then, that many nineteenth-century Americans craved both the authentic experience outside the bounds of Victorian respectability and the intense spiritual ecstasy of communion with God. It was not surprising that they yearned to resurrect a solid sense of self by recapturing the "real life" of the premodern craftsman, soldier, or saint.

Neither in Europe nor in America was that antimodern impulse wholly regressive. On the contrary, far from encouraging escapist nostalgia, antimodern sentiments not only promoted eloquent protest against the limits of liberalism but also helped to shape new modes of cultural authority for the oncoming twentieth century. In Europe, where discontent with liberalism was more pervasive and severe, antimodernism formed much of the emotional basis for communitarian critiques of capitalism as well as for fascist and Nazi ideology. In America, where antimodern protest was more idiosyncratic, the transformation of cultural authority was subtler and longer lasting. American antimodernism unknowingly provided part of the psychological foundation for a streamlined liberal culture appropriate to twentieth-century consumer capitalism. If in Europe liberal culture was sometimes openly rejected, in America it was more often revitalized and transformed.[1]

Part of the reason for this difference was that liberal culture was more firmly established in America than in Europe: its individualism was less openly challenged, its optimism more brazen and banal. Throughout much of our history, the voices of doubt have been drowned (though never stilled) in a resurgent chorus of national self-congratulation. Puritan and republican jeremiads have often served to reinforce the dominant culture by reducing social conflicts to questions of individual morality and providing troubled Americans with an innocuous means of discharging half-conscious anxieties about the effects of expanding market capitalism. Periodically relieved of doubt, the fretful bourgeoisie have returned to the official belief that everything will work out in the long run. In a sense antimodernism falls into this recurring pattern of mingled doubt and reaffirmation.[2]

But only in a sense. The playing out of antimodern impulses was far too complex a process to fit any schematic patterns. Above all, it is important to remember that antimodernism, despite its role in revitalizing and transforming capitalist cultural authority, was far more than a response to the effects of market capitalism; it contained a critique of modern culture applicable to all secular, bureaucratic systems, whether socialist or capitalist. The antimodern impulse stemmed from revulsion against the process of rationalization first described by Max Weber—the systematic organization of economic life for maximum productivity and of individual life for maximum personal achievement; the drive for efficient control of nature under the banner of improving human welfare; the reduction of the world to a disenchanted object to be manipulated by rational technique.[3] At its most profound, antimodernism attacked the hubris of this bureaucratic "rationality" and subverted progressive pieties of any political stripe. Yet despite this common front, the particular varieties of antimodernism were shaped by particular national circumstances. To begin to understand American antimodernism, we need first of all to explore the modern American culture which provoked it—to listen, in effect, to what was being said at the banquets.

# A Pattern of Evasive Banality: Official Modern Culture in Industrial America

At bottom the official doctrines were progressive.* Faith in the beneficence of material progress has always been a central tenet of modern culture in America: today it survives among real estate developers, corporate planners, and unreconstructed Keynesian economists; a century ago it rang from pulpits and platforms across the nation. The Reverend Henry Ward Beecher expressed the dominant mood of self-assurance in a centennial speech at Peekskill, New York on July 4, 1876. The Revolutionary generation built a great nation, he said, but we are building a greater one. "We not only wear better heads, but we have better bellies [great laughter], with better food in them."[4] Beecher himself embodied the change. His father Lyman Beecher was a gaunt defender of Calvinism and republican virtue; Henry Ward was a genial, portly creature of urban comfort and affluence. His belief in progress was the stuff of banquet oratory. It was an afterdinner creed, meant to be consumed with Courvoisier and La Coronas.

*Throughout this study, I use "progressive" to refer to a general belief in progress and "Progressive" to refer to the reformers who applied that term to themselves around the turn of the century.

Late-nineteenth-century enthusiasm for material progress is difficult to chart because it was omnipresent and often implicit in the emergent modern culture. It united businessmen, politicians, ministers, journalists—all the stout thought-leaders of the urban bourgeoisie. Even many labor leaders, socialists, and dissident farmers accepted the progressive faith: they attacked the maldistribution of wealth, not the fundamental beneficence of economic growth; they accepted the conventional link between technological development and national greatness. Americans who despised the steel magnate Andrew Carnegie would have echoed his claim in *Triumphant Democracy* (1886): "The old nations of the earth creep on at a snail's pace; the Republic thunders past with the rush of the express." Carnegie revealed a major foundation of the belief in progress: the idea that nations (like individuals) can never stand still. They must always be growing, changing, improving their material lot; life is a race to be won by the swiftest. Like the progressive faith itself, this notion was often left implicit. Yet its impact has been incalculable. It accounts for the relentless dynamism at the heart of capitalist development, spreading an obsessive need for change throughout modern culture. And for most educated and affluent Americans in the late nineteenth century, "change" meant "progress."[5]

The chief engine of progress was industrial technology. Throughout the nineteenth century, middle- and upper-class Americans grew increasingly enthusiastic about the possibilities of applying technology to the practical concerns of making a living. Entrepreneurs, engineers, and economists hailed the whole industrial apparatus of advancing capitalism, from factory town to gritty city. By the 1880s on both sides of the Atlantic, industrial and urban growth had entered a new phase which has been called a "second industrial revolution" to distinguish it from Britain's experience over a century earlier. The second industrial revolution struck more rapidly than the first; its reach was broader, its technology more sophisticated. Until the 1870s the tracks of progress had been laid with iron; after that decade they were laid with steel. It was not accidental that Andrew Carnegie chose "the rush of the express" to epitomize the pace of American progress; for many Americans the railroad was the first among many machines which embodied the new primacy of their country's industrial might. But there were other equally striking mechanical emblems. The great Corliss steam engine at the Philadelphia Centennial Exposition of 1876, which developed up to 2500 horsepower, stood thirty-nine feet tall, weighed 680 tons, and inspired thousands of tourists to crowd into Machinery Hall and pay homage to the machine as "that wonder of the modern era . . . the highest embodiment of a man's power. . . ." The Brooklyn Bridge was another monument to American technology—born in the mind of John Roebling, raised amid the graft and intrigue of Tammany Hall politics, finally completed in May 1883 as several thousand New

Yorkers gathered to hear the world's largest suspension bridge solemnized at the opening ceremonies. To one speaker, the Reverend Richard Storrs, the bridge's steel construction was particularly significant because steel embodied "the bolder temper which is natural here, the readiness to attempt unparalleled works, the disdain of difficulties." Steel represented the triumph of the American will, the conquest of nature by technology.[6]

Yet the second industrial revolution meant more than technology in the saddle. It also meant that the nation's technical expertise was being placed in the service of big business. The second industrial revolution was entwined with the shift from the disorganized entrepreneurial capitalism of the earlier nineteenth century to the organized corporate capitalism of our own time. The rationalization of economic life—the drive for maximum profits through the adoption of the most efficient forms of organization—was moving into high gear, especially in the United States. Instead of the small workshop, the dominant mode of economic organization was becoming the monopolistic corporation—organized in accordance with precisely calculable and strictly functional procedures, managed by a hierarchical bureaucracy of salaried executives, geared to dominate an ever-larger share of an emerging national market. In matters of organization technical "rationality" was becoming the dominant mode; the older local enterprises, run by the boss's whims or rules of thumb, were settling into the interstices of the economy. By the post–Civil War era, the most successful large businesses were beginning to organize both production and marketing on a national basis. Canals, telegraphs, and railroads had extended the web of the national market to the remoter rural communities; the growth of cities in the Northeast and Midwest had created inviting target areas for more intensive selling efforts. Though popular rhetoric spoke of "subduing nature," business leaders embraced the functional rationality and technological innovations of organized capitalism for more precise reasons: to stabilize production and consolidate control over a national market.[7]

Rationalization was not a neutral or impersonal process; it was primarily furthered by the dominant social groups who stood to benefit, however indirectly, from corporate expansion; it threatened many who did not stand to benefit from that expansion. (This is an obvious point, but it has been overlooked by historians and social scientists for whom "modernization" is a *deus ex machina* hovering over several centuries of economic growth.) While old inequalities of wealth and power persisted, the growing ascendance of larger corporations brought to prominence a more nationally oriented bourgeoisie. The Marxist idiom, shopworn though it may be, is inescapable: rationalization promoted many interests but primarily those of an emergent national ruling class—still embryonic, torn by tension, sometimes barely cohesive, but an incipient ruling class nonetheless.

The process of rationalization did more than transform the structure of economic life; it also affected the structure of thought and feeling, of culture in the broadest sense. The rationalization of culture, too, served the interests of the national bourgeoisie, but in subtler ways than those specified in most Marxist analyses. The rationalized, modern culture was not merely a static "superstructure" reflecting ruling class interests; nor was it simply a product of deliberate attempts to indoctrinate a hapless populace. Modern values and attitudes served the interests of the bourgeoisie in more oblique ways as well. The cultural dominance of the bourgeoisie was partly an unintended consequence of sincere (though often self-deceiving) efforts to impose moral meaning on a rapidly changing social world—efforts led not by bankers and industrialists but by ministers and other moralists. The best term for this process is not social control but cultural hegemony.[8]

I use this term reluctantly because it is easily misconstrued as a mechanistic formula. But a few historians in the Marxian tradition, particularly Raymond Williams, have pointed the way to more complex usages.[9] Handled with care, the concept of hegemony offers the best way to understand the role of culture in sustaining inequalities of wealth and power. (For my purposes, it is more narrowly focused on class relations than the related but broader concept of authority.) The concept of hegemony has led me to underscore the unconscious self-deceptions among ruling-class custodians of culture as well as the unintended consequences of their attitudes and ideas—which were often far removed from issues of class relations. Indeed these people themselves were often unaware of their hegemonic role. Confronting moral and psychic dilemmas in a modernizing society, they joined in creating the doctrines of modern culture for largely personal reasons. Yet their private struggles had unintended public consequences. They led to the formation of values and beliefs which gave meaning and purpose not only to individuals but to the dominant bourgeoisie as a whole —and which also inspired trust and allegiance from much of the rest of American society. This modern synthesis was unstable and diffuse: it was often congenial to the older localism as well as the newer "rationality"; it ranged from fully articulated ideas to half-conscious perceptions. But for a time, however precariously, it helped to sustain the cultural hegemony of the ascendant bourgeoisie. We need now to examine this modern culture in more detail, beginning with one of its most basic components—the perception of time.

With the growth of industrial capitalism during the post–Civil War years, more and more Americans were feeling the pressure to be "on time." (The phrase itself was a colloquialism which did not appear until the 1870s.) The corporate drive for efficiency underwrote quantified time as a uniform standard of measurement and reinforced the spreading requirement that people regulate their lives by the clock. The heaviest pressure

came from employers in factories and bureaucracies who increasingly demanded rigid adherence to quantified schedules. And though there was
much resistance, especially among workers from preindustrial backgrounds, the triumph of clock time seemed assured by 1890, when the time
clock was invented. While premodern people simply passed the time,
modern Americans saved it, spent it (the money metaphor is significant),
and finally packaged it in discreté, repeatable units. The "pace of modern
life," a staple of popular sociology, is a direct result of the bureaucratic
imperative in organized capitalism—the demand for disciplined, systematic work.[10]

If modern life promoted a new sensitivity to clock time, it also generated
a new intolerance for physical discomfort. As early as the 1830s, the perceptive French observer Alexis de Tocqueville had noted the American
democrat's obsession with material comforts. By the later nineteenth century, technological advance had made it increasingly possible for the urban
bourgeoisie to satisfy that obsession. Improvements in public health had
increased longevity and sharply reduced infant mortality, and the widening
use of anesthesia (introduced in 1842) made painless surgery an everyday
occurrence. Progress in transportation technology had decreased the like-
lihood of steamboat or railroad disaster; it also eliminated much minor
discomfort. After 1865, George Pullman's "palace cars" became a standard feature on every railroad in the country, and for $2.00 a night the more
affluent traveller could insulate himself in Victorian luxury, far from the
dirt and disorder of the coach. Back at home, the spread of central heating
and indoor plumbing were further protecting the urban bourgeoisie from
physical unpleasantness. And developments in organic chemistry were
increasing the supply of narcotics available to Americans. Before 1914,
Americans could buy cocaine, opium, morphine, laudanum, and heroin in
patent medicines or soft drinks. Numerous men and women followed the
example of Mary Boykin Chesnut, who in 1863 "took opium to relieve the
tedium" of a long and uncomfortable carriage ride. The earliest and most
successful national advertising campaigns were waged by manufacturers of
patent medicines, nearly all of which contained large doses of narcotics.
In general, Americans by 1880 were far more able—and eager—than their
ancestors to avoid both physical and emotional discomfort.[11]

Both the craving for comfort and the triumph of clock time were key
components in the emergent modern culture. Both are still very much with
us, so pervasive that they go almost unnoticed—except in passing references to "our pill-popping society" or "the pace of modern life." In the
nineteenth century both marked important changes in sensibility, changes
wrought by the urban-industrial transformation we now take for granted.

Yet the recoil from physical discomfort was more than a sign of dramatic material progress. It also points us in profounder directions, toward a more extended consideration of the values which shaped modern

character. Material progress alone cannot explain Americans' preoccupation with escaping discomfort. The flight from pain reflected larger tendencies in Western beliefs and values. It was part of an increased sensitivity to suffering in general—to the plight of slaves, prisoners, mistreated animals, and the insane. Among the nineteenth-century bourgeoisie, in both England and America, humanitarian concern for others' suffering coincided with a personal revulsion from pain and a distaste for violence in general. These attitudes undergirded the bourgeois cult of respectability; they also helped persuade Victorians that material progress meant moral progress as well.

An idea of progress had existed in Western culture for centuries, but in the nineteenth century it became more sweeping in its implications and more widely held than ever before. Of all Victorian habits of mind, this tendency to equate material and moral progress is perhaps most difficult to swallow today. Among later generations, it has helped earn Victorian moralists a reputation as consummate hypocrites. One can easily see why by looking (for example) at a symposium called "The Moral Drift of Our Time," sponsored by the Congregational Club of New York and held at the Vienna Café, corner of Tenth Street and Broadway, on May 25, 1883. After a huge seven-course meal (which included salmon à la hollandaise, sirloin of beef braisé, breaded breast of lamb, and stewed prunes), the symposium participants settled down to a chorus of sober self-congratulation. Judge Noah Davis noted the elevated tone of politics since the banishment of the "slave power;" the literary critic Hamilton Wright Mabie applauded the application of the scientific spirit to literature; Professor William Tucker of Andover Theological Seminary was sure that religious sentiment was on the rise because church membership was up. From the banquet vantage, the "moral drift of our time" seemed hardly drift but inevitable, calculable ascent.[12]

This sort of optimism is difficult to credit today, when it survives only among a few vapid futurologists. But it epitomized the pattern of evasive banality which pervaded modern culture. To try to catch the significance of this pattern, we need to see the equation of material and moral progress not simply as complacent hypocrisy but as a natural outgrowth of nineteenth-century bourgeois morality.

The center of that morality was the autonomous individual, whose only moral master was himself. For centuries, the internal dynamic of bourgeois individualism had been undermining all the older, external forms of moral authority—the authority of king over subject, priest over communicant, master over slave. Freed from older constraints, each masterless man needed a moral gyroscope to keep him on course or else market society might dissolve into a chaos of self-seeking individuals. The destruction of old oppressive forms created new problems of social control; in order to preserve any semblance of public order, oppression had to yield to repression. Even as they attacked the old, external forms of moral authority, bourgeois moralists labored to create a new, internalized mode of moral authority. As Weber brilliantly suggested, Protestant ministers played a major role in beginning the work; they were joined in the more secular nineteenth century by medical men, public educators, and social reformers of all sorts. Health and morality became intertwined. By the 1880s, whether sanctioned by secular or religious authority, an internalized ethic of self-control had become the unquestioned norm for the middle and upper classes as well as for much of the rest of society.[13]

The ethic of self-control had been embodied in American moralists from Cotton Mather to Benjamin Franklin, but the nineteenth century gave it a further turn. The Victorian world view, spreading among the educated and affluent in Britain and America, intensified the ethic of self-control and extended it into new areas of personal conduct. Not only aggression but also sexuality were placed under the strictures of the conscience. This prudery has provoked the enlightened twentieth century's contempt, but if we move beyond sneers we can begin to see the historical significance of this unprecedented extension of self-control. It was the strongest attempt yet made to extend the process of rationalization from the outer to the inner life; it meant that systematic methods of self-control would press beyond the workplace into the most intimate areas of daily experience—perhaps even into unconscious wishes, dreams, and fantasies. In other words, the Victorian extension of self-control meant the triumph of a modern superego, more thoroughly internalized, more systematically demanding than any of its historic predecessors.

The creation of a modern superego had been a slow process, as the sociologist Norbert Elias shows in his magisterial book *The Civilizing Process.* But the late-Victorian period represented the modern superego at its apogee. The point can be made with reference to one of the most extreme (perhaps pathological) examples of Victorian sexual respectability, John Harvey Kellogg. Besides putting Battle Creek on the map as the home of Rice Krispies, Kellogg wrote success manuals for boys. His popular *Man, the Masterpiece, or Plain Truths Plainly Told, About Boyhood, Youth and Manhood* (1886) dwelled on the dangers of sensual self-indulgence: in food, in sleep, and above all, in sex. For Kellogg as for many of his contemporaries, the greatest single danger was the "secret vice," masturbation. To enable men to conquer the secret vice, Kellogg proposed a regimen aimed at eliminating not only conscious masturbation but even unconscious erotic dreams. The key agent in this program (as indeed in all of modern character formation) was the will. During the waking hours, Kellogg advised, young men should keep the will in fine trim by practicing self-denial; properly disciplined, the will might even be applied to unconscious temptation, snapping the youth awake and out of his dream in time to prevent nocturnal emission. Like many of his contemporaries, Kellogg provided medical as well as moral advice. His physiological agenda included:

1. Kneading and pounding on the abdomen each day to promote evacuation before sleep and thus avoid "irritating" congestions.
2. Drinking hot water, six to eight glasses a day (same end in view).
3. Urinating several times each night (same end in view).
4. Avoiding alcohol, tobacco, and tea because they stimulated lecherous thoughts.
5. Taking cold enemas and hot sitz baths each day.
6. Wearing a wet girdle to bed each night.[14]

Silly as it seems, Kellogg's regimen was more than just another example of bizarre Victoriana. It paralleled Frederick Winslow Taylor's time-and-motion studies of the labor process, which were beginning to appear at about the same time. (Taylor performed his first experiments in 1882.) By breaking down each task into its smallest component parts, eliminating all wasted motion and energy, and recombining the parts into a more efficient whole, Taylor promoted the "scientific management" of the workplace. (Indeed in the hagiographical literature of management seminars, Taylor is acclaimed as the "father of scientific management.") While Taylor sought the full rationalization of human work, Kellogg yearned for the full rationalization of the human psyche. The aspirations of both men represented a high point in the development of the modern superego.[15]

The extremism of men like Kellogg and Taylor makes them problematic models for a whole society. In fact a number of historians have challenged the whole concept of a "Victorian consensus" in nineteenth-century America. Evidence from moral tracts themselves suggests that they were written to combat looser patterns of behavior in the larger society. The question inevitably arises: how representative were men like Kellogg and Taylor? Were they and the many more moderate apostles of self-control actually members of a Victorian "counterculture?" Was their repressive ideology profoundly at odds with prevailing social practice?[16]

On balance, I think the answer is no. There was, to be sure, widespread dissent from Victorian norms among immigrants from premodern cultures and native-born Americans from less modernized areas of the United States. There was also a great deal of half-conscious discontent among the educated and affluent avatars of modern values—that is what this chapter will later explore in some detail. Yet for all that, the Victorian ethic of self-control was engrained widely and deeply enough to constitute the mainspring of the dominant culture. I am not suggesting that Victorian respectability constituted a monolithic moral system uniting all of American culture. That would be a gross simplification. I am arguing that Victorian respectability undergirded the values disseminated by the educated bourgeoisie. Those values were not descriptions of actual behavior; they were official standards of conduct. But evidence suggests that many Americans of all classes tried hard to conform to them.[17] In other words, Victorian respectability did not create a genuine cultural consensus; rather, it played a key role in sustaining the hegemony of the dominant social classes. Originating among the middle and upper bourgeoisie, Victorian ideals formed a collective conscience which inspired allegiance from subordinate groups and brought coherence to a potentially fragmented society.

A number of sensitive historians have underscored the social importance of Victorian morality by illuminating its focal point, the bourgeois family.[18] The family marked the chief arena for the creation of a modern superego, the chief agent of acculturation in a volatile culture. Though respectable Americans paid increasing attention to medical moralists like Kellogg, they placed their highest hopes for the preservation of moral order on the family itself. Their expectations surfaced most clearly in a sentimentalized picture of domestic life. The Victorian domestic ideal pervaded nineteenth-century culture; it was commemorated in the novels of Charles Dickens and Harriet Beecher Stowe, the poetry in women's magazines like *Godey's Ladies Book* (1830–1898), the lithographs of Currier and Ives. The conventional image of Victorian family life—pompous patriarch, submissive and angelic mother, sickly-sweet children—has been the focus for much popular discussion of the family throughout the twentieth century. Nostalgic conservatives have imagined the Victorian domestic ideal to be an emblem of emotional harmony amid disruptive social change; feminists have assailed it as a piece of ideological mystification designed to keep women in their place; social activists have attacked it as the source of "privatization" which has lured Americans away from public commitments. None of these views gets at the full complexity of Victorian domestic life.

To be sure, many Victorian ideologues did imagine the family to be a haven in the heartless world of capitalist competition. The domestic ideal was inextricably tied to the growth of modern market capitalism. As subsistence farming gave way to an urban market economy throughout the nineteenth century, the family steadily lost its productive role but acquired new psychological and ideological burdens. Under urban conditions of life, "work" became radically separated from "home" and that separation reinforced another: between productive adult males and nonproductive women and children. According to the conventional wisdom, the male world of work was tough and demanding; the female world of home was comfortable, reassuring, and adorned by "the finer things of life." In the transition to an urban market economy, women gave up the many productive duties they had performed on the farm and became the guardians of culture and morality. Remaining aloof from the emerging market society, Victorian housewives were encouraged to shelter their children from the corruptions of the marketplace and comfort their exhausted husbands.

The new female role reflected both demographic and economic change. On the farm children had been an economic asset; in the city they became a liability. The urban birthrate dropped steadily beginning in 1810, and mothers found it possible to devote more attention to each child. The paucity of children made it easier to sentimentalize them as sacrosanct individuals; the isolation of the home made it easier to imagine both children and their mothers as embodiments of moral innocence. The innocent child, epitomized by Little Eva in Stowe's *Uncle Tom's Cabin,* joined the maternal "Angel in the House" atop the domestic pedestal. Populated by fewer children, cut off from the public realm as never before, the Victorian home focused longings (particularly male longings) for escape from the rigors of an expanding commercial society. In the bourgeois imagination, the home became an oasis of tenderness and affection in a desert of ruthless competition.

But a genuine "privatization" of family life never occurred. The problem was not just that expectations of domestic tranquility were inflated beyond hope of fulfillment; there were also contradictions at the heart of the domestic ideal. It was impossible for the home to remain altogether isolated from the market society. Inevitably the haven embodied many values of the heartless world outside. If the home was meant to be a refuge from the marketplace, it was also meant to socialize people (particularly males) to succeed in that competitive realm. If it encouraged mutual harmony, it also taught the aggressive traits of the self-made man.

The domestic ideal contained further complexities as well. Victorian sex roles were not nearly as simple as their twentieth-century critics have suggested; they were full of contradictory expectations. Victorian women were expected to be not only submissive helpmates but pillars of strength in times of trouble and repositories of moral and cultural authority. Their roles simultaneously prescribed self-effacement and self-reliance. Men faced a similar problem. Outside the family they were urged toward autonomous competition; within it they were expected to conform to domestic models of social harmony. And many did conform; even in the early-Victorian period Tocqueville noted that by European standards American men were exceptionally dependent on their families for emotional sustenance. Far from being a mere mystification designed to keep women under male domination, the domestic ideal was a reflection of male self-doubts and dependent impulses. Men who worshipped at the domestic shrine created an image of serene womanhood, free from the erotic and aggressive impulses they distrusted in themselves. At the same time, by underscoring specific male responsibilities the domestic ideal provided a means by which women could exert cultural and psychological influence over men. As the historian Daniel Scott Smith points out, "the literature of the utopian home demanded that husbands consult their wives, avoid sexual assault on them, and even consciously structure their own behavior on the model of their spouses." One need only think of Kellogg to realize that the ideologies of domesticity tried to create sexless men as well as sexless women. Both the Christian Gentleman and the True Woman faced rigid and contradictory sexual roles; both faced the rivalrous claims of autonomy and dependence.[19]

But from the viewpoint of the dominant culture, the modern family presented no problems. On the contrary, it was the highest moral achievement of man, the emblem of his ascent from barbarism. The repressive aspects of the modern family were treated as signs of moral progress; the insoluble conflicts it helped to generate were ignored or evaded.[20]

One can see this same quality of evasive banality in much of the literature spawned by Victorian culture. As the United States became the most aggressively expansionist society in the world, American literature increasingly celebrated a sentimental vision of mutually dependent social relations. In the name of "realism," fiction concerned itself largely with decorous conversations and parlor intrigues; the domestic problem novel became the self-proclaimed "modern" mode. The most distinguished realist, William Dean Howells, urged that American writers focus on "the more smiling aspects of life, which are the more American." Though Howells's own best work far transcended this formula, many more popular novels did not. Genteel literature, like the idealized domestic circle, became a portal of escape from the economic realm of strife and struggle.[21]

For generations, historians and critics have vilified the genteel tradition in literature for its failure to confront the reality of a brutal new industrial civilization.[22] What most have missed is that sentimental literature, by contributing to the evasive banality of the official culture, actually helped to legitimize modern industrial capitalism. The common pattern of culture involved a denial of the conflicts in modern capitalist society, an affirmation of continuing harmony and progress. Sentimental literature performed the same function as the domestic ideal: both were part of an overall pattern of evasion in the dominant culture.

It is important to be clear on this point. The word "evasion" might suggest a conscious process, deliberately planned by bourgeois moralists and literati to further the interests of their class. Nothing could be more mistaken. In fact, the process of evasion was half-conscious, a matter of instinctive self-deception rather than deliberate duplicity. Its social consequences were unintended yet profound. By underwriting the equation of material and moral progress, the pattern of evasion strengthened the cultural hegemony of dominant social groups throughout the nineteenth century.

Evasiveness underlay a central tenet of the modern world view: faith in individual autonomy. The official creed held not only that progress was inevitable but that the key to it was the disciplined, autonomous self, created in the bosom of the bourgeois family. From the dominant view, the autonomous self was a Promethean figure, conquering fate through sheer force of will. Faith in autonomous selfhood required a denial of inner conflict and an insensitivity to actual social conditions; it epitomized the evasiveness of modern culture.

This faith emerged most clearly in nineteenth-century success ideology, which held aloft the example of the self-made man. In the popular imagination, that figure possessed neither intellectual brilliance nor unusual physical prowess; what he had in abundance were industrious work habits, extraordinary moral discipline, and above all an indomitable will. "To the man of vigorous will, there are few impossibilities," said a clerical success adviser in 1878. "Obstructions melt before his fiat like spring snowflakes." The career of the self-made man embodied the dynamism inherent in all capitalist development. Autonomous achievement required perpetual motion; the modern self never stood still. Like the heroes of Horatio Alger's novels, the self-made man would forever *Strive and Succeed;* he would always be *Struggling Upward.* [23]

The image of the Promethean self-made man was mythic in a double sense: it was part of a world view which provided many Americans with meaning and purpose; and it was false. Social historians have conclusively demonstrated that gross inequalities of opportunity existed in the United States during the Jacksonian era; by the 1880s the growth of organized corporate capitalism had made genuine economic independence a near impossibility. Yet the ideal of self-made manhood persists. One can find traces of it today at all levels of our culture, from the calls for "self-starters" in the want ads to the fascination of ego psychologists with autonomy to the assertions of sociologists about workers in modern industrial societies. According to Clark Kerr, for example, the modern worker is fully committed, "dedicated to hard work, a high pace of work, and a keen sense of individual responsibility for performance of assigned norms and tasks"; he is moved not by grudging acquiescence but by "an ideology and an ethic." He is, in other words, an embodiment of autonomous achievement. [24]

Faith in autonomous selfhood has also survived in economic thought. The autonomous Economic Man still stalks the pages of textbooks, rationally making choices in accordance with his own self-interest. But during the nineteenth century autonomous selfhood received its most forthright formulation in the economic theories spawned by classical liberalism. And here too the quality of self-deceiving evasion was apparent. Nineteenth-century liberal economists consistently side-stepped the social implications of their theories, which sanctioned an atomized society composed of autonomous members, each engaged in the untrammeled pursuit of his own material welfare.

Liberal theory had not always been so obtuse. Thomas Hobbes, writing in the seventeenth century, had confronted the social meaning of liberal individualism: all men were crowded onto the same narrow roadway where they jostled for success in the race of life. But many of Hobbes's intellectual descendants in the liberal tradition shrank from his bleak view. Popularizing Adam Smith's famous argument in *The Wealth of Nations* (1776), nineteenth-century liberal theorists insisted that the autonomous individual's pursuit of private gain somehow promoted the welfare of the whole society. Behind the Hobbesian war of all against all lay the natural laws of political economy, which transformed private vice into public benefit and guaranteed that a harmony of interests would unify an apparently atomized society.

This optimistic liberalism was especially popular in the United States. In 1876, some Americans celebrated the centennial of *The Wealth of Nations* as enthusiastically as that of the Declaration of Independence. If one document declared political freedom, it was said, the other affirmed economic freedom; the two were intertwined. On December 12, 1876, 100 people attended a banquet at Delmonico's to commemorate the centennial of Smith's book. Following dessert, speaker after speaker arose to acclaim the continuing validity of Smith's insights. *The Wealth of Nations* was a monument to the triumph of classical liberalism among the American bourgeoisie. As the *Bankers' Magazine* declared in a review of the event: "[The book's] usefulness is now as great as ever."[25]

Americans managed to avoid the brutal implications of classical liberalism by embedding it in a framework of optimistic moralism. Embracing the basic principles set forth by Smith, they rejected the more pessimistic dimensions of classical theory developed by David Ricardo (who held that wages in the long run would never rise above subsistence level) and Thomas Malthus (who held that population would always tend to outstrip food supply). Both Ricardo and Malthus recalled the Hobbesian vision of conflict; Americans preferred the sunnier views of Frédéric Bastiat, a French economist whose *Harmonies of Political Economy* (1850) attempted to demonstrate that competitive free enterprise would ultimately create a harmony of interests.[26] Bastiat, like Smith, was a moral philosopher as well as a political economist: nineteenth-century Americans could not take their economics undiluted by moralism. To justify an ethos of autonomous achievement, to sustain moral authority in a fragmented market society, they had to banish the Hobbesian specter of amoral struggle.

For decades that task fell to academic moral philosophers. Typically they were college presidents who taught the graduating seniors; typically they solved difficult philosophical problems by bland assertion. Drawing mostly on Scottish moral philosophy but also on German idealism and British utilitarianism, referring all disputed matters to the "common sense" of mankind, men like Noah Porter of Yale and Francis Bowen of Harvard insisted that economic and moral laws were fundamentally similar. According to Bowen, the economic arrangements of society "manifest the contrivance, wisdom, and beneficence of the deity, just as clearly as do the marvellous arrangements of the material universe, or the natural means provided for the enforcement of the moral law and the punishment of crime." A man's conscience informed him about the moral universe just as empirical observation informed him about the natural universe; since ethical truth was knowable, the problem of morality was simply a matter of will: one chose one's duty or one shirked it. And duty, in every case, involved autonomous achievement. The disciplined pursuit of individual self-interest was a moral imperative; prosperity was dependent on virtue.[27]

With their views summarized baldly, these moral philosophers sound like moral idiots. They were not. They were sincere moralists who were desperately trying to reconcile traditional Christian ethics with the corrosive individualism of an expanding market society. Seeking to vindicate an ethos of autonomous achievement, they preached the war of the individual against his baser nature, not a Hobbesian war of all against all. Even into the late nineteenth century academic moral philosophy continued to provide ethical ballast for a capitalism pledged to economic growth and material progress.

But during the second half of the nineteenth century, many educated Americans began to look toward more dynamic, more self-consciously "modern" sanctions for autonomous achievement in a liberal society. Though common-sense idealism persisted even in the precincts of early social science, a number of social scientists, journalists, and even clergymen became progressively intrigued by an outlook which can loosely be labelled "positivism." I am not concerned here with the social positivism of Auguste Comte nor with the logical positivism of twentieth century analytical philosophers. The positivism in question was less a systematic philosophy than a cultural tendency, a habit of mind shared by educated Americans and Europeans alike and persisting from the nineteenth century to our own time.

At bottom, this diffuse positivism involved a belief that the entire universe—including all human life—was governed by deterministic laws discoverable only through scientific inquiry. Science, in other words, was a kind of Easter-egg hunt; once the eggs were gathered the game would be over: the laws governing the universe would be fully known. Despite the deterministic implications of this positivist "block universe," many educated Americans found it not a depressing but an exhilarating prospect. In the dominant view the advance of positivist science presented no threat to familiar religious beliefs or moral choices; on the contrary, science underwrote Protestant Christianity at every turn.

The credit for the accommodation belongs to the British positivist Herbert Spencer, whose works were widely popularized in the United States. Joining his liberal individualism to his belief in scientific law, Spencer grafted his whole system of thought onto an evolutionary framework. The law of evolution, he believed, explained the transformations at work in every state of being—social as well as biological. All of life was evolving from a state of primitive homogeneity to complex heterogeneity. The process was inexorable and beneficent; its widest-ranging social result was the shift from a warlike or militant stage of development to a pacific industrial stage, from the isolated clan or tribe to the interdependent market societies of Great Britain and the United States. As society became more complex, older conflicts slipped away; social sympathy played a larger role in securing group security which in turn guaranteed the well-being of each individual. In heterogenous societies, egoism and altruism were no longer at odds; in fact, they complemented one another. The pursuit of individual self-interest led not to Hobbesian chaos but to Spencerian harmony as militant conflict gave way to industrial peace.[28]

It ought to be clear from this brief summary that Spencer was no "social Darwinist," as many historians have claimed. He had a great deal of trouble fitting Darwinian notions of struggle and arbitrary brutality into his orderly, progressive scheme. Instead of systematically appropriating Darwin, Spencer drew eclectically on a variety of evolutionary ideas to buttress his essential vision: a lawful cosmos evolving inexorably toward Something Better. Contrary to his critics' charges, Spencer did not write apologetics for laissez-faire capitalism; he provided a social-scientific sanction for the popular tendency to link material and moral progress.[29]

Despite Spencer's agnosticism, he presented no threat to dominant religious beliefs. Wedded to a positivist world view, he did not deny God; he denied the possibility of ever knowing God's existence. In place of Providence, Spencer posed an Unknowable power manifesting itself in the unfolding process of evolution. It was only a short step to a sort of cosmic optimism. From his Olympian vantage atop the evolutionary process, Spencer could dismiss the suffering and death of individuals as unimportant, the necessary friction on the high road of progress. This evolutionary optimism pervaded Anglo-American thinking during the second half of the nineteenth century. As one of Spencer's critics wrote in 1882, "the philosophers of the ultra-evolutionary school put out of sight, in the scientific sweep of their social theories, two commonplace facts—individuality and death." While the philosophers of the Enlightenment hoped death might be abolished, "those of the present appear to think that, if we will all be quiet and refrain from ill-omened words, it may be hushed up."[30]

Spencer's hushing up of death, his evasion of conflict and tragedy in the name of perpetual progress, accounted for his appeal to the educated bourgeoisie in the United States. Popularized by Edward L. Youmans of the *Popular Science Monthly* and the corpulent cosmic optimist John Fiske, Spencerian phrases decorated banquet oratory and editorial pronouncements throughout the later nineteenth century. Ignoring the darker, deterministic implications of Spencer's thought, Americans embraced his concept of a transition from militant violence to industrial peace and his insistence that the "heterogenous" societies produced by modern capitalism were models of altruistic harmony. Spencer appealed, not because he addressed the issue of social conflict but because he evaded it. Hobbesian (or Darwinian) views of life as a struggle dissolved in the broth of evolutionary optimism.[31]

Spencerian optimism has by no means disappeared from contemporary social theory. Spencer's intellectual descendents can be found among the social scientists engaged in the current revival of evolutionary thinking, for whom all class conflict and cultural dislocation in "developing" countries is obscured by the magic of "modernization." Yet this sort of evasiveness lacks the broad appeal it once had. Persistent as it is, Spencer's evolutionary optimism had a special resonance in the aggressively entrepreneurial culture of the late-nineteenth-century United States.

This was clear on the evening of November 9, 1882, when Youmans held a banquet in Spencer's honor at Delmonico's. The audience was a distinguished group of clergymen, lawyers, physicians, businessmen, and bankers; it included such luminaries as Henry Ward Beecher and Andrew Carnegie; it constituted, in effect, the honor roll of the educated bourgeoisie. After the Mumm's Dry and the Roederer Imperial, a series of speakers paid homage to the British philosopher. None revealed much knowledge of his system in its details; none referred to it as a sanction for Darwinian struggle in the business world; most praised Spencer in general terms as "benevolent," "serious," and "reverent." As the former Secretary of State William M. Evarts said approvingly, Spencer's system "treats evil not as eternal, but as evanescent, and it expects to evolve at what is sought through faith in the millennium—that condition of affairs in which there is the highest morality and the greatest happiness."[32]

To most Americans, Spencerian positivism was not a bleak necessitarianism but a secular religion of progress, a social scientific version of the optimistic, liberal Protestantism which pervaded the educated bourgeoisie. Spencer's American disciples sought consciously to join evolutionary positivism and Protestant Christianity; this effort appeared earliest in Fiske's *Outlines of Cosmic Philosophy* (1874). Writing to his mother on the eve of its publication, Fiske made clear that there was no tension between his own evolutionary optimism and her religious beliefs: "If I were to say that my chief comfort in affliction would be the recognition that there is a Supreme Power manifested in the totality of phenomena, the workings of which are not like the workings of intelligence but far beyond and above them, and which are obviously tending to some grand and worthy result, even though my individual happiness gets crushed in the process . . . you would probably reply, 'why this is Christianity.' Well, so it is, I think."[33]

The marriage of positivism and Christianity, proposed by popularizers like Fiske, was consummated in the writings of American theologians.

Beecher made the connection explicit in *Evolution and Christianity* (1884) but even those liberal Protestants who never mentioned Spencer genuflected before the altar of progressive optimism. Discarding Calvinistic severity, they formulated a Christ-centered evolutionary creed which married spiritual to material progress and preached universal salvation. Ministers like Beecher, Lyman Abbott (editor of the *Christian Union*), and Phillips Brooks (Episcopal bishop of Massachusetts and rector of Boston's Trinity Church) as well as secular moralists like Fiske blunted all the sharp edges in Protestant tradition and produced a bland religion of reassurance. God, as Brooks wrote, was no longer "fitful omnipotence" but "essential law," immanent and unfolding in Nature. "Conversion is not something strange and unnatural. To be the new man in Christ Jesus is merely to be more fully and thoroughly a man."[34] Nor were miracles any longer to be considered violations of natural law, cataclysmic interventions by an arbitrary Monarch. Rather, they were present in the most ordinary events of each day. In Emerson's "Divinity School Address," that view had seemed radical; forty years later it had become a liberal commonplace. A poem in the *Christian Union* in 1882 summarized the emergent view of "progressive orthodoxy,"

> We need not wait for thunder peal
> Resounding from a mount of fire
> While round our daily paths we feel
> Thy sweet love and Thy power to heal
> Working in us Thy full desire.[35]

Confronted by the challenges of positivist science, liberal Protestants sought to exorcise the last vestiges of shadow and magic from their creeds, to create a clean, well-lighted place where religion and rationalist optimism could coexist in harmony. The triumph of what was called "modernism" in theological circles signalled the submergence of religion in secular modes of thought. Liberal Protestantism lost much of its power as an independent source of moral authority and became a handmaiden of the positivist world view.

A sentimental, optimistic religiosity conformed to the common pattern of evasion pervading the dominant culture. In the inspirational literature of liberal Protestantism, all conflicts were resolved, all tensions relaxed—even the tension between life and death. Elizabeth Stuart Phelps's popular religious novel *The Gates Ajar* (1868) presented the afterlife as the fulfillment of the domestic ideal. Aunt Winifred, the voice of wisdom in the novel, predicts that her hair will no longer be gray in heaven, that her niece Mary will have her favorite cookies to eat and a piano to play, and that heaven will look (at least to Winifred) like Kansas (her favorite state).[36] The modern euphemistic approach to death, by now a staple of our popular culture, was already well-established among the educated bourgeoisie of

the late nineteenth century. And from the outset its effects were perni-
cious. By scaling down the afterlife to domestic proportions, moralists like
Phelps denied death and trivialized life. Their self-deceptions and evasions
stamped many liberal Protestants as of a piece with ideologues of domesticity, genteel literati, success mythologists, and Spencerian positivists—by
denying personal and social conflict, all promoted a vision of progress and
harmony that sanctioned status quo social arrangements. Embracing official doctrines for a wide variety of personal reasons, they unwittingly
reinforced the cultural dominance of their own class, the educated bourgeoisie.

The hegemonic role of liberal Protestantism could be seen most clearly
in the churches' growing absorption by business culture. A rapprochement
between business and urban Protestantism had become apparent as early
as the great Revival of 1857–1858, which had revealed that Protestantism
had begun to compete with commercial civilization on the latter's terms.
With businessmen in charge, revival meetings had been scheduled to coin-
cide with lunch hours; lay leaders ensured efficiency by limiting speakers
to five minutes and prohibiting denominational controversy. Ancient tensions between piety and profit were beginning to relax. By the late nineteenth century, business values permeated the pulpit itself. "Indeed, so far
has the church caught the spirit of the age," Rollo Ogden observed in the
*Nation* in 1886, "so far has it become a business enterprise, that the chief
test of ministerial success is now the ability to 'build up' a church. Executive, managerial abilities are now more in demand than those which used
to be considered the highest in a clergyman."[37]

Protestant pastors, catering to their affluent flocks, dismissed the complaints of the underpaid and jobless. Brooks reassured his congregation
that in America "excessive poverty, actual suffering for the necessities of
life, terrible as it is, is comparatively rare." Beecher was more specific. It
was not that striking railroad workers were poor, he announced in 1877,
but that they refused to live within their means.

> It is said that a dollar a day is not enough for a wife and five or six children. No,
> not if the man smokes or drinks beer. It is not enough if they would live as he
> would be glad to have them live. It is not enough to enable them to live as
> perhaps they would have a right to live in prosperous times. But is not a dollar
> a day enough to buy bread with? Water costs nothing; and a man who cannot
> live on bread is not fit to live.[38]

For his own congregation, Beecher had different advice. He enlarged
upon "The Moral Uses of Luxury and Beauty," discouraged fasting except
for hygienic reasons, and praised Lent as a "social vacation" for too-
hurried society ladies. Beecher's enthusiasm for upper-class pleasures reflected a more general tendency among urban ministers and their flocks.
Numerous observers noted that churchgoing had become little more than

a social event, an occasion to see and be seen. As a *Christian Union* contributor put it, "people are looking at each other and not at Christ, and they want the spice of worldly life introduced into the churches."[39] In many urban congregations, the critical distance between God and Mammon—maintained with some difficulty by earlier Protestants—had disappeared altogether.

The accommodation between religion and wealth was never complete; nor was it unprecedented. Many ministers refused to issue apologetics for social display and material consumption; some actively protested such practices. And in any case, religions have often been enmeshed in the dominant mores of their historical situation. What was different this time was that the emerging ethic of an expanding commercial society was less a framework for values than a means of doing without them. However diluted with progressive bromides, liberal individualism remained a betrayal of traditional Christianity.

Liberal Protestantism, like other official doctrines of nineteenth-century America, came to terms with modernity by denying its darker side. The specter of class conflict, the pain of passions thwarted, the spiritual sterility of the positivist world view—all were overlooked on the highroad of progress. The pattern of evasive banality pervaded the modern outlook from the "feminine" sentimentality of genteel literature and the domestic ideal to the "masculine" progressivism of liberal economics and Spencerian social science. While the growth of industrial capitalism created a society torn by social and psychic conflict, the modern view evaded conflict at every turn.

Historians have long castigated Gilded Age culture for its failure to grapple with the realities of a raw, new industrial society; in actuality that "failure" served an important social purpose.[40] By denying the dilemmas posed by modernization, the official doctrines provided both a source of escape from unprecedented conflict and a means of legitimizing continued capitalist development in a liberal polity. In the official doctrines of our own time, the same bland reassurances serve the same social purpose: they legitimize the hegemony of capitalist proprietors and managers. But the reassurances are cast in a new moral and cultural mold. According to the conventional wisdom, we have thrown aside the cumbersome mental furniture of our Victorian ancestors and liberated ourselves from the burden of our puritan past: a cultural "revolution" has taken place. The problem with this view is that the "revolution" has done little or nothing to alter the structure of social relations. Despite momentous changes in manners and morals, wealth and power remain in the hands of a few. Everything has changed, yet nothing has changed.

The key to this anomalous situation lies in the late nineteenth century, when modern culture began to show signs of strain, cracks in the surface of official optimism. Among educated Americans there was a growing sense of dis-ease, a barely articulated feeling that denial and evasion were inadequate strategies for containing the unprecedented social and psychic conflict in the emerging industrial society. It was not so much that late Victorians reacted consciously against modern culture as that they began half-consciously to perceive its limitations and contradictions, its failure to live up to its claims of perpetual progress and perfect autonomy. Ultimately that critical perception helped to generate a crisis of cultural authority, rooted in the social and psychic turmoil of the late nineteenth century.

The social dimensions of the crisis were the clearest. By the early 1880s, it became apparent that the evasive banality of modern culture might no longer be adequate to maintain social order. The technical rationality of industrial capitalism was *merely* technical; the irrationalities of the business cycle continued to generate mass unemployment and heightening class conflict. As upper-class orators denounced labor unrest and fretted publicly about "impending revolution," their audiences began to rethink official optimism and resurrect an alternative cultural tradition: the darker strain of Puritan and republican moralism. Subterranean but strong even at the apex of mid-Victorian optimism, the republican tradition allowed troubled Americans to make moral sense of the social conflicts bred by industrial capitalism. From the republican vantage, historical development was not linear but cyclical; material progress contained the seeds of moral decline. Every paean to economic growth evoked, in many minds, the old republican fears of overcivilization.

# A Social Crisis:
# The Republican Tradition and
# the Radical Specter

American ambivalence toward material progress dated from earliest Puritan times. Puritan divines urged diligence and frugality, then fretted over the prosperity resulting from those habits. Wealth was a sign of God's blessing but also an agent of corruption. Freed from adversity, men inevitably sank into slothful ease. Economic success contained the seeds of moral failure. As the historian Edmund Morgan has observed, "it was [the Puritans'] lot to be forever improving the world, in full knowledge that every improvement would in the end prove illusory."[41]

Morgan has shown the vitality of the Puritan ethic in the Revolutionary era, when republican ideologues had begun to enjoin diligence and frugality for political as well as religious reasons. English Whigs had taught their

American counterparts that every republic had been destroyed by success. Whig historiography established a common pattern: the flourishing of trading centers inevitably bred an irresponsible leisure class and a vicious urban mob; the martial virtues declined among the elite, which soon established a hireling standing army; finally, demagogues led the populace on a chaotic crusade against their erstwhile leaders.[42]

American republicans were determined to avoid such a fate. They inveighed tirelessly against urban corruption; they imagined effeminate fops on street corners, potential *canaille* in public squares. Suspicious of wealth but impressed by the ability to acquire it, they urged men of property to cultivate sober responsibility and public duty. With the success of the Revolution, such fears slackened. Post-Revolutionary orators hailed the United States as "Nature's Nation," a land of fresh starts and pure hopes, unsullied by old Europe's dark past.[43]

Yet a nagging anxiety persisted: European corruption might yet be imported; America might yet follow the example of earlier, failed republics. Republican moralizing remained a major tradition in American cultural criticism throughout the nineteenth century, widely disseminated in school curricula. Whig history was embodied in elementary and advanced texts, republican principles in McGuffey readers and college moral philosophy courses. For generations, in classrooms at all levels, republicanism continued to temper the official creed of progress. The Mugwumps received much the same instruction as their grandfathers.[44]

It was not surprising, then, that many late-nineteenth-century critics of overcivilization stood squarely within the republican tradition. Its rhetoric united such diverse figures as the patrician art historian Charles Eliot Norton and the mystical democrat Walt Whitman. As early as 1856, Norton worried whether America would follow the path of Renaissance Italy: "she had lost the capacity for moral suffering, and she sought relief from harass in self-forgetfulness among the delights of sensual enjoyment." Surveying the post–Civil War cultural landscape in *Democratic Vistas* (1871), Whitman found only "numerous congeries of conventional, over-corpulent societies, already become stifled and rotten with flatulent, infidelistic literature, and polite conformity and art."[45] The problem with American culture, Whitman insisted, was that it was too dandified, too European. Theodore Roosevelt echoed that complaint almost twenty-five years later. Throughout the last two decades of the nineteenth century, critics warned against the effects of European luxury and fashion on national character. They agreed that Americans, whether artists or ordinary citizens, should not be ashamed of their provincialism but should wear it proudly as an emblem of their freedom from aristocratic foppishness. Despite such exhortations, fears persisted that America would repeat the classical republican pattern. As George Frederic Parsons of the *New York Tribune* mused in 1887: "Poverty, thrift, prosperity, wealth, luxury, corruptness, degradation: in these seven words the fate of many great empires is told. No nation following in that track has escaped the common destiny. Shall we?"[46]

Though Parsons's worries recalled those of John Adams, a century of industrial transformation separated the two men. By the 1880s urban landscapes blotted out pastureland from the Atlantic to the Great Lakes. The folkways of the countryside began to succumb to the standardized "chromo civilization" of the city. And the city was the republicans' *bête noire;* it offered no fertile ground for the growth of righteous leaders. In republican mythology, the virtuous husbandman had long been counterposed to the corrupt cosmopolitan, but as rural populations declined, urban writers increasingly idealized farm life. A host of "local color" writers imagined republican virtue in a wide variety of preindustrial communities. In 1888 a pathologist writing in the *North American Review* summarized the conventional wisdom: "Once let the human race be cut off from personal contact with the soil, once let the conventionalities and artificial restrictions of so-called civilization interfere with the healthful simplicity of nature, and decay is certain."[47]

Concern about urban luxury was intensified by embryonic but momentous changes in the economy. As the leaders of organized capitalism solved the problems of mass production by adopting technical innovations, they began to face new problems of marketing and distribution. For many the central question became: how could one persuade people to consume the articles now being mass produced? (The example of the tobacco magnate James B. Duke is illustrative. In 1882 he adopted the Bonsack machine for mechanically rolling cigarettes; within two years he had saturated the market and moved from North Carolina to New York, where he concentrated his attention on marketing, distributing, and advertising cigarettes rather than producing them.) Major enterprises began to place heavier emphasis on advertising consumer goods for an expanding urban market. As the economy started slowly to shift from a producer to a consumer orientation, the urban bourgeoisie were encouraged to place an even higher premium on purchasing material comfort and convenience—or "luxury" from the old republican view. Thorstein Veblen's famous satire of "conspicuous consumption" in *The Theory of the Leisure Class* (1899) was rooted in part in republican outrage over sybaritic waste among an overcivilized elite.[48]

Most critics of overcivilization were more overtly moralistic than Veblen and more worried about social disorder. They feared urban comfort as a source of both bodily and spiritual enervation, and their fears were reinforced by intersecting racial and class anxieties. Worry about an irresponsible elite's destruction by an unleashed rabble, always a component of republican tradition, intensified in the face of unprecedented labor unrest, waves of strange new immigrants, and glittering industrial fortunes. An overcivilized bourgeoisie was vulnerable to "race suicide" on the one hand, revolutionary overthrow on the other.

The mingling of race and class fears emerged most clearly in the hysterical response to the explosion during an anarchists' assembly at Haymarket Square, Chicago, in 1886, when a policeman was killed and six other persons wounded. "The enemy forces are not American [but] rag-tag and bob-tail cutthroats of Beelzebub from the Rhine, the Danube, the Vistula and the Elbe," a typical editorial trumpeted. Another advised that "if the master race of this continent is subordinated to or overrun with the communistic and revolutionary races, it will be in grave danger of social disaster." Surveying the class strife of 1886, which included not only Haymarket but also numerous clashes between strikers and police, the Reverend Theodore T. Munger concluded: "This horrible tyranny is wholly of foreign origin."[49]

That conclusion offered cold comfort, even to Anglo-Saxon chauvinists. The radical specter, whether imported or domestic, continued to haunt the bourgeois imagination throughout the late nineteenth century. As early as 1877, striking workers burned millions of dollars worth of B. & O. and Pennsylvania Railroad property in cities from Philadelphia to Chicago; federal and state militia killed scores of people in retaliation. During the next several decades, periodic social upheavals kept bourgeois hysteria at white heat: the Haymarket Affair and the giant Knights of Labor strike in 1886, the violent class confrontations at Homestead in 1892 and Pullman in 1894, the assassination of President McKinley by a self-proclaimed anarchist in 1901—these were only the best-publicized incidents. To frightened men of property, even William Jennings Bryan seemed an "agrarian revolutionist."[50]

If such language was hyperbolic, it is nevertheless important to stress the extent to which social disorder actually existed in the second half of the nineteenth century. Americans had always been a restless people, but never before had so many crowded in polyglot cities, or attached themselves to class-oriented social movements like populism, trade unionism, socialism. However entangled with bourgeois aspirations, such movements presented frightening spectacles to the middle and upper classes: torchlit mass meetings, fire-breathing denunciations of economic injustice, bloody battles between policemen and civilians. In the speed with which labor organizations grouped, disbanded, and regrouped elsewhere, one can see the impact of a rootless proletariat, wandering over entire regions in search of work. That floating population, as demographic historians have recently shown, constituted a huge proportion of the nineteenth-century work force.[51] The long depression, lasting with only a few letups from 1873 until the late 1890s, further swelled the ranks of transient jobless. It was during this period that "the tramp problem" was first discussed by social commentators; the light-hearted hobo of Hollywood folklore was drawn from life, but his actual model was most likely grimmer.[52]

Much of this ferment has received ample attention from political and social historians, but it has not been clearly connected to the contemporaneous cultural crisis. That connection illuminates the largest significance of late-nineteenth-century social disorder. Class warfare seemed particularly threatening to settled urban elites preoccupied by their own physical and moral decay.

Evidence for physical decay was largely impressionistic. The increase of sobriety, applauded by the *Nation,* seemed to other observers a cause for concern; they felt that the disappearance of the legendary "two-bottle man" suggested a decline of physical stamina among the urban bourgeoisie. Numerous critics pointed to the increase of pallor and flab among citydwellers, whose occupations "do almost nothing to make one sturdy and enduring. . . ." Nor was recreation any help. As William Blaikie, a New York lawyer and former Harvard crew hero, told *Harper's Monthly* readers, "about all our play is mental or emotional, adding hardly anything to bodily vigor." It was a common view that urban artifice and mechanical convenience had transformed the apple-cheeked farm boy into the sallow "industrial man."[53]

Such impressions were strengthened by more precise evidence: a declining birthrate among old-stock Americans. Respected statisticians like Francis A. Walker and Frederick L. Hoffmann warned that decadent Anglo-Saxons were being replaced by inferior immigrant stock. The increasing authority of scientific racism buttressed arguments for immigration restriction. Drawing on Walker, Gustave Le Bon, and other racial theorists, restrictionists like Henry Cabot Lodge insisted that the newer Latin and Slavic immigrants, unlike their Nordic predecessors, were biologically inassimilable to American life. Lodge's views gained wide support as the century drew to a close, but the most influential critic of overcivilization in the context of immigration was Theodore Roosevelt. Though he rarely sniped at immigrants, Roosevelt interpreted Walker's thesis as a warning that Anglo-Saxons were on the road to "race suicide." The phrase was widely incanted by cultural critics; Roosevelt used it as a stick with which to chastise birth control advocates and exhort the Better Sort to greater fecundity.[54]

Among the overcivilized, critics charged, moral as well as muscular fiber had softened. In the familiar cycle, the industrious had been corrupted by the fruits of their own success; wealth brought flaccidity and self-indulgence. Noticing the mutation of Puritan villages into luxurious resorts, cultural critics flayed a nascent leisure class well before Veblen's satire appeared. The disappearance of Spartan public spirit among the elite became a journalistic commonplace. Dr. James Weir's 1894 comment on the social effects of such degeneration was typical: "The rich become effeminate, weak, and immoral, and the lower classes, taking advantage of this moral lassitude, and led on by their savage inclinations, undertake strikes, mobs, boycotts and riots." Hope, he concluded, lay in the sober, native-born middle class, not yet corrupted by prosperity.[55]

Even many well-intentioned respectables, others felt, were hampered by reluctance to dirty their hands in practical politics. In the *Atlantic,* the lawyer Henry Childs Merwin scolded mugwumps for "being civilized too much": their effete intellectualism had cost them any influence with the multitude. To the *Century,* a more serious result of elite fastidiousness was the undermining of law enforcement. While "the vicious and disorderly classes . . . constitute a positive, aggressive, implacable element in our politics," an editor wrote in 1883, "the intelligent, virtuous, and well to do citizens are not at all aggressive. Some are too busy, and some too fastidious, to take any active interest in the administration of justice." As a result, laws approved by "the class that ought to rule" went unenforced.[56]

Yet as labor troubles continued, increasing numbers of affluent citizens grew determined to fight. They armed themselves and their police as never before. President Charles W. Eliot of Harvard pointed the way when he began drilling the Harvard riflemen in 1877, to defend propertied New Englanders against the eastward spread of rioting workers. Concerned community leaders banded into a number of vigilante "Law and Order Leagues" during the 1880s. By the end of that decade, massive armories brooded at the center of every American city—testimony to the official fears of domestic insurrection. Amid such precautions, warnings against the dark designs of labor leaders and anarchist assassins proliferated in the established press, and expectations of apocalyptic class warfare pervaded both fiction and journalism. The publisher Henry Holt employed a dominant image when he wrote in 1895 that "the large majority of intellectual people . . . are peacefully sitting reading physical science and the classics, on a crust covering a mephitic chasm or, as many think, a volcano."[57]

The Volcano under the City embodied the social sources of the crisis of cultural authority. Concern about overcivilization was heightened by ethnic and class antinomies, impossible to ignore, in the emerging industrial society. Earlier republican moralists, though they expressed concern about restive lower orders, had never faced such widespread evidence of lower-class discontent. Even by the 1890s, when urban elites were extraordinarily well organized and prepared to meet any disturbance, working-class discontent still seemed volcanic in its white-hot explosiveness— unpredictable and unmanageable. Despite all ruling-class precautions the forces of social chaos smoldered; modern culture seemed unable to contain them.

Yet many problems involved in this crisis of cultural authority were even less manageable than the threat posed by the Volcano under the City. Threats came from aboveground as well—not merely the familiar urban danger of physical and moral decay but a subtler menace, unknown to earlier moralists. The spread of technical rationality bred more than social chaos; it also produced spiritual and cultural confusion. In an emerging national market dominated by bureaucratic corporations, the bourgeois ideal of the independent self seemed barely tenable. As new theories in sociology and psychology gave scientific sanction to the notion of an over-civilized, diminished human personality, the bourgeois vision of individual autonomy began to seem sharply circumscribed. And if autonomy was circumscribed, personal moral responsibility was undermined as well. Familiar ideas of character and will were shaken by the triumph of organized capitalism.

These difficulties were exacerbated by religious changes. As Calvinism softened into platitudinous humanism, Protestant Christianity lost the gravity provided by older, sterner creeds. Lacking spiritual ballast, bourgeois culture entered what Nietzsche had called a "weightless" period, marked by hazy moral distinctions and vague spiritual commitments. Gradually personal identity itself came to seem problematic. Part of the difficulty was that individual will and action were hemmed in by the emerging iron cage of a bureaucratic market economy. But the trouble ran deeper: the rationalization of urban culture and the decline of religion into sentimental religiosity further undermined a solid sense of self. For many, individual identities began to seem fragmented, diffuse, perhaps even unreal. A weightless culture of material comfort and spiritual blandness was breeding weightless persons who longed for intense experience to give some definition, some distinct outline and substance to their vaporous lives.

This sense of unreality has become part of the hidden agenda of modernization. Throughout the twentieth century, a recoil from the artificial, overcivilized qualities of modern existence has sparked a wide variety of quests for more intense experience, ranging from the fascist fascination with violence and death, to the cults of emotional spontaneity of avant-garde artists to popular therapies stressing instinctual liberation. Antimodern impulses, too, were rooted in longings to recapture an elusive "real life" in a culture evaporating into unreality.

# Unreal City: Social Science, Secularization, and the Emergence of Weightlessness

During the second half of the nineteenth century, the city became an emblem of modern unreality. From Baudelaire's "Swarming city, city full of dreams/ where the spectre in broad daylight accosts the passerby" to Eliot's "Unreal City" where crowds of people shuffle to work "under the brown fog of a winter dawn," the most sensitive observers imagined the modern city as the breeding ground of a vapid, anonymous existence—a death-in-life.[58] Yet the perception of urban culture's unreality was not simply the property of isolated literati. In various forms, that perception was shared by the educated bourgeoisie on both sides of the Atlantic; it was rooted in sweeping social changes which affected ordinary people as well as poets of genius.

The most obvious of these changes was the transformation of the visual environment. It was not just that the cityscape had isolated late-nineteenth-century Americans from the old-shoe "reality" of the rural landscape, but that familiar architectural and decorative forms had dissolved in a riot of eclecticism. As early as the 1850s, at least among the urban bourgeoisie, the simple and straightforward designs of the colonial period had been swept away by waves of imitative "revivals": Greek, Gothic, Tuscan, even Egyptian. In the post–Civil War American city, eclectic ornament bedecked nearly everything in sight, from public buildings to the most ordinary objects in private households. There were Egyptian gateways on Protestant cemeteries, Greek gods on teapots, Gothic facades on railway stations. The late-nineteenth-century citydweller was confronted by a new and bewilderingly various visual environment.

It is difficult but not impossible to speculate on the larger cultural significance of eclecticism in the visual arts. While a few historians have seen this jumble of pseudohistorical styles as a sign of American energy and exuberance, I suggest that it was energy which often lacked a controlling purpose and which embodied the cultural confusion of men who no longer possessed a coherent vocabulary of symbols. Eclecticism was both a symptom and a source of the process Siegfried Giedion has called "the devaluation of symbols"; it both reflected and reinforced feelings of diffuseness and disorientation.[59] Reaching for the legitimacy conferred by traditional symbols (and celebrating their vitality), eclectic designers unwittingly undermined the power of these earlier forms. Uprooting once-sacred symbols from their appropriate time, place, and purpose, the eclectic approach trivialized them—reduced them to commodities in the marketplace of taste. Eclecticism signified the impoverishment of a culture which lacked resources for creating its own symbols. The grab bag of symbolic forms had a profound (though perhaps largely unconscious) impact on the minds of Americans. It intensified the feeling, peculiarly resonant in republican America, that the urban environment was somehow artificial and unreal.

While the devaluation of symbols affected perceptions of the external environment, other related processes were undermining the individual's sense of selfhood; inner as well as outer landscapes seemed increasingly ghostlike. Both Baudelaire and Eliot caught the spectral quality of urban existence; by the later nineteenth century many lesser minds had also come to sense it. Not only the modern city but also its inhabitants seemed unreal. The reasons for these perceptions are extraordinarily diverse and complex. Let us begin with the most mundane, the everyday workings of an urban market society.

The growth of American cities was inextricably entwined with the growth of a national market economy. For most Americans, urban living increasingly meant entanglement in the web of the market. As market relations spread, they undermined individual autonomy and promoted social interdependence. Ordinary people's livelihood depended increasingly on decisions made in distant cities, on circumstances largely beyond the individual's control. The increasing specialization of labor in factories and bureaucracies reinforced the tendency toward interdependence; people in ever narrower occupational specialties grew more dependent on others to supply their basic needs. As the sociologist Edward A. Ross exclaimed in 1905, "Under our present manner of living, how many of my vital interests must I entrust to others! Nowadays the water main is my well, the trolly car my carriage, the banker's safe my old stocking, the policeman's billy my fist."[60]

Before sociologists like Ross grasped the impact of interdependence on selfhood, other Americans had begun to sense it. While the dominant perception of the interdependent urban market was that man had broken loose from preindustrial isolation and poverty, there was a paradoxical underside to official optimism: a sense that individual causal potency had diminished, a growing doubt that one could decisively influence one's personal destiny. And this perception promoted another: the dawning recognition that social interdependence had fatally weakened individual autonomy. In the emerging social system, the autonomous self seemed no longer Promethean but fragmented, defined according to the needs and demands of others. By the turn of the century, more than a few Americans had begun openly to declare that independent selfhood was an illusion.

The assertion struck at the heart of the liberal creed. Liberalism was being outstripped by the events it had helped to generate. The urban-industrial transformation, stemming from faith in individual autonomy, was undermining that faith at the moment of its triumph. As autonomous selfhood seemed increasingly troublesome, classical liberalism offered a less than adequate account of human action. One of Emerson's aphorisms summarized the dilemma of nineteenth-century Economic Man. "Every spirit makes its own house," he wrote, "but afterwards the house confines the spirit."[61]

Doubters glimpsed an interdependent mass society in which exceptional talent was hemmed in by mediocrity and even simple independence seemed an outmoded ideal. It was time to admit that individual character, even the greatest, was not self-created, wrote Louise Imogen Guiney, a Boston poet, in 1897. Rather, "we are the poor relations of every conceivable circumstance." Charles Eliot Norton, among others, believed it had not always been so: autonomy had been greater in preindustrial times. As he put it, "the man of to-day is less independent than the Greek; he cannot get along alone, he is more helpless by himself with every advance of our complicate civilization." The assumption that earlier folk could control their own destinies was curious but often unquestioned.[62]

To combat such pangs of insecurity and helplessness, middle- and upper-class citydwellers made psychic adjustments to economic and social interdependence. New tendencies in metropolitan character began to appear, and formed the kernel of some new notions about selfhood. Individual character began to seem neither so permanent nor so unified as liberal theory held. Among educated Americans, the idea of a divided or discontinuous self gained currency. To some observers, modern man seemed to lack any irreducible core of individuality; selfhood consisted only in a series of manipulatable social masks.

It was around the turn of the century, David Riesman points out in *The Lonely Crowd,* that "other-directed" character traits first emerged among the educated strata in larger cities. The older, "inner-directed" character, in Riesman's scheme, clung to values implanted at a tender age by parents and Protestant ministers; inner-direction was rooted in a solid ground of selfhood which, however repressive and conformist, seemed at least firm and unchanging. According to Riesman, inner-directed morality characterized an industrializing economy not yet honeycombed with bureaucracy. The rapid bureaucratization of industry and government removed more and more individuals from direct involvement in the production process; bureaucratic jobs demanded involvement with people rather than things. Increased geographic mobility among business and professional people required them to adjust their attitudes and behavior to varying localities and social situations. A hypersensitivity to the feelings and impressions of others, an ability to shift one's psychological stance to meet the needs of specific circumstances—these other-directed traits became useful means of advancement in a mobile, bureaucratic society.[63]

It would be gross exaggeration to claim that late Victorians bore much resemblance to the glad-handing "impression managers" described by contemporary sociologists like Riesman and Erving Goffman. Yet the concept of other-direction does offer some useful insight into tendencies which were embryonic in the late nineteenth century and have become common in our own time. In particular, other-direction seems to fit the dawning awareness that there might be "no clear core of self" (in Riesman's phrase), that individual identity might be just a collection of social roles.[64]

That notion had been abroad for centuries. In his *Autobiography,* Benjamin Franklin proposed manipulation of various "selves" as a means of professional advancement. The technique became common in the relatively fluid, mobile market society of antebellum America. A dread fascination with deceit and imposture pervaded nineteenth-century American culture. Herman Melville's *The Confidence Man* (1857) was the most penetrating documentation of wheedling insincerity in a democratic, capitalist society. But in the antebellum era, despite widespread fears of confidence men, only deep-dyed dissenters like Melville could doubt the existence of a "simple, genuine self" beneath the layers of convention.[65]

It was only toward the end of the nineteenth century that a thoroughly discontinuous self was discussed. In *The Portrait of a Lady* (1881), Henry James implicitly connected the phenomenon with the growth of a mature and complex civilization. As Madame Merle, the worldly European, tells the intelligent but somewhat provincial American, Isabel Archer:

> When you've lived as long as I you'll see that every human being has his shell and that you must take the shell into account. By the shell I mean the whole envelope of circumstances. There's no such thing as an isolated man or woman; we're each of us made up of some cluster of appurtenances. What shall we call our "self"? Where does it begin? Where does it end? It overflows into everything that belongs to us—and then it flows back again. I know a large part of myself is in the clothes I choose to wear. I've a great respect for *things!* One's self—for other people—is one's expression of one's self; and one's house, one's furniture, one's garments, the books one reads, the company one keeps—these things are all expressive.

Like a good Emersonian, Isabel disagrees. She "was fond of metaphysics, but was unable to accompany her friend into this bold analysis of the human personality."

> I don't agree with you. I think just the other way. I don't know whether I succeed in expressing myself, but I know that nothing else expresses me. Nothing that belongs to me is any measure of me; everything's on the contrary a limit, a barrier, and a perfectly arbitrary one. Certainly the clothes which, as you say, I choose to wear, don't express me; and heaven forbid they should![66]

As American society became more urban, more "European," increasing numbers of Isabel's countrymen were willing to side with Madame Merle. In 1886, an *Atlantic* writer traced the feeling of discontinuity to the increasing mobility of a cosmopolitan civilization.

> No doubt there are lives that do go on with apparently unbroken coherence—tranquil, native, or village lives, whose sun always rises over the same horizon, and whose radii of interests, from year to year, go out to the same unchanged circumference. Here the constantly overlapping continuity of the neighborhood existence helps to keep a man's own thread of personality unbroken. But when we once cut loose from geography, make friends and break with friends, become the very opposite of "Bourbons" in that we are always "learning" and always "forgetting," then how far backward over our days can the uninterrupted "I" be said to extend?

"In truth," he concluded, "this whole matter of the individual identity—the I-ness of the I—is thick with difficult questions."[67]

Contemporary writers agreed. Identity seemed far more fragmented and problematic than earlier generations had imagined. In the success literature of the period, especially that derived from mind cure and New Thought, authors described other-directed techniques for achieving economic and psychic well-being—what Riesman calls "modes of manipulating the self in order to manipulate others."[68] Such techniques presupposed a fragmented self, defined according to the needs of the moment.

At the highest theoretical levels, too, Americans showed a fascination with social role playing. In *Principles of Psychology* (1890), William James wrote that "a man has as many social selves as there are individuals who recognize him and carry an image of him in their mind." Several years later, George Herbert Mead began to formulate a social definition of selfhood. If Mead was correct, identity was a product of interdependence, rooted in the continuing dialectic of cognition and re-cognition between self and other.[69]

The fragmentation of selfhood was rooted in the process of urbanization but also shaped by the social relations of a maturing capitalist society. In the interdependent urban marketplace, the fragmented self became a commodity like any other, to be assembled and manipulated for private gain. And as the self became commodified, it was also expressed more often through the consumption of commodities. Veblen erroneously described "conspicuous consumption" as an anachronistic cultural style confined to a predatory elite—the American equivalents of James's Madame Merle. Actually, a broad range of middle and upper class Americans (not merely a parasitic leisure class) was becoming more oriented toward consumption, their outlook affected not only by the democratization of comfort but by the increasingly sophisticated strategies of advertising.[70] In the embryonic consumer culture of the late nineteenth century, more and more Americans were being encouraged to "express themselves" (like Madame Merle) not through independent accomplishment but through the ownership of things. It was a far different and in many ways diminished sense of selfhood from that embodied in the image of the headstrong self-made man.

The notion of a newly evanescent selfhood stemmed from moral as well as social and economic sources. The tensions in bourgeois morality also intensified the growing sense of personal fragmentation and discontinuity. The contradictory expectations promoted by the domestic ideal—the sharp distinction between work and home, the rivalrous claims of autonomy and dependence—these strengthened an emerging distinction between public and private "selves." At the same time another and broader development occurred. As moralists like Kellogg pressed the rationalization of the inner life, they brought a repressive ethic of self-control to ever more intimate areas of experience. It was no accident that countertendencies set in: a return of repressed impulses to consciousness, a growing realization that selfhood was far more riven by conflict than liberal theory had acknowledged. If from without, the self began to seem fragmented into social roles, from within it seemed divided into conscious will and unconscious impulse.

As early as the 1880s, the unconscious mind had become a common topic of conversation among educated Europeans and Americans. The lay public was fascinated by hypnotic trances and multiple personalities, by any psychiatric experiment revealing a state of mind outside normal waking consciousness. By 1908, a *North American Review* contributor, citing the experiments in hypnotism performed by Boris Sidis, Pierre Janet, and Morton Prince, could assert that "the human self is a much more complex and unstable affair than has generally been supposed. . . . Indeed, the self of which a man is normally conscious is but a self within a larger self, of which he becomes aware only in moments of inspiration, exaltation, and crisis."[71]

If unconscious motives and impulses undercut traditional notions of human will and choice, hereditarian ideas further complicated the problem. During the late nineteenth century, the role of heredity began to loom larger in discussions of human personality. Influenced by the Italian criminologist Cesare Lombroso, a number of psychiatrists and social critics claimed that antisocial behavior such as alcoholism was a congenital deformity like a club foot or a harelip; the individual had not chosen depravity but inherited it.[72] Both the discovery of the unconscious and the rise of hereditarian psychiatry undermined the plausibility of the liberal Economic Man, rationally directing his life in accordance with his own self-interest.

All the new social and psychological theories had this in common: they suggested the need for profound revision in the concept of the self. By the end of the nineteenth century, the self seemed neither independent, nor unified, nor fully conscious, but rather interdependent, discontinuous, divided, and subject to the play of unconscious or inherited impulses. The older conception of the self had been the foundation of the bourgeois world view; the newer one undermined that foundation at every point. The older conception was solid, the new one insubstantial.

To be sure, the new image of the self did not invariably cause alarm. The whole pattern of evasive banality within modern culture had obscured the erosion of autonomy in the emerging industrial society, and that pattern has persisted throughout the twentieth century. Spencer, in the nineteenth-century mode, celebrated social interdependence and popularized the idea that great men were products of their environment while he clung to a faith in liberal individualism. Mead, prefiguring many present-day sociologists, used his social definition of selfhood as a Magna Charta for worldly activism. The mind-cure movement, anticipating the self-help literature of our own time, pointed hopefully to the unconscious as a reservoir of psychic strength to be drawn on in times of need. All continued to evade the conflict between the newer theories of the self and older notions of autonomy.

Yet during the late nineteenth century, the newer notions of selfhood did embody a subtle threat to familiar moral conventions: a flickering if often unstated recognition that human character was largely shaped by forces beyond conscious control. To many social scientists, determinism seemed the inevitable conclusion of their work. As the ethnologist Daniel G. Brinton wrote in the *Century* in 1898, "that master magician Nature practices no greater deception on us than when she persuades us that we are free agents." The following year another author announced that "the time is passing when a man of any education will throw his arms wildly about and say, 'I at least am no automaton. I do all that entirely of my own accord.'"[73] William James knew that such statements were the logical outgrowth of Spencerian positivism. He spent his entire career wrestling with the determinist Minotaur, because he understood what Spencer and other positivists overlooked: the ethical implications of a deterministic world view.

If people were largely creatures of social circumstances or psychological drive, then personal moral responsibility was seriously eroded. That recognition impelled James as well as numerous other Americans to resist the deterministic implications of the new social science. In 1883, for example, the *Century* noted "the close relation between what is sometimes called the 'advanced' thought of the day and the rude notions of the lowest stratum of society." In both seminar and saloon, men mouthed "a doctrine that denies free will, and makes of man only a bundle of appetites and impulses and propensities whose law is in themselves. . . ." Such a view of human nature "destroys not only religion and morality, it destroys also the foundation of education, and makes discipline a solecism."[74] A fragmented, diminished self was not simply a problem in liberal theory but a challenge to familiar sources of moral action, a threat to cultural authority with both public and private consequences.

The public consequences surfaced earliest and most clearly at the trial of President Garfield's assassin Charles J. Guiteau, in 1881. Guiteau, a shabby-genteel Illinois swindler, had become convinced that God had appointed him to "remove" Garfield in order to heal a factional dispute within the Republican party. Guiteau admitted and in fact boasted of the killing; the only possible defense his counsel could devise was based on an insanity plea.[75]

The trial became a sparring match between two bitterly rivalrous schools of psychiatry. On one side were the prosecution witnesses, led by the widely respected John Gray, superintendent of the Utica, New York, asylum. His definition of insanity was hemmed in by his belief in the vigor and omnipresence of evil. Sin, he believed, not "neuropathic weakness," caused crime. Witnesses for the defense, on the other hand, took a mechanistic, hereditarian approach to insanity. The more outspoken, men like Charles Edward Spitzka and James Kiernan, insisted that Guiteau's family history ensured his assassin's role and absolved him of all criminal responsibility.[76]

Their argument outraged not only conservative psychiatrists like Gray but also nearly all lay observers. Ministers and editorialists, warning that Spitzka's European materialism only aided "the criminal and revolutionary elements" in society, demanded an end to sentimental psychologizing and a speedy hanging. For the brash psychiatric determinists, moralists reserved a special scorn. As the *Nation* put it, "according to the experts, the penal justice of society should exist only for the occasional lapses of the class to which it owes nearly everything of value in it—the steady, soberminded, upright, industrious, and successful."[77]

Guiteau's conviction and execution brought relief to arbiters of the public conscience, and the criteria used to evaluate insanity pleas remained narrow.[78] Yet the issue of criminal responsibility has persisted. In the 1880s and 1890s (as today), editorialists continued to fantasize that materialistic scientists and hair-splitting lawyers had formed an unholy alliance to promote sentimental concern for the rights of criminals. Soon after Guiteau's death, the psychiatrist William A. Hammond attacked the resort to the insanity plea. "A man with murderous tendencies which he is unable to restrain, is as much an enemy of society as a ferocious tiger or a mad dog, and ought to be dealt with in quite as summary a manner as we deal with these animals," he asserted. Nearly twenty years later, the *Nation* concluded that the "Lesson of the Czolgosz [President McKinley's assassin] Trial" was the value of swift, sure punishment—in refreshing contrast to "our general looseness and slackness in criminal procedure [which] are undoubtedly on the increase...."[79] The embryonic spread of laws authorizing parole and indeterminate sentencing convinced many respectable Americans that criminals were released daily, beneficiaries of modern confusion over moral responsibility.

The increasingly problematic quality of moral responsibility involved more than the threat of runaway street crime. It also raised serious questions about personal ethics even for paragons of respectability. Concern for salvaging moral responsibility in a determined universe had been implicit in the romantic reaction against the "mechanical philosophy" of the eighteenth century. For most nineteenth-century Americans, academic moral philosophy had solved the problem by assertion: moral responsibility was ensured by self-interest. As Archibald Alexander, a Princeton moralist, wrote in 1852, "virtuous conduct is generally productive of pleasure and peace of mind; and immoral conduct generally a source of misery."[80] In a morally governed universe, individual duty was neither difficult to discover nor arduous to fulfill.

By the later 1800s, perceptive Americans began to find these "common sense" notions wholly inadequate. They felt they had to join the free will-determinism debate once more, not only in the philosopher's study but also in the new and more challenging arena of social science. The stakes were far more than intellectual; they involved profound psychological and moral issues. Determinism eroded the psychic center of Victorian moral character, the individual will; it left man a fragile and dependent creature, unreal by comparison to the autonomous self of liberal mythology. And there was a further difficulty as well. Educated Americans, facing dilemmas they could scarcely define, lacked the religious certainty of their grandparents. Ancestral theological armor lay in disuse, corroded by secularization.

The process of secularization exacerbated the problem of personal moral responsibility and contributed significantly to the sense of unreality underlying the crisis of cultural authority. Lately it has become fashionable —at least among Panglossian apologists for modern industrial society—to deny that any genuine "secularization" has occurred. At its most simpleminded, this point of view trivializes human experience by denying the destructive effects of historical change.[81] We need to understand the process of secularization as a cultural strain experienced by individuals in specific historical contexts. During the late nineteenth century, for educated Americans, secularization meant primarily a particular dis-ease: a sense that American Christianity had begun to lose moral intensity and that as a result, the entire culture had begun to enter what Nietzsche had called a "weightless" period. Nietzsche had seen the secularizing process as part of a larger tendency in modern culture—a general blurring of moral and cultural boundaries and loosening of emotional ties, a weakening of the conviction that certain principles, certain standards of conduct, must remain inviolable, and a loss of the gravity imparted to human experience by a supernatural framework of meaning. With the decline of Christianity, he had predicted, "it will seem for a time as though all things had become weightless."[82]

The adjective was elusive but apt. It recalled the "melting vision" of the *Communist Manifesto,* in which the inner dynamic of capitalism dissolves all stable social relations and settled convictions: "All that is solid melts into air, all that is holy is profaned. . . ." Both Marx and Nietzsche sensed the disintegrative effects of bourgeois culture—the diffusion of identity, the pervasive feeling of unreality. But while Marx tied these effects to the everyday workings of the bourgeois economy, Nietzsche looked toward the changing structure of belief.[83] His insight could be applied not only to the Protestant accommodation with bourgeois culture and the flaccid state of liberal theology but also more specifically to the individual's loss of meaning and purpose in a secularizing cosmos. From the Nietzschean perspective, secularization had both social and personal meaning.

The social meaning was the possibility of revolution. Increasingly absorbed by business culture, Protestant churches steadily lost influence over a restive urban proletariat. In the bourgeois imagination, "atheistical" anarchists plotted in secret while immigration swelled their ranks. Both anarchists and their opponents knew that a doctrine of rewards and punishments in a future life acclimated the poor to their meager lot. A weightless Protestant culture, without force or bite or broad appeal, could no longer be a bulwark of status quo economic arrangements. Religious decline threatened the rending of the social fabric.[84]

The personal meaning of secularization was more important, at least for my purposes. As the sociologist Peter Berger has argued, religion has traditionally played a key role in the social construction of reality—the process by which people construct frameworks of meaning to extract an ordered sense of reality from the blooming buzzing confusion of sense experience. As supernatural frameworks of meaning become problematic, individuals slide into anomie; the sense of a coherent universe wavers; reality seems to slip out of focus and blur into unreality. This was the most profound effect of secularization on late-nineteenth-century Americans: they sensed that familiar frameworks of meaning were evaporating; they felt doomed to spiritual homelessness.[85]

The most poignant examples of this spiritual plight were the plaints of unwilling doubters. "Oh, for one look of the blue sky, as it looked when we called it heaven!" cried James Froude in 1849, and generations echoed him. Despite the official truce between Protestantism and science, many educated persons realized that the positivistic outlook had made deep inroads on traditional Christian belief. Biblical criticism had challenged scriptural authority; Darwinian biology had shattered the "common sense" argument from design for God's existence. (I see orderly design in the universe; therefore there must be a Grand Designer.) As a result, many were left bereft of spiritual consolation. In the United States, this sort of *angst* especially afflicted those most sensitive to European currents of thought. Like Matthew Arnold, they saw the ebbing of "the sea of faith" and heard "its melancholy, long, withdrawing roar." Striking the elegiac note of "Dover Beach," they longed hopelessly to recover the lost innocence of a childhood faith.[86]

These overt religious anxieties have been much discussed by cultural historians, but there was another sort of disquiet that was subtler, more difficult to chart, and ultimately more significant for understanding the spiritual unrest in the wider culture. This was the disturbance bred by a new kind of doubt—late Victorians called it "modern doubt." Modern doubt was not openly atheistic; on the contrary it might well conform outwardly with the pious progressivism of a Beecher or a Fiske. But its effects were insidious. According to the Reverend Theodore T. Munger, writing in 1887, modern doubt "destroys the sense of reality." Questioning truth itself, it "envelops all things in its puzzle,—God, immortality, the value of life, the rewards of virtue, and the operation of conscience. It puts quicksand under every step."[87]

This uncertainty was the underside of the accommodation between Protestantism and modern culture. Subjecting religion to positivistic standards of truth, subordinating Christian stoicism to progressive optimism, liberal Protestants deprived their faith of emotional power, moral force, even of independent ontological status. It became a religion *banalisé*, its psychological impact barely distinguishable from that of modern doubt. Like modern doubt, liberal Protestantism put quicksand under every moral step. Nowhere was this clearer than in the changing Protestant views of Satan and hell.

For centuries, Christians had dreaded Satan as a monstrous, palpable Tempter, and had shuddered at hell as a tangible reality, a place of preternatural torment. Satan and his minions were virtually omnipresent; they swarmed even into such godly precincts as Massachusetts Bay, as Jonathan Mitchell warned in 1677: "New England is but Earth and not Heaven; no place on Earth is exempt from molestation by the Devil and his Instruments." The belief in witchcraft, the persistent conviction that the devil could take entire possession of an individual's personality, suggested how deeply his power was respected. While notions of witchcraft faded in the early eighteenth century, belief in a real and personal devil did not. The Black Man, the Man of Sin, persisted in sermons and schoolbooks well into the nineteenth century. Whatever form he took—from grotesque demon to unctuous manipulator—he lay always in wait, ready to challenge God for the ownership of the individual soul.[88]

For the Protestant, the outcome of that struggle was eternal and absolute. Strait was the gate to heaven, and for the unregenerate there was no purgatorial way station on the road to hell. Generations of preachers dwelled on hell's terrors. Jonathan Edwards's warnings were atypical only in their rhetorical skill.

> Do but consider how dreadful despair will be in such torment. How dismal will it be, when you are under these racking torments, to know assuredly that you shall never, never be delivered from them; to have no hope; when you shall wish that you might be turned into nothing, but shall have no hope of it; when you shall wish that you might be turned into a toad or a serpent, but shall have no hope of it. . . . The smoke of your torment shall still ascend up forever and ever; and . . . your souls, which shall have been agitated with the wrath of God all this while, yet will still exist to bear more wrath; your bodies, which shall have been burning and roasting all this while in these glowing flames, yet shall not have been consumed, but will remain to roast through an eternity yet, which will not have been at all shortened by what shall have been past.[89]

While few of Edwards's successors could match his ferocity, traditional conceptions of hell and Satan survived even among the most optimistic evangelicals. In 1836, Charles Grandison Finney could assert that "the world is divided into two great political parties; the difference between them is, that one party choose Satan as the god of this world. . . . The other party choose Jehovah for their governor. . . ." Finney's political metaphor suggested an appeal to the secular concerns of his audience, but his confident division of the world reflected the persistence of orthodox notions. Yet throughout the early and mid–nineteenth century, theologians like Friedrich Schleiermacher and Horace Bushnell had been dismantling the orthodox devil's personality and power, reducing him to a metaphor for evil. Bushnell's liberal successors not only rejected the devil but chafed at any notion of endless punishment after death. Traumatized in childhood by orthodox hellfire, they began openly to scorn the Westminster Confession's definition of hell. It was "Spiritual Barbarism," Beecher charged. The Reverend Lyman Abbott's shifting stance typified the growing liberalism. Beginning in scriptural conservatism, by the 1880s he had become deeply sympathetic to Universalist views. "The more I study my Bible," he wrote in 1882, "the more unscriptural seems to me the conception of endless sin; the nearer I come into fellowship with God my Father, my Saviour, my Comforter, the more intolerable grows the thought of it to me."[90]

By the late nineteenth century, liberal ministers had grown weary of the crabbed and joyless qualities of old-style evangelicalism; they had seen too many people scarred by the endless agonized wait for a conversion experience which never came, or by constant imaginings of imminent damnation. So they trimmed both God and the devil down to size and stressed what Brooks called "The Safety and Helpfulness of Faith," rather than its demands. As for hell, by 1898, as William Gladstone pointed out, it had been "relegated . . . to the far-off corners of the Christian mind . . . there to sleep in deep shadow as a thing needless in our enlightened and progressive age."[91]

But enlightenment had unanticipated consequences. The disappearance of hell and Satan paved the way for profound emotional change. When educated Americans began to imagine Satan as merely the personification of a shadowy Evil Principle, when they began to reject the very thought of eternal damnation, they won freedom from fear but lost possibilities for ecstasy. As heaven became less an urgent necessity than a pleasant inevitability, the intense yearning for salvation waned. To many late Victorians, the depth of emotional life seemed shallower, the contours of spiritual life softer, than ever before.

These perceptions were intensified by the softening of material conditions of life. The escape from physical pain paralleled the escape from hell: both resulted from the desire to maximize human happiness; both generated an unforeseen vexation of spirit. The unprecedented insulation from danger and discomfort reinforced the sense of educated Americans that life had become too soft, too civilized. Prophets of race suicide complained that modern women were no longer willing to suffer in childbirth and that their oversensitive husbands backed them up.[92] Other observers were more circumspect but still troubled. As a *Century* editorial pointed out in 1888, "modern civilized man is squeamish about pain to a degree which would have seemed effeminate or worse to his great-grandfather, or to the contemporary barbarian."[93] The recoil from pain, whether physical or spiritual, was a symptom of overcivilization.

To William James, the matter was more complex: the changing attitude toward pain constituted a fundamental shift in sensibility. In 1902, he marvelled that "a strange moral transformation has within the past century swept over the Western world. We no longer think that we are called upon to face physical pain with equanimity. It is not expected of a man that he should either endure it or inflict much of it, and to listen to the recitals of cases of it makes our flesh creep morally as well as physically."[94] This revulsion was a corollary of the optimistic, tolerant liberal Protestant view of human nature. It marked a significant departure—away from the fatalistic stoicism enshrined in the Jewish and Christian traditions, and toward a theology of formulized benevolence and personal well-being. For many this was cause for cheer. For others (including James), both physical and moral life began to seem suffocating in their ease, weightless in their lack of significance.

By the 1880s and 1890s, American culture's drift toward weightlessness had begun to arouse widespread concern in both conservative and liberal religious circles, and among secular commentators as well. To some, the disappearance of Satan and hell seemed to have serious consequences. It was not merely the social threat of an unchurched multitude which troubled cultural critics, but a subtler process: a general uncoiling of the springs of moral action. George Santayana, in his essay "The Poetry of Christian Dogma" (1900), pointed directly to the problem. "The Christian doctrine of rewards and punishments," he wrote, "is . . . in harmony with moral truths which a different doctrine might have obscured. The good souls that wish to fancy that everybody will be ultimately saved, subject a fable to standards appropriate to matters of fact, and thereby deprive the fable of that moral significance which is its excuse for being."[95]

Other critics, while refusing to reduce dogma to "fable," shared Santayana's view that the decline of hell undercut moral action. "What Has Become of Hell?," a *North American Review* contributor wondered in 1900, and four years later another had a disturbing reply: "the New Hell is often made so pleasant that it is liable to be chosen by bad men as a place of residence . . . like some of our reform prisons, which by unintelligent zeal in goodness, are made so comfortable and honorable as to fail of the purpose of prisons." Critics noticed the connection between the increasing reluctance of the churches to grapple with evil as a palpable, omnipresent reality and emergent theories that sin was socially determined rather than individually chosen.[96] Both liberal theology and positivistic social science seemed grave threats to personal moral responsibility. For that reason, a *Scribner's* editorial mourned "The Passing of the Devil" in 1899.

> The old doctrine was stern and terrible enough in principle, and trivial enough in some of its workings out; but it encouraged the idea that each man must bear his own burden and fight his own fight. It developed the martial virtues; it trained a race of men, austere and narrow, but so virile, so indomitable and forceful, that their impress is even yet stamped deep upon our national character. Will the new attitude do as much? The man who believes that he is tempted by a definite spirit of evil whom he may resist and ought to resist may yield, or even take sides with the tempter and sin with a high hand, and yet be of heroic mould; but what hope is there for the man who holds himself blameless because his course is shaped by a power too strong for resistance? Is there for him any possibility of brave living or genuine effort? *"Courage, tout le monde; le diable est mort!"* Is his disappearance an unmixed good?[97]

The editor's stress on the devil's role in promoting character would have seemed strange to earlier, believing Christians. To them, Satan had no such instrumental value; he was an object of dread, the chief obstacle to their salvation. But by 1899, after belief in an actual devil weakened, he was prized as a buttress of secular morality. The problem with secular humanism, from this view, was not that it was theologically mistaken, but that it failed to generate the zeal for struggle inspired by older, sterner creeds.

Other observers, less resolutely activist, attacked liberalizing tendencies from a slightly different direction. Sensing that contemporary moral issues had become indistinct and unintelligible, they traced the problem to the growth of indiscriminate toleration. They began to ask: has our vaunted tolerance become a mask for ethical indifference? The *Nation* assailed "The Open Mind" and listed "Some Blessings of Intolerance," while an *Atlantic* writer complained that "conscience has lost its strong and onpressing energy, and the sense of personality lacks sharpness of edge." Among the educated, spiritual resolution seemed dissipated in "distracted, wavering, confused thought"; tolerance for a bewildering variety of beliefs had become so general that many felt baffled, immobilized. "I lately found myself questioning if it were worth while to have any convictions about anything," an *Atlantic* writer admitted, "when everybody differs from everyone else, and each one's opinions hold good for one's self alone, of what particular use are they to the individual, after all?"[98]

The author's quandary suggested that the emergence of weightlessness engendered a deep disquiet. Many Americans, after prying their inherited creed loose from the rocky subsoil of evangelical orthodoxy, realized that their paths led not into a theological New Jerusalem but rather into a wilderness of moral uncertainty. The sense of ethical and spiritual dislocation added another dimension to the emerging image of the overcivilized modern character. Physically enervated, an easy target for lean and hungry radicals, that figure was also lost in oversubtle thought. Eager for enlightenment, he was nonetheless troubled by deterministic social science; aspiring to be tolerant, he was nonetheless baffled by the modern confusion of voices. Unable to choose or even to act, he wandered through the Unreal City, drifting away from the moral arena—or at least so his detractors charged. It seemed that modern character, as well as modern culture, had become weightless.

# A Psychic Crisis: Neurasthenia and the Emergence of a Therapeutic World View

The sense of weightlessness blurred the outlines of the autonomous self and pointed toward the psychic dimensions of the crisis of cultural authority. Internalized, private authority seemed threatened as gravely as external, public authority. As personal moral responsibility became increasingly problematic, the repressive constraints of a modern superego became less tolerable, its conflicting demands more difficult to fulfill. As respectable Americans slipped into immobilizing, self-punishing depressions they called "neurasthenia," many sought relief in a proliferating variety of therapies. The spread of therapies involved more than faddishness; it signified a shift toward new secular modes of capitalist cultural hegemony. To understand the beginnings of this therapeutic world view, we need first to look more closely at criticism of the enervated modern character.

To many critics, late-nineteenth-century American culture revealed "a lowering of the mental nerve" among the urban bourgeoisie. The typical respectable American was now, according to Henry Childs Merwin, "a creature who is what we call oversophisticated and effete—a being in whom the springs of action are, in greater or less degree, paralyzed or perverted by the undue predominance of the intellect."[99] The problem was not just hypertrophied intellect, a young *Chap-Book* writer complained. His contemporaries seemed mired in cynicism and affectation, with every natural drive repressed.

> Idealism is our perversion, and the Soul depraves us. We are drinking the dregs of the immaterial and have touched the dingiest bottoms of purity. . . . Nature and commonsense crumble, and sincerity has long since withered away. Cabaret conversations are of the stupidity of sex and small-talk in drawing rooms runs on the idiocy of love. Mating is a platitude, begetting an absurdity, and mother-

> hood has the quaintness of things obsolete. . . . Complexions are of wax when
> feminine; when masculine, of pale peach-blossom!

Contemporary American youth, *Scribner's* agreed in 1896, presented a new phenomenon: "a generation that is more interested in questions about life than in living."[100]

Even among those just coming of age, late Victorian sexual and social propriety seemed to stifle every genuine impulse and emotion. The spread of respectability impressed William Dean Howells, who admitted wryly in 1889 that "people now call a spade an agricultural implement. . . ." Toward the end of the century, other critics began scorning such prim decency as the morality of "a weak and snivelling race." "Everyone," said a *Forum* contributor, "is afraid to let himself go, to offend the conventions, or to raise a sneer." The buttoned-up, humorless urban bourgeois became a stock figure of cultural criticism. Critics deplored "the decay of sentiment," "the disuse of laughter," "the decadence of enthusiasm," and "the decay of personality." The essayist Agnes Repplier summarized a widespread view in 1887 when she wrote: "the old springs of simple sentiment are dying fast within us. It is heartless to laugh, it is foolish to cry, it is indiscreet to love, it is morbid to hate, and it is intolerant to espouse any cause with enthusiasm."[101]

For the late-Victorian bourgeoisie, intense experience—whether physical or emotional—seemed a lost possibility. There was no longer the opportunity for bodily testing provided by rural life, no longer the swift alternation of despair and exhilaration which characterized the old-style Protestant conversion. There was only the diffuse fatigue produced by a day of office work or social calls. Bourgeois existence seemed a narrow path, with no erratic emotional detours.

No wonder, then, that late Victorians began to feel that they had been cut off from "reality," that they experienced life in all its dimensions at second hand, in books rather than action. The impatient impulse to smash the veneer of Victorian convention, the frustrated desire to lash out at a moral void—those emotions pervaded the cultural criticism of the late nineteenth century. They stemmed from two related historical anomalies. First, the softening of theological rigor had not produced any parallel loosening of the bourgeois morality of self-control. As the code of respectability lost supernatural sanctions, its demands for fastidious conduct seemed more onerous, its contradictory expectations less easy to bear. "What an awful pity it is that you can't say damn," said Alice James's friend Miss Loring. "I agreed with her from my heart," James confided to her diary. "It is an immense loss to have all robust and sustaining expletives refined away from one! At such moments of trial refinement is a feeble reed to lean upon."[102]

James's devotion to diary-keeping suggested a second anomaly: Protestant habits of introspection persisted while their supernatural and even ethical justifications evaporated. Introspection, indeed, was very much alive at the turn of the century, celebrated by literary men like Hamilton Wright Mabie as the quality distinguishing the modern from the medieval mind. Yet even Mabie began to feel that the healthy self-consciousness spawned by the Reformation had turned wholly inward and sickened.[103]

To some observers, the clearest example of "morbid self-consciousness" was the Decadent movement in art and literature. While few Americans took seriously Max Nordau's shrill anti-Decadent tract *Degeneration* (English translation, 1895), many felt that the introspective meandering of Oscar Wilde, Joris Karl Huysmans, and other Decadents was an extreme case of a more general malady infecting both Europe and America.[104] To be sure, few Wildean poseurs appeared in the United States, yet critics believed that American culture displayed symptoms of Decadent lassitude and self-absorption. In literature, as the vigorous outdoor romance gave way to the modern mode of domestic realism, action lagged while characters lapsed into endless self-analysis. Many attributed this enervation to the increasing dominance of a female audience in a society where women had become the keepers of the cultural flame; others insisted the difficulty ran deeper. "The oppressiveness of modern novels," they felt, reflected not merely "feminization" but the more general malaise of "a civilization grown over-luxurious, over-inquiring, too languid, . . . too uncertain. . . ." Noting the eclipse of landscapes by human subjects, the art critic Royal Cortissoz exclaimed: "Verily, in the Palace of Art [as in politics, journalism, and theater], we have grown so morbidly self-conscious, so enamored of ourselves, that we are dissatisfied if our explorations bring us face to face with any image but our own!"[105]

As larger frameworks of meaning weakened, introspection focused on the self alone and became "morbid." Among earlier Protestants, for whom salvation was a definite goal, self-scrutiny had sometimes produced intense feelings of guilt; among their uncertain descendants, for whom salvation had become unreal, self-scrutiny more often engendered a diffuse anxiety. Plagued by doubt but still driven by a Protestant conscience, introspective late Victorians felt compelled to seek relief from decision-making and responsibility. One woman habitually took six-hour train rides because "it is such a comfort not to have the fireman come in to ask whether he shall put any more coal on the fire, and the engineer pulls his throttle without looking to see if I signal him; and even if the train runs off the track, it is none of my business, and nobody will think of blaming me for it."[106] That, of course, was an idiosyncratic flight from anxiety. More often, the escape route led not to the railroad station but to bed with nervous prostration— "the disease of the age."

The earliest full-length description of nervous prostration was George

Miller Beard's *American Nervousness* (1880). Beard, a New York neurologist, had earlier coined the term "neurasthenia" to describe what he felt was a new nervous malady, characterized by "lack of nerve force" rather than excitability. Besides a bewildering variety of physical signs including dyspepsia, insomnia, nocturnal emissions, and tooth decay, Beard listed such mental symptoms as "desire for stimulants and narcotics . . . fear of responsibility, of open places or closed places, fear of society, fear of being alone, fear of fears, fear of contamination, fear of everything, deficient mental control, lack of decision in trifling matters, hopelessness. . . ."[107]

Beard's lumping together of disparate phenomena suggested that neurasthenia was a catchall term, encompassing what present-day psychiatrists would classify as various neurotic symptoms. They were unified, however, by a common effect: a paralysis of the will. Tortured by indecision and doubt, the neurasthenic seemed a pathetic descendant of the iron-willed Americans who had cleared forests, drained swamps, and subdued a continent. In fact, Beard claimed, neurasthenia was virtually unknown among his grandparents' generation; the disease was a product of the post–Civil War era.[108]

Other observers agreed. Physicians like Silas Weir Mitchell and Robert Edes, as well as numerous lay commentators, pointed to the novel prevalence of neurasthenia.[109] Such eminent cultural figures as William James, Charles Eliot Norton, and Henry Adams suffered from neurasthenic symptoms. The poet Thomas Bailey Aldrich spoke for them and for legions of their anonymous contemporaries when he cried:

> Work on me your own caprice,
> Give me any shape
> Only, Slumber, from myself,
> Let myself escape![110]

The anxious desire to flee "morbid self-consciousness" often fed on itself and generated further immobilizing introspection. By the early twentieth century, the problem seemed general; references to "our neurasthenia epidemic" proliferated in the established press. "On every street, at every corner, we meet the neurasthenics," a *North American Review* writer observed in 1908.[111]

Insanity and suicide—both outgrowths of nervousness, it was believed —appeared to be rising as well. *Munsey's* wondered "why, when life is continually made more worth living," people should increasingly want to abandon it. In Europe as well as America, nervous disorders seemed to be spreading. What Westerners called "the civilized world" seemed afflicted by a collective nervous crisis.[112]

Yet some groups were more nervous than others. American commentators agreed that neurasthenia predominated in metropolitan areas, especially those north of the Potomac and east of the Mississippi. Educated business and professional men and their wives were far more likely—and able—than their employees to lie abed with nervous prostration. Modern suicide, too, was felt to be "less the custom of the barbarous than of the cultivated man." In general, observers concluded that more "civilized" individuals and peoples were the most susceptible to the new varieties of nervousness; neurasthenia was a product of overcivilization.[113]

Neurasthenia was historically important not because nervous ailments had actually increased—that point is impossible to substantiate—but because observers *believed* nervousness was on the rise, and treated its spread as a cultural problem. Some, it is true, dismissed neurasthenia as a spurious leisure-class complaint, confined primarily to society ladies who were either too coddled or too dissipated to shoulder their duties as wives and mothers. Such critics counselled rededication to duty and hard work.[114] More often, however, Americans viewed neurasthenia as a result of impersonal historical forces, not to be easily exorcised by injunctions to bourgeois virtues.

Most commentators traced the rise of nervous illness to "modern civilization." The unprecedented speed with which railway and telegraph allowed people to transact business, the barrage of information from magazines and newspapers, the monotony of routinized, subdivided labor—all were cited as causes of nervousness or insanity. Perhaps most apparent, to Americans with rural backgrounds, were the discordant noises of urban life. "How can we be happy when the nerves are kept jangling day after day and night after night?" one of many disgruntled citydwellers asked. Beard had no comforting words for the questioner. Jangled nerves, he argued, were the necessary price of progress. America was the most nervous country in the world because she was at the advance guard of modernization; other countries were becoming nervous to the extent they were Americanizing.[115]

Beard mistook the cultural development of the United States for a universal historical process. The modernizing trend he and others saw behind neurasthenia was, more precisely, *embourgeoisement*. That became clear when analysts shifted their attention from technological to cultural causation.

Beard, for example, listed "repression of emotion" as a contributing cause of nervousness. "Constant inhibition, restraining normal feelings, keeping back, covering, holding in check atomic forces of the mind and body, is an exhausting process, and to this process all civilization is constantly subjected." Beard's "all civilization" was actually late-Victorian civilization. Its severest repressions were not barriers against barbarism, as Dr. Robert Edes recognized, but social conventions. "Would it not be better if our customs and 'good form' permitted a patient to scream, as she so often wants to, instead of restraining her feelings for propriety's sake, and developing a neuralgia or paralysis, or an attack of nervous prostration?" Edes asked the Boston Medical Society in 1895. His question recalled Alice James's frustration, and suggested a connection between repression and neurosis—a connection Freud would later make explicit. But Edes pulled back from his insight when he concluded that the most effective cure for nervous invalids was "mental and moral control."[116]

To most critics, the "struggle for existence," rather than repression, seemed the chief cause of nervousness in bourgeois culture. "The struggle between civilized men for the world's goods is becoming more and more a struggle of intellectual strength, ingenuity, and skill," the literary critic William Mathews told *North American Review* readers in 1891, "and as the brain is the weapon with which the fight is made, it breaks down under the strain to which its forces are unequal." One source of strain was the new tyranny of the clock, "the unremitting persistency of effort to be 'on time' " for business or social appointments. More fundamental, in the eyes of most observers, was the compulsion to work itself. When Herbert Spencer stepped to the dais at Delmonico's on November 9, 1882, his paean to progress contained an unexpected leitmotif: a doleful warning against overwork. Spencer, broken by years of battling with nervous exhaustion, was alarmed by the frequency of suicide and nervous collapse among American businessmen. "Everywhere I have been struck with the number of faces which told in strong lines of the burdens that had to be borne," he said. Americans did not know how to relax; they were bored out of harness, driven within it; they were even passing on their nervousness to their children, through high pressure public schooling. "In brief," Spencer concluded, "I may say that we have had somewhat too much of the 'gospel of work.' It is time to preach the gospel of relaxation."[117]

Throughout the late nineteenth century, numerous Americans echoed Spencer's warnings. "Overpressure," it seemed, bedeviled every arena of American life: schools, homes, and offices. Critics charged that middle-class children were physically stunted and intellectually precocious, that their mothers sacrificed health to social duty, and that their fathers were hopelessly tied to their desks. "Something must be done—this is universally admitted—to lessen the strain in modern life," announced *Harper's Monthly* in 1894.[118]

By the 1880s, a wide variety of remedies for nervousness had begun to appear. Many advisors simply exhorted Americans to cultivate relaxation and repose, to learn from "Oriental people, the inhabitants of the tropics, and the colored peoples generally." Americans had had enough moral and intellectual strenuosity; they needed to husband their psychic resources. Silas Weir Mitchell codified this advice into a protracted "rest cure" designed to isolate his patients from nervous stimuli, to "fatten" and "redden" them until they could return to active life.[119]

Mitchell's regimen, like much of the advice urging Americans to slow down, was based on an assumption of psychic scarcity. Mental hygienists often compared a person's supply of nervous energy to a bank account: psychic wastrels could easily overdraw and bankrupt themselves. The money metaphor underscored the link between this "scarcity therapy" and the expanding capitalist economy. If productive energies seemed to be exhausted at precisely the moment when economic development had moved into high gear, the scarcity therapists' solution was to reassert a more prudential version of the familiar achievement ethos: avoid all undue excitements, prudently save your psychic energies and you can continue carefully to exert your will. From this view, the autonomous self was not problematic but only in need of even heavier doses of self-control.[120]

For many neurasthenics, this therapy was worse than the disease. Charlotte Perkins Gilman's autobiographical short story "The Yellow Wall Paper" (1892) typified one response. The story described a woman slowly driven mad by the benevolent tyranny of her husband, a physician who prescribes a thinly disguised version of Mitchell's rest cure. Confined in a single room, denied books or pen and paper, she becomes imprisoned by the fantasy that there are other women creeping through the grotesque floral labyrinth printed on the walls. Her husband discovers her quite mad, on her hands and knees, scratching furiously at the yellow wallpaper.[121] It was not surprising that scarcity therapy often only exacerbated longings for liberation from the stifling closed room of late-nineteenth-century culture. Alluding vaguely to "the strain of modern living," repeating the shibboleths of bourgeois morality, therapists like Mitchell often left the neurasthenic mired in helpless passivity.

But by the turn of the century, one begins to see a new style of therapy based not on the assumption of psychic scarcity but on a new faith in psychic abundance. Spawned primarily by the mind-cure movement, these newer style therapies paralleled the growing fascination with economic abundance among the educated bourgeoisie. More suited than scarcity therapies to the emerging culture of consumption, abundance therapies did not simply reassert the claims of character and conscious will. Rather, they recognized the problematic qualities of the self and particularly the role of the unconscious mind. According to many mind-curists, the existence of unconscious mental powers suggested new approaches to nervous illness. By tapping the unconscious as a wellspring of psychic strength, nervous individuals could actually cultivate *Power Through Repose*—the title of a popular mind-cure manual by Annie Payson Call. Mind-cure panaceas proliferated towards the end of the century. Their specific programs varied but many advised the overstrained to put themselves in touch with "the great everlasting currents" of psychic energy in order to win back and perhaps even increase lost mental and emotional vigor. Many also elevated release over control, "personality" over character, "letting go" over striving, continual psychic growth over adherence to prescribed norms. Embodiments of widespread longings for liberation, these abundance therapies suggested a loosening of the constraints of the modern su- perego.[122]

There were hidden affinities between the spread of abundance therapy and the emergence of a new moral orientation in the culture as a whole. Mind-curists were brothers under the skin to a new breed of corporate liberal ideologues—social engineers who spoke of economic rather than psychic abundance but who shared the interest of mind-curists in liberat- ing repressed impulses. The economist Simon Nelson Patten, for example, argued at the turn of the century that the era of economic scarcity was over and that the "new basis of civilization" would be self-expression rather than self-denial. "Men must enjoy," would be the watchword of the emerg- ing economy of abundance. "The new morality does not consist in saving but in expanding consumption," he asserted. Patten's deification of "self- expression" and "experience" as ends in themselves, his rejection of ulti- mate values in favor of perpetual growth and process—these qualities allied him with abundance therapists and with other social theorists like John Dewey and Walter Lippman. Whatever their individual interests, all helped to create a new climate of educated opinion about matters of personal morality. By 1908 a contributor to a symposium on divorce could say that "virtue no longer consists in literal obedience to arbitrary stand- ards set by community or church but rather in conduct consistent with the demands of a growing personality."[123] The shift from "arbitrary stand- ards" to "the demands of a growing personality," from fixed values to values in constant process, marked the beginnings of a culture stressing self-fulfillment—the dominant culture of our own time.

Most historians have seen this change as a liberation. The problem with this view is that the rhetoric of liberation concealed new patterns of self- manipulation and new modes of accommodation to the emerging corpo- rate system. Rejecting the excessive rationalization of modern culture, therapists and social engineers promoted subtler forms of rationalization for the twentieth century. Part of the difficulty stemmed from their limited objectives. They urged that "liberated" impulses be channeled into "con- structive" purposes: not only the consumption of goods (as Patten sug- gested) but also the re-creation of mind and body for more efficient service in factory and office. Whether counselling a neurasthenic bourgeoisie or prescribing remedies for working-class unrest, they offered novel means for achieving familiar ends of discipline and productivity.

Yet it was not simply a case of old wine in new bottles. The social engineers rejected all fixed values, deifying "growth" and "experience" as ends in themselves; their strategies corroded larger ethical and religious frameworks of meaning outside the self. The growing influence of thera- pists, whether old-style moralists like Mitchell or mind-curists like Call, pointed in the same direction. Whatever the therapy prescribed, the neurasthenia epidemic—itself a product of secularization—led numerous troubled Americans to seek solace not from ministers but from mind-curists and mental hygenists whose cures for nervousness frequently lacked a supernatural dimension. References to salvation dropped from view; psychological well-being became—though often only implicitly—an entirely secular project.

A longing for psychic harmony as an end in itself, rather than as a byproduct of religious faith, was a new development in the history of Western Christianity. It pervaded both older and newer style therapies; it was the profoundest symptom of late-nineteenth-century cultural crisis. By the 1880s and 1890s, the confluence of weightlessness and persistent introspection had helped to pave the way for the contemporary therapeutic world view recently described by Philip Rieff—an outlook adopted by those for whom all overarching structures of meaning have collapsed, and for whom there is "nothing at stake beyond a manipulatable sense of well-being."[124]

This was hardly a liberation. As larger ethical and religious frameworks blurred, the quest for well-being was often doomed to self-defeat. By emphasizing techniques rather than ultimate values, and by encouraging the neurasthenic to focus on his own immediate emotional requirements, the therapeutic orientation often left him mired in "morbid introspection." Personal moral responsibility remained more problematic than ever; neither the mental hygienist's counsel of restraint nor the mind-curist's advice to "let go" broke the circle of self-absorption.

There was a further difficulty as well. Both older and newer style therapies had been formulated in response to the spreading weightlessness of late-Victorian culture: neither provided a genuine alternative to it. The older therapies (like Mitchell's) simply reaffirmed a regime of emotionless aridity; the problem with the newer therapies was more complex. Loosening the restrictions of bourgeois morality in the name of "a growing personality," therapists and social engineers actually accelerated the devaluation of emotional life. Their exaltation of unconscious impulses depended on the insistence that those impulses were benign. Before instinct could be celebrated it had to be deprived of its darker dimensions. Like the afterlife in liberal theology, human emotions lost their power to exhilarate as well as their power to strike fear. Yearning for instinctual liberation, Americans began to achieve it by reducing instincts to banality and reinforcing the drift toward weightlessness.

Both older and newer styles of therapy have persisted throughout the twentieth century, as formalized regimens and more importantly as the most self-conscious manifestations of a cultural tendency, a therapeutic world view which has become part of the continuing pattern of evasive banality in modern culture. Celebrating spurious harmony, the therapeutic outlook has further undermined personal moral responsibility and promoted an ethic of self-fulfillment well attuned to the consumer ethos of twentieth-century capitalism. And it has provoked such perceptive critics as Rieff and Christopher Lasch.[125]

But neither Rieff nor Lasch has quite grasped the full historical complexity of the therapeutic world view. Both tend to tie it too closely to psychoanalysis and other formal therapeutic regimens; both sometimes treat it almost entirely as a product of the post–World War II era. Actually the therapeutic world view was less a formal regime than a way of life embraced by people sometimes only dimly aware of psychiatry. And its roots stretch not merely into the counterculture of the 1960s and the suburban affluence of postwar America, but into the cultural turmoil of the late nineteenth century—above all the effort to reconstruct a coherent sense of identity in a culture which was rendering all identities (and all values) vaporous and unreal. Further, the therapeutic world view was not simply imposed on a hapless working class by the "helping professions" (as Lasch sometimes suggests); it was also the product of an unconscious collaboration between professionals and their clients among the bourgeoisie. The professional self-interest of therapists and social engineers meshed with the unfulfilled longings of middle- and upper-class Americans —longings which were shaped and sustained by the late-nineteenth-century crisis of cultural authority.

The therapeutic world view, in other words, has a long history. Goethe had foreseen it as early as 1782, when he wrote: "Speaking for myself, I do believe humanity will win in the long run; I am only afraid that at the same time the world will have turned into one huge hospital where everyone is everyone else's humane nurse." A century later, the American bourgeoisie had begun to establish that huge hospital. By 1899, *Scribner's* complained that life no longer seemed a battlefield but rather "a kind of infirmary" where "moral invertebrates" sought emotional security by avoiding responsibility for their actions.[126] And the most conspicuous "moral invertebrate" was the neurasthenic. Indeed, the neurasthenic embodied Rieff's therapeutic mode in embryo: paralyzed by introspection and self-doubt, obsessed with easing his own psychic tensions.

The neurasthenia epidemic epitomized the crisis of cultural authority. For the American bourgeoisie, their dilemma involved more than the recognition that modern culture was inadequate to maintain social order, though that concern was surely present. More important was the dawning perception that the spread of bourgeois values had begun to undermine rather than promote individual autonomy. "Industrial man" seemed physically and morally enfeebled. Physical enervation was disturbing but more easily cured than the host of problems besetting familiar ideas of personal moral responsibility. New deterministic theories made free will seem little more than a convenient fiction; a liberalized Protestant theology softened convictions and promoted ethical confusion. Yet habits of introspection and rigid notions of social propriety persisted and drove many "morbidly self-conscious" Americans to nervous prostration. "The disease of the age" afflicted its victims with a sense of frustrated helplessness, an extreme version of the feeling pervading the educated bourgeoisie.

In large measure, the antimodern impulse was a reaction against that helpless feeling. Transatlantic in scope and sources, antimodernism drew on venerable traditions as well as contemporary cultural currents: republican moralism, which promoted suspicion of urban "luxury"; romantic literary convention, which elevated simple and childlike rusticity over the artificial amenities of civilization; a revolt against positivism, gathering strength toward the end of the century, which rejected all static intellectual and moral systems, often in the name of a vitalist cult of energy and process; and a parallel recovery of the primal, irrational forces in the human psyche, forces which had been obscured by the evasive banality of modern culture. Given this variety of sources, it is not surprising that the antimodern impulse led in a variety of directions. To a bourgeoisie which seemed stagnant and vulnerable to revolution, some antimodern cultural critics exalted robust simplicity, moral certainty, and the ability to act decisively. This activist version of antimodernism preached regeneration through preindustrial craftsmanship and a pastoral "simple life," or posed the violent lives of medieval warriors as a refreshing contrast to the blandness of modern comfort. Other more inward-turning antimodernists escaped the emotional constraints of bourgeois life and the spiritual limitations of a positivistic or therapeutic outlook by exploring the joys and terrors of medieval or Oriental religious belief. Those who recognized the problematic qualities of modern identity sought a wider selfhood by embracing the "childlike" or "feminine" aspects of premodern character. Disparate as their odysseys were, these critics shared a common view that modern culture had narrowed the range and diffused the intensity of human existence. They longed to rekindle possibilities for authentic experience, physical or spiritual—possibilities they felt had existed once before, long ago.

This preoccupation with recovering intense experience unified a wide variety of antimodernists but rendered their protest ironic and muddled. In part, this muddle was due to the ambivalence of the antimodernists themselves—an ambivalence shaped by class interest and personal commitments. Half-committed to modernization, antimodernists unwittingly allowed modern culture to absorb and defuse their dissent. Unable to transcend bourgeois values, they often ended by revitalizing them. Ambivalent critiques became agenda for bourgeois self-reformation: antimodern craft ideologues became advocates of basement workbench regeneration for tired corporate executives; antimodern militarists became apologists for modern imperialism. Because they were among the most influential cultural leaders of the American ruling class, antimodern thinkers played a key (albeit often unknowing) role in revitalizing the cultural hegemony of their class during a protracted period of crisis.

Antimodernists did more than revitalize older bourgeois values of activism and achievement; they also helped to transform those values. This transformation stemmed less from class determinants than from the nature of the dissent itself. In a secularizing culture, where larger frameworks of meaning were fading, the antimodern quest for "real life" often focused on the self alone; intense experience became an end in itself. Sentimentalizing emotional spontaneity and instinctual vitality, much antimodernism displayed the limits common to *fin-de-siècle* vitalism; it also melded with new-style therapies of abundance and some versions of corporate liberal social engineering. All these responses to cultural crisis promoted the same circular and self-defeating quests for intense experience; all were rooted in personal disquiet but had unintended social results: they helped ease the transition to secular and corporate modes of modern culture—new forms of evasiveness for a new social world.

Yet there was this difference. Antimodern dissent more often contained a vein of deep religious longing, an unfulfilled yearning to restore infinite meaning to an increasingly finite world. The more profound antimodernists recognized the hopelessness of those yearnings but they acknowledged and indeed embraced them just the same. They accepted the insoluble conflict at the heart of their human condition; they rejected the evasive banality of modern culture in either its Victorian or its streamlined, therapeutic modes. Informed by this stubborn stoicism, antimodernism became more than a path to accommodation: it also preserved an enduring witness against the flatulent pieties of our progressive creed.

# ·2·

# THE FIGURE OF
# THE ARTISAN:
# ARTS AND CRAFTS
# IDEOLOGY

IN AMERICA THE WORK ETHIC HAS ALWAYS BEEN A touchstone of national morality. The contemporary cant about "lagging productivity" is only the most recent example of a long tradition of upper-class complaints about shiftless workers—now translated from the language of republican moralism to the jargon of social science. Yet there has also been a minority tradition extending from Henry David Thoreau to Studs Terkel, joining a wide variety of critics who have sensed the benumbing busyness of modern work and have tried to locate alternatives. The revival of handicraft at the turn of the century partook of both these traditions; it was meanspirited and largehearted, suffused with upper-class forebodings and utopian aspirations. Its contradictions mirrored more than the tensions in the national mythology of work; they also reflected the social and cultural confusion of the late nineteenth century.

In work-obsessed America, it was not surprising that the recoil from overcivilization generated a critique of modern work. Despite shopworn paeans to the nobility of toil, a number of sensitive observers began to see that labor in industrial America was being degraded as never before. In the factories and bureaucracies of organized capitalism, even the more fortunate workers were being reduced to the status of machine tenders or paper shufflers. Contrary to Daniel Bell and other present-day prophets of "postindustrial society," the rationalization of economic life did not primarily promote new skills; more often it destroyed old ones. Even before Taylor introduced "scientific management," the drive for maximum productivity and control led managers to divide labor into repetitive, minute tasks. Individual workers could neither envision the larger purpose of their labor nor exert much control over their working lives.[1]

For white collar clerks and professionals there was a further problem. Despite their relative security their work seemed strangely insubstantial. The new bureaucratic world of work often fragmented their labor and reduced their sense of autonomy: more important, it isolated them from the hard, substantial reality of things. Among the middle and upper classes, the transformation of work reinforced difficulties pervading the wider culture; the splintering sense of selfhood, the vague feelings of unreality. Yearning to reintegrate selfhood by resurrecting the authentic experience of manual labor, a number of Americans looked hopefully toward the figure of the premodern artisan. His work was necessary and demanding; it was rooted in a genuine community; it was a model of hardness and wholeness. Or so it seemed.

The revival of handicraft originated and flourished primarily among the educated bourgeoisie—the class most troubled by the crisis of cultural authority during the late nineteenth century. To be sure, industrial workers from agrarian or craft backgrounds often clung valiantly to traditional skills and resisted modern work discipline. But they did not self-consciously resurrect an ideal of craftsmanship as an antidote to modern ills. They did not have to; craftsmanship was their birthright.[2] Arts and Crafts ideologues, on the other hand, came usually from among the business and professional people who felt most cut off from "real life" and most in need of moral and cultural regeneration.

These people believed they were part of an "Arts and Crafts movement," but that phrase encompassed a wide variety of social types and reform enterprises. Craft ideologues ranged from the aloof patrician Charles Eliot Norton to the flamboyant former soap salesman Elbert Hubbard. Their activities varied even more widely: organizing communes dedicated to the "simple life" of craftsmanship and subsistence farming, making and marketing craft goods, lecturing and writing on the craft ideal, arranging craft exhibits, or simply collecting *objets d'art*. The "Arts and Crafts movement" was less a cohesive social phenomenon than a catchall polemical phrase.

Despite their differences, Arts and Crafts spokesmen had much in common. Most came from an educated and relatively affluent background; most shared the world view of America's metropolitan bourgeoisie at the end of the nineteenth century. Though their differing personal circumstances led to various angles of vision, their cultural criticism stemmed from common concerns, addressed similar themes, and led to closely interrelated consequences. It is possible to view their underlying unity of outlook as an ideology—a collective mode of consciousness shaped to the actual or imagined needs and interests of a social group under particular historical circumstances, designed not only to legitimize a version of reality but also to mobilize action.[3]

In forming that ideology, craft leaders were partly influenced by indigenous social circumstances and cultural traditions. Like many others among the educated bourgeoisie, they felt that their class had become enervated and vulnerable to social upheaval. To make moral sense of this situation, they drew heavily on Puritan and republican tradition—particularly the deep distrust of urban "luxury" and the faith in the ennobling powers of hard work. And to focus their identities as reformers, they drew on another resource as well: the ethos of evangelical reform which had infused republican moralism with missionary zeal during the antebellum era, spawning innumerable utopian communities and benevolent societies designed to mitigate social chaos by promoting self-improvement. The individualist and idealist assumptions of the republican tradition and its evangelical variant played a dominant role in shaping the antimodern stance taken by the craft leaders.

Yet American craftsmen were also affected by several varieties of European antimodernism: the pastoral doctrine of the "Simple Life" preached by Leo Tolstoy and the British poet Edward Carpenter; the decentralized communitarianism of the anarchist Prince Kropotkin; and above all the critique of labor under modern capitalism developed by the British polemicists John Ruskin and William Morris. For a number of American craft leaders, exposure to the ideas of Ruskin and Morris was the catalyst for their embrace of the Arts and Crafts ideal. The two Britons were widely cited in Craft publications; their antimodern aphorisms were essential components of many American craft polemics. Before turning to American Arts and Crafts ideology, it is worth looking briefly at Ruskin and Morris in their British context. The fate of their ideas and of the movements they inspired suggests some interesting comparisons between British and American antimodernism.

Ruskin was the key forerunner, the antimodern Jeremiah. Beginning with *The Stones of Venice* (1853), he juxtaposed the creative improvisation allowed the medieval craftsman at work in the irregular Gothic style with the superhuman demands made by the Renaissance architects who insisted on recapturing classical symmetry. In Ruskin's view, the Renaissance rage for order led ultimately to the regimentation of the modern factory system, where mechanization and minute subdivision of labor had reduced the worker to "a heap of sawdust." By splitting the population into "morbid thinkers and miserable workers," the factory system created a situation that was both morally and socially dangerous. Warning that revolution was imminent, Ruskin argued that medieval cathedral builders (unlike modern factory hands) remained satisfied with their material lot because they found joy in their labor. Ruskin's class fears mingled with his moral convictions and led him to propose voluntaristic remedies. He exhorted affluent Britons to boycott machine-made goods, sought to spread enthusiasm for manual labor by leading Oxford undergraduates on road-mending expeditions, and, in *Unto This Last* (1860), urged fatherly benevolence from captains of industry as well as minimum welfare guarantees from a paternalistic state. Finally he tried to re-create a microcosm of medieval society in his St. George's Guild. The Guild epitomized the quixotic quality of Ruskin's reform. It was to be a miniature feudal kingdom on twenty acres of wooded land, but Ruskin's encroaching mental instability doomed his sporadic organizational efforts.[4]

Despite his failure at reform, Ruskin's antimodern critique had intellectual consequences. Most importantly, it shaped the antimodern vision of William Morris. Morris read Ruskin while he was an undergraduate at Oxford in the 1850s. The experience led him from the dreamy aesthetic medievalism of the university to a career as a reformer of mid–Victorian taste who designed neomedieval furniture and textiles for wealthy clients —and ultimately to a second career as a socialist agitator whose efforts were still animated by an antimodern impulse. "Apart from the desire to produce beautiful things," Morris wrote in 1894, "the leading passion of my life has been and is hatred of modern civilization."[5]

Convinced by the 1880s that Ruskin's schemes were pathetically inadequate, Morris sought to wed his mentor's antimodernism with Marxian socialism. Unlike Ruskin, Morris admitted the violence and exploitation in medieval society. But he argued that the medieval guilds were communal islands of "production for use," resistant to feudal and capitalist oppression alike. And he further insisted that the abolition of medieval despotism had exacted a fearful price: for the vast majority, intellectual and political liberty had been vitiated by industrial slavery and aesthetic impoverishment. In modern England, capitalism's "ceaseless creation of wants" and the excessive division of labor had produced a nation of "wretched lopsided creatures." Abandoning the elitism of Ruskin's critique, Morris kept its moral core—the insistence on the worker's right to joyful and useful labor. That insistence separated Morris from the Fabians and other leading British socialists. With unerring accuracy he foresaw one of the central failures of the socialist Left in the twentieth century: he warned that bureaucratic state socialism promised only a "quasi-socialist machinery" of improved administration, rather than a humane socialist community. Distrusting the preoccupation with efficiency in all bureaucratic systems, Morris could direct his fire at the stifling overorganization common to both capitalist and socialist versions of modern industrial society.[6]

In Britain, the antimodern visions of Ruskin and Morris suffered at the hands of their audiences. Ruskin's social criticism was widely scorned as the product of mental imbalance and approaching senility. His admirers preferred to remember him as a benevolent arbiter of mid–Victorian taste. Morris's critique, on the other hand, was not so much dismissed as distorted and diffused. Many of the British were inspired by Morris's earlier design work to promote the revival of handicraft, but this British Arts and Crafts movement largely ignored his career of socialist agitation. By 1888, Morris was attacking the movement for its "empty grumbling about the continuous march of machinery over dying handicraft" and its "various elegant little schemes" for encouraging public appreciation of handicraft—none of which touched the heart of the matter, the degradation of work. In the minds of most craft revivalists (and indeed of the British generally), Morris shed his revolutionary mantle and became the patron saint of nostalgic aestheticism. And even for those seeking to transcend aestheticism, Morris's critique became diffused among the Simple Lifers, vegetarians, and dress reformers who clustered in the backwaters of the British Left, organizing "rustic gatherings" and entertaining fantastic visions of social regeneration through the abandonment of corsets and mutton. The Arts and Crafts crusade against the "crinkum-crankum" spread by Victorian taste somehow attracted the crinkum-crankum of Victorian society.[7]

Meanwhile, the mainstream of socialist thought flowed away from Morris, following the route charted by the Fabians Beatrice and Sidney Webb.

The Webbs envisioned a technocratic society run by enlightened managers who were devoted to the disinterested service of the community. Criticizing capitalism's excesses, they clung to the positivist faith in the link between material and moral progress, anticipating an "inevitable" transition from corporate capitalism to bureaucratic state socialism. Ultimately most British socialists (whether intellectuals or rank and file) accepted the Webb view, ignored Morris's warnings, and became enmeshed in the "quasi-socialist machinery" of Labour Party politics.[8]

Yet antimodern sentiments survived and sustained important intellectual and social developments. The desire to reintegrate a fragmented sense of self led to many more plans to promote satisfying labor in an "organic" community of face-to-face relationships. One can see that desire in manifestoes like A. J. Penty's *The Restoration of the Guild System* (1907), as well as the guild socialism of G. D. H. Cole, the distributism of Hilaire Belloc and Gilbert Keith Chesterton, and the organicist cultural criticism of T. E. Hulme and F. R. Leavis. Whether egalitarian and secular (like Cole's), or hierarchical and religious (like Chesterton's), all these visions of community sought to create islands of wholeness in a fragmented capitalist society. Outside of intellectual circles, the influence of the British antimodern impulse was vaguer but longer lasting. A distaste for the ugliness spread by industrial capitalism, a nostalgia for a "green and pleasant land"—these sentiments have survived throughout the twentieth century. Originating in aristocratic court literature but later widely popularized, persistent pastoralism has united Tories and Labourites, helping to dull popular enthusiasm for unrestrained capitalist development. In Britain, the antimodern critique personified in Ruskin and Morris's medieval artisan lost much of its force but survived.[9]

The same was true of the American craft ideal, but here the picture was messier from the beginning because the American craft leaders were neither as articulate nor as clearheaded as Ruskin and Morris. Drawing on a wider variety of cultural resources, the American critique seemed eclectic and muddled by comparison to that of the British forerunners—though not by comparison to that of their disciples. American craft leaders were hampered from the outset by their class interests and anxieties, their individualist and idealist assumptions about the nature of social reform, and above all by their own underlying ambivalence toward modern culture and its progressive creed. These difficulties loomed larger as the craft movement spread, ultimately transforming it from a critique of modern culture to a new kind of accommodation.

In the public realm the craft revival revealed its accommodationist bent by sponsoring manual training in public schools as a safe mode of socializing the rebellious working class. But accommodation meant more than devising new forms of social control; it meant evaporation of the hopes of the craft leaders for a truly alternative culture. Afflicted by the spiritual uncertainties of their age, ambivalent in their antimodern dissent, American craft leaders quickly lost sight of religious or communal frameworks of meaning outside the self. Like many of their British counterparts, they allowed their quest for wholeness to center on the self alone. The ideal of joyful labor, when it was not submerged by aestheticism, became a means of personal revitalization rather than a path to renewed community. In part a reaction against therapeutic self-absorption, the revival of handicraft ultimately became another form of therapy for an overcivilized bourgeoisie.

By World War I, the craft ideal had largely been reduced to a revivifying hobby for the affluent: the nervous businessman would return refreshed to the office after a weekend of puttering at his basement workbench. In subsequent years and especially since World War II this therapeutic approach to manual labor has spread from the comfortable bourgeoisie throughout much of the American population. "Do-it-yourself" projects have provided innumerable Americans with a sense of autonomy and a chance to confront the substantial reality of material things. For people whose working lives seem beyond their control and permeated by the barrenness of a bureaucratic civilization, this is no small achievement. Yet it perpetuates the fragmentation decried by Ruskin and Morris: the split between work for pay and work for joy.

Despite this accommodation, the American craft ideal has also preserved its critical edge. The communal efforts of the Arts and Crafts movement, however disastrous in the end, were part of a continuing tradition that looked backward to antebellum utopians and forward to the agrarian communities of the New Deal era and the 1960s. Seeking the "hard reality" of life on the land, these communitarian ventures have sometimes borne eloquent witness against the stifling complacency of an overstuffed and overorganized society. And besides promoting this popular protest, Arts and Crafts leaders also served as the intellectual ancestors of decentralist intellectuals in our own time—men as diverse as Paul Goodman, Lewis Mumford, and E. F. Schumacher, who have had to remind us once more of the deadening effects of rationalization and the desperate need for creative, useful labor. The American craft revival, in other words, displayed the characteristic antimodern blend of accommodation and protest.

To begin exploring the complex fate of the craft ideal in America, we need to look first at the movement's leaders. A disparate lot of educators, designers, and visionary entrepreneurs, they shared a common perception that America had become somehow overcivilized. But the way they defined overcivilization depended on their various social and personal circumstances.

# Origins of the American Craft Revival: Persons and Perceptions

The chief American precursor of Arts and Crafts ideology was Charles Eliot Norton, a close friend of Ruskin and first Professor of Fine Arts at Harvard. Throughout his life Norton tried to meld his aesthetic concerns with his deep-dyed republican moralism. His *Historical Studies of Church Building in the Middle Ages* (1880) joined Ruskin and republicanism. To Norton the achievement of the medieval artisan typified the power of religious faith and communal pride in an age before rationalism had destroyed one and individualism the other; the coming of the Renaissance marked the decay of both art and morality. In Norton's view the Renaissance in Italy—like his own post–Civil War era in America—marked "a gilded not a golden age." Both periods showed the destruction of a virtuous community by the obsession with private gain and by the decline of any unifying belief system.[10]

As Norton grew older his fears of working-class unrest deepened; his republican moralizing grew more intense, his aestheticism more fastidious. There had always been a powerful countercurrent of aestheticism in Norton's work; his attacks on what Morris had called "the Age of Shoddy" were directed as much at vulgarity as at immorality. (According to Harvard legend, upon admission to heaven Norton shrank in horror from the pearly gates crying: "Oh no! So vulgar! So Renaissance!") By the 1890s aestheticism and republican elitism had become the dominant strains in Norton's thought. Preoccupied by artistic and moral decadence, he overlooked the plight of the individual worker.[11]

In 1897, Norton joined a number of prominent Bostonians in founding the Boston Society of Arts and Crafts, and became the society's first president. (Enfeebled by age and illness, however, he always served as elder statesman rather than active member.) Regretting "the loss of a sense of personal elegance as expressed in articles of common use," revering "costly but precious products, with something of human life in them," Norton inveighed against "the popular impatience of law and form and the desire for overornamentation and specious originality." His elitism and aestheticism reflected the majority views of the society's membership, which was dominated by architects, museum administrators, professors of design, and their civic-minded wives. Larger and more active than any other craft organization, the Boston Society debated social and cultural issues in its magazine *Handicraft* (1902–1904, 1910–1912) and survived long after its first president stepped down.[12]

The year 1897 also marked the founding of the Chicago Arts and Crafts Society, which included prominent business and professional people, members of the University of Chicago faculty, and the cofounders of Hull House, Jane Addams and Ellen Gates Starr. The Chicago Society helped to provide an audience for the Chicago Art Institute journal *Brush and Pencil* (1897–1905) and a forum for the polemicist Oscar Lovell Triggs of the University of Chicago English department. A charter member of the Chicago Society, Triggs founded the Industrial Art League in 1899 and the Morris Society in 1903 (both in Chicago), but he made his national reputation largely through free-lance lecturing and writing. Triggs's academic odyssey had taken him from Cornell College in rural Iowa to Oxford, Berlin, and finally back to Chicago. With his deepset eyes, bushy moustache, and earnest manner, he became a familiar figure on public platforms throughout the Midwest. Triggs tried to preserve Morris's vision but gradually succumbed to writing corporate liberal apologetics for giant factories and bureaucracies. His work was widely reprinted and praised by Arts and Crafts leaders in other parts of the country.[13]

Among those leaders was Horace Traubel, like Triggs an admirer of both William Morris and Walt Whitman. Whitman had been a friend of the Traubel family in Camden, where Horace was born in 1858. Unlike most craft leaders, Traubel came from a modest social background. His father was a German–Jewish printer who passed that trade to his son. Traubel worked as a printer's devil, lithographer, and journalist until 1902 when he began to devote full time to free-lance writing. A burly stub of a man, he lived one step ahead of the bill collector, devouring great quantities of cheap food and tirelessly coining afterdinner aphorisms. In 1903, Traubel joined two Philadelphia architects, Will Price and Hawley McLanahan, to found the community of Rose Valley. Located in the Pennsylvania countryside about thirteen miles from Philadelphia, Rose Valley discussed its aims in the *Artsman* (1903–1906). The community combined subsistence agriculture and cottage industry in an effort to attract dissatisfied citydwellers, especially skilled craftsmen, to a life of vigorous and profitable labor.[14]

A similar colony had appeared in the western Massachusetts hills in 1900. Its founder, Edward Pearson Pressey, was a Harvard-educated Unitarian minister who had begun an effort to revive local craft traditions during his pastorate at Rowe, Massachusetts, in 1897. Discouraged by local indifference, he trudged westward to Montague and began preaching in an abandoned church. Pressey soon proclaimed the founding of a new community. He and his wife, their two children, and three adult friends planted subsistence crops and started operating a small printing press, with which they published *Country Time and Tide* (1901–1909). Following Edward Everett Hale's suggestion, Pressey christened the colony "New Clairvaux," to recall the cultural revival led by St. Bernard during the twelfth century.[15]

Such monastic overtones were repugnant to Elbert Hubbard, the most visible and eccentric craft leader in America. In 1893, Hubbard sold his profitable half-interest in the Larkin Soap Company, enrolled briefly at Harvard, and then toured England's literary shrines. Among them was the home of William Morris, whose Kelmscott community so impressed Hubbard that he styled himself a Morris disciple when he returned to the United States. He began to print, bind, and sell Kelmscott-style books at East Aurora in western New York. He also started publishing a pocket-size magazine, the *Philistine* (1895–1915), in which he denounced marriage, Christianity, and the "leisure class," and printed aphorisms designed to promote himself and his business.[16]

Not far from East Aurora, in Syracuse, Gustav Stickley opened his United Crafts furniture workshops in 1898. No flamboyant self-advertiser like Hubbard, Stickley was the stolid, ambitious son of Scandinavian immigrant farmers in Osceola, Wisconsin. After his father abandoned the family, they moved to Brandt, Pennsylvania, where Stickley worked in his uncle's chair factory. He rose rapidly, became manager and foreman, and soon accumulated enough capital to start his own business. As a young journeyman woodworker, his passion for self-improvement had led him to read Carlyle, Ruskin, and Morris, and he had been moved to propagandize the value of craftsmanship. For that purpose, he started publishing the *Craftsman* (1901–1916).[17]

These publicists—Stickley, Hubbard, Pressey, Traubel, Triggs, and Society leaders in Boston and Chicago—were the chief shapers of Arts and Crafts ideology. In nearly every case, exposure to the ideas of Ruskin and Morris marked a key moment in the emergence of their commitments to the craft revival. But those commitments were always ambiguous. Craft leaders were both prepared to heed Ruskin and Morris and predisposed to reinterpret their message. The attitude of the Americans stemmed from their immediate historical situation and from venerable cultural inheritance.

The heritage of republican moralism framed the assumptions of craft revivalists about American culture. They feared cities as the breeding grounds of corrupting luxury and "unnatural," foppish fashion. Pressey warned summer boarders at Montague against "the sin of urbanity," and craft journals railed often against "the vulgar struts, male and female, who parade our streets"—pretenders to the throne of High Society. Leisure-class amusements seemed a national danger. Alarmed by a magazine's midsummer cover which showed a young woman slouched in a veranda chair, partaking of bonbons and romantic stories, Stickley charged that such diversion was "a real peril to the country; too subtle to be met by legislation, too well disguised to cause suspicion, and too attractive to be resisted by those it makes mad and destroys."[18]

Alongside such traditional complaints, craft reformers struck some new notes as well. It was not only moral and physical deterioration which threatened American life, but the appearance of a new and disturbing mentality among the middle and upper classes. Stickley called it "premature old age." "We are losing the charm of youth; we have forgotten how to play; we can only joke," he complained.[19] At its most extreme, this repression of spontaneity and freshness led to neurasthenia—the severest symptom of overcivilization.

To craft reformers, neurasthenia seemed in part a product of modern urban life. "As cities grow bigger," Ernest Crosby wrote in a 1904 *Craftsman* article, "asylums, hospitals, sanitariums . . . grow still more rapidly." Yet the malady was also an occupational disease, affecting primarily what Pressey called "our intellectual dilettante class." No longer forced to work with their hands for a living, "brain-workers" slipped into introspection and ennui. In Hubbard's mythical city of Tagaste, "those who used only their heads suffered from Bright's Disease, Paresis, and Nervous Prostration."[20]

Behind this widespread plight, some felt, was technological growth. Earlier republican moralists, though they distrusted material progress, had nevertheless often joined the national chorus of praise for machines and labor-saving devices. But after a century of staggering technological advance, craft revivalists had begun to fear that mechanization was unnerving even the most affluent Americans. Stickley's observation was typical. "Originally intended to make simpler and easier the doing of necessary things," he wrote, "the introduction of machinery with its train of attendant evils has so complicated and befuddled our standards of living that we have less and less time for enjoyment and for growth, and nervous prostration is the disease of the age."[21]

On this point, the language of Stickley's critique pointed to its ultimate assimilation. He assailed the machine as a threat to "enjoyment" and "growth"—two key terms in the developing vocabulary of the therapeutic world view. For Stickley as for other craft revivalists, craftsmanship would provide a means of rehabilitating neurasthenics; it promised not social transformation but therapeutic self-renewal within a corporate structure of degraded work and bureaucratic "rationality."

Yet mechanization also bred a subtler dis-ease, immune to therapeutic solutions: a feeling that unprecedented comfort and convenience diminished the stature of the individual will. From this view, the most privileged beneficiaries of technological growth were also its secret victims. As Douglas Volk complained in *Brush and Pencil,* "We no longer walk upstairs, but are hoisted up, and we have only to press a button in order to have performed for us countless services that we once undertook for ourselves."

The profusion of labor-saving devices caused Triggs to fear the coming of "a perfect mechanical world and impotent humanity, an engine complete on all its sides, and a man shorn of all his quondam greatness."[22]

This sense that modernity meant encroaching impotence was the most important psychic impetus for Arts and Crafts ideology. It haunted craft leaders, sharpening their suspicion that they had lost touch with the tangible reality of the material world. Like other educated professionals, they had been spared the necessity of scuffling for survival by the sweat of their brows; yet that liberation bred self-doubt and even self-disgust. "You do not know what life means when all the difficulties are removed!" Jane Addams cried as a young woman. "I am simply smothered and sickened with advantages. It is like eating a sweet dessert the first thing in the morning."[23] Other craft leaders shared Addams's revulsion. They felt suffocated by the stale gentility of modern culture; they longed to flee the library and the cushioned parlor into "real life."

Given the self-doubts of many craft leaders, it was not surprising that their quest for reality led them to idealize manual labor. Many seemed convinced that experience was not genuine unless it was physically demanding. That conviction heightened their republican horror of leisure-class dilettantism as well as their tendencies toward anti-intellectualism. Few go as far as one Harold E. Gorst, whose dictum "books are absolutely dangerous to healthy mental development" Stickley amended by adding: "This is true the moment we turn to books as a substitute for, instead of as a supplement to, life and experience." But the distinction between intellect and "life" became an article of faith for many craft ideologues. "We have dealt with words and symbols so long that we have no understanding of reality," Triggs told fellow members of the overcivilized bourgeoisie. A highly educated literary critic and editor himself, Triggs questioned the authenticity of his own career: "It is doubtful if the literary man can ever be sincere, for not having experienced life he must be haunted by doubts and self-questionings." Pressey banished those doubts by his flight to New Clairvaux, where he jeered at "leisure-class" journalists and ministers. "Loafing is called work and made a profession—editorial and sermon writing," he announced.[24] The contempt for intellect as a leisure-class commodity revealed a vein of self-distrust characteristic of intellectuals in a democratic, utilitarian culture; it also joined craft leaders with other educated Americans who sought authentic experience in the physical or emotional intensity of an imagined premodern past.

If the craft leaders' reverence for the premodern artisan stemmed from their psychic needs, it was shaped by their social circumstances. Arts and Crafts ideology was entwined with the class and racial anxieties common among affluent Americans at the end of the nineteenth century. Worry about proliferating socialists, anarchists, and immigrants energized the craft revival and powerfully influenced the reform proposals offered by its leaders. Their definition of the labor problem often recalled Ruskin at his most elitist. They agreed that the intelligent skilled worker, bored with his factory job, found the only outlet for his ambition in clamoring for higher wages. From this view, the revival of craft possibilities for skilled artisans promised the best answer to the irresponsible demands of labor agitators.

Yet most craft leaders recognized the problem ran deeper: factory work involved not simply boredom but dehumanization and degradation. In Hubbard's Tagaste, factory hands became "dispirited, dissipated, and vicious. . . ." Will Price warned from Rose Valley that "civilization is not strong enough to stand the strain of an ever-increasing population of unthinking laborers."[25] It was bad enough that such laborers developed a boundless craving for wealth; far worse was the threat they posed to social order itself.

In the minds of many craft ideologues, brutalized workers crowded into socialist meeting halls, raptly absorbing the gospel preached by revolutionary demagogues. Irene Sargent, professor of art history at Syracuse University, made the connection between degraded work and revolution explicit in a 1901 *Craftsman* article. What is to be expected, she asked, "from a man, the play of whose intelligence is confined to the endless repetition of a single mental process, and whose physical exercise is restricted to the working of certain unvarying muscles?" He "will develop morbidly, and his mind will offer a resting-place for destructive and chaotic ideas. . . ." The result seemed inevitable: "being not without personal claims to dignity and power, he becomes an insurrectionist, perhaps even a pervert and a criminal." Stickley, Sargent, and other *Craftsman* contributors feared crime and insurrection among the urban poor generally, but they worried particularly about the strange new immigrants—"the vicious yet cowardly Sicilian with his ever-ready knife," even the hard-working Jewish pushcart man. Ethnic and class animosities merged to sharpen the dread of revolution, and to heighten concern about the vulnerability of an overcivilized bourgeoisie.[26]

In their attacks on the urban masses, as in their critique of modern culture in general, craft leaders drew heavily on the republican tradition. But to formulate solutions for social problems, to define their own role as reformers, they required related cultural resources as well. Chief among them was the heritage of antebellum romantic reform. Romantic reformers had been animated by two major impulses in evangelical Protestantism: the perfectionist longing for complete holiness or "perfect sanctification," and the millennialist belief in the imminence of the Kingdom of God on Earth.[27]

The perfectionist impulse sometimes sparked challenges to existing institutions, notably slavery. But more often perfectionism was absorbed into the desire for self-improvement common among an ascendant bourgeoisie. For example, Arthur and Lewis Tappan's Society for Promoting

Manual Labor in Literary Institutions (1829–1833) included clergymen, college presidents, and businessmen, all of whom testified to the invigorating effects of physical toil on "brain-workers." In such groups, perfectionism revealed a this-worldly function: men hewed wood and carried water not to save themselves, but to increase their professional efficiency.[28] Among social reformers and advocates of "self-culture," such secular emphases increased throughout the nineteenth century. For educated Americans, perfectionism survived as a habit of mind if not as a path to salvation. It sustained the delusion that social problems were entirely soluble through individual moral betterment; it also reinforced the spread of the therapeutic world view. "Self-culture" easily became "personal growth."

Millennialism also persisted in secularized form, as Jean Quandt has made clear.[29] With the growth of religious uncertainty among the educated, millennialist beliefs lost theological content. Faith in the kingdom as the culmination of the unfolding divine plan gave way to evolutionary schemes of inevitable linear progress. The belief that Christians could make straight the way of the Lord became the conviction that gradualist social reform would eventually smooth the path to a secular utopia. The secularized millennial dream, along with the perfectionist stress on "self-culture" and individual moral change, pervaded the imaginations of American reformers well into the twentieth century.

Craft reformers were no exception. With their "Progressive" contemporaries, they shared the evangelical heritage of antebellum reform; they also revealed how much that heritage had been secularized. Pressey preserved the religious emphasis most self-consciously. He placed himself in the perfectionist tradition by announcing that New Clairvaux was modelled on such antebellum experiments as Adin Ballou's Hopedale and George Ripley's Brook Farm, and he recounted his decision to found the colony in the language conventionally used to describe conversion experiences.

> Six years ago I saw a vision from the north slope of Adam's mountain in Rowe, overlooking the wilderness of Rowe, Heath, and several other towns. "And this," I exclaimed, "is the Holy Land, and I knew it not." For I saw the remarkable lives that had been lived there in one hundred and fifty years and what was to come hereafter. And a hot coal was in my heart for the poor dying race of the present day. My life work passed in vision before me. And I veiled my eyes, for I was yet too weak to know the Glory of God for a season.[30]

As a result of his vision, Pressey left his Unitarian congregation to preach in the deserted church at Montague. He never quit the ministry, and he continued to print his magazine "for the glory of Christ." But he insisted that the Montague building was "a meeting house, not a church"; he justified Sabbath observance on therapeutic grounds of "sanity and health"; and he opened the pages of *Country Time and Tide* to the mind-curist Horatio Dresser.[31] The evangelical heritage blended with the emerging therapeutic world view.

Other craft leaders showed the same secularized religiosity. They shared an admiration for antebellum utopias and a ministerial style of exhortation. (Triggs, Norton, and the *Artsman* contributor William Sloane Kennedy were all ministers' sons.) They used the language of the pulpit to extol "the religion of the home," "the new doctrine of work," and "the sacrament of common things." The most specific religious connections survived at Rose Valley. Although the perfectionist prophet most often cited in the *Artsman*'s "Rose Valley Scriptures" was Whitman rather than Wesley, the perfectionist mentality persisted among Traubel and his friends. Traubel explicitly acknowledged the community's spiritual debt to Brook Farm, and the Rose Valley meeting house sheltered an ethical humanism which met Washington Gladden's criterion for "Progressive" religion: it was "less concerned about getting men to heaven than about fitting them for their proper work on the earth."[32] Salvation in the next world had given way to self-improvement—or perhaps only "adjustment" —in this one.

The crafts reformers' evangelical legacy surfaced most clearly not in specific references, but in the assumptions they shared with contemporary humanitarian "Progressives": an individualist indifference to the collective dimension of political life, an idealist disregard for the inertia generated by existing institutions, a secularized millennial faith in the inevitability of progress, and a therapeutic concern with psychic well-being as an end in itself. The evangelical ethos, theologically a pale reflection of its antebellum ancestry, nevertheless persisted and shaped responses to the crisis of bourgeois values. Arts and Crafts ideology reflected not merely the social and cultural tensions felt by a specific group at a particular historical moment, but also the changing uses of time-honored republican and Protestant traditions. To explore the full significance of that ideology, we need to examine its social functions in detail.

Arts and Crafts ideology, like other manifestations of the antimodern impulse, served both to revitalize and to transform modern bourgeois culture. While Simple-Lifers stressed familiar virtues of discipline and work, aesthetes embodied a new style of high consumption appropriate to the developing consumer economy and educational reformers offered manual training as a therapeutic mode of adjustment to the corporate world of work. Yet it is important to emphasize that Arts and Crafts ideology was not reducible to these social functions, and that the revitalization and transformation of capitalist cultural hegemony were not consciously plotted programs but largely unforeseen results of half-conscious yearnings for "real life."

# Revitalization and Transformation in Arts and Crafts Ideology: The Simple Life, Aestheticism, Educational Reform

True to the republican tradition, many craft leaders remained deeply suspicious of urban "luxury." Seeking a wider significance for their hatred of modern tawdriness, they agreed that social and moral decay revealed itself in the decline of American taste—the "metallic, nervous, and discordant effect of commercial dyes," the clutter of Victorian interiors.[33] Rather than merely embracing aesthetic reform, many craft revivalists warred on bric-a-brac to promote what was in some ways an old-fashioned republican solution to the problem of overcivilization: "the simple life." Resisting the emergent style of consumption, Simple-Life advocates sought to revitalize older producer values. Calls for the simplification of life stressed the sanctity of hearth and home, the virtues of life on the land, and the ennobling power of work.

For decades ministers and conservative cultural critics had been decrying family decline, but by the turn of the century the conflicts in the domestic ideal had produced a vast literature of complaint, not only from male moralists worried about "race suicide" but from "New Women" for whom the bourgeois home was a stifling prison. Respectable Americans had more reason than ever to fret about the fate of the bourgeois family. This private dimension of the crisis of cultural authority provoked craft leaders as well as other social critics to reassert the values enshrined in the domestic ideal. Craft ideologues tended to infer the social problem from its aesthetic effects. Recoiling from "feminized" Victorian interiors, Pressey complained that "masculine interest in the home has declined, almost vanished. . . ." Others charged that the "tyranny of mere things" in Victorian living rooms desecrated the dwelling's inner sanctum, where "the mind and soul of the house" should reside. Invoking standards of health as well as morality, they urged housewives to banish "dust-catching, insect-breeding, microbe-sheltering plush furniture and hangings" from the family home. That task accomplished, "no litter of things could confuse, distress, or annoy the mind of its inmates," a *Craftsman* writer predicted. Redecoration only scratched the surface of the home problem, as most craft leaders admitted. Recognizing that the growth of an urban market economy had undermined the home's economic role, they failed to see that the same developments had generated the domestic ideal they sought to preserve. They mistakenly connected bourgeois domesticity with a subsistence farming economy. "Rejuvenation of the home instinct," in their view, required regeneration of the agrarian countryside.[34]

Return to the soil promised more than domestic revival; it also meant the return of a flaccid bourgeoisie to virtuous and productive life. Drawing on late-nineteenth-century agrarian revivalists like Prince Kropotkin and Edward Carpenter, and on the indigenous example of antebellum utopians, craft revivalists envisioned rural life as a path to moral regeneration. To be sure, there was a practical argument for the agrarian revivalist: to raise enough food for his own needs and still have time to work at his craft. But more important, the rehabilitation of rural life seemed essential to national revitalization. Craft leaders believed that the decline of country life posed its most serious threat to "the mental and moral fibre of the rising generation, especially its young men." City upbringing created only cleverness, not "the bone and blood that a man needs for his fighting days in the world." The emphasis on rural life as socialization led not to a rejection of modern culture but to a revitalization of it: only farm experience could provide that "centralization of purpose" demanded by modern work at all levels. Perhaps most disturbing was the effect of rural decline on leadership. Often observing that all America's greatest leaders had had rural boyhoods, craft leaders sought to revive the community life of the countryside. Pressey aimed to instill a new seriousness into rural social life, to revive local trades and local pride throughout New England. Other craft revivalists looked hopefully beyond the Berkshires, to the Kentucky mountains, where civilization had bypassed backwoods craftsmen and left them "strong and lithe of body," or to the arid regions of the Southwest, where a battle against a hostile environment was "producing a new type of American," resourceful, tough, and optimistic. Sweet were the uses of adversity. The chief value of life on the land was that it required hard work.[35]

A deep reverence for the work ethic was the third and most important component of arguments for the simple life. At Rose Valley, Traubel wrote, work was worship, the workbench an altar, and bad work blasphemy. His first *Artsman* editorial insisted that the Arts and Crafts movement was "no mere return to simple or archaic methods of production, but an assertion of the dignity and necessity of productive work." Work's greatest value lay in its strengthening of individual character. Diligent workers escaped from "that double-mindedness to which feeble or excitable natures are subject" and slept well without "malt extracts or strong waters."[36]

Enthusiasm for the work ethic led craft leaders sometimes to ignore Morris's distinction between "useful work and useless toil."

> Labor! all labor
> Is noble and holy

Pressey proclaimed, and pointed out that boys and girls learned "the blessedness of drudgery" at the New Clairvaux manual training school. How should a worker approach mere drudgery? Percival Wiksell asked in the *Artsman.* He should "pull himself together, and, taking the fat with the lean, keep his face lighted and his hand willing"—a proper attitude was the key to true craftsmanship. "Like the sailor we must do the hard work with a song—make prose into poetry by external means." An *Artsman* editorial told a story with a similar moral: any work can be artful if done in the proper spirit. The author had told a shoeshine boy he could stop. " 'Boss,' he protested, 'I want you to let me go on till I'm done.' The boy was an artsman."[37]

By shifting their attention from conditions of labor to the laborer's frame of mind, craft ideologues could acclaim the value of any work, however monotonous. Uncritical devotion to the work ethic blurred the figure of the artisan in American Arts and Crafts ideology. The character extolled by Ruskin and Morris had been decidedly preindustrial: unhurried, patient, absorbed in his work because it was enjoyable and unhampered by managerial schedules or discipline. The portrait was only partially accurate but it provided a sharp polemical focus. American craft reformers lost that focus by neglecting any distinction between premodern and modern work habits. The medieval artisan became indistinguishable from the modern bourgeois.

The merger of medieval and modern character was eased by the whiggish historiography of the craft leaders. Irene Sargent's interpretation of the decline and fall of the Florentine guilds described the guildsmen as a nascent middle class crushed between upper and nether millstones. That argument no doubt appealed to reform-minded Americans in 1901, when Sargent wrote the essay. Paralleling Sargent, other crafts leaders presented the medieval artisan as a harbinger of bourgeois values among dissolute nobles and swinish serfs. Craftsmen's search for bourgeois forerunners led them to identify St. Francis of Assisi as a proto-Protestant and St. Bernard of Clairvaux as "a medieval hero of simplicity" who "exalted afresh the power of manual work under spiritual forethought." To Pressey, Bernard was a worthy antecedent of John Wycliffe and Oliver Cromwell.[38]

Whig history provided a noble lineage for reform. Craft leaders stressed continuity between the medieval guild and their own efforts to revive what Sargent called the "gild spirit"—sobriety, discipline, and hard work, combined with deep suspicion of luxury, leisure, and sensual self-indulgence.[39] Those values, recalling republican moral tradition, formed the bedrock of the simple life. The simple life, in other words, was less a rejection of modernity than a means of revitalizing the modern morality of self-control during a period of social and psychic stress.

Aestheticism, on the other hand, pointed toward transformation rather than revitalization, toward a new culture of consumption rather than a revival of republican moralism. In republican America, aesthetic enterprise of any kind had long been eyed suspiciously. Pleasure in aesthetic creation or contemplation seemed perilously close to sensuality; art collecting seemed a vice of the European aristocracy. Yet by the second half of the nineteenth century, urban elites had begun to forget puritanical scruples. Wealthy Americans endowed museums, bedecked their homes with costly paintings and statuary from Europe, and established a network of patronage for a favored few artists. The burgeoning of an art establishment did not banish moralistic doubts overnight but it did encourage a more open admiration for aesthetic activity as an end in itself.[40]

This new attitude affected the entire Arts and Crafts movement, but especially the Boston Society. Most members lacked Norton's moral concerns. From the beginning they focused primarily on the artisan's product rather than his character. "If Arts and Crafts Societies stand for one particular thing more than another, is it not for the promotion of 'good taste' or the fitness of things in matters of decorative art—by exhibitions, by keeping a shop, by making themselves felt in the community?" one member asked in 1904. Morris had done more good through his actions than his words; his socialist rhetoric encouraged irresponsibility among craftsmen. "The craftsmen must himself change the conditions under which he works if he wants them changed. The Public won't do it and the Society can't, but the Public will soon or late buy his goods if they are good. The evils of Commercialism as affecting art are the evils of bad taste and can be cured only by the example of good taste."[41]

The elevation of public taste became a Boston Society shibboleth. A 1910 *Handicraft* editorial cited evidence for the Arts and Crafts movement's progress during the previous six years: "improved standards of taste" and "the finer qualities of design and workmanship displayed" at exhibits and salesrooms. Other editorials discussed criteria for evaluating an article as handicraft and warned the juries of other societies not to lower standards during the Christmas rush. Despite artistic advancement, the ever-present threat of dilettantism remained. Jury reports complained about shrewd craftsmen's affectation of "happy accidents," the deliberate creation of lumps and irregularities in otherwise symmetrical pottery, metal, or glassware. That practice reassured buyers that the article was indeed handmade but sometimes spoiled its functionality.[42]

The Boston Society's aestheticism led to trivial discussions like the talk about "happy accidents" or the long and pointless debate on the question: should machines be allowed to imitate handmade ornament? Such discussions left the Arts and Crafts movement vulnerable to critics like Thorstein Veblen. Veblen attacked the mania for bumpy vases and cockeyed plates as another leisure-class search for emblems of conspicuous consumption, and many articles in *Handicraft* unwittingly provided evidence for his view. The *reductio ad absurdum* of the flight from modern vulgarity appeared in 1911, when the magazine reported the Twelfth Night revels of the Detroit Society of Arts and Crafts.

> Of the individual garments it would be impossible to speak, else one would be tempted to linger over certain wonderful garments which most faithfully reproduced the spirit of a by-gone age; there was, for instance, a Princess of France wearing her coat of arms with royal dignity; and a Prioress who might have stepped straight from the pages of an illuminated missal. But after all, it is the picture of the whole that remains in the memory; the long table with its lighted candles and the guests in their quaint costumes; the grouping and passing of shadows on the tapestried wall; above all, the complete absence of any touch of modernity, any "spectators" who "just came to look on," that gave the unity of effect which makes an artistic whole, and made the occasion one long to be remembered.[43]

The Detroit Society's antics suggested that Arts and Crafts aestheticism was not confined to Boston. Editor Charles Francis Browne announced that *Brush and Pencil* "stands for good taste, and hopes to be an influence in this vast sea of ugliness for better things and higher arts." Most of the magazine's Arts and Crafts reportage simply evaluated the quality of exhibitions by the Chicago Society and other Midwestern groups. In both the *Artsman* and the *Craftsman,* contributors often discussed the quality of craft goods without reference to their makers. Their articles showed that for a number of participants, the Arts and Crafts movement was nothing more than an aesthete's pursuit of *objets d'art.* By elevating that pursuit into a moral crusade for "good taste," some craft leaders helped to legitimize the emerging cultural style of conspicuous consumption.

Yet contrary to Veblen's assumption, Arts and Crafts aestheticism did not always preclude wider concerns. At the least, aesthetes were plagued by the anxieties of their class; more often they shared with other craft leaders a concern for proper character formation among working class and "leadership class" alike. Like many other educated and affluent Americans, nearly all craft ideologues embraced educational reform as the solvent for social tension. By the turn of the century, John Dewey had begun to propagandize the "new education" from the University of Chicago and leading educators from Charles William Eliot to Felix Adler were forming the vocational training movement. Many middle- and upper-class Americans felt that if only the proper educational balance could be struck, immigrants could be assimilated, angry workers calmed, and an incipient leisure class returned to productive life.[44] The fascination of

Arts and Craft leaders with the possibilities of education stamped them
of a piece with their "Progressive" contemporaries. Because they defined
collective problems in individual terms, both craft revivalists and progressive educators drew back from fundamental social change and ended
by fitting individuals into the bureaucratic hierarchy of the emerging corporate system. Seeking to put both the immigrant urchin and the effete
rich boy in touch with "real life," they joined corporate liberal social
engineers in promoting a new kind of reform aimed not at achieving
social justice but at manipulating psychic well-being. Losing sight of antimodernism, they too promoted the transformation of modern American
culture.

The process of accommodation operated even at Hull House, where
Jane Addams and Ellen Gates Starr pioneered the tailoring of education
to the needs of immigrants. Starr began by lecturing on art at the settlement, studied bookbinding in London under Morris's associate, T. J.
Cobden-Sanderson, and returned to add a bindery to the Hull House
crafts program. Her essay "Art and Labor" (1895) acknowledged her
intellectual debt to Ruskin and Morris and revealed an accurate understanding of their work.

"Only by re-creation of the source of art can it be restored as a living
force," Starr announced at the outset. Restoration would come only
through "the freeing of the art power of the whole nation and race by
enabling them to work in gladness and not in woe. . . ." How that was to
be accomplished, Starr left unclear. She hopefully assumed that the
transformation of labor would occur at some misty future point, but argued that in the meantime, "one must always remember the hungering
individual soul. . . ." On that ground, Starr shied away from the logical
consequences of her original position, the need to eliminate alienated
labor in order to revitalize art. She devoted herself to providing "the
solace of art" to weary factory hands in evening classes and to their children in the public schools. Her efforts no doubt lightened many lives,
but her individualist and idealist assumptions paved the way to a conception of art as little more than uplift. As she put it, "The nourishment to
life of one good picture to supplant in interest vicious story papers and
posters; of one good song to take the place of vulgar street jingles, cannot, I believe, be estimated or guessed."[45]

Addams's educational ideas led to an equally manipulative conclusion.
As a young woman, she had read and admired Ruskin, and in *Twenty Years
at Hull House* (1910) she wrote movingly about the plight of factory workers
driven to alcoholism and suicide by the tedium of their jobs. But in *The
Spirit of Youth and the City Streets* (1909), she had already dismissed the
Ruskin-Morris attack on the factory as an impractical "first reaction against
our present industrial system." Accepting the inevitability of mass produc-

tion, she sought to educate factory hands to a self-conscious role in the industrial process.

> If a child goes into a sewing factory with a knowledge of the work she is doing in relation to the finished product, if she is informed concerning the material she is manipulating and the processes to which it is subjected; if she understands the design she is elaborating in its historic relation to art and decoration, her daily life is lifted from drudgery to one of self-conscious activity, and her pleasure and intelligence is registered in her product.

The key to this process was the Hull House Labor Museum, where workers learned the historical and industrial significance of their jobs. Addams called it "a beginning toward that education which Dr. Dewey defines as 'a continuing reconstruction of experience.'" She believed that by encouraging a spirit of teamwork among factory hands employed on the same product, the fragmenting effects of the division of labor might be overcome altogether. "A man who makes, year after year, but one small wheel in a modern watch factory, may, if his education has properly prepared him, have a fuller life than did the old watchmaker who made a watch from beginning to end," she wrote.[46]

Here again one can see the surfacing of a therapeutic approach in Arts and Crafts ideology, the same approach that has vitiated much twentieth-century educational reform despite the noble intentions of the reformers. Addams's effort to create a "fuller life" for factory hands paralleled the longings of her own class for more intense experience; in a way it was a projection of those longings. Eager to escape the suffocating protectiveness of her Victorian girlhood, Addams embraced the hard reality of settlement-house work and prescribed that same solution for other young women who felt smothered by material advantages. The recoil from over-civilized gentility pervaded the ethos of reform at the turn of the century. Determined to revitalize their own lives, reformers became convinced they could revitalize working-class lives as well. Their focus began to shift from social justice to personal fulfillment. This was a key moment in the reformation of capitalist cultural hegemony: humanitarian reformers, even the perceptive Addams, began unwittingly to accommodate themselves to the corporate system of organized capitalism. Assuming that education alone could overcome alienated labor, Addams ended in an intellectual position scarcely different from the unctuous paternalism of the "job enrichment" programs now run by giant corporations.

Though other craft leaders admired Addams's Labor Museum, they approached educational reform differently. To close the modern caste division between "blunt, brutish human tools" and "super-sensitive esthetic weaklings," they urged the introduction of manual training into public school curricula. Our present educational system is crippled by its European origins, they argued. It fills students with useless learning, appropriate for an old-world leisure class but not for practical members of an industrial society; it educates mediocrities beyond their station by encouraging vain and destructive ambitions. Craft ideologues claimed that curricula emphasizing useful work met the needs of both the Arts and Crafts movement and American society as a whole. Manual training would bridge the gap between the movement and the production process by endowing workers with good taste and aesthetes with physical strength and technical expertise. More important, proper educational reform would relax class tensions by diffusing the values of self-control and service among both rich and poor.[47]

For nearly all craft reformers, manual training became *the* solution for industrial problems. Elbert Hubbard's expectations were only slightly more inflated than those of the movement as a whole. "If college education were made compulsory by the state, and one-half of the curriculum consisted of actual useful manual labor," he predicted, "most of our social ills would be solved, and we would be well on the highway towards the Ideal City." In their enthusiasm for manual training, craft leaders transformed the revolutionary visions of Morris and Kropotkin into tepid advocacy of educational reform. Kropotkin's communitarian-anarchist antidote to the division of labor was reduced by Sargent to "integral education by the state"—the reunion of brain and hand in public technical schools. Triggs interpreted Morris's plea for "Education towards revolution" as proof that the Briton had converted to the cause of manual training by the 1890s. Turning Morris on his head, Triggs preached socialization, not revolution. Unlike labor unions, which bred only selfishness and party strife, Triggs asserted, his workshop method of education would restore "that courtesy and sympathy once so common, but now so rarely met with" among workers. The children of factory workers, particularly immigrants, might well be saved from a life of idleness and crime through manual training.[48]

Addams's starting point had been the factory hand's need for fulfillment; other Arts and Craft leaders began with the factory owner's need for efficiency. They presented manual training as a practical business proposition—a way to replace shiftless or incompetent employees with conscientious graduates of trade schools. They argued that such training should be specialized and geared to factory work—not the preindustrial "play-work" idealized by Ruskin and Morris. Using democratic rhetoric for elitist ends, manual training advocates railed against "feudal" and "aristocratic" schooling while they sought to train the lower classes for a subordinate role because "too many parents educate their children out of their proper sphere of usefulness. . . ."[49]

Yet manual training also served as therapeutic socialization for the bourgeoisie. Arts and Crafts leaders claimed that it provided affluent children—especially boys—with nourishing roughage amid the sweetmeats served up by polite education. "There is a custom, if not a law, in the royal households of Prussia that every boy shall learn a trade," observed Daniel Coit Gilman, first President of Johns Hopkins University and an early supporter of the Baltimore Society of Arts and Crafts. He advised the American leadership class to adopt the Prussian example.[50]

Other craftsmen agreed that leadership ability depended on the "conquering spirit" engendered by manual labor, especially on the farm. After "being sent into the country to 'rough it' on the farm," Stickley maintained, upper-class children "would come back to their books invigorated, broadened, and with a new zest for life." Stickley's Craftsman Farms School for Citizenship (tuition $1000) sought to implement this idea. Pressey started a similar but less expensive school at New Clairvaux (tuition $150). Both combined farming and craft training in an effort to discipline teenagers during their formative years; neither expected students to make a life's work of farming or craftsmanship.[51] Like the many other summer camps and boarding schools appearing among the upper class at the turn of the century, these craft schools aimed to promote smoother socialization rather than social alternatives.

While manual training toughened wealthy children for leadership roles, it revitalized their parents for continuing achievement. Pressey applauded the rehabilitation of two Deerfield neurasthenics through weaving and an *Artsman* editorial predicted that home furniture making had paved the way for "the future banishment of that dreaded foe of society, ennui." Recalling the antebellum crusade for manual labor led by the Tappan brothers, Arts and Crafts leaders pointed out that business and professional people could escape from depression or boredom through home training in cabinet work, pottery, or some other handicraft. But the moral note of the antebellum era gave way to a new and exclusive emphasis on health. As Stickley announced in 1904, "the age of handicraft is gone beyond recall," a victim of commercial efficiency, but "the value of handicrafts for the numberless thousands of men and women who are leading ill-balanced, abnormal lives" remained incalculable. The *Craftsman* carried articles testifying to the therapeutic effects of manual labor. A typical story lauded a bank president whose "antic of 'fooling' in his little shop adds cheer to his arduous work in the bank, and, he believes, postpones old age indefinitely."[52] Here one can see the origins of the present-day "do-it-yourself" hobbyist, whose revitalizing stints at the basement workbench are rooted in the assumption that the work he does for pay will continue to be unsatisfying.

The Arts and Crafts approach to manual training reinforced the belief that the work people do for a living will be tedious or excessively demanding and will drive them to seek the satisfactions of firsthand experience off the job. That belief has become a tacit assumption pervading our contemporary culture; its presence in Arts and Crafts ideology suggested a significant departure from Morris's ideas. He had deplored the growing gap

between work and leisure in industrial societies, and had sought the restoration of joy in work. American craft publicists, by treating craftsmanship
(in the diluted form of manual training) as an agent of socialization, abandoned Morris's effort to revive pleasurable labor. Manual training meant
specialized assembly line preparation for the lower classes and educational
or recreational experiences for the bourgeoisie; in neither case did it
challenge the separation of productive labor from joyful labor, nor protest
the modern organization of work. Instead it eased adjustment to our twentieth-century world of organized capitalism, where "work" and "life" exist
in separate spheres. The fascination of craft leaders with education reform,
like their enthusiasm for *objets d'art,* led toward transformation of modern
culture rather than protest against it.

The transformation furthered by aestheticism and educational reform,
the revitalization embodied in the cult of the strenuous life: these social
functions of the craft movement epitomized its drift toward accommodation. Despite its origins as a reaction against modern overcivilization, the
craft revival served to intensify the modern preoccupation with individual
fulfillment. Though some craft leaders resisted incorporation, most were
too easily enraptured by progressive pieties and too comfortably situated
in the bourgeois social structure to become consistent critics of modern
culture. Ambiguous from the outset, their antimodern critique became
progressively diluted within only a few years. Ultimately most applauded
mechanization, the division of labor, the gap between urban work and
suburban leisure—in short, the whole range of modern ills condemned by
Ruskin and Morris. The American craft movement's long-term value as
antimodern protest lay less in its dominant themes than in its quieter
leitmotifs—the still small voices of its minority of dissenters, the half-
conscious motives and unrealized intentions of its leaders. Considered as
an intellectual critique, the Arts and Crafts movement was a confused and
circular reversal of antimodernism.

# Reversing Antimodernism: The Factory, the Market, and the Process of Rationalization

One example of this reversal was the way craft reformers recast Morris's
critique of the factory system. Their implicit acceptance of modern work
conditions, combined with their individualist and idealist assumptions, led
Arts and Crafts leaders to a position which would have seemed strange
indeed to the British socialist whom many still acknowledged as an inspira-

tion. By stressing the ennobling qualities of even the dullest work, they melded preindustrial craftsmanship with the assembly line, collapsed the critique into the thing criticized, and legitimized modern factory labor as a form of character building. By ignoring the external conditions of labor to concentrate on the formation of proper attitudes, they transferred responsibility for shoddy workmanship from the proprietors and managers to the worker himself. Rather than criticize industrial capitalism, they attacked individual performance within capitalism. Both the *Craftsman* and the *Artsman* gave prominent space to Bliss Carman's lament: "We are ineffectual because we are slovenly and lazy and content to have things half done."[53]

It was only a short step from "we" to "they," from self-accusation to castigation of workers for their inattention to craftsmanship. The process was especially clear in Stickley's *Craftsman.* The magazine's early discussions of poor workmanship partially exonerated the worker by pointing to his joyless position. Irene Sargent pointed out in 1901 that "he practices the petty deceptions, the small thefts of time, the dishonesties which creep into the work of one whose labor is not made light by hope."[54]

An emphasis on moral shortcomings was present even in such sympathetic accounts, and it grew as Stickley became more successful in his business and more alarmed by labor violence. By 1904, he was arguing that the factory's harm lay less in dull work than in high wages, which discouraged self-reliance and ambition. The more Stickley distorted or ignored the capitalist framework of labor, the less sympathy he had for the workers' plight. "A carpenter working at his bench is told by the foreman not to stop to pick up the nails that have slipped through his fingers, as his time is worth more than the nails," he wrote. The anecdote could have illustrated the imperatives of rationalized production under capitalism, but Stickley ignored the foreman's role as the employer's agent and developed a sermon on the carpenter's irresponsibility. The carpenter "is taught a slipshod carelessness toward the property of his employer, that finally extends to everything. If he were a good, conscientious, thoroughly trained workman of the old school, he would be as careful of small things as of great, and would no more waste the property and time that belong to his employer than he would steal from him." Though no craft leader insisted as often as Stickley on that point, others agreed that industry's greatest problem was the shiftless worker.[55]

Character defects alone were not responsible for the modern worker's failure to meet preindustrial standards. The Boston architect C. Howard Walker identified another major problem: "the absolutely stultifying effect on skilled work of the trades unions, which are the apotheosis of mediocrity." Craft reformers at first argued that the trusts and the trade unions shared equally the blame for division of labor and decline of craftsmanship, but alarm quickly shifted to the unions alone. Triggs assailed the "factionalism" bred by unions; Stickley argued that they were not the heirs but the antitheses of medieval guilds. The guilds had fostered self-reliance and cooperation; the unions bred only selfish grumbling about "oppression." The guild stamp had guaranteed excellent workmanship, and symbolized a "religion of industry"; its modern descendant was the manufacturer's label. The union label guaranteed nothing except that a group of men had successfully monopolized production of that article by "forcing some manufacturer to come to their terms." Of course, Stickley admitted, labor unions were by no means alone to blame for the meaninglessness of their label. The root of the problem was that modern workers had no stake in individual productivity. As a result, they sought only "shorter hours and higher wages in return for careless and incompetent service. . . ." To revive the worker's interest in the quality of his work, "a thorough reorganization of our whole industrial system" was necessary. This did not include reorganization of the trusts, which for all their greed still embodied a devotion to quality products, but the reorganization of labor unions on a new basis of dedication to efficient workmanship.[56]

Until that halcyon day, the revival of craftsmanship could counter the class consciousness of unions by channeling social unrest into constructive, individualized solutions. Stickley wrote that "when a useful thing is beautifully made, and the user and maker have equal interest in the making, a point of contact is at once established between the one who has the power to make it and the other who has the means to possess it, and mutual respect and friendliness spring up between the two." As an example of this process, Stickley presented the comradeship that had developed between the Reverend Phillips Brooks, a fancier of fine furniture, and an Irish cabinetmaker. Here craftsmanship served the same social purpose traditionally met by pastoral literature: it insinuated what the literary critic William Empson once called a "beautiful relation" between rich and poor.[57] Stickley proposed a bourgeois version of pastoral; the solvent of class tensions was not bucolic leisure but hard, useful work.

Despite the *Craftsman* short stories which told of menacing tramps made into useful citizens through woodchopping, the radical specter would not go away. Concern about labor unrest led some craft reformers to further revisions in the image of the ideal artisan. For Norton and Sargent, the medieval artisan had been vigorously involved in his local polity; for other craft leaders, the artisan's chief virtues began to seem absorption in his work and contentment with his lot. Amid labor strife, traditional, hierarchical societies emerged as seedbeds of "simple goodness" in contrast to the "blind assertiveness" engendered by American democracy. To some craft revivalists, the most appealing model was "that land of . . . divine obedience to authority," Japan. In their view, neither the Tokugawa woodcarver nor the contemporary Japanese showed the restless discontent of American workers; both seemed content with their "simple life." For Stickley, the medieval artisan shared similar admirable qualities. His third-person editorial persona extolled "his predecessors in the Middle Ages, whom he strives in all things to imitate: in enthusiasm for his work, in contentment with his lot, in gaining pleasure with the small things."[58]

In contrasting the contented premodern artisan with the ill-humored labor agitator, some craft revivalists joined such defenders of capitalism as Columbia University president Nicholas Murray Butler, whom Stickley quoted admiringly. The movement's affinity for business apologetics suggested a more general entanglement in market values. In discussions of two related subjects, the high price of Arts and Crafts goods and the problem of the artisan's livelihood, craft reformers revealed their inability either to confront difficulties raised by the pressures of a market economy or to transcend the values of their class. Eager for a wider reality, they nevertheless allowed the market to define the boundaries of the possible.

For a movement with egalitarian aims, the exorbitant cost of hand-wrought wares was an embarrassment. Some solved the problem by taking the high road of aesthetic superiority. Stickley, for example, argued that the average wage-earner ignored craftsman furniture because "it doesn't conform to his machine made standards." Others admitted a problem. Traubel warned that craft revivalists would fall into dilettantism if they could not learn how to make good things cheaply, but he never proposed specific ways to accomplish that goal. Hubbard did. In his early years at East Aurora, he styled himself a socialist. When a critic charged that Roycroft books on socialism were too expensive for the average workingman, Hubbard replied, "Socialism does not consider it desirable to supply cheap stuff to anybody. The Socialist aims to make every manufactured article of the best quality possible. . . . Then sell it at a price that affords something more than a bare existence to the workmen who put their lives into the making of it." Hubbard's socialism, which he soon repudiated, turned out to be little more than enlightened capitalism. Rather than confront what Traubel called "the problem of cheap and dear," other craft leaders preferred to sidestep it altogether. As Traubel's Rose Valley colleague Will Price put it, "It is a proof of the growth of artsmanship to be able to make a living making things for use, even if only the few can afford to buy them."[59]

To concentrate on the artisan's livelihood was to recast the problem, not solve it. In Boston, despite most of the society members' determination to focus on aesthetics alone, the question of the artisan's survival in a market economy continued to surface. The discussion stemmed from a feeling of uneasiness, a sense that the society during its early years had been engaged in ineffectual, dilettantish activity. When *Handicraft* began publication in 1902, aestheticism still dominated but had become a minor theme of the society's discussions. Arthur Carey, Professor of Design at Harvard and Norton's successor as president, worried that commercial motives eroded the artisan's creativity. The society should help him rid himself of commercial motives by prohibiting secret commissions and setting up cooperative craft shops where the craftsmen divided profits according to the value of their works, Carey suggested. These cooperatives would be best located in the country, where they could follow Morris's example in providing models for a society where "in order to produce the best possible work, the laws of commercialism might be reversed." Yet in Carey's cooperative shops, market values still set the prices. He admitted that "there is a real antagonism between business for the sake of gain and art for the sake of use and beauty, but the antagonism is between the motives, not between the business and the art." Indeed, Carey insisted, success in art and in business both depended on the same character traits. "Order, promptness, and accuracy are valuable sources of economy and power both in artistic and commercial work."[60] Bestowed with bourgeois values, the figure of the artisan lost polemical power—as at other points in Arts and Crafts ideology.

Carey's mishmash of vague proposals typified the efforts of most Boston Society members to connect aesthetic and social problems. Within a single article, paeans to the creative stimulus provided by the medieval guilds coexisted with admonitions to "make the best of conditions as they are." But for Mary Ware Dennett, leatherworker, wife of the architect Hartley Dennett and later a leading suffragist and birth control pamphleteer, such confusion was pathetically insufficient. In Dennett's view the refusal to consider fundamental social change confined craft organizations to frivolous pursuits. She urged Arts and Crafts Societies to take Ruskin and Morris seriously, to "spend less time on rag-rugs, baskets, and what a sign recently seen in a shop window called 'burnt goods,'" and more on challenging the commercial economy which poisoned the wellsprings of artistic creativity. The "elevation of public taste" was impossible as long as the majority of workers was too bored and exhausted to make or enjoy beautiful things. If the craftsman is to get an adequate livelihood, Dennett told her affluent audience, *we* will have to pay for it. "And indeed if we have no other wish than a mere selfish desire for beauty . . . we shall be forced to arrange just conditions, simply in order that the supply of art may not be choked at its source," she warned.[61]

Dennett's blueprints for just conditions were admittedly vague—she drew tentatively on Ruskin, Kropotkin, and Henry George—but they were enough to provoke the architect Herbert Langford Warren, who succeeded Carey as president of the Boston Society in 1903. The Arts and Crafts movement's association with socialism has made "the great world" look askance at societies like our own, he cautioned. The Boston group's success was due to its avoidance of such distractions. "It is commercialism, the subdivision of labor, and the machine that have made the nineteenth century and are making the twentieth century what it is, that have brought larger opportunities to so much larger numbers than at any other time in the world," Warren announced. It would be "not only futile but wrong" to crusade against "those great systems." Instead, the Arts and Crafts movement should stick to its last: the elevation of public taste. If the public learned to appreciate beautiful things, he concluded, craftsmanship would become commercially viable.[62]

Given automatist economic assumptions, the problem of the artisan's livelihood solved itself. As Sylvester Baxter of the *Boston Transcript* put it, "Reduced to the plainest terms, the work of the artist will be seen to be a pursuit like any other pursuit, and amenable to the laws of supply and demand." Baxter went on to point out ways in which the artist could accommodate himself to the marketplace without compromising the quality of his work—such as painting signs for taverns and restaurants.[63]

The notion of an independent artisan, skipping about the interstices of the economy, was comforting but delusive. Letters from artisans unable to make even a subsistence living from the sale of their work continued to appear in *Handicraft*. Soon after the magazine began republication in 1910, Carl Purington Rollins assumed the editorship and attempted to revive controversy. Rollins had worked with Pressey at New Clairvaux and had shared the minister's individualist approach in their 1904 pamphlet, *The Arts and Crafts and the Individual*. But by 1911 Rollins had become a Marxian socialist. In his first article, he complained that the American Arts and Crafts movement was far behind its predecessor in England, where Morris's ideas culminated logically in socialism. We craftsmen "belong, by all that is decent, to the working class," Rollins declared.[64]

> We make articles of use and beauty for the rich, but we seldom wear or use these articles ourselves: we cannot, by our very birthright, be members of the bourgeoisie, for their god is trade, and we do but deny our god in so strange a one. The logical class for us, then, is the proletariat, the last great class now emerging into conscious life.[65]

Rollins's "we" was an illusion. He was a printer, albeit a former Harvard student. But his readership was dominated by professional men and club women. The Boston Society asked for Rollins's resignation from its executive committee, but it allowed him to stay on as editor—perhaps because he printed the magazine and the Society stationery free of charge. Subsequent *Handicraft* articles on the artisan's livelihood were less defiant than Rollins's original manifesto. Dennett continued to attack "Special Privilege" and suggest populist alternatives; other contributors more commonly called for rural cooperatives which could promote art and fellowship while enabling participants to produce *"the most salable work."* The tendency of crafts to merge with commercial trades illustrated "a law of survival"; if handmade products could not pass the test of the market, they were not worth producing.[66]

Those assumptions continued to frame Arts and Crafts debate, within both the Boston Society and the movement as a whole. Will Price looked forward to the abolition of privilege, but his ideal society was "governed by the laws of supply and demand" as well as "the law of natural cooperation. . . ." While Stickley preached "the commercial value of design," Hubbard became a flamboyant prophet of business prosperity and an enemy of socialism's supposed threat to it. Pressey, dazzled by the "simplicity" of Marshall Field's department store, placed "leaders of private enterprise" at the head of his mythic "Altrurian Army of Production."[67]

The assumption of the market's inevitability led most craft reformers to embrace some variant of "industrial relations" as the key to improving the worker's lot. Pressey, hoping for "some form of Christian socialism" as his ultimate goal, urged profit sharing as an interim solution. The *Craftsman* continued articles on "The Social Secretary—an Opportunity for Employer and Employee to Understand Each Other" and on "A Co-operative Village for Working People—Beautiful and Practical and a Four Percent Investment." The path to the future, Stickley was convinced, lay along the lines of the National Cash Register Company's factory betterment program. Like the Hull House Labor Museum, such reforms betrayed Morris's vision while pretending to refine it. They promoted not social justice but social engineering.[68]

As accommodation with the corporate system became more complete, the impulse to revitalize older producer values grew fainter. Even the sanitized petit-bourgeois version of the antimodern impulse, the Simple-Lifers' vision of a land dotted with villages, small farms, and cottage industries, became unsatisfactory to many craft leaders. Influenced by a developing corporate liberal ideology, they sought to heal the wounds in the modern psyche not through a reassertion of autonomous will but through smooth adjustment to the "inevitable" process of rationalization. For many, what began as a reaction against rationalization ended in therapeutic assimilation to it; Morris's "hatred of modern civilization" became transformed beyond recognition.

A key to this reversal of the antimodern impulse lay in the craft reformers' faith in the inevitability of progress. Mary K. Simkhovitch, a settlement-house worker who shared Addams's privileged background, invoked a favorite theme of all craft ideologues when she reminded *Craftsman* readers that "no one must expect in any way to stem the tide of the historical process." Convinced that the current of progress flowed inexorably, Stickley, Traubel, and Boston Society leaders all sought to dissociate themselves from the "antimachine rantings" of Morris and his followers. "The railroad, the factory, and the mine are the sources of the strength of the modern world, and it should be our task to convert this strength from ugliness and injury to beauty and beneficence," the architect Claude Bragdon wrote in the *Craftsman*. Some craft leaders defended not only specific machines, but even the fragmentation of tasks endemic to the process of rationalization—the very problem which had first provoked the craft revival. Even during the *Craftsman's* early years, when the ghosts of Ruskin and Morris stalked on almost every page, there were hints of apostasy. Committed to a belief in progress, critics like Sargent admitted the factory system was "a necessary step in social evolution." Specialization, the *bête noire* of Ruskin and Morris, soon won Stickley's ultimate accolade of "inevitability."[69] It was Triggs, however, who was the most influential advocate of rationalization. In 1897, even as he invoked the bleak vision of "a perfect mechanical world and an impotent humanity," he checked his pessimism by musing on the machine's inscrutable, godlike purposes.

> It may be, of course, that the machine is preparing the world for an event it knows not of—an event that requires the subjection of the individual for its accomplishment, some such event as universal competency. In itself the machine is an object of wonder, one of the special triumphs of the age, and worthy of all homage.[70]

This sort of technocratic determinism, though not expressed as vapidly, has marked corporate liberal thinking from Walter Lippmann to Rexford Guy Tugwell. Triggs came by it easily, working as he did in the heady "Progressive" atmosphere of turn-of-the-century Chicago. By 1903, fellow Chicagoans like Frank Lloyd Wright and John Dewey had convinced Triggs that rationalized technological growth did not destroy individual dignity, but enhanced it. Whatever misgivings Triggs may have had evaporated. Still claiming allegiance to Morris's goals, he had become a prophet of mechanization and corporate capitalism. "We want machinery," he announced.

> We want more and ever more of it. But when machinery has done its work, when all our common and primitive needs are satisfied by quantitative production, when everything that is really mechanical in conduct is mechanized, then we escape into a transcendental sphere where the will is free, where conduct is vital every moment.[71]

Trigg's valuation of "escape" reflected the belief—repugnant to Morris—that personal fulfillment existed only in a "transcendental sphere" cut off from mundane necessities. The means of escape remained vague. Only under perfect organization along the lines suggested by the trusts, Triggs argued, could the individual become truly free. Then, by a strange alchemy, "under conditions of freedom industry changes its character and becomes aesthetic."[72]

Triggs's enthusiastic predictions of a "new industrialism" were often quoted in Arts and Crafts journals. He helped to inspire a hopefulness toward giant corporations, even among craft leaders claiming to be Christian Socialists. It was left to Stickley to produce the apotheosis of rationalization. In 1911, he published a lead editorial entitled "Waste: our Heaviest National Liability," in which he praised the "amazing results" Frederick Winslow Taylor had achieved through his system of scientific management. The system was particularly valuable, Stickley alleged, because it might persuade labor unions to abandon their wasteful practices. Concluding with a paean to Nature's efficient use of resources, Stickley reminded citydwellers that they could live far more efficient lives by periodically recharging their batteries at Nature's "great powerhouse of being."[73] As at other points in Arts and Crafts ideology, social control of the working class coincided with personal regeneration of the bourgeoisie.

Stickley had abandoned Morris completely, although the *Craftsman* still printed his aphorisms—incongruous alongside praise of Taylor. Stickley's embrace of Taylorism was only an exaggerated version of the entire movement's fate. By compromising with modern industrial capitalism at a number of key points, Arts and Crafts leaders blunted the polemical edge Morris had given to the figure of the artisan. In Arts and Crafts ideology, the premodern artisan variously embodied a model bourgeois, a docile employee, and—most importantly—a source for therapeutic revitalization. Only a few craft ideologues tried to sustain the image of the artisan as a model of joyous labor in a community. For most, the critique of degraded labor and the vision of humane community slipped away; craftsmanship became a means of social control and self-fulfillment in a rationalizing capitalist society.

# The Fate of
# the Craft Ideal

While assimilation of rebellious workers remained an important leitmotif in Arts and Crafts ideology, the most persistent theme was not social control but psychic self-renewal: the rejuvenation of the overcivilized personality. By 1908 the journalist Alvan F. Sanborn could identify the Arts and Crafts movement's chief effects as the improvement of industrial design and the rehabilitation of society ladies with "overstrained nerves" and of "tired, nervous businessmen. . . ."[74] Reporting on handicraft instruction at Ipswich, Massachusetts in 1903, Sylvester Baxter wrote of the rejuvenation process, describing it in language which underscored the link between the craft revival and other antimodern efforts to recover a primal authenticity of thought, feeling, and action.

> . . . the student goes back to the primitive beginnings of an art, and is shown how to put himself in place of the ancient worker, so far as possible; doing the

thing as it was done in the beginning and, by following the primal instincts for art, to develop his work according to natural indications and without the sophistication that comes with beginning a lesson in the middle. Knowing what we know, we cannot, of course, return to the primitive state of mind and feeling, and hence do things in just that same way, any more than the grown man can return to childhood. But while from our twentieth century civilization we may not return to the childhood of the race, we can in great measure bring into play the primitive springs of thought, impulse, and action that exist in every human being and so put ourselves *en rapport* with the primitive state of mind and primitive view of things, just as the adult can bring himself into sympathetic relations with the child.[75]

Baxter realized that the flight from modernity was partial and temporary. Setting the "natural" over the "sophisticated," he sentimentalized the "childhood of the race" but sought only fleeting contact with it. His careful primitivism typified the revitalizing and transforming functions of both the craft movement and antimodernism in general. By returning to "the primitive springs of thought, impulse, and action," whether at the carpenter's workbench or the wilderness weekend cottage, modern men and women could refresh themselves for more effective action in the workaday world; familiar bourgeois virtues could be revitalized. At the same time the very stress on escape—however temporary—from adult constraints suggested that craftsmanship could fit the newer mode of leisure and self-fulfillment. Whether it pointed toward revitalization or transformation, the craft ideal contained a new and secular emphasis on personal well-being as an end in itself. What began in reaction against the "morbid self-consciousness" of the therapeutic world view ended as another self-absorbed therapy, promoting adjustment rather than dissent.

The path of adjustment can be clearly seen in the craft reformers' redefinition of the simple life. Implicitly accepting the modern distinction between city work and country leisure, many reduced the simple life to a vacation cottage or a rustic exurban home. In the *Artsman,* William Sloane Kennedy waxed lyrical over his lakeside cabin, where he escaped on weekends from flaccid ease and oversubtle thought. Other backwoods enthusiasts refused to sacrifice urban comfort even temporarily. Bliss Carman contributed a *Craftsman* article on his Adirondack retreat where he had "all the privacy of the wilderness, and yet all the essential luxuries of the town," including a laundress. Stickley thought that the simple life could be aided by professionalized training of servants and the growing popularity of annual vacations—"recognized as a necessity by all classes of our people. . . ." He became a prophet of a tasteful, bucolic suburbia, joined to the city by trolley car and automobile.[76]

Tolstoy, Kropotkin and Carpenter, the originators of the simple life, would all have been dismayed by such a vision. But it flowed naturally from an idealist redefinition of the simple life as a state of mind. As Traubel put it, "simplicity of life has nothing necessarily to do with living on a farm. Our cry is not: Back to the land! Our cry is: Back to yourself!" Stickley reassured his readers that the simple life "is not necessarily the humble life."[77] Whoever worked hard with a fixed purpose truly lived the simple life. Voluntary poverty was not on the agenda.

Faithful adherence to bourgeois values, in mansion or tenement, became the key to simplifying one's life. The *embourgeoisement* of the simple life pointed to the Arts and Crafts movement's fundamental compromises with modernity. Confronting the fragmenting impact of economic rationalization, American craft leaders transformed what might have been an alternative to alienated labor into a revivifying hobby for the affluent. The craft movement became less a critique of modern culture than a means of reaffirming it—including its great factories and corporate bureaucracies. How had craft revivalists, still claiming to be followers of Morris, come to embrace institutions so abhorrent to him?

The fate of Arts and Crafts ideology resulted in part from the class position and interests of its adherents. It was not just that they accepted laissez-faire economic assumptions; they were personally involved in business ventures. Their accommodation with bourgeois culture grew more apparent as their business concerns became more dominant. By 1908, Sanborn observed: "Nearly all the Crafts furniture and much of the pottery is now put on the market by business partnerships and corporations. . . ." Yet from the beginning craftsmen had shared the anxieties common to a business and professional class. They feared their own weakness in the face of restive workers and "swarming immigrants." Their concern about overcivilization combined with their commercial entanglements and led them to play conflicting roles. They sought business success at the same time they preached social regeneration. Hubbard's entrepreneurial ambitions smothered his "socialism" as early as 1899, when he discovered the profit to be had from propagandizing business. Stickley sought a more dignified stance. He built an impressive "Craftsman building" in Manhattan to show Mission furniture and house his magazine's offices, joined several fashionable clubs, and voted Republican. The organizers of Rose Valley were equally frank about their commercial purposes. The community was "not an impractical or visionary undertaking but a concrete business proposition," said Hawley McClanahan. Traubel's editorials continually solicited investment dollars. Investors ought not to have profit as their primary motive and it would be best of all if they contributed work as well as dollars, but we will, of course, take dollars alone, Traubel admitted. Pressey did not embrace commercialism so willingly but he was determined to free New Clairvaux from its Boston benefactors. Financial self-sufficiency required a cash income from the print shop, the farm, and the school. Advertisements for the school announced that at New Clairvaux, "We carry on a *Productive* Business. It is therefore practice, not theory."[78]

But it would be an oversimplification to claim that class interest alone thrust Arts and Crafts ideology toward accommodation. There were other pressures at work as well. One was the legacy of antebellum romantic reform, the individualist, idealist approach to social change. Hostile to socialism's "indifference to ideals," intent on improving the worker's lot by "spiritualizing business," or molding his mind and character, craft revivalists remained unable to conceive problems in collective terms and fatally indifferent to questions of power.[79] At the same time, their hostility to existing institutions was softened by their millennial faith in the inevitability of progress.

The heart of the thrust toward accommodation was neither class interest nor the evangelical legacy but the psychic needs of craft ideologues themselves. Their quest for authentic experience embodied yearnings for a larger life, a wider selfhood than the modern superego allowed. But the vagueness of the complaint left the question open: how was "real life" to be embraced? A few, like Pressey, immersed themselves in subsistence farming. But nearly all agreed in the end that the bedrock of reality was the process of industrial production. The modern world of work was finally inescapable. Jane Addams spoke for an entire generation when she said:

> You may remember the forlorn feeling which occasionally seizes you when you arrive early in the morning a stranger in a great city: the stream of laboring people goes past you as you gaze through the plate-glass window of your hotel; you see hard-working men lifting great burdens; you hear the driving and jostling of huge carts and your heart sinks with a sudden sense of futility.[80]

"The Subjective Necessity for Social Settlements," Addams declared, was that they counteracted that sense of futility by giving useful work to sheltered young women. Addams did not address herself to the subjective necessities of males; other craftsmen assumed that young men would dispel youthful anxieties through immersion in productive labor.

The love affair of craftsmen with productivity led them to the marketplace, which the Harvard Design professor Denman Ross admired as "the big world of hard work and real work." Anything less than full acceptance of industrial capitalism, Ross told the Boston Society, reduced craftsmen to dilettantism or sentimental utopianism. The only "real work," apparently, was work sold for profit. That was the standard at Triggs's People's Industrial College where "Everybody works practically and not in a playing, dilettante manner. Everything must stand the test of the market." If the Arts and Crafts movement was to be work and not play, Ernest Batchelder warned in the *Craftsman,* it must prove itself commercially.[81] For many craftsmen, to reject industrial capitalism was to risk evading the "real life" they longed to face. Their flight from modernity led always in circles.

Or almost always. It would be mistaken to assert that Arts and Crafts ideology had no other significance than as a source for revitalizing and transforming the dominant culture. To be sure, the organized Arts and Crafts movement was moribund by the First World War: Rose Valley folded for lack of funds in 1908; New Clairvaux followed in 1909; Hubbard died on the *Lusitania* in 1915; Stickley and the *Craftsman* went out of business in 1916; the Boston and Chicago Societies survived by restricting their attention to aesthetic matters. Yet the craft impulse has become dispersed in millions of do-it-yourself projects and basement workshops, where men and women have sought the wholeness, the autonomy, and the joy they cannot find on the job or in domestic drudgery. If the result of this craftsmanship has been to accommodate them to everyday routine, the motive behind it provides a touching commentary on the nature of work in contemporary society. One can hardly presume to "explain" such a vast and complex phenomenon, but it is at least possible to suggest that the contemporary craft hobbyist shares some of the motives of his turn-of-the-century forebears. He—or she—may sometimes feel a similar longing for individual identity and measurable accomplishment in a culture where all meanings seem to be evaporating into weightlessness.[82]

Besides spawning this mute protest, the craft movement also prefigured a more systematic intellectual challenge to the stifling overorganization of life in factories and bureaucracies. The decentralized communitarianism preached sporadically by Pressey and Traubel (and more consistently by Dennett and Rollins) foreshadowed the critique of the modern megastate formulated by Mumford, Goodman, and Schumacher—critics who have warned Americans all over again about the dangers of galloping technological growth and gluttonous consumption of resources. Easily caricatured as Luddites by their progressive opponents, these critics have not been "against technology" any more than Morris was. They are Morris's true heirs, focusing their attack not on abstractions like "the machine" but on the rationalizing elites who remain obsessed with efficient productivity at the expense of satisfying labor and humane community.

By now, "small is beautiful" has become a catchword on the Left; the decentralist critique has been popularized by the antinuclear activists and back-to-the-landers who constitute the remnants of the 1960s counterculture. Like Morris's views in Britain, the American decentralist critique has been diffused among the "crinkum-crankum" on the fringes of intellectual respectability. It has been denied any real legitimacy in a political "debate" dominated by barely distinguishable corporate liberals and "neoconservatives." For both these groups, economic productivity remains a panacea for social ills.

Yet despite the contemporary political impotence of decentralized communitarianism, the communal impulse is an important and recurring phenomenon in our popular culture. It represents a persistent effort to reject a modern way of life split between routine work and passive leisure, to seek the restoration of wholeness by living a hard but satisfying life on the land. Using different slogans and enjoying varying degrees of success, several generations of Americans have reenacted this antimodern dream. The most recent were the countercultural communards and craft revivalists of the 1960s; the earliest (at least in this century) were the Simple-Lifers of the Arts and Crafts movement. Though they looked toward antebellum antecedents, craft leaders like Pressey and Traubel were among the first communitarians to confront problems of fragmented selfhood and anomie that still plague Americans today. Despite its ineffectuality and its accommodationist tendencies, the Arts and Crafts movement was parent to a powerful strain of antimodern discontent.

At bottom that discontent was religious. The deep dissatisfaction with labor-saving devices and bourgeois notions of comfort, the lust for "hard reality" and the deification of work, all suggested that the Arts and Crafts movement had religious overtones—not simply in its secularized perfectionism and millennialism, but also as a faint, unconscious protest against an emergent secular civilization based on material consumption. As the theological core of Protestantism slipped away, craftsmen clung to the husk of puritanical habit. Having grown up in the lap of affluence, they agreed with Pressey that "to enter life we all need a fearful challenge, something hard to do."[83] The revival of handicraft reflected a kind of vicarious atonement for unprecedented physical comfort. This religious disquiet lay at the root of all the profounder varieties of antimodernism; at best, it helped to sustain a stoical cast of mind amid the evasive banality of modern culture.

But among craft ideologues stoicism was nearly always submerged by progressive cant. The final irony was that, despite the craft movement's origins in antimodern discontent, most of its leaders worshipped at the national shrine of economic growth. And most fell victim to the evasions and self-deceptions of the dominant culture. In the name of individualism, many hailed the vision of a future society modelled on the giant corporation. They shared that enthusiasm with the corporate liberal ideologues who had formed the National Civic Federation in 1900 and had begun to coalesce around Theodore Roosevelt. Roosevelt's advocacy of the strenuous life jelled with the Arts and Crafts program for individual regeneration. Both urged the cultivation of supposedly primitive traits as a path to greater efficiency in modern life. Both responded to the crisis of cultural authority, which reached a flash point in the 1890s. But Roosevelt's strenuosity remained inextricably tied to militarism, and militarism required a fiercer premodern focus than the peaceful artisan could supply.

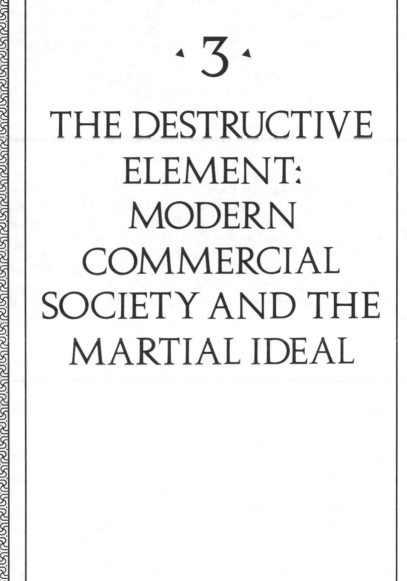

# ·3·
# THE DESTRUCTIVE ELEMENT: MODERN COMMERCIAL SOCIETY AND THE MARTIAL IDEAL

T HE MARTIAL IDEAL IS VIRTUALLY TIMELESS. FROM Odysseus to Lancelot, from samurai to citizen-soldier, the figure of the warrior has preoccupied the human imagination. It is a risky business to link such a universal image to particular historical circumstances. Yet for cultivated Americans during the late nineteenth century, concern with martial virtue did help to focus many of the particular dilemmas generated by the crisis of cultural authority. To bourgeois moralists preoccupied by the decadence and disorder of their society, the warrior's willingness to suffer and die for duty's sake pointed the way to national purification; to those who craved authentic selfhood, the warrior's life personified wholeness of purpose and intensity of experience. War promised both social and personal regeneration.

This militarist idea may have existed for millennia, but it has acquired particular force in the twentieth century—the century of mass politics and total war. As the rationalization of culture increasingly has reduced more and more existence to banal routine, life at war has sometimes seemed to promise authentic experiences no longer available in everyday life: the opportunity for moral and physical testing, the sheer excitement of life amid danger and death. Above all, war has offered men the chance to escape the demands of bourgeois domesticity and reintegrate a fragmented sense of self by embracing a satisfying social role. As heroic actors in a "theater of war" and members of a tight-knit (though manufactured) male community, men have sometimes temporarily eluded the contradictions and confusions of modern culture. (Only in this light can one begin to understand the nostalgia some men seem to feel for their military experience.)

Besides this private dimension, twentieth-century militarism has had a more obvious public side. Since the 1880s, cults of violence have inspired imperialists, fascists, and revolutionary guerillas throughout the Western world and perhaps beyond. During the same period in the United States, a more respectable and insidious militarism has infected the thinking of opinionmaking elites. One can hear it today in the "nuclear superiority" cant of Reaganite Republicans, in the assaults of Cold War Democrats on "sentimental McGovernism," in all the "tough-minded realism" that passes for wisdom in the established press. Whether markedly aggressive or softened by a patina of respectability, most varieties of twentieth-century militarism—at least in the West—share a common cultural origin in the late-nineteenth-century recoil from a weightless modernity.

In the United States, antimodern militarism was energized by the tensions between the regnant commercial society and an inherited martial ideal—tensions shaped by the process of rationalization but originating in the republican ambivalence toward material success. For centuries, republican moralists had insisted that spartan virtue was a necessary antidote to the corruption bred by commercial "luxury." As the historian J.G.A. Pocock has pointed out, English libertarians of the seventeenth and eighteenth centuries posed virtue against commerce, the country against the court, the independent landed warrior citizen against the bureaucrat and the mercenary. Loyal to a static, agrarian vision, "country" ideologues transmitted their fears of growth to republican thinkers in America. For Jefferson as for Harrington, the landed gentry were the foundation of political liberty and a counterforce to the corruptions of the town. From the Revolutionary era on, the "country" strain in republican thought exalted the freeholding warrior-citizen as a redeemer of modern comfort and complacency.[1]

During the early nineteenth century, under the influence of romantic literary convention, the warrior's cultural uses became more various. Recalling the traditional antithesis between the burgher and the knight, Sir Walter Scott and his imitators transformed the landed gentleman into a chivalric knight—at once a purifier of commercial corruption and a charming alternative to urban grayness. For Scott's avid American audience in the antebellum decades, the martial ideal fused republican and romantic tradition, moral and aesthetic appeal.

The fusion seemed most compelling to slaveholding Southerners, whose chivalric posturing and enthusiasm for Scott have become proverbial. Though the political importance of Southern medievalism has been exaggerated, there is no doubt that proslavery critics of Northern commercialism held aloft the image of the aristocratic country gentleman, who fought hard and rode hard and cared not a fig for money matters. The image was more than a piece of ideological mystification; it was grounded in Southern customs and traditions which were reinforced by the Civil War. The widespread obeisance to notions of personal honor, the persistence of dueling, and the proliferation of military schools designed to produce "officers and gentlemen"—all underscored the importance of premodern martial ideals among upper-class Southerners well into the twentieth century.[2]

In the North the martial ideal faced a more problematic future. From the early nineteenth century it was overshadowed by a spreading sentimental ethos, a compound of romantic sensibility and evangelical benevolence. To be sure, Scott was more widely read above the Mason-Dixon line than below it. Flutterings of anxiety over Yankee chicanery led a few Northern writers (such as Sarah Josepha Hale, the editor of *Godey's Lady's Book*) to look southward in search of an antidote. And some Northern intellectuals rejected the sentimental ethos, hailing the Civil War as an opportunity to revive Spartan virtue. But in general, the Northern martial ideal remained largely covert.[3]

By midcentury, sentimentalism had spawned the modern literary style, proclaiming itself "realism" but largely concerned with the limited spheres of polite society and domestic intrigue. "Realistic" authors were usually female; they preferred analysis to action, the parlor to the battlefield. After the Civil War, within the "feminized" Northern culture, the spread of domestic realism was reflected in the declining popularity of Scott. By the 1870s, his sun had set. His flowery style and trumpet-and-drum subject matter found little favor among admirers of Howells, Eliot, or their imitators. It was a common view that Scott was an "early romanticist" whose attachment to the Great Man had become anachronistic in an age which recognized the press of heredity and environment on character.[4]

Social theorists and literary critics alike believed that the emergence of an interdependent, commercial society signalled the displacement of the romantic warrior by the peaceful bourgeois. During the 1870s and 1880s, in fact as well as fiction, the chivalric hero seemed on the verge of extinction. It was not simply that mass democracy rendered "exceptional men" unimportant, but that modern commerce required perpetual peace. That at least was the view of many Northern observers in the post–Civil War decades. In the excitement of postwar economic expansion, it seemed to many that commercial necessity had rendered the martial virtues obsolete.

That notion may seem curious today, when business and military interests are so often allied rather than opposed, but in the nineteenth century it received scientific sanction from Spencerian and other progressive models of social change. Nearly all postulated some variation on the three-stage development from savagery through barbarism to civilization. And nearly all agreed that modern civilized man was rational, self-controlled, and anxious to avoid violence—a being altogether superior to his aggressive ancestors. The republicans' cyclical view of history was overshadowed (though never wholly obscured) by schemes of linear progress. From the progressive view, economic growth did not stifle Spartan virtue—as republican moralists had feared—but allowed it to develop into the "more elaborate moral organization" of the urban bourgeoisie.[5]

Such comforting beliefs pervaded post–Civil War American culture, but even Spencerian "social science" could not fully ease the fear that prosperity required a Spartan solvent. Traditional republican doubts combined with *fin-de-siècle* worries that a pacifistic "higher moral organization" might be merely a symptom of cultural anemia. A reaction against the sentimental ethos had been building for decades; by the 1890s it became a revolt. The martial ideal emerged as a popular antidote to overcivilization. Joining transatlantic currents of romantic activism, it animated cults of strenuosity and military prowess; it influenced literature and social thought, education and foreign policy. Though conventional wisdom dismissed war as an anachronism, many conventionally wise Americans began to hope that the warrior might return to redeem them from enervation and impotence.

There were several avatars of martial virtue in the late-Victorian imagination, but the most prominent was the medieval knight. The image of the slaveholding cavalier, restored to national mythology in the sentimentalizing of the Lost Cause, was weakened by entanglement in recent political controversy. Critics of overcivilization required a clearly premodern alternative to lackluster "industrial man." The Japanese warrior was fascinating but culturally remote—and also an emerging international rival. The figure of the knight presented fewer difficulties. Unlike Japan or the antebellum South, medieval Europe seemed a quintessentially warlike culture: common assumptions about social progress contrasted medieval violence with modern gentility. In the popular imagination, the medieval gentry spent much of their time "feasting, hunting, and hacking one another to pieces. . . ." Their chivalric code was a matter of "ferocity partly restrained by etiquette."[6] Antimodern militarists, reversing the progressive framework, equated the decline of ferocity with encroaching enervation. Noting that medieval warriors were "butchers maybe, but they carved provinces and kingdoms," militarists argued that medieval violence had been the midwife of national greatness. They offered Spartan redemption in medieval guise.

The late-Victorian image of the medieval warrior could be Galahad or Saxon knight. Rooted in Spartan tradition and the literary conventions of Malory, Scott, and Tennyson, the Galahad figure could embody purity and honor, and point toward moral regeneration. Infused with newer currents of racism, the Saxon warrior could provide a leaven of ferocity and suggest possiblities for physical revitalization. While both Galahad and Saxon reaffirmed familiar Victorian values, Saxon also personified emergent cultural modes: a therapeutic stress on authenticity in personal relations, a tough-minded rationale for force in foreign relations. These two dominant images were united by their anticommercial potential; they overlapped and sometimes merged in popular historical romances. The chivalric hero of romantic fiction could be a brute fighter, a man of honor, or both at once. Moral or amoral, he was never a common tradesman.

It would be a mistake, though, to overemphasize the opposition between commercial society and the martial ideal. The republican antithesis between virtue and commerce had always been unstable. Antimodern militarists, like their ideological forebears, applauded economic growth while they feared its cultural consequences. Wedding virtue and commerce, they invoked the warrior image—an image born in opposition to mercantile expansion, bureaucracies, and professional armies—to animate an ideology of empire. This ideological confusion has become familiar in our own time, when imperialist adventures in the interest of modernizing corporate elites are routinely justified with reference to traditional values of honor and patriotism. In republican America, the innovator has frequently presented himself as traditionalist. Like present-day imperialist apologetics, antimodern militarism reflected the self-deceptions of its spokesmen. Merging medieval and martial ideals, antimodern militarists transformed their nostalgia for the past into a complex movement toward regeneration in the present.

The regeneration was at once social and personal. On the one hand, antimodern militarists longed to toughen a flabby bourgeoisie against the threat of anarchists, immigrants, strikers, tramps, and criminals. Interpreting the triumph of domestic realism as a symptom of upper-class enervation, they not only promoted a revitalized "literature of action"; they also urged stricter socialization of children through athletics and military drill, a revival of capital punishment and retributive penology in general, and imperialist crusades for the welfare of the entire nation. On the other hand, this whole movement toward class revitalization was energized not only by a conscious program of social control but also by barely articulated psychic needs—the yearning for a scientifically sanctioned racial identity in a society where all identities seemed in dissolution, the desire to recapture the ever-elusive "real life" that modern culture hid. Anglo-Saxon racism melded with the antimodern quest for authentic experience; both powerfully accelerated the spread of militarism. The archaic warrior typified the racial superiority of the "pure Nordic strain" as well as the intensity of life amid danger and death. He fired the imaginations of tough-minded liberals in America and fascists in Europe.

Antimodern militarism, like the craft revival, served as revitalization, transformation, and protest. Reasserting familiar Victorian values of self-improvement and self-control, militarism merged with Theodore Roosevelt's cult of the strenuous life and revitalized the bourgeois achievement ethos. But if duty grew vague, the risk-taking demanded by the strenuous life sometimes became a path to psychic well-being rather than a byproduct of moral ardor. The exaltation of the premodern warrior's authentic experience cleared the ground for a current shibboleth of popular psychology: at the turn of the century, as now, to be aggressive was to reassure oneself that one was "really alive." Yet the militarist search for authenticity sometimes pointed in more profound directions as well. It merged with the recovery of primal irrationality pioneered by thinkers as diverse as Nietzsche, Lawrence, and Freud; it led toward the recognition that life was more tragically complicated, more ridden with inescapable pain and conflict, than the liberal imagination understood.

In what follows here, I explore the continuing dialectic between commercial society and the martial ideal, beginning with the literary critique of domestic realism. The critical evidence in many briefs against modernity was the Victorian novel. According to a number of observers, an overcivilized literature required regeneration through romance. What they sought was not the romance of encrusted convention and pale idealism, but the romance of fierce emotions and manly action—of "real life."

# From Domestic Realism to "Real Life"

During the 1890s, historical romances full of heroic exploits flooded American magazines and bookstores. A subliterature of adventure stories for boys had existed for decades; the 1890s witnessed its spread to a wider adult audience. In part, the process resulted from the "magazine revolution," the proliferation of cheaper periodicals with larger circulations and more sensational contents. Such magazines as *Munsey's* and *McClure's* attracted a growing middle-class readership, less affluent and less educated than the reading public of previous decades. Yet romantic adventure pervaded the "quality magazines"—*Harper's Monthly*, *Scribner's*, the *Century*, the *Atlantic Monthly*—as well as the upstarts. The popularity of historical romance signified not only a larger audience but also a shift in taste within the traditional audience, the educated Northern bourgeoisie.[7]

That shift is difficult to chart precisely. Literary historians, labelling it a resurgence of "neoromanticism," have dismissed it as the death rattle of an outmoded genre. According to Edwin Cady, historical novelists were "wringing the last drops of the fantastic and *outré* out of the romantic tradition."[8] Cady's description typifies the belief that late-nineteenth-century literary history was a Manichean struggle between progressive realists and reactionary romantics. The problem with this view is that it accepts at face value the comments of contemporaneous observers like Hamlin Garland, Jack London, and Frank Norris—all of whom denounced historical romance for its subservience to convention and tradition. These men overlooked the fundamental tie between themselves and advocates of historical romance: the shared conviction that domestic realism was not realistic enough, because it failed to embrace the reality of life as struggle. Both groups contributed to a resurgent "literature of action," which encompassed sea-fights, shipwrecks, and Wild West adventure as well as more archaic violence. A common undercurrent of romantic activism united historical novelists like F. Marion Crawford with naturalists like London and Norris and even (for a time) with the "veritist" Hamlin Garland. Whether or not they explicitly voiced the opinion, all agreed that the world of Howells's novels lacked physical and emotional conflict, that it neglected the harsh experience of pain inflicted or endured, that it was devoid of "real life."

One common form of activist criticism was an assault on the "feminization" of American culture. William Dean Howells accepted this condi-

tion as a fact of literary life, but by the 1880s, even realists like his friend
H. H. Boyesen had begun to attack the female reader as "the Iron Madonna who strangles in her fond embrace the American novelist." Silas
Weir Mitchell expressed the male conventional wisdom when he complained that "the monthly [magazines] are getting so lady-like that naturally they will soon menstruate."[9] Such comments revealed less about the
publishing industry than about the anxieties of male observers. To be
sure, women had gained more influence over literary taste, but that fact
alone did not alarm cultural critics. What did concern them was the apparent result of feminization: a decline of vital energy in art and life. The
problem afflicted men as well as women—especially the educated men
who had chosen literary or intellectual careers. Distrusting their own usefulness in an activist society, they traced enervation to feminization because they equated masculinity with forcefulness. To men who feared a
loss of will, both in themselves and in the culture generally, women offered a convenient target.

The fundamental difficulty was both wider and deeper than the feminization of taste. The ascendance of domestic realism, it was said, marked
the displacement of Gothic romanticism by a new and distinctively modern
style.[10] A drab and oversubtle fiction reflected the rise of an interdependent mass society, where will was emasculated and selfhood diminished.
Confident that literature could regenerate life, many activist critics called
for a return to premodern tales of adventure. It was necessary to rediscover
the Middle Ages, when "men sang a manlier way." Magazine versifiers
lamented the decline from "those old, true gallants" of Robin Hood's time
to the nineteenth century's "modish swains through monocles that stare."
Antimodern critics urged a redefinition of literature. In their view it was
not a criticism of life but a temporary refuge from life. The oversubtle,
analytic domestic novel gave no respite from everyday cares; it only mired
the reader more deeply in "morbid self-consciousness." But the chivalric
romance, as the essayist Agnes Repplier pointed out in 1896, presented
an opportunity "to leave the present, so weighted with cumbersome enig-
mas and ineffectual activity, and to go back step by step, to other days,
when men saw life in simpler aspects, and moved forward unswervingly to
the attainment of definite and obvious desires." The contemplation of
medieval willfulness might jolt modern readers into more effective action
in the present.[11] Here again one can see the revitalizing, therapeutic function of premodern character, reaffirming the bourgeois ethic of autonomous achievement.

The regenerative powers of chivalric romances made them appealing to
moralists alarmed by overcivilized childrearing. Many of the psychologist
G. Stanley Hall's contemporaries shared his belief that medieval legends
and folk tales, like "primitive" literature generally, would enlarge and
elevate the adolescent imagination. Contemporary juvenile fiction seemed

inadequate to those tasks. An *Atlantic* contributor complained in 1882 that fairy tales had been replaced by a "flavorless" reading fare for children. Unless they received a healthy dose of fairy tales and Robin Hood, of the Waverley novels, of Froissart and Malory, their minds would become like those of their parents: "flabby, nerveless, and inactive." It was not surprising, then, that reviewers welcomed juvenile literature like Sidney Lanier's *Boys' King Arthur* as a bracing alternative to modern boys' books. Nor were boys alone to benefit from reading about medieval vigor. Critics offered Scott's strong-willed and active young heroines as healthy models to modern girls who were kept in adolescence too long, performing empty academic and social exercises.[12]

Scott was more than a prod for female aspirations; he became the central figure in the literary polemics of the late nineteenth century. To apologists for domestic realism, his work embodied outmoded theories of human nature and the social order. To advocates of romance, he seemed the potential savior of American character and society. Toward the end of the century the latter view triumphed, but there were straws in the wind as early as 1880, when the literary critic Thomas Sargeant Perry explained that while Scott had packed his novels full of "living people," realists described "commonplace people" with "tepid passions"—characters more suited to modern taste.[13] Perry's contrast foreshadowed the arguments used by Scott revivalists during the 1880s and 1890s. To them, he became not just a brilliant novelist but the emblem of a larger, fuller life. A *Century* verse of 1899 suggested Scott's wider cultural significance.

> Rhymers and writers of our day,
> Too much of melancholy!
> Give us the old heroic lay;
> A whiff of wholesome folly;
> The escapade, the dance;
> A touch of wild romance.
> Wake from this self-conscious fit;
> Give us again Sir Walter's wit;
> His love of earth, of sky, of life;
> His ringing page with humor rife;
> His never-weary pen;
> His love of men![14]

Scott's admirers stressed common themes of activism, morality, and health. For some, the novelist's value lay in his elevation of strenuous effort over self-absorbed thought. "He believed in action, and he delighted in describing it," Repplier wrote. " 'The thinker's voluntary death in life' was not, for him, the power that moves the world, but rather deeds,—deeds that make history and that sing themselves forever." He allied his activism with lofty sentiments, and inspired litanies of praise. He was "bracing, animated, moral, never degenerating into sentimentality, too deep to be cynical, animated throughout by the very spirit and essence of manliness," a *Munsey's* writer exclaimed. Numerous critics agreed that Scott's life and work were alike "eminently healthy." Scott offered invigoration at once mental, moral, and physical.[15]

Scott's resurgent reputation among the educated bourgeoisie paralleled a renewed scholarly interest in folk tales of archaic courage and strife. William Morris's pathbreaking translations from the Icelandic, begun in the 1860s and 1870s, inspired a host of similar projects. At first only occasionally, then more frequently, updated versions of Norse, French, and English medieval sagas appeared in Britain and America. Critics fretting over modern introspection praised the old tales for their "vigorous and healthy objectivity" and recommended them for both adults and children.[16] Like Scott's works, folk tales promised therapeutic revitalization.

The spread of newly translated medieval sagas coincided with the renascence of martial motifs in fiction and poetry. During the 1880s and especially the 1890s, historical romances like Charles Majors's *When Knighthood Was in Flower* led the best-seller lists, martial lyrics like those of Louise Imogen Guiney and Richard Hovey filled magazines, and periodical fiction turned from domestic problems to battlefield heroics. "The story of action, or romantic novel, appears for the time to be in complete possession of the popular field of fiction," a *Century* editor wrote in 1900, noting that "the juvenile air and vigor of the novel of action has had a mollifying effect on our introspective and analytical realists." The premier American realist, William Dean Howells, complained that same year that "truth in fiction" was everywhere in eclipse. "In our own country," he wrote, "where every genuine talent, young as well as old, is characterized by the instinct if not the reason of reality, nothing of late has been heard but the din of arms, the horrid tumult of the swashbuckler swashing on his buckler."[17]

As part of the broader literary shift toward "the plain tale of high adventure"—whether set in medieval England or the American West—the revival of historical romance embodied longings for psychic rejuvenation. To Bliss Carman, the popularity of Kipling, Stevenson, and other "masculine world wanderers" suggested a widespread desire for spontaneity. "We had become so over-nice in our feelings, so restrained and formal, so bound by habit and use in our devotion to the effeminate realists, that one side of our nature was starved," he wrote in 1894. "We must have a revolt at any cost." For proof of the vitalizing results of that revolt, Frank Norris advised in 1901, one need only "look into some of the magazines of the 70's and 80's. It is astonishing to consider that we ever found an interest in them. The effect is like entering a darkened room. And not only the magazines, but the entire literature of the years before the 90's, is shadowed and oppressed with the bugbear of 'literature.' " Norris overlooked the gradual development of the reaction against domestic realism—the translations of medieval sagas, the returning popularity of Scott. For him, the 1890s alone marked a breakthrough into "real life."[18]

We do not need to accept Norris's sharp periodization to see that toward the end of the century, the yearnings of romantic activists for more intense, immediate experience became common among educated Americans. Editors and publishers claimed their preference for violent subjects was simply a response to popular demand. As evidence for the public appetite for violence, a *North American Review* writer cited an occurrence in the office of "a well-known magazine of large circulation." "A genially written story of acceptable length had been forwarded by a frequent contributor to the best monthlies. In an interview which followed the article's rejection the editor stated frankly: 'Your story was well written, but, unfortunately, it was too quiet and lacked vim. Our readers want blood and vim.' "[19]

The editor's explanation is partially accurate but it oversimplifies his own role in determining literary taste. As Levin Schücking points out in *The Sociology of Literary Taste*, "art is dependent on certain propagators of taste and . . . the ability of such groups to assert themselves is again dependent on the degree of power they can exercise within the social structure or, to be more exact, on the extent to which they control the mechanism of artistic life. . . ."[20] Schücking's observation suggests a fuller explanation for the rise of romantic activism: influential leaders of the educated bourgeoisie, urging romantic activism as a cure for overcivilization, effected a shift in literary taste by collaborating with a wider audience which shared enthusiasm for the literature of action. The wider audience may also have shared the motives behind that enthusiasm—the yearning for release from introspection and ennui. Literary arguments entwined with social and moral unrest. The revolt against domestic realism was rooted in the crisis of cultural authority.

Viewed in the context of late-nineteenth-century cultural crisis, literary warrior-heroes assume larger significance. In fiction as in social criticism, the romantic man on horseback focused growing admiration for the martial virtues. And that sentiment was part of a wider fascination with physical power.

# Class, Race, and the Worship of Force

During the 1890s, crusades for physical vigor swept the educated bourgeoisie in both Europe and America. By 1900, the *Atlantic Monthly* noticed "a sort of satiety of civilization, which is leading in all the departments of life to a temporary reversal of the softening of manners made during the century. The revived love of war is not an isolated phenomenon." Martial bellicosity paralleled the growing enthusiasm for boxing, football, bicycling, and outdoor life in general. All those tendencies coalesced in the cult of the strenuous life, whose most vigorous exemplar and prophet was Theodore Roosevelt. He and other advocates of strenuosity repeatedly listed "the ethical functions of football" and lauded sport as "the modern chivalry." Through athletics, a "delicate, indoor genteel race" might receive "a saving touch of honest, old-fashioned barbarism. . . ." The historian John Higham has perceptively discussed the cult of strenuosity but he has not connected it to the social tensions of the late nineteenth century. To a bourgeoisie feeling enervated and fearful of lower-class unrest, the worship of force presented paths to class revitalization.[21]

The mania for sport reinforced bourgeois values of discipline and productivity. Observers claimed that football instilled self-reliance and regularity—habits which would later prove useful in a business career. Others pointed out that a weekend of camping returned fitter men to the office on Monday. Outdoor exercise seemed the perfect antidote to "morbid self-consciousness" and excessive mental work.[22] Said to recapture preindustrial vigor without sacrificing the benefits of industrial progress, sport revealed a strain of careful primitivism. Sport's regenerative effects quickly became a staple theme in the official culture of the twentieth century. Roosevelt's cant anticipated Nixon's. The notion that sport toughened "the leaders of tomorrow," by now a television cliché, originated in the *fin-de-siècle* worship of force.

This impulse toward class revitalization was strongly reinforced by an unprecedented outpouring of racism among the middle and upper classes. Within the popular culture as well as scholarly circles "Nordic" ethnocentrism spread; antiblack and particularly anti-Semitic views became more overt, more fashionable, and more pervasive than ever before. During the 1890s vaudeville comics shifted from the "two Irishmen" joke to newer routines involving "two Jews"; belief in the superiority of the Anglo-Saxon (or Aryan) "race" permeated the writings of social scientists and their popularizers.[23]

In America as in Europe, racism intertwined with the recoil from modern softness. Anglo-Saxon racism offered a rationale for imperialist crusades against "inferior" overseas foes and also met less obvious social and psychic needs. Racism reasserted the cultural authority of the WASP bourgeoisie; it may also have provided many WASP Americans with a kind of negative identity—a means of shoring up selfhood by disowning impulses they distrusted in themselves. Defining idleness, irresolution, avarice and other moral shortcomings as "race traits" confined to inferior stock, racists reaffirmed a masterful, virtuous mode of identity for those who had lost a solid sense of self. Private needs had public consequences. In a variety of ways, racism revitalized the hegemony of the dominant WASP culture at a critical historical moment.

The growing fascination with martial vigor, as part of the wider revitalizing process, tells us a great deal about some important efforts to resolve social and cultural tensions. Two of these efforts closely paralleled those of craft revivalists: the attempt to toughen the flaccid children of the WASP bourgeoisie (albeit through military models rather than manual labor) and the drive to control a restive working class (albeit through harsher penology rather than education reform). A third item on the militarist agenda was different: moral regeneration through military adventure and the creation of an overseas empire. This last had the most important and ironic results. It was a betrayal of republican tradition which had been intended to revive it.

One can see the martial ideal at work, first of all, in the changing patterns of socialization which developed during the late nineteenth century. Enthusiasm for sport combined with admiration for martial heroism to influence upper-class education. At elite boarding schools and colleges, the growth of organized athletics paralleled the rise of military drill: both were praised as builders of character. And the quest for disciplined vitality led beyond the preserves of the wealthy, into the Christian youth organizations of middle-class Protestantism.

During the 1880s and 1890s, Protestant youth groups proliferated; a disproportionate number adopted military organizational models and described their activities in military language. Many unwittingly caricatured medieval precedents. The Church Temperance League was divided into Young Crusaders (ages 8–16) and Knights of Temperance (ages 16–21); the Princely Knights of Character Castle, founded in 1895 for boys 12–18, had offices such as "herald" and "keeper of the dungeon"; the Knights of King Arthur enlisted college boys, who could graduate from "page" to "esquire" if they read eight thousand pages of heroic adventure tales.[24]

Silly as they seem, these groups—like the demands for martial rejuvenation of children's literature—represented part of an important shift in socialization. The Christian youth leaders preached a cult of strenuosity softened by benevolence and suffused with morality. Yet despite their moral concerns, they were not simply reviving Spartan republicanism; in fact their work embodied significant departures from tradition. During the antebellum era, paramilitary youth groups—voluntarily formed by the young men themselves—were associations for the training of militia; their swaggering drunkenness often provoked clerical hostility. The late-nineteenth-century groups were formed by men for the benefit of boys; they had no civil functions; they enjoyed ministerial sponsorship and endorsement. Abandoning voluntarism, they encouraged unquestioning obedience to authority: the "watchwords" of the Knights of King Arthur were "adult-leadership" and "hero-worship." Designed solely to socialize the young, the late Victorian groups sought to wean youth away from what one leader called "unwholesome introspection and self-analysis" toward immersion in disciplined group activity. Though it recalled premodern chivalric ideals, youthful paramilitarism reinforced adjustment to the regimented, hierarchical organization of work under corporate capitalism.[25]

The success of such socializing efforts remains an open question. No doubt many younger Americans ignored or resisted their elders' injunctions to chivalry. My point is not that youth groups reshaped late-Victorian culture into a paramilitary mold, but that they reflected adult anxieties about childrearing in a secularizing culture. Stressing character formation rather than salvation, Christian youth leaders replaced the conversion experience with the ironclad pledge to live life "in earnest." One Christian Endeavour enthusiast wrote in 1892 that members "treat the pledge as a knight of old treated his knightly vow." Insistence on the pledge's sanctity obscured the vagueness of its purpose. As Joseph Kett has ably demonstrated, the most striking fact about Christian paramilitarism was its lack of any clear goals.[26] Activity was an end in itself; the only commitment was to the idea of commitment. One can sense some of the same circularity in the youth groups of suburban Christianity today. The Christian paramilitarism of the 1890s foreshadowed the spiritual confusions of contemporary childrearing. The paramilitarist pledge, despite its associations with medieval chivalry, was a rite of passage into a peculiarly modern culture where ultimate purpose was absent. Formed in opposition to modern moral flaccidity, paramilitary youth groups unknowingly exacerbated it.

Christian youth groups embodied the "soft" side of the martial ideal; the "hard" side had more obvious social causes and consequences. On the domestic scene, it included not only agenda for strenuous outings but also a return to "barbarous" methods of social control. To Americans who believed that inferior immigrants were overrunning native stock, that socialist revolution was imminent, and that vicious crime was openly condoned, medieval brutality grew more attractive. The iron fist of the feudal lord, once scorned as a relic of medieval barbarism, now seemed the only alternative to social chaos. The swift sword of medieval punishment appealed strongly to moralists who were sick of ethical confusion and impatient with the "sentimentalism" of penal reformers.

Railing against judicial weakness, numerous cultural critics urged a revival of retributive justice based on medieval models. Medieval punishment, an *Atlantic* writer observed in 1880, treated brutes as men responsible for their misdeeds; modern punishment views them as irresponsible brutes, impelled into crime by psychical forces beyond their control. A rediscovery of "the hemp cure" would be an appropriate antidote to modern permissiveness, he concluded. Other observers shared his concern. Some, citing the precedent of the medieval *posse comitatus,* praised the formation of vigilante groups by wealthy urban citizens. Others called for the resurrection of the whipping post for wife-beaters, tramps, and "the off-scourings of the criminal classes of Europe" who were crowding into American cities. Confronted by "the menace of the discontented," many affluent Americans abandoned any pretense of concern for due process.[27]

Racist currents reinforced the reaction against liberal traditions. Even lynching was justifiable as a return to rough but honest Saxon justice, a reaction against the "dilettantism" of the "educated legal class. . . ." As the *Century* editorialized in 1889:

> A Saxon hue and cry, hailing a fugitive criminal before the hundred for punishment, would be a picturesque historical spectacle, while the Indiana or Mississippi lynching mob is a subject for reprobation only. Yet the latter may be only a reversion to an ancestral type, caused by the practical breakdown of the more civilized and artificial type which has succeeded it.[28]

Insisting that "it is better that ten innocent men should suffer than that one guilty man should escape," upper-class moralists pleaded for a hardening of modern attitudes toward criminality and a tightening of judicial discipline. Judge J. A. Jameson in 1883 admitted that Spencerians could deplore such a change as "a relapse from industrialism to 'militancy.' " But "if modern liberalism . . . is to land us in anarchy, then welcome the return of militancy . . . for the sake of its accompanying social restraints." To a bourgeoisie under siege, the certainty of medieval rank and the savagery of medieval punishment alike held strong appeal.[29]

It is difficult to say how these shifting attitudes affected the actual treatment of criminals. The "return to militancy" was no doubt largely rhetorical. Throughout the late nineteenth and early twentieth centuries, penology continued a gradual if halting shift from retribution to rehabilitation. There was a decline in the number of capital offenses, and in the severity and publicity of punishment. There was no clear pattern of approach to capital punishment until the decade after 1910, when seven states abolished the procedure. In general, moralist pronouncements in national magazines probably had only an indirect impact on state legislatures, whose debates reflected local conditions and issues. (Maine, for example, abolished capital punishment in 1876, restored it in 1882 after a convict attacked a prison guard, and reabolished it in 1887 in response to the governor's argument that the death penalty had not reduced the number of murders committed in the state.)[30]

The impact of bourgeois militance on social dissidence was another matter. The rejection of due process and the advocacy of quick, retributive punishment no doubt reinforced the tendency to gun down strikers and other enemies of the economic status quo. Further, the admiration for archaic violence pointed toward the self-reformation of the bourgeoisie through heroic defenses of property at home and imperialist crusades abroad. Besides destroying dissidents, reversion to medieval violence might purify their executioners.

In their efforts to recapture fading national prominence, antimodern militarists pointed American leaders to medieval examples. Degeneration was common to all periods of declining faith and spreading wealth, said Mayo W. Hazeltine, the literary editor of the *New York Sun:* nineteenth-century America might be profitably compared to thirteenth-century Provence. There, "a carnival of lust and blasphemy" was excised by "the rough but needful surgery of the Albigensian crusade. . . . Thenceforward the troubadours ceased to sing, but men lost nothing from restriction to the relatively pure and high ideals [of] . . . the 'Song of Roland,' the 'Nibelungen Lied,' and the 'Morte d'Arthur.' " Americans might hope for a similar turn toward Spartan virtue, Hazeltine concluded, if enough of the nation's moral leaders heeded Max Nordau's warnings. From Hazeltine's discussion, it was unclear whether the new crusade should be directed against unruly American citizens or an overseas foe. But his fundamental point was clear: military adventure could lance the festering sore of luxury and return overcivilized Americans to simpler, purer ideals.[31] And on that point, numerous cultural critics began to agree. The militarism of the 1890s was in large measure a manifestation of elite yearnings for self-purification. Though the militarist impulse was expressed in antimodern rhetoric, it had modernizing effects. Recalling republican commitments to Spartan virtue, militarism helped to create the republican nightmare of commercial empire.

It is true that militarism met emotional needs and relaxed social tensions outside the urban bourgeoisie. Besides purifying the educated and affluent, war distracted less fortunate Americans from their economic worries; it disbanded the army of the discontented and regrouped its ragged recruits under the American flag. Social conflict was temporarily submerged in the rhetoric of national unity.[32]

But among the educated and affluent, militarism seemed more than a solvent for social unrest. War promised reestablished social dominance not just because it distracted populists and socialists from their grievances but also because it offered a stronger, purer sense of selfhood to a flaccid urban bourgeoisie. "Idleness and luxury have made men flabby," a *North American Review* contributor observed in 1894, wondering "if a great war might not help them to pull themselves together." Imperialist adventures offered a chance for enervated young men to follow Francis Parkman's prescription: "to realize a certain ideal of manhood—a little medieval." As the *Century* wrote in 1898, the contemporary passion for war signified a yearning for purification: "we think of war, nowadays, not so much as being a means of making others suffer as an occasion for giving ourselves up to suffering." To worried members of the cultural elite, war seemed a "moral medicine," a purgative for overcivilization.[33] Militarism reached its zenith during the 1890s, but it has persisted throughout the twentieth century as a continuing response to the fear of enervated refinement. Now as at the turn of the century, war appeals to moralists who fear a "failure of nerve" has crippled the will of the nation's "leadership class."

In seeking alternatives to modern softness, American militarists drew on a variety of resources. They recalled their countrymen to the heroism of the Civil War generation; they joined the French in their renewed glorification of Napoleon. (Twenty-eight American books on Napoleon were published in the three years 1894–1896.) But for those who felt that timid gentility was a peculiarly modern phenomenon, the exaltation of strife required a more archaic focus. Many cultural critics looked longingly to the feudal warrior, the product of a traditional hierarchical social order. One such feudal type was the Japanese warrior, surviving amid the remnants of his traditional culture well into the late nineteenth century. A few Americans posed the lean and duty-bound samurai against the overweight, nervous Western businessman. But the figure of the samurai was ultimately too alien and threatening to energize American militarism.[34] Historical romances, set in more familiar European territory, offered more appropriate leadership models for the affluent and educated. In chivalric fiction, authors highlighted the strengths of the warrior-hero by contrasting him with weaker specimens: the courtier, the saint, and the scholar.

Combining purity and ferocity, the chivalric hero triumphed because he plunged headlong toward his goal, avoiding the pitfalls of fashion, impractical religiosity, or intellectual fastidiousness. The contrast between warrior and courtier emerged most clearly in *When Knighthood Was in Flower.* Though Major's protagonist Charles Brandon is nobly born, he knows not the practiced flatteries of court life. Even before Brandon demonstrates his appetite for violence, young Mary Tudor spots his distinction. After years of dalliance with dilettantish noblemen, she cries, "For once I have found a real live man, full of manliness." Manliness precluded saintliness as well as foppery. In *Via Crucis* (1898), F. Marion Crawford juxtaposed his protagonist Gilbert Warde to the pious King Louis IX, whom he depicted as a ridiculous figure, ineffectual in both military and martial duties. Gilbert, while remaining oblivious to Louis's seductive wife Eleanor, "practiced virtue in a rough-and-ready fashion which would not pass muster in modern society, though it might in heaven." Gilbert is strong-willed, decisive—a sharp contrast to the pathetic king. The same decisiveness characterized a recurring protagonist in chivalric romance, Joan of Arc. She was the subject of novels by Mark Twain and Mary Hartwell Catherwood, a verse drama by Percy MacKaye, a widely read biography by Francis C. Lowell, and numerous poems and magazine articles. Joan's appeal was manifold: many felt drawn to her "rural simplicity and rhapsodical faith" as well as her forceful leadership. But to Americans fretting over an elite's supposed failure to lead, Joan's most impressive talent was her ability to organize a nation from a crowd of nerveless and disunited Frenchmen. For the protagonist of historical romance, sainthood was acceptable only if it did not conflict with military duties.[35]

Indeed, some chivalric heroes disdained moral distinctions altogether. Saxon displaced Galahad; the brute fighter overrode the man of honor. In Justus Miles Forman's "The Maid of Landevennec," the maid Azilicz refuses the marriage proposal of Count Dènés, because he is a notorious pirate who "preys on the weak." He captures and imprisons her; she remains adamant. In despair, and still insisting that his love transcends his violent ways, he releases her. She relents, won by his rough justice and simple love. In the end, piracy and a habit of victimizing the weak seemed minor flaws in Dènés's character.[36]

The lesson taught by many stories was that an intensely lived existence requires a certain indifference to conventional morality. However hedged with platitudes, militarism contained the doctrine that might makes right. As Agnes Repplier said, when mounting for battle—whether actual or imaginary—"it is best to leave ethics alone, and ride as lightly as we can." The worshipper of force scorned the benevolent ethics of the educated bourgeoisie. In Repplier's words, "fighting is not a strictly philanthropic pastime, and its merits are not precisely the merits of soup kitchens and emigration societies."[37] Such disdain typified the common militarist fear that modern industrial conditions promoted pacifism and sentimental coddling of the weak.

There was hope for regeneration, though, in the persistence of Anglo-Saxon "race traits." Racism reinforced the militarist tendency to confuse physical and moral courage; it pervaded historical romance as well as social debate. Chivalric fiction displayed a conventional ethnic hierarchy: Italians were cowardly and treacherous; Frenchmen were effete; and Anglo-Saxons were brave and indomitable. They were, in Gilbert Warde's words, "men who had the strength to take the world and to be its masters and make it obey whatsoever laws they saw fit to impose."[38]

Besides strengthening the covertly amoral strain in the worship of force, late-nineteenth-century racism affirmed a tough, secure sense of autonomous selfhood and offered the cheering thought that Anglo-Saxons were potentially as masterful as ever. A belief in the unity and continuity of the Anglo-Saxon "race" preserved a certain optimism even among critics of overcivilization. To them, the latent survival of Saxon force and vigor offered cause for hopefulness even in a flabby commercial age.

For old-stock Americans, it was encouraging to think that rough Saxon ways had not altogether succumbed to the "livery-like mannerisms" of the Victorian parlor. Cultural critics took comfort from scholarly arguments tracing New England town meetings to Aryan folkmoots, and applauded a new interest in "simple and indigenous" Saxon diction among philologists and writers of fiction. Anglo-Saxon continuity included not only politics and language, but individual character traits as well. In the common view, a heritage of Saxon ferocity survived in the heart of the most placid bourgeois. Anglo-Saxon chauvinism decreed that such "racial characteristics" as endurance, courage, and determination persisted despite the vicissitudes of culture and custom. Brander Matthews, professor of dramatic literature at Columbia, was certain that the English-speaking people were as "self-willed and adventurous" in 1901 as in Alfred's time, "in old England and in the newer England here in America."[39] Possibilities for heroism survived, even amid unheroic getting and spending.

The assumption of Anglo-Saxon continuity allowed militarists to transfer the martial ideal from the Middle Ages to the present. Insisting that the quest for the Grail was not dead, they urged the cultivation of traditional "race traits" among the old-stock, Protestant bourgeoisie. In their view, their task was to wean Americans away from fondness for material comfort toward higher and more bracing goals.

One of the most active in that effort was the poet Richard Hovey, whose work merged medieval and martial ideals in a continuing attack on commercial complacency. His *Songs from Vagabondia* (1894), written in collaboration with Bliss Carman, mingled the comradeship of sword and buckler with the contemporary camaraderie of the open road. And in Hovey's play *The Marriage of Guenevere* (1891), King Arthur's counsellor Godmar voices a warning aimed at the late-nineteenth-century United States.

> I am for war.
> . . . For men in peace,
> Lacking brave emulation, and the zeal
> Of a great cause, fall to their petty ends
> And, letting their high virtues atrophy,
> Wallow in lust and avarice, till the heart
> And nobler functions rot away and leave
> A people like an oyster, all stomach.

Throughout the public debate over entry into the Spanish-American War, Hovey flayed the "pompous prattlers" mouthing "idle platitudes of peace." When the declaration of war finally came, Hovey was jubilant: to skeptical Europeans, Americans had shown that they were not "soulless money-getters" but seekers after honor and righteousness. "Who now are they whose God is gain?" he asked. "Let Rothschild-ridden Europe hold her peace!"[40]

By elevating the soldier over the businessman, Hovey, as well as a number of his contemporaries, joined a long militarist tradition. Contempt for the "money changer," often charged with anti-Semitic overtones, had characterized apologetics for war since the Middle Ages. But the sentiment became especially strong in a *fin-de-siècle* cultural atmosphere overheated by racism and fears of social decay. Anticommercial rhetoric accelerated the growth of fascist and Nazi ideology, and also pervaded the American militarism of the turn of the century. Theodore Roosevelt, railing against the "ignoble ease" produced by the "base spirit of gain," typified patrician distrust of the peace-loving plutocrat.[41]

Men like Roosevelt, Henry Cabot Lodge, and Brooks Adams considered themselves public-spirited warrior-aristocrats. They were from old families with old money, and they had been raised in an atmosphere of republican moralism. It was only natural that they should disdain "men of means who have always made the till their fatherland. . . ." Though their values and status were eminently bourgeois by European standards, they enjoyed attacking "the bourgeois type" as "a miracle of timidity and short-sighted selfishness." They agreed that the American bourgeoisie needed a dose of aristocratic dash and daring. As Crawford pointed out, only well-born warriors like Gilbert Warde had preserved Saxon courage down to the present by "again and again rousing the English-speaking races to life and conquest, when they were sunk deep in the sordid interests of trade and moneymaking."[42]

Such anticommercial sentiments have led historians to describe the emergence of a "warrior critique of the business civilization" during the 1890s. The phrase is misleading because it overstresses the militarists' hostility toward capitalism. Unlike some of their European counterparts, American "warrior critics" did not despair of commercial civilization altogether. Rather, they insisted that martial vigor complemented business success. Roosevelt told a group of Chicago businessmen in 1900 that "if we are to hold our own in the struggle for naval and commercial supremacy, we must build up our power without our borders." And Benjamin Harrison (a former Union Army general as well as a former president) argued in 1894 for universal military training because "a free, erect, graceful carriage of the body is an acquisition and a delight. It has a value in commerce, as well as war." The clearest example of this rapprochement between commerce and the martial ideal was an exhibit at the Chicago World's Fair of 1893—a statue of a medieval knight on horseback, made entirely of prunes, and set up by the state of California. The World's Fair brochure noted that

> The knight on horseback made of prunes . . . was distinctly a unique departure in statuary. It was exhibited in the California building, and metaphorically impressed the fact that the prunes of that state are being introduced victoriously into all lands, to the discomfiture of the products of other countries.[43]

For all its absurdity, the knight of prunes pointed to an important cultural fact: the assimilation of the militarist critique. Convinced of the persistence of Anglo-Saxon virtue, American militarists believed bourgeois society could remain intact—provided it was imbued with a renewed martial spirit. Rather than demanding root and branch institutional change, they called for moral reform within existing frameworks of bourgeois values and organized capitalism. Exalting premodern courage, they urged its recovery in their own time, by members of their own class.

By discussing American militarism as an effort toward cultural revitalization, I do not mean to deny its economic origins and effects. The more public-minded militarists, men like Brooks Adams and Alfred Thayer Mahan, urged war as a path to overseas economic expansion as well as moral revival. The roots of the modern American empire were intertwined in economic interest and cultural crisis: the desire for foreign markets drew strength from elite fears that America was becoming a sterile, stagnant nation. The effects of imperialism, too, were at once cultural and economic. *Scribner's,* examining the fruits of war in 1899, observed that imperialism was not only an antidote to commercial success, but also its handmaiden.[44] The acquisition of empire reinforced the self-confidence, the economic power, and the cultural authority of a bourgeoisie which felt threatened by internal decay and lower-class discontent. Even though antimodern militarism was not institutionalized in a large standing army, it became a form of class regeneration—whether achieved through hardened domestic social control or through foreign conquest. And the stage was being set for the full-scale militarism of the later twentieth century: the interests of the dominant class were being redefined as an ever-expansive "national interest," global and virtually limitless.

But for many among the educated bourgeoisie, class regeneration was not a conscious goal at all. Often it was an unsought byproduct of an impulse rooted in private concerns: an instinctive rebellion against late-Victorian comfort and complacency. The worship of premodern force was not reducible to its social functions. Upper-class strenuosity, Anglo-Saxon racism, and vagabond boisterousness contained hints of a yearning for intensified experience, a yearning left unfulfilled by imperialist adventures or violent methods of social control. A search for personal meaning and purpose persisted, though the seekers remained ambivalent and their destinations seemed uncertain.

# The Psychological Uses of the Martial Ideal: The Cult of Experience and the Quest for Authentic Selfhood

Ever since the earliest Puritan-Indian wars, upright Americans had periodically looked to violence as a means of personal regeneration.[45] By the 1890s, among educated, urban Easterners who faced an increasingly onerous standard of respectability, longings for regeneration through violence became particularly acute. The enfeeblement of liberal Protestantism combined with the fragmenting sense of selfhood to create widespread feelings of personal disorientation and anomie among educated Americans. Fears that autonomy and even identity had become problematic lay behind yearnings for a reintegrated personality, for a self made whole again. The desire for wholeness, often focused on the archaic warrior, underlay romantic activism. Militarists and advocates of the strenuous life deified action not only for its social value but for its own sake. They helped to create a cult of experience with martial activism at its core. In popular fiction and poetry, the cult of experience became a cult of violence. Lurid descriptions of bloodshed appeared in best-selling novels; fantasies of violence, sometimes fused with elements of sublimated sexuality, became a staple of the culture-consuming public. Aggression, at least in the forms of disciplined vitality or vicarious amusement, became respectable.

The fascination with aggressive impulses involved more than cheap thrills or an anti-intellectual cult of machismo. It contained a moral critique of modern culture. Fantasies of aggression could sometimes turn inward, dwelling on the experiences of pain and death. In part the vestige of an older, harsher Christian conscience, this tendency suggested an embryonic discontent with utilitarian standards of morality. Though the bourgeois ethic still paid homage to instinctual renunciation, in practice it sanctioned an overriding commitment to the continual increase of material consumption and physical comfort. In the United Stats, the idea that human happiness was the highest good spread steadily throughout the nineteenth century. Tocqueville noted it as the unofficial creed of the American democrat; American moral philosophers sought to harmonize it with Christianity; many liberal Protestants and social scientists made it the cornerstone of their convictions.[46] The fascination with pain of martial antimodernists was one of the early manifestations of an attempt to move beyond the pleasure principle of a democratic, industrial culture. It was a groping for transcendance, an effort to restore some superhuman dimension of meaning to the moral life. But because it was surrounded by spiritual confusion, its purpose remained vague and its denouement unsatisfying. Like other varieties of romantic activism, it often ended in a self-defeating quest for authentic selfhood.

To trace the circuitous path of the cult of martial experience, we need to begin with the militarist drive for mastery and delight in action for its own sake. We fight "because we want to realize our spontaneity and prove our power for the joy of it," said Oliver Wendell Holmes, Jr. Agnes Repplier attributed the same zest for instinctual life to the medieval warrior, and that assumption underlay contemporaneous chronicles of archaic warmaking. Short stories presented twelfth-century fighters as bumptious schoolboys, unable to resist a flagon, a song, or a scuffle. Medieval heroes often mingled mischief and bravery.[47]

The boyish leavening of chivalric virtue joined martial antimodernism to the romantic activism of the 1890s. Carman and Hovey's Saxon warriors, who

> Greet the morn
> With a double horn,
> When strong men drink together!

were scarcely different from their collegiate vagabonds crying

> Midnights of revel,
> And noondays of song!
> Is it so wrong?
> Go to the devil![48]

The twelfth-century warrior and the nineteenth-century student were alike exuberant in their animal spirits and their disdain for Victorian decorum.

Carman and Hovey's revolt against respectability seemed inoffensive and even appealing to some respectable reviewers. Despite their bohemian pose, one noted, Carman and Hovey had "no real objection to a bathtub and clean linen. . . ."[49] They shared the values and self-doubts of the educated bourgeoisie. Their romantic activism was rooted in a deliberate anti-intellectualism: as highly educated men of letters, they feared estrangement from "real life." Hovey, for example, jeered at opponents of the Spanish-American War as bookish half-men.

> Back to your world of books, and leave
>     the world of men
> To them that have the habit of the real
> Nor longer with a mask of fair ideal
> Hide your indifference to the facts of pain![50]

The flight from intellect could lead to an embrace of the medieval warrior, who embodied unselfconscious physical action. As Repplier wrote, "The Wandering Knight is well-nigh as disencumbered of mental as of material luggage. He rides as free from our tangled perplexity of introspection as from our irksome contrivances for comfort."[51] The Wandering Knight was an emblem of unmediated experience, a manifestation of the late-Victorian urge to strip away convention and live at full throttle.

For some, the attack on convention became an apotheosis of violence. The ability to kill became a sign of total virility. Bloodshed marked emancipation from effeminate weakness. Warriors in "genteel" magazine verse consumed their victims' blood in sacramental rites of passage. The poet Eugene White's Saxon swordsmen "drank manhood up from the Battle-cup, the wine of the gods' own brew." A similar initiatory motif appeared in Bryan Hooker's "Swanhild" (1910). The story revolves around the developing manhood of Randver, son of a fierce Scandinavian king. Through ten years of peace and comfortable upbringing by the courtier Bikki, Randver has become a shy and sensitive lad. His father, disgusted with the boy's inability to fight, sends for Swanhild, whom he hopes will sire *real* sons. The king despatches Randver, Bikki, and an armed company across the sea to Swanhild's castle. En route, Randver wins the respect of the crew by strangling an oarsman who had insulted him. Returning with Swanhild, Randver attains full manhood by slaying a score of mutineers and taking command of the ship. Having thwarted Bikki's domination and won the heart of Swanhild, Randver heads for the open sea and a career of plunder. But fog closes in, and Bikki steers the ship back to the king. Prodding the king's jealousy, Bikki persuades him to have Randver beheaded. Swanhild refuses the king's marriage proposal. Randver, she says, had outstripped his father in courage and manhood. The outraged king orders her trampled to death by horses. *Exeunt omnes.*[52]

The pervasive violence in Hooker's story typified much "genteel" literature during and after the revolt against realism. As early as 1885, the mild-mannered Hamilton Wright Mabie, retelling a Norse legend for juvenile readers of the *Christian Union,* described how "the terrible hammer struck Hrungner in the very center of his forehead, crushed his head into small pieces, and threw him with his foot across Thor's neck." Crawford's Gilbert Warde rained "blow upon blow, with clash of steel, thrust after thrust as the darting of serpents, till the dead lay in heaps, and the horses' hoofs churned blood and grass to a green-red foam. . . ."[53] And Charles Major presented the following scene in *When Knighthood Was in Flower:*

> Young Brandon replied, "Stand your ground, you coward! . . . If you try to run, I will thrust you through the neck as I would a cur. Listen how you snort. . . ." Judson tried to keep the merciless sword-point from his throat. At last, by a dexterous twist of his blade, Brandon sent Judson's sword flying thirty feet away. The fellow started to run, but turned and fell upon his knees to beg for life. Brandon's reply was a flashing circle of his steel, and his sword-point cut lengthwise through Judson's eyes and the bridge of his nose, leaving him sightless and hideous for life.[54]

The gratuitous killing and maiming in the historical romances suggested a parallel with the contemporaneous "pornography of pain" astutely analyzed by the historian Neil Harris—the newspapers' lurid dwelling on the human suffering caused by railroad and steamship accidents, fires, floods, and other disasters. For the comfortable bourgeoisie, bloodshed and pain were becoming unfamiliar enough to be titillating, yet as subject matter they remained within the bounds of Victorian propriety. By detailing what Crawford called the medieval warrior's "half-deadly, half-voluptuous longing for bloodshed," the romancer offered safe stimulation to his readers. Whether in books or on the battlefield, violence allayed the lust for immediate experience.[55]

While most activist polemics centered on the image of the Saxon fighter, those with a moral dimension sometimes emphasized the pure heroism of the Galahad figure. By fulfilling traditional Christian ideals, the medieval warrior seemed to rebuke the flaccid ease of the nineteenth-century bourgeois. That criticism was implicit in the Reverend Cameron Mann's 1907 contrast between the values of the *Morte Darthur* and those of the *Arabian Nights*. According to Mann, the Arabian warriors had "no magnificent aspirations, no heroic resolves." They wanted only "luscious food . . . beautiful women . . . gay music and wanton verses." The Arthurian legends, on the other hand, presented an ennobling pageant of "souls which the bodies serve." The Round Table was not "laden with all cakes and confectionaries; there are bread and meat and wine." There were sins in Camelot, but they never went unpunished; in Bagdad there was neither good nor evil, only animal sensuality. All in all, Mann concluded, "we have on the one hand the fruit of the Koran, on the other the fruit of the New Testament."[56] Mann's faith in the Biblical origins of medieval chivalry underlay his hope that heroism would persist wherever Western Christianity prevailed.

Mann's discussion suggested two related functions of martial antimodernism. A stress on the medieval warrior's pure aspirations and disdain for sensual pleasure could reinforce a Victorian moral code which had grown brittle and vulnerable. For Americans who felt that ethics had deteriorated into social convention, the knight's rejection of immediate gratification for "some unselfish yet all-repaying end" reaffirmed a familiar morality of instinctual renunciation. And for Americans reared in a republican distrust of luxury, the apotheosis of the martial ideal provided a way to discharge anxieties produced by modern comfort. This resolution of psychic tension eased critics of commercial society into peaceful coexistence with it. For many, antimodern militarism became less a focus for dissent than a means of revitalizing their class's cultural hegemony.

Yet a residue of discontent remained, born of continuing religious disquiet. The cult of martial experience had psychic significance which transcended its social consequences. It was ultimately entwined with an effort to endow weightless modern experience with gravity and purpose. This impulse was clearest in discussions of the medieval capacity for suffering. American fascination with the stoic endurance of the warrior reflected not only penitence for material abundance but also a need to protect moral and spiritual meaning from the acids of modernity.

It was a common view that the knight's willingness to suffer resulted from his soaring aspirations. Short stories and verses told of crusaders who rejected the earthbound pleasures of the pastoral life to embrace "their deeper heritage of pain, the divine right to suffer." Gilbert Warde epitomized a central aspect of the martial ideal, "the belief of that age in something far above common desires and passion, dwelling in a temple of the soul that must be reached by steps of pain; . . . the spirit of men who starved and scourged their bodies almost to death that their souls might live unspotted." For Crawford's Warde, suffering was an agency for salvation; for Major's fifteenth-century narrator, suffering was "that great broadener, in fact, maker of human character." That was the conventional

Victorian view. Many late-nineteenth-century Americans, uncertain in their supernaturalism, treated medieval and modern suffering alike as bulwarks of this-worldly morality.[57]

The cult of experience, though it was rooted in religious needs, gave this secularizing process a further turn. For seekers of authenticity, suffering became less an instrument of salvation or character formation than an opportunity to sharpen an otherwise dull existence. A *Century* poet's apostrophe to pain typified this feeling.

> You eat the heart of life like some great beast,
> You blacken the sweet sky that God made blue,
> You are the death's-head set amid the feast,
> The desert breath that drinks up every dew. . . .
>
> And yet—oh Terrible!—men grant you this:
> You work a mystery. When you are done
> Lo, common living turns to heavenly bliss,
> Lo, the mere light is as the noonday sun![58]

Recognizing pain's power to heighten experience, the medieval warrior not only endured pain but sometimes enjoyed it. When Gilbert Warde was thrown from his horse, he got up, "shook himself and stretched his long arms as if awaking from sleep and dreaming. The motion hurt him, and he felt all his bruises at once, but there was a sort of pleasure in the pain, that accorded with his strange state of heart, and he did it a second time in order to feel the pain once more."[59]

Pain was both exhilarating and exalting: it could give new hope to those who felt imprisoned and helpless, as L. H. Hammond's "Knights Errant" (1898) suggested.

> Thou Pain, before whose strength I reel,
>   Thou of the iron grip,
> Beneath thy mailed clutch I feel
>   My life-blood slowly drip. . . .
>
> Fettered, I watch in the slow dawn
>   The free knights riding by,
> The knights to whom men's hopes are drawn,
>   Who neither yield nor fly.
>
> They beckon, and I learn at length
>   The price for knighthood paid:
> Thy fetters are their secret strength,
>   Thy clutch their accolade.[60]

Through the experience of pain, the poet bids farewell to a sense of futility and joins the iron-willed knights who "neither yield nor fly." Pain bought freedom, self-worth, a revitalized sense of autonomous identity.

The renewed valuation of pain extended ultimately to death itself. To a number of observers, the sheer uncertainty of medieval existence, the ever-present possiblity of sudden death through plague or violence, seemed to breed a reckless exuberance unknown in modern life. The crusader who faced death daily experienced "an instinctive and illogical delight in living," Agnes Repplier claimed. Militarists of the 1890s extolled the authenticity of life in the presence of imminent destruction.[61] In *Songs from Vagabondia,* the gaiety sometimes revealed a kind of desperate urgency, a sense that activism derived its meaning from a doomed struggle with death. "The Buccaneers" cried:

Wine for the weaklings of the town,
Their lucky toasts to drain!
Our skoal for them whose star goes down,
Our drink the drink of men!
No Bacchic ivey for our brows!
Like Vikings, we await
The grim, ungarlanded carouse
We keep tonight with Fate.[62]

There was an element of romantic posturing in such verse, but it derives greater importance in the context of cultural crisis. However conventional the poem's language, it expressed pervasive yearnings. The courting of pain and death, the cultivation of courage and self-sacrifice, seemed urgent necessities in a modern culture where personal meaning had dissolved in comfort and complacency, where experience seemed weightless and death a euphemism.

Even William James, pacifist and anti-imperialist, idealized the intensity of life at war. To him, contemporary visions of a world without war lacked the "moral spur" provided in earlier times by fear of the Lord or fear of the enemy; they seemed concerned only with this-worldly well-being. As James said, "the whole atmosphere of present-day utopian literature tastes mawkish and dishwatery to people who still keep a sense for life's more bitter flavors." Drawing on the economic theories of Simon Nelson Patten, James suggested that militarists sensed America's imminent transition from a scarcity economy energized by avoidance of pain to an economy of abundance based on the seeking of pleasure. They feared the ubiquitous mediocrity of a civilization dedicated to no higher goal than material well-being. Because James shared that fear and at the same time abhorred militarism, he groped for a "moral equivalent of war" in dedication to ideals of civic duty.[63]

Few critics of overcivilization shared James's horror of war. To some, war-making alone seemed to offer a restoration of purpose in a universe barren of supernatural or even ethical meaning. Oliver Wendell Holmes, Jr., recalled his generation's Civil War experience as a secular conversion, a collective initiation into larger life. "Through our great good fortune," he told a Memorial Day audience in 1884, "in our youth our hearts were touched with fire. It was given to us to learn at the outset that life is a profound and passionate thing." Holmes's language made war appear a kind of Pentecost, from which disciples went forth to preach a stoic gospel. But that gospel lacked content. Holmes was left with an empty affirmation of militarism as a substitute for religious faith. "I do not know the meaning of the universe," he said in 1895. "But in the midst of doubt, in the collapse of creeds, there is one thing I do not doubt . . . and that is that the faith is true and adorable which leads a soldier to throw away his life in obedience to a blindly accepted duty, in a cause which he little understands, in a plan of campaign of which he has no notion, under tactics of which he does not see the use."[64] Holmes's persistent popularity among "realists" and "pragmatists" in the twentieth century is a comment on the moral hollowness of contemporary liberalism.

That hollowness can be traced to the *fin-de-siècle* cult of experience. Amid spiritual confusion, intense experience became an end in itself. Discontented Victorians embarked on a frustrating quest for authentic selfhood. Unable to preserve larger meanings outside the self, they remained enmeshed in the "morbid self-consciousness" of the therapeutic world view—the cultural malady which had provoked their discontent in the first place. Hemmed in by secular values and institutions, their antimodern impulses ended in reaffirmation of modern culture, or in futility and despair. Their rebellions seemed encircled by a slack rope in a slip knot. If they moved beyond a prudential range the knot tightened. The pattern emerged in the relationship between women and the martial ideal, particularly as expressed in the poetry of Louise Imogen Guiney, and in the careers of Frank Norris and Brooks Adams.

# The Psychological Uses of the Martial Ideal: Guiney, Norris, Adams

By the late nineteenth century, middle- and upper-class women were openly chafing at the bonds of propriety. Astride bicycles or clutching tennis rackets, they fled from suffocating gentility into the open air; they took up athletics as never before; they clamored for the vote in unprecedented numbers. Fearful that Victorian culture had reduced them to passive, useless ornaments, many embraced the activism of the 1890s with special fervor.[65]

For some, the martial ideal promised fresh possibilities. Even if military adventure remained a male prerogative, as in the polemics of Agnes Repplier and Elizabeth Bisland, idealized war-making could embody desires for intensified experience. But military adventure did not remain a male pre-rogative, at least not in the realm of historical romance. The heroines of chivalric fiction could sometimes ride, fight, and organize an army as well as any man. Joan of Arc was one such figure; another was Crawford's Eleanor of Guienne, who rides unflinchingly to face the Turk. Bored by her giggling ladies-in-waiting, she cries, "Oh, I often wish I were born a man!" That sentiment haunted educated women at the turn of the century, and suggested one reason for the popularity of self-willed chivalric heroines: they represented liberation from restrictive femininity.[66]

The life of the chivalric warrior, male or female, ranged far outside the realm of reading circles and parlor chitchat. "Oh, to be a wild Kossack!" Emily Greene Balch wrote in her commonplace book after reading *Taras Bulba*, "Fight hard and drink hard and ride hard. . . . Our clothes grow strait. Oh, for a horse between the knees, my blood boils, I want to fight, strain, wrestle, strike. . . . To be brave and have it all known, to surpass and be proud, oh the splendor of it!" For women as well as men, fantasies of aggression could fuse with sublimations of repressed sexuality. More important, by symbolizing a masculine world of action and achievement, the martial ideal counterposed meaning and purpose to a feminine world of empty formalities.[67]

The connection between the martial ideal and a woman's search for sustaining purpose was clearest in the work of Louise Imogen Guiney. She was born in Boston in 1861, the only child of respectable Irish immigrants. As a young girl she grew deeply attached to her father, the Union general Robert Patrick Guiney. Wounded in the Wilderness campaign, he returned home a spectral figure, an invalid unable to play with his adoring daughter. At eleven, after Louise entered a convent school in Providence, she began to write him long, affectionate letters suggesting a comradeship in arms. She addressed him as "Big Brother" and mentioned her mother only as an afterthought.

Though her father remained a shell-wracked, sickly man the rest of his short life, Louise stayed largely innocent of what she called "the painful side of war." From childhood, she rejected the porcelain world of Victorian girlhood for boyish fantasies of military adventure. Ask Santa Claus to bring me a toy sword, she wrote her father in 1872, "because we play soldiers here and I have a gun and flag, and a sword is all I want." As late as 1876, when she was fifteen, she added a postscript: "Please send my Scottish chiefs." A year later, General Guiney died, and entered his daughter's imagination as an embodiment of vitality and martial nobility. Forgetting his long infirmity, Louise recalled him as "my playfellow father." She kept his sword, spurs, and regimental scarf mounted on her study wall, beside the flag which had draped his coffin. Years later, she wrote that sorrow over her father's death had brought "the hardest discipline of my life."[68]

General Guiney cast a long shadow. No other man so affected Louise's work: though she had many male friends, she remained single and apparently celibate throughout her life. In her mind, he continued to express the essence of manhood. He was the source of his daughter's reverence for the martial ideal, and his memory brooded over many of her lyrics.[69]

To Louise Guiney, disaffected and discouraged throughout her literary career, the image of the chivalric warrior offered sustaining personal identifications. Largely self-educated after secondary school, she began publishing poetry and literary criticism in national magazines during the 1880s. But her father's death left the family in financial straits, and Louise was forced to support herself and her invalid mother by working at the Auburn, Massachusetts, post office. Since the job was dull and left little time for writing, Guiney's literary productivity fell sharply. The setback intensified her distaste for the modern world. Guiney had been raised as a Roman Catholic, and loyalty to her childhood faith sometimes left her ill at ease in a Protestant culture. Connecting Protestantism and modernity, she longed "to emigrate to some hamlet that smells strong of the Middle Ages, and put cotton wool in my ears, and swing out clear from this very smart century altogether." Convinced of "the happy conditions England enjoyed in the days of the great Guilds when Faith was in the saddle," she found a focus for her antimodern discontent in the figure of the knightly warrior.[70]

Guiney's martial lyrics joined her masculine identity, derived from her father, with visions of a pre-Cromwellian "merrie England." More important, her consistent stress on the premodern warrior's indomitable will suggested her poetry's wider connections with the late-nineteenth-century cultural crisis. Her martial lyrics stemmed from idiosyncratic personal needs and from concerns she shared with many educated Americans. Suffering insomnia and neurasthenia, she worried about the diminution of individual potency in a determined universe. Her poem "The Kings" (1894) dramatized this concern in a dialogue between a man and his guardian angel.

> A man said unto his Angel
> "My spirits are fallen low,
> And I cannot carry this battle.
> O brother! where might I go?
>
> "The terrible Kings are on me
> With spears that are deadly bright;
> Against me so from the cradle
> Do fate and my fathers fight."

The Kings represent the press of heredity and environment, which generates paralyzing self-doubt. The angel replies:

"Thou wavering witless soul,
Back to the ranks! . . .

"Thy will is the sovereign measure
And only event of things:
The puniest heart, defying,
Were stronger than all these Kings. . . .

"While Kings of eternal evil
Yet darken the hills about,
Thy part is with broken sabre
To rise on the last redoubt;

"To fear not sensible failure,
Nor covet the game at all,
But fighting, fighting, fighting,
Die, driven against the wall."[71]

The remedy for modern self-doubt was a life of constant action. In Guiney's work, as in that of other romantic activists, renewed dedication to a life of constant striving redirected the antimodern impulse toward contemporary life. In "Of the Golden Age" (1897), a child complains:

"Once, gods in jewelled mail
Through greenwood ways invited;
There now the moon is blighted
And mosses long and pale
On lifeless cedars trail."

His mother responds by urging him to "keep this good unrest" that he may help to usher in a future "time more true and ample. . . ." Guiney's longing for medieval splendor was always cut short by a reaffirmation of heroic potentialities in the present. Despite her distaste for imperialism, she admitted that the heroism of Roosevelt at San Juan Hill and Dewey at Manila Bay "is mighty thrilling, and makes one swagger to be in the same world with them."[72]

Guiney's swaggering activism, combined with the martial motifs in her verse, reflected a general attraction to a masculine role. In her correspondence, Guiney adopted the romantic activists' what-ho tone of male camaraderie. She saluted addressees with a "heigho!" and referred to correspondents, male and female, as "good fellows." This was a common practice among young Victorian women, but Guiney's notions of masculinity were narrower than most. Influenced by her father and by the late-nineteenth-century cult of strenuosity, she defined male identity almost entirely in military terms. The definition surfaced in her poetry and her criticism alike. In an 1897 essay on Prosper Mérimée, Guiney wrote: "You feel wroth at him that he went out of the world, not like a veteran from the battlefield, but like a girl from the ballroom, in smiling weariness, and without a scar."[73] Life was a battle, in which women did not participate. To live fully was to be a man, to fight.

Ultimately, the activist imperative proved too exhausting for Guiney. Unnerved by frenetic American life, she sailed for England in 1902. The following year, having settled in Oxford, she confided to a friend:

> I can't go home: it gives me the most genuine and involuntary fit of trembling to think of it, much as I long for the faces of my friends. The pace at which everything goes there, the noises, the publicity, the icicles, the mosquitoes, the extreme climatic conditions,—I am not equal to face them now; and I fall back, as on and into, a mossy bank, to the peace, the utter simplicity, the anonymity, of my life in England, and feel that I cannot give it up, and more, that I actually have some right to it.[74]

Guiney remained in England until her death in 1921. Despite the peacefulness of Oxford, she wrote little more poetry. As her literary productivity declined, the tone of male camaraderie disappeared from her letters. The urge to achieve and create seemed to require a masculine identity, which Guiney could not sustain.

Guiney's difficulties reflected those of many late-Victorian women who were caught between rigid sexual roles. It may be, as Carroll Smith-Rosenberg suggests, that midcentury women found alternatives to masculine aggressiveness in enduring female friendships.[75] But by the end of the century, at least to many ambitious women, relationships in the feminine sphere seemed schoolgirlish and silly. Recoiling from their sisters' china-doll existence, female rebels often idealized the masculine vision of life as a struggle among individuals. Untrained to compete in the male arena, lacking sufficient ego strength, they ended their rebellions in personal frustration. Their efforts toward liberation, while they may have temporarily opened some space for personal autonomy, ultimately reinforced the culture they had set out to criticize.

For Frank Norris and Brooks Adams, as for Guiney, the archaic warrior presented an enticing but finally problematic character ideal. Their quest for wider selfhood melded with the interests of their class: both moved from antimodern nostalgia to imperialist apologetics. But the personal significance of both men's odysseys transcended their role in the revitalization and transformation of bourgeois culture. Norris and Adams's intellectual careers intermingled the social and psychological dimensions of martial antimodernism.

From early youth, Frank Norris sought success outside the boundaries of commercial society. His father was a self-made San Francisco jeweler aptly named Benjamin Franklin Norris, a pillar of rectitude and strength who dominated the sensitive and introverted young Frank. Norris's mother was a former actress who indulged his shyness. Cherishing artistic ambitions for her son, she encouraged him to practice drawing. Since the boy showed some talent, his father agreed to send him to the atelier Julien in Paris. But when young Norris began to neglect painting in order to write chivalric poetry, his father ordered him home. Back in San Francisco, Norris enrolled in the University of California. When his parents were divorced while he was a student, his father eliminated Frank from his will, depriving him of a sizeable inheritance. The divorce left his mother free to encourage his literary enterprises. But the influence of Benjamin Franklin Norris persisted, shaping Frank's notions of manhood.[76]

Norris's early writing showed a persistent fascination with the martial ideal in medieval settings. He published several poems in the student literary magazine, most of them extolling the medieval warrior in conventional romantic language. In 1891, his mother arranged to have the long verse romance *Yvernelle* privately and sumptuously printed. The narrative itself was insignificant, a tedious tale in which Sir Caverlaye of Vosvenel thwarts the dark sorceress Guhuldraha and her murderous brother just in time to marry the fair Yvernelle before she enters a convent. But the poem's prologue revealed Norris's undergraduate disaffection from the modern world, and foreshadowed most of his later concerns.

After recounting the medieval lord's mistreatment of his vassals, Norris added: "The feudal baron yet remains today . . . changed into the modern moneyed lord. . . ." The destruction of the feudal social order had brought not justice but utilitarian grayness. Medieval pomp and pageantry were now "undervalued by a colder race." For his contemporaries' coldness, Norris had a familiar diagnosis: modern man was unromantic because he had insulated himself from death and danger, setting himself at one remove from immediate experience.

> Real blood—real death—real gasp and dying moan—
> Aroused the equite's mind, the baron's heart;
> While we, a dainty age, and milder grown,
> Find our diversion in the mimic art . . .[77]

Fascinated by "real blood—real death—real gasp and dying moan," Norris returned often in his early work to the violence of the premodern warrior. In "Grettir at Drangey" (1892), one of several Norris short stories modelled on Morris's Icelandic tales, Norris extolled the masculine camaraderie of Grettir and Illugi on the "lonely, rock-ribbed island" of Drangey. They live "a brave life" until it ends in an orgy of bloodletting. The villainous Thorbjorn the Hook, claiming the island as his own, storms Grettir's homestead with twenty men. Illugi dies early, but Grettir lasts an unearthly time as arms are hacked off, eyes gouged, and heads speared from ear to ear. Having maimed all and killed most of Thorbjorn's men, Grettir "died as he would have wished to, in battle, his harness on, his sword in his grip."[78]

Ultimately, Norris transferred his tales of brute force from medieval Iceland to the contemporary American West. At Berkeley, he could not preserve his antimodern pessimism amid an intellectual climate pervaded by optimistic evolutionism and Anglo-Saxon racism. Heartened by the discovery that "somewhere in the heart of every Anglo-Saxon lies the predatory instinct of his Viking ancestors—an instinct that a thousand years of respectability and taxpaying have not quite succeeded in eliminating," Norris decided that the winning of the American West was every bit as heroic a subject as those which inspired the *Song of Roland* or the *Nibelungenlied.* The problem, as a character in one of Norris's later novels said, was "to get back to that first clear-eyed view of things" because "we have been educated away from it all. We are out of touch."[79]

Norris, seeking renewed contact with "primeval epic life," repeatedly assailed tendencies toward overcivilization. He feared that educated Americans were mired in "Other People's books" and "Other People's notions"; he railed against the timidities of domestic realists who failed to deal with "real life." Norris's hostility toward "the bugbear of 'Literature' " suggested a distrust of his own vocation—a vocation nurtured by his mother and susceptible to such "feminine" maladies as intellectualism or aestheticism. Like other twentieth-century novelists from Hemingway to Mailer, Norris equated artistic creativity with virility and feared losing both. He seemed haunted by the fear that thought unmanned the thinker. The United States, he insisted, "does not want and does not need Scholars, but Men—Men made in the mould of the Leonard Woods and the Theodore Roosevelts."[80]

Norris's insistent manliness reflected his ambivalence toward women. Long dependent on his mother, he was fearful and covertly hostile toward his father. Reared in the "civilized" sexual morality dissected by Freud, he endured a long engagement until he was financially able to marry at thirty. He idolized his fiancée and all respectable women, but his writing revealed a resentment of their asexual sanctity. His admirable female characters were all "masculine" in their bluff heartiness and Amazonian strength. The rest of his feminine figures embodied traditional male fears: they were seductive but treacherous, like the sorceress Guhuldraha in *Yvernelle.* For Norris, the feminization of culture bred moral and physical weakness. The task facing American novelists was to resist feminization by rekindling masculine potency.[81]

The sexual dimension in Norris's worship of force emerged most clearly in "Lauth" (1893). The title character, a withdrawn university student in fourteenth-century Paris, is caught up in a riot, much against his will. In the tumult he is somehow given a weapon. Defending himself, he undergoes an exhilarating transformation.

> At the sight of blood shed by his own hands all the animal savagery latent in every human being awoke in him,—no more merciful scruples now. *He could kill.* In the twinkling of an eye the pale, highly cultivated scholar, whose life had been passed in the study of science and abstruse questions of philosophy, sank back to the level of his savage Celtic ancestors. His eyes glittered, he moistened his lips with the tip of his tongue, and his whole frame quivered with the eagerness and craving of a panther in sight of his prey. He could not stretch his arbalist quickly enough again, and his fingers shook as he laid the bolt in the groove.[82]

The sensual details and suggestions of phallic imagery underscored the connection between the violence and repressed sexuality in Norris's work. For him, the realm of instinct harbored aggressive and sensual impulses. The latter seemed particularly dangerous. The key to avoiding overcivilization was not release of inhibition but careful channeling of instinctual forces into constructive pursuits. One such pursuit was war; another—at least toward the end of Norris's career—was business.

By the time of his death in 1902, Norris had overcome most of his youthful distaste for commercial society. He despised the rich and idle, but he admired active businessmen for their commitment to a disciplined life of productivity. Norris's accommodation with industrial capitalism emerged clearly in his essay, "The Frontier Gone at Last," written just before his death.

In the Middle Ages, Norris wrote, the battle of life had been joined by knightly warriors; in the twentieth century it was fought by businessmen. But the "race impulse" was the same. It was the Anglo-Saxon urge to push ever westward in search of new frontiers to conquer. In Norris's mind, the medieval warrior and the modern businessman finally merged, joined by the assumption of Anglo-Saxon continuity. "Had the Lion-Hearted Richard lived to-day he would have become a leading representative of the Amalgamated Steel companies," Norris wrote, "and doubt not for one moment that he would have underbid his Manchester rivals in the matter of bridge-girders." The latest frontier was "our present commercial crusade to the East." As Norris said, "we cannot speak of it but in terms borrowed from the glossary of the warrior. It is a commercial 'invasion,' a trade 'war,' a 'threatened attack,' on the part of America; business is 'captured,' opponents are 'seized,' certain industries are 'killed,' certain former monopolies are 'wrested away.' " Norris concluded with the pious hope that American patriotism would develop into a wider world-embracing spirit, but the emotional thrust of his essay was all in the opposite direction. The Anglo-Saxon destiny was conquest, and "races must follow their destiny blindly. . . ."[83]

The Anglo-Saxon activism of the 1890s, coupled with Norris's psychic need to embrace a conventional manliness, led him to shift the martial ideal from past to present. Seeking an identity outside bourgeois society, he found its values difficult to escape. His antimodern impulse led not to dissent or even nostalgia but to the revitalization and transformation of modern culture. Beginning in romantic medievalism, Norris ended by affirming modern imperialism. A similar pattern, arising from different sources, characterized the career of Brooks Adams.

From Charles Francis Adams's viewpoint, his youngest son Brooks was a troublesome youth. By comparison to his quick-witted older brothers, Brooks seemed easily confused, unable to sustain concentration. To his fretting father, the boy seemed unable to apply himself. When Brooks left home for Harvard, his father wrote him regular didactic letters—constantly correcting his spelling and lecturing him on habits of self-discipline. As the youngest son in an old and illustrious line, Brooks Adams felt the double burden of family tradition and family expectation.[84]

Adams's early intellectual interests may have signified a protest against paternal domination. His father was a good nineteenth-century liberal, contemptuous of medieval culture and of Pre-Raphaelite efforts to revive it. But as early as 1868, when Brooks was twenty, the youth confessed to his father that "the dawning of *our* civilization . . . has interested me more than all the splendour of the ancient."[85] The interest must have seemed heterodox if not heretical to Charles Francis Adams, who cherished the teachings of classical republicanism. But Brooks's most ringing declaration of intellectual independence came in 1887, when he published *The Emancipation of Massachusetts.* Determinedly iconoclastic, the book celebrated rebellions against the Puritan "theocracy," and raised a storm of protest among New England filiopietists. More important, the *Emancipation* marked a critical period in Adams's developing emotional life.

The *Emancipation* culminated several years of drift and psychic turmoil. After graduation from college, Brooks had followed his brothers into the political arena, jousting at corruption as a mugwump journalist. Troubled more than his brothers by their collective ineffectiveness, Brooks fell victim to a prolonged attack of nervous exhaustion. During the winter of 1880–1881, he abandoned all efforts to work, claiming he could only read Walter Scott. Brother Henry was sympathetic but impatient. "I *order* you to get well," he said. "I shall expect great things of you."[86] Brooks was back on his feet by spring, snappish and gloomy but ready to rejoin Boston society.

Two discoveries lightened the gloom of the 1880s for Adams. One was his encounter with the martial ideal, in the old-world grandeur of M. de Bussigny's riding academy and in the stoic militarism of Oliver Wendell Holmes, Jr.'s, early lectures to Boston audiences. The other was the glory of the medieval cathedrals of France. As he told Henry, "everything pales before my discovery of the meaning of Gothic in 1888, which was to me a revelation. My intense excitement when I first began to read Chartres, and Le Mans, and all the rest, could never be equalled again by anything."[87] To Adams, medieval character seemed an exhilarating fusion of martial virtue and religious faith, a sharp counterpoint to the sordid commercial ethic of the Gilded Age.

During the early 1890s, medieval character provided a focus for Adams's growing discontent. The panic of 1893 endangered the Adams family fortune and convinced Brooks that a plutocratic conspiracy was manipulating the currency to the ruin of the American people. Predicting imminent revolution if Wall Street's power were not broken, he railed against "the rotten, unsexed, swindling, lying Jews represented by J. P. Morgan and the gang which have been manipulating our country for the last four years."[88] Like other antimodernists in both Europe and America, Adams was attracted to anti-Semitism. In some ways the Jew became a negative identity for him, defining by negation his uncertain sense of self and reaffirming his republican suspicions of commercial prosperity. Ultimately Adams embraced the medieval soldier as the emblem of a culture undefiled by commerce or its allegedly Jewish agents. That notion was historically confused but polemically powerful. It energized Adams's major work, *The Law of Civilization and Decay* (1895).

The *Law* traced the gradual shift from the imaginative mentality of the Middle Ages, when fear was the dominant human emotion, to the sordid commercialism of modern times, when fear had been superseded by greed. According to Adams, the social disorganization and physical danger pervading early medieval Europe generated a widespread fearfulness which in turn produced the highest religious, military, and artistic development the West had ever seen. As the Roman Empire disintegrated and life became more uncertain, men cowered before the unknown, seeking to propitiate the lowering darkness with the fetishes and rites of medieval Christianity. The waxing of the magical world view produced the characteristic medieval type: hot-blooded, fanciful, fearful of unseen powers but capable of great physical courage. Such traits spread widely during the tenth and eleventh centuries, when "commerce nearly ceased," science was forgotten, and "the imagination had full play." The stage was set for the great flowering of the emotional type, the first crusade.[89]

From Adams's viewpoint, the crusader's approach to war had to be sharply distinguished from that of the modern mercenary: "A crusade was no vulgar war for a vulgar prize, but an alliance with the supernatural for the conquest of talismans whose possession was tantamount to omnipotence." Whole villages, aflame with religious enthusiasm, followed the noble chivalric warriors, "the originals of the fairy knights, clad in impenetrable armour, mounted on miraculous horses, armed with resistless swords, and bearing charmed lives."[90]

The charm did not last long. As Adams pointed out, the first crusade met only indifferent success; the second ended in disaster. The emotional temperament promoted courage but undermined tactics; its declining influence was apparent in subsequent crusades, begun for economic rather than religious motives. To soldiers dreaming of plunder rather than salvation, miraculous visions came less frequently. In Adams's view, the sacrilegious debauch at the fall of Constantinople in 1204 portended the eclipse of emotional civilization.[91]

As trading centers grew, society became more centralized and life more secure. With "the transformation of physical force into money . . . individual strength or courage ceased to have importance." According to Adams, the Reformation marked the decisive victory of economic civilization. Religion grew cheap: "as the tradesman replaced the enthusiast, a dogma was evolved by which mental anguish, which cost nothing, was substituted for the offering which was effective in proportion to its money value." And, in Adams's view, a new character type emerged: "subtler, more acquisitive, more tenacious of life" than the feudal lord had been. The remainder of the *Law* recounted the continuing ascendance of the economic character type, up to his most recent and powerful incarnation in Adams's *bête noire*, the nineteenth-century banker.[92]

Throughout Adams's sketch of world history, he preserved a facade of scientific neutrality. Yet his emotional commitments were clear in the breathless excitement with which he described the first crusade, and in the bleak tones of his conclusion. To Adams, the decline of the emotional type had led to a host of contemporary problems: the disintegration of the family unit, the decline of the birthrate, the drying up of artistic inspiration, the desecration of religious feeling. The last seemed particularly galling to Adams: "the ecstatic dream, which some twelfth century monk cut into the stones of the sanctuary hallowed by the presence of his God, is reproduced to bedizen a warehouse, or the plan of an abbey, which Saint Hugh may have consecrated, is adapted to a railway station." The devaluation of symbols portended the collapse of the modern West—a collapse more total than Rome's, because "we lack the stream of barbarian blood which made the Middle Age."[93]

Adams's pessimism, like his personality, was unstable. Even the *Law* betrayed a fundamental ambivalence between devotion to the emotional type and admiration for the sheer force exerted during the centralizing process. Appealing to this latter tendency, Theodore Roosevelt cheered his friend's spirits. Adams, respecting Roosevelt's opinion and influence, asked him to review the *Law* in the *Forum*. Roosevelt agreed, insisting in his review that martial virtue was alive and well in America. On that point, Adams was open to persuasion—because he shared Roosevelt's belief in the regenerative powers of war. Ultimately Adams was content to follow Roosevelt's example and make peace with commercial society in hopes of an imminent imperialist crusade. In militarist circles Adams's calls for a "centralized" navy second to none elicited growing respect. After war with

Spain was declared, the naval victories at Santiago and Manila Bay established Adams as a serious strategist, a confidante of such influential militarists as Alfred Thayer Mahan. Excited by the war and no doubt flattered by the attention from the powerful, Adams began to abandon his pessimistic stance. When Roosevelt succeeded to the presidency in 1901, Adams became convinced that a thoroughgoing revival of the martial ideal was at hand.[94]

Military revival did not involve the crushing of the Economic Man, but his regeneration through imperialistic adventure. Adams made that clear in *America's Economic Supremacy* (1900) and *The New Empire* (1902). Both books were blueprints for world domination, economic and military. In these imperialist polemics, economic determinism relaxed the tension between medieval and modern culture. If war was "the final stage of economic competition," martial virtue no longer seemed antithetical to commercial success.[95]

In domestic policy, too, Adams grew progressively optimistic. "I cannot share your expectation of a breakdown," he told Henry in 1903.[96] The two brothers drifted apart, Henry remaining obstinately pessimistic while Brooks advanced a plethora of proposals for the remaking of society. In Brooks's mind, the ideal warrior began to merge with the ideal administrator. He still warned that the United States must develop the military temperament or perish but his reverence for authority and fear of social disintegration led him to intellectual spadework for corporate liberalism. In his enthusiasm for efficient administration, he joined such nationalist "Progressives" as Roosevelt, Herbert Croly, and Walter Lippmann. Like them, Adams began to advocate a streamlined capitalist state directed by an elite corps of administrators. As the *Law* had stated, the only alternative to chaos was forceful centralization. Adams had reversed his antimodern critique, easing the ideological transition to the twentieth-century corporate system.

Yet the urgency with which Adams urged administrative reform betrayed his continuing uneasiness in modern industrial society. He saw disintegrative forces everywhere. In modern childrearing, he charged in 1908, "the first lesson taught the infant is no longer to control the attention of the will." Medieval leaders had willfully imposed order on their chaotic world, said Adams (forgetting his earlier descriptions of a disunited medieval culture); their modern descendants, lacking educational discipline, fell into moral and physical lassitude. "The old society is rotting everywhere," Adams complained in 1909. Both sexes evaded duty: women avoided childbearing while men shrank from military service. "The object of democracy, of course," Adams said, "is to relieve itself of military duty, in order that it may have more time and money for self-gratification." Like George Will and other present-day militarists, Adams counterposed military ideals against the "democratic" obsession with comfort and well-being. Imperialistic adventures, it seemed, had not spread martial virtue after all.[97]

Adams's continuing attacks on materialist complacency revealed the psychological and religious roots of his martial antimodernism. He was not merely a militarist; he imagined himself both soldier and saint. As he told Henry in 1895, "I am in feeling absolutely at one with Saint Anselm, or Godfrey de Bouillon." Throughout the *Law*, Adams had stressed that martial virtue was the product of an ecstatic spirit light years away from modern rationality. His imperialist polemics overlooked that point, but distaste for the modern "economic type" continued to shape Adams's thinking. Despite the aggressive positivism of his theories, he remained impatient with rationalist optimism and depressed by his bouts of "morbid introspection." He sought release in an imaginary realm of color, spontaneity, and sacred passion, a realm embodied by the Gothic cathedral. In 1895, Brooks returned to Chartres, on the brink of nervous collapse. Writing to Henry of the experience, Brooks made clear he was no aesthetic dabbler, but a lost pilgrim.

> Even the artistic men like [the painter John] La Farge don't see the heart of the great imaginative past. They see a building, a color, a combination of technical effects. They don't see the passion that this means, or meant, and they don't feel that awful tragedy, which is the sum of life. The agony of consciousness.[98]

Adams's longings brought him to the threshold of Catholicism, but no farther. In the end, the weight of family tradition prevailed. As he grew older, Adams sought to make his peace with ancestral memory, to join his idiosyncrasies with family tradition. He grew fond of saying that if his grandfather John Quincy Adams had lived during the twelfth century, he would have been one of the crusaders. And he began to make the Old House at Quincy "a sort of memorial" to the Adams line. In 1914, Brooks Adams publicly renounced his private judgment and professed adherence to the Congregational faith.[99] The profession of faith did not soothe Adams's troubled mind—he remained an anxious and embittered man until his death in 1927—but it did suggest that an unfulfilled religious longing lay behind his antimodern dissent. For Adams as for other Americans, the new empire temporarily eased social fears but failed to satisfy spiritual discontent.

The diverse strains in Brooks Adams's thought pointed to the complex and various meanings of martial antimodernism. The fascination with archaic strife revealed idiosyncratic psychic needs and also embodied a recurring activist impulse among American intellectuals: a desire to escape feelings of isolation and impotence by immersing themselves in their bustling, democratic society. Further, the American reverence for military force was part of the transatlantic current of romantic activism. From

Nietzsche to Kipling to Sorel, to name only three, European men of letters celebrated violence as a protest against overcivilized gentility and intellectualism.

Originating largely in individual rebellions, the worship of force had important social consequences on both sides of the Atlantic. In Europe, martial antimodernism undermined parliamentary liberalism and laid the intellectual groundwork for fascism and Naziism. In America, where anti-Semitism and contempt for democracy were less overt, the martial impulse produced different results. It strengthened the will of a nervous bourgeoisie and provided intellectual antecedents for liberal votaries of *realpolitik*. As advisors to the well-placed and powerful, twentieth-century American intellectuals have sanctioned military force with an aura of inevitability. Though they have advocated "realism" rather than fascism, they—like a number of their European counterparts—have become servants rather than critics of power.

Martial antimodernism was more than another chapter in the history of the love affair of intellectuals with power. The transatlantic revolt against overcivilization had an enduring psychological and religious significance. Preoccupation with violence stemmed from a more general rediscovery of what D. H. Lawrence called the "primal, dark veracity" underlying conventional pieties and civilities. That rediscovery may have led to an exaltation of brute force, but it also included a number of strikingly parallel intellectual formulations, all of which appeared within a few decades: Nietzsche's apotheosis of the will to power, Freud's exploration of id-processes, Bergson's celebration of the *élan vital*, Jung's concept of the archetypal mind-state Moira—a gratification-world presided over by a prehistoric earth-goddess. Writing in the *Century* in 1898, the ethnologist Daniel Brinton expressed a common view when he defined "the alleged progress of man" as "a superficial veneer, a deceptive surface on society, burnishing its exterior, while the most of each man remains the pristine savage that his remote ancestor was, with the same hopes and fears, wants and wishes."[100]

The revaluation of primal irrationality was closely entwined with the widespread gropings toward "real life." Desperate quests for authentic experience led often to the discovery of the "pristine savage"—uncivilized, uninhibited, and aggressive. The link between the *fin-de-siècle* fascination with primal, aggressive impulse and the emerging search for authenticity discloses one of the most important undercurrents in twentieth-century cultural history: the desire to recombine a fragmented self and re-create a problematic reality through aggressive action. That desire has lain behind fascism as well as the mass-market murder story; it has persisted to our own time. One can see it, for example, in the continuing fascination with combat among some military men (including such articulate veterans as Philip Caputo and William Styron)—a fascination with a world beyond the boundaries of modern safety and routine, where moral distinctions still seem sharp and death is not a euphemism but a daily adversary. One can see it as well in the current cant of popular psychology, in advice on "winning through intimidation" and in the constant praise of "risk-taking." "To be aggressive is to be alive—so many now seem to believe," Richard Sennett wrote recently. "Why is aggression now seen as life?" The answer may lie in a continuing revolt against the modern sense of unreality, a revolt which has exalted masterful (and sometimes violent) action as a path to "real life."[101]

Like the craft revival, antimodern militarism revitalized familiar bourgeois values but also transformed them. The protestant urge for self-improvement survived but its ultimate purpose became progressively unclear. As middle- and upper-class life seemed increasingly insulated from danger and immured in institutionalized routine, the educated and affluent felt a persistent need for the manly testing the quotidian world no longer allowed. But the test increasingly took place in a moral void. The stage was set for a new kind of heroic act with no larger purpose beyond itself. Philip Caputo has much in common with his spiritual ancestors Holmes and Hemingway: all seem to see "toughness," "manhood," and the "rapture" of combat as ends in themselves. This is an understandable and eloquent commentary on the platitudinous banality of official apologetics for modern war; it contains an admirable streak of honest stoicism, but at bottom it is assimilable to the nihilism of our dominant culture. The militarist obsession with authenticity, like other cults of risk-taking, became a circular and self-defeating quest for intense experience—a characteristic mode of adjustment to a secular culture of consumption. Reacting against therapeutic self-absorption, the cult of martial experience proved unable to transcend it.

Yet this antimodern quest for authenticity is not reducible to either the raptures of military men or the slogans of contemporary self-help manuals; it resisted as well as reinforced the modern obsession with personal fulfillment. As Lionel Trilling has observed, the late nineteenth century witnessed the beginnings of a split between Western politics, which promoted a socialist or liberal vision of increasing material comfort for all, and Western literature, which increasingly sought to transcend the progressive pleasure principle and attain a kind of spiritual heroism.[102] In the light of Trilling's observations, the antimodern fascination with suffering revealed important connections with avant-garde literature. Dostoevsky and Lawrence shared some concerns with middlebrow moralists like Hamilton Wright Mabie, who wrote in 1895:

> In our slippered ease, protected by orderly government, by written constitutions, by a police who are always in evidence, we sometimes forget of what perilous stuff we are made, and how unseparable from human life are those

elements of tragedy which from time to time startle us in our repose, and make us aware that the most awful pages of history may be rewritten in the record of our own day. . . . A stable world is essential to progress, but a world without the element of peril would comfort the body and destroy the soul.[103]

The duty of the artist, he concluded, was to remind us of "the tragic background of life" by confronting the realities of violence, danger, and sudden death as medieval romancers had done.

Mabie rarely engaged the "perilous stuff" of humanity in his essays, and never applauded the recovery of primal irrationality. Concerned about spiritual enervation, he nevertheless remained committed to material progress. Yet his words were a significant if pale reflection of profounder impulses. The exploration of the irrational contained, at bottom, a renewed appreciation of the terror and mystery of life. You cannot shut your eyes to "the real trouble—the heart pain—the world pain," said Joseph Conrad's Stein in *Lord Jim* (1900).

> A man that is born falls into a dream like a man who falls into the sea. If he tries to climb out into the air as inexperienced people endeavour to do, he drowns —*nicht wahr?* . . . No! I tell you! The way is to the destructive element submit yourself, and with the exertions of your hands and feet in the water make the deep, deep sea keep you up.[104]

For Conrad, "the destructive element" was not violence but experience in all its tragic dimensions. To live fully was not to make war but to accept "the heart pain—the world pain."

A number of American antimodernists groped toward that insight. Even worshippers of force seemed faintly aware that their difficulties transcended military solution. If discontent with modernity persisted, then the problem lay beyond the battlefield. Brooks Adams sensed it when he described "the agony of consciousness" at Chartres. For him, as for other Americans, medieval character embodied not merely craftsmanship or martial virtue, but a fundamentally different sensibility. The search for meaning and purpose led ultimately to the medieval mind and soul.

· 4 ·

# THE MORNING
# OF BELIEF:
# MEDIEVAL
# MENTALITIES
# IN A MODERN
# WORLD

TO LATE-NINETEENTH-CENTURY AMERICANS, MEDIEVAL character presented an ever-changing face. It was wraithlike, evanescent, its outlines dependent on the observer's personal and social circumstances. This complexity was nowhere more apparent than in perceptions of medieval thought and feeling. By reconstructing those perceptions, I hope to cast light on the hovering soul-sickness which emerged in the late nineteenth century and which has spread throughout the twentieth —the sense that modern life has grown dry and passionless, and that one must somehow try to regenerate a lost intensity of feeling.

This is obviously not a task that lends itself to precise measurement. The job of reconstructing these antimodern perceptions involves piecing together casual references, tacit assumptions, and common themes from the voluminous late-Victorian writings on medieval beliefs and values. The result is not a monolithic medieval "mind," but a group of overlapping mentalities—that is, shared character traits mingling various qualities of intellect and emotion. Pale innocence, fierce conviction, physical and emotional vitality, playfulness and spontaneity, an ability to cultivate fantastic or dreamlike states of awareness, an intense otherworldly asceticism: those were medieval traits perceived by late Victorians and embodied in a variety of dramatis personae.

Peasants, saints, and seers haunted American imaginations around the turn of the century. Journalism, fiction, and verse celebrated the simple faith of the charcoal burner and the ecstasy of the mystic. Biographies of medieval saints and translations of their writings proliferated as never before. From Francis of Assisi to the humblest communicant at Chartres, the souls of the Middle Ages fascinated the American reading public.

Among this cast of medieval characters, there was one figure missing: the scholastic philosopher. In the popular press Thomas Aquinas, Duns Scotus, and their fellow schoolmen received virtually no attention. The omission underscored the links between the American fascination with medieval mentalities and the crisis of cultural authority. People who felt overburdened by intellectuality and cut off from "real life" did not want the scholastics' rational system, however elegantly constructed. Some wanted simple faith, others spontaneous feeling, others sacred mystery— anything, in other words, except logical order. So logic disappeared from the popular view of the Middle Ages. To feel drawn toward medieval mentalities was to participate in the recovery of primal irrationality, to share the primitivist impulse of the late nineteenth century.

The recovery of primal irrationality was a complex cultural phenomenon, with diverse and far-reaching implications. A stress on the nonlogical sources of human conduct cast doubt on libertarian beliefs in rational choice but also undermined determinist models of human action. By the early twentieth century, a widespread questioning of determinism permeated nearly every area of Western culture, from the empyrean reaches of philosophy and physics to popular therapies and cults of strenuosity. On both sides of the Atlantic, a diffuse but pervasive sentiment spread: a sense that nineteenth-century science had not explained the universe, a quickening hope that mystery was alive in the world. Feeling a wind in positivist stillness, reflective religious people felt that they could breathe again. They looked hopefully toward the revival of neoidealism and intuitionalism in philosophy, particularly the vitalist gospel according to Henri Bergson, or toward the cult of simplicity preached by the British poet Edward Carpenter.[1] Late-nineteenth-century Americans drew on all those sources, as well as on indigenous republican tradition, in articulating discontent with modern thought and feeling. The primitivist impulse, in other words, led in a variety of directions: toward an apotheosis of pious simplicity, toward a reasserted republican morality of self-control, toward a fascination with the uncivilized, the uncanny, the inexplicable.

Here as elsewhere, the antimodern impulse revitalized existing cultural modes, created new ones, and preserved an edge of dissent. While the admiration for medieval simplicity and sincerity merged with "Progressive" efforts to regenerate a bourgeois morality of self-control, the vitalist fascination with medieval energy melded with newer tendencies which undermined that morality—indeed which threatened all familiar bases of moral action. Despite their many differences, antimodern vitalists shared one important trait with avant-garde bohemians, corporate liberal ideologues, and early therapists: all tended to elevate becoming over being, the *process* of experience over its goal or result. Though it originated in religious longing, much antimodern vitalism reinforced the process of secularization by dissolving larger frameworks of meaning in the flux of "pure experience." And by sentimentalizing the "primitive" traits of premodern people, some antimodern vitalists contributed to maladies they had hoped to cure. They brought primal irrationality to light, but in doing so they sanitized it, integrating instinctual impulses into a therapeutic ethic of "self-expression." Weightlessness clung to the vitalist critique like a mocking shadow. Yet some, the true dissenters, recognized that primitivism recalled not only spontaneity and innocence but also dread and awe—emotions altogether alien to the enlightened optimism of the emerging twentieth century.

Among those who felt the antimodern impulse, the common strand of primitivism was especially clear in numerous references to medieval "childishness." Though not all writers described medieval traits as "childish" or "childlike," the terms recurred often enough to constitute a leitmotif in discussions of nearly all medieval mental traits, from innocence to spontaneity to fantasy. The notion that the Middle Ages were the "childhood of the race" linked medieval people to other childlike premodern types, notably to the nineteenth-century Japanese. The same impulse which led some Americans to medieval Europe led others to the Orient.

The stress on premodern childishness stemmed not only from *fin-de-siècle* primitivism but also from time-honored literary traditions and common habits of mind. To understand the full significance of childlike mentalities for antimodern thinkers, we need first to glance at the developing imagery of childhood and youth during the nineteenth century. The image of the child had two distinct but related social uses. On the one hand, an exaltation of childishness pointed to a critique of adult conventions; on the other hand, it accommodated adults to those conventions by providing a brief, imaginary escape from them. Both tendencies emerged fullblown during the late nineteenth century, when interest in childhood and youth reinforced fascination with the medieval childhood of the race.

# The Image of Childhood and the Childhood of the Race

The history of nineteenth-century attitudes toward children is an enormous subject. I can only suggest its complexity here, as a brief but necessary prelude to an analysis of medieval "childishness" in late-Victorian thought. The logical starting point is the New Testament. "Except ye be converted, and become as little children," Christ said, "ye shall not enter into the kingdom of heaven" (Matt. 18: 3). But for nearly two millennia, reverence for childhood remained only an undercurrent in Christian thought. Under the shadow of Original Sin, children seemed closer to Satan than to God. A widespread apotheosis of childhood awaited the early nineteenth century, when cultural and demographic developments had combined to promote a sense that childhood constituted a separate sphere of being.

One key to the growing differentiation between adults and children lay in the history of manners, which Norbert Elias has brilliantly analyzed in *The Civilizing Process*. After the sixteenth century, Elias notes, there was a widening gap between behavior expected of adults and behavior perceived as childish. Having not yet fully internalized prohibitions against impulse, children were still likely to blow their noses on their sleeves, to spit on the dinner table, or to fly into uncontrollable rages. "Civilized" adults increasingly forbade themselves such practices. The new fastidiousness in social relations extended into the home, as adults and children began to sleep in separate rooms. By the end of the eighteenth century, in family and in company, the child seemed more and more a being apart.[2]

As Elias points out, the civilizing process was more than a matter of fashion. It involved a radical restructuring of conduct and feeling, the gradual development of a modern superego. However trivial in its details, the concern with manners furthered the rationalization of Western culture. The growing gap between adults and children was part of the differentiation of roles which accompanied the rationalizing process; the growing organization of the minutiae of social relations was part of the systemization of all human conduct.[3]

Childhood began to seem a playful prelude to the careful business of life. During the eighteenth century there was a key shift in middle- and upper-class attitudes toward children. No longer "miniature adults," English children became "superior pets" on whom their parents lavished clothes and toys.[4] Toward 1800 a literary cult of childhood coalesced, linking latitudinarian Christianity and romantic primitivism in uneasy alliance. By transforming Original Sin into Original Innocence, liberalizing theologians made the idea of an uncorrupted child nature more acceptable to educated Protestants. They began to juxtapose the child's sincerity against the adult's artifice. Romantic thinkers shared the Christian admiration for childlike innocence but added a primitivist stress on the child's capacity for spontaneous feeling and intense experience. To Blake and Rousseau, freedom from social convention and utilitarian calculation made the child an emblem of a fuller sensuous and imaginative life—a focal point for a potentially sharp critique of the modern superego.[5]

Though that critique became explicit in Blake and Rousseau, it remained muted in Wordsworth, whose ideas were more widely popularized in England and America. His ode, "Intimations of Immortality from Recollections of Early Childhood," (1806) became a central text for Anglo-American attitudes toward children.

> Heaven lies about us in our infancy!
> Shades of the prison-house begin to close
>   Upon the growing Boy,
> But He beholds the light, and whence it flows,
>   He sees it in his joy;
> The Youth, who daily farther from the east
>   Must travel, still is Nature's Priest,
>   And by the vision splendid
>   Is on his way attended;
> At length the Man perceives it die away,
> And fade into the light of common day.[6]

For Wordsworth and his readers, utilitarian adulthood assumed an aura of inevitability. Protest often became elegiac regret.

Throughout the nineteenth century, Wordsworthian sentiments drew strength from the developing domestic ideal. The spread of capitalist social relations made the family seem a psychic refuge where intimacy and emotional warmth could survive amid the ruthless competition of the marketplace. By midcentury, middle-class children were no longer "fostered out" to relatives or wet nurses. Unlike their colonial predecessors, they stayed increasingly at home, shielded by their mother from the market's corrupting influence. In the common view, women and children—especially children because they were untainted by social artifice—embodied the moral innocence and emotional spontaneity which seemed increasingly absent from the public realm.[7]

It was no accident, then, that toward the end of a century of capitalist expansion the image of the sickly-sweet child pervaded popular novels, plays, and poems. Its appeal was intensified during the 1880s and 1890s by the crisis of cultural authority. As social conventions stiffened, their religious basis weakened, and the psychic demands of adulthood grew more onerous. As familiar definitions of selfhood and maturity became less trustworthy, childlike traits became more alluring.

In popular late-Victorian images of the child, two tendencies dominated: a liberal Protestant nostalgia for innocent sincerity and a primitivist veneration for vitality. The two tendencies overlapped and often merged, but they were potentially distinct and even contradictory in significance. Deriving from longstanding Protestant anxieties about commercial prosperity and from the romantic heritage of the "Ode," nostalgia for childish innocence was readily assimilable to the dominant culture and social arrangements; it concentrated on the past but eased adjustment to the present and future by providing a temporary, after-hours escape from the rigors of bourgeois adulthood. The innocent child was a vision of psychic wholeness, a "simple, genuine self" in a world where selfhood had become problematic and sincerity seemed obsolete.

Persistent primitivism generated different notions about childhood with more complex social meanings. When vitality joined sincerity, the child's image provided a focus for revitalization rather than escape. In fantasies of childlike energy, the self was not only made whole but made vigorous. The exaltation of childhood merged with the cult of the strenuous life. At the same time, admiration for childish vitality began to join late-nineteenth-century fascination with irrational, unconscious mental processes. In the popular imagination, a link between childhood and the unconscious emerged. A growing number of "overcivilized" Americans idealized the child's capacity for unrepressed emotional and imaginative experience.

This resurgent critique of the modern superego had a variety of effects. At bottom, it registered a protest against the emotional impoverishment of bourgeois culture. But the protest led to a quixotic quest for alternatives, damaged by internal contradictions: a self-conscious effort to escape self-consciousness. Stemming in part from moral anxieties, that effort nevertheless lacked moral content. Acclaiming spontaneity and vitality as ends in themselves, the assault on the superego helped pave the way for a nonmorality deifying immediate experience and self-gratification—an outlook well suited to the developing consumer orientation of corporate capitalism. The spontaneous child served to reinforce accommodation to new, secular modes of capitalist cultural hegemony. Yet the protest also preserved a philosophical importance, underscoring the inadequacies of nineteenth-century positivism and pointing toward profounder conceptions of "reality."

Late-Victorian perceptions of medieval childishness revealed similar social and philosophical significance. By the 1880s, the link between the childhood of the individual and the childhood of the race was firmly established in the bourgeois imagination. The notion had become a nineteenth-century commonplace, used by Spencerians and Hegelians, positivists and idealists; it was less a product of self-conscious analysis than an outgrowth of widespread prejudices and habits of mind. Its usage arose from the common tendency to analogize individual and social development, coupled with the assumption that nineteenth-century liberalism was the maturest outlook known to man. From this dominant view, childish traits characterized any society which did not conform to the model of Western industrial capitalism. The "civilized world," having put childish things in its medieval past, had reached social adulthood.

As suspicion grew that social adulthood might be indistinguishable from overcivilization, admiration for childhood, both individual and "racial," began to receive scientific sanction. As a *Nation* reviewer noted in 1896, "scientists have informed us that the child alone possesses in their fullness the distinctive features of humanity, that the highest human types as represented in men of genius present a striking approximation to the child type" —that is, to the personality type predominating in primitive cultures. From this view, personal and social maturation was "to some extent progress in degeneration and senility."[8]

The "scientists" mentioned by the *Nation* reviewer were the leaders of the burgeoning child study movement, whose most influential spokesman was the psychologist and educator G. Stanley Hall. Hall's theories authoritatively joined the cult of the child and the fascination with the childhood of the race. They also showed how an interest in childlike mentalities could lead both to a critique of the dominant culture and to an effort to revitalize it.[9]

Drawing on the dubious biological theories spawned by German romanticism, Hall restated the common analogy between the child and the race in an influential formula: ontogeny recapitulates phylogeny.[10] To reach vigorous adulthood, he argued, schoolchildren should repeat the experiences and emotions of their primitive ancestors. Adolescents, in particular, should imaginatively relive the deeds of Homeric and medieval heroes. To promote the full flowering of spiritual sentiment, the budding youth should encounter the religious forms of the medieval past, through exposure to Catholic ritual. In general, Hall urged the loosening of rigid curricula and teaching methods to allow for the natural playfulness and curiosity of students.

Hall preached the cultivation of primitive vitality, not for its own sake, but in order to create more productive adults. His goals differed little from those of earlier educators. Like them, Hall wanted to produce disciplined, responsible members of bourgeois society. In his view, exposure to Catholic ritual would smooth "progress from Rome toward reason"; early release of primal energies would allow them to flow, under proper guidance, in healthy directions. Hall's version of "the new education" used antimodern means for modern ends.[11]

Despite the conventionality of his purpose, Hall's writings disclosed a deep distrust of modern industrial society. He was haunted by the suspicion that "civilization is at root morbific and sure to end in reaction and decay"—a fear reinforced by his reading of Prince Kropotkin and Edward Carpenter. Hall admired their proposals for the agrarian "simple life." He fretted continually that nineteenth-century schools were transforming children into miniature overcivilized adults, worldly-wise and self-conscious before their time. "Childhood," Hall believed, "is the paradise of the race from which adult life is a fall." He insisted that "in those halcyon days we were more complete and all-sided, more adequate representatives of the race." Like Wordsworth (and Freud), Hall pulled back from absolute primitivism. In his view specialization was "inevitable"; it was "necessary in becoming a member of the community. . . ." Yet Hall's emphasis on the wholeness and sensuous intensity of the child's experience implied a critique of a stale, self-conscious Victorian culture and a "bitter struggle for existence."[12]

Hall's anti-intellectual attacks on bourgeois education illustrated an important shift from moral to medical standards of value. "What shall it profit a child if he gain the whole world of knowledge and lose his own health?" Hall asked, replacing the biblical concern for the soul with a modern concern for the body. Searching for examples of minds untainted by schooling, he pointed out that "The knights, the elite leaders of the Middle Ages, deemed writing a mere clerk's trick beneath the attention of all those who scorned to muddle their wits with others' ideas, feeling that their own were good enough for them." Premodern character animated a program of reform carried out under modern, therapeutic auspices. Like others who felt the antimodern impulse, Hall feared that modern intellectualism was destroying possibilities for unmediated experience. His antidote, like many others, was self-contradictory: the deliberate cultivation of spontaneity. Hope lay in temporarily recapturing the outlook of children, medieval knights, and contemporary primitives.[13]

Mingling medieval character with that of contemporary children and primitives, Hall's imprecise primitivism typified the wider preoccupation with childishness at the turn of the century. Educated Americans sought childlike mental traits from a variety of sources, including Japanese as well as medieval culture. To nearly all Western observers, Japan was a "toy land" and her people "in many respects a race of children." Lafcadio Hearn, the most influential popularizer of Japanese culture in America, ignored the educated, urban elites in order to create a nation peopled entirely by "fairy-folk" of childlike grace and simplicity. Other observers followed Hearn's lead in applauding the absence of labor unrest and nervous prostration among the "sweet children" of Japan. But after 1905, it was hard to see an international rival, capable of a surprise attack on the Russians at Port Arthur, as a model of childish sincerity.[14] In any case the lure of Japan had always been as much exoticism as antimodernism. Medieval character, culturally more familiar and historically more remote, exerted a more profound imaginative influence. And for many Americans, the key to medieval character was its childlike straightforwardness.

# Medieval Sincerity: Genteel and Robust

Recoiling from the complexity of modern thought to an ideal of premodern mental simplicity, overcivilized Americans hailed the "big children" of the Middle Ages as models of naiveté. Reviewers agreed that medieval sagas revealed a "simple directness of thought and expression which is as difficult to catch and keep when it concerns the childhood of a nation as when it concerns the childhood of an individual; so wide, in either case, is the distance back to it from the grown-up mind." One could see that distance in the contrast between modern fiction and the Norse sagas, or between the rhetorical tricks of post-Renaissance writing and the "childlike grace and sweetness" of Plantagenet prose. But what accounted for the distance? The essayist Davida Coit supplied a typical answer in 1885. In her view, "The thought of our day has little sympathy with childlike straightforwardness or unquestioning delight in the present." Medieval authors preserved those qualities because in their time "the age of introspection" had not yet begun.[15]

Literary simplicity implied an extreme literalism, a tendency to accept the mythic and fanciful as material fact. While that quality seemed the chief reason for the power of religious belief among the medieval populace, many American travellers also found it surviving among European Catholics in the late nineteenth century. The celebration of medieval sincerity included veneration for the persistence of peasant belief. "There is no faith like this in Protestantism!" the illustrator Joseph Pennell exclaimed after visiting the Provençal Feast of the Two Marys in 1892. He was only one of many Americans who haunted the holy places of Europe, recording their impressions in an abundant travel literature. One of the chief attractions was the Passion Play at Oberammergau, which some visitors left in a chastened spirit, doubting "the superiority of enlightened, emancipated, cultivated intellect, with all its fine analyses of what God is not. . . ." The Catholic peasant worshipped a tangible deity, not a Spencerian "Unknowable."[16]

Yet even Americans who admired the peasant's faith viewed it as a fading anachronism. To Edith Wharton, writing in 1893, the handful of worshippers in Chartres cathedral seemed a pathetic remnant of a medieval multitude.

> On the prayer-worn floor,
> By surging worshippers thick-thronged of yore,
> A few brown crones, familiars of the tomb,
> The stranded driftwood of faith's ebbing sea—
> For these alone the finials fret the sky.[17]

As late as summer, 1914, when Randolph Bourne visited Chartres, he discovered "the inevitable band of black-bonneted old women performing their devotions before the altars." To Bourne, too, they represented "a sort of last desperate bulwark against the encroachments of the modern spirit."[18]

Admiring the peasant only from a distance, unable to embrace his literal-minded faith, most American observers viewed popular Catholicism as a pale reflection of its medieval past. Wearied by struggles with religious doubt, impatient with the vagueness of liberal optimism, Americans hailed the "childlike faith" of the Middle Ages "in the reality of the visions that peopled the heavens and the earth." The key word was "reality." Admiration for the sincerity of the medieval peasant was tied to longings for "real life." Among the educated, Protestant theology had reduced dogma to weightless unreality; medieval literalism seemed refreshingly authentic by comparison. The novelist James Branch Cabell underscored the distinction in the preface to *Chivalry,* a collection of his short stories published in 1909, when he described the religious faith of his medieval characters. "It is not merely that they are all large children consciously dependent in all things upon a not foolishly indulgent Father," Cabell wrote, but that "the Father is a real father, and not a word spelt with capital letters in the Church Service; not an abstraction, not a sort of a something vaguely describable as 'the Life Force,' but a very famous kinsman, of whom one is naively proud, and whom one is on the way to visit."[19]

Cabell's fond bemusement reflected a common attitude toward medieval belief, particularly when it was conceived of as childlike. Paeans to premodern sincerity often degenerated into sentimental nostalgia. An elegiac mood suffused evocations of static, passive innocence. Remaining diffuse, such sentiments merged easily with the pale idealism of the dominant culture. The imagery of premodern belief lost polemical force.

The difficulty was particularly apparent in late-nineteenth-century treatments of medieval saints. Their symbolic functions were complex; their meanings varied widely. For many late-Victorian authors, the saints embodied instinctive communion with nature, simple faith unhampered by learning, and sexual purity. Personifying shibboleths of romantic liberal Protestantism, they entered the pantheon of the genteel tradition.

To an extent, Joan of Arc met that fate. In the *fin-de-siècle* imagination, she was most at home with the beasts of the field and the fowls of the air; her untutored piety confounded the learned inquisitors at Rouen. Nearly all accounts stressed her virginity and her girlish asexuality. Joan's sexual immaturity and early death linked her to other figures in late-nineteenth-century hagiography. One was the Holy Fina (1238–1253), virgin of Santo Giminiano, whose legend was translated for American readers in 1908. The Holy Fina died at fifteen, after lying on a bare board for four years, praising God. In a sense, she and Joan resembled the innumerable dying children in Victorian novels—descendants of Little Eva and Little Nell. All died young and undefiled, their innocence preserved forever. Their common fate suggests that the image of childhood—medieval or modern— could offer a vicarious escape from adult moral and sexual anxieties.[20]

Dying virgins were not the only medieval saints to reappear in late-Victorian culture. Probably the most popular saintly figure was St. Francis of Assisi. He had long been praised as an early protestant against the mummified formalism of the medieval Church and an embodiment of undogmatic Christian charity. (The French Protestant Paul Sabatier fixed that notion firmly with his influential *Vie de St. Francis,* which was translated into English in 1894.) But for a number of Americans, Francis had more specific emblematic meanings as well. By the early twentieth century, many hagiographers would have agreed with the historian Henry Osborne Taylor, who claimed in 1911 that "Francis . . . would not have been what he was but for certain childlike qualities of mind which never fell away from him." In the Franciscan literature, fear of intellect's corrosive effects on religious belief joined with romantic nature worship in a celebration of childlike sincerity. Ignorance, from this view, was not a shortcoming but a prerequisite for natural piety. The point was dramatized in Henry Maugham's play, *The Husband of Poverty* (1897). The lady Clare, founder of the Franciscan sister order, the Poor Clares, at first protests her unworthiness to organize a sisterhood. "I am an ignorant and simple maid," she says. Francis replies:

> That is a merit in the works of God
> What knowledge has the bird that sings His praise?[21]

The exaltation of ignorance stemmed from the Wordsworthian notion that, as another hagiographer put it, "children and the simple-hearted are nearer to God than most of us." Such sentimentality betrayed the fundamental weakness of much hagiographical literature. Reducing medieval saintliness to childlike simplicity and sincerity, hagiographers diminished the challenge to secular modes of thought and feeling offered by the saints. Products of modern spiritual confusion, the images of premodern belief were bound to become indistinct. The blurring process occurred on both sides of the Atlantic. It was aptly described by the French historian Gabriel Monod in 1895,

> Our age has lost faith and admits no other source of certainty than science, but at the same time it has not been able to resolve, as positivism would wish, not to reflect and to remain silent about what it ignores. . . . It has the feeling that, without faith or hope in invisible realities, life loses its nobility, and it demonstrates for the heroes of religious life, for the mystical souls of the past, a tenderness composed of futile regrets and vague aspirations.[22]

The childlike sincerity of medieval saints became a focus for "futile regrets and vague aspirations," but not for cultural criticism.

For late-nineteenth-century Americans, medieval sincerity was not just a childlike state of grace. It had a more active, demanding side as well— a dimension deriving from republican moralism. In the lives of the saints, innocence was not always innate; it was sometimes won through force of will. An individual hagiographer might treat his subject as both an ethereal child of nature and a robust moral activist. The two notions coexisted and intermingled, often within the same mind.

Mark Twain, for example, extolled Joan of Arc's innate sanctity but also revered her iron will. As George Bernard Shaw once pointed out, Twain's Joan was an "American school teacher in armor"—an incarnation of disciplined bourgeois virtue. According to Twain, Joan's motto was "Work! Stick to it!" That activist strain pervaded his *Personal Recollections* as well as other treatments of Joan and pointed to her role as a focus for bourgeois revitalization. Nearly all authors subordinated Joan's private piety to her public genius. She became an emblem of nationalism sanctified by religiosity.[23]

Francis of Assisi had no such political connotations; his appeal was entirely moral and religious. But for late-nineteenth-century Americans, Francis, like Joan, combined genteel and robust sincerity. In him, childish and republican versions of simplicity merged; the Franciscan image implied a personal morality of self-control and a freedom from elitist conventions and social display. Maugham's *Husband of Poverty* intertwined the themes. In that play, Francis's childlike piety is the result of mature self-discipline, a redirection of his lust for Clare into saintly service. He joins republican virtue and childish innocence. Francis, from this view, was not just an object of sentimental veneration but a rebuke to the self-indulgent and irresolute. His piety was a triumph of the moral will. "To have complete control of himself," the Presbyterian Reverend J. H. McIlvaine wrote in 1902, "was his great desire." As a gilded youth, Francis had learned that "a life of pleasure leads only to satiety and self-contempt." That lesson led Francis to enforce a puritanical discipline on himself and his brethren: "he insisted rigorously on the duty of work; he was inflexibily severe on idleness." McIlvaine concluded that Francis achieved "complete self-forgetfulness" in virtuous action.[24]

By removing the Catholic framework of medieval sainthood, and concentrating on morality rather than belief, Protestants like McIlvaine could transform saints into acceptable models for reviving the bourgeois ethic of self-control. Many American hagiographers reduced the medieval world view of their subjects to a severe moral outlook, full of sharp distinctions between reward and punishment, right and wrong. From the liberal standpoint, that ferocious sincerity had long seemed a vestige of barbarism, the source of innumerable persecutions and martyrdoms. By the turn of the century, for many educated Americans, what had once appeared intolerance emerged anew as healthy moral enthusiasm. To those troubled by a paralysis of the will or by flickering doubts about personal moral responsibility, it was enough that medieval saints held convictions—even narrow ones—and acted on them.[25]

One can see this longing for moral revitalization in the Reverend Richard S. Storrs's approach to St. Bernard of Clairvaux. In a series of lectures, delivered in Boston, Princeton, and Baltimore in 1892 and published the following year, Storrs presented Bernard as a proto-Protestant moralist and an avatar of republican virtue. Like his oration at the Brooklyn Bridge, Storrs's lectures laid heavy stress on the primacy of the individual will. In Bernard's case, the will was bent toward the conquest of sin rather than nature (which "revived his spirit.") Fortified by pastoral interludes, Bernard went forth, "always in lofty earnest," to face the luxurious and licentious—above all, to face Abelard. In Storrs's lectures, Bernard's rationalist opponent became an early apostle of weightless theology who deprived religion of all mystery and divinity.[26]

In contrast to Abelard's rational humanism, Bernard's ecstatic supernaturalism did seem decidedly antimodern. But Storrs was quick to point out that there was "nothing morbid and nothing debilitating" in Bernard's longings for union with the Divine. Rather, his meditations had a tonic effect, "simply exalting and quickening to whatever in him was most heroic." To Storrs, Bernard's contemplation was redeemed by his activism: he transmuted mysticism into practical morality by exercising "his overwhelming and incalculable will." That was why, in the end, Storrs could praise Bernard as enthusiastically as he had the builders of the Brooklyn Bridge. Embodiments of will, they rebuked the indolent and the timid. Here as elsewhere, reverence for the premodern past melded with a drive toward moral regeneration in the present. Like other saints, Storr's Bernard provided "uplift from depression" and "encouragement to duty"; he suggested a critique of bourgeois values in crisis, and a model for their revitalization.[27]

Bernard, Francis, and other saints expressed fierce sincerity in their preaching and personal morality; the anonymous cathedral builders left more visible monuments to their firmness of conviction. To the Ruskinian observer, Gothic architecture might suggest a passive, childlike acceptance of the spiritual world; or it might imply a more vigorous, active effort to enshrine one's faith in visible form. In other words, sincerity of the cathedral builders might be genteel or robust. More often it was the latter. Struck by the oxlike labors required to erect a cathedral, Americans could only marvel at the builders' fanatical zeal. Yet as Bourne said, "if it was the madness of fanaticism that caused the peasants to yoke themselves to the carts and drag the stones to rebuild their church in the twelfth century, what a divine madness, and how divine the reach and imagination of that social soul of theirs which inspired that splendid form!"[28]

Divine madness had yielded to rational calculation. That was the Ruskinian view, and it was widely accepted by Americans at the turn of the century. Numerous commentators agreed with James Russell Lowell that

> Fagot and stake were desperately sincere:
> Our cooler martyrdoms are done in types
> . . . . . . . . . . . . . . . . . . . . . . . . . . . .
> This is no age to get cathedrals built . . .[29]

The architect Henry Brewer told *Scientific American* readers in 1900 that during the Middle Ages

> the men must have been grown-up schoolboys, retaining the ardor, generosity, and intense partisanship of the boy, together with his thoughtless cruelty and complete indifference to the feelings of others; ready to "go through fire and water" for his friends, but unmerciful in his views regarding boys of an opposition school; firmly convinced of the absolute correctness of his own views and the rectitude of his own principles.[30]

Like Maugham's St. Francis, Brewer's "grown-up schoolboy" melded childlike spontaneity and republican virtue. Such a child-man, as a medieval citizen, would win lifelong friends and enemies, enforce strict laws, erect magnificent monuments to his own beliefs, and eventually throw away his life in defense of a principle or a comrade in distress. He stood in sharp contrast to his modern descendants.

> Our ideas are to do away with partisanship as much as possible, to do away with violent contrasts, to allow everyone to think as he likes, to tone down everything, and rather to suspect enthusiasm, whether it is found among our friends or enemies. . . . We make our laws and legal tribunals so lenient that they often

become a greater terror to the innocent than to the guilty party. In fact, we dislike contrast and enthusiasm.[31]

It was no wonder, Brewer concluded, that modern architects no longer designed great cathedrals, for "how can you express, in brick and stone, the wants of an age which simply 'wants to be let alone,' or the feelings of a people whose whole study is how to subdue sentiment?"

To many observers, the decline from medieval convictions to modern opinions seemed painfully apparent. In the cultural criticism of the turn of the century, saints and cathedral builders emerged to rebuke ethical confusion and to dissipate an enveloping feeling of impotence. Since their Catholicism was reduced to Ruskinian "sincerity," they personified an unambiguous sense of personal moral responsibility. They seemed to vindicate familiar ideas of will and choice against the spreading hegemony of a therapeutic world view—an outlook which corroded moral accountability by invoking social and psychic determinisms. Admiration for medieval sincerity was a response to the crisis of cultural authority.

One can see the full complexity of that response in discussions of Dante Alighieri. Throughout the nineteenth century, the admiration of educated Americans for the Tuscan poet had been growing steadily. Among major intellectual figures, the chief devotees were James Russell Lowell, Henry Wadsworth Longfellow, and Charles Eliot Norton. Lowell wrote an influential appreciation of Dante in 1876; Longfellow published several similar pieces during his early career, as well as a verse translation of the *Divine Comedy* in 1867; Norton followed with a prose rendering in 1892.[32] In 1881, they founded the Dante Society, which met weekly in Norton's Cambridge home to read and discuss passages from the text. After Longfellow and Lowell died, Norton kept the society alive. His reverential readings continued to attract an audience of Harvard undergraduates.

Dante was more than the object of an aesthetes' cult.[33] Reverence for his poetry could represent not withdrawal from the world but entanglement with contemporary moral dilemmas. Nor was fascination with Dante confined to the Brahmin few. The poet was acclaimed and interpreted by critics in the established press, eulogized and imitated by dozens of magazine versifiers. The Dante vogue pointed not only to aestheticism or vaporous romanticism, but to widespread moral and religious concerns. While it was difficult to describe the *Divine Comedy* as the achievement of a childish mind, late-Victorian interpretations of Dante nevertheless valued his work primarily for its moral simplicity and sincerity—the same qualities assigned to his childlike medieval contemporaries. By ignoring the scholastic superstructure of the *Divine Comedy,* commentators were able to join Dante with simpler medieval types. Like the saints and peasants, he became a prophet of spiritual certainty in an uncertain, excessively tolerant age.

Dante's prophetic role did not emerge clearly until the final decades of the nineteenth century. During the early- and middle-1800s, Americans had praised him primarily as a precursor of the Reformation who "used Rome's harlot for his mirth."[34] Insofar as he embodied a distinctively premodern sensibility, Dante received short shrift. In 1872, Eugene Benson revealed a typical strategy of dismissal in his contrast between Shakespeare, "the first great secular genius," and Dante, the poet of medieval Christianity. Juxtaposing the rigidly moral Dante with "serene and complacent Shakespeare," Benson decided that humanity had sacrificed "exalted and intense feelings" for "prosperity and tolerance." The medieval moral type had disappeared, he believed, because the ills of Dante's time had been peacefully resolved. Shakespeare represented the triumph of the more humane modern point of view.[35]

But by the 1880s and 1890s, Dante's fierce conviction had grown more attractive. As Frances Sanborn wrote in 1882, "the intense reality of Dante's faith is in refreshing contrast to the indifferent half-belief of the present day, which assumes certain religious attitudes because they are the proper, the most respectable thing."[36] In an age when religious belief seemed reduced to a social amenity, Dante's vision shimmered in clear-eyed certainty, another version of the ever-elusive "reality."

Dante's freedom from modern doubt and hesitation accounted for his poetry's particular appeal around the turn of the century. According to the Reverend Charles Dinsmore, a Boston Congregationalist and influential popularizer of Dante, the poet's genius was to catch the spirit of "those hot, stormy, creative centuries—centuries which, with all their crudeness and barbarism, followed the highest spiritual ideals with a passionate enthusiasm which has never been equalled, and, with a vision clearer than our own, realized the presence of the eternal. . . ." The forthright supernaturalism of the *Divine Comedy* inspired the admiration of the fretful religious. "No poem ever written has left the reader so impressed with the reality of the unseen world," Oscar Kuhn noted in 1897. "Surely never were such lessons needed more than in the present materialistic age."[37]

It was not simply a matter of spiritualism versus materialism. What attracted some Americans to Dante was his conviction that he could know the infinite varieties of good and evil, that he could map out the topography of the undiscovered country. On any subject, George Santayana wrote in *Three Philosophical Poets* (1910), Dante wanted "to think straight, to see things as they are." In Santayana's view, that desire was typical of the Middle Ages, and it produced results far superior to liberal theology's metaphors and evasions. Instead of confronting doubt, Santayana charged, modern Christianity had retreated to "the cheap fictions that alone seem to us fine enough for poetry or for religion."[38] It was easy—and meaningless—to believe in a metaphor.

Though other critics were less hostile to "cheap fictions," they also admired Dante's clarity of moral vision—particularly his sharp sense of evil. Study of Dante revealed how completely we had rejected "the Christian theory of sin," wrote Susan Blow in 1886. She was one of a number of Dantists among the St. Louis Hegelians, but her words could have been written by any number of her contemporaries. "We live in an age which is rapidly losing the consciousness of sin," Blow charged. "Equally alien to our feeling are the physical self-scourgings of the medieval saint and the spiritual agony of the Puritan." Earlier conviction of sin had been rooted out by the notion of evolutionary progress. "Whatever else this theory may or may not be," Blow observed, "it is distinctly anti-Christian." Dante overshadowed evolutionary optimism with his complex awareness of human weaknesses and possibilities.[39]

For some critics, this comprehensive, tragic vision—an ability to see humanity in its extremes of folly and nobility, a sense of an infinite frame of meaning for human action—lay behind Dante's power. The literary critic Vida Scudder preferred the *Divine Comedy* to Shelley's *Prometheus Unbound* because while Shelley's hope for human perfectibility offered only "the unlimited extension of limited conditions," Dante's hope was boundless. And though Santayana could not accept Scudder's theism, he shared her admiration for the range of Dante's imagination and for the keenness of his moral insight. In Santayana's judgment, Dante saw "the various pitfalls of life with intense distinctness"; indeed Dante was "the master of distinction."[40]

Santayana's choice of "distinction" as a value in itself implied a critique of the modern blurring of ethical boundaries. Other Dantists were concerned about that difficulty, but they lacked Santayana's sophistication. To them, the only important distinction was between permissiveness and moral order. According to Dinsmore, Dante's chief legacy was his stress on "the accountability of man, the supremacy of moral law, the certainty of its rewards and punishments." And behind all those related ideas was a belief in free will and personal moral responsibility.[41] Dante was an emblem of resistance to the evasive banality of modern culture in either its nineteenth-century form or its streamlined therapeutic mode. As positivistic science and a fragmenting sense of selfhood made man seem neither free nor responsible, Dantists embraced the *Divine Comedy* as a powerful reminder of human dignity. Only Santayana dissented, deriding the poem's "fond delusion that man and his moral nature are at the center of the universe." That anthropocentric assumption lay at the root of the *Divine Comedy*'s appeal to the educated bourgeoisie. It impressed one above all with "the actual and potential greatness of man," said Dinsmore. The reverse side of man's greatness was embodied in the inscription over Hell's gate: "Abandon hope, all ye who enter here." As Blow pointed out, "the sense of that inscription is so alien to the sentiment of to-day, that it is hard for our minds to grasp. Its implicit argument is this: if man is free he is responsible." If, to late Victorians, medieval saints and cathedral builders were practitioners of the moral will, Dante was its philosopher.[42]

To interpret Dante as a philosopher of the moral will was to underscore his potential as a "tonic for to-day"—a model for revitalizing familiar ideas of moral accountability. While some Dantists, such as Norton, remained convinced that the study of the poet could only reveal inexorable decline, by the end of the century many felt they were at the crest of a moral and spiritual wave. In their view, Dante's thought was no longer anachronistic but "essentially modern" because it harmonized with a widespread recovery of man's inner life.[43] Dinsmore summarized this phenomenon, and Dante's relation to it, in 1901:

> The prophets of materialism and agnosticism have had their day, and now the clearest voice that in modern times has spoken the soul's deep consciousness of its mastery over matter and fate is being heard. To Dante the physical is fleeting, the spiritual is the real. . . . This is the steadily growing conviction of the world. In a time of vanishing materialism, with its attendant fatalism, we exult in this superb reassertion of the freedom of the will. . . .
>
> The great revival of interest in him is also due to the splendid sincerity of his convictions, which quicken those moods that our minds, troubled with doubt, crave. We are living in a time of intense spiritual desire. We are stretching our hands toward the gloom and calling into the unknown. Our representative poets are struggling for a faith, and the strong tide of interest in our best literature is toward spiritual problems.[44]

Dinsmore referred hopefully to the widespread dissatisfaction with nineteenth-century science, common on both sides of the Atlantic by 1900. Yet his tone revealed his own religious uncertainties. The battle against positivism seemed incomplete; further struggle seemed necessary. It was almost as if Dinsmore planned to will the rebirth of supernaturalism by writing about it. And the outlines of that supernaturalism were hazy: Dinsmore wrote of "the unseen," "the gloom," "the unknown." Dante's assumption that "the spiritual is the real" offered only the vaguest of hopes.

But Dante's stress on human freedom presented firmer grounds for optimism. Dinsmore wrote more confidently and specifically about the decline of "fatalism," the renewed awareness of "the soul's deep consciousness of its mastery over matter and fate," and the relevance of Dante's "superb reassertion of the freedom of the will. . . ." Dinsmore's emphasis on will rather than faith suggests that it was easier to assimilate Dante to Rooseveltian activism than to contemporary religious belief. While liberal Protestantism had become a shapeless void, bourgeois morality remained strong enough to be revitalized—at least for a time.

For some, the Dantean vision of salvation became reduced to a program for secular achievement. As Dinsmore said, Dante's "conception of the strenuousness of life" was particularly resonant for modern readers. In "Nel Mezzo del Cammin" (1895), a *Scribner's* poet appended Dante's phrase to a poem with an onward-and-upward moral: in the middle of life's journey, don't waste time looking back; keep struggling forward. Such incongruities were common. By the turn of the century, Dantean ideas were often interpreted as agenda for character formation. As one Methodist author said, "Dante's conception of personal salvation" was "nothing less than the winning of holy self-control. Salvation is character."[45] Its theological framework dismantled, the *Divine Comedy* became a Victorian tract—a program for the moral rehabilitation of an overcivilized ruling class.

The late-Victorian reinterpretation of Dante paralleled the treatment of saints and cathedral builders. By ignoring the substance of medieval belief and concentrating on the sincerity and firmness of medieval conviction, Americans transformed the Catholics of the Middle Ages into proto-Protestant moralists. As apostles of will power and duty, the "big children" of the Middle Ages became more than the objects of nostalgia. As advocates of moral strenuosity, they focused longings for purification and solidified commitments to moral revival among the middle and upper classes. Looking backward for inspiration, the admirers of medieval sincerity looked forward to "Progressive" reform. Rejecting the problematic qualities of the autonomous self, they preached an activist gospel linking childish innocence and republican virtue. Their emphasis on the primacy of the moral will reappeared in Anglo-Saxon crusades against urban corruption and in the evangelical imperialism of Theodore Roosevelt. Their antimodern quest led to a revitalization rather than a critique of dominant values.

Besides revitalizing dominant values, the turn toward medieval character could also transform them. For many antimodern thinkers, medieval figures represented neither pale innocence nor fierce conviction, but rather physical and emotional vitality—a trait also perceived as childlike. The vitalist strain linked perceptions of medieval character to popular cults of youth and athletic vigor, movements designed to toughen a flabby bourgeoisie. But antimodern vitalism had personal as well as social meanings. As part of the recovery of primal irrationality, the apotheosis of youthful spontaneity pointed toward the celebration of intense experience in the work of such philosophers as Henri Bergson and William James, toward the cultivation of extreme sensibilities among the nascent European avant garde, and toward the exploration of the unconscious mind.

Stressing the emotional extremism of medieval character, antimodern vitalists imagined a medieval epoch pervaded by *eros*—by perpetual excitement born of boundless desire. Their attack on the constraints of the modern superego could lead in two directions. Channelled by conventional morality and progressive optimism, it could revitalize the producer ethos of the nineteenth-century bourgeoisie. Or, if the moral framework sagged and optimism weakened, the impulse could generate an obsession with the *process* of intense experience rather than its larger purpose. This emphasis on process joined antimodern vitalists with pragmatists, avant-gardists, and therapists on both sides of the Atlantic. In Europe it sometimes underlay fascist cults of experience; in America it pointed toward a looser bourgeois morality more suited to the dawning era of consumer capitalism. Whether antimodern vitalism revitalized or transformed dominant values, its supernatural dimension was frequently submerged, borne under by the vitalist imperatives of inner or outer experience. In part a protest against secularizing tendencies, antimodern vitalism also helped to reinforce them. Far from reflecting escapism or defeatism, antimodern vitalism was (ironically) entwined with some of the most "forward-looking" tendencies in the wider culture. A close examination of the vitalist impulse places those tendencies in a clearer light.

By focusing here on the erotic appeal of medieval character, I want to underscore one of my major arguments: the twentieth century's "revolution in manners and morals" was scarcely a revolution at all. It was not an overnight result of post–World War I disillusionment but the outcome of gradual, almost imperceptible fits and starts of cultural change stretching back into the late nineteenth century. It was not a plan deliberately carried out by defiant bohemians and "flaming youth," but a culmination of half-conscious wishes and aspirations among the respectable bourgeoisie. And most important, it posed few challenges to the dominant pattern of social relations. Justifying the quest for intense experience as a therapeutic release, this "revolution" eased adjustment to the emerging system of consumer capitalism and bureaucratic "rationality." Through the prism of antimodern vitalism we can see the hidden affinities between two apparently contradictory strands in recent American cultural history—between the liberationist ideology of avant-garde bohemians and the acquiescent leisure ethic of the mass society they deplored. Both sanctioned a new nonmorality of self-gratification.

# Medieval Vitality: The Erotic Union of Sacred and Profane

In part, the perception of medieval vitality stemmed from a liberal Protestant assumption that Catholic practices bred undisciplined emotion. In the dominant view, the immoderation of excitable Catholics immersed in pointless piety was another childlike trait inherited from the medieval past. A wide range of commentators agreed that the Middle Ages was a period of extremes—a "mixture of religious fervor and blatant sensuality," as a

*Nation* reviewer said in 1891. Nurtured by Catholic emotionalism, medieval character was character *in extremis*. Medieval extremism might lead to gross self-indulgence or fanatic asceticism; in liberal Protestant eyes, either result was intolerable, Bourgeois society demanded moderate citizens; the Catholic search for perfection bred seekers who violated the Protestant ideal of useful service and the Victorian cult of domesticity.[46]

That set of majority assumptions influenced the views of antimodern vitalists, who accepted the superiority of Protestant moderation. Nonetheless, they felt a contrary, often unacknowledged longing for the emotions engendered by Catholic piety. What seemed childish indiscipline from one view could seem childlike spontaneity from another. By the turn of the century, religious practices which had seemed barbarous or bizarre were winning renewed attention and respect. In 1901, William James devoted his Gifford lectures to "those religious experiences which are most one-sided, exaggerated, and intense." Many were the experiences of medieval saints. To James, saints of all faiths shared an ability to sustain a "pitch of intensity . . . which, if any emotion reach it, enthrones that one as alone effective and sweeps its antagonists and all their inhibitions away." Many of James's contemporaries, too, were fascinated by the bursting of spiritual limits. Though most held to a belief in spiritual progress, they fondly described the "heedless grace" and "careless rapture" generated by medieval religion. In an atmosphere permeated by feelings of psychic imprisonment, the exploration of the soul's farthest reaches evoked a new admiration.[47]

Impatient with the stodginess of bourgeois virtue, many Americans imagined an ecstatic medieval piety—soaring to summits of spiritual exaltation, dropping to abysses of self-abasement, burning always with a white-hot flame. The historian Henry Osborne Taylor, contrasting classical and medieval sensibilities in 1902, claimed that the medieval Christian attained "heights and depths of emotion undreamed of by antiquity." Nor were they dreamed of by modernity, Taylor implied.[48] Medieval piety, apparently producing unique emotional energy, appealed to seekers of psychic regeneration.

At bottom, the appeal was erotic in the strict etymological sense. That is, the emotional extremism of the Middle Ages embodied boundless, unfulfilled desire rather than sexuality per se. It is true that a number of authors noted the intermingling of religion and sexuality in medieval culture. They pointed out that during the Middle Ages, "the worship of the Virgin was not always to be distinguished from an earthly human love" or from primitive fertility rites, and that even monks and nuns "dreamed of salvation . . . with an erotic tinge." But the important point about such dreams is that they remained physically unconsummated. They lifted the soul to perpetual, feverish yearning. In a 1910 *North American Review*, William Smyser, professor of English at Ohio Wesleyan University, pointed to the erotic attraction of the medieval temper in his admiring list of monastic traits: "the practice of ascetic life even to the point of perversion of bodily sensibility, in consequence of which hunger and thirst, cold and all bodily pain becomes pleasurable, the experience of mystical religious rapture, the breathless ecstasies of a mystical union in absolute maidenhood with the Heavenly Bridegroom. . . ." For late Victorians like Smyser, medieval eroticism implied a state of passionate longing, fulfilled rarely and fleetingly, never resting, aspiring ever upward. To the novelist Henry Blake Fuller, writing in 1896, the mentality expressed in Gothic architecture was "panting aspiration." The phrase captured the union of physical and spiritual excitement in the erotic appeal of medieval emotionalism.[49]

Emphasis on the erotic qualities of medieval piety suggests that many vitalists were attracted to premodern religion for secular reasons. In the orthodox Christian view, the saintly practice of piety transforms *eros* into *agape;* the saint transcends boundless desire and attains sovereign serenity.[50] Antimodern vitalists, for whom intense feeling was its own reward, stressed becoming rather than being, *eros* rather than *agape.* What attracted these Americans was the process of medieval piety, not its fulfillment. From the vitalist perspective, the medieval believer exerted much the same appeal as the chivalric warrior and the legendary lovers like Guenevere and Lancelot, Paolo and Francesca, or Tristan and Isolde. All lived at a high pitch of emotional intensity; all seemed emblems of "real life." Sacred and profane vitality melded in the turn of the century cult of experience.

Fearful of living at secondhand, many late Victorians extended medieval emotionalism beyond the cloister to the culture as a whole. An emerging consensus described a passionate medieval temperament, "restless, impetuous, and unreasonable . . . and ready at a fiery breath to give up all or seize all." Such descriptions were double-edged. Dismissing the "unreasonable" quality of medieval character, they nevertheless betrayed esteem for its intensity of feeling. In many minds, admiration for the emotional vitality of the Middle Ages could coexist alongside progressive dogma. Even the positivist historian Henry Charles Lea believed that in thirteenth-century Europe, "passions were fiercer, convictions stronger, virtues and vices more exaggerated, than in our colder and more self-contained time."[51] Medieval Europeans, like contemporary children, were appealing because they had not yet internalized the dictates of the modern superego.

Moralists who lauded restraint and self-control nonetheless felt the pull of undisciplined fervor—partly because any sort of ardor seemed in short supply among the educated bourgeoisie, and partly because rampant emotion possessed the charms of childishness. Many descriptions of medieval character began to suggest that in the transition to social adulthood something of value might have been lost. While some chronicled a decline of virtuous enthusiasm, others discarded any moral framework for medieval vitality. Among the latter, perhaps the most revealing was Elizabeth Robins's "Mischief in the Middle Ages," which appeared in the *Atlantic Monthly* in 1881. (Robins was an essayist who later married the illustrator Joseph Pennell and wrote under her married name.) In Robins's view, "Wanton playfulness—mischief for the sake of mischief" was the key to the Middle Ages, "when the world was young."

> Artists and nobles, peasants and serfs, high and low, all dearly loved a jest, and went laughing through life as if it were a carnival, and one's only aim was to be jolly. There was a grotesqueness, a quaintness, a certain irresistible charm, about the mischief of those days which had never been before, and which can never be again.[52]

It could never be again because the Renaissance had witnessed Europe's passage into manhood: "It was time to cast off the childish state and with it the cap and bells, and all savoring of mischief." Men grew conscious of their ignorance; "the Renaissance and the Reformation brought with them a new seriousness and thoughtfulness that made wanton playfulness for the many an impossibility."[53]

For Robins, more than innocuous fun had been lost. That was clear from her definition of mischief as "selfish wantonness or indulgence of animal spirits; that is, the desire of action not guided by reason, or the desire to feel one's own power, often inspired by humor. . . ."[54] From this view, medieval childishness offered the opportunity to express irrational and often aggressive impulses. It was not simply an uncorrupted prelude to modern adulthood, but a more intense, immediate experience of the world. This vitalist version of medieval childishness recalled romantic tradition and prefigured Hall's paean to the child's sensuous "paradise." The stress on spontaneity and exuberance as ends in themselves arose from contemporaneous romantic activism, and pointed toward an emerging new image of medieval culture.

By the late nineteenth century, American authors and illustrators were limning a novel version of medieval Europe—brighter and more colorful than their countrymen had ever seen. The medieval world of the magazines was populated by jolly friars, winning jongleurs, passionate lords and ladies. Paolo and Francesca, Lancelot and Guenevere, Tristan and Isolde were the most familiar lovers whose legends were retold by writers like Richard Hovey, Louis Anspacher, and Edith Wharton. The legendary lovers embodied the emotional vigor pervading the new imagery of the Middle Ages. As one writer said in 1908, the Middle Ages "stand before us a dazzling vision of beauty and of youth, of children gamboling in the forenoon of enthusiasm, belief, fancy, and desire."[55] These twentieth-century personifications of medieval children were the descendants of Blake's boys and girls on the Echoing Green; they signified not just intense piety but a range of imaginative and emotional life which seemed impoverished in modern society.

The youthful vision of medieval character suggested a critique but not a repudiation of the modern cultural superego. Products and beneficiaries of modern society, antimodern vitalists clung to faith in the possibilities of the present. In 1881, Robins had declared that medieval vitality was irrecoverable, but by the early twentieth century, after romantic activism had swept the American cultural elite, it was possible to believe that the animal spirits of the Middle Ages again flowed freely. Social adulthood seemed at least partly leavened by laughter at "stuffed shirts" and "sissies"—two slang terms which first appeared at the turn of the century—and partly rejuvenated by cults of youthful vigor.[56] In the heady atmosphere of "the strenuous era," longings for medieval vitality could reinforce zeal for modern achievement.

The coexistence of medieval and modern enthusiasms appeared most clearly in the work of Howard Pyle and Mark Twain. Their approaches to the problem of dual allegiance differed sharply. Pyle, having apparently internalized the demands of the modern superego, put medieval childishness behind him and embraced conventional adulthood. He assimilated his admiration for premodern vitality to progressive optimism. Twain, on the other hand, remained torn between respectability and childish impulse. The unresolved tensions between medieval and modern character in *A Connecticut Yankee in King Arthur's Court* (1889) betray the continuing battle in its creator's mind. Pyle and Twain, by illustrating the two poles of smooth adjustment and tortured ambivalence, underscore the wide-ranging psychic significance of antimodern vitalism.

Pyle, who illustrated the medieval fiction published by *Harper's Monthly,* had begun his career as a writer and illustrator of children's books; his *Merry Adventures of Robin Hood* (1883) established the outlaw's puckish pranks as a fit subject for children. As an artist, Pyle rejected the half-tones and quarter-tones popular among academic painters. Using brilliant primary colors, he did much to fix a sunlit vision of the Middle Ages in the minds of Americans. The dazzling directness of Pyle's illustrations recalled the effects of medieval stained glass—far different from the opalescent olives and mauves favored by contemporaneous glassworkers like John La Farge. Though Pyle respected the conventions of academic realism, he resembled European postimpressionists in his abandonment of somber for vibrant colors. In a sense, Pyle's work constituted a careful effort toward artistic rejuvenation, an aesthetic analogue of the vitalist impulse.

If Pyle's writings and drawings betrayed his fondness for an imaginary medieval realm of youthful vigor, he nevertheless embraced a creed of perpetual, evolutionary progress. As he told the Boston Society of Arts and Crafts in 1902, medieval primitivism was charming but out of date. He cautioned the Society against sentimental reverence for the art of the past.

> I do not believe that we of this time can ever paint Madonnas, and Angels, and Saints with the ardent and childlike enthusiasm that medieval Italians painted such things. . . . I believe that the possibilities and source of the achievements

of our Art are greater and nobler and more God-like than those of the past. Those old masters of Art were big children, powerful in their vitality, vivid, if false, in their perceptions. We of to-day are not children, but men, each of us with a man's work to do, and, though we love those old paintings painted by our ancient brethren with a great and passing love, they do not belong to our adult purposes.[57]

Powerful vitality, vivid perceptions, and ardent enthusiasm would refine and deepen as man became more Godlike. For Pyle, as for many of his contemporaries, a secularized postmillennialism strengthened faith in progress, checked nostalgia, and transmuted antimodern vitalism into a rallying cry for action in the contemporary world.

For Mark Twain, optimism was more problematic. As Justin Kaplan and Henry Nash Smith have shown, Twain wrote *A Connecticut Yankee* during a critical period in his career. Anticipating huge profits from his publication of General Grant's memoirs, he began the novel in a burst of enthusiasm. It was to be a comic contrast between two civilizations, recounting the incongruous adventures of a nineteenth-century democrat bringing industrial capitalism to sixth-century Britain. But the comedy soon fell victim to Twain's misfortunes. For several years, he had been investing heavily in the Paige typesetter, a Rube Goldberg contraption of eighteen thousand moving parts, hopelessly vulnerable to breakdown and superseded almost as soon as it was begun. To Twain, it was a symbol of the great "machine culture" of the nineteenth century. As he struggled with the writing of *A Connecticut Yankee,* he sank more and more of his publishing house's earnings into the doomed invention. The machine's protracted failure shook Twain's faith in progress and aggravated his suspicion that he was a mountebank masquerading as a respectable bourgeois. Hemmed in by financial reverses and restive among the genteel literati whose favor he courted, Twain escaped to the medieval childhood of the race. Arthurian England became at once the object of his progressive scorn and the repository of his fantasies of liberation.[58]

The novel abounds in the imagery of antimodern vitalism. To the Yankee, King Arthur's court first appears as a delight of color and commotion, with "much greeting and ceremony and running to-and-fro, and a gay display of moving and intermingling colors, and an altogether pleasant stir and noise and confusion." Like any nineteenth-century progressive bringing civilization to the barbarians, the Yankee patronizes the Arthurians as "big children." But the phrase, as usual, is double-edged. It is not just that monks display a "childish wonder and faith"—the Yankee can dismiss that as superstition. There is also a sense that the Arthurians have much in common with Huck Finn. They are free from the self-consciousness, the restraints and decorum, of Victorian "sivilization"; their animal spirits flow freely; their lives, though bounded by ignorance, seem fluid with possibilities. They are inveterate pranksters, convulsed with laughter at the stalest of jokes, "just like so many children." They are reckless and improvident, continually embarking on fantastic adventures which dismay the prudent Yankee. In general, their childish traits reflect the Eden of Twain's youth, the mother lode of memories he mined for his greatest work, as well as the sunlit medieval world imagined by other late Victorians.[59]

The "big children" of Camelot aroused contradictory impulses in Twain—fantasies of instinctual liberation on the one hand, of apocalyptic destruction on the other. The violence and confusion in the novel reflect unresolved tensions in its author's mind. Fond references to the childlike vitality of the Arthurians appear alongside diatribes against medieval oppression. Descriptions of childish behavior diminish during the second half of the book, and the overall tone turns grimmer as the plot moves toward the climactic Battle of the Sand Belt. The Yankee, now a dictatorial "Boss," kills 35,000 knights with the push of a button, but he must then watch his own band die one by one, "made sick by the poisonous air bred by these dead thousands." Cast into a 1300-year-sleep by Merlin, the Yankee awakes in the troubled present. He longs for his fair maid Sandy; he dies unable to distinguish modern reality from his medieval dream. It is possible to imagine the Yankee as Twain himself, tossing on his bunk, torn between loyalty to the respectable morality of the bourgeoisie and longings for the lawless realm of childhood.[60] His quest for medieval "reality," like that of a few other antimodern vitalists, led to the beginnings of a recognition that reality was far more problematic than the progressive mind could imagine.

*A Connecticut Yankee* illuminated Twain's personal ambivalence; it also pointed to deepening conflicts in the wider culture—not just the public conflict between technological progress and republican pastoralism, but also private conflicts between overt commitments to rationality and half-conscious yearnings for a realm of fantasy and instinctual vitality. For Twain and for many of his contemporaries, an imaginary medieval realm focused those yearnings, and medieval mentalities—like primitive mentalities in general—took on many characteristics of the unconscious mind. Like the individual child, the medieval childhood of the race seemed to represent unconscious mental life at its least repressed. A web of connections joined childhood, the unconscious, and the childhood of the race in the late-Victorian imagination.

Those connections suggested the largest significance of the fascination with premodern mentalities. Yearnings for unconscious vitality underlay a mounting challenge to the modern superego. This rebellious impulse animated avant-garde art and literature; it also had a wider social significance. Therapeutic quests for well-being proliferated, focusing often on premodern models, forming an inchoate cult of inner experience. Though they aimed to recover primal irrationality, devotees of inner experience frequently trivialized unconscious mental and emotional life by denying its darker dimensions of aggression, rage, and conflict. Stemming from reaction against a modern sense of weightlessness, the cult of inner experience often reinforced that feeling by producing a sentimentalized version of the unconscious—a version well in tune with the developing therapeutic orientation of the wider culture. Ignoring Freud's stress on the inevitability of repression and inner conflict, popular therapists presented "personal growth" and "self-expression" as solutions for all psychic ills. Like these more systematic therapies, the cult of inner experience had an ironic effect: its devotees reinforced the evasive banality they had intended to escape.

There was a further affinity between the turn toward a premodern unconscious and the therapeutic world view. Even if it descended deep into the unconscious, the quest for inner experience—like the more profound therapies spawned by early depth psychology—seldom transcended the self. The spreading desire to sustain a manipulatable sense of well-being displaced earlier, higher loyalties—to particularist ideals of family or community; to universalist ideals of humanity, fraternity, or duty; to God. The process was only embryonic around the turn of the century, but it eased the transition to a consumer culture based on the imperative of self-fulfillment and instinctual gratification. Here as elsewhere, dissent from modernity paved the way for modernity.

Yet some antimodern dissent preserved a firm religious framework. By focusing on otherworldly fulfillment, religious antimodernism discredited the cult of inner experience and reinforced loyalties outside the self. Sometimes obliquely, sometimes overtly, it protested the therapeutic orientation of the emerging corporate system. As at other points in twentieth-century American cultural history, the most radical critics of capitalist culture were at bottom the most conservative.

# The Medieval Unconscious: Therapy and Protest

The late nineteenth-century interest in multiple modes of perception, in dream, trance, and hypnosis, joined with curiosity about the workings of primitive or archaic minds—especially medieval minds. The two preoccupations overlapped and sometimes reinforced one another. Explorations of medieval thought processes intersected with a revaluation of fantastic, oneiric, and visionary experience. By focusing on these intersections, we can illuminate the links between antimodernism and the artistic search for new structures of thought and expression—the "modernism" which was so often a protest against the evasive banality of of modern culture. We can also clarify the role of antimodernism in the formation of a therapeutic world view and in the shaping of antitherapeutic dissent.

Like the recovery of the unconscious, the resurrection of medieval thought processes revealed both collective and individual dimensions. Among many late Victorians, there was widespread inquiry into what might be called a European folk mind, a realm of magic and myth preserved in popular tales and superstitions. Among a smaller number, there was a growing fascination with spiritual exercises and aspirations of Oriental, medieval, and Counter-Reformation mystics. To turn-of-the-century observers, mysticism and folk mind sometimes intermingled, but for analytical purposes the two must be considered separately. Before the fascination with mystics can be explored, we need to examine the common assumptions about the medieval folk mind, then to analyze its appeal.

From the dominant nineteenth-century view, the fundamental quality of premodern folk thought was its melding of fact and fantasy. In the eyes of Mark Twain's Yankee, Arthurian thinking is a hopeless muddle; the "big children" are unable to separate external reality from the projections of their own minds. Their confusion reflected a commonplace of educated opinion about medieval thinking. Americans agreed that systematic empirical thinking had not emerged until the seventeenth century. "For our ancestors," wrote William James, "dreams, hallucinations, revelations, and cock-and-bull stories were inextricably mixed with facts."[61] And Vida Scudder observed that the early Arthurian romancers did not grasp "the principle of causality": they simply strung episodes together, willy-nilly. "Probably the attempt to depict a universe governed by chance will never be repeated," Scudder mused, "for the race has outgrown its childhood, and only childhood can try the experiment of freedom uncontrolled."[62]

The only logic in many medieval tales—particularly the earlier ones—was the logic of children, madmen, or dreamers. Americans often stressed the dreamlike irrationality of the Middle Ages. To the positivist historian Ephraim Emerton, medieval culture was "that strange middle world where men moved like the half-demented victims of terrible delusions." Hamilton Wright Mabie took a milder position. He admired the medieval spirit because "it had a naiveté and unconsciousness which we sadly and fatally lack." At the same time, that "priceless quality of unconsciousness" meant medieval personality was in a "deep sleep" which produced "splendid dreams and heavenly visions, but . . . no deep and vital sense of reality."[63]

Yet if "reality" was more problematic than Mabie recognized, medieval fantasies might be worth closer examination. The psychiatrist Boris Sidis thought so. To study the medieval mind, he argued in 1896, was to unearth the origins of "mental epidemics," for the Middle Ages displayed unequalled afflictions of mass insanity. "Men went mad in packs, by the thousands." Surveying the chaotic evidence, Sidis concluded that *"the medieval man was in a state of light hypnosis."* Animated by religious ecstasy, he was especially susceptible to self-hypnosis, because "ecstasy is mono-ideism, the intense concentration of attention on one object, an essential condition of hypnosis." Sidis believed that the hypnotic state of mind produced the "pilgrimage mania," the "crusade mania," and the "flagellant mania" during the Middle Ages. His ultimate point was not that modern people had outgrown episodes of mass hysteria. Though man had cast off the yoke of medieval authority, he remained "a suggestible animal, *par excellence."* In the nineteenth century as in the twelfth, Sidis warned, "man carries within him the germ of the possible mob, of the epidemic."[64]

Sidis's article linked interest in medieval folk belief to the more general rediscovery of human irrationality—latent in modern man, manifest in his premodern ancestors. *Scribner's* underscored the connection in 1909. An editorial described archaic man as "a mere bundle of susceptibilities" dominated by "fear, passion, and the sense of mystery"; his world view, preserved in folklore, was composed of stammerings . . . in the face of cosmic events." Only a few gifted artists could consciously recapture those stammerings; but ordinary people could recover them in their dreams. What had been a constant state of awareness for primitive man became, for his modern descendants, a brief and unconscious descent into nocturnal fantasy. to explore the folk mind of our ancestors, the editorial concluded, was to delve into "our own subconscious life."[65]

It would be a mistake to follow *Scribner's* too literally, to suggest that investigators of the European folk mind unconsciously sought to replicate or stimulate their own fantasies. Their motives were too many and complex to support such a speculative generalization. Yet there is a sense in which the turn toward medieval irrationality was part of an effort to recover a larger mental inheritance, a storehouse of myths, fantasies, and folk beliefs—a collective unconscious, to use Jung's term.

By the late nineteenth century, that inheritance was receiving systematic attention. Europeans and Americans had begun to study primitive mentalities as never before. In the United States, scholars organized the American Folk-Lore Society in 1888 and the American Anthropological Association in 1899. Research publications proliferated. Sir James Frazer's *The Golden Bough* was the most ambitious and influential compendium of primitive lore (both ancient and modern), but numerous lesser works appeared as well. (The first two-volume edition of *The Golden Bough* appeared in 1890; the third, expanded to twelve volumes, between 1911 and 1915.)

Many seemed animated by a sense of urgency, for as more cultures developed secular habits of mind, the primitive legacy seemed to be slipping away. This seemed especially true in Europe, where medieval traditions survived only in peasant backwaters. As John Fiske, an early folklorist, noted in 1890, "it is well that this work has been carried so far in our time, for modern habits of thought are fast exterminating the old world fancies."[66]

Most early folklorists, like Fiske, collected "fancies" in a positivistic spirit. They remained contemptuous of or bemused by the material they amassed. But the impact of their work crossed the boundaries of professional scholarship, spreading ultimately throughout the educated middle and upper classes. The nonacademic audience, approaching magic and mystery in a different spirit, showed unambiguous fondness for popularized translations of folk and fairy tales.

In part, enthusiasm for fairy tales reflected an effort to revitalize children's literature in accordance with spreading notions about the mystery and sanctity of childhood. As early as 1868, John Ruskin had complained that modern nursery stories had succumbed to a leaden didacticism, and that only a revival of traditional fairy tales would restore freshness and vigor to the child's imagination. During subsequent decades, as if in response to Ruskin's summons, brownies, sprites, and elves of all description returned to Anglo-American children's literature. Some roamed the pages of reissued traditional tales; others were newly invented. Nearly all, in their impish irrationality, embodied the romantic conception of children's minds—which bore important resemblances to the psychoanalytic conception—the belief that children lived in a discrete mental realm, unbounded by the restrictions of rational adulthood. Like primitive tellers of tales, children believed in wish-fulfillment and the omnipotence of thoughts; they clung to an animistic conception of life. It was only fitting that they should be offered fantasies from the childhood of the race.[67]

The fairy-tale vogue involved more than the redefinition of children's minds; it pointed to popular tastes among older people as well. In England and America, J. M. Barrie's *Peter Pan* (1904) played to enthusiastic adult audiences. Hoping their applause would save Tinker Bell, the crowds clapped furiously at the line "Do you believe in fairies?" Many who admired medieval character also felt the lure of Elfland. In 1888, Louise Imogen Guiney lovingly described *Brownies and Bogles* for juvenile readers. Charles Eliot Norton, who edited the *Heart of Oak* series for children, was careful to include a volume of fairy stories. A taste for fairy tales often accompanied a distaste for modernity.[68]

Adult enthusiasm extended beyond fairy stories to include all manner of popular legends and superstitions, gleaned from the remote corners of Europe. The fascination filled magazines and bookstores with folklore; it influenced not only scholars and the general reading public but also artistic innovators like William Butler Yeats and Richard Wagner. After wandering about the hills, "talking to half-mad and visionary peasants," the young Yeats published *The Celtic Twilight* (1893), a collection of Irish lore. The book met praise in both England and the United States, and provided Yeats with material for much of his greatest work. Ultimately Yeats transmuted folk tradition into enduring art, as Wagner had done before him. Wagner's operas brooded on legends from Germany's medieval past. In

1876, he established a summer theater at Bayreuth for their performance. By the 1880s and 1890s his work had achieved international acclaim and the place had become a cultural shrine, a mandatory stop for reverent tourists. The Wagnerian cult was of a piece with the fairy and fantasy vogues. All pointed to a widespread impulse among the educated and affluent: a desire—sometimes timid, sometimes intoxicated—for escape from a demanding modern superego and immersion in the European collective unconscious.[69]

There are several ways we can explain this "fondness for old follies," as the *Nation*'s Hammond Lamont called it. It is possible to agree with Lamont and dismiss the popularity of fairies and fantasy as a "regressive" escape to static childishness. This is the view of the evolutionary progressive, recently expressed by the literary historian Peter Coveney in *The Image of Childhood*. From this one-eyed perspective, every cultural phenomenon must be judged by its contribution to "growth" and "adult responsibility" —vague criteria which, in the United States, have usually implied adjustment to dominant values and social arrangements.[70]

Aside from its inherent bias toward complacency, another problem with the evolutionary view is that the impulse toward fantasy could also be defended as an instrument of adjustment. G. Stanley Hall, for example, argued that if the fancy was allowed free play in childhood, the adult could more effectively perform his duties in modern society. (Bruno Bettelheim has recently made a similar argument in *The Uses of Enchantment*, defending fairy tales as aids to "growth.") Others assigned fantasy a similar role in the leisure time of adults: after office hours, a wander through the celtic twilight might revive the brain-worker for further efforts in the battle of life. Fantasy, like the new historical romances, could provide a mental holiday for the overcivilized bourgeoisie. Bryan Hooker, an author of medieval romances, hinted at this function in 1908.

> The present day is exhibiting a curiously vivid interest in fairy tales; curious because that passionate self-consciousness which is always with us finds the foreground of its mirror filled with machinery, busy under a canopy of smoke; and it seems strange to discover the livid vapor shadowing forth the wings of dragons, or the faces of the little people glimmering between the wheels. Perhaps our very materialism is responsible for this new hunger after fantasy. Because the world, never so bluntly actual as now, is too much with us, we spend our vacations upon the foam of perilous seas.[71]

Hooker's reference to "vacations" pointed to an emerging ethic of leisure. He linked fantasy to the growing acceptance of "the gospel of relaxation," the belief that an overworked bourgeoisie required brief respites from toil. And what Hooker saw as vacation might also become therapy. It was no accident that the hunger for fantasy coincided with widespread alarm over nervous prostration. Beset by self-doubts and anxieties, the neurasthenic felt drawn into Merlin's wood, and beyond to the White Isle "where is no death/and dreams come true"—the realm of wish fulfillment celebrated in turn-of-the-century magazine verse.[72]

The most forthright invocation of this fantasy world occurred at Bayreuth, where the Wagnerian cult offered what the historian Carl Schorske has called "theatrical psychotherapy for the cultivated operagoer." As Schorske has shown, the therapy differed according to the piece performed. *Parsifal* presented a parable for the overcivilized: the opera's characters, at first mired in psychological paralysis, are freed through exposure to Parsifal's pre-oedipal innocence and medieval ideals of heroism. *Tristan und Isolde* celebrated the triumph of instinctual wish over rational reality, though that victory requires the lover's death.[73]

However Wagner's themes varied, his operas created a mood of submission to a surging, oceanic realm of feeling. The American poetess Ella Wheeler Wilcox, writing in 1894, described her reaction to *Tristan und Isolde* in these terms:

> . . . in the flood of music swelling clear
> And high and strong, all things save love were drowned.
> A clamorous sea of chords swept o'er my soul,
>     Submerging reason. Mutinous desire
>     Stood at the helm; the stars were in eclipse;
> I heard wild billows beat, and thunders roll;
>     And as the universe flamed into fire,
>     I swooned upon the reef of coral lips.[74]

Though devoted Wagnerians complained that the mass of visitors to Bayreuth were simply fashionmongers, Wilcox's response suggested that, for Americans as well as Europeans, Wagnerianism was more than an aesthetic fad.[75] Shorn of its romantic melodrama, her oceanic imagery recalled the language of mind cure and pointed to the therapeutic possibilities of the collective unconscious. Jung would later codify those possibilities, but around the turn of the century they remained diffuse. The exploration of the collective unconscious was a tentative probing of a neglected mental realm—in many respects another form of mind cure.

But there were important differences. The recovery of fantasy was not reducible to a balm for the "sordid troubles" of life. Wilcox's language, for all its hackneyed qualities, suggested unsettling emotions foreign to the passive tranquillity of mind cure. Legend and folklore, in their unsanitized versions, could evoke fear and awe. Hooker mentioned "the foam of perilous seas" in 1908; three years earlier, the Scottish literary critic Andrew Lang had more directly discussed the dimension of fear in the fantasy vogue. Why, he asked in 1905, were modern men and women so anxious to feel "the stirring of ancient dread in their veins?" He thought he had an answer: "As the visible world is measured, mapped, tested, weighed, we seem to hope more and more that a world of invisible romance may not be far from us."[76]

While mind cure either lacked supernaturalism or reduced it to platitudinous vagueness, premodern superstition possessed an overt otherworldly dimension, insistent and sometimes disturbing. As Freud pointed out in his essay on "The Uncanny" (1919), the folk tale's capacity to evoke dread depended on the existence of "something familiar and old-established in the mind which has been estranged only by the process of repression"—that is, on the animistic outlook of children and primitives. Educated late Victorians, in the process of internalizing an "enlightened" world view en route to adulthood, repressed their fantastic fears of malevolent sorcerers with evil eyes, of secret powers activated by wish alone. Yet the process was never complete. It is possible in part to see the folk-tale vogue as a return of repressed childhood fantasy in respectable form.[77]

In its capacity to inspire dread, the folk tale contained an erotic appeal similar to that of saintly "excess." Both fascinations revealed a longing for intense feeling. They betrayed a taste for titillation but also constituted implicit critiques of the spiritual blandness diffused by liberal Protestant culture. The growing popularity of ghost stories, for example, suggested not only a "pornography of the occult" but also a revival of traditional fear and awe of the dead—an ambivalent attitude which had gradually etherealized into vague reverence.[78] To many Americans the "stirring of ancient dread" may have seemed a more appropriate response to death than the optimistic pieties of the modern "memorial service."

It is possible to see this same dual significance in the waves of popular occultism which have repeatedly washed over the American cultural landscape from the turn of the century to our own time. On the one hand, satanist cults and horror films offer mass-produced thrills to a society satiated with routine; on the other they reflect a widespread suspicion that modern enlightenment can never fully banish the terror and strangeness from the universe. Theological formulae have faded but the impulse behind them persists. Popular occultism, however simpleminded or sleazy in its expression, embodies longings which can only be called religious.

Like contemporary occultism, the late-nineteenth-century fascination with archaic fantasy and myth suggested an inchoate protest against the disenchantment of the world, a muted insistence that mystery could survive in a rationalized universe. As Elizabeth Robins Pennell observed in 1884, belief in fairies, dryads, and dwarves originated in primitive animism but flowered most fully among common folk in the Middle Ages. This "child-like stage of belief" could not withstand the rise of rationalism. "The whole tendency of modern culture is antagonistic toward the animistic conception of nature," she wrote. "As the voice of Science increases in strength, the horns of Elfland blow fainter." A recalcitrant impulse remained, a desire to recapture the breath of "untutored childhood" in medieval fantasy.[79]

Among the most determined seekers was the critic and essayist Agnes Repplier, who extolled "the benefits of superstition" in the *Atlantic Monthly*. In 1886, she complained that "the whole wide world is painted gray on gray/ and Wonderland forever is gone past." The most offensive destroyers of wonder, Repplier charged, were positivistic myth-collectors like Fiske.

> "Where the modern calmly taps his forehead," explains Mr. Fiske, "and says 'arrested development!' the terrified ancient made the sign of the cross, and cried, 'were-wolf!'" *(Myths and Mythmakers)*. Now a more disagreeable object than the "modern" tapping his forehead, like Dr. Blimber, and offering a sensible elucidation of every mystery, it would be hard to find. The ignorant peasant making the sign of the cross is not only more picturesque, but more companionable—in books, at least—and it is of far greater interest to try to realize how *he* felt when the specimen of "arrested development" stole past him in the shadow of the woods.[80]

Repplier's phrase "in books, at least" pointed to a central dilemma which has endured to our own time. Those who craved the mysterious, however strongly they reviled positivism, were nevertheless often unable to embrace the beliefs of the past. Disdaining a diluted sense of the supernatural, longing to experience faith at firsthand, many could enter the premodern spiritual world only in books, or as spectators at "picturesque" shrines. They might remain only tourists of the supernatural. (You do not need to be a Roman Catholic to enjoy the Passion Play at Oberammergau, a traveler told *Christian Union* readers in 1880: "You do not, indeed, need to be anything.") Or, like many European aesthetes, the American admirers of fantasy might become religious dilettanti, fleeing from ennui in search of the delicate *frisson* which only premodern superstition could provide.[81] Wandering between two worlds, many antimodern seekers remained outsiders in both.

For all that, the risks of dilettantism did not discredit the will to believe. The profoundest religious documents of the age betrayed an aspect of secondhand observation. William James's *Varieties of Religious Experience* (1902), though it was in part a personal testament, was primarily a report on spiritual ecstasy from the outside, by an observer who had not shared the experiences of his dramatis personae. In regard to mystical states, for example, James acknowledged that "my own constitution shuts me out from them almost entirely, and I can speak of them only at second hand."[82] But for James, as for many of his contemporaries, the exploration of the religious experience of others was more than a detached research project. It was rooted in emotional necessity, and it constituted an important protest—sometimes embryonic and oblique, sometimes thorough and straightforward—against a desanctified, weightless universe.

James's interest in mysticism, though it transcended the Middle Ages, pointed toward a general preoccupation with medieval and Counter-Reformation mystics. By the turn of the century, translations of their spiritual exercises and meditations were proliferating in both Europe and America. In magazines and bookstores, such strangers as John of the Cross and Theresa of Avila, Meister Eckhart and Ignatius Loyola, appeared alongside more familiar figures like Francis, Joan, and Catherine of Siena. Catholic mystics, like Catholic saints in general, laid unprecedented claim on the educated Protestant imagination.[83]

At the same time, some Americans turned toward Oriental mysticism. Literature like Lafcadio Hearn's essays and Sir Edwin Arnold's *The Light of Asia* (1880), coupled with growing awareness of China and especially Japan, helped to generate a wave of Western interest in Buddhism and Oriental religion in general. Vedanta, popularized at the 1893 Chicago World's Fair and after by Swami Vivekenanda, and Theosophy, preached by Madame H. P. Blavatsky and Annie Besant, also won many American adherents during the late nineteenth century.[84] As early as 1886, Elizabeth Stuart Phelps noted the growth of Orientalism among the fashionable bourgeoisie. She described the vogue of Eastern religion as part of a general reaction against positivism.

> Carried along upon a roller of reaction from the explicit, the world is well-nigh going over a cataract after the mysterious. Silken society seeks what it is pleased to call the esoteric, as it would seek a new waltz or an original dinner card. It is *au fait* to be a Buddhist, at least we hear of a Chela served up for lunches, as if he were the last new poet or a hummingbird on a half-walnut shell. A live Theosophist is a godsend in a dead drawing room.[85]

Popular Orientalism was unsystematic and diverse; its adherents were often ignorant of the traditions they claimed to embrace. Like the current wave of interest in Oriental mysticism, late-nineteenth-century Orientalism could easily be dismissed as a trivial exercise in exoticism. But it would be a mistake to do so. Then as now, the popularity of Eastern religion signified more than a fad. Even the hostile Phelps hinted at its larger significance. Orientalism, like the mind-cure movement, the fascination with the European folk mind, and the turn toward medieval mysticism, was a response to the spiritual turmoil of the late nineteenth century.

Besides a common exploration of nonrational thought processes, there were more specific connections between mysticism and emerging secular therapies. Like mind-curists, mystics employed a kind of self-hypnosis—what Sidis called "mono-ideism"—to release the mind from normal waking consciousness. James pointed out that both mind cure and mysticism sought to submerge individual identity in union with the cosmos, and that both produced "an immense elation and freedom as the outlines of confining selfhood melt down." (Freud later called this an "oceanic feeling.") Rejecting Faustian self-reliance, the mystic and the mind-curist alike cultivated an awareness of their dependence on the universe. That awareness, together with the longing to escape "confining selfhood," linked Western and Eastern mysticism, and made both appealing to Americans for whom liberal ideas of individuality and autonomy had become problematic. Paul Carus, who popularized Buddhism in his *Open Court* magazine, also translated the meditations of Angelus Silesius, a German mystic of the Counter-Reformation who believed that "the thought of self—nothing else—is hell."[86] To neurasthenic Americans, the idea no doubt struck close to home. By "letting go" into the unconscious, they avoided a self-conscious flight from self-consciousness. Both mind cure and the mystical wave seemed genuine liberations.

For many, the sense of liberation was illusory. As belief in the supernatural faded and ethical commitments wavered, religion and morality shrank to conform to the individual's immediate emotional requirements. If admirers of mind cure or mysticism sought renewed meaning through fulfillment of psychic needs, rather than through submission to higher religious or ethical commitments, their efforts remained self-centered. In the emerging therapeutic culture, the flight from the self returned often to its starting point.

Although they had therapeutic potential in common, mind cure and mysticism revealed important differences. Mind cure overtly promoted a therapeutic orientation. Its devotees sought to nurture their own psychic well-being in the secular world, and to revitalize the individual will for continued achievement. The mystical wave, on the other hand, primarily involved proliferation of religious tracts, most of which preserved an otherworldly orientation. For those unable to accept supernaturalism, mystical literature may have provided another self-absorbed therapy; for the believing few, it may have had genuine religious significance. In both Oriental and medieval mysticism, a supernatural dimension generated pessimism toward earthly existence and hostility toward secular self-fulfillment. Those attitudes formed an important barrier to the assimilation of the antimodern impulse; for some readers they may have provided an important resource for resistance.

Otherworldly resistance was less marked in popular Orientalism, partly because certain ethical traditions in Buddhism lent themselves to progressive reinterpretation. Carus reconciled his Orientalism and his belief in progress by presenting Buddhism as optimistic, monistic idealism, a sort of benign Ethical Culture. Yet Carus and other Orientalists remained hostile to liberal individualism. The notion of the autonomous self moved Carus to confused and contradictory denunciation. "The existence of self is an illusion; and there is no wrong in this world, no vice, no sin except what flows from the assertion of self," he insisted. Lafcadio Hearn pointed troubled Americans toward the Buddhist Nirvana, which he interpreted as "the extinction of individual sensation, emotion, thought,—the final disintegration of conscious personality,—the annihilation of everything that can be included under the term 'I'. . . ." Such notions attracted the neurasthenic, horrified the Protestant polemicist, and suggested that, for some Americans at least, a fascination with Oriental mysticism might signify a quietistic withdrawal from a disenchanted universe.[87]

But to most educated Americans, Catholic mysticism seemed more insistently otherworldly. Its asceticism and pessimism toward the things of this world made it less susceptible to progressive or therapeutic reinterpretation. In the common view, the self-flagellation practiced by mystics reflected the dominant medieval contempt for secular well-being. As Randolph Bourne said, the Middle Ages were "a time when it must really have been believed—O miracle of the western world! that the body and its comforts were as nothing, and only the soul had life."[88] Henry Osborne Taylor summarized the typical sense of medieval otherworldliness in 1911, when he defined the medieval spirit as

> . . . a spirit different from that of any other period of history—a spirit which stood in awe before its monitors divine and human, and deemed that knowledge was to be drawn from the store house of the past; which seemed to rely on everything except its sin-crushed self, and trusted everything except its senses; which in the actual looked for the ideal, in the concrete saw the symbol, in the earthly Church beheld the heavenly, and in fleshly joys discerned the devil's lures; which lived in the unreconciled opposition between the lust and vainglory of earth and the attainment of salvation; which felt life's terror and its pitifulness, and its eternal hope; around which waved concrete infinitudes, and over which flamed the terror of darkness and the Judgment Day.[89]

The most striking embodiments of this otherworldly spirit were the mystics, who starved and scourged themselves that they might see God. Their asceticism was not simply the physical endurance of the soldier, or the moral discipline of the ordinary pious Christian, but a severe preparation for union with the divine—an *askesis*, to borrow a neologism from the French theologian Denis de Rougement.[90] How does one account for the power of this *askesis* over American imaginations? Any answer must be speculative, but I want to suggest three related explanations.

First, like so many alleged medieval traits, the ascetic practices of the mystics appealed to the longing for intense experience. Denials and lacerations of the flesh, if confined to the realm of the imagination, grew exciting to Americans who felt overfed and overcivilized. At the Chicago World's Fair of 1893, the most popular painting depicted a group of fifteenth-century Spanish flagellants; the painting's appeal no doubt involved titillation as much as spiritual aspiration.[91] For some Americans, the *askesis* of the mystic possessed an erotic attraction like that of medieval piety in general; it suggested not fulfillment but perpetual excitement of body and soul.

The second possible explanation involves the ethical dimension of the medieval *askesis*. The ascetic practices of many Catholic mystics were too obsessive and severe to assimilate to a proto-Protestant morality of self-control. Yet, in an age when the churches seemed absorbed in "oysters, ice cream, and fun" (as one religious paper put it), the medieval *askesis* presented an important moral force. It recalled not Victorian "duty" but an earlier, fiercer stoicism, rooted in the stratum of hardness that runs through the Christian tradition. Henry Osborne Taylor pointed to that stoical temper when he mentioned the medieval spirit's willingness to live in "unreconciled opposition" between finite and infinite worlds; the medieval *askesis* involved an acceptance of the insoluble conflict at the heart of human existence. William James nearly captured the stoical spirit from a different perspective when he defended even the most extreme ascetic practices against secular critics. Asceticism, James said, "symbolizes, lamely enough no doubt, but sincerely, the belief that there is an element of real wrongness in this world, which is neither to be ignored nor evaded, but which must be squarely met and overcome by an appeal to the soul's heroic resources, and neutralized and cleansed away by suffering."[92] James's assumption that evil could be "cleansed away" obscured the darker meaning of Christian stoicism, the recognition that evil was an irreducible element of the human condition. But his emphasis on "real wrongness" revealed his dissent from progressive optimism. Further, James's defense of otherworldly asceticism reasserted the value of self-sacrifice and even self-abasement as paths to commitment to a higher loyalty. By symbolizing a genuine disregard of self, the medieval *askesis* could focus discontent with the emerging therapeutic world view.

Third, American interest in the medieval *askesis*—particularly its fulfillment in union with the divine—suggested a longing for spiritual liberation, a desire to break the bonds of finitude which were beginning to encircle late-Victorian culture. As Max Scheler has pointed out, Christian asceticism had always ideally been "positive, not negative asceticism—aimed fundamentally at a liberation of the highest powers of personality from blockage by the automatism of the lower drives."[93] By the late nineteenth century, for many educated Americans, that renunciatory mode had lost much of its supernatural sanction; it was becoming a secular creed of self-control and self-reliance, a means of accepting rather than transcending mundane limits. To idealize the fulfillment, as well as the process, of mystic aspiration was to yearn for release from anomie and restoration of an infinite dimension of meaning.

Henry Osborne Taylor pointed to that desire when he contrasted classical and medieval sensibilities in *The Classical Heritage of the Middle Ages* (1901). His descriptive terms suggested that, in his own mind, there were important affinities between classical and late-Victorian cultures. According to Taylor, the antique spirit stressed "self-control, measure, limit"; it suffered from "the inherent limits of self-reliance. . . ." Medieval Christianity, on the other hand, "did not recognize limit. Its reach was infinite." Medieval believers, particularly the mystics, achieved release from self-reliance and "liberation resting upon the power of God. The human spirit . . . became conscious of the measureless reaches of the soul created for eternal life by an infinite and eternally loving God."[94]

Much of Taylor's language reflected the diffuse idealism of the genteel tradition, but his stress on boundlessness suggested the largest significance of the turn toward Catholic mysticism and underscored its manifold relation to the crisis of cultural authority. Late Victorians felt hemmed in by busyness, clutter, propriety; they were beset by religious anxieties, and by debilitating worries about financial insecurity. (According to James, "the prevalent fear of poverty among the educated classes is the worst moral disease from which our civilization suffers.") It was only natural that the more reflective among them should turn to saints whose genius was to be rather than to have or to do. " 'The true monk,' " James wrote, quoting an Italian mystic, " 'takes nothing with him but his lyre.' "[95] The life of a mystic embodied liberation from the tyranny of material things and trivial social duties.

As part of a more general exploration of the unconscious, the popularity of mysticism also had wide-ranging philosophical and religious significance. Like other fantastic and visionary experiences, unearthed and revalued around the turn of the century, mystical states of mind pointed to the inadequacies of positivism. They suggested that consciousness was not static and unitary but dynamic and multiple, and that "reality" was far more complex than nineteenth-century science had imagined. Those suggestions were enough to revive faith in "the reality of the unseen."[96] The late-Victorian turn toward mysticism, like the many more recent waves of mystical enthusiasm in our popular culture, demands serious attention rather than condescending dismissal. For Scudder, James, and other reflective believers, the mystics' vivid experience of eternity preserved some supernatural meaning in a secular world, some vestige of gravity in a weightless universe.

On both sides of the Atlantic, the fascination with medieval mentalities revealed the complexities of the revolt against positivism. Often perceived as displaying childlike traits, the peasants, saints, and seers of the Middle Ages focused reactions to the crisis of cultural authority: an apotheosis of simplicity, a reassertion of moral will, an exaltation of vital energy, a revaluation of visionary experience. In offering temporary escapes to a realm of innocence or wish-fulfillment, or in stressing action as an end in itself, some antimodern impulses revived the modern ethos of achievement even as they recast it in a looser therapeutic mold. Here again antimodernism served to revive familiar cultural modes while easing the transition to new ones. Yet antimodernism also nurtured critiques of modern culture, applicable to both its older and newer versions: by restating claims of moral responsibility against the ethical flaccidity of social and psychic determinisms and by ennobling otherworldly asceticism over the secular preoccupation with this-worldly well-being. In Europe and America, the resurrection of medieval mentalities possessed similar social, psychic, and religious dimensions.

But there were significant differences, too. In France and Germany, medieval mentalities energized rightist ideologies. French nationalists idealized Joan of Arc, and Catholic reactionaries like the Vicomte de Vogüé held the simple faith of the peasant masses above the anticlericalism of the *lycée*. German anti-Semites deified the Aryan folk soul of the Middle Ages, and endowed the Wagnerian cult with political meaning. Richard Wagner was not only a theatrical psychotherapist for the affluent; he was also Hitler's favorite composer, the master who immortalized the German *Volksgeist*. [97]

Beyond their political functions, medieval mentalities also helped to crystallize several tendencies within the emerging European avant-garde. Admiration for primitive childishness underlay the self-image of the avant-garde artist as a spontaneous "child man" and nurtured the twentieth-century style which Roger Shattuck has called "serious whimsey"—the style of Henri Rousseau and Erik Satie. Fascination with premodern myth and fantasy, by reinforcing interest in the unconscious mind, accelerated rejection of linear narrative and discursive logic. Shattuck has perceptively noted the parallels between premodern mystical practices and the techniques of hallucination and composition used by Alfred Jarry, Erik Satie, and Guillaume Apollinaire. In general, their cultivation of life *in extremis* paralleled the preoccupations of antimodern vitalists. Pushing vitalism to its secular limits, the avant-garde ignored or rejected supernaturalism, replaced God with deified man, and embraced a cult of risk-taking and self-fulfillment. [98]

Among turn-of-the-century primitivists, European extremism contrasted with American moderation. The European movement toward premodern mentalities led toward opposite ends of the cultural spectrum: toward Catholic royalism at one extreme, a Nietzschean cult of the self at the other. Reactionaries and avant-gardists were united by a common hatred of the moderate bourgeois—Zarathustra's "last man," the apex of mediocrity Nietzsche foresaw at the end of the evolutionary process. In the United States, where those in power were more firmly committed to bourgeois values, critics of modern sensibility remained cautious. Their careful primitivism became reformist rather than radical, a means for revitalizing and transforming capitalist cultural hegemony rather than posing fundamental challenges to it. Privileged heirs to a liberal and Protestant culture, they were unable to renounce their inheritance.

The generalization must be qualified. Antimodern dissent was too complex to be fully explained by invoking class and cultural determinants. At bottom, the turn toward medieval mentalities was animated by a religious impulse—an impulse which varied with each individual's circumstances. The dominance of the religious motive, of the longing to locate some larger purpose in a baffling universe, helps to explain the personal, idiosyncratic qualities of much antimodern protest. God lives, Blake wrote, in the details. The details of American antimodernism disclose its most enduring significance, as a *cri de coeur* against the evasions and self-congratulations of the oncoming twentieth century.

# · 5 ·

# THE RELIGION
# OF BEAUTY:
# CATHOLIC FORMS
# AND AMERICAN
# CONSCIOUSNESS

THE MEDIEVAL SOUL LEFT TRACES IN ART AND RITUAL. Housed in massive cathedrals, preserved in solemn sacraments, the aesthetic legacy of medieval Catholicism charmed increasing numbers of nineteenth-century American Protestants. Only a few entered the Church of Rome; more commonly they embraced some variety of Anglo-Catholicism. Most often, Protestants separated ceremony from doctrine and embellished spare services without reviving sacramentalism.[1] Outside the churches, collectors filled museums and homes with artifacts of the medieval church. The fascination with Catholic forms paralleled more general interest in premodern art and ritual and merged, at its periphery, with *fin-de-siècle* aestheticism. Rooted in the antebellum decades, the movement toward Catholicism flowered in its full complexity toward the turn of the century. The motives of its adherents were diverse; the cathedral had many doorways.

Perhaps more than any other antimodern impulse, the movement toward art and ritual displayed a Janus face. It accelerated tendencies republican antimodernists deplored: the accumulation of "luxury" in the form of premodern *objets d'art,* the "feminization" of Protestantism through the new emphasis on decorative and theatrical elements in public worship. By generating a cult of taste in churches as well as secular society, it promoted a consumption ethos appropriate to the coming era of corporate capitalism. Yet at the same time, the fascination with Catholic forms was in many ways a reaction against the same diffuse anxiety and "morbid self-consciousness" which provoked republican strenuosity and romantic activism. If premodern art and ritual possessed supernatural sanctions, they could focus genuine dissent from the dominant culture. At its profoundest, the movement toward art and ritual resembled the interest in premodern mysticism. Neither sought "real life" through militarism or rural simplicity; both explored a more complex reality than the nineteenth century had imagined.

I want to analyze the movement toward Catholic forms in three contexts: the growing enthusiasm for premodern (and especially medieval) *objets d'art* among the cultural elite as a whole, the efflorescence of art and ritual (though not distinctly Catholic observance) among urban Protestant congregations, and the spread of Catholic tendencies within the American Episcopal Church. This is neither a narrative of denominational controversy, nor a descriptive account of American art collecting, nor a formalist history of the American Gothic Revival: all are available elsewhere.[2] My approach concentrates not on art but on what people thought and felt about certain kinds of art, in an effort to connect those sentiments with the late-nineteenth-century crisis of cultural authority. By looking carefully at late-nineteenth-century ritualism and aestheticism, we can see a nervous ruling class discovering premodern emblems of unity, exclusivity, and cultural authority; we can also see educated and affluent Americans confronting private dilemmas of personal moral responsibility and individual identity. Like other forms of antimodernism, the fascination with Catholic forms had both social and personal significance; it eased adjustment to a streamlined modern culture even as it sustained protest against that culture.

My argument is beset by the danger of making oversimplified inferences from art to society—as many historians have previously done. They have linked the growing interest in medieval artifacts, along with the rise of art collecting in general, to two related social phenomena: the retreat of a Brahmin caste from social responsibility to dilettantism, and the effort of wealthy capitalists to surround themselves with baronial elegance. The first notion derives from the observations of contemporaries like Charles William Eliot. "One of the most discouraging phenomena of the last twenty years," he wrote in 1896, "has been the reaction in the New England community toward ritualism and aestheticism, a reaction which has accompanied increase of luxury." The second idea draws on Thorstein Veblen's belief that, toward the end of the nineteenth century, an American "leisure class" began indulging in "conspicuous consumption" to establish social prestige.[3]

Both these notions contain a measure of accuracy (Veblen was especially acute on the link between aestheticism and an emerging consumption ethos); neither provides sufficient insight. Veblen and Eliot were utilitarian moralists, impervious to the psychological and religious attractions of "barbaric" art and ritual. The same ideological blinders have narrowed the perspective of more recent historians, who have seemed virtually obsessed by moral decline and status concerns among the late-nineteenth-century cultural elite. To illuminate the social, psychological, and religious functions of the fascination with Catholic forms, we need to abandon stale and mistaken assumptions about "dying elites" as well as a reductionist sociology that dismisses most upper-class cultural forms during this period as expressions of "status anxiety." We need to take art and religion seriously, to separate aestheticism from explicit sacramentalism, and to trace the significance of each in individual lives. And the point to begin is the earliest interest in Catholic art, among the travellers and tastemakers of the antebellum era.

# The Rise of Catholic Taste: Cultural Authority and Personal Regeneration

During the years after 1816, when the first steam-packet service between New York and Liverpool was established, the stream of American tourists swelled steadily. Recording their experiences in an abundant travel literature, they created images of European culture for their less fortunate countrymen. The most pervasive presence in that culture was the Roman Catholic Church. In brooding cathedrals and ruined abbeys, at wayside shrines and village festivals, the traveller confronted the Church's influence.

Though traditional hostilities ebbed slowly, the encounter could provoke the admiration of Americans even during the early years. Romantic aesthetics had linked Gothic architecture with savage Nature and labelled both "sublime" in contrast to the utilitarian grayness of the nineteenth century. At the same time, the massive solidity of Gothic architecture and the orderly behavior of peasants at religious festivals attracted upper-class moralists anxious to maintain deference and stability in Jacksonian America. Both personal and social concerns led more and more Americans to share the sentiments of Washington Irving, who yearned "to escape . . . from the commonplace realities of the present, and lose myself amid the shadowy grandeurs of the past."[4]

Among midcentury travellers, grounds for admiration broadened. Besides social order and "shadowy grandeurs," Catholic art and ritual embodied a feast of color and incense and music unknown in meeting houses. "Oh, that we had cathedrals in America," Nathaniel Hawthorne confided to his notebook, "were it only for the sensuous luxury." The growing enthusiasm for Catholic forms reflected a wider revaluation of aesthetic experience, which grew symbiotically with foreign travel. As early as 1873, according to a Swiss economist cited in *Appleton's Journal,* 25,000 American tourists were visiting Europe annually. The cathedral pilgrimage became a staple of their itinerary. Proliferating handbooks detailed the beauties of Chartres, Rouen, Beauvais, likening their appeal to that of other ancient monuments. Elizabeth Robins Pennell reassured her readers at the turn of the century that even if Beauvais cathedral were taken over by the state and "handed over a prey to the tourist," its beauty would not be lost. "Art is the rock on which the cathedral of St. Peter [at Beauvais], in the gray North, is as firmly set as the pyramids of the Egyptian desert, as the broken stones of the Parthenon under the sunlit skies of Greece."[5] Aesthetes like Pennell detached Catholic and other religious monuments from specific historical meaning and transformed them into relics of a cult of taste.

Pennell's aestheticism was symptomatic. Throughout the later decades of the nineteenth century, the art fever rose steadily. It animated not only aesthetic pilgrimages abroad but also unprecedented institutional activity at home. The Metropolitan Museum of Art, the Boston Museum of Fine Arts, and the Corcoran Gallery in Washington, D.C., all were founded in 1870, the Chicago Art Institute in 1879. Private collections proliferated, their range widening as travellers added the Near East and the Orient to their itineraries. Charles Langdon Freer, Denman Ross, and William Sturgis Bigelow assembled Japanese prints and porcelain; Isabel Stewart

Gardner crowded her Boston home with Oriental and medieval acquisitions; J.P. Morgan combined medieval and Egyptian enthusiasms in forming his huge collections; the sculptor George Gray Barnard spent years acquiring the paintings, sculpture, and stained glass for the Cloisters, which he opened in 1914. (The Metropolitan Museum bought the collection in 1925 with funds provided by John D. Rockefeller.) Earlier and more enthusiastically than their European counterparts, American collectors rescued Tokugawa pottery from modernizing Japanese, unearthed twelfth-century Madonnas from roadside ditches, and in general tried to prevent the sacred relics of the past from becoming the detritus of the present.[6]

The enthusiasm for collecting premodern art does not fit neatly into an antimodern framework, partly because so many collectors were forward-looking millionaires and partly because interest in medieval or Oriental art was part of a more diffuse aestheticism. In general, the collecting impulse reflected the contradictory tendencies of American antimodernism. A taste for the exotic, a desire to preserve the old—these sentiments could coexist with a zeal for industrial growth, even with an ability to build financial empires. Acquisition of the art of the past could buttress one's prestige in the present, as Veblen pointed out. Without doubt, much late-nineteenth-century art collecting was an exercise in conspicuous consumption performed by the beneficiaries of modern capitalism.

But this view oversimplifies the collecting impulse. Most collectors, however wealthy, were not mindlessly acquisitive. They discriminated; they preferred some objects, some periods, to others. They were methodical, not megalomaniacal. To understand the larger significance of their efforts, we need to look more closely at both their methods and their preferences.

As the French historian René Brimo has suggested, late Victorians approached the art of the past with a new concern for archaeological correctness. Like the Beaux-Arts architects who aimed for precise historical re-creations of Gothic and other styles, collectors rejected mid-Victorian eclecticism as an amateurish muddle. They turned to scholarly authority in an effort to establish standards of historical accuracy and aesthetic coherence. Gardner sought advice from Charles Eliot Norton and Bernard Berenson, Bigelow and Ross from Edward Sylvester Morse and Ernest Fenollosa, Morgan from Roger Fry.[7]

The quest for aesthetic models was part of a broad response to the late-nineteenth-century sense of crisis—an effort to shore up cultural authority through the establishment of professional standards. Upper-class conservatives had long been alarmed by the impact of majority opinion on intellectual and artistic achievement. Determined to rout amateurs and charlatans from scholarship, law, and medicine, educated Americans began to found professional associations even before the Civil War. Toward the end of the century, as social tensions deepened, such efforts intensified and broadened. Like other cultural enterprises, artistic connoisseurship became professionalized.[8]

The professionalization of connoisseurship affected public museums as well as private collections. The Boston Museum of Fine Arts offers a suggestive example. Its founders intended to depart from aristocratic European traditions by exhibiting a modest collection of reproductions for pedagogic purposes. But during the 1890s, under the leadership of Benjamin Ives Gilman, the Museum's directors began to transform it into an elegant shrine. Beginning with the Japanese collections of Bigelow and Ross, they selected objects on the basis of their rarity, authenticity, and aesthetic quality. The new museum establishment, confident of its expertise, expected to render judgments with scientific precision.[9]

The transformation of the Boston Museum reflected general tendencies in the institutionalization of art. The great collections, like the museums which ultimately housed them, were organized on the basis of professional advice. Their authenticity was undeniable; their beauty had received scholarly sanction. In their impressive new institutional homes, collections of premodern artifacts became new and striking emblems of upper-class cultural authority.

One can see the social significance of the collections most clearly in the light of a more general enthusiasm for premodern emblems of authority. There was, for example, an unprecedented interest in genealogical pedigrees and coats-of-arms around the turn of the century. Genealogy merged class-consciousness with racism. As class and racial fears heightened, many Americans longed for the Nordic purity supposedly guaranteed by medieval antecedents. Genealogical societies multiplied: the Aryan Order of St. George (1892) and the Baronial Order of Runnymede (1897) were two of many formed during this period. The Lenox Library in New York set aside a genealogical room in 1896. With the same professional care displayed by artistic connoisseurs, genealogists justified claims to coat-armor. Intended only to satisfy their wealthy clients, their work nevertheless had wider social consequences. It provided an upper class under stress with valuable emblems of unity and exclusiveness.[10]

A similar conjunction of premodern symbols with modern class needs occurred at elite boarding schools and universities. The most influential and prestigious Northeastern prep schools were nearly all founded between 1881 and 1906. Eton or Harrow was the standard model, Gothic the approved mode of construction. Consciously recalling medieval English traditions, these schools trained the proprietors and managers of the modern capitalist state.[11] During the same period, as elite colleges became modern universities, their leaders turned to Gothic architecture and medieval ceremonial with unprecedented eagerness. Despite the scorn of utilitarians like Eliot, a number of prominent schools—including Yale, Princeton, Chicago, Cornell, and West Point—housed laboratories in

Gothic castles and clothed professors in archaic regalia on official occasions. In education as in social relations and art, the urban upper classes' use of premodern symbols promoted a sense of continuity with aristocratic traditions and eased the transition to more secular and specialized modes of cultural authority.[12] Far from signifying defeatist withdrawal, the turn to premodern educational symbols represented an important and successful response to the crisis of cultural authority. Looking backward to the fourteenth century, upper-class educators could more easily move forward to the twentieth.

As part of this wider search for premodern emblems of authority, the collecting and institutionalizing of medieval and Oriental art performed an important social function. It is important to emphasize, though, that collectors were largely unaware of that function. Their motives were private rather than public. They sought official sanctions for personal tastes. And their preferences were rooted in the psychic turmoil of the late nineteenth century.

Amid the jumble of periods and styles in late-Victorian collections, there was a common thread of fascination with the primitive. Allied with archaeological methods, the primitivist impulse sparked interest in Egyptian, Oriental, and early medieval work, as well as that of colonial American craftsmen. It signified a preference for monochrome ceramics over ornate *chinoiserie,* for Chartres or the Pyramids over the Crystal Palace. In general, as Brimo writes, late-Victorian collectors "were especially attracted by those epochs in which art was calmest, most monumental, most massive, those in which 'tactile values' dominated: the twelfth century in France rather than the fifteenth or even the fourteenth century."[13]

It is possible to exaggerate the shift to primitivist taste. Both travellers and collectors still displayed a yen for the ornate. Primitivist tendencies coexisted with older admiration for "refinement"; at Fenway Court, Gardner placed Italian Renaissance furniture around the corner from a twelfth-century altarpiece. But the important point is that the altarpiece was there, signifying a primitivist countercurrent which would have baffled an earlier generation of collectors. During the 1860s, James Jackson Jarves had been unable to interest Americans in his outstanding collection of early medieval Italian paintings. By the turn of the century, medieval "primitives" formed an important part of many American collections, including those of Gardner and John Graver Johnson; they became a fashionable commodity after a well-publicized exhibit at Bruges in 1902. The new interest in early medieval painting not only reflected the transatlantic current of primitivism, but also marked a dramatic shift in American taste.[14]

The spread of primitivist taste was in part a collective change of mind, reinforced by scholarly authority—a turn away from assumptions of progress in art, an abandonment of the obsession with great names. But it was also a change of heart. The tastes of collectors stemmed from emotional

needs as well as intellectual fashion. Mere ownership provided only transient pleasure, as the experience of William Randolph Hearst suggested.
("Every time Willie feels badly [*sic*], he goes out and buys something,"
Hearst's mother said, while he filled warehouses with his acquisitions.)
What many collectors sought instead was a religious surrogate. It was not
just that they sometimes spoke in religious language of their duty to preserve the "sacred flame" of Western tradition. Such notions of the aesthete's public role became increasingly important during the late
nineteenth century, but they were stronger among professors like Norton
or curators like Gilman than among collectors. Turning to the religious art
of premodern cultures, some collectors sought not fulfillment of public
duty but release from chronic anxiety.[15]

There were a number of neurasthenics among the most prominent
late-Victorian collectors. Bigelow graduated from medical school, but then
spent most of his life travelling in Europe and the Orient or in bed with
nervous prostration. After Gardner's first baby died, her second miscarried
—the result of a mysterious malady brought on by her sister-in-law's death.
Gardner remained a periodic victim of nervous exhaustion for the rest of
her life. Even Freer, a self-made railroad millionaire, was fragile and
neurasthenic. Retiring at forty-four, he was increasingly plagued by debilitating fears and inexplicable bouts of intense irritability.[16]

All these collectors used premodern art to create a realm of beauty
where they could withdraw—however temporarily—from nervous strain.
Bigelow arrived in Japan in 1882, immersing himself in the study of Buddhism and the acquisition of lacquer, sword guards, and paintings. His
Bostonian friends, who remembered him as a restless, anxiety-ridden
young man, marvelled at his transformation to serenity. After Bigelow
returned to America in 1887, he clung to Japanese art and Buddhism as
his chief sources of spiritual sustenance. Gardner, who visited Bigelow in
Japan, also found "tranquillizing" qualities in Oriental culture. But while
she collected ninth-century Buddhas along with twelfth-century Madonnas, she remained a devout Anglo-Catholic. Her religious convictions were
reflected in the medieval chapels at Fenway Court. Freer, too, sought
serenity amid premodern *objets d'art.* After his early retirement, he withdrew for the rest of his life into an exquisite realm of Japanese porcelain
and Persian pottery. His secretary recalled that toward the end of Freer's
life, while he was continually wracked by nervous ailments, "he would cling
to certain jade pieces with deep satisfaction and with almost religious faith
in their restorative powers." Premodern art promised spiritual comfort
and therapeutic restoration.[17]

Not only the proud possessors, but also the culture-consuming public
might derive psychic benefit from art collections. Around the turn of the
century, cultural commentators began using a new vocabulary to describe
the effects of aesthetic contemplation. The older didacticism persisted but

a new approach emerged as well, stressing that aesthetic experience was primarily psychological rather than moral. One logical next step was the notion of art as therapy. Henri Matisse took it in *Notes d'un Peintre* (1908). Matisse hoped for "an art which might be for every mental worker, be he businessman or writer, like an appeasing influence, like a mental soother, something like a good armchair in which to rest from physical fatigue."[18]

In approaching art as therapy, most Americans were neither as straight-forward nor as secular as Matisse. But his remarks were symptomatic of changing attitudes toward aesthetic experience on both sides of the Atlantic. Slowly disentangling themselves from didacticism, Americans began to appreciate art not because it stirred them to heroic thoughts and deeds but because it calmed them, provided them with respite from the constant demands of the modern superego. The change was halting and half-conscious, as the ambiguous responses of visitors to Fenway Court suggested. In one letter, Ida Higginson hailed the lifelong devotion to "beauty and duty" manifested in the Gardner collection; in another, she thanked Gardner for bringing "happiness and refreshment to us all." A similar ambiguity characterized William James's reaction to the opening of Fenway Court on January 1, 1903. He used moral terms to describe a psychological phenomenon. From his view, the "moral influence" of Fenway Court was not the ennoblement sought by didactic art critics but the transformation of spectators from busy, self-conscious adults to docile, self-forgetful "children." Morality and therapeutic "refreshment" mingled in late-Victorian views of aesthetic experience.[19]

The notion that art could provide release from bourgeois anxieties emerged most explicitly among the young aesthetes who clustered at Harvard around the turn of the century. Scorning athleticism, a few students gathered at the Stylus Club, where they quoted Huysmans and composed Wildean sonnets. For exemplars, they looked to Santayana or Pierre Chaignon La Rose (a book designer who helped to arrange the redecoration of the Museum of Fine Arts in 1904). Like Santayana, they sought liberation from the "straitened spirit" of the late-Victorian bourgeoisie by tasting beauty in its many guises. Chalice and crucifix, Buddha and *kakemono,* all became relics in the cult of aesthetic experience. Disdaining strenuosity, the aesthete nevertheless shared the romantic activist's suspicion that possibilities for authentic experience had diminished if not disappeared in late-Victorian culture.[20]

Both activist and aesthete rejected routine. In quest of intensity and immediacy, the activist took to the open road or the battlefield, while the aesthete hoped for a more exquisite *frisson* in the contemplation of premodern art. As a reaction against the dictates of a modern superego, the Harvard cult of aesthetic experience shared the psychic origins of the more general fascination with premodern forms. It also had some of the same results. Though they railed against modern culture's lack of "spirituality," the aesthetes detached premodern *objets d'art* from any traditional religious meaning, creating a surrogate religion of taste well suited to a secular culture of consumption.

The emergence of art as a religious surrogate posed a significant dilemma for liberal Protestants. Traditionally hostile toward graven images, they nevertheless increasingly felt the emotional power of Catholic art and symbolism. For many, the central question was posed by the heroine of Henry Adams's *Esther* (1884). Impressed by an Episcopalian service in a Gothic revival church, she wondered, "was the moral equal to the aesthetic effect, or was the former paralyzed or overshadowed by the latter . . . was the worship spiritual or simply dramatic?"[21] During the later nineteenth century, the problem became acute as Protestant congregations built Gothic churches, decorated their interiors, and elaborated their services with music and ritual.

# Art, Ritual, and Belief: The Protestant Dilemma

Most antebellum Protestants damned Catholic art and ritual as a "barbarous pageant" designed to keep "the senses captive." But a few glimpsed a favorable relation between art and religion, concealed beneath layers of Catholic corruption. By the 1840s and 1850s, ministers and laymen were heeding Ruskin's plea to adapt Gothic architecture for Protestant purposes. During the post–Civil War years, old suspicions subsided steadily.

Religious art and ritual flowered most fully toward the turn of the century, when even such committed antiritualists as the Congregationalist minister Lyman Abbott were acknowledging that "perhaps we Puritans have reacted too far from the sacerdotalism of medaevalism and need to retrace our steps." And what to Abbott was a matter for conjecture was to lay commentators a cause for celebration. William B. Chisholm, writing in the *Century* in 1893, hailed "the evolution of a new reign of taste, and . . . beneficent estheticism in the matter of form and ceremony itself." In Chisholm's view, "the sharpest religious reaction this country has ever witnessed" was "rapidly extending over the country and taking in all shades and descriptions of believers." Others agreed that music, ritual, decoration, and architecture had transformed a "bare order of service" to one of "elaborate aesthetic import." Externally, at least, many urban Protestants had buried their Puritan past.[22]

One common explanation for the efflorescence of art and ritual is that it expressed the *embourgeoisement* of urban Protestantism, the increasing fondness of affluent congregations for "sensuous luxury." This notion harmonizes with the church-sect typology developed by Max Weber and Ernst Troeltsch and first applied to the United States by H. Richard Niebuhr. Within that framework, the growth of "aesthetic religion" reflects the transformation of rural sects into urban churches: the growing acceptance of wealth, worldliness, and priestly authority. Late-nineteenth-century Protestantism, from this view, was a gilded religion for a gilded age.[23] The church-sect interpretation embodies the outlook of many nineteenth-century Protestants. Certainly a circuit rider of the 1830s would have been shocked by the Gothic churches his grandchildren accepted with equanimity. And many late-Victorian observers, still wedded to republican moralism, also perceived churchly aestheticism as worldly accommodation—another form of overcivilization.

The description of aestheticism as accommodation is partially accurate. It underscores the point that religious art forms could conceal secularizing tendencies. The notion that religious preference was a matter of "good taste" reduced religion to a commodity in an emerging culture of consumption. In religious aestheticism as in secular connoisseurship, devotion to art and ritual could ease the transition to twentieth-century affluence. But church embellishment is not reducible to a symptom of accommodation. By linking religious aestheticism to rising social status, church-sect typology clarifies the larger outlines of denominational change but obscures the importance of art and ritual for the individual Christian. The rise of Protestant aestheticism revealed widespread, complex dissent from modern culture.

One dimension of that dissent involved the spread of theatrical elements in Protestant worship. In *The Fall of Public Man*, Richard Sennett has linked the growing privatism of the later nineteenth century to the increasing dearth of public rituals. His argument is overstated, but it does suggest that theatricality in religion could have partially compensated for the withdrawal into self-absorption. The Protestant movement toward ritual may have been a recoil from habits of introspection which had lost supernatural sanction. As Chisholm pointed out, "Ritualism is not necessarily in the direction of distinctly Catholic observance. It means the substitution of the scenic for the introspective, the putting away of that rather morbid religious overzeal and self-inspection of old for the eminently social exercises of the modern assemblage."[24] The new enthusiasm for the decorative and theatrical was an effort, half-conscious and rarely articulated, to ease modern anxieties by reviving public ritual.

At the same time, the growth of Protestant aestheticism reflected the revision of familiar modes of religious belief. The liberal retreat from dogma, conducted in the name of reason, nevertheless made rational assent seem an inadequate form of religious commitment. Having abandoned theological rigor, Protestants hoped to surround vapid sermons with emotional passion. "Religion is dying out in our churches," a Unitarian minister complained in 1892, "because it has no lyrical lift, no aroma of poetry, no wings of spiritual imagination, no vital communion with sublime natures."[25] Both ministers and laymen thought art and ritual might provide a "lyrical lift" to the faltering claims of urban Protestantism.

Toward the end of the nineteenth century, cultural commentators increasingly stressed the salutary effects of art and ritual on the "instinct of worship." Their examples were invariably Catholic. In magazine verse, poets used Catholic artifacts to evoke a religious atmosphere. Katherine Coolidge's "In the Cathedral" (1899) typified a popular *fin-de-siècle* genre, and pointed to the role of art and ritual in newer modes of Protestant worship.

> The city's burning heart beats far outside
> This dim cathedral, where the mystic air
> Vibrates with voices of impassioned prayer,
> From generations that have lived and died
> . . . . . . . . . . .
> Soft from the jeweled windows falls the light,
> Touching the incense-laden atmosphere
> To glory, while a deep antiphony
> Rolls from the organ to the arches' height.
> To soul and sense a Presence liveth here,
> Instinct with power of immortality.[26]

The fundamental appeal of the cathedral lay in its separation from the secular urban world. "Jeweled windows" and an "incense-laden atmosphere" insulated worshippers from "the city's burning heart," creating a self-contained perceptual universe. Unlike the Unitarian meeting house, the cathedral was discontinuous with its modern surroundings; entering it, one beheld a different world.

This quality of "otherness" suggested two divergent religious developments. First, the rise of Protestant aestheticism reinforced a growing tendency to praise cathedrals (and churches generally) for their capacity to provide temporary refreshment amid urban chaos. By virtue of their insulated charm, they became gardens of cool repose—therapeutic antidotes to feverish modern haste. The Protestant aesthete could return, revitalized, to his daily tasks. Second, the desire to create a religious environment wholly different from that outside suggested an embryonic uneasiness with liberal theology. Postmillennial progressivism assumed that God was immanent in Nature, and that men could discern and implement His will. At the turn of the century, those assumptions still pervaded Protestant churches—but they were more compatible with meeting houses than with cathedrals. The movement toward art and ritual, by elevating church atmosphere beyond mundane human affairs, suggested a reluctance to divinize human purpose and a longing for a deity who was wholly other. The fascination with Catholic forms not only eased adjustment to the emerging therapeutic ethos but also embodied religious longing for transcendence.

Hope that art could restore transcendence depended partly on the Ruskinian assumption that the greatest art originated in and reinforced religious faith. Many American ministers, artists, and cultural critics embraced this notion during the later decades of the nineteenth century. Accepting the bond between art and religion, they found both in decay in a secularizing culture. "Why have the arts of design steadily and everywhere fallen off in excellence and influence during modern times?" the painter William J. Stillman asked in 1886. He traced the difficulty to the corrosive effects of scientific empiricism on "that entire range of spiritual faculties, perceptions, emotions" which had always formed the basis for both religion and art.[27]

According to Ruskin, artistic and religious regeneration had to await the reconstruction of society. Americans like Stillman resisted Ruskin's radicalism and instead suggested that art and religion could save themselves by uniting to promote "spiritual faculties, perceptions, emotions." And according to many the best example of that union was the premodern artist, whose achievement stemmed from his subordination of self to God in the task of illuminating a mysterious yet providentially ordered universe.[28] The secularized postmillennialism pervading the churches undermined this premodern attitude at every point. It questioned self-abnegation and supernaturalism; it proclaimed a knowable, improvable universe; it deified human purpose. To the extent that religious aestheticism sought to rekindle a sense of transcendence, it embodied an attempt to recapture a vanishing, God-centered world view.

In 1905, *Scribner's* underscored the connection between a fondness for ritual and a premodern world view. An editor contrasted the ritualized Orient to the modern West. "The last word on modern civilization," he announced, "defines it as that social order which confers 'the maximum of bodily comfort on the average man'—a conception peculiarly alien to Oriental thinking." And, he might have added, to medieval thinking as well. As many visitors observed, both the Gothic cathedral and the Buddhist shrine generated a sense of human insignificance—a conviction of the need to adapt to one's physical and spiritual environment, rather than attempt to master it. This stoical fatalism underlay many of the "religious sentiments" engendered by art and ritual. By symbolizing "the spirit of reverence," said the *Scribner's* editor, ritual not only "lends charm to life" but also "gives it meaning." Even at its least self-conscious, in the embellishment of Protestant services, religious aestheticism may have signified a murmur of protest, a demand for meaning in a darkening universe.[29]

Yet the link between aesthetics and belief remained problematic. Ruskinian assumptions about the religious value of art and ritual could not be taken for granted. The "instinct of worship" stirred by ritual might be only emotional or sensuous excitement. Religious aestheticism could point toward unconscious realms of vitality; it could have a primitivist appeal. *Fin-de-siècle* primitivism revalued ritual for its enlargement of sensuous experience and its aid in cultivating nonrational mental processes.[30] This primitivist approach to ritual contained possibilities for deepening religious experience, but it might also blend with a secular cult of inner experience. And whatever the long-term results of ritualism, the immediate, personal impact was sometimes catastrophic. For Protestants who were adrift from older theological moorings and still clinging to liberal formulas, the encounter with premodern art and ritual engendered confusion and even despair.

The most penetrating account of this dilemma was Harold Frederic's novel *The Damnation of Theron Ware* (1896). As an *Atlantic* reviewer perceived, *The Damnation* explored the appeal of "what may be called the feudal or medieval theory of the higher life" by dramatizing the difficulties of the Reverend Theron Ware.[31] Disdaining the hellfire of primitive Methodism, Theron preaches a vaguely optimistic gospel of moral and material progress. But his enlightened creed cannot survive confrontation with the older world view of European Catholicism, personified by the learned parish priest Father Forbes and his friend Celia Madden. Theron's Emersonian optimism begins to disintegrate when he stumbles onto the last rites of an Irish workman. Father Forbes arrives to administer the sacrament, and Theron feels drawn into the ceremony.

> He found himself bowing with the others to receive the sprinkled holy water from the priest's white fingers; kneeling with the others for the prayers; following in impressed silence with the others the strange ceremonial by which the priest traced crosses of holy oil with his thumb upon the eyes, ears, nostrils, lips, hands, and feet of the dying man. . . . moved by the rich novel sound of the Latin . . . with its soft Continental vowels and liquid r's.[32]

Theron's sensuous encounter with ritual leads him into intellectual and emotional entanglements with Forbes and Celia. To Theron, who believes that "the more we know, the nearer we shall approach the Throne," Forbes insists that man cannot escape his primitive inheritance. "Just as the material earth is made up of countless billions of dead men's bones," Forbes says, "so the mental world is all alive with the ghosts of dead men's thoughts and beliefs; the wraiths of dead races' faiths and imaginings." In Forbes's view, to speak of religious progress is absurd. "Where religions are concerned, the human race are still very much like

savages in a dangerous wood in the dark, telling one another ghost stories around a campfire. They have always been like that."[33] Forbes pre-
fers Catholicism to Protestantism because he believes Catholic ritual
satisfies primal impulses. It touches the substratum of irrationality underlying all religious belief.

It is Celia, the organist at the Catholic church, who arouses Theron's
irrational impulses—not just sexual desire but more importantly a childlike urge for maternal domination. In Theron's mind, Celia's image
merges with the stained-glass Madonna in the village church, and with
the figures of Venus, Isis, and Horus enshrined in her boudoir. Self-
consciously and almost to the point of caricature, she embodies archaic
feminine principles of fecundity and maternity. Theron's most ecstatic
moment occurs when he gives way to his childlike longings and buries
his face in her lap.

> The thing that came uppermost in his mind, as it swayed and rocked in the
> tempest of emotion, was the strange reminiscence of early childhood in it all.
> It was like being a little boy again, nestling in an innocent, unthinking transport
> of affection against his mother's skirts. The tears he felt scalding his eyes were
> the spontaneous, unashamed tears of a child; the tremulous and exquisite joy
> which spread, wave-like, over him, at once reposeful and yearning, was full of
> infantile purity and sweetness.[34]

Theron's joy is short-lived. In the end, Celia proves a false mother. She
tells Theron that his shameless fawning and affectations of learning have
made him "a bore." Despairing, he seeks solace from another maternal
figure, an opportunistic revivalist named Sister Soulsby. Ultimately he
achieves ambiguous redemption. United with his wife, Alice, he prepares
to head West, hoping for success in real estate or politics. He has become
thoroughly secular and cynical; his romantic liberal Protestantism has
disintegrated.

While it is easy to make unwarranted inferences from literature to cultural history, one can nevertheless argue that *The Damnation* is an historically significant document. Frederic strove for realistic social observation,
and his novel perceptively explored important psychic tensions among
the educated bourgeoisie. It not only dramatized lingering republican
fears of aestheticism, it also illuminated the primitivist appeal of Catholic
art and ritual. The desire for fuller sensuous life, the longing for submission to a nurturing Mother Church—these emotions may well have
linked the interest in Catholic forms to the more general recovery of
primal irrationality. As Theron's fate suggested, without a supernatural
framework such sentiments could destroy belief. To become an articulate
religious protest, ritualism required theology. And for American Protestants, the source of that theology was the Anglo-Catholic movement in
the Episcopal church.

# American Anglo-Catholicism: Legitimation and Protest

American Anglo-Catholicism originated in the early antebellum years. Well before English High Church ideology surfaced at Oxford and Cambridge in the 1830s, American churchmen had begun adapting medieval art and Catholic ritual to Episcopalian liturgical purposes. But from the 1830s on, the English ideologies helped to crystallize inchoate American tendencies by powerfully expressing High Church views. The Oxford Tractarians urged a renewed sense of Christian worship and holiness based on return to Catholic literature and discipline; the Cambridge Ecclesiological Society disseminated the "laws" of church architecture and promoted the resurrection of medieval liturgical practices. The emphasis at Oxford was primarily theological, at Cambridge primarily aesthetic. In American Anglo-Catholicism, theology and art were often intertwined. Under the influence of the Oxford and Cambridge movements, Episcopalians in Boston, Philadelphia, and New York organized for Anglo-Catholic worship. In 1844, some prominent Boston laymen founded the Church of the Advent in an effort to put into practice the principles of the Oxford movement. In 1848, under the influence of the Cambridge Movement, High Churchmen formed the New York Ecclesiological Society and St. Mark's parish in Philadelphia. The London Ecclesiological Society drew the plans for St. Mark's Gothic church, which was designed to suggest a fourteenth-century abbey. The infusion of English ideas transformed American Anglo-Catholicism from a diffuse impulse into a coherent ideology animating major congregations in the largest American cities.[35]

Toward the end of the nineteenth century Anglo-Catholic growth paralleled a general rise in Episcopalian church membership. Between 1860 and 1900, for example, St. Mark's communicants increased 550 percent, while Episcopalian churches showed a 318 percent growth. Philadelphia's population, meanwhile, grew 130 percent. Citing such statistics, historians have lumped Anglo-Catholicism with Episcopalianism and have treated both as symptoms of upper-class status seeking. Anglo-Catholicism, from this view, was simply a more self-conscious form of Episcopalian elitism. It was conspicuous consumption with a theological patina, a religion for Anglophile snobs and ecclesiastical milliners.[36]

The cliché is partially accurate. Anglo-Catholicism involved a fondness for pomp and a reverence for social hierarchy. It exaggerated the decorative tendencies in Broad Church Episcopalianism, which, like nonliturgical denominations, sought to avoid excessive display and explicit replication of medieval splendors. But Anglo-Catholics were less restrained in both their aestheticism and their medievalism. The rector of St. Mark's typified their attitude in 1895 when he assailed "cheapness" in church decoration and reminded his parishioners that medieval people, unlike their modern descendants, were eager to fill churches with costly treasures.[37] This war on "cheapness" allied Anglo-Catholicism with other efforts to locate upper-class emblems of unity and exclusiveness. Anglo-Catholic vestments and decorations shared the social functions of medieval university ceremonials, coat-armor, and premodern *objets d'art:* all promoted a sense of continuity with aristocratic traditions. It was no accident that a number of Anglo-Catholics also played at royalism. In Boston, for example, Isabel Stewart Gardner and the architect Ralph Adams Cram joined William H. Van Allen (who became rector of the Advent in 1902) in drinking seditious toasts on the Fourth of July and offering expiation on the Feast of St. Charles. However frivolous, royalist antics underscored the elitist implications of American Anglo-Catholicism.[38]

But the preoccupation of historians with elitism and social display has led them to neglect the full range of connections between the High Church movement and late-nineteenth-century cultural crisis. Anglo-Catholicism was not simply a more ornate and snobbish version of Protestant aestheticism. There were important institutional and theological distinctions between Anglo-Catholics and other Protestants, including Episcopalians. Far more strenuously than their Broad Church brethren, Anglo-Catholics required submission to ecclesiastical authority as an antidote to modern confusion. Amid a welter of therapeutic creeds and nostrums, a number of educated Americans embraced the institutionalized certainty of High Church authority. More socially acceptable than Roman Catholicism, High Church Anglicanism offered an equally authoritative alternative to weightless tolerance.[39]

The High Church movement had a subtler psychological appeal as well. Weber observed that "the God of Calvinism demanded of his believers not single good works, but a life of good works combined into a unified system." By the late nineteenth century Calvinism had dissolved in an Emersonian haze, but its inner imperatives persisted in the unforgiving introspection of the modern superego. Lacking supernatural sanctions, the drive to live a systemized moral life was further exacerbated by new uncertainties about personal moral efficacy. Anglo-Catholicism offered relief not merely in its elevation of the theatrical over the introspective—that appeal was common to much of urban Protestantism—but more especially in its stress on sacramental observance. Sacramentalism reinstated what Weber called "the very human Catholic cycle of sin, repentance, atonement, release, followed by renewed sin." To the Anglo-Catholic believer, sacramental observance became an end in itself: it withdrew the practitioner from the market morality of secularized Calvinism and cancelled the necessity of spiritual bookkeeping. The Anglo-Catholic, like his medieval predecessor, was able to live ethically from hand to mouth.[40]

By easing ethical strenuosity and loosening the dictates of the modern superego, the flight from market morality promoted worldly accommodation. High Church Anglicanism seemed a perfect religion for the man of affairs. George Wharton Pepper, a Philadelphia lawyer and vestryman at St. Marks' for more than fifty years, typified the activist Anglican. Throughout his life he urged vigorous action and the cultivation of manly virtues as antidotes to paralyzing self-consciousness. As Pepper wrote in his autobiography, "it is not in analysis but in actual experience that the power of the Sacrament is to be found." Having abjured introspection he was free to make his way in the world. Pepper's attitude illustrates the sociological commonplace that highly institutionalized, sacramental religions legitimate the communicant's place in the existing social order.[41]

The problem with this commonplace is that it applies primarily to homogenous, traditional societies. To be sure, there were many Anglo-Catholics like Pepper, combining sacramentalism with acceptance of the modern world. But in a complex, secularizing society like the late-nineteenth-century United States, where many public rituals were either disappearing or becoming civil rather than religious, Anglo-Catholicism could focus a variety of challenges to the dominant culture. Many Anglo-Catholic churchmen, dissenting from mainstream traditions in Episcopalian theology, fought hard against the Broad Church establishment; a number used sacramentalism as a polemical weapon against modern industrial society. American Anglo-Catholicism frequently led not to legitimation of the secular order but to rebellion against it—a rebellion that, like other dissents from modernity, often remained intertwined with the culture it attacked.

Anglo-Catholics led in developing an Episcopalian social gospel. Unlike evangelical reformers, who attacked slavery and alcohol for contaminating the sanctity of the individual will, Episcopalians stressed group rights and duties. High and Broad Churchmen alike insisted on the responsibilities of the rich for the poor, of workingmen for one another, and of the church for the entire society.[42] But for Anglo-Catholics especially, there remained important tensions between Catholic corporatism and the centrifugal tendencies of liberal culture.

One can see those tensions in the difficulties of Anglican monasticism in America. The Society of St. John the Evangelist, founded in 1866 at Cowley (near Oxford) by British and American priests, was a monastic order devoted to missionary preaching and conducting retreats; it required the traditional vows of poverty, chastity, and obedience. But obedience broke down when the Americans returned to this country and found themselves caught between conflicting loyalties toward their American bishop and their monastic superior in England. Ambivalent toward medieval precedents, the American Cowley Fathers longed for religious community but feared an autonomous monastic order as a potential source of corruption. They remained a loosely organized band of individuals, whose vows of obedience were complicated by a dual system of authority.[43]

The most successful Cowley Fathers were two Englishmen, Arthur C. A. Hall and Charles Neale Field. Hall retained close ties to Boston's Anglophile elite but also widened S.S.J.E. concerns to include the back streets and slums near his Bowdoin Street church, where he organized reading rooms and liturgical festivals for the poor. Field was sent to St. Clement's, Philadelphia, where in 1883 he and twelve workingmen founded the Guild of the Iron Cross—an organization which backed labor unions, campaigned for shorter work weeks, arranged holiday outings for factory hands, and in general sought "to unite capital and labor in a spirit of mutual understanding and good will." Sometimes naively paternalistic, Field and Hall tried hard to wed traditional monastic asceticism and the nineteenth-century humanitarianism of the nascent social gospel.[44]

The difficulties of sustaining that union emerged clearly in the other monastic order founded during the late nineteenth century, the Order of the Holy Cross. James Huntington, son of the Broad Church bishop Frederic Dan Huntington, professed his vows as the Order's first member in 1884. A disciple of Henry George, Huntington moved to the slums of lower Manhattan, joined the Knights of Labor, and organized the Church Association for the Advancement of the Interests of Labor—the first Protestant group to defend labor's right to organize. Huntington hoped for a monastic order devoted to social justice, but after ten years he had attracted only two other monks. He decided to withdraw with them into a more contemplative life. On small farms near Westminster, Maryland, and later near West Park, New York, the Order of the Holy Cross grew slowly, conforming increasingly to traditional patterns of otherworldly monasticism.[45]

Huntington's experience, together with the difficulties of the S.S.J.E., suggests that Anglican monasticism may have been more effective as a means of religious protest than as a vehicle for social reform. Even successful reformers like Hall and Field were hampered by idealistic and individualistic assumptions. Like the postmillennial dreams of the craft leaders, the Cowley Fathers' hopes for Christianizing the social order easily degenerated into a bland faith in "industrial cooperation." But monasticism as a disciplined, ascetic way of life offered an eloquent witness against the emerging culture of comfort and convenience. As William James said, monastic asceticism insisted that the "real wrongness in the world" was not to be exorcised by progressive incantations.

A similar point can be made about Anglo-Catholicism in general. It was strongest where it was most concerned with religious convictions. Secular-minded historians have missed a fundamental point: many Anglo-Catholics took both their morality and their theology seriously. They were implacable enemies both of the incipient "fun morality" preached by Smooth-It-Aways like Beecher, and of the evolutionary Broad Church theology embodied in *Lux Mundi* (1889). In part, Anglo-Catholic protest recalled traditional republican moralism. In his sermons at New York's Trinity Church, the Reverend Morgan Dix included traditional complaints about "overindulgence" and "selfish luxury" alongside a newer attack on "the whole machinery which builds up cold, heartless, highly-cultured, conceited, voluptuous lovers of themselves, despisers of the brethren, doubters of God."[46] By the late nineteenth century, this was standard language for backcountry fundamentalists, but not for the shepherds of fashionable urban flocks.

Unlike fundamentalists or other republican moralists, High Churchmen allied their attacks on modernity with Catholic theology. Their ritualism exalted not spectacle but sacrament. Insisting on the objective validity of the sacraments as "the perpetual Incarnation of God on earth, wrought by the marvelous miracles of Font and Altar," they believed that the sacraments were the limbs of Christ's Mystical Body, redeeming man from spiritual powerlessness. Anglo-Catholic sacramentalism counteracted feelings of moral impotence by affirming the possibility of mediation between God and man. Long denied by the Calvinist tradition, mediation not only broke the endless chain of "morbid introspection"; it also restored some tension between the natural and the supernatural. Immanentist theology had relaxed that tension by postulating a Divine plan unfolding in Nature. Sacramentalist theology, by providing rituals to propitiate a God Who was wholly Other, revived the transcendent dimension of worship. High Church theologians believed that Anglo-Catholic services generated "an unspeakable awe, derived from realization of the supernatural" which was unavailable in the "decorated Humanitarianism" of liberal Protestantism.[47]

At its most profound, Anglo-Catholic sacramentalism suggested premodern alternatives to liberal theology. Like the fascination with fairy tales and folk beliefs, sacramentalism embodied an effort to preserve a sense of the miraculous in a disenchanted world. Yet, while Anglo-Catholicism and the folk tale vogue overlapped, there was an important difference between them. Many folk tale enthusiasts remained vicarious participants in a vague supernaturalism; Anglo-Catholics wanted not Wonderland but heaven, and they sought it through their sacraments, especially the Eucharist. Though they stopped short of transubstantiation, Anglo-Catholics insisted that the consecrated bread and wine contained the "Real Objective Presence" of God. The distinction between transubstantiation and the Real Presence was important to theologians, but the same hunger for the miraculous characterized both beliefs. The Anglo-Catholic priest, though more prudent in his claims that his Roman counterpart, was nonetheless a miracle worker. And that was an honorable task amid the spiritual devastation wrought by modern culture. In the largest sense, Anglo-Catholicism can be linked to the crisis of cultural authority not merely as a device for easing social and psychic tensions, but also as part of the transatlantic revolt against positivism.

For a fuller understanding of the fascination with Catholic forms, we need to move beyond historical generalization and examine biographical details. I have chosen to look closely at Ralph Adams Cram and Vida Scudder, two Anglo-Catholics who used their similar religious convictions to formulate two very different critiques of modern culture and society. Remaining enmeshed in modern culture while struggling to transcend it, their careers not only reveal characteristic dilemmas of antimodern dissent but also illuminate the complex meanings of Catholic forms in the lives of individual Americans.

# The Poles of Anglicanism: Cram and Scudder

Ralph Adams Cram was one of the most prolific American architects of the last hundred years; he was also an ardent Anglo-Catholic and medievalist who left dozens of Gothic monuments throughout the United States. The Graduate Center at Princeton; the Post Headquarters at West Point; the Westhampton campus at the University of Richmond; the chapel of St. George's School in Newport, Rhode Island; the cathedrals of St. Alban's in Washington, D.C., and St. John the Divine in New York City—these were only a few of Cram's many designs. He also left a score of books, nearly all filled with firebreathing polemics against modern culture. Since Cram's death in 1942, historians have dismissed him as an elitist crank, a reactionary in art and politics. In doing so, they have oversimplified Cram's lifelong work and overlooked its connections with the wider antimodern response to the crisis of cultural authority.[48]

Cram was born in Hampton Falls, New Hampshire, in 1863. His family background shaped his adult thinking. The grandson of a farmer he revered as "the last of the squires," the son of a Unitarian minister with transcendentalist leanings, Cram later displayed a consistent fondness for rural patriarchy and a tendency toward Platonic idealism. But his early passion was for drawing, and since his family could not afford to send him to college, he went to Boston in 1881 to learn architecture through apprenticeship.[49]

In Boston, Cram fell in with other young men from the provinces who had professional or artistic ambitions. With the architect Bertram Good-hue (who later became his partner), and the publishers Herbert Copeland and Fred Holland Day, Cram dabbled in royalism and Christian socialism, burned incense in honor of the Lady Isis, and composed imitative verse *pour épater le bourgeoisie*. Though Cram wrote short stories espousing a decadent "gospel of inaction," he was buoyed by the optimistic belief that he was beginning his career during a period of renewed idealism and religious faith. "We felt that we were surrounded by a cloud of witnesses, and so we were," he recalled. The cloud of witnesses included such influential medievalists as Norton, Ruskin, Morris, the English Pre-Raphaelites, and Wagner.[50]

Yet Cram remained a religious doubter, vacillating between "a respectable Deism" and "Oriental occultism of the Madame Blavatsky type" until he went to Europe in 1886. As a cathedral pilgrimage, the trip became "not only apprenticeship, but revelation" for Cram. In religious disputes with an Anglo-Catholic companion, Cram admitted that "I could not argue with any deep confidence, because all the art of a thousand years, in which I was fast becoming immersed, was getting in its deadly work, and I was beginning to realize that, if it had validity, if it related itself to life, it was not the life of rationalism and physical science and liberal Unitarianism, but very specifically the life of the Catholic Church."[51] At midnight mass in a Roman Church, art and religion fused in a Catholic conversion experience.

> Suddenly came the bells striking the hour of midnight, and with the last clang the great organs and the choir burst into a melodious thunder of sound; the incense rose in clouds, filling the church with a veil of pale smoke; and the Mass proceeded to its climax with the offering of the Holy Sacrifice of the Body and Blood of Christ. I did not understand all of this with my mind, but I *understood.*[52]

Unwilling to embrace Roman Catholicism, the church of the immigrant, Cram adopted the more fashionable solution of High Church Anglicanism. He returned to the United States, joined the Church of the Advent, and became a close friend of Arthur Hall and other Boston Anglo-Catholics. His religious convictions coalesced into polemical zeal. In 1893, together with Goodhue and Copeland, Cram began to publish the *Knight Errant,* a short-lived magazine which briefly united a number of Boston medievalists. The first issue contained contributions from Norton and Guiney, as well as Cram's "On the Restoration of Idealism."[53]

Cram's essay set forth ideas he repeated and elaborated the rest of his life. During the Middle Ages, he assumed, a superior art had been rooted in a vital religious community; the modern decay of art resulted from the double destruction of religion and communal life. Though "the change from the spirit of the fourteenth to that of the sixteenth century came soft and unnoticed," its consequences were incalculable. By the nineteenth century, the West had fallen prey to "a riot of individualism" in artistic as well as intellectual and economic life. Yet Cram insisted that a "restoration of idealism" was underway. Pointing to Wagner, the English medievalists, and the Anglo-Catholic revival, he argued that the restoration would gather strength and power, "until at last, when that chaos has come which is the *reductio ad absurdum* of current individualism, the restored system of idealism shall quietly take its place, to build on the wide ruins of a mistaken civilization a new life more in harmony with law and justice."[54]

Like other antimodernists, Cram found alternatives to modern fragmentation in traditional Japan as well as medieval Europe. He visited Japan in 1900 and celebrated its culture in *Impressions of Japanese Architecture and the Allied Arts* (1905). Japanese art, in Cram's view, reflected the same communal religious feeling embodied in the Gothic cathedral. But Westernizing influences, by pulling up the roots of Japanese culture, were destroying the sources of art. Beauty was disappearing from modernizing Japan. "In three centuries we have sold our birthright for a mess of pottage," Cram wrote. "Japan bartered hers in less than forty years."[55]

Even if Japanese art had been flourishing, it was still too remote from Western Christianity to represent a directly inspiriting example. Instead, Cram declared, antimodern idealists must turn to the Middle Ages. In scores of polemics published between the turn of the century and World War I, Cram presented medieval Europe as an aesthetic, religious, and social paradise lost where all men were artists, all women revered, and all social classes bound in an "organic," deferential social order.[56]

Ironically, Cram's medievalist fantasies animated an increasingly successful architectural career. During the early years of the twentieth century, his firm steadily built a national reputation, winning contracts with West Point, Princeton, and the Episcopal Diocese of New York. His assaults on modern culture continued. His Gothic architectural designs allowed him to join his polemical concerns with his professional role. Seeking his father's vocation through aesthetic achievement, Cram proclaimed "the ministry of art" and spiritualized his work in Platonic terms as an effort to achieve absolute Beauty. Like republican and Ruskinian moralists before him, Cram held that aesthetics and morality were inseparable. In general, "the unbeautiful or the ugly thing is the thing of the wrong or evil shape, whether in art or religion, philosophy, government, or the social fabric."[57]

Cram's aesthetic emphasis betrayed a new relation between art and morality. He departed from the conventional insistence that art must justify itself as uplift. In his view, one did not proceed from absolute moral principles to an evaluation of art. Instead one reversed the procedure: aesthetic judgments preceded and shaped moral judgments. Beauty was an infallible gauge of moral worth.

Cram's developing outlook undergirded aestheticism, Ruskinian moralism, and Platonic idealism with Anglo-Catholic theology. He embraced with Lewis Mumford, the Nashville Agrarians, and other critics of industrial society. Still a prolific designer, he remained hopeful that his buildings not only symbolized a dissent from modernity, but also heralded a postmodern spiritual revival.[63]

In the 1930s as in the 1890s, Cram's antimodernism was a response to cultural dilemmas which had first surfaced during the late nineteenth century. Rising to sacramental heights, his polemics were rooted in traditional republican fears of luxury. From his earliest essays, he assaulted modern culture for its deification of "purely material and enervating bodily comfort." He hoped that the First World War might purify an overcivilized Western world, and in *Walled Towns* he warned that "the suffocating qualities of gross luxuriance are sometimes more fatal than the desperate sensations of danger, adversity, and shame."[64] The vision of a flaccid "mass man," morally enervated and glutted with convenience, haunted Cram throughout his career.

Scarred by elitism, Cram's dissent nevertheless articulated widespread and still unresolved dissatisfactions. His faith in sacramental mediation spoke to widespread feelings of moral and spiritual impotence. For the politically impotent, he had less to offer. In formulating his decentralist alternatives, he revealed a concern for salvaging personal morality and an indifference to lower-class powerlessness—qualities shared by many European critics of mass society. The growth of giant organizations, Cram charged, had reduced the individual to "a negligible point in a vast and abstract proposition where all personal relationship, personal duty, personal obligation are impossible." He urged the renovation of the "small, manageable, and personal group," not to empower people rendered politically helpless, but to restore in them a sense of individual moral responsibility. Like the post–World War II sociologists for whom the "community" and the "voluntary association" became panaceas, Cram remained insensitive to class domination in capitalist societies.[65] Yet his political aims, though narrow, were not trivial.

Cram's sacramental eclecticism embodied an equally important purpose: the regeneration of traditional Christian symbols amid a corrosive eclecticism. The late-Victorian concern with archaeological correctness represented a general reaction against the devaluation of symbols, but Cram fought that process more explicitly by insisting that Gothic be used only for appropriate institutions. Like Jung, Cram understood the importance of inherited cultural symbols. "Without these, men cannot live, nor can society endure," he wrote in 1918. His polemical efforts involved far more than a crusade for "good taste"; they were a protest against the symbolic impoverishment of a secularizing culture. And, unlike Jung, Cram knew that the revaluation of Christian symbols was not enough. Christian belief had to undergird them. Cram's Anglo-Catholic commitments reinforced and completed his antimodern dissent.[66]

An irony remained. Cram's sacramental rationale for his professional role concealed entangling alliances with modernity. Against the background of his busy firm, his primitivist pretensions sometimes seemed a little hollow. When he designed the chapel at Whitehall, his country estate, in 1910, he claimed that "the guiding idea was to think and work as would pious but quite ignorant peasants who knew nothing about architecture. . . ." The affectation was apparent. Cram knew a great deal about architecture—both as an art and as a business. Though he sought to emulate the medieval artist's service to God, he often resembled the Renaissance artist, whom he stigmatized as a "mouthpiece and servant" of wealth. Indeed, Cram sustained an exceptionally warm relationship with the patronage establishment. He refused to recognize that his patrons may have preferred Gothic for reasons different from his own, refused to acknowledge that he often designed premodern buildings to house modern institutions. Clinging to his sacramental self-justification, Cram overlooked the indissoluble links between "Gothic" institutions and the commercial society he professed to despise.[67]

However entangled with bourgeois institutions, Cram's Anglo-Catholic medievalism nevertheless generated a thoroughgoing corporatist critique of centrifugal liberalism. The same corporatist emphasis marked the work of Cram's contemporary, Vida Dutton Scudder. But while Cram took corporatism in a conservative direction, toward an exaltation of hierarchy and stability, Scudder declared herself a Christian socialist. In her political and religious polemics, as well as in her popularized biographies of medieval saints, she used Anglo-Catholic sacramentalism as the basis for an assault on "Protestant individualism." Scudder's social criticism also had psychological significance. Her career reveals characteristic late-Victorian tensions between activism and quiescence, mastery and surrender—tensions which Anglo-Catholicism focused but left unresolved. By looking briefly but closely at her life, we can begin to see some connections between the public and private dimensions of the crisis of cultural authority—between the evasive banality of modern culture and the questionings it provoked in individual lives.

Scudder's family background linked her to changing New England traditions. Her uncle, Horace Scudder, was an editor of the *Atlantic Monthly;* her father, David Coit Scudder, was a Congregational missionary to India, a student of Max Müller's translations of Oriental lore. Vida was born in India in 1861. Three months later her father drowned there, and her mother, Florence Dutton, returned with her to Auburndale, Massachusetts. The Dutton family professed a benevolent Broad Church creed. "The stern terrors of Calvinism . . . passed me by," Scudder wrote in her autobiography, recalling her mother's devotion to the teachings of Phillips Brooks. The young girl slipped almost effortlessly into Episcopalian adulthood.[68]

Yet she became troubled by religious doubts during her college days at Smith, and a gradual movement into Anglo-Catholicism brought only partial relief. Unlike Cram, Scudder remembered no immediate, momentous conversion. But in both cases exposure to European art and ritual proved the catalyst for Catholic belief. "Cathedrals, sacred art, liturgies, biographies, bore a witness I could not repudiate," Scudder recalled. "They pointed me toward a life which had been neither chaotic, negative, nor suffocated by formulae, but sweetly ordered through the acceptance of supernatural verities."[69]

Though Scudder made her first trip abroad when she was eight years old, her crucial encounter with Europe occurred after she graduated from college in 1883, when, with her best friend Clara French and their mothers, she journeyed to Oxford. For Scudder, Oxford brought "a passionate sense . . . that the middle ages rather than the nineteenth century were my natural home, but she also paradoxically brought initiation into the mood of prophecy." Homesickness for the Middle Ages stemmed from the Anglo-Catholic revival, "the mood of prophecy" from the lectures of John Ruskin, who was still promoting discontent with bourgeois modernity. Scudder, feeling "a desperate wish to do violence to myself" and "an intolerable stabbing pain" at her privileged lot, joined the Salvation Army. But the pain soon subsided to a "dull ache," and Scudder returned to Boston with a love for Catholic tradition and a vague desire to write.[70]

She wrote magazine essays, travel sketches with medieval settings, even a fairy tale. But she remained dissatisfied. The polite culture of literary appreciation and lectures to women's clubs oppressed her.[71] Like so many of her contemporaries, Scudder felt that authentic experience was eluding her. Her drive to link Anglo-Catholicism and social action was not simply an attempt to assuage the guilt she felt about her privileged status, but an effort to escape from the web of words into "real life."

"From my babyhood on," Scudder wrote, "I had encountered too much at second hand. I had saturated myself with the records of life at its most dramatic and passionate; novels, poetry, drama, religious treatises, biographies, heaped up pell-mell in my girlish mind." Gradually she realized that she had never experienced the "great emotions" described in those books; the recognition underlay her youthful attacks on the "imitative life" fostered by polite education. In 1890, writing in the *Andover Review,* she complained of her college generation that "We lead sham lives in our youth, and the sham knowledge deadens for us the reality." For Scudder as for other late Victorians, the word "reality" had a talismanic significance.[72]

Scudder's quest for reality involved more than a recoil from literature to life. It had a metaphysical dimension as well. A dread of solipsism, a "puzzling, distressing sense of unreality" haunted her from earliest childhood. As a little girl, she would often disconcert her mother by running her hands through a bed of nettles, "dancing up and down with the sting. 'I *like* it so!' the child would cry. Delicious, reassuring sting, witnessing to actual existence outside oneself!" By the time Scudder was sixteen the sense of unreality "took definite nightmare form." "Oh God, if there be a God," she prayed, "make me a real person!" She repeated that prayer throughout her adult life.[73]

Ambiguous prayers were not enough. Scudder sought other ways of allaying her solipsistic dread. One was a traditional solution to problems of epistemological doubt: involvement with other people. David Hume, when he began to doubt his own existence, fled from the solitude of his study to the conviviality of his billiard room. Scudder, with characteristic late-Victorian intensity, turned to more intimate personal relationships. "Marriage, as I had always serenely expected, without regrets, was not for me," Scudder wrote—but friendship was another matter. Scudder's bond with Clara French became her chief source of psychic stability. When both received teaching appointments at Wellesley, they were exhilarated. From earliest days at Smith they had dreamed of working together. Then, in 1888, French died of typhoid fever. From that day, Scudder said, "the door to what is called passion swung to in my heart." She formed other friendships, but none as intense as that with French. She never had a love affair or "sex interests." Though she continued to maintain that "friendship is a definitive experience of reality," Scudder sought reality elsewhere.[74]

One path led toward social activism. This was the way of the young Salvation Army member and the little girl grasping the nettles. During the 1890s, Scudder immersed herself in settlement-house work. She spoke frequently to religious and academic groups on "The Relation of College Women to Social Need"; she helped organize the College Settlement Association and Denison House in Boston. Like Jane Addams and other educated late-Victorian women, Scudder embraced settlement work as a "subjective necessity." The "gracious manners, regular meals, comfort, security, good taste" of bourgeois life created a pleasant atmosphere. "Yet sometimes it suffocated me," Scudder recalled. "Were not the workers, the poor, nearer perhaps than we to the reality I was always seeking?"[75]

But settlement work did not provide the hard, physical test Scudder was searching. She began to crusade for the Simple Life. In 1898, she complained that "our comfort stifles us, the elaborate forms and objects that surround us lay on us an unbearable burden, and we realize that would we gain once more the free heart of the child, we must return to child conditions." The most appropriate model of childlike simplicity was St. Francis of Assisi, who seemed to unite Scudder's Catholic and socialist ideals. She read Sabatier's *Vie,* and later journeyed reverently to Assisi. By 1900, "the call of Lady Poverty rang clear. . . . The comfort and security of my life, the beauty of the Wellesley campus, the charm of my pleasant home, filled me with loathing."[76] Yet Scudder remained at Wellesley, in order to provide financial support for her mother. The decision left her anxious and filled with uneasy self-mockery.

If neither social activism nor friendship proved satisfactory routes to reality, religion pointed a third way. Soon after Clara French died, Scudder joined the Companionship of the Holy Cross, a group of Anglican women dedicated to intercessory prayer. In later years, while she was torn between her life at Wellesley and some more exacting (but undefined) social commitment, she sought spiritual guidance from Arthur Hall and James Huntington. She remained a faithful member of St. Stephen's Anglo-Catholic Church in Wellesley, though incapable of personal certitude.[77] Her developing religious thought pervaded her writings from the 1890s on. It underlay her efforts to link socialism and Anglo-Catholic sacramentalism; it informed her treatment of medieval character. An examination of Scudder's polemical themes reveals the complex relation between her medievalism and her continuing quarrel with modern unreality.

In her early essays, Scudder juxtaposed medieval vitality against modern enervation; the contrast had both moral and psychological significance. On the one hand, it was a rebuke to institutional Christianity for losing the sense of evil, and declining into evasive banality. "We are suffering," she wrote in 1902, "from a diffusion of Christianity at the cost of its intensity." The Middle Ages, in her judgment a time of "violent contrasts," were in some ways preferable to "these days, when we are all reduced to one apparent level of moral respectability, and great saintliness and dramatic guilt are alike seldom conspicuous. . . ." Where sin was banished, saintliness grew obsolescent.[78]

On the other hand, Scudder's fondness for medieval vitality was a primitivist antidote to her own recurrent bouts of neurasthenia. During her postgraduate Oxford days, whenever she had shown signs of an impending breakdown, her mother had whisked her off to Cornwall or Devon. In those places, Scudder recalled, "the spirit of Arthurian romance first became potent in me." She devoted much of her teaching, and in 1917 a lengthy book, to the study of the *Morte Darthur*. Seeking the breath of "untutored childhood," she found it in medieval fantasy, which seemed "a spontaneous product of primitive man with its inexplicable world." The Middle Ages provided temporary escape from self-conscious adulthood.[79]

Around the turn of the century, Scudder began to focus on a certain kind of medieval mysticism—"not of the Celtic type, nurtured on fantastic shadows, far less of that Oriental type which creates around itself a void," but rather a mingling of mysticism and realism which "charges . . . facts with a vision-like solemnity, and uplifts them into enduring significance." It was, in other words, a sacramental mysticism. As she wrote of a disciple of Catherine of Siena, "the earth was to him no finality on the one hand, no illusion on the other, but image or sacrament of the Unseen." The medieval characters Scudder most admired—William of Langland, Catherine of Siena, the early Franciscans—all were sacramental mystics.[80]

For Scudder, sacramental mysticism seemed to reconcile her impulse toward social engagement with an emerging desire for mystical quiescence and retreat. This latter feeling had remained latent during much of her youth, but it surfaced and strengthened as she grew older. Since adolescence, perhaps influenced by her father's death in India (a land of mystical passivity in religion), Scudder had had a recurring dream of drowning. She resisted, only to be swept further down until she obeyed an inner voice which told her to "Let go!" Then she awakened, at peace. The dream became more meaningful for her in March, 1901, during the period she was struggling with her desire for activist social commitment. "On the train home one evening," she recalled, "something crashed in my head." She was bedridden for weeks with shooting pains in her head, for which the doctors could find no organic cause. Gradually, she began to heed the advice of Charles Brent, rector of her church, who "told me not to whip myself into any activity, even spiritual; bade me sink as far as I could into non-existence." Ultimately, the lesson of both dream and breakdown seemed clear to her: the profoundest reality was attainable not through struggle but through surrender; the "acceptance of emptiness and the negation of desire" alone brought lasting peace.[81]

Yet that conclusion was never fully satisfying to Scudder, even in her old age. And during her middle years she groped continually to synthesize struggle and quietistic withdrawal, using the sacramental mystics to focus her efforts. Catherine, in Scudder's eyes, "is one of the purest of contemplatives; she knows, what we to-day too often forget, that the task is impossible without the vision. But it follows directly upon the vision, and this great medieval mystic is one of the most efficient characters of her age."[82] She felt the same was true of Francis and his followers. These syntheses were intellectually complete but emotionally unsatisfying. Scudder remained divided between contemplative urges and the desire to be an "efficient character" in the service of social reform. She never embraced Lady Poverty; she remained outside the mystic experience. In her approaches to both mysticism and social activism, Scudder remained tormented by the demon of secondhand experience.

Yet in her writing, she continued her synthesizing efforts. From *Socialism and Character* (1912) to the hagiographical *Father Huntington* (1940), Scudder tried to wed Catholicism and Marxism in sacramental union. Equating Marxism with economic determinism, she argued that "more and more, Christians recognize that a sacramental conception of reality involves acceptance of much truth in economic determinism." The linkage never involved more than vague assertions: Scudder was no theorist. She insisted that the physical basis of life, as the embodiment of divine Reality, must not be ignored by those concerned with "higher" things. At the same time she feared moral enervation under "the monotonous level of external well-being which socialism proposes." Life without struggle was unthinkable, even in a socialist utopia.[83]

There remained the difficulty of reconciling a stress on material determinants with a Catholic faith in free will. Scudder solved it by embracing a kind of evolutionary idealism. "These 'determined,' these automatic forces, which mechanically generate our passions and power—may they not themselves be messengers, fulfilling a central Will?" she asked. In this Will was her peace. "Paradoxical as it may seem," Scudder announced, "we can become intelligent co-workers with destiny only when we abandon belief that we are responsible for creating it." To be free was to cooperate in the unfolding divine plan.[84]

Scudder's ambitious design lacked polemical force; it suffered from a pervasive blandness. This difficulty stemmed in part from her limp prose style, in part from her continual efforts to harmonize opposites in ever-hopeful conclusions. Behind the synthesizing impulse lay a persistent faith in progress. Despite her use of Catholic theology, she shared with liberal Protestants a faith in "that mighty sweep of the ages which, as we trust, is carrying the race upward." Belief in progress narrowed her approach to the Middle Ages; her medievalism focused on figures who seemed to anticipate twentieth-century enthusiasms for socialism and mysticism. Past and present, like Catholicism and Marxism, blended in the broth of progressive optimism.[85]

Fear of isolation from "reality" combined with idealist postmillennialism to blunt Scudder's social criticism. She endowed virtually all "practical" activity—"Scientific efficiency, the conservation of natural forces, the study how to increase riches most sanely, abundantly, and swiftly" with an aura of spirituality. For leaders of her cooperative commonwealth, she looked not to socialist agitators but to practical reformers—the managers and administrators of philanthropic enterprises. Nor could she join other socialists in opposing World War I. Sensitive to "the stages in the slow ethical ascent of humanity," Scudder was "unwilling to cast on the scrap heap the ancient record of the glorious virtues engendered by war." Arthurian knights, as well as American doughboys, had convinced her that "fighting is the condition of real living. . . ." Fretfully yearning for submission to an oceanic realm of passivity, Scudder always pulled up short. A "haunting sense of futility and uselessness" revived her zest for struggle and led her to crucial compromises with modern culture.[86]

But if the impulse to struggle vitiated Scudder's social thought, it deepened her religious witness. Despite her lifelong hopes, she was unable to attain spiritual peace through surrender—partly because she rejected the passivity of the conventional female role, partly because she remained a religious doubter. Flight to the arms of a nurturing Mother Church never stilled her fears of a "blank nescience" surrounding all human action. Like other late Victorians, she admired but could not share the faith of the medieval peasant. Yet she was no tourist of the supernatural. If she failed to experience the mystical raptures she described, she was frank to acknowledge her difficulty. Ultimately she sought neither to banish doubt nor to play at belief. Alongside Miguel de Unamuno, with whom she claimed a spiritual kinship, Scudder occupied the territory between despair and hope.[87] Rejecting the evasive banality of modern culture, she accepted inner conflict as the essential condition of religious life in the modern world. This was her most lasting achievement.

Probably Scudder's fortitude was idiosyncratic, but her stoical faith undercuts reductionist interpretations of High Church Anglicanism. Neither church-sect typology nor evolutionist psychology explains the fascination with Catholic forms. Energized by a serious search for faith, the movement toward Catholicism could be more than a quest for prestige or authority, more than a flight from "mature" autonomy to "childish" dependence. It could be an effort to overcome doubt by encountering the mystery of faith, in the daily miracle of the Eucharist. In the emerging culture of the twentieth-century United States, that effort had profound religious significance. Scudder's example, however lonely, remained formidable.

If Scudder's stoical faith was idiosyncratic, her vacillation between engagement and withdrawal was a common late-Victorian phenomenon. It affected the eminent and the obscure, the housewife and the man of affairs. At its most extreme, this pattern could be characterized as manic-depressive psychosis, which according to one psychiatric study has been particularly widespread among prominent Northeastern families since the mid–nineteenth century.[88] More commonly it emerged in lives of relentless achievement punctuated by frequent bouts of nervous prostration. The devotee of action was also the helpless neurasthenic. People of prodigious energy and omniverous curiosity, who filled bookshelves with their collected works, were liable to lapse into bedridden immobility for weeks or months at a time—sometimes plagued by mysterious pains, sometimes simply too weak to move.

Whatever its specific pattern, the pervasive ambivalence had far-reaching significance. It energized the shifts of antimodernists between premodern will and premodern quiescence; it pointed to some of the most profound tensions in late-Victorian culture. The origin of those tensions lay in the contradictory dictates of the modern superego, which were internalized but also challenged in the bourgeois family. Family conflicts shaped the dominant pattern of Victorian ambivalence and the quest for antimodern alternatives to it. In what follows, by exploring the paths to adulthood chosen by several antimodern thinkers, I hope to illuminate the connections between widespread psychic ambivalence and Janus-faced antimodernism—between tensions in individual families and the wider crisis of cultural authority.

# ·6·

# FROM PATRIARCHY TO NIRVANA: PATTERNS OF AMBIVALENCE

A S A SEEKER OF DOUBLE MEANINGS, FREUD FOUND
ambivalence everywhere. The concept grew from one of his most
important insights: the recognition that character traits were not
fixed and separate but fluid and intermingled. Convinced that personality
embraced opposites, Freud emphasized the inner rage behind the meek
demeanor, the desire for submission behind the wish to be free. Exploring
the dialectic between latent impulse and manifest behavior, he insisted that
ambivalence is woven into the structure of the self.[1]

But if ambivalence is universal, certain patterns of ambivalence resonate
with special force at particular historical moments. During the Victorian
era, the conflict between engagement and withdrawal was one such pattern. It embodied profound cultural tensions—between the conflicting
ego-ideals of autonomy and dependence, between commitment to the
superego and resentment against its contradictory demands. In the triumphant bourgeois culture of the nineteenth century, to be engaged in practical affairs was to be in the world of men, where conscious control and
autonomous achievement were most highly prized. To withdraw from that
realm was to enter the feminine sphere, which had its own restrictive ideals
but which tended to sanction passive leisure and emotional dependence.
Within most Victorians, impulses toward both autonomy and dependence
jostled for predominance. Those who outwardly conformed were often
inwardly ambivalent. Even the most conventionally successful male might
harbor longings for absolute quiescence.

At its most extreme, withdrawal was animated by the desire to abandon
autonomous selfhood and sink into a passive state of boundless union with
all being, by the wish to experience what Freud called an "oceanic feeling."
That yearning has existed at least as long as religious aspirations have been
recorded, but during the nineteenth century it acquired new psychological
and cultural significance. As the "feminine" side of the newly dominant
achievement ethos, it promised liberation from the systematic morality of
the male bourgeoisie. As the psychic counterpart of pantheism, it helped
to energize the romantic assault on the modern superego. Goethe advised
his followers to abandon futile striving and "Live in the All." Emerson took
up the cry, drawing on Oriental mysticism as well as Western idealism,
exalting union with the unconscious life of maples and ferns. By midcentury, many educated Americans had embraced an Emersonian revision of
republican pastoralism, accentuating man's dependence on a deified Nature.[2]

Yet the oceanic impulse remained only half of a double consciousness.
In the wider culture as well as the individual psyche, a drive toward autonomous action coexisted with a longing for dependent passivity. Alongside
pastoral poetry, magazines printed hymns to material progress. Maples
and ferns acquired greater romantic appeal as more were uprooted by
enterprising frontiersmen. Goethe's pantheism did not slow his productiv-

ity, nor did Emerson's paeans to Nature prevent him from venerating the frontiersman who subdued it. By remaining linked to activism, oceanic feelings helped to generate the pastoral haze which obscured the rise of industrial capitalism; they also incorporated temporary, revitalizing respites from achievement. They reinforced accommodation as well as protest.[3]

The same doubleness survived into the late-nineteenth-century crisis of cultural authority. Afflicted by a fragmenting sense of autonomous selfhood, late Victorians yearned increasingly for oceanic dependence—on the "great, everlasting currents" of mind cure, on the sacraments of a nurturing mother church, on mystical union with God. Though they often idealized premodern thought (especially its "unconscious" dimension), they remained committed to nineteenth-century values of autonomous achievement and conscious control.

Rooted in continuing ambivalence, the desires of antimodernists for dependence had complex effects. Like other antimodern vitalists, those who longed for oceanic boundlessness revealed an inchoate hostility to the modern superego—the internalized set of inhibitions which had become the articulated moral system of the ascendant bourgeoisie. By loosening rigid character ideals and creating more fluid possibilities for self-definition, the antimodern turn toward dependence helped to ease the transition from a Protestant to a therapeutic orientation within the dominant culture. Experiencing boundlessness in homeopathic doses, antimodernists vacillated between strenuosity and quiescence. Rejecting total dependence, they achieved revitalized autonomy. At the same time, their quests for boundless union had more than social significance. By exploring unconscious modes of perception, they joined both the revolt against a narrow positivist "reality" and the avant-garde search for new expressive forms. By reviving the *askesis* used in mystical practice, they bore witness against the spiritual desiccation of a rationalizing culture. Resistance as well as assimilation persisted; a Janus-faced antimodernism mirrored the ambivalence of the late-Victorian psyche.

At many points, the antimodern oscillation between autonomy and dependence reinforced the dominant pattern of ambivalence. To illuminate the variety of those connections, to suggest the relationships between cultural tensions and individual lives, we need to examine biographical detail. But before turning to individual antimodernists, I want to place the origins and development of their inner struggles within the wider realm of modern culture. The conflict between autonomy and dependence involved public ideology as well as private circumstance; it embodied questions of authority which were arising in both polity and family—and which have persisted to our own time. By concentrating on recurring patterns of ambivalence, I hope to realize one of my larger conceptual aims: to connect psychic with social change, the resolution (or nonresolution) of personal dilemmas with the revitalization and transformation of the dominant culture.

# The Problem of Victorian Ambivalence: Sources and Solutions

The problem of ambivalence reflected the dilemmas of authority in a liberal, democratic society. As feudal patriarchy had given way to bourgeois democracy, Protestant emphasis had shifted gradually but inexorably from God the Father to Christ His Son. In ways difficult to specify but nonetheless palpable and profound, the modernization of authority penetrated the family as well as the wider culture, providing unprecedented legitimacy for the revolt of democratic children against authoritarian fathers. Unprecedented, but not sufficient: traditional patterns of deference persisted; oedipal rebellion remained shrouded in moral ambiguity.

Protestant and liberal ideology corroded habits of deference to external authority, replaced them with an internalized morality of self-control, and enshrined the autonomous individual whose only master was himself. Contrary to the current popularizations of ego psychology, the individual's need to establish an independent identity is not a universal, timeless drive; it is largely a product of Western, bourgeois cultural norms. Yet those norms have never been wholly consistent. While liberalism and Protestantism required that one form an unshakable will, Christian tradition and social stability required that one continue to submit to the wills of others —not only to the electoral majority but also to parents. The father, especially, demanded allegiance. It was not surprising that many of the most intense conflicts over authority were fought in the bourgeois family.

Tensions were particularly severe within the family because nineteenth-century moralists had burdened it with huge and contradictory expectations. Embracing the family as the key agency for internalizing authority in a volatile culture, ideologues of domesticity expected the home to wall off children from a corrupt marketplace and to prepare them (especially if they were male) for success in that marketplace. In the bourgeois imagination, the family was both a haven of social harmony and a schoolhouse for competitive aspiration. On the one hand it encouraged dependence and filial loyalty; on the other it promoted self-assertion and achievement.[4]

Amid dual expectations, an independent identity—as much a shibboleth of liberal ideology in the nineteenth century as it is today—became a precarious accomplishment. It could often be established only by suppressing rebellious impulses and internalizing parental values. Autonomy was morally acceptable, in many cases, only on terms defined by the family. For many Victorians the process of identity formation generated intense and sometimes insoluble conflicts between autonomy and dependence.[5]

Those conflicts often persisted throughout life, because the contradictions in the domestic ideal affected adults as well as children. For Victorian women, the official role simultaneously demanded obedience to masculine will and the assertion of maternal strength. Men, too, faced problematic expectations—even though the father remained an unambiguous emblem of authority. Victorian males, constantly urged toward aggressive achievement in the public realm, were at the same time counselled to conform to female definitions of personal morality at home. The Christian Gentleman, like the True Woman, confronted a continuing conflict between individual assertion and domestic harmony.[6]

The dilemma was further exacerbated by the nineteenth-century division of sexual roles. The tendency to define autonomy as male and dependence as female made ambivalence especially severe among those for whom gender identity was most problematic: women who sought "masculine" careers in public life, men who nurtured "feminine" aspirations toward literature, art, or the increasingly "feminized" ministry. These were scrupulous and sensitive people. Perhaps more thoroughly than most of their contemporaries, they had internalized the dictates of the modern superego—including the contradictory domestic ideal.[7] And they were the most likely victims of nervous prostration.

Neurasthenia sometimes proved an appropriate means of sustaining the tensions in Victorian character. For those still plagued by lingering fears of material prosperity, invalidism helped to preserve a secularized, republican ethic of suffering in an expanding commercial society. The commitment to suffering as an end in itself generated enough moral energy to preserve the balance between engagement and withdrawal, as the ambivalent Victorian self oscillated between those two poles. By providing obstacles for the willful to overcome, nervous invalidism surrounded self-assertion with an aura of self-sacrifice. Under the shadow of neurasthenia, literary enterprise could seem as heroic as business enterprise. At the same time, neurasthenia could also provide medical sanctions for escapes into idleness. ("Sir Michael had gone to his dressing-room to prepare for dinner after a day of lazy enjoyment; that is perfectly legitimate for an invalid," wrote a Victorian novelist in 1862.)[8] Symbolizing inescapable pain, nervous invalidism could legitimize both autonomy and dependence. For many mid-Victorian neurasthenics, the orientation of the self became an emotional balancing act, energized by moral ardor derived from the ethic of suffering.

During the later decades of the nineteenth century, the balance proved increasingly difficult to maintain. Though the ethic of suffering was revived by Civil War ideologues and later by advocates of the strenuous life, it nevertheless seemed too weak to counteract the growing aversion to pain, the spreading material comfort, and the unprecedented confusion over personal moral responsibility among the urban middle classes. "Industrial man" lacked the stoical temper of his grandparents. By corroding faith in the moral will, social and psychic determinisms weakened the ethic of suffering; by blurring the boundaries of personal identity, the disintegration of the sense of autonomous selfhood undermined the ethic of suffering at its core.[9] Without a clear sense of self to sacrifice, how could one embrace a doctrine of self-sacrifice? If one felt driven to create (or make whole) a sense of selfhood, then self-denial was impossible and a quest for self-fulfillment a psychic necessity.

The decline in the ethic of suffering exacerbated the persistent problem of authority in the wider culture. The weakening sense of selfhood and personal moral responsibility undermined possibilities for internalizing authority; the softening of a supernatural framework of meaning cut off opportunities for submitting to external authority. By the 1880s and 1890s, neither autonomy nor dependence seemed any longer to possess moral or spiritual sanction. The individual seemed increasingly adrift in a boundless, weightless universe without the older bedrock of "reality."

In the context of a developing sense of moral crisis, the cultural significance of nervous invalidism changed. It could still provide opportunities for heroism, but its role as a rationalization for idleness became more suspect. As neurasthenia spread, and the duration of immobility lengthened, moralists interpreted the "epidemic" not only as a sign of overwork but also as a symptom of moral decay. By the turn of the century, to many observers, the Victorian balance seemed tipped from disciplined action toward self-indulgent passivity. The loss of equipoise made selfhood seem more diffuse and problematic than ever before.

Amid this spreading confusion, the fascination with premodern character had complex effects. For some, it reasserted the ethic of suffering, reestablished equipoise, and reaffirmed activist commitments. "How dull it is to pause, to make an end, to rust unburnish'd, not to shine in use!" Tennyson's Ulysses had complained in 1833, and many American critics of overcivilization repeated the sentiments at every opportunity. (In 1900, Theodore Roosevelt used the passage from "Ulysses" as the epigraph to *The Strenuous Life*.) But by the turn of the century, suffering was often less a means of character formation than another path to intense experience. As ethical frameworks softened, vitalism replaced stoicism. Action became its own reward; to pause was to risk falling prey to paralyzing self-doubts and anxieties.[10] Bounded by familiar moral values, the activist imperative helped to sustain the bourgeois ethic of self-control; energized by amoral vitalism, it promoted an activist version of therapeutic self-absorption—a fascination with "risk-taking" and "winning through intimidation" as ends in themselves.

At the same time, the vitalist apotheosis of spontaneity and energy could lead in less familiar directions, toward a "feminine" submission to an oceanic realm of feeling as well as a "masculine" reassertion of will. Merged with antimodern vitalism, the "feminine" ideal of dependence acquired a new cultural resonance. In the *fin-de-siècle* imagination, many of the "childlike" qualities associated with premodern character, and with the unconscious, were also linked with femininity: fantasy, spontaneity, aesthetic creativity. The premodern unconscious generated androgynous alternatives to bourgeois masculinity. Those options especially appealed to the men and women who were most restive under bourgeois definitions of gender identity, and who suffered most acutely from the fragmenting sense of selfhood.

If Americans were succumbing to a loss of conscious will, it was possible to discover in that loss a gain; if culture had been "feminized," it was possible to redefine femininity as a source of strength. The origins of that redefinition lay in the ideology of domesticity, which elevated the serene and self-possessed woman over the striving and ultimately self-defeated man. The *fin-de-siècle* imagination infused the pallid domestic ideal with vitalist imagery, merging images of childhood and femininity in a cult of inner experience which encouraged the shedding of rigid ego ideals through immersion in mystical or aesthetic contemplation. Often focusing on the "unconscious" qualities of premodern mental life, this cult of inner experience accelerated a subtle shift in the modernization process—a shift away from the producer values of self-control and autonomous achievement toward a more passive, leisure-oriented ethos appropriate to the maturing economy of consumer capitalism. Eager for liberation from Victorian constraints but lacking firm moral commitments outside the self, many Americans transformed mysticism and aestheticism into therapeutic cults of personal fulfillment. Far from being the nostalgic representatives of a "dying elite," these antimodernists were harbingers of important cultural change. The twentieth century's "revolution in manners and morals" was prepared unintentionally by religious seekers unable to transcend their immediate experience; and it proved less a "revolution" than a means of adjusting to a new and secular capitalist culture.

For all that, the antimodern cult of inner experience had complex personal meaning as well. One of my main purposes in this chapter is to show that the lure of the premodern unconscious cannot be fully explained either as a "reaction against modernization" or as a means of accommodation. It must be understood in all its idiosyncratic detail. For many *fin-de-siècle* seekers, the contemplative mode promised refuge from the endless dualisms of Victorian culture—subject and object, free will and determinism, mastery and submission—in a boundless union of self with all being.

Yet the turn toward dependence could create problems as well as solutions. Besides the fear of overstepping conventional gender boundaries there were more serious difficulties as well. Premodern mystical practice required ascetic discipline as well as "letting go"—a discipline affluent Americans found hard to sustain. Even if they ignored asceticism, the profoundest problem remained. The association of premodern character with the warm enveloping darkness of unconscious life suggested not only revivified life but also the unconsciousness of death. To submit to the oceanic feeling was finally to drown. Whatever their discontents, antimodern thinkers had internalized the achievement ethos. Those who failed to meet its demands were tormented by self-accusing, sometimes self-destructive impulses. Equating oceanic and suicidal impulses, they feared self-extinction in an oceanic unconscious. Despite premodern examples, the impulse to "let go" was rarely more than fleeting. The premodern unconscious proved less a resolution of ambivalence than a means of recasting it in new cultural forms.

The recasting process emerged in various ways. As I suggested in the previous chapter, Harold Frederic dramatized late-Victorian ambivalence in Theron Ware's vacillation between childlike dependence and intellectual autonomy, while Scudder embodied ambivalence in her oscillating attractions to engagement and withdrawal, progressive optimism and antimodern dissent. This chapter is concerned with six antimodernists whose lives revealed comparable patterns of ambivalence: William Sturgis Bigelow, George Cabot Lodge, Percival Lowell, Charles Eliot Norton, G. Stanley Hall, and Van Wyck Brooks. Since Bigelow and Brooks are in many ways the most suggestive for my purposes, I will deal with them at greatest length. But even my longer sketches do not pretend to be full psychological portraits. At the risk of seeming too schematic, I have bypassed some revealing details and some enticing opportunities for psychological speculation—all in an effort to highlight the larger pattern of ambivalence behind the individual variations.

These were all educated, middle- or upper-class men with a fondness for contemplation. Though most lacked the spur of necessity, all faced compelling family expectations of practical achievement in the world. All experienced periodic neurasthenia and ambivalent urges toward both autonomy and dependence; all felt constrained by conventional definitions of masculinity. And as familiar conceptions of selfhood eroded, all turned to premodern modes of mystical or aesthetic contemplation.

It would be absurd to suggest that these men were "representative Americans." Four were extraordinarily wealthy; all were highly educated and articulate. In fact, their privileged position makes their lives peculiarly significant for the history of the wider culture. As members of professional and cultural elites, they represented the highest aspirations of earlier republican ideologues; they constituted, in a sense, the "natural aristocracy" envisioned by Jefferson. Yet they felt ambivalent toward republican tradition and constrained by dominant values. Educated, articulate, they were the "point men" of modernization—the most polished products of a modern culture coming into its maturity. Yet they felt profoundly dissatisfied with that culture. As they groped for alternatives, their private struggles sometimes developed unintended public consequences. They portended a shift from republican moralism toward a twentieth-century culture of consumption. Here, at the level of individual conduct, one can most clearly see the interplay of accommodation and resistance in antimodernism.

As sensitive and self-conscious observers, these six men also articulated psychic needs felt by many of their less privileged contemporaries. Sometimes overtly, sometimes half-consciously, they sought to resolve contradictory impulses toward autonomy and dependence, to unify a fragmenting sense of selfhood, to preserve some ethical or religious framework amid evaporating creeds. In other words, they all confronted the crisis of cultural authority, yet each adopted a different strategy. Their antimodern dissents (like all antimodernism) resisted facile generalization. Their lives embodied six variations on a common theme, six varieties of antimodern experience.

Among these six men, the desire for oceanic dependence appeared in both medieval and Oriental forms, serving several functions. Norton, Hall, and Brooks all felt drawn to the aesthetic legacy of the medieval church; Bigelow, Lowell, and Lodge—the first three to be considered here—were all lured by visions of Nirvana. For all six, an ambivalent attraction to the unconscious qualities of premodern thought illuminated tensions between masculine and feminine ego ideals, and helped them to form new self-definitions at crucial points in their lives. And for each of the three Orientalists, difficulties in identity formation stemmed from conflict with paternal authority.

# The Lotus and the Father:
# Bigelow, Lowell, Lodge

## WILLIAM STURGIS BIGELOW

William Sturgis Bigelow (1850–1926) is remembered, if he is remembered at all, as an eccentric and faintly ridiculous Bostonian. To historians, his fascination with Japanese art and Buddhism has symbolized the spreading dilettantism of elite culture in the late nineteenth century. Notions of Bigelow's *préciosité* originated with his contemporaries. Edith Wharton marvelled that his "erudition so far exceeded his mental capacity"; Margaret Terry Chanler recalled him as a religious dandy and something of a fake: "Prematurely bald, he had a carefully tended beard and looked indescribably clean. At once an epicure and a mystic, he professed an ascetic religion and wore beautiful Charvet haberdashery and handsome English clothes. He was full of Buddhist lore and emanated a peaceful radiance mingled with a faint suggestion of toilet water."[11]

The image of Bigelow as dilettante is accurate but superficial. It caricatures the religious longings which led him to Buddhist lore; it ignores the complex sources and significance of his spiritual quest. A closer acquaintance with Bigelow's faith reveals important connections with the wider antimodern response to the crisis of cultural authority. A more thorough investigation of his life suggests strong parallels with the psychic conflicts of his antimodern contemporaries; it also discloses an element of tragedy.

Bigelow was born in Boston in 1850, under the heavy weight of ancestral accomplishment. His grandfather was Jacob Bigelow, an eminent physician and botanist, Professor of Applied Science at Harvard and President of the American Academy of Arts and Sciences. His father was Henry Jacob Bigelow, a distinguished surgeon at Massachusetts General Hospital, professor at Harvard Medical School, and almost a caricature of the self-reliant individual. Henry's obsessive struggle to get clear of his own father's shadow and establish an independent identity set an example which young Sturgis was unable to follow.[12]

When family friends advised Henry to follow his father's path and enter medical rather than surgical practice, the boy snapped, "I'll be damned if I won't be a surgeon!" By his late twenties, Henry was already establishing a reputation as an exacting martinet in the hospital. After he married Susan Sturgis in 1849, he abandoned social life for full-time pursuit of professional prominence. In Sturgis's memoir of his father, one glimpses a driven man who "intended to be the founder of his own fortune and to be dependent upon no one but himself for promotion."[13]

His father's brusque manner might have been counterbalanced by his mother's gentleness, but she died when Sturgis was three years old. One can only imagine the long-term effect of this loss on the small child. It may well have constituted the early trauma which predisposed Sturgis to his later depressive withdrawal. It may also have led him to fantasize a "feminine" ideal which focused his adult longings for the boundless dependence of Nirvana. In any case, it is clear that Susan Bigelow's death drove her husband even further into his work. His professional dedication, Sturgis remembered, made him seem "unmindful of the joys and sorrows of those among whom he was born and died." But his indifference to personal relations involved more than professional dedication. Henry Bigelow was a compulsively busy man, whose proliferating hobbies ranged from passenger pigeons to mechanical toys. On the rare occasions when he felt overworked, he "dropped everything and cleared out" on a shooting vacation.[14] His career of relentless achievement punctuated by occasional withdrawal fit the dominant pattern of Victorian ambivalence.

For young Sturgis, an only and motherless child, life with father must have been difficult. He grew up a shy and sensitive boy, surrounded by adoring aunts. Even when he and his father were on vacation together, the older man played a stern and monitory role. He discouraged Sturgis's tendency to create an elaborate fantasy life, gave him a shotgun and urged him to hunt, and in general shackled him to a narrow ideal of manliness.[15]

By his late teens, Sturgis seemed content with conventional upper-class education and ambitions. At Harvard, he was prankish and secular-minded, scientifically and socially adept. Upon graduation, he left Boston to study in Europe. He learned German in Dresden; anatomy, pathology, and microscopy with Waldzer in Strasbourg; and bacteriology with Pasteur in Paris.[16]

Bigelow's experience with Pasteur was the most important. By focussing the young student's professional ambitions, it generated the conflict with his father that shaped the rest of his life. When he had first applied to work in Pasteur's laboratory, Bigelow had admitted that he had no special skills. Pasteur declined his application. But while Bigelow was waiting to see Pasteur, he had noticed that the laboratory assistants were bungling their glassblowing. He apprenticed himself to a Parisian glassblower for several months, returned to Pasteur, and announced, "Now, Monsieur, I can blow glass." Pasteur accepted him, and Bigelow began the happiest and most productive period of his life.[17]

But when Bigelow returned to Boston in autumn of 1879, afire with enthusiasm for bacteriology, he faced the formidable obstacle of paternal opposition. Sturgis opened a private bacteriological laboratory at Pemberton Square, but his father gave him no encouragement and soon prevailed upon him to take the post of surgeon to outpatients at Massachusetts General Hospital and assistant in surgery at Harvard Medical School. The position presented several serious problems for Sturgis. He had no time for his primary research interests, no stomach for a surgeon's duties, and no respect for the antiquated surgical procedures followed by his father and the hospital staff. Henry Bigelow was so opposed to the teachings of Pasteur that Sturgis was not allowed to use the antiseptic techniques he had learned in Paris.[18]

Sturgis quickly lost interest in his work. As early as December, 1879, Marian Adams noted that he "sigh[ed] for Europe" during a visit to her Washington home. In January, 1881, according to Bigelow's biographer, "a breakdown of health necessitated giving up work." The nature of that breakdown was unclear. Throughout 1881, Bigelow drifted between Washington and Boston; he also managed to visit Vienna, where Wagner provided balm for his troubled spirit. It was a curiously mobile existence for a man whose health had supposedly broken down, but it was no stranger than many other cases of neurasthenia. Bigelow's problem was not paralysis of the body but paralysis of the will, an inability to act decisively. His withdrawal from active engagement with the world, like that of many other affluent invalids, took the form of protracted, restless travel.[19]

There is only fragmentary evidence about this crucial period in Bigelow's life. No correspondence with his father has survived. But it is possible to reconstruct the process which led to the breakdown. The basic clue lies in Erik Erikson's observation that often a parent selects "one child, because of an inner affinity paired with an insurmountable outer distance, as the particular child who must *justify the parent.*" Through an "all pervasive presence and brutal decisiveness of judgment," the parent pressures the child into a "fatal struggle for his own identity." Henry Bigelow, seeking to justify his own rebellious choice of surgery over medicine, may have blocked his son's aspirations toward autonomy in bacteriological research.[20]

In Paris, far from paternal authority, Sturgis's ambitions had flowered. But they remained vulnerable to his father's disapproval. When Sturgis returned to Boston he resumed the familiar posture of filial submission, even though he could have little professional respect for his father. But Sturgis could not sustain the tension between the duty of filial loyalty and the desire for professional self-esteem. He had to leave the medical profession to preserve some sense of his own worth. Yet ultimately he preserved very little. Judging by Bigelow's subsequent behavior, I would suggest that his repressed feelings of rebelliousness against paternal authority generated a sense of guilt, which turned his rage against himself. After his confrontation with his father, Bigelow became a lifelong nervous invalid. His protracted depressions and his persistent hypochondria served a dual purpose: they were rationalizations for his escape from the achievement ethos; they were also self-inflicted punishments for his failure to meet ego ideals. Lacking sufficient ego strength to chart his own course in bacteriology, Bigelow could only disengage himself, and drift.[21]

During the winter of 1881–2, the drifting stopped for a time. At the Lowell Institute in Boston, Edward S. Morse gave a series of lectures on Japan, and Bigelow was captivated. By May, 1882, he had arranged to join Morse on his return voyage to the Orient. In retrospect, Bigelow called the decision "the turning point of my life."[22] It temporarily ended the long period of depression and aimlessness; it promised escape from the tension between autonomy and dependence.

In Japan, Bigelow's vestigial commitments to achievement melted away. He stayed first with Morse and later with Fenollosa, both of whom worked tirelessly while he enjoyed a life of repose and aesthetic contemplation. He visited temples and museums, collecting superb *objets d'art* and donating vast sums for the promotion and preservation of Japanese art. But he never sought to meet Western standards of productivity. In July, 1884, Fenollosa wrote Lodge: "I wish you could stir up the Doctor [Bigelow] to the point of writing on the decorative arts. He has an immense amount of material, but is deficient in ambition."[23] Bigelow's apparent inactivity baffled his ambitious companions.

To be sure, Bigelow felt some twinges of conscience. The Japanese climate, he told Lodge in 1883, was "a little like Capri in the moral effect of making you not want to stir. And yet I suppose that stir I must, in a year from now, if not sooner." Vaguely uneasy at his own inactivity, Bigelow also feared that he had been morally abandoned by Boston society. He related a revealing dream to Lodge: "I was standing in Japanese summer dress—a cotton wrapper, with no hat nor shoes—in deep snow—about up to my knees—in front of your house, watching the people come out and get into their carriages after a party and thinking that the time had been when you would not have let me stand out there in such weather."[24]

But such misgivings were only a momentary mood. To most of his visitors and correspondents, Bigelow seemed profoundly at peace; he had embarked on a serious and satisfying Buddhist pilgrimage, foreign to all his American experience. According to Margaret Terry Chanler, "he had never, before going to Japan, had any spiritual experience whatever. He knew more about the mountains in the moon than he knew about his own soul." Now he was far from the demands of the achievement ethos and deep in lore of esoteric Buddhism. As Marian Adams said to her father, "I am so glad Bill Bigelow is so happy in Japan; Boston is so depressing to him that I doubt if he can ever live there; and why should he?"[25]

Bigelow had found a particularly congenial variety of esoteric Buddhism. After studying under Sakurai Keitoku, an Ajari, or teacher, in the temple at Hōmōyōin, he received the precepts of the Mikkyō sect on September 21, 1885. Esoteric Buddhism met Bigelow's psychic needs in two ways. First, it prescribed a series of ascetic practices and meditative exercises with the ultimate purpose of extinguishing individual desire and transcending the sense of autonomous selfhood. To Bigelow, for whom autonomy had become a burdensome ego ideal, esoteric Buddhism promised a welcome immersion in what his teachers called the *ku,* or void. (Bigelow later recognized the correspondence between the *ku* and "what is called the subliminal consciousness or subconsciousness by modern psychologists in the West.") Second, esoteric Buddhism placed almost total authority in the hands of the Ajari. As the living repository of the secret doctrines, he alone was empowered to pass their meaning on to others.[26] In embracing esoteric Buddhism, Bigelow preserved his dependent role by leaving a stern father for a benign Ajari. The Ajari embodied paternal wisdom and maternal solace; he symbolically unified Bigelow's ideal father and his lost mother.

For Bigelow, a Buddhist commitment meant more than self-indulgent passivity. To be sure, the ultimate goal of meditation was an oceanic feeling of oneness with the universe. But it could be reached only through rigorous ascetic discipline—a discipline the hedonistic Bigelow found difficult to maintain. Moreover, dependence on the Ajari also implied duties toward him. According to a Japanese observer, when Sakurai fell ill, Bigelow nursed him "as a filial child would his benevolent father." During the years after Sakurai died in 1889, Bigelow remained loyal and obedient to his teacher's successors.[27]

The problem for Bigelow became a conflict between Eastern and Western ideals of duty, neither of which he could fulfill because of his inherent passivity. Drawn to Buddhism by his longings for boundlessness and his desire to submit to a benevolent father-mother, he was unable fully to accept Buddhist discipline. Nor could he abandon his conflicting Western ideals of autonomous achievement and filial loyalty.

The East-West dilemma surfaced in 1887. Henry Bigelow had hit his head when he fell from a carriage, and Sturgis dutifully returned home to nurse his father. After the older man had remained in bed for weeks, the nature of his ailment began to seem unclear. According to Henry Adams, Sturgis's father was "either dying or pretending to die; I think the former, although the doctors have hinted the latter, because H. J. B. is so bent on his own way that they can never tell what else ails him." It is possible that the elder Bigelow was prolonging his invalidism to extract continued devotion from his son. Sturgis did not return to Japan for over a year; after he did, his father stayed on his mind. When his visitor Phillips Brooks left for Boston, Bigelow asked him to "please report me of sound and disposing mind to my father, if you see him. He does not take any stock in Buddhism, and thinks that I am hovering on the verge of lunacy, because I do not come home and get up some grandchildren for him, like a well-regulated Bostonian."[28]

In the spring of 1890, the old man's health was definitely failing and Sturgis came home again. Henry Bigelow died in October. In response to condolences from friends, Sturgis's replies were formal and heavily conscious of ancestral ties. To Lodge, Bigelow wrote: "I know you were one of the ones who would feel my father's death, both from your own associations and from those you inherit."[29] He prepared a memoir of his father which epitomized filial self-effacement. It was published anonymously; it commemorated a father to whom the son owed little professional respect and much personal frustration.

The ties of affection and loyalty held. After his father's death, Bigelow remained in Boston, though his old symptoms of depression returned. The rebellious flight to Japan had provided peace for a time, but it ultimately rekindled Bigelow's need for self-punishment. He became increasingly withdrawn, and by 1900, his biographer writes, "chronic breakdown of health had become a recurrent theme of his life." Besides suffering from dyspepsia, insomnia, shingles, and other nervous ailments, Bigelow periodically "broke down" and stayed in bed for weeks. Even in Japan, he had been haunted by a sense of uselessness as he approached middle age. "I am 39 this year," he wrote Lodge in 1889, "and nothing done yet." After Bigelow returned to America his self-doubts intensified, while he drifted between his Boston clubs and the Tuckernuck retreat he had inherited from his father.[30]

For a time Bigelow transcended self-absorption by forming a fatherly relationship with George Cabot Lodge, the senator's son, known to family and friends as "Bay." During the mid-1890s Bigelow initiated Bay Lodge into Buddhist meditative practice while they spent long hours together in the oceanic solitude of Tuckernuck. Nearly all visitors felt drugged by an eerie sense of timelessness there; history and personal identity seemed to dissolve in the "all" of sea and sky. To Bigelow and Lodge, the island retreat became a this-worldly embodiment of Nirvana. For Bigelow especially, it provided opportunities for both meditation and leisure in an atmosphere permeated by memories of his father; it symbolically reconciled his Buddhist commitments with a sense of ancestral continuity.[31]

The reconciliation was unstable at best. Around the turn of the century, Bigelow began trying to arrange another visit to Japan. But he was hindered by his own self-doubts. In the worldly atmosphere of Beacon Hill, his commitments to regular meditation had slipped away. He felt inadequately fitted for Buddhist discipline. "Bonno's [lusts] are strong and hard to kill," he complained to Naobayashi Kanryō, Sakurai's successor. When Naobayashi urged him to visit Japan in the spring of 1899, Bigelow replied, "This I should gladly do, but I hesitate a little, remembering the fatiguing effect on body and mind of former practice. I should be glad of your advice." For three years Bigelow postponed his return. "He doesn't want to go a bit," Bay Lodge told his mother, "and for that very reason I imagine feels as if he ought to." Finally Naobayashi insisted, and Bigelow left for Japan in the summer of 1902. Arriving in Yokohama in August, he wrote Naobayashi that "when you wrote me—'please overcome all obstacles and come' I felt that such a request from an Ajari should have but one answer, and I obeyed." Besides performing an act of filial piety, Bigelow was also trying to recapture the peace of the 1880s. On that count, his visit was only a mixed success. Throughout his stay he felt oppressed by a sense of his own inadequacy. As he told Senator Lodge, "I have everything done for me that anybody can—but I feel like a five-year old child entrusted with a Masamune sword."[32] Dyspeptic and neurasthenic, Bigelow drifted back through Europe, arriving in Boston in 1904.

He had by this time developed a reputation as a patron of the arts and an authority on Buddhism. The trustees of Harvard asked him to give the 1908 Ingersoll lecture on Immortality. "Buddhism and Immortality" became Bigelow's most sustained effort to explain his faith to an American audience. Since the 1880s, he had conceived Buddhism as "a sort of Spiritual Pantheism—Emerson, almost exactly. . . ."[33] Alluding to Emerson frequently, restricting his comments to the Tendai and Shingon traditions of Northern Buddhism, Bigelow presented his faith as a form of monistic idealism.

Like many mind-curists and mesmerists, Bigelow exalted an impersonal personality. "The separate personal consciousness with its offshoots is . . . the only obstacle to complete freedom of the will," he said. "The only will that is not free will is the personal will." The only restrictions on selfhood are bodily, he claimed; consciousness is infinite, and the self only seems to be separate because of the overwhelming preponderance of sense experience in our lives. In reality, said Bigelow, "The self is co-extensive with the universe. The difference between organic beings is merely how much of themselves they realize."[34]

If Bigelow's words prefigured a therapeutic orientation toward "self-realization," he nevertheless clung to altruistic commitments. "Consciousness is continuous," he said; "there is but one ultimate consciousness. All beings are therefore one; and when one man strikes another, he strikes all men, including himself. . . . The difference in beings, is how much they realize of this universal consciousness." In Buddhism, Bigelow said, there were two ways to increase universal consciousness: Kengyō, the simple everyday practice of unselfish morality, and Mikkyō, the far more difficult effort to combine ordinary morality with meditative practice. Whatever path one chose, the ultimate object of life "is to acquire freedom from the limits of the material world by substituting volitional for sensory consciousness." That freedom underlay the serene wisdom of Emerson; it promised "the peace which passeth understanding trained on material things,—infinite and eternal peace,—the peace of limitless consciousness unified with limitless will. That peace is NIRVANA."[35]

Bigelow's idealist paean to Nirvana sanctioned his repudiation of the achievement ethos; it also merged with the mystical wave in the urban Northeast. Despite his reputation as an idiosyncratic dilettante, Bigelow was actually in the tide of an important popular movement. Throughout the years around the turn of the century mind-curists and interpreters of Eastern mysticism were leading less privileged Americans on similar quests for Nirvana.

There was much in esoteric Buddhism to support Bigelow's quietistic interpretation, but there was much to support other interpretations, too. Fenollosa, who had studied with Bigelow under Sakurai, drew from the Ajari a lesson of ethical service. As Fenollosa told Isabel Stewart Gardner, "Mysticism is not *the only* 'way'; not necessarily even the *best* 'way'; certainly not the *normal* 'way.' " Bigelow acknowledged that even in Mikkyō there was an ethical emphasis, but he preferred to view it simply as a stress on kindness to others; Fenollosa Westernized it into a crusade for democratic art education. "There are many roads up the mountain." Bigelow said.[36]

Yet Bigelow's road remained rough. He was too fond of upper-class leisure to embrace Buddhist discipline, too imbued with ideals of activism to rest content with quietistic withdrawal. Nor could he stick at work in the world. He was appointed Lecturer at Harvard after delivering "Buddhism and Immortality" in May, 1908, but he delivered only four lectures that autumn. He stayed the following summer in Paris. On September 9, George Cabot Lodge died of a heart attack at Tuckernuck. Bigelow was crushed by the news; he never again enjoyed the Nirvana-like calm of Tuckernuck. When Bigelow returned to the United States, his successful friends continued urging him into some productive activity, particularly a study of Buddhism. "I have been at him to write a book on the subject, and last autumn felt very hopeful of success," a medical school classmate wrote in May, 1912. "I arranged that he was to see nobody in the morning, and he made a start. He is, however, so desultory, and so liable to interruptions of systematized and stated work by headaches, etc. that he has not accomplished much. . . ."[37] Long after his father's death, the achievement ethos surrounded Bigelow, embodied in his productive friends. His "headaches, etc." remained his most effective rationalization (as well as his severest self-punishment) for escape from paternal ideals.

In 1915, Bigelow contributed a sum to the Boston Surgical Society for the establishment of a Henry Jacob Bigelow medal. The Bigelow medal was to be periodically awarded to one chosen for his "contribution to the advancement of surgery."[38] It was a final, ironic act of filial loyalty, and it suggested how thoroughly—despite all obstacles—Sturgis Bigelow had internalized the ideal of domestic harmony.

His spiritual and physical health seemed to decline together. Torn between Eastern and Western ideals, neither of which he could fulfill, Bigelow raged increasingly against himself. Channelled by self-destructive impulses, his longing for boundlessness became a longing for death. In 1921 he wrote a long and moving farewell to Naobayashi's successor: "As you are doubtless aware, I died spiritually in the third month of last year." In a passage full of self-contempt, he expressed his desire for complete nonexistence.

When a bronze founder casts a statue of Buddha, there are sometimes flaws in the work. When these are not large, the defective part is cut out and sound metal put in its place; but when the defects are very large, the statue must be melted over again and cast afresh; but if the metal itself is bad, nothing can help. The statue will be full of defects no matter how many times it is cast. So with human beings also. It is easier to make bronze Buddhas than real ones. Bonnos may be cut out, but if the metal itself is soft and weak, there is nothing to be done. It is not possible to make a rope of sea-sand nor to make a wet towel stand on end no matter how long one tries, and there is no place in the universe for wet towels. Therefore, I hope and pray for obliteration, not of my Bonnos, but of myself.

Physical suicide was not enough, because in the Buddhist view it did not interrupt the cycle of reincarnation. "What I want," said Bigelow, "is a spiritual seppuku [hara-kiri] that will finish me once and for all, but unfortunately I am so ignorant that I do not know how to do it."[39]

Bigelow's dilemma epitomized the tragic contradictions of antimodern dissent. Estranged from his father but imbued with paternal ideals, longing for boundlessness but unable to extinguish the urge for autonomous selfhood, admiring renunciation but too fond of comfort to accept ascetic discipline, Bigelow remained spiritually homeless throughout his life. His wanderings in Europe and Japan reflected his restless spirit. When he died of a cerebral hemorrhage in 1926, an Episcopal service was held at Trinity Church, Boston, and half of his ashes were buried beside his mother, in the Mt. Auburn cemetery founded by his grandfather. The other half, by direction of his will, were sent to the Hōmōyōin temple in Japan and buried there, on the shores of Lake Biwa. "The soul follows its strongest ties," Bigelow had said in 1908. "These are generally the family ties, but not always. . . ."[40] Even in death his soul was divided.


## PERCIVAL LOWELL

Not all Oriental pilgrimages left family conflict unresolved. Percival Lowell (1855–1916) shared Bigelow's enthusiasm for Morse's Lowell Institute lectures, and he followed Bigelow to Japan in 1883. Like Bigelow, Lowell was restless and uncertain about his direction in life. But for him the Orient acquired a very different meaning. The journey to the East dispelled his "feminine" desire for withdrawal, eased his accommodation with paternal authority, and reinforced his commitment to conventional male ego ideals. The encounter with Oriental character provided a negative background against which he could focus his own diffuse sense of identity.

Lowell was born in Boston in 1855, the first of three children born to Augustus and Katherine Lawrence Lowell. By all accounts his mother was kind, matronly, and absolutely subservient to her husband. Augustus Lowell was a slightly built, tight-lipped, impeccably dressed businessman, the owner of several textile mills which he managed with cool efficiency. Like Henry Bigelow, he epitomized bourgeois productivity and expected it from his children. "Somehow he made us feel that every self-respecting man must work at something that is worth while, and do it very hard," Percival's brother recalled. "In our case it need not be remunerative, for he had enough to provide for that; but it must be of real significance." Yet Percival was not at first able to comply. For years he was restless and discontented with conventional upper-class prospects. After graduation from Harvard, he managed trust funds for his grandfather and cotton mills for his father. Living comfortably on his investments, he remained a troubled young man. Amid ancestral shadows, he longed on the one hand for independent achievement that would please his father and on the other hand for escape from business routine.[41]

After hearing Morse's lectures in 1883, Lowell booked passage to Japan. He hired a house in Tokyo, entertained lavishly, and quickly won a reputation in academic and diplomatic circles. His letters home revealed a mingled fascination and contempt for things Oriental. In Japan, he wrote, "Everyone is a poet, just as he is an artist in embryo." A few weeks later he was complaining that "the far eastern peoples might aptly be described as impossible peoples. The impossibility of obtaining anything like exact information is only equalled by the impossibility of ever getting anything done." Unlike Bigelow, Lowell reaffirmed his activist commitments in the Far East. His restless energy made him impatient with what he saw as Oriental lethargy; his commitment to autonomy made him deplore "the strange lack of individual variation" among Far Eastern people.[42]

Still plagued by self-doubts ("I wish I could believe a little more in myself," he wrote his mother), Lowell temporarily found a stable identity as a writer. His most popular book, *The Soul of the Far East* (1888), inflated his prejudices into principles explaining the superiority of the individualist West over the "impersonal" Orient. Instead of idealizing the "childish" elements in Oriental culture, Lowell ridiculed them—for important psychic reasons. Elevating consciousness over unconsciousness, separate selfhood over oceanic unity, Lowell reaffirmed his allegiance to conventional definitions of male adulthood. The same process was even clearer in Lowell's *Occult Japan or the Way of the Gods. An Esoteric Study of Japanese Personality and Possession* (1894). In this analysis (and crude satire) of Shinto trances, Lowell argued that the ease with which Japanese lost conscious personality in trance states signified a "feminine" trait: "absence of Ego." Indeed, "Japan is the feminine half of the world."[43]

Femininity, childhood, and the unconscious merged in Lowell's vision of premodern character; all represented tendencies he needed to repudiate en route to male adulthood. Identifying dependence and loss of conscious will with the "inferior" Japanese, Lowell revitalized his commitment to autonomous Western manhood. A racist condescension toward Oriental character helped create a negative identity against which Lowell could define a stronger sense of self.

Lowell's repudiation of the unconscious as "feminine" underscored the crucial role he assigned to disciplined intellect. Noting in *Occult Japan* "how ill the self fares under these illusions and disillusions of the trance," Lowell became increasingly concerned with the precariousness of selfhood. Like many of his contemporaries he concluded that "self, indeed, would seem to be an illusion; and the bundle of ideas in that mass of machinery, the brain, alone to constitute the I."[44] Conscious thought alone was the basis of personal identity.

At thirty-nine, Lowell reaffirmed allegiance to conscious intellect by choosing a life of scientific research in astronomy. After completing *Occult Japan* he organized an expedition to Flagstaff, Arizona, to build an observatory. He worked at high speed until May 1897 when he returned to Boston "nervously shattered." Lowell remained a helpless neurasthenic for three years, convinced that the doctors' decision to confine him to bed in his father's house had exacerbated his condition.[45] The stringent demands of the modern achievement ethos had been intensified for Lowell by his father's insistence on accomplishment "of real significance." A virtually unattainable paternal ideal, embodied in a father who was difficult if not impossible to please, may ultimately have contributed to the breakdown of the striving son. For Lowell as for others like him, neurasthenia was a passive but painful rebellion against the moral authority of both the bourgeois family and the wider culture. A sign of weakness to the conscientious, neurasthenic invalidism could not be prolonged indefinitely—at least not by the dutiful Lowell.

In Spring 1901 Lowell returned to the Observatory, where he became a model of punctuality, order, and productivity.[46] When he died in 1916, Percival Lowell had forged an identity which was not only rational and scientific but strenuous and "Western." Besides promising clear air and good weather, Lowell's choice of Flagstaff implied his rejection of the effete, urban Northeast, where paternal claims were strong and selfhood problematic; it signified his embrace of the open frontier, where autonomy seemed available in the old familiar way.

Both Lowell and Bigelow faced problems of identity formation in patriarchal families. Henry J. Bigelow made clearcut demands on his son, who internalized them, later resisted them, and ultimately fell victim to the chronic dis-ease generated by his rebellion; for Sturgis Bigelow, Buddhism focused his desire for a benevolent father-mother and functioned as a temporary but ultimately unsatisfying respite from the paternal will. Augustus Lowell's demands were less precise but still compelling; for his son, the Orient provided a way to clarify and reaffirm commitment to paternal expectations. Both fathers were near caricatures of male ego ideals—autonomous, righteous, and aloof. Their rigidity precipitated the anxious quests for self-definition undertaken by their sons: in Bigelow's case, "a fatal struggle for identity," in Lowell's, a more conventionally successful one.

But what happened when the parent-child confrontation was not so clearcut, when patriarchy was softened by domesticity? Since the antebellum era, ideologues of domesticity had been urging that parents govern through the manipulation of affection rather than through authoritarian fiat. And as early as the 1830s, Tocqueville had noted the intertwining of the achievement ethos and the domestic ideal among American men; they seemed to need "the deep, regular and quiet affection" of family life as a counterweight to a life of striving. By the second half of the nineteenth century, at least in some families, the "feminine" dimension of domestic ideology was beginning to reshape fatherhood. (The process was accelerated by the softening of Old Testament Calvinism, with its emphasis on a stern patriarchal God, into the Christ-centered sentimentality of liberal Protestantism.) Among the bourgeoisie, a number of fathers were trying to cultivate patience and understanding, even with an intractable child—to rule through the orchestration of love rather than through patriarchal command.[47]


## GEORGE CABOT LODGE

The life of the poet George Cabot Lodge (1873–1909) illustrates the difficulties of male identity formation under the aegis of affection. Henry Cabot Lodge, scholar and senator, was more accomplished than Henry Bigelow or Augustus Lowell; yet unlike them he sought to mold Bay's character through affection rather than sovereignty. And his influence was balanced by his wife's. Anna Cabot Mills Lodge maintained an extraordinarily close relationship with her son. Bay Lodge grew up amid the tender encouragement of his parents and the adulation of family friends —Bigelow, the Adams brothers, Theodore Roosevelt. Edith Wharton perceptively observed that this hothouse atmosphere of affection "kept Bay in a state of brilliant immaturity."[48] Financially and emotionally dependent on his parents throughout his life, he never developed a firm sense of adult identity. Though the father was patient and forgiving, he embodied an unattainable ideal for his son. And young Lodge's sense of inadequacy was exacerbated by the dictates of the modern superego—more stringent than his parents' demands. He sank periodically into immobilizing depression, torn between respect for the achievement ethos and rage against its constricting influence. As his continuing dependence deprived him of self-esteem, Lodge turned his rage not only against himself in periodic depressions, but also, in poetic fantasies of omnipotence, against his parents and all sources of respectable moral authority. Unable to meet the standards for male achievement set by familial and cultural authority, Lodge took refuge in a private cult of Promethean masculinity.

Bay Lodge was born in 1873, the second of three children, the first son. Though both parents doted on the boy and marvelled at his intellectual precocity, from childhood he was closer to his mother than to his busy and often absent father. Indeed those long absences may have increased Bay's tendency to elevate his father's achievements to an inaccessible, ideal plane. At Harvard, Bay performed badly, in large part (he claimed) because he felt overshadowed by his eminent father. Disappointed by Bay's academic performance, his father hid his impatience and fretted privately about the boy's future. Bay "seems to have no interests or ambitions and to love mere stupid idling beyond anything," Lodge told Henry Adams. "What can one do? Be friends with the boy and trust to fate is the only answer I find."[49] The desire to "be friends with the boy" reflected a domestic rather than a patriarchal notion of fatherhood, and foreshadowed the twentieth century image of the father as a companion to his children. It led Lodge to cultivate an attitude of patient encouragement unknown to Henry Bigelow or Augustus Lowell. Grateful for this forebearance, Bay always promised to redouble his efforts. Towards graduation, he began to identify more closely with his father. He wrote to him more frequently and affectionately; he also began enclosing his poetry, which his father sympathetically criticized and sometimes rewrote.[50]

Bay remained more dependent on his mother, to whom he confided his anxieties and aspirations. His letters to her reveal nascent religious yearnings. He read Thomas à Kempis, felt the attraction of Roman Catholicism ("the most religious sect in all Christendom"), and discovered Carlyle's "Spiritual Optics" ("the most wonderful things I have seen written in English"). Disdaining "unhealthy and fetid" realism, Lodge grew more confident in the nobility of his purpose: to become a poet. But he was still plagued by fears of failure. "I do so want to do something that will last, —some man's work in the world,—that I am constantly depressed by an awful dread that perhaps I shan't be able to."[51]

Tension between doing "a man's work in the world" and being "a miserable little poetaster" existed throughout Lodge's college years. Stemming from his ambivalent response to his father's values, it was reinforced by the divergent examples of his father's two best friends, Roosevelt and Bigelow. Roosevelt took Bay camping in the Bad Lands, praised his poetry and showed it to publishers; he embodied a vigorous parallel to Bay's father. But Bigelow's contemplative life proved more alluring. Roosevelt had been bored by Tuckernuck and left after twenty-four hours; Bigelow and Bay Lodge spent endless summer days there, exploring the quiescence of the oceanic "all." Bigelow was eager to instruct Lodge in Buddhism, and sought advice on how to proceed from Kanyro Naobayashi. But neither pressed for an immediate pilgrimage to the East. Even if Bigelow had been ready, Lodge was not. Though he longed for Nirvana, he was determined to establish a separate sense of self. Hoping to acquire a ticket to financial independence, Lodge arranged to take a *degré d'études supérieures* in French literature at the Sorbonne. But after arriving in Paris in September 1895, Lodge soon fell into a prolonged personal crisis.[52]

Lodge's anxiety had religious as well as psychic roots. He had made a cathedral pilgrimage with Henry Adams during the summer of 1895, and had read Brooks Adams's *Law of Civilization and Decay* soon after. By December, Lodge was lamenting the passing of religious belief in a commercial society. "I love aspiration. I love the men who painted on their knees," he wrote his mother. "I abhor my own incapacity for faith, my utter skepticism, all that makes of me a man of this end of the nineteenth century." Yet there were other more mundane difficulties for Lodge as well. Above all, he was torn by "the continual thought of money and my crying inability to adapt myself to my time and become a moneymaker."[53] Discrediting "the tide of life" by identifying it with moneymaking (rather than military or public service), Lodge ruled out his father's path and left possibilities open for contemplative withdrawal.

Lodge's impulses toward both autonomy and dependence were exacerbated by his sense that he was suffocating in a stifling climate of overcivilization. As he told his mother, "One feels a crying need for actual physical action and contact sometimes and the impossibility of it in a world of machine-guns and machine-everything-else makes one want sometimes to go quietly down and drop off the Pont d'Alms or do anything to be able to take a long breath."[54] For Lodge as for many other Americans, a feeling of weightlessness intensified the desire for "actual physical action" on the one hand, oceanic oblivion on the other.

For a while the oceanic impulse was stronger, especially when he withdrew with Bigelow to Tuckernuck, where the two men practiced meditation. In 1897 Lodge sent the older man "Nirvana," a poem reflecting their common spiritual aspirations, which concluded that only the extinction of desire brought one face to face with the "white, uncovered breast of peace." (The maternal connotations were significant.) Nirvana, for Lodge as well as for Bigelow, meant release from a finite world of conflicting desires into a cosmic sense of unity.[55]

Ultimately, the impulse toward engagement with "real life," strengthened by the desire for worldly recognition, overbalanced Lodge's craving for Nirvana. Though he remained close to Bigelow, he was increasingly swept up in the romantic activism of the 1890s—the obverse side of oceanic antimodernism. As a naval cadet, in the Spanish-American War, he was exhilarated by life under fire; the experience reaffirmed his commitment to conventional ideals of manliness. He returned from the war more eager than ever to achieve financial autonomy as a professional author.[56]

The problem was that none of Lodge's work sold. He remained financially dependent on his father, emotionally dependent on his mother—even after his marriage to Elizabeth Frelinghuysen Davis in 1901. Unable to achieve autonomy in his life, Lodge exalted it in his work. His poetic themes moved away from Nirvanic "will-lessness" and toward a Nietzschean apotheosis of will—from one pole of antimodern dissent to the other. The new emphasis marked most of Lodge's *Poems, 1899–1902*. The design of the book foreshadows Lodge's later theme that the artist's quest for transcendence required the dissolution of family ties. Woman appears as the supreme consoler, but also as a temptress, using "love's euthanasy" to lure the artist-hero away from moral combat. Purging himself of the earthbound "feminine" world, he finally achieves a kind of apotheosis in the last line of the book: "And vast beyond all and inclusive of all things, my God is Myself!"[57]

By the time he wrote *Cain* (1904), Lodge had turned entirely from Nirvana toward a vision of all-consuming selfhood. Lacking firm belief in a supernatural framework of meaning, preserving his commitment to a separate sense of self, Lodge tended ultimately to equate the oceanic feeling with annihilation—especially since his longings for Nirvana so often coincided with his depressions. Like Lowell, Lodge repudiated Nirvana as part of a larger effort to transcend "feminine" elements in his character. He elevated conscious intellect over instinct, autonomy over dependence. But unlike Lowell, Lodge in actuality remained dependent. His achievement of autonomy was imaginary, and therefore more sweeping and intense. His dramas sought to vindicate his artistic role by presenting it as the purest form of masculine activism—more complete, more sublimated and "spiritual" than the mundane activism of the businessman, the soldier, or the politician.

Lodge's rhetoric of rebellion concealed his persistent commitment to his father's values. He admitted to his mother in 1901 that "there are remains of ambitions for worldly success in me. . . ." Though he had a weak heart, he drove himself continually, writing far into the night. His work received mixed praise from reviewers, enthusiastic encouragement from his parents and their friends. Telling himself that "these are my great years," he still vacillated between elation and despair. He suffered several mild heart seizures during 1907 and 1908, but told no one in his family. In August, 1909, his heart weakened and finally failed. He died on Tuckernuck, in his father's arms.[58]

The significance of the young poet's life reaches well beyond his Washington circle; it involves the complex origins and functions of the antimodern impulse. Rooted in his distaste for commercial society and his longings for an infinite sense of purpose, Lodge's dissent from bourgeois modernity was conditioned by cultural and family circumstance. Unable to embrace a supernatural framework of meaning, ambivalent toward his father's authority, Lodge turned toward oceanic withdrawal, then toward activist engagement, finally toward rejection of bourgeois familial and cultural authority in the name of absolute self-fulfillment. Shifting between poles of antimodernism, Lodge remained a misfit in the modern world. His friend Cecil Spring-Rice thought Lodge was "the sort of stuff that in the middle ages would have made a great saint or a great heresiarch—I dare say we have no use for such people now. . . ." The comment paralleled Frederick Shattuck's remark of Bigelow that, in another time, his medical school classmate might have been a "medieval saint." Both observations underscored the profound religious disquiet Lodge and Bigelow shared.[59]

Yet both men's religious discontent ultimately served to reinforce secularizing tendencies in the wider culture. Torn by doubts and conflicting loyalties, Bigelow sank into permanent nervous invalidism. Seeking to transcend "morbid self-consciousness" through meditation, his seasons in Nirvana were brief and ever less frequent. His endless visits to health resorts, his agonized inability to make decisions, his fretful preoccupation with his own well-being—all prefigured the therapeutic "hospital culture" of twentieth-century America. And if Bigelow's self-concern was covert and intermittent, Lodge's was explicit and pervasive. His cry "My God is Myself!" looked backward to Emersonian subjectivity, forward to avant-garde literature and consumer capitalism. While Lowell illustrated the revitalization of older bourgeois values, Bigelow and Lodge unknowingly pointed to new and secular cultural modes. The tension between the lotus and the father involved a continuing dialectic between protest and accommodation.

The social consequence of that dialectic—the shift from a Protestant to a therapeutic basis of capitalist cultural hegemony—was an unforeseen, unintended result of the efforts of individual men to locate meaning amid cultural confusion. The idiosyncratic quality of each effort contained the kernel of dissent. Personal protest led to social accommodation. Troubled by secular habits of mind and conflicting ego ideals, yearning for boundlessness only in their most self-destructive moods, many seekers of Nirvana conceived it as annihilation. Reasserting strenuosity, they turned to an activist cult of experience; or, lacking even a secularized ethic of suffering, they retreated to a debased version of the dependent feminine role, a state of chronic anxiety and self-absorption. But the accommodationist outcomes neither discredited the protest nor undercut its long term significance. However uncertain and ultimately circular, the search for Nirvana exposed the emotional limitations of bourgeois masculinity and the spiritual bankruptcy of nineteenth-century positivism.

# Aesthetic Catholicism and "Feminine" Values: Norton, Hall, Brooks

The same blend of personal, philosophical, and social significance characterized the turn toward Catholic art and ritual. In the late-Victorian imagination, Catholicism was joined with both childishness and femininity. It signified contemplative passivity rather than humanitarian action, emotional dependence rather than moral autonomy, aesthetic responsiveness rather than intellectual rigor. For some, the Church embodied the "feminine" values of the cult of domesticity. To Protestants influenced by the domestic ideal, who began to speak of "the Womanly in God," the Church's Mariolatry enshrined the worth of woman. To antimodern vitalists, the rich aesthetic tradition surrounding the Madonna and Child suggested a revitalized imagery of maternal sustenance. By promising refreshing "feminine" alternatives to desiccated male ideals, Catholicism threw into relief the conflicting claims of the modern superego and suggested avenues of escape to oceanic boundlessness.[60]

For Norton, Hall, and Brooks, aesthetic Catholicism played a crucial counterpoint to the "masculine" theme of autonomy. Though the three men grew up in various cultural milieus and under differing historical circumstances, they shared a number of characteristics. None became Catholics, but all were drawn to the Church's aesthetic legacy as the focal point of a wider Old World charm. All identified Catholic Europe with "feminine" values of repose, contemplation, and emotional dependence; all finally sublimated their aesthetic longings into some form of accommodation with the dominant culture. And for all three, the catalyst for successful sublimation was a psychic crisis arising during middle age.

Despite common themes, there were also significant differences among these men's responses to "feminine" values. Norton (1827–1908) preserved the most self-conscious ethic of suffering. It stemmed from his religious upbringing in Cambridge during the early-Victorian era, when commitments to self-denial were still comparatively strong; it checked his longings for quiescence and ultimately sustained his oscillation between autonomy and dependence. Hall (1844–1924) was born seventeen years later than Norton, on a farm in western Massachusetts. Like Norton, Hall achieved an ambivalent fusion of "masculine" and "feminine" values in middle age. But while Norton's ambivalence was undergirded by a republican ethic of suffering, Hall's was energized by antimodern vitalism. The residue of moralism was slipping away.

The process took a further turn with Brooks (1886–1963). He was born nearly sixty years after Norton, in the Wall Street suburb of Plainfield, New Jersey. He grew to manhood in the ripe afterglow of *fin-de-siècle* aestheticism, when the ethic of suffering was fading among the urban bourgeoisie. Unlike Norton or Hall, Brooks slipped first into an aesthete's role. But he felt the press of activist ideals. Like Lodge, he shifted between the poles of antimodernism, trying to merge aesthetic withdrawal with moral engagement. The process proved difficult because by the early twentieth century, amid the fascination with the unconscious and the cult of inner experience, aestheticism had acquired some new and disturbing connotations. To Americans like Brooks, it suggested not only bizarre or effeminate behavior, but also oceanic passivity and loss of the self. Like the Orientalists' desire for Nirvana, Brooks's longing for oceanic dependence was most intense when he was most depressed; it seemed ultimately to point toward suicide. Equating aestheticism with annihilation, Brooks (like Lowell) pulled back from passivity and reaffirmed a rigid ideal of autonomy.

The careers of Norton, Hall, and Brooks reveal the complex functions of the antimodern impulse at a variety of historical moments. Energized by a secularized ethic of suffering or by a vitalist cult of experience, it could revivify familiar values by sustaining ambivalence. Associated with oceanic oblivion, it could provoke a repudiation of ambivalence through reassertion of autonomy. The result, in all three cases, was renewed accommodation with the dominant culture. But where ambivalence remained, so did a measure of moral criticism.

## CHARLES ELIOT NORTON

Norton was the third of six children in a tightknit family. He was close to both his parents, but his moral instruction came almost exclusively from his father, the Reverend Andrews Norton, Unitarian "Pope" and archenemy of transcendentalism. By all accounts the child learned his lessons too well. He became a priggish parody of his father, mocked by his schoolmates as "Pope Charles." Lying on a sickbed at age ten, the boy announced: "I wish that I could live, so that I could edit Father's works." Young Norton's eagerness for paternal approval reinforced his intellectual bent and drove him to long hours of study.[61]

At fifteen Charles developed eye strain and was sent to New York for treatment. It was the first of many ailments which incapacitated him for months at a time, and it suggested the dual role invalidism would play in his later life. Like his later bouts of neurasthenia, the eye strain legitimized a vacation from the achievement ethos but also reinforced young Norton's commitment to an ethic of suffering. In contrast to his mother's "newsy" notes, his father's didactic letters drove home the value of suffering as a means of character formation and as "part of our discipline for the future life." Charles Norton later lost his faith in a future life, but not in the character-building powers of suffering. In his later years, a secularized ethic of suffering helped him to work in the world despite his tendency toward depressive withdrawal.[62]

But almost from the beginning, some of the elder Norton's expectations presented difficulties. Concerned about his son's prodigious bookishness (and perhaps keeping his *bête noire* Emerson in mind), Andrews Norton warned his son against the perils of a "merely literary life" which lured one from "exertion and self-improvement" amid "the business of the world." While the ministry was apparently not a live option, literature required explicit repudiation. Upon graduation from Harvard in 1846, Charles embraced his father's activist ideals by entering the countinghouse of Bullard and Lee. Bored by business routine, he wrote essays and reviews in the evenings.[63]

When Bullard and Lee offered Norton a post as supercargo on its ship *Milton,* bound for India, Norton accepted. There was no problem maintaining loyalty to his father's ideals in India, where Norton had preoccupying business duties. But when he returned through Europe in the spring of 1850, he encountered a new world of aesthetic experience. His letters rhapsodized over mountains, cathedrals, even Roman Catholic festivals. He delayed his return for several months, claiming he hoped to do "something worthwhile" but admitting he was enjoying himself as never before.[64]

In January 1851, Norton returned to America and business—but only for a time. Family expectations, as well as office routine, began to seem oppressive to him. After his father died in September 1853, Norton began to "edit Father's works" in the evenings. An act of filial piety, the editorial project was also the beginning of Norton's decisive turn from his father's activist ideals. His rebellion was covert, passive, and painful. Financially but not psychologically able to quit business outright, Norton experienced "a rapid decline in his health" (according to his biographer) with no organic cause. In the summer of 1855, Norton left Bullard and Lee, claiming he needed more time for his editorial work. But instead of turning to scholarship, he left for Europe with his mother and two of his sisters.[65]

Describing the journey from Nice across the initial heights of the Riviera into Italy, Norton revealed the network of associations Italy—and ultimately all of Europe—came to have in his mind.

> One of the first . . . promontories is that of Capo Sant'Ospizio. A close grove of olives half conceals the old castle on its extreme point. With the afternoon sun full upon it, the trees palely glimmering as their leaves move in the light air, the sea so blue and smooth as to be like a darker sky, and not even a ripple upon the beach, it seems as if this were the very home of summer and of repose. It is remote and secluded from the stir and noise of the world. No road is seen leading to it, and one looks down upon the solitary castle and wonders what stories of enchantment and romance belong to a ruin that appears as if made for their dwelling-place. It is a scene out of that Italy which is the home of the imagination, and which becomes the Italy of memory.[66]

Memory and imagination; aesthetic, sensuous, and emotional experience—all were joined in Norton's vision of Italy. At bottom, it evoked an oceanic feeling, but it remained far from Norton's consciousness. He sublimated his sensuous response to Italian art into a concentration on moral lessons and images of ideal beauty; he suppressed his admiration for Italy's Catholic culture by denouncing superstition and papal corruption. Yet a tension persisted between his ingrained commitment to male ego ideals and his awakening attraction to this seductive "home of the imagination."

Pleading poor health, Norton postponed a return to America to resume work on his editorial project. As his biographer writes, "Poor health did not seem to enfeeble his energies for study, however." Not, that is, if study meant contemplating cathedrals or translating Dante's *Vita Nuova*. In August 1857 he returned to Boston and joined the staff of the new *Atlantic Monthly*. But for a year Norton was out of touch with the magazine, living as a semi-invalid.[67] His attention to his father's papers also lagged; he never completed the project. As Norton moved from Unitarianism to agnosticism, and from paternal ideals to European alternatives, the editorial work became laden with insurmountable inner conflicts. Yet he could not abandon it without suffering from insomnia, dyspepsia, and a host of other neurasthenic symptoms.

The coming of the Civil War temporarily roused Norton from neurasthenia, rekindled his enthusiasm for paternal ideals, and redirected his ethic of suffering outward, toward republican preaching as editor of the *North American Review*. But as republican virtue succumbed to the Grant "barbecue," Norton's optimism and energy waned together. Again citing his failing health, he resigned the editorship of the *Review* and embarked with his family for Europe in summer, 1868. Loitering through the English countryside, he called it "grandmother's garden"; the domestic and maternal connotations were significant. So was the water imagery he habitually used in his letters. "I am gradually getting rid of some American angularities and drynesses," Norton reported to Howells. "My roots feel the refreshment of unfamiliar waters flowing from the deep old-world springs of culture and imagination." His vitalist vision was widening to include all Europe. Norton increasingly associated the Old World with the repressed "feminine" elements in his own character—with emotional spontaneity and aesthetic responsiveness, but also with indolence. Insisting on his allegiance to "American" values of achievement, he eluded them for four years in Europe.[68]

As always, Norton's escape from the achievement ethos was accompanied by neurasthenia. Here again, the disease may have functioned both as legitimation and as expiation for a son's failure to meet the actual or imagined demands of paternal authority—demands, in this case as in many others, for a life of "exertion and self-improvement." Immersing himself with Ruskin in the study of thirteenth-century cathedrals, Norton was plagued by what he called "failing strength" which prevented him from completing any scholarly projects. Supported by his mother's wealth in passive leisure, he felt "useless and disappointing" but unable to return to America.[69]

The encroachment of middle age may well have heightened Norton's tendency toward drift and self-accusation. He seemed to lack the component of maturity Erik Erikson has called "generativity"—the ability to establish and guide the next generation, not only through childrearing but also (especially given Norton's intellectual background) through "fathering" books, ideas, or some altruistic aim outside the self.[70] By the early 1870s, Norton was in his mid-forties; outside his family, his generative capacities seemed stillborn. His crusading journalism seemed a failure, lost in the moral confusion of the Grant era. His scholarly projects seemed dilettantish; he did not even have the strength to sustain them. Losing faith in the future of both Europe and America, he felt little commitment toward the next generation. He faced the onset of old age without having secured the fruits of maturity. Yet from his point of view, securing them meant internalizing the ego ideals he found most oppressive—the bourgeois values which were troubling his leisure and spoiling Europe's charm.

Norton remained indecisive until his wife died in childbirth in 1872. Perhaps the shock made him eager to recover some sense of generativity and avoid declining into self-absorbed old age. In any case he refused Ruskin's invitation to stay and embraced "regular compulsory occupation" as Professor of Fine Arts at Harvard. Repudiating retreat into helpless passivity, Norton joined masculine and feminine ideals in his lectures by defining beauty as "the ultimate expression and warrant of goodness" and in his *Historical Studies of Church Building in the Middle Ages* (1880) by presenting the medieval artisan as a republican bourgeois. His assaults on modern civilization focused on corruption of character in both feminine and masculine modes—the "maudlin sensualisms" of Wilde and the "bastard imperialism" of Roosevelt.[71]

Norton sustained the conflicts in this ambivalent fusion by reaffirming a secularized ethic of suffering which stressed personal moral accountability. Confronted by his wife's death as well as the senility of his mother and Ruskin, Norton pondered "the inexorable cruelty of Nature." Charging that "the long traditions of Heaven, paradise, and happiness have enfeebled the spirit of manliness in us," Norton characterized the position of the freethinking stoic as "the manliest which has yet been attained." Norton's stress on manliness revealed his continuing suspicion that his own role was somehow effeminate. But his stoical creed generated the moral ardor which energized his ambivalence and blocked his retreat to the debased mode of passive aestheticism.[72]

Sometimes the lines of defense wavered. Norton was still periodically neurasthenic, still tormented by longings for release from conflict in the sheltering arms of Catholic Europe.[73] But on the whole he adjusted to modern ego ideals, sublimating his "feminine" impulses in socially acceptable forms. Given his moral commitments, Norton conceived aesthetic experience not as permanent escape but as temporary renewal, a process he described in the organic or liquid imagery of antimodern vitalism. The process of renewal had an antimodern dimension because Norton viewed aesthetic creativity as a premodern phenomenon, no longer available in work-obsessed America or "Americanized" Europe. The pilgrim to the past could not linger; he had promises to keep in the present. Immersion in the oceanic realm of beauty was only a therapeutic respite from contemporary cares.

Yet Norton's antimodernism preserved a moral edge. If his ambivalence allowed accommodation with a conflicting superego, it also reflected his greatest strengths. Unable to rest content with rigid male ideals, Norton sought a wider selfhood. But confronted with the aesthetes' cult of experience, he hesitated. Loyal to inherited ideals of duty, he could not accept as a model the self-absorbed aesthete—the harbinger of the androgynous, leisure-oriented personality appropriate to consumer capitalism. Turning to aesthetic contemplation but preserving an ethic of suffering, Norton embodied an implied rebuke to the rigid morality of the nineteenth century as well as to the nonmorality of the twentieth. Standing between two worlds, his was a solitary example of stoical integrity.

As supernaturalism waned, stoical endurance became more difficult. The dictates of the superego seemed more onerous, their contradictions more apparent. "Real life" seemed ever farther out of reach. To energize the self in its ambivalence, something more than stoicism seemed necessary. Norton's austere version of "manliness" was not enough; the next generation surrounded it with vitalist imagery and called it the strenuous life. Beneath the tide of respectable strenuosity there were currents of fascination with primal irrationality and instinctual vitality. G. Stanley Hall was one antimodern vitalist who embraced both Rooseveltian activism and irrationalist primitivism. A generation younger than Norton, he sustained his ambivalence not through stoical endurance but rather through a vitalist apotheosis of intense experience.

## G. STANLEY HALL

In many ways, Hall's inner life paralleled Norton's. The lives of both men followed cyclical patterns, in which periods of passive withdrawal alternated with periods of active achievement. Neither was able to control this manic-depressive oscillation until he had integrated "feminine" values into a stable professional identity. Both associated those values with aesthetic Catholicism. For each, the catalyst for successful integration was a psychic crisis during middle age, precipitated by the death of his wife. And in both cases, the result was renewed accommodation with the dominant culture as well as a measure of personal protest.

Since Dorothy Ross has written a thoughtful biography of Hall, the details of his development need only be sketched here. He was born in 1844 in Ashfield, Massachusetts, where Norton spent many summers. (The two men later became good friends.) Hall's mother was an ardent Congregationalist who hoped her son would enter the ministry; his father was a farmer of modest means who hoped his son would stay home and help him scratch a more substantial living from the soil. Young Stanley was deeply dependent on his mother, fearful and covertly hostile toward his father. Drawn as a boy toward music and literature, he was terrified by the prospect of mediocrity and fiercely ambitious to enter a larger world than his father's. Ultimately his ambitions led him to physiological psychology, which he embraced as a secular quest for Truth and the first clear pathway to a masculine identity.[74]

As Ross shows, Hall successfully suppressed his admiration for "feminine" values until the early 1890s, when a series of disasters combined to produce a prolonged psychic crisis. Like Norton, Hall seemed to feel a frustrated desire for generativity. His efforts to build a first-rate scientific research center at Clark University had dissolved in internecine quarrels. William James, whom Hall considered his chief professional rival, had just published *Principles of Psychology*; Hall had been planning a similar synthesis for years, but he had nothing to show except disconnected notes. He felt old, useless, and impotent, one among many pedants unable to create.[75]

Hall's feelings of isolation and worthlessness were deepened by personal misfortunes. In 1887 his parents died; three years later his wife and eight-year-old daughter were accidentally asphyxiated. He had not been particularly close to his wife, who remained in the shadow of his professional aspirations. But after she died, he may well have formed an idealized vision of her in his mind. In any case, after her death Hall increasingly venerated an idealized feminine principle, derived from the domestic ideal but surrounded with vitalist imagery.

Among artists and intellectuals during the late nineteenth century, that principle played an increasingly important role. From Rossetti's Blessed Damozel to Baudelaire's Giantess to Henry Adams's Virgin of Chartres, images of female vitality pervaded the Western imagination. (This movement reached its apogee during the early twentieth century, in Joyce's Molly Bloom.) For Hall, the clearest embodiment of the feminine principle appeared in his story, "How Johnnie's Vision Came True" (1902). It recounts a young boy's mountain climb where he vows to achieve greatness—as Hall had done when he was fourteen. He prays first to the sun, the emblem of masculine intellect: "Don't set, but rise in my soul." But the sun does set, and when the moon rises he sees in it his mother. "Take me up to you now, now," he pleads. Uncertain whether he has heard a reply, he nevertheless feels "some new inner rapport established between them so that henceforth the moon would mean something more to him." Then Johnnie falls asleep, dreaming of a woman with "the mingled charm of mother, sister, and bride" who "resembled no one he had ever seen before, unless it was a rude woodcut of the Holy

Mother that he saw in a Catholic church he had visited months ago in a little village." They embrace, and "soon his lips met hers in a moment of such ecstacy as he had never dreamed of before." Johnnie never forgets that moment: late in his life, a widower and a successful man of affairs, he meets the woman of his vision and marries her.[76]

The story dramatized Hall's mature allegiance to the moon-goddess, a vitalist emblem of generativity. In later life, he satisfied some generative urges by turning from the sun-god of mechanistic science to a more capacious role as educator, speculative theorist, and counselor to youth. His movement from despair to regeneration involved a loosening of his sense of individuality in a grand cosmic scheme of evolutionary biology, which Hall identified with nature—the "all mother." In his paeans to maternity, Hall looked most frequently toward Catholicism for the supreme emblem of "feminine" values. "I keenly envy my Catholic friends their Maryolatry," Hall admitted.[77]

The revitalization of domestic values culminated in *Adolescence* (1904). Hall's sprawling two volumes joined childhood and femininity with the unconscious, presenting a vitalist alternative to male ego ideals, viewing maturation as a fall from unconscious unity to conscious fragmentation. For Hall, the androgynous adolescent symbolized his own effort to recast sexual ambivalence. His program for adolescent education was a revealing litany: "repose, leisure, art, legends, romance, idealizations, in a word, humanism." The moon-goddess presided over the curriculum. It embodied a "feminine" alternative to male ego ideals, an alternative with links to a mythopoeic unconscious. Yet Hall remained committed to the masculine ethos, insisting that the exposure of male adolescents to feminine values was only a temporary, vitalizing preparation for adulthood.[78]

Both Hall and Norton energized their ambivalence with moral ardor, but Hall moved closer to full accommodation. Lacking a coherent ethic of suffering, committed (though uncertainly) to progress, Hall devised a secular program for bourgeois revitalization. Like Walter Lippmann and other "Progressive" theorists, Hall wanted to free instinctual impulses in order to channel them toward social usefulness. His outlook epitomized the two hegemonic functions of the antimodern impulse. In his strenuosity and devotion to discipline, Hall looked backward to the achievement ethos; in his efforts to loosen character structure and his apotheosis of the "healthy personality," he looked forward, toward a therapeutic orientation of the self. Though he remained personally committed to the older ideals —both "masculine" achievement and "feminine" nurturance, Hall's vitalist apotheosis of domesticity pointed in new directions. His popularization of a benign unconscious paved the way for a therapeutic cult of "letting go" and a spurious cultural radicalism that labelled instinctual repression the central problem of capitalist society. His fatuities anticipated those of

Wilhelm Reich, Hugh Hefner, and the more deluded among the counter-cultural radicals of the 1960s. Sentimentalizing instinctual vitality, they exacerbated the weightlessness they tried to escape. In general, Hall's valuation of leisure, physical vigor, and psychic health was hardly the stuff of rebellion; it was well suited to the emerging outlook of twentieth-century consumer capitalism.

For all that, Hall himself remained a complex man, far more than a therapeutic social engineer. His interest in fantasy, dream, and visionary experience linked him with the European avant-garde and with the burgeoning psychoanalytic movement. (He arranged Freud's visit to America in 1909.) A pioneer popularizer of psychoanalysis, Hall was also groping toward some of Freud's profounder insights. From his own experience, Hall knew the complexities of a mind forever divided against itself: "the many-voiced comments, the sense of assent and dissent, pleasure and pain, the elation of strength or the aesthetic responses, the play of intuitions, the impulses to do or not to do . . . the mild or incipient insanities [which anyone] that is honest and has true self-knowledge will . . . confess to recognizing in his own soul."[79] Hall shared a glimmering of Freud's stoical self-awareness—which was, in a sense, a psychoanalytic version of Norton's ethic of suffering. It involved the recognition that the human mind was a tissue of tragic contradictions: ambivalence was an inescapable part of the human condition. In his public affirmation and private discontent, G. Stanley Hall shared in the failures and triumphs of the revolt against positivism.

The revolt offered an inexhaustible variety of pathways to regeneration. Often circular and self-defeating, they nevertheless preserved a philosophical and religious significance. Hall's vitalist vision of "feminine" values, though ultimately assimilated to the emerging therapeutic ethos, embodied a sharp critique of mechanistic science and restrictive masculinity. It joined maternal nurturance, emotional spontaneity, aesthetic responsiveness, and mythopoeic creativity—a constellation of ego ideals more fluid than their male counterparts, but ideals nonetheless. Yet the vitalist revision of "feminine" values increasingly associated them with the unconscious—explicitly in Hall, implicitly in the popular imagination. The linkage suggested an unfamiliar conclusion: the "feminine" realm might signify not another set of ideals, but release from all ideals and all ambivalence into an oceanic realm of passivity.

The connection between the oceanic feeling and the "feminine" realm of aesthetic Catholicism was especially strong among *fin-de-siècle* aesthetes. They sometimes sought a kind of secular Nirvana, a loss of separate selfhood in the soothing contemplation of Catholic art and artifacts. This kind of quest was more pervasive in Europe than in America, but for a number of years around the turn of the century, it flourished at Harvard. There, the young Van Wyck Brooks encountered the fullest American flowering of what he later called "pre-Raphaelite aestheticism and dilettantish Catholicism."[80]

## VAN WYCK BROOKS

Recoiling from an enervated Protestant culture and his own "morbid self-consciousness," the young Brooks vacillated between cults of outer and inner experience. Yearning to participate in the bustling "real life" of American democracy, Brooks was also eager for some transcendant belief and drawn toward the boundlessness of aesthetic contemplation. Yet to the periodically depressed youth, who sometimes longed for self-obliteration and who lacked a firm supernatural framework of belief, the Nirvana of the aesthetes ultimately suggested death. Confronted with a sense of imminent nonexistence, Brooks finally reaffirmed "masculine" activism and began a lifelong effort to deny his own ambivalence. Lacking any trace of inner conflict or tension, his optimistic creed met his deepest psychic needs and typified the persistent evasive banality of modern culture.

Like Hall, Brooks was dependent on his mother, indifferent and covertly contemptuous toward his father. But his contempt, unlike Hall's, was mixed with pity rather than fear. Charles Brooks was a failed mining speculator and semi-invalid who worked as a clerk in a Wall Street brokerage house. To the young Van Wyck, his father seemed a weak and pathetic man, whose plight symbolized the price exacted by the "morbid excitements" of business life. Brooks's wealthy and domineering mother, Sallie Ames Brooks, presented an alternative to the dull and destructive world of business. While her husband stayed home, preserving his fictitious role as provider, she led her two sons to the cultural shrines of Europe. Brooks's early impulse toward an artistic career was inextricably connected with reverence for the Old World and with memories of his mother's commanding presence.[81]

From early youth, Brooks imagined his mother's domestic realm as a haven from the masculine world of competition. He recalled a sense of "endless time" in her family home, where he grew up—an eternal present filled by cultivated indolence. But the neurasthenic businessmen on Plainfield park benches were haunting reminders of the masculine ethos, and even Brooks's mother equated masculine success with business success. Vaguely troubled by such expectations, Brooks read poetry and fiction through long afternoons in his mother's house. For decades, men and women alike had exalted this domestic alternative to aggressive masculinity. Like sensitive males before him, Brooks responded warmly to the "feminine" values enshrined in the domestic ideal.[82]

For Brooks, as for Hall, the "feminine" realm was linked to the unconscious. Other than Europe, the most sustaining source of "feminine" values was his own fantasy life. In adolescence, after he had formed an androg-ynous conception of the perfect soul, he wondered: "Is it preposterous to think that Jesus Christ was half-woman?" His youthful poems to Eleanor Stimson (whom he later married) were filled with fantasies of escape, expressed in the imagery of the sea and of Europe.[83] And from early childhood, he had a recurring dream.

> . . . I was on the lawn when a Hindu, suddenly appearing, in a coat of many colors, chased me with a knife,—a glittering knife that he held in his out-stretched hand, and, just as he approached me, running, I soared into the air and floated away, free, aloft, and safe. On other occasions the fiend was not an Oriental, he was merely a nondescript minatory figure that pursued me, and I was not even anxious when I saw him approaching, for I knew I possessed the power to float away.[84]

Brooks interpreted this dream as an allegory of his escape from the menacing world through writing. As David Brion Davis has suggested, one can spin a more complex web of associations among the Hindu, whom Americans of the early twentieth century might well have linked to the Black Hole of Calcutta; the coat of many colors, for which the Biblical Joseph was cast into a hole; and Brooks's father, who was figuratively in the "hole" of a menial clerkship. Viewed this way, the dream symbolized Brooks's triumph over his father, who was potentially threatening (even castrating), but actually weak. Brooks was "not even anxious" about the "minatory figure" approaching, for he knew he could "float away" with his mother to Europe.[85]

Yet reassuring fantasies were not enough. Though his father posed no threat, Brooks still felt oppressed by the world of destructive competition where one's manliness was constantly tested. His mother and brother chided him for his moody self-absorption, and he longed to do productive work. As he confided to his diary, "beyond all others, my faults are indo-lence downright, and half-heartedness in everything."[86] The desire to "float away" from male responsibility engendered persistent feelings of guilt and periodic self-accusations.

Brooks's ambivalence was heightened by the *fin-de-siècle* cultural milieu, in which antimodern vitalism sanctioned both withdrawal and activism. For Brooks, one pole pointed toward contemplative aestheticism, the other toward spontaneous creative achievement. As a child in Plainfield, Brooks had served as an altar boy at an Anglo-Catholic church, had placed an altar in his room, and had dreamed of entering the priesthood. He was naturally drawn to the aesthetic Catholicism flourishing at Harvard around the turn of the century. Yet he could not emulate the languorous aesthetes clus-tered around George Santayana and Pierre La Rose. He began to worry that aestheticism was an excuse for indulging his "morbid and mawkish" tendencies.[87] Ingrained activist ideals led Brooks to suspect that "feminine" values sanctioned irresponsible emotionalism and dependent passivity.

There remained a deeper problem. Brooks associated the realm of Europe and the arts not merely with effeminate withdrawal but with impotence and self-annihilation. As early as adolescence, his fantasies of escape had included thoughts of suicide. His encounters with Catholic art in Europe also generated the fear that he might be swallowed up by a sea of beauty. As Brooks later remembered, after having "filled my diary with Ruskinian pages about ambones and medieval pulpits covered with mosaics. . . . I felt the danger of what Melville described as 'falling into Plato's honey head' and, as he added, sweetly perishing there."[88]

Brooks revealed that fear in *The Wine of the Puritans* (1908), published soon after his graduation from Harvard. The book opens on an Italian midsummer afternoon, with the two protagonists lounging amid "flowering glooms of dusty verdure. Here and there a line of yellow columns stood out like rich candles among the silks of a splendid altar." "There is something I don't quite like about this," says one. "I feel as if a great many things had suddenly come together to brush me out of existence. I think we had better have a discussion!"[89] Brooks's "discussion" was his first effort to resist self-annihilation in European aestheticism, and to heal the split in his psyche by affirming hopes for American culture.

After railing against the hyperrationality of American culture, Brooks nonetheless refused to abandon it. Despite his pessimism about the immediate prospects for Americans, Brooks's reverence for "life" as a value in itself led him to reject expatriation as the refuge of the dilettante. "Every degree of fastidiousness is also a degree of stagnation," he warned. The intellectual's greatest danger lay in avoiding "vital contact with American life." Brooks's affirmation was rooted in his own psychic need, not in his evidence. After his bleak assessment of contemporary American culture, his prediction that "a day will come when the names of Denver and Sioux City will have a traditional and antique dignity like Damascus and Perugia" seemed hollow and unconvincing.[90]

Nor had Brooks convinced himself. He remained drawn toward Europe and dependent passivity. *The Wine of the Puritans* was his declaration of independence, but he feared "the possibility of its hurting mama," through its sharp criticism of genteel culture. Returning to New York after a year of sporadic attempts at journalism in London, Brooks was forced to take a job on the *World's Work,* an embodiment of the business culture he despised. His fascination with religious art and ritual persisted, and he often stretched his lunch hour to two in order to linger in Catholic churches. His fiancée dismissed the Church as a refuge for moral "cowards and weaklings," but for Brooks, it nurtured his impulses toward aesthetic contemplation and emotional dependency.[91]

During 1909, while he drifted from the *World's Work* to various other hack jobs in literary New York, Brooks composed *The Soul: an Essay Towards a Point of View*. The pamphlet dramatized the polarities overshadowing his entire life—"feminine" dependence and "masculine" autonomy, aesthetic withdrawal and social action, European Catholicism and American Protestantism. Behind Brooks's ambivalence, there was one consistent purpose: a desire to experience the "real life" concealed by literary and social conventions. "How much of life I had faced through the veil of other men's opinions!" Brooks exclaimed at the beginning of *The Soul*. He insisted that there was a cosmic unity behind that veil. By discovering "such laws as . . . the indestructibility of matter, the conservation of matter, and the evolution of species," Brooks claimed, modern science has confirmed the intuitions of medieval mystics.

> As I thought of that cry of St. Thomas a Kempis: 'How sweet it is to love, to be dissolved, and to swim in love!', I saw in this very sense of the sweetness of dissolution precisely that which animated St. Francis at the moment of death. By some quick intuition of precisely those laws of science, a passionate love for the elements composing his body and soul become articulate in him at the moment of dissolution. We are told that he stretched forth his hands and cried with joy, 'Welcome, Sister Death!'[92]

This sense of unity with all being made St. Francis superior to Luther, Brooks decided. Luther spent his life in action, dying in frustration and despair. Francis (and Mary Magdalene) withdrew from the world to a life of contemplation; they lived and died in joyous identification with the universe. This line of argument led toward endorsement of Catholic contemplation, but Brooks pulled up short. The problem with Catholicism, he said, was that the Church institutionalized otherworldliness and tried to shackle it to a particular social order. In the end, though Catholicism seemed attractively composed of "all that is unexpected, bizarre, exaggerated, and unconventional," neither form of institutional Christianity seemed sufficient.[93]

Between reflections on religion, Brooks kept returning to primitivist fantasies of boundlessness. He traced the origin of poetry to primitive man's desire to express his identity with the universe; he attributed poetry's decline to the loss of that sense of elemental unity "in love and in dreams," as words became playthings of conventionality. He imagined recovering the sense of unity while swimming in the sea, or lying in long grass, entering a world where "there is no such thing as failure. . . ." "And if all action exists for this," he wondered, "why laboriously translate into action experience that has been lived already . . . ?"[94] In other words, why write criticism?

In the circling prose of *The Soul*, Brooks always checked these reflections with another tribute to "reality." He kept insisting that "a man, so long as he is real, can have in him the dream of a world." The question remained:

Which was more "real," individual assertion or cosmic unity? Brooks continued to waver. His attempt to give form to the flux of events made him "like one who has engaged a sculptor to make a mask of his face," Brooks concluded. I fear the distorted impression of stasis the mask will leave, he wrote; "yet under the plaster as it grows gradually cold I am free all the time."

> I release my lips. I open my eyes. Oh the silence! oh, the dark solitude! and all that whirls within me.

> O pondus immensum;
> o pelagus intransnatabile:
> ubi nihil de me reperio quam in toto nihil.
> Ubi est ergo latebra gloriae;
> ubi confidentia de virtute concepta?[95]

The suggestion that he was being fitted for a death mask, perhaps being buried alive, along with the lines from à Kempis—all undercut Brooks's attempt at an affirmative conclusion. Though he longed for union with the infinite, his uncertain religious faith led him to connect boundlessness with death. Though he admired the "feminine" realm of contemplation, his male ego ideals led him to associate it with total passivity and unconsciousness. His fantasies of boundlessness contained the suspicion that all individual assertion might be a futile exercise to stave off thoughts of death. Brooks counteracted that anxiety by stressing his need to express "all that whirls within me!" The will toward literary creation became his antidote to suicidal despair.

After struggling with *The Soul*, Brooks moved steadily away from aestheticism. He married Eleanor Stimson in 1911, secured a teaching position at Stanford, and tried to exorcise his otherworldly tendencies by attacking *The Malady of the Ideal* in a book of that title in 1913. His best book, *America's Coming-of-Age* (1915), was an effort to harmonize his own ambivalence by confronting what he saw as the basic division in American life—between "masculine" business and "feminine" culture. Calling for a "genial middle ground" between enervated ideals and "catchpenny realities," Brooks satirized the lowbrow culture of success ideology, but also flayed his fellow American writers for "their disinclination to take a plunge, reckless and complete, . . . into the rudest and grossest actualities."[96] His moral ardor sustained this ambivalent stance throughout the book. Brooks never again orchestrated his inner tensions so skillfully.

During subsequent years, while he wrote for the *Seven Arts* and the *Freeman*, Brooks's balance began to slip. Stubbornly sticking to America, he felt "a frequently acute homesickness for the European scene." His oscillation between elation and despair sharpened to "ridiculous ups and downs"; his depressions deepened and lengthened. With Randolph

Bourne, Brooks denounced the "futility and empty verbalism" of avant-garde poetry—the shortcomings he feared in his own work. Haunted by a growing sense of his own ineffectuality and emotional dependence, Brooks became obsessed with writing as an act of will. "Literature is nothing but the expression of power, of the creative will, of 'free will,'" he wrote in 1922.[97] "Free Will" and "Life" became talismanic words to him as he felt more helpless and isolated.

Brooks's sense of helplessness arose partly because he was divided against himself, partly because he had boxed himself in intellectually. Throughout his career, he had insisted that an artist's creative powers could flower only in the soil of his native country, surrounded by a supportive community of creators. As a seedbed of literary tradition, this community preserved the writer's "usable past." The problem was that to the younger Brooks so much in America's past seemed useless. Impressed by the barrenness of the American cultural landscape, but convinced that expatriation was futile and irresponsible, Brooks could only write such chronicles of failure as *The Ordeal of Mark Twain* (1920) and *The Pilgrimage of Henry James* (1925). Iconoclasm cut Brooks off from the bearers of the genteel tradition; nationalism set him apart from the cosmopolitan avant-garde. Sinking into frustrated isolation, he was tormented by a sense of failure—by the feeling, as he said in his autobiography, that all his early efforts had merely "ploughed the sea."[98]

The image crystallized the generative elements in what Brooks called "my *crise à quarante ans.*" In his own mind, he had been sowing his seed where it could not grow, where not even a furrow would remain. His commitments to achievement in America seemed fruitless; he had not escaped effeteness after all. His oceanic impulses returned—now definitely suicidal, connected with fears that he might be swallowed up by the sea of European culture, or crushed by the weight of its tradition. Brooks could not exorcise the Old World demon of his youth, that compound of pessimism, fastidious withdrawal and self-destructive impulses. He was haunted by the "great, luminous menacing eyes" of Henry James, the personification of "feminized" European aestheticism. "I was half aware, in connection with him, of the division within myself," Brooks later wrote.[99] He drifted from one sanatorium to another for five years. He was unable to write or sleep; he sometimes grovelled on the ground and ate grass; he thought constantly of suicide.

During this period (1926–1931), while Brooks still associated Europe with helpless passivity and a "death drive," he increasingly identified America with free will and the determination to survive. Nationalism, always essential to his public role, became the lodestar of his psychic well-being. Returning to work, he began the rigorous schedule of writing and reading which resulted in the Makers and Finders series (1936–1952). He set about the creation of a usable past, less for the inspiration of contemporary writers than for the preservation of his mental stability.

During his later years, almost everything Brooks wrote revealed an effort to disown his youthful impulses toward aestheticism and pessimistic withdrawal. In the Makers and Finders series, Brooks invented a native literary tradition, rooted in the doctrines of free will, progress, and the natural goodness of man. For the old goal of cosmic unity he had nothing but contempt. In *The Opinions of Oliver Allston* (1941), Brooks attacked the "infantilism" and "death-drive" of avant-garde artists and intellectuals. "Many held the view that man had steadily deteriorated since the Middle Ages"; others accepted some cyclical theory of history. In all cases their lack of faith in progress cut them off from democratic roots and walled them up in stifling coteries. They were "children sucking their thumbs," Brooks charged.

> . . . was it not *immature* . . . to throw up the sponge of life as they did? Was it not immature to "break away" from the mould of life and seek for death, or the primitive, or a nihilist Nirvana? Was it not immature to whine, with Eliot and Pound, about the "pure" past and the "vulgar" present?[100]

The virulence of Brooks's attack on antimodernism as a form of childish regression suggested how urgently he needed to disown his own antimodern tendencies in order to preserve a stable adult identity. His career illuminates the circuitous path from antimodern dissent to revitalized accommodation. Recoiling from a stale and enervated culture and from his own "morbid self-consciousness," Brooks alternately sought oceanic peace and activist rejuvenation. Like George Cabot Lodge, Brooks oscillated between the "feminine" and "masculine" poles of antimodernism. Unable to sustain ambivalence, he fell into suicidal despair. He finally reintegrated some sense of selfhood by reaffirming activist ideals of modern culture. Brooks's activism was not, to be sure, the activism of the avant-garde—the cult of experience embraced by men like Rimbaud or Apollinaire. Indeed, it was only a pale reflection of the romantic activism of the American 1890s. There was little exuberance, and no worship of instinctual vitality, in Brooks's activist outlook. There was only the tired reiteration of nineteenth-century optimism—a creed devoid of tension or conflict, little more than a strategy for psychic survival.

To draw wider inferences from these six lives, one must first meet the objection that these were only a handful of intellectuals, whose conflicts have no relevance to the larger culture. They comprised an exceptionally well-educated group, but they shared common tensions with many less articulate and privileged members of the bourgeoisie. The neurasthenia epidemic spread far into the middle class; so did the ideology of domesticity, with its high valuation of the "feminine" realm, and its contradictory expectations of autonomy and dependence. Fundamentally, these men's conflicts were rooted in the modern superego, the moral orientation pervading all of bourgeois culture. Victorian ambivalence was hardly restricted to Beacon Hill. Yet the fact remains that antimodernism developed mainly among the affluent and educated. It was socially significant not because it affected the entire population but because, in some of its forms, it reinforced the cultural hegemony of dominant groups—partly by reaffirming their commitments to familiar bourgeois values, partly by promoting new values which later became diffused throughout all of American culture. In these six lives, antimodernism revealed its two major social functions: the revitalization and transformation of the dominant American culture.

In many ways, antimodernism provided cultural forms which allowed troubled Americans to sustain an ambivalent stance during a difficult time. With the softening of supernaturalism and the waning of an ethic of suffering, the conflicting demands of the modern superego became more burdensome. The oscillation between autonomy and dependence—between "masculine" and "feminine" ideals—became more difficult to sustain. Antimodernism provided a variety of cultural resources for grappling with ambivalence: it surrounded autonomy with the imagery of romantic activism, dependence with oceanic passivity; it revitalized both "male" and "female" ideals.

But in the end, for these six men, "male" ideals proved stronger. In every case, they served to thrust antimodernism toward accommodation. Having internalized the "masculine" ethos, these men tended to identify "feminine" values with irresponsible dependency and sometimes even self-annihilation. For Lowell and Brooks, male ego ideals shaped a repudiation of ambivalence and a more rigid identity. For Lodge, they provoked an imaginative rejection of actual dependence and fantasies of total autonomy. For Norton and Hall, they channeled "feminine" impulses toward ambivalent fusion in conflict-ridden identities: Norton as republican aesthete; Hall as national therapist. And for Bigelow, unable to form any coherent alternative to them, male ego ideals accelerated his slide into a chronic, helpless dependence—a debased caricature of the "feminine" mode.

In these six men's lives, we can glimpse the psychic basis for the revitalization and transformation of ruling class cultural hegemony—a link between Freud and Gramsci, so to speak. At the basic level of their individual psyches, attachment to autonomy conditioned their antimodern impulse, pressing it toward circularity and accommodation. Even the quest for boundless union with the cosmos stemmed from the desire to add substance to a "weightless" personal identity. That desire was rooted in psychic needs and religious longings; all six of these men sought some transcendent meaning for human action. Their religious yearnings were often reinforced by desires for oceanic dependence. Yet of the six, only

Bigelow could rest content with Nirvana—even temporarily. Returning from Japan to the United States, he became paralyzed by self-doubt and ended in despair. The profoundest hopes for boundlessness often coincided with the most self-destructive moods. Lacking firm belief, all but Bigelow equated union with annihilation and retreated to autonomy.

But the circularity was not complete. The various paths to readjustment revealed important transitions in the dominant culture. Of the six, only Norton (who was born earliest) sustained his ambivalence through the republican ethic of suffering. Lowell and Brooks repudiated ambivalence altogether, but their rigidified commitment to autonomy suggested a reaffirmation of nineteenth-century hegemonic culture. On the other hand, Lodge's imaginative rejection of ambivalence pointed toward the avant-garde cult of self-fulfillment, as well as its popularized version in the twentieth-century culture of consumption. Hall sustained his ambivalence, but through a vitalist exaltation of energy rather than a republican ethic of suffering; his paeans to vitality helped pave the way for the twentieth-century obsession with psychic health. And if Hall represented the official optimism of the incipient therapeutic world view, Bigelow embodied its underside of helpless dependence and perpetual anxiety: its paralysis of will.

Though these men were not "representative men," they do represent six varieties of antimodern experience. And their psychic careers suggest the working out, in individual lives, of cultural tensions which pervaded the educated bourgeoisie. Further, their solutions to the problem of ambivalence can metaphorically imply larger shifts in the structure of thought and feeling. The older achievement ethos persisted, but with a new rigidity and brittleness—at least for sensitive men like Brooks. As the ethic of suffering waned, vitalism replaced republican moralism as a source for ardor. But without a religious or even an ethical framework of meaning, the oscillating self lost the capacity to sustain ambivalence. Desires for total release —for escape from all inner conflict—began to proliferate among the educated bourgeoisie. In the emerging secular culture of the early twentieth century, the modern superego softened. Both "masculine" and "feminine" ideals lost moral content; they became different ways of savoring experience—one active and "risk-taking," the other passive and leisure-oriented, both self-absorbed. By generating cults of outer and inner experience, the antimodern impulse reinforced those tendencies and promoted a therapeutic basis for the cultural hegemony of an emerging managerial bourgeoisie.

Men like Lodge, Hall, and Bigelow prefigured various aspects of the new therapeutic mode: self-fulfillment, obsessive "vitality," chronic depression. Neither they nor other antimodernists were part of a nostalgic "dying race"; rather they embodied embryonic developments come to fruition only recently. Though most did not know it, they were at the forefront of cultural change.

Brooks himself popularized the idea that dissent from modernity constituted a decline from antebellum belief in progress to *fin-de-siècle* nostalgia. Preoccupied with sustaining his postbreakdown identity, Brooks caricatured antimodern aestheticism as a flight from "reality" and minimized his own attraction to contemplation. (He never mentioned *The Soul* in his memoirs.) Obsessed with disowning his "hyperaesthetic youth," Brooks overlooked the Janus-faced quality of antimodern dissent—including his own. His errors have influenced a generation of cultural historians.

Yet the most serious error involves not the social significance of antimodernism, but its moral and religious importance. Even as the antimodern impulse helped to spread a therapeutic orientation, it also promoted antitherapeutic protest. The very effort to sustain ambivalence contained moral significance; it suggested a recognition that schemes for psychic harmony were fated to be quixotic, that unresolved conflict was the essence of the human predicament. This tragic sense of life gave Norton's stoical endurance a certain gravity and grandeur. Despite the smugness of his claims to "manliness," he preserved an ethic of suffering in an increasingly self-absorbed age. There were also those, like Bigelow, for whom stoicism was not enough. His persistent quest for union with the Divine, however confused and ultimately frustrated, marked an heroic protest against the encroaching restraints of a secularizing culture. More insistently religious than the others considered here, Bigelow's antimodernism was not only an implied critique of the modern superego but a doomed desire for the infinite—in the end, a cry for cooling water from an old man in a dry month.

# ·7·

# FROM FILIAL LOYALTY TO RELIGIOUS PROTEST: HENRY ADAMS

EVEN AS RELIGIOUS PROTEST, ANTIMODERNISM WAS often more a matter of half-conscious aspiration and vague regret than of explicit sentiment. Among Americans who felt the antimodern impulse, only Henry Adams transmuted it into a coherent and enduring critique of modern culture. Early ingrained with male ego ideals, he was increasingly attracted toward "feminine" values. Recasting his ambivalence in antimodern cultural forms, he personified civility while he assaulted overcivilized manhood and womanhood alike. His life and work embodied all the major themes of antimodernism.

I intend to revise two misinterpretations which have dominated discussions of Adams. Following Van Wyck Brooks's lead, historians have dismissed Adams's later work as the product of a "displaced patrician" who projected his personal and political disappointments onto the cosmos. Literary critics have praised the later work as the product of a skeptical "modern consciousness"; they have revered Adams as an early example of Lévi-Strauss's *bricoleur*—an intellectual who values only the free play of ideas for their own sake. The historians veer toward reductionism, the critics toward intellectualism. Though both perspectives are illuminating, neither quite grasps the emotional dilemmas behind Adam's literary symbols or the religious significance of his writings. To understand more fully the psychic and religious dimensions of his work, I want to place it within the contexts of late-Victorian ambivalence and the wider antimodern response to the crisis of cultural authority.[1]

Adams's ambivalence was profound and persistent. From earliest youth, he had internalized male ego ideals, reinforced by republican moralism and the family tradition of public service. But Adams's unusually accomplished family background intensified the conflicts of authority in the modern superego—particularly the ambiguous relation between individual achievement and domestic harmony. In a culture committed to autonomy, a distinguished family might be a burden as well as a gift. Like other late Victorians, Adams faced a central moral question: How did one reconcile the drive toward autonomy with filial loyalty, especially if the father allowed independence only on his own terms? More imaginatively than any of his contemporaries, Adams explored modern dilemmas of authority.

For Adams, as for the men in the preceding chapter, the conflict between autonomy and dependence within the wider culture was exacerbated by parallel conflict within his own inner life. Here again, public and private dilemmas intermeshed. And for Adams, too, conflict took the form of tension between "masculine" and "feminine" ideals. Committed to active engagement, he was nevertheless a sensitive boy who detested "the strife of the world" and longed for a quiet literary life. He alternated between manic ambition and depressive withdrawal. The "feminine" realm of nurturance and repose, idealized in the cult of domesticity, grew more attractive as Adams grew older. He moved away from his father's activist ideals. Frustrated in his desires for generativity, lonely and childless after his wife's suicide, he began to create a personal mythology centering on an archaic feminine principle. Yet his longings for maternal comfort were joined with fears of self-obliteration. Like other late-Victorian men, Adams viewed the Great Mother as both creator and destroyer. His male ego ideals survived, resurfacing in geopolitical fantasies and a Faustian fascination with science. As he wrote in *The Education,* "Life was a double thing."

Increasingly aware of his own ambivalence, Adams sustained it with a vitalist apotheosis of energy and a persistent desire for a supernatural framework of meaning. Like other expressions of antimodernism, his was rooted in the crisis of cultural authority. Adams shared the neurasthenia of the upper bourgeoisie as well as its class and ethnic prejudices. He betrayed the patrician's contempt for the socialist and Jew, the republican's suspicion of luxury (including his own), and the religious doubter's distaste for the bland reassurances of liberal Protestantism. The social and spiritual unrest of the 1890s heightened the tensions in his own ambivalent psyche. Ultimately he sought not to banish tension but to endure it. Dialectic became the fundamental principle of his late work. Intelligence and instinct, Dynamo and Virgin, appeared and reappeared in the ferment of his imagination.

But the proliferating dialectics in Adams's late thought were not the playthings of a *bricoleur.* Stemming from his ambivalent psyche, they carried heavy emotional weight. His revaluation of dependence became the path to a profounder autonomy—a declaration of independence from his father's values. His scientific speculation was driven by a desire to turn science against itself, to discredit positivist certainties by widening the cracks in the "block universe." Adams's belated rebellion against the authority of his father became a rebellion against the authority of his father's cultural universe—the confident platitudes of progressive optimism. Raising personal issues to a philosophical plane, Adams joined the revolt against positivism. However cosmic his speculations became, all originated in the turmoil of his divided self.

# Early Manhood: the Meandering Track of the Family Go-Cart

The parents of Henry Adams cast a long shadow over his career. Abigail Brooks Adams was effusive in her affection but disposed to dark imaginings about the future—a trait which may have reappeared in Henry. In raising her sons she deferred to her husband, Charles Francis Adams. He was a pillar of self-control, given to demanding introspection and periodic depressions. Like his own father, John Quincy Adams, he appeared detached and cold in family relations. A hectoring moralist to his sons, he hid his affection and withheld his praise. "He never wrote to nor even spoke to me in his life about any production [i.e., accomplishment] of mine," Henry recalled. In politics a classical liberal, in religion a Unitarian, Charles Francis Adams distrusted enthusiasm in public as well as private affairs. His mind, like his character, was a model of moderate, mildly optimistic decorum.[2]

Young Henry Adams grew up in a suffocating atmosphere of paternal expectation and family pride. If his father was stubborn and self-righteous, his older brother Charles caricatured those traits. He became a kind of surrogate father to Henry, perpetually urging him toward self-improvement and filial loyalty. It was no wonder Henry preferred Harvard to home. Upon graduation he departed for Berlin. To his father and brother, Henry tried to justify the sojourn as a rigorous program of study in Civil Law. Once abroad, he slipped into prolonged depression, floundering from one project to another. He thought of editing his grandfather's works, then abandoned the plan because "it is not in me to do them justice." Soon convinced he was unfit for law, Adams dabbled in journalism. But he feared failure and the disapproval of his father, who thought magazines "ephemeral." Finally he rejoined his parents in Washington, where he resumed the study of law. As he wrote his mother, "If Papa and you approve this course, and it's found easy to carry out, you can have at least one of your sons always with you." Eager for an independent career but haunted by the fear of "making a slump" in journalism, Adams chose the path of filial loyalty.[3]

When President Lincoln appointed Charles Francis Adams minister to England, Henry followed as his private secretary. Father and son were "as merry as grigs" in the office together by day, but Henry was despondent by night. He felt useless and dilettantish in contrast to Charles, an officer in the Army of the Potomac. As his depressions deepened, his self-accusations engendered an emerging sense of doubleness. As he wrote Charles: "Do you understand how, without a double personality, *I* can feel that *I* am a failure? One would think that *I* which could feel that, must be a different *ego* from the *I* of which it was felt."[4]

The feeling of double personality reflected Adams's "morbid self-consciousness"—his developing awareness of his own ambivalence. In an effort to escape ambivalence, he turned first to disciplined intellectual endeavor, later to longings for dependence on an oceanic Great Mother. Neither solution proved sufficient to the problem of ambivalence, but both signified an important break with family ideals of public activism. As early as 1867, he had written to Charles:

> John [the oldest brother] is a political genius; let him follow the family bent. You are a lawyer and with a few years' patience will be the richest and most respectable of us all. I claim my right to part company with you both. I never will make

a speech, never run for office, never belong to a party. I am going to plunge under the stream. For years you will hear nothing of any publication of mine —perhaps never, who knows. I do not mean to tie myself to anything, but I do mean to make it impossible for myself to follow the family go-cart.[5]

Henry's attitude alarmed Charles, who sensed his brother's drift from politics to a literary "Bohemianism." After Henry returned to Washington and plunged into a bewildering variety of intellectual projects, Charles wrote him the customary lecture on singleness of purpose. Henry shot back: "I see you are getting back to your old dispute with me on the purpose of life. . . . You like the strife of the world. I detest and despise it. You work for power. I work for my own satisfaction. You like roughness and strength; I like taste and dexterity. For God's sake, let us go our ways and not try to be like each other."[6]

Like it or not, Adams was harnessed to the family go-cart, to the ego ideals embodied in his father and brother. The pressure toward active engagement led him from literary projects to political commentary. The demand for regular employment—a moral if not a financial necessity for the upper bourgeoisie—led him from free-lance journalism to a teaching position at Harvard. At first resisting the offer of an assistant professorship in history, he finally accepted at the urging of his father and brother, again sacrificing autonomy to filial loyalty.

The cultural atmosphere of Boston deepened Adams's depressive tendencies. It seemed anemic, overcivilized. "In this Arcadian society sexual passions seem to be abolished," he wrote wryly, just before his engagement to Marian Hooper in 1872. Four years later he complained that "Everything is respectable, and nothing amusing. There are no outlaws. There are not only no convictions but no strong wants." As Adams formed his dissent from modernity, he expanded his indictment of Boston's bourgeois culture to include all of Western civilization. But for the moment he wanted only to escape.[7]

He did in 1877, when he and Marian moved to Washington. Offered the editorship of the Albert Gallatin papers, Adams welcomed a chance for relief from the familial air of Boston. His father sensed that Henry was breaking family ties. "I feel," the old man wrote in his diary, "as if he was now taking a direction which would separate us from him gradually forever."[8] Henry Adams was groping toward a new identity as a speculative artist of ideas.

The process was slow. Through the early 1880s, many of his attitudes still reflected his father's liberal belief in progress. Though Adams was alarmed by working-class unrest, he remained convinced that in general "Man is still going fast upward." Writing to John Hay, Adams jeered at Lord Acton's forebodings: "Tell my lord to come over here and live for the future, not for the middle ages." Life in Washington seemed full and good, with plenty of satisfying work, political gossip, and dinner table repartee. In all, it struck a nice balance between "Bohemian" impulses and family ideals.[9]

But for all the surface complacency in Adams's outlook, a change was taking root. In part, it involved a deepening of philosophical concerns. The expositor of Anglo-Saxon law now sought more speculative historical issues. He pondered the fate of individual autonomy in a mass democracy; he resumed his struggle to reconcile liberal voluntarism with philosophical determinism. In a moment of adolescent iconoclasm, Adams had declared himself a "full-blown fatalist"; now his research in early American history forced him to confront the implications of the claim.[10]

The implications were personal as well as intellectual. The growing sense of man's inability to challenge the decrees of fate stemmed partly from his recognition that the intentions of individual policymakers were nearly always thwarted by the historical process; but it also arose from the turmoil in Adams's own psyche. His darkening speculations reflected his own cyclical tendency toward depression, the frustrations of his childless marriage, and the feelings of sterility that began to surround his historical labors. In his early forties, his sense of identity still seemed uncertain. Generativity had eluded Adams; entering middle age, he had fathered neither a child nor the major historical work he planned. Restive in his roles as husband and historian, Adams sought release from his father's male ego ideals. He never abandoned them, but he began tentatively to nurture "feminine" alternatives—implicit in his own character, sanctioned culturally in the domestic ideal. His wife's suicide threw his generative longings into relief, transforming his vague discontent into profound depression.[11]

# Husband, Historian, Novelist: Adams's Crisis of Generativity

As early as 1880, while he was still immersed in the research for his *History*, Adams was faintly self-contemptuous. "Aridity grows on me," he wrote to his former graduate student, Henry Cabot Lodge. "I always felt myself like Casaubon in Middlemarch and now I see the tendency steadily creeping over me. This makes me all the gladder to see you plunged into active life."[12] In part this comment reflected an intellectual's envy for a man of affairs, but there was more to it than that. By referring to Casaubon, the pedantic historian and pathetically inadequate husband in Eliot's novel, Adams betrayed a deeper source of dis-ease: a fear that he was entering an impotent and sterile old age without having generated ideas, books, or children.

The deepest source of Adams's anxiety was his childlessness. On Henry's wedding day, his father noted the event in his diary, adding: "I trust the issue will be propitious." The propagation of children was a proud duty among most upper-class Victorian families; to the Adamses it seemed particularly important. Imbued from childhood with a sense of family continuity, Henry accepted his childlessness with bitter disappointment. "One consequence of having no children is that husband and wife become very dependent on each other and live very much together," he admitted to an English friend. "This is our case, but we both like society and try to conciliate it."[13]

One can only imagine the secret pain involved in that effort. Since the opening of the Adams Family Papers, historians have discovered a few revealing details: that the couple became attached to their two Skye terriers, that Henry's father grew increasingly hostile toward Marian, that Henry owned *Clinical Notes on Uterine Surgery with Special Reference to the Management of Sterile Conditions*. An old friend recalled that Marian had "all she wanted, all this world could give, except children—and not having any was a greater grief to Mr. Adams than to her."[14]

Without children Adams attached an even greater personal significance to the completion of his *History*. Complaining that "weariness and langour" had settled over the writing, he began habitually to refer to the nine-volume project as a protracted process of childbirth. "Do you know," he wrote Hay in 1882, "a book to me always seems a part of myself, a kind of intellectual brat or segment, and I never bring one into the world without a sense of shame. They are naked, helpless, and beggarly, and the poor wretches must live forever and curse their father for their silent tomb." Henry's own father had become senile and the younger man was troubled by a "nervous fear of losing time" before his own generative powers declined. "I have only one offspring," he told Lodge, "and am almost forty-four while it is nothing but an embryo."[15]

Scholarship alone could not satisfy Adams's frustrated urge for generativity. Chafing at the bonds of a masculine superego, he explored the feminine realm of cultured leisure. He wrote two novels, both of which had female protagonists; he also courted the companionship of women: his young friend Elizabeth Cameron, his nieces, above all his wife. Fastidious, diffident, Adams had never conformed to Victorian stereotypes of manliness. By the 1880s he preferred the company of women to that of most men. Adams was only slightly exaggerating when he told Hay in 1883: "Man delights me not. Woman is my only solace."[16]

Adams's preference for female society had complex origins. Among women he found "taste and dexterity" corresponding to his own. More important, women provided maternal comfort which nurtured his dependent impulses. The domestic ideal enshrined childhood as well as femininity; Adams's flight from male ego ideals pointed in both those directions. Woman was the model for his behavior but also the mother who nourished his childlike needs. And the most powerful maternal figure was Marian Adams. From her vigorous letters, Ernest Samuels has observed, "one senses something of the way in which she mothered Henry Adams, providing that domination at the hands of women which he craved."[17] Marian was not only comforting; she was aggressive, with a reputation for barbed wit. In many ways, Marian Adams was the prototype for Henry's vitalist mother-goddess—at once consoling and fierce, creative and destructive.

The problem was that Marian seemed to draw all her strength from her father, none from her husband. When her father died, she entered a downward spiral of depression. On December 6, 1885, she committed suicide. Her death shattered Adams's precarious sense of selfhood and intensified his yearning for "feminine" alternatives. He felt cut adrift at midlife. "I am left alone in the world at a time when too young to die and too old to take up existence afresh," he wrote Hay two days after the suicide. More preoccupied than ever with an urge for generativity, Adams struggled to give some meaning to a life "cut in halves."[18]

In part, this effort involved the task set by male ego ideals: the completion of the *History*. Still referring to the volumes as "children," Adams returned with rigorous self-control to his writing schedule. Yet he found no solace in the work. The process of composition seemed dreary and mechanical; the project as a whole seemed the product of his "past life." He could not shake the demon of ennui. Except for a trip to Japan in 1886, he remained in self-imposed isolation for five years—withdrawn into his study, cut off from all but a few friends, forbidding even the mention of Marian's name in his presence.[19]

Adams's mourning was extreme even by Victorian standards. Judging by his growing obsession with "feminine" values, the mourning may have involved the process described by Freud in "Mourning and Melancholia" (1917): "an *identification* of the ego with the abandoned object. Thus the shadow of the object fell upon the ego, so that the latter could henceforth be criticized by a special mental faculty like an object, like the forsaken object."[20] Marian may have entered Adams's mind as a kind of idealized superego, an emotionally-charged embodiment of the "feminine" values associated with the domestic ideal. The "feminized" superego reinforced Adams's longings for maternal consolation and forgiveness, for relief from moralizing introspection, and for a wider sense of selfhood than the "masculine" ethos allowed.

But for Adams, mourning was more than a matter of identification with a lost love object; it was also a protracted exercise in self-reproach and a desperate search for expiation. The sources of this self-punishing guilt (which also strengthened Adams's desire for release) were complex and difficult to specify. They probably lay in puritan habits of mind and in the (mostly unknown) circumstances surrounding Marian's death. She had taken her life by drinking the potassium cyanide she used in photography; Henry may have blamed himself for leaving poison within reach of a suicidally depressed woman. He may also have half-suspected that he had desired her father's death, the catalyst of her final depression. That thought was inadmissible to consciousness, but there is some evidence of tension between Adams and his father-in-law. Since the bond between Marian and her father was unusually strong, Adams, resenting the barrier it placed between him and his wife, may have wished for its dissolution. Yet when Marian's father finally died, Henry seemed unable to provide emotional support; he had depended on her too long to reverse the relationship. Sensing his own inadequacy, he may have felt doubly responsible for her death.[21]

An exaggerated sense of individual moral responsibility, often defined in narrowly personal terms, lay at the heart of modern culture. By the years of Adams's maturity, the foundations of that sense were eroding—weakened by the fragmenting of familiar notions of selfhood and the waning of supernatural sanctions for morality. For Adams as for many of his contemporaries, personal moral responsibility became an increasingly burdensome ideal; autonomy became problematic. Adams's difficulty was reinforced by idiosyncratic personal circumstances—the extra weight of filial loyalty in a distinguished family, the anxious introspection heightened by his wife's death. The "feminine" realm of dependence, always an appealing alternative to men influenced by domestic ideology, acquired a special significance for Adams.

Drawn to "feminine" values, Adams remained ambivalent. Amid the antimodern vitalism of the late nineteenth century, he embraced cults of outer and inner experience, Mont-Saint-Michel and Chartres. The latter impulse proved stronger; he finally subordinated the warrior archangel to the Virgin Queen. What gave his work point and force, what made it more than a therapeutic quest for authenticity, was the religious longing behind it. In his efforts to overcome depression, he sought generativity not only by exploring the "feminine" realm of unconscious creativity, but also by transcending self-absorption and reestablishing an infinite framework of meaning. Turning first to Orientalism, later to medievalism, Adams could neither fulfill his aims nor abandon them. In the end, he transformed his inner conflict between autonomy and dependence into a cosmic struggle between skepticism and belief.

# The Antimodern Quest:
# From Niagara to the Virgin

The first evidence of Adams's developing religious concern was *Esther*. Published a year before Marian's death (under a revealingly feminine pseudonym), the novel satirizes the secularization of mainstream Protestantism and tentatively explores Oriental and medieval alternatives. It opens with a wry description of the fashionably dressed, complacent congregation at St. John's Episcopal Church, New York (modelled on Trinity Church, Boston). There was, Adams's characters agree, "a terribly grotesque air of the theater" about the place. "It *is* a theater," complains the artist Wharton, who has been commissioned to paint the church murals. "That is what ails our religion. But it is not the fault of our art. . . ."[22] To Adams, the embellishment of Protestant churches signified an empty theatricality, devoid of genuine belief. The book's major characters stand apart from the fashionable aestheticism of St. John's parishioners; they pray in a different spirit.

The novel's thin plot is a scaffolding for discussion of religious issues. The Reverend Stephen Hazard, first pastor of St. John's, falls in love with the freethinking Esther Dudley. After her father's death, when she longs for religious consolation, Esther accepts Hazard's marriage proposal. She soon regrets it, realizing that she can share neither his faith nor his devotion to the "stupid crowd of people" in the church. Hazard enlists the aid of his friend, the geologist George Strong—an uncertain ally because he is an agnostic. Despite Strong's efforts, Esther cancels the engagement. Spirited off to Buffalo by an aunt, she finds temporary refuge in contemplating the falls at Niagara, then rejects Hazard once more. Strong, impressed by her firm will, proposes marriage. Esther's reply concludes the book: "But George, I don't love you, I love him."[23] The inconclusive conclusion reflected Adams's own unresolved conflict between belief and doubt.

Through his major characters, Adams explored alternatives to mainstream banality. Hazard, unlike his frivolous flock, is a "high churchman with thirteenth century ideas"; he believes in free will and personal immortality. As for laying doubts to rest: "It is a simple matter of will!" In spite of Hazard's dogmatism, Adams admires his intellectual fiber. "Like most vigorous-minded men, seeing that there was no stopping place between dogma and negation, he preferred to accept dogma. Of all weaknesses he most disliked timid and half-hearted faith. He would rather have jumped at once to Strong's pure denial, than yield an inch to the argument that a mystery was to be paltered with because it could not be explained."[24] Like others who felt the antimodern impulse, Adams scorned the vacuity of the Spencerian Unknowable.

While Hazard and Esther are theologically at odds, they share a mystical sensibility. After Esther's father dies, Hazard's comforting words promise the ultimate dissolution of selfhood and its earthly ties in an infinite realm of Being. But his theology, particularly its domesticated heaven where loved ones reunite, seems "all personal and selfish" to Esther. With its High Church rituals, St. John's seems to cry " 'flesh, flesh, flesh,' at every corner. . . ." Esther yearns to transcend her instinctual life; Hazard's creed builds faith on it. "All religion does nothing but pursue me with self even into the next world," she cries.[25] Craving boundlessness, Esther reluctantly rejects Hazard's "medieval" notions of personal immortality.

The major alternative to Hazard's outlook emerges at Niagara. For Esther, the falls become an emblem of eternal Being and a challenge to Hazard's anthropomorphic conceptions of immortality. She is drawn toward Strong's declaration that thought alone is eternal. "If you can get hold of one true thought," he tells Esther, "you are immortal as far as that thought goes." A crucial exchange follows:

> "Does your idea mean that the next world is a sort of great reservoir of truth, and that what is true in us just pours into it like raindrops?"
>
> "Well!" said he, alarmed and puzzled: "the figure is not perfectly correct, but the idea is a little of that kind."
>
> "After all I wonder whether that may not be what Niagara has been telling me!" said Esther, and she spoke with an outburst of energy that made Strong's blood run cold.[26]

Dissolution in the "great reservoir of truth" promises final release from autonomous selfhood. Adam's water imagery connects Niagara with Nirvana; late-Victorian Orientalists commonly used the metaphor of dewdrops dissolving in an ocean to express the attainment of Nirvana. Adams had intellectual and personal reasons for an interest in Oriental mysticism. Popularized in magazine treatments of Oriental culture, "Nirvana" became a catchword within his circle of friends—which included William Sturgis Bigelow.[27] Both Adams and Bigelow longed for liberation from rigid ego ideals; both confronted intensifying psychic dilemmas during the 1880s. *Esther* suggested that Adams, too, was pondering the escapes from autonomy promised by Oriental mysticism.

But Adams was unable to share Bigelow's enthusiasm. The ambiguities in the lesson of the falls reflected Adams's own uncertainty. If Hazard's "thirteenth-century ideas" were intellectually unsatisfying, Strong's pallid doctrine offered little emotional solace. Even the scientist's blood runs cold when Esther reveals the underlying implication of his doctrine: that individuality and immortality are incompatible.[28] Immersion in the "reservoir of truth" liberated the seeker from confining self-consciousness, but only by annihilating all but the most abstract component of individuality. The idea that thought is eternal—itself an intellectualist distortion of Oriental mysticism—could have at best a mixed appeal to a man who felt "like Casaubon in *Middlemarch*."

But there was a third path, winding between the dogmatism of Hazard and the intellectualism of Strong. Adams embodied it in Wharton, whose spiritual turmoil reflected the anxieties behind antimodern vitalism. Ravaged by private demons, eager for childlike innocence but unable to recover it, Wharton is drawn less to Oriental quiescence than to medieval emotionalism. "To me religion is passion," he cries. "To reach Heaven, you must go through hell, and carry its marks on your face and figure." Wharton's conception of religion as Dantean pilgrimage was rooted in his desire for a faith with infinite emotional range. Contemptuous of the theatricality admired by St. John's parishioners, Wharton wants "to go back to the age of beauty and put a Madonna in the heart of their church. The place has no heart." The desire for emotional intensity, the double yearning for maternal consolation and childlike innocence, the belief that religion involves a terrible inner struggle between faith and doubt—Wharton's outlook epitomized many currents in antimodern vitalism.[29]

It also reflected the most enduring impulses of Henry Adams. Though Wharton remained on the periphery of the novel's plot, his choric commentary suggested Adams's future direction. Admiring Hazard's certitude but unable to share it, burdened by self-consciousness, Adams looked hopefully toward absorption in the "reservoir of truth." But this intellectualist version of Nirvana remained emotionally unsatisfying. A sense of individual selfhood persisted, sustaining the hope of spiritual consolation and personal immortality. Even at this early stage, Adams was drawn toward a heterodox medieval Christianity. Like Wharton, Adams would conceive religion as passion, and would put a Madonna in the heart of his private church.

During the 1880s, Adams continued to ponder the path to Nirvana. Obliteration of self still held a certain appeal, especially after his wife's suicide had intensified his anxious introspection. Accompanied by the painter John La Farge, Adams embarked for Japan in 1886. In the Orient, his perceptions remained stereotypically Western: he dismissed Japan as a "child's country." Immersing himself in Buddhist lore, he finally decided it was "a trifle flat and unsatisfactory," By the end of the decade, Adams had rejected Nirvanic self-extinction.[30]

In part, his disenchantment stemmed from a continuing commitment to Western ideals of autonomous achievement—a commitment which counterbalanced his longings for quiescence. Adams dramatized his conflict between activism and withdrawal in "Buddha and Brahma" (1891). The poem explores the spiritual dilemma of a young disciple of Gautama Buddha. Perplexed by Gautama's refusal to discuss metaphysics, the disciple seeks wisdom from his own father, a Brahman activist "who cannot fly the world" as the Buddha does but instead seeks

> To live two separate lives; one, in the world
> Which we must ever seem to treat as real;
> The other in ourselves, behind a veil
> Not to be raised without disturbing both.[31]

The poem arrives at a protestant conclusion: one may be in the world but not of it. The Brahman's insistence that "Gautama tells me my way too is good" reflected Adams's attempt to sustain his ambivalence. In a sense the Brahman way embodied the "worldly asceticism" of Charles Francis Adams, Sr. Henry Adams's inner loyalty to his father's moral authority blocked the path to Nirvana.

Yet the Brahman's ideal was as problematic as the father's. The idea of a double life was too schematic to sustain ambivalence; it was no more emotionally energizing than Esther's "reservoir of truth" had been. Bigelow's Nirvanic version of Paradise was equally unsatisfactory: Adams preferred what Bigelow dismissed as "the Fireside"—the domestic ideal of married love. Neither Buddha nor Brahma met Adams's need for generativity; he turned with increasing fascination to a vitalist cult of domesticity.[32]

Adams's devotion to the domestic ideal intensified strongly after his wife's death. More preoccupied than ever with natural processes of generativity, he built a greenhouse and "took to learning roses." Perpetually anxious, he was "amused and tranquillized" by his feminine companions. Writing letters to his nieces, Adams sometimes pretended he was a small child at his mother's knee; he became their "Dear Dordy," their little boy. His letters to Elizabeth Cameron were less fanciful; they revealed a genuine and deepening dependence. "Please, how are you, today?" he asked in one of the dozens of notes he sent to her home across the square. Or: "The roses are sweet. I feel very belle. How about our ride? Is it off?" Ultimately Mrs. Cameron became the initial focus for Adams's vitalist cult of domesticity.[33]

In Adams's imagination, Mrs. Cameron epitomized "feminine" values. He vied with Hay and the British diplomat Cecil Spring Rice in praising her beauty and fecundity. A sonnet by Spring Rice, headed "HA to EC," compared her to a "fair magician" bringing "spring in her smile and summer in her eyes" to winter, turning January drabness to "deep green and gold and creamy white." Floral and generative imagery proliferated in the tributes. After she gave birth to a daughter, Martha, in 1887, the maternal symbolism seemed complete. Pathetically devoted to the infant Martha, Adams became passionately obsessed with her mother. Touched by his affections but aware of her delicate position as a senator's wife, Mrs. Cameron realized that the situation threatened to embarrass them both. Finally, in 1891, she fled to Europe, urging her suitor to start his long-planned voyage to the South Seas. Adams reluctantly agreed.[34]

For Adams, the enforced separation was an emotional ordeal but also a crucial catalyst in widening his sense of selfhood and preparing him for his exploration of medieval Catholicism. Polynesia provided sensuous regeneration. In Japan, Adams had commented wryly on phallic worship, appreciatively on a few nude bathers, and admiringly on the temple of the Goddess Kwannon. But for the most part he had remained inert to unfamiliar sense impressions. Polynesia transformed him, largely because he was ready to be transformed. Visiting Japan, he had faced three more years of work on the *History*. Now he was finished and eager to "plunge into another existence. . . ."[35]

The hallmark of Adams's new existence was his unprecedented sensuous responsiveness. His letters revealed a new sensitivity to color and light, a new vocabulary of concrete shapes and images. Again accompanied by La Farge, he began experimenting with the artist's watercolors, trying to capture this new world "full of life and color." No longer nervous, Adams was eating and sleeping better than he had since Marian's death. "I enjoyed myself, and the sense of living, more than I have in five years," he reported. "I am glad to be dead to the old existence, which was a torture, and to forget it, in a change as complete as that of another planet."[36]

Infused with a renewed sense of youth, Adams revised his attitude toward the "childlike" traits of primitive peoples. Japanese childishness had been cause for contempt; Samoan childishness was cause for indulgent affection and sometimes admiration. The Samoans were spontaneous, healthy, free from "our idiotic cant about work. . . ." They were neither nervous nor self-conscious. Indeed, "I have never lived in so unselfconscious a place," Adams wrote. The limits of Samoan civilization "are a matter of course, but so are those of a delightful child. I still prefer the child and the limitations, as I prefer La Farge's unfinished sketches."[37]

Adams's enthusiasm for Samoan childishness was more than a tourist's fancy; it revealed his own rediscovery of childlike traits within himself. Before he left America he had begun to connect childhood not only with emotional dependence but also with a vital sensuous life. After his mother died in June, 1889, Adams spent several weeks at the family home in Quincy. Revisiting childhood haunts, he concluded that his senses had been "cut down to a kind of dull consciousness": he could not recover the acute sensuous experience of his youth. When his senses reawakened in the South Seas, Adams felt a childlike exuberance return. He repeatedly told his correspondents: "La Farge and I are schoolboys on a lark." At the same time, in the old Tahitian chiefess Marau Taaroa he found another focus for his dependent impulses. He became her adopted son, celebrating her family traditions in *Memoirs of Marau Taaroa* (1891). His veneration for the domestic ideal was turning toward primitive matriarchy and acquiring a vitalist tinge.[38]

Rediscovering sensuous experience among the childlike Samoans, Adams moved toward a reverence for natural fecundity and instinctual vitality. Antimodern vitalism channelled Adams's private cult of domesticity into public cultural currents. Like many of the upper bourgeoisie, Adams suffered from what he called "our common epidemic of neurasthenia."[39] He shared the neurasthenics' sense of helpless anxiety (particularly during his periodic depressions) and their yearnings for psychic regeneration. By the 1890s, antimodern cultural forms were focusing those yearnings, directing them toward cults of inner and outer experience. Originating in his urge for generativity, Adams's antimodern vitalism linked his personal quest with the wider antimodern response to the crisis of cultural authority.

Adams's developing antimodern outlook, like that of his contemporaries, was shaped by class fears and ethnic prejudices as well as by lingering republican moralism. His *History* had discussed the enervating effects of luxury, the purgative powers of war, and the decline of the hero in mass society. The economic and social unrest of the 1890s reinforced those concerns and led Adams toward apocalyptic fantasies of destruction. Lamenting that "our old-fashioned liberalism" was obsolete, he joined the patrician chorus denouncing goldbugs, Jews, and socialists. "I want to put every money-lender to death, and to sink Wall Street and Lombard Street under the Ocean," he wrote in the panic year of 1893. "Then perhaps, men of our kind might have some chance of being honorably killed in battle and eaten by our enemies."[40]

Henry's fantasies paralleled those of his brother Brooks, whose *Law of Civilization and Decay* focused Henry's rage. Identifying the goldbug as the embodiment of modern greed and unearned luxury, the *Law* seemed to provide a historical justification for anti-Semitism. Like the clerical reactionaries of Europe, the Adams brothers merged capitalist, usurer, and International Jew, declaring a plague on all their houses and exalting the Christian knight of the Middle Ages as an untainted alternative. In the Adams's updating of republican mythology, the ascendance of the goldbug symbolized the sterility of a civilization unmanned by prosperity.

For a time, Henry followed Brooks's lead in seeking a revitalized identity through a racist cult of violence. Imperialist adventures temporarily leavened his despair—but only temporarily. Unlike Brooks, Henry quickly concluded that military adventure was only a palliative for the modern malaise. By 1901, he was cautioning Brooks that "violence is always waste."[41]

As early as 1895, when Henry was discovering medieval culture in

French cathedrals as well as in the *Law,* his letters revealed that his anti-modern impulse was far more than the reflex of a "displaced patrician." To be sure, they betrayed the provincial ethnocentrism of a Brahmin who fancied himself a descendant of Norman warrior-farmers; but they also showed that class and ethnic prejudice was only one component of a vitalist sentiment with aesthetic, psychological, and religious dimensions.

The aesthetic concern manifested itself in several ways. Adams was so impressed by the artistry of Coutances, Mont St.-Michel, and Chartres that he persuaded Brooks to include a chapter on aesthetic decline in the *Law.* The stained glass alone convinced Henry that "modern man has lost at least one sense; that of color." He railed against the overcivilization of contemporary professional artists: "never a picture or a figure is *felt,*" he complained to a niece in 1897. The loss of artistic feeling betokened a more general enervation. The twelfth century, Adams grew fond of saying, "never knew ennui." The violent tenor of life, the deep contrast between wealth and poverty, saint and sinner, all made the Middle Ages "more amusing" than modern times.[42] The desire to be "amused," to savor experience as spectacle and titillation, was an outgrowth of Adams's sensuous reawakening in Samoa. It connected him with Harvard dandies and Wildean poseurs.

But it would be a mistake to stress that connection too strongly. Despite his epicurean pose, Adams (like Norton) remained wary of *fin-de-siècle* aestheticism. In *Esther,* he had attacked the substitution of theatricality for religion; he continued to do so during the 1890s. As he told his niece, "Art and religion are really states of mind. They become bric-à-brac the moment they are made a show."[43] To Adams, medieval artifacts were less important as amusements than as keys to medieval "states of mind."

The complexity of Adams's fascination with medieval mentalities appeared in a letter to John Hay, recounting a visit to Coutances cathedral in 1895. As in other letters, Adams fancied himself a medieval warrior-farmer.

> I was a vassal of the Church; I held farms—for I was many—in the Cotentin and around Caen, but the thing I did by a great majority of ancestors was to help in building the cathedral of Coutances, and my soul is still built into it. I can almost remember the faith that gave me energy, and the scared boldness that made my towers seem to me so daring, with the bits of gracefulness that I hasarded with some doubts whether the divine grace could properly be shown outside. Within I had no doubts. There the contrite sinner was welcomed with such tenderness as makes me still wish I were one. There is not a stone in the whole interior which I did not treat as though it were my own child.[44]

Adams's language suggested the diverse impulses behind his antimodern vitalism. Like other late-Victorian neurasthenics, he admired the medieval cathedral as an emblem of triumphant will; medieval religion was admirable not because it was true but because it gave men energy and purpose. Strengthened by the *fin-de-siècle* sense of cultural crisis, Adams's desire to transcend self-absorbed ennui was rooted in his private longings for generativity: it was not accidental that he imagined treating each stone as "my own child." At the same time, Adams's wish for divine forgiveness revealed his continuing need for expiation—the aftermath of the long self-punishing depression that had followed Marian's death. His personal plight combined with a dis-ease typical of the wider culture, leading him to yearn for spiritual as well as sensuous authenticity.

In Adams as in his contemporaries, the desire for spiritual authenticity stemmed from dissatisfaction with liberal Protestantism—from the feeling, articulated most clearly by Nietzsche, that Protestant culture had evaporated into "weightlessness." After his Unitarian upbringing, Adams revealed a deepening respect for older, sterner creeds. Though their visions of damnation were terrifying, they seemed to possess greater intellectual depth and profounder emotional range than their liberal successors. This new attitude was evident in the satire of *Esther*, in the critique of Unitarian vacuity at the conclusion of the *History*, and in the growing sympathy Adams showed toward medieval Catholicism during the 1890s. By 1900, Adams was criticizing St. George Mivart for his attempt to liberalize the orthodox Catholic conception of hell. "In my view," Adams wrote, "Hell is all there was to make life worth living. Since it was abolished, there is no standard of value. Hell is the foundation of Heaven, and now costs nothing and measures nothing."[45] Without a supernatural framework of meaning, ethical boundaries seemed blurred and spiritual experience merely self-referential.

Adams's reaction against liberal Protestanism had both philosophical and personal significance. It signified his revolt against the authority of modern culture as well as his belated rebellion against his father, who embodied that authority and instilled it in his sons. While Henry grew increasingly hostile toward secular progressivism and the male achievement ethos (the basis of modern authority), he also cooled toward the memory of his father and toward his brother Charles—his surrogate father since early manhood. Eager to elude Charles's hectoring "family lectures," Henry began to avoid him at every turn. When Charles began to prepare a memoir of their father, Henry's revulsion was acute—and revealing. Extracts from the father's diary betrayed traits Henry sought to expunge in himself: morbid introspection, pointless repression of passion. "The stale smell of dead anxieties makes me sick," he confided to Brooks. "The effect of reading Charles's book is only to make this feeling keener, and to stimulate all my twelfth century instincts." Flying to the twelfth century was an acceptable form of revolt against paternal values;

writing the memoir would have involved an unendurable symbolic confrontation with the father. Even reading it was painful: for Henry, the memoir called up a host of buried aggressive impulses. "Now I understand why I refused so obstinately to do it myself," he wrote Elizabeth Cameron. "These biographies are murder, and in this case, to me, would be both patricide and suicide. . . . I have sinned myself and deeply, and am no more worthy to be called anything, but, thank my diseased and dyspeptic nervous wreck, I did not assassinate my father."[46]

Adams's impulse toward a kind of symbolic patricide took the subtle, sublimated form of antimodern cultural criticism—animated by a vitalist cult of domesticity, focused on an archaic feminine principle. The apotheosis of "feminine" values was not exactly a model for Adams's behavior: it was a maternal complement for his desire to recover his own childlike traits of sensuous vitality, emotional dependence, and innocent faith. Etherealizing his passion for Elizabeth Cameron into a veneration for the Virgin of Chartres, Adams joined his private cult of domesticity to wider currents of fascination with a primitive Great Mother.

Like G. Stanley Hall, Adams was familiar with the matriarchal theory of social development originated by the Swiss anthropologist J. J. Bachofen and disseminated in the English-speaking world by such scholars as Lewis Henry Morgan, Lester Frank Ward, and Sir James Frazer. For some readers, matriarchal anthropology might meld with antimodern vitalism. The primitive matriarchies were peaceful, agricultural societies: they enshrined woman as the emblem of the tilled and holy earth; they embodied the principle of fecundity tamed by maternal love. From the "masculine" and progressive view, patriarchal society was superior because it was more "spiritual," more given to science and abstract thought; from the view of antimodern vitalism, matriarchy was superior because it was more firmly rooted in unconscious, instinctual reality. Like Hall, Adams adopted the latter view.[47]

Yet Adams, too, remained wary of the "feminine" realm. For him as for early depth psychologists, the association of femininity with the unconscious suggested not only mythopoeic inspiration but also uncontrolled, amoral impulse—and ultimately the smothering unconsciousness of death. The Great Mother was both creator and destroyer. As early as 1876, in a lecture on "The Primitive Rights of Women," Adams had noted the ferocity shown by women of "the heroic age," whose aggressiveness contrasted with "the modern type of Griselda,—the meek and patient, the silent and tender sufferer, the pale reflection of the Mater Dolorosa. . . ." Vitalism uncovered alternatives to the pallid mid-Victorian ideal, but they were threatening as well as reassuring.[48] Like other late-Victorian dissenters, Adams preserved vestigial commitments to male ego ideals, to individual autonomy and conscious control. He felt a mingled longing and fear toward the "feminine" realm—longing for release from his father's values, fear that release might mean oceanic oblivion. Projecting his ambivalence onto his personal mother-goddess, the Virgin of Chartres, Adams fashioned his most deeply felt work.

# Between Father and Mother, I: The Virgin, The Dynamo, and the Angelic Doctor

Adams's first invocation of a vitalist Virgin was also his first effort to transmute ambivalence into art. The "Prayer to the Virgin of Chartres" (1901) juxtaposed the Virgin and the Dynamo, the "feminine" realm of faith and the "masculine" realm of reason. In its tension between maternal and paternal values as well as its underlying religious yearning, the poem foreshadowed both *Mont-Saint-Michel and Chartres* (1904) and *The Education of Henry Adams* (1907).

Identifying himself with Western Christianity, Adams begins by begging pardon for having abandoned the Virgin Mother. Like all children—like Christ himself—he has left the Mother to seek the Father. For Adams, as for Western man in general, the Father-search has been the "masculine" quest for knowledge and secular power.

> So I too wandered off among the host
>   That racked the earth to find the father's clue.
> I did not find the Father, but I lost
>   What now I value more, the Mother,—You!

The rejection of the Mother, the impulse toward "masculine" world mastery, has been strongest among Protestant Americans.

> Crossing the hostile sea, our greedy band
>   Saw rising hills and forests in the blue;
> Our father's kingdom in the promised land!
>   —We seized it, and dethroned the father too.
>
> And now we are the Father, with our brood,
>   Ruling the Infinite, not Three but One;
> We made our world and saw that it was good;
>   Ourselves we worship, and we have no Son.

Their efforts to claim "the father's empire" have ended in self-absorption and sterility. True generativity has eluded them; they pray only to the silent Dynamo, uncertain whether it is their salvation or the agent of their final destruction. Convinced that the prayer to the Dynamo signifies a spiritual void, Adams rejects the Father-search and returns to the Mother.

> Waiting I feel the energy of faith
>> Not in the future science, but in you!
>
> . . . . . . . . . . . . . . . . . . . . . . . . . . . . . .
>
> . . . years, or ages, or eternity,
>> Will find me still in thought before your throne,
>
> Pondering the mystery of Maternity,
>> Soul within Soul,—Mother and Child in One![49]

Rejecting the "futile folly" of rational attempts (whether scientific or theological) to probe the infinite, Adams penned a vitalist paean to instinctual life and intuitive faith. He also presented a sharp critique of a secularizing culture absorbed in self-worship and oblivious to the destructive effects of scientific progress. Choosing the Mother over the Father, Adams remained aware of the Father's powerful appeal—the Faustian drive for knowledge embodied in the Dynamo. Adams's "Prayer to the Virgin of Chartres" revealed the religious *angst* and psychic ambivalence which shaped his mature antimodern outlook.

Now openly committed to "feminine" values, Adams explored "the mystery of Maternity" in *Chartres,* exhumed his own Father-search—only to dismiss it as a "failure"—in the *Education,* and completed his rejection of male ego ideals by turning science against itself in both *The Education* and his last speculative essays. Yet all these writings betrayed Adams's continuing ambivalence. In their complex dialectics, in their fascination with science and metaphysics, they revealed that he was drawn to the masculine principle of rationality even as he sought to disown it.

*Mont-Saint-Michel and Chartres* contained the many voices of antimodernism: the fretful patrician who boasted of his Norman ancestry and created an anti-Semitic Virgin Mary; the world-weary aesthete who sought only tasteful amusement; the romantic primitivist who delighted in the childlike simplicity and intensity of twelfth-century emotion; the skeptical believer who doubted Thomistic theology and trusted Franciscan mysticism. Ultimately ethnocentrism and aestheticism faded; what remained was both a complex paean to the primitive and a heterodox profession of faith.

*Chartres* began in Wordsworthian nostalgia, with the hope that "granting a fair frame of mind, one can still 'have sight of that immortal sea' which brought us hither from the twelfth century; one can even travel thither and see the children sporting on the shore." The early chapters alternated between aestheticism and "masculine" antimodernism. With Viollet-le-Duc as guide, Adams delighted in the play of light and shadow, the grace and finesse of vaulting. "Taste is free, and all styles are good which amuse," he said. Yet at Mont St.-Michel, he clearly preferred the eleventh-century nave to the sixteenth-century choir. The latter showed the fatal mark of modernity: it was "self-conscious." Adams exalted the "directness, simplicity," and "intensity of purpose" embodied in both Mont St.-Michel and the *Chanson de Roland.* This was the "masculine" realm of the round arch and the drawn sword; God the Father presided over it as feudal seigneur; Mary was nowhere to be seen.[50]

In these early chapters, the tone was playful, sentimental. For a time, Adams sustained a tourist *persona:* an uncle conducting his nieces on a cathedral pilgrimage. But as the pilgrimage moved toward Chartres, there was a growing seriousness. Sometimes it surfaced in waspish irritation at modern enervation, sometimes in nostalgic regret for declining religious passion. Gradually, a commonplace lament for lost feeling became an original work of cultural criticism.

The originality stemmed from Adams's vision of medieval culture—a more complex vision than that of other antimodernists. Unlike Ralph Adams Cram, for example, Adams imagined no static utopia, but rather a culture in constant process, riven by tension. To be sure, he sometimes evoked the sunlit medieval world of the late-Victorian magazines—the same world evoked by James Branch Cabell or Howard Pyle. The Gothic, Adams insisted, signified not "age and decrepitude" but "exuberant youth, the eternal child of Wordsworth"; not gloom but light and color. Indeed, medieval man's "natural colour-sense"—so evident in the twelfth-century glass—was only part of "the fun of life" common in the Middle Ages but lost to modernity.[51] All this was standard antimodern vitalism, the exaltation of childlike intensity for its own sake. But by developing a vitalist cult of domesticity as a complement to his celebration of medieval childishness, Adams not only underscored his commitment to "feminine" values; he also dramatized the tensions within himself and within the wider culture.

The fundamental tension arose between individual autonomy and boundless dependence. In *Chartres,* the underlying motif was Adams's desire to escape a restless, fragmenting sense of selfhood in union with eternal Being. "Man is an imperceptible atom always trying to become one with God," he said. "Energy is the inherent effort of every multiplicity to become unity."[52] His own fascination with the energy spawned by medieval faith reflected his discontent with autonomy and his longings for boundlessness. He elevated instinct over intellect because "feminine" values embodied a more satisfying mode of unity—a return to childlike dependence on a vitalist mother-goddess. Yet like other late-Victorian men, Adams pulled up short; boundless union seemed indistinguishable from death. For him as for other antimodernists, autonomy blocked dependence. The conflict between Father and Mother persisted.

That conflict became more explicit as the unity of Mont-Saint-Michel gave way to the unity of Chartres. "The church is wholly given up to the Mother and the Son. The Father seldom appears. . . . Chartres represents, not the Trinity, but the identity of the Mother and Son."[53] It embodied a symbolic revolt against the Father, in the name of a vitalist domestic ideal. And the quiet strength of the Virgin Queen signified a religion of infinite forgiveness, suited to Adams's deepest needs.

> People who suffer beyond the formulas of expression—who are crushed into silence, and beyond pain—want no display of emotion—no bleeding heart—no weeping at the foot of the Cross—no hysterics—no phrases! they want to see God, and to know that he is watching over His own.[54]

Although Adams's vitalist cult of domesticity was rooted in his private longings for expiation, it also suggested a broader critique of mainstream Protestantism. Chartres, he said, was not a human-centered hall of worship but a shrine intended for the Virgin Queen, "as the Temple of Abydos was intended for Osiris." The desire for restored transcendence not only fired Adams's admiration for the Virgin's "apartments" at Chartres, but led him to outbursts of scorn against modern mentalities. "You may, if you really have no imagination whatever, reject the idea that the Virgin herself made the plan [for the apse]; the feebleness of our fancy is now congenital, organic, beyond stimulant or strychnine, and we shrink like sensitive-plants from the touch of a vision or a spirit; but at least one can still sometimes feel a woman's taste, and in the apse of Chartres one feels nothing else."[55] Adams's vitalist cult of domesticity, despite its elements of sentimentality, transcended the banalities of liberal Protestantism; rejecting accommodation with "masculine" intellect, it sought the recovery of irrational faith.

In the second half of the book, as Adams moved from cathedrals to medieval culture in general, the masculine-feminine conflict became overtly religious. Having linked Mary with archaic Great Mothers—Astarte, Isis, Demeter, Aphrodite—Adams also paired her with medieval mystics against the Trinity and its scholastic expositors. On one side was the oceanic unity of the infant and his mother, the believer and his God; on the other was the metaphysical unity of the Church Intellectual, resting on law and logic rather than love. Unlike other antimodernists, Adams included scholasticism in his image of medieval culture; but his discussion of Aquinas's philosophy served ultimately to show what for him was its inadequacy. In the conflict between "masculine" logic and "feminine" love, Adams left no doubt where his sympathies lay. Like the medieval people he imagined as "children," Adams "yearned for protection, pardon, and love." In his view, "this was what the Trinity, though omnipotent, could not give. Whatever the heretic or mystic might try to persuade himself, God could not be Love. God was Justice, Order, Unity, Perfection; He could not be human and imperfect, nor could the Son or the Holy Ghost be other than the Father. The Mother alone was human, imperfect, and could love. . . ."[56] The most emotional passages in the book evoked the Virgin's superiority to the Trinity.

> True it was, although one should not say it jestingly, that the Virgin embarrassed the Trinity; and perhaps this was the reason, behind all the other excellent reasons, why men loved and adored her with a passion such as no other deity has ever inspired; and why we, although utter strangers to her, are not far from getting down on our knees and praying to her still. Mary concentrated in herself the whole rebellion of man against fate; the whole protest against divine law; the whole contempt for human law as its outcome; the whole unutterable fury of human nature beating itself against the walls of its prison-house, and suddenly seized by a hope that in the Virgin man had found a door of escape.[57]

All Adams's need for expiation, all his gropings for a "door of escape" from burdensome ego ideals, focused in the emblem of the Virgin. Her power embodied the boundless union with all Being celebrated in St. Francis's "Cantico del Sole"; like the church door at Chartres, the chant of the Sun was "another 'Pons Seclorum'—or perhaps rather a 'Pons Sanctorum'—over which only children and saints can pass." Childlike dependence was the key to unity; rational autonomy brought only discord. Between the chapters "Les Miracles de Notre Dame" and "The Mystics," Adams placed "Abelard." The sterile debates of Abelard and his opponents threw the message of the Virgin and the mystics into high relief.

> In essence, religion was love; in no case was it logic. Reason can reach nothing except through the senses; God, by essence, cannot be reached through the senses; if He is to be known at all, He must be known by contact of spirit with spirit, essence with essence; directly; by emotion; by absorption of our existence in His; by substitution of His spirit for ours.[58]

In other words, God could be known only if the seeker abandoned autonomous selfhood.

Much as Adams shared the longings of the mystics for boundlessness, he believed their ascendancy had been short-lived. Though "the Church drew aside to let the Virgin and St. Francis pass and take the lead—for a time," it soon reasserted the prerogatives of rational dogma. The genuine (though precarious) unity of Chartres gave way to the spurious unity of the *Summa Theologica*. In Adams's scheme, scholasticism was a portent of modernity. "St. Francis of Assisi was not more archaic and cavedweller than Thomas of Aquinas was modern and scientific." The assertion was confusing because Adams knew that scholastic logic-chopping was anathema to empirical scientists. He meant that Aquinas was "scientific" in his determination to reduce all creation to the unity of rational law. But on this point, too, there was room for argument. Adams was aware that, by the turn of the century, the positivist attempt to formulate all-encompassing scientific laws was under attack even within the scientific community; he acknowledged that "modern science, like modern art, tends, in practice, to drop the dogma of organic unity."[59] To Adams, Aquinas was not so much the first "modern scientist" (though he used that term) as the first positivist, imposing arbitrary laws on an unruly cosmos.

Adams's discussion of Aquinas in the conclusion of *Chartres* was another chapter in the revolt against positivism. By referring all motion to a Prime Motor, Adams charged, Aquinas had "reduced God to a mechanism and man to a passive conductor of force." Like many positivists, the angelic doctor had stripped man of free will; like them, he clung inconsistently to belief in personal moral responsibility. That at least was Adams's view. However questionable in its interpretation of Thomism, it underscored his vitalist conviction that the free will-determinism debate was finally insoluble, and that "true religion felt the nearness of God without caring to see the mechanism." The *Summa* was satisfying in its architectural completeness but no more than an empty husk without the foundation of faith. When men tried to reason their way into heaven, when they abandoned the childlike ways of the mystics, the medieval synthesis broke down.[60]

Yet the synthesis had always been precarious. Adams symbolized its uncertainty in the apparent instability of the Gothic cathedral: ". . . never let us forget that Faith alone supports it, and that, if Faith fails, Heaven is lost. . . . The delight of its aspirations is flung up to the sky. The pathos of its self-distrust and anguish of doubt is buried in the earth as its last secret. You can read out of it whatever else pleases your youth and confidence; to me, this is all."[61] By elevating faith over reason, by repudiating all closed systems of belief (whether Thomist or positivist), Adams joined William James, Henri Bergson, and a host of other rebels against the nineteenth-century world view.

Adams's revolt, like many others, was tied to the values he sought to exorcise. Though he differed from most antimodern vitalists in emphasizing the result as well as the process of medieval piety—the attainment of unconscious unity through acceptance of total dependence on the Divine —he remained ambivalent toward his own dependent impulses. Clinging to conscious control, longing for dependence in his most depressive phases, he associated dependent union with punishment as well as liberation. The archaic feminine principle was more than a source of consolation; it signified amoral instinctual power. "Perhaps the best starting point for study of the Virgin would be a practical acquaintance with bees, and especially queen bees," Adams wrote. As an embodiment of feminine superiority, his Virgin could be strong, aggressive, even cruel. Pairing her with the tough earthly queens Eleanor of Guienne and Blanche of Castile, Adams admitted that when his Virgin was criticized, or when her will was crossed, she took quick revenge. She tongue-lashed knights, sledgehammered monks, and consigned hapless bishops to hellfire for overlooking her whims.[62] In many ways, she focused Adams's self-punishing depressive impulses and his half-conscious recognition that unconscious unity implied the destruction of individual selfhood.

That recognition emerged most clearly in Adams's chapter on the mystics. He sensed that the mystical quest for boundlessness fulfilled itself only in " 'our sister death,' the long-sought, never-found sister of the schoolmen, who solved all philosophy and merged multiplicity in unity." The schoolmen never found her because they preserved "masculine" commitments to consciousness; mystics abandoned those commitments and sank into unconscious unity. "The mind that recoils from itself can only commit a sort of ecstatic suicide; it must absorb itself in God," Adams wrote.[63] But while his own mind recoiled from itself, he was unable to follow the mystics' path. Fears of "ecstatic suicide" held him back; mystical unity eluded him.

Unable to join the mystics, Adams remained suspended between autonomy and dependence, father and mother. But that tension paralleled a profounder private struggle between faith and doubt. As his chapters on scholasticism suggested, Adams sustained a logician's love for the thrust and parry of argument and a rationalist's admiration for the integrated philosophical system. Despite his admiration for emotional spontaneity, he was incurably self-conscious and cerebral. Like other antimodern vitalists, Adams hesitated at the doors of mystical perception, unable to enter. Though he knelt before the Virgin, he confessed he was an utter stranger to her. Adams's Virgin looked "down from a deserted heaven, into an empty church, on a dead faith."[64] Yet the very act of writing *Chartres* underscored his refusal to despair; the impulse toward resignation coexisted with the will to believe. Projecting his own "self-distrust and anguish of doubt" onto the Gothic cathedral, Adams continued to hope for faith even as he preserved the analytical attitude which corroded it.

For Adams, the analytic attitude finally provided a major path to self-discovery as well as another major work of cultural criticism. In the circling sentences and aphoristic insights of *The Education*, Adams transformed his own inner conflict into the cosmic historical dialectic between Dynamo and Virgin. Though he adopted the detached pose of a *bricoleur*, referring to himself in the third person, *The Education* was an intensely personal book. Charles Francis Adams, Sr., played a critical role. Around his father, Henry Adams ranged a whole constellation of modern values—a liberal faith in rationality, a Victorian commitment to decorum, a positivist belief in orderly progress through discovery of scientific laws—all central to the nineteenth-century bourgeois world view. Much of the book was an effort to discredit both his father and the wider modern outlook through ironic deprecation. Against the nineteenth-century Father, Adams arrayed vitalism and postpositivist science—both the Virgin and the Dynamo. Rejecting the false unity of positivist law, he embraced a world of contradiction and ambivalence.

# Between Father and Mother, II: The Antimodern Modernist

Adams adopted an oblique and sometimes baffling rhetorical strategy for *The Education.* In particular, his attempt to link his own retrospective sense of failure with the failures of bourgeois culture has created confusion. His references to the "mechanical consolidation of force which ruthlessly stamped out the class into which Adams was born" were full of hyperbole and distortion, but they have led historians to treat *The Education* as the quintessential product of a "waning patriciate."[65] In actuality it was the most sophisticated manifestation of the antimodern impulse toward cultural regeneration among the upper bourgeoisie. In its cruder forms, that impulse revitalized ruling class hegemony by reaffirming familiar values or reinforcing newer tendencies toward a therapeutic orientation of the self. In its subtler forms—as in *The Education*—the regenerative impulse preserved a critical edge, and embodied the more profound insights of the emerging European avant-garde. Adams, like the men considered in the previous chapter, was not only a nostalgic elitist but also a harbinger of cultural transformation.

In the Preface to *The Education,* Adams began by distinguishing his project from Rousseau's *Confessions,* "a monument of warning against the Ego."

> Since his time, and largely thanks to him, the Ego has steadily tended to efface itself, and, for purposes of model, to become a manikin on which the toilette of education is to be draped in order to show the fit or misfit of the clothes. The object of study is the garment, not the figure. The tailor adapts the manikin as well as the clothes to his patron's wants. The tailor's object, in this volume, is to fit young men, in universities or elsewhere, to be men of the world, equipped for emergency; and the garment offered to them is meant to show the faults of the patchwork fitted on their fathers.[66]

In the manikin figure, Adams symbolized the modernization of self-hood. The manikin was the spiritual heir of Melville's Confidence Man, epitomizing the problematic nature of the modern self.[67] Since Rousseau's time, Adams suggested, the Ego had become hollow, manipulable according to the needs of the moment, socially constructed. The modern self had become a flexible manikin. The fit of various garments reflected the appropriateness or inappropriateness of various patterns of socialization. In

Adams's case, the garment presented him by his father was only a patchwork. He set out to dissect its faults and suggest alternatives.

Adams opened the first chapter in the accents of the displaced patrician. "Had he been born in Jerusalem under the shadow of the Temple and circumcised in the Synagogue by his uncle the high priest, under the name of Israel Cohen, he would scarcely have been more distinctly branded, and not much more heavily handicapped in the races of the coming century, in running for such stakes as the century was to offer; but on the other hand, the ordinary traveller, who does not enter the field of racing, finds advantage in being, so to speak, ticketed through life, with the safeguards of an old, established traffic."[68] Reflecting on the circumstances of his birth, Adams was characteristically ambivalent. His family background was both a burden and a gift. In any case, it was not the Adams name which proved to be the severest handicap, but rather the point of view the Adams family adopted—the classical liberalism of the educated bourgeoisie. (Historians and critics have persistently overlooked this fundamental distinction.) Adams's quarrel with his paternity was a means of raising larger philosophical questions.

At first, the terms of Adams's dialectic were personal: the extremes of New England climate, shaping the double consciousness of a sensitive Boston boy. "Winter and summer . . . were two hostile lives, and bred two separate natures. Winter was always the effort to live; summer was tropical license. . . . Winter and summer, town and country, law and liberty, were hostile, and the man who pretended they were not, was in his eyes a schoolmaster—that is, a man employed to tell lies to little boys." Adams associated winter with the false education of mechanical recitation, summer with the spontaneous learning he acquired in the old farmhouse at Quincy, reading Walter Scott (like brother Brooks), and "raiding the garden at intervals for peaches and pears."[69]

Winter was the sphere of male ego ideals; summer prefigured the "feminine" realm of sensuous and aesthetic experience. In Adams's account of his youth, "feminine" values were ineffectual, shackled to a pallid domestic ideal and subordinated to masculine authority. Though Adams called his mother "the queen-bee of the hive" (recalling the vitalist Virgin of *Chartres*), he mentioned her only perfunctorily, noting that she was unable to control her children. But the other side of the dialectic, the father, was another matter.[70]

In large measure, *The Education* recounted Adams's efforts to free himself from the authority of his father's liberal, progressive values—whether couched in the eighteenth-century language of the Enlightenment or the nineteenth-century language of positivism. The book's early chapters were pervaded by ironic deprecation of the elder Charles Francis Adams and his cultural milieu. Though Henry acknowledged that his father "never preached and was singularly free from cant," the faint praise concealed contempt for his father's mentality.

> To his son Henry, the quality that distinguished his father from all the other figures in the family group, was that, in his opinion, Charles Francis Adams possessed the only perfectly balanced mind that ever existed in the name. . . . His memory was hardly above average; his mind was not bold like his grandfather's or restless like his father's, or imaginative or oratorical—still less mathematical; but it worked with singular perfection, admirable self-restraint, and instinctive mastery of form. Within its range it was a model.[71]

Adams restricted the range of his father's mind to a narrow and insignificant compass. He excluded from it all the qualities he valued most highly —memory, imagination, speculative boldness, even analytical precision. When he had finished there was little left to emulate or admire. As Henry wrote, "such perfect poise—such intuitive self-adjustment—was not maintained by nature without a sacrifice of the qualities which would have upset it." Henry and the other Adams children never realized "how rare and complete was the model before their eyes. A coarser instrument would have impressed them more." Adams recalled that he had been unimpressed by the "common sense" advice his father wrote him in Germany: "the young man would listen to no sense at all, but insisted that Berlin was the best of educations in the best of Germanies; yet, when, at last, April came, and some genius suggested a tramp in Thuringen, his heart sang like a bird. . . ."[72]

The "yet" did not lead backward toward recognition of his father's advice, but forward to an exploration of sensuous, aesthetic, and religious experience. Straying from his father's path of systematic legal study, Adams claimed to learn most outside the classroom, in music halls and thirteenth-century cathedrals. At Antwerp, "he was only too happy to feel himself kneeling at the foot of the Cross; he learned only to loathe the sordid necessity of getting up again, and going about his stupid business."[73] As in the "Prayer to the Virgin of Chartres," Adams contrasted religious longing with the "stupid business" of masculine achievement.

Adams soon linked his father's defects with those of bourgeois cultural leaders in Paris and London as well as Boston. On both sides of the Atlantic the "upper-class *bourgeoisie*" was characterized (according to Adams), by balance, decorum, bland faith in human goodness, and progress. The Boston Unitarians were especially self-assured. "For them, difficulties might be ignored; doubts were waste of thought; nothing exacted solution." To Adams, growing up under the vaporous tenets of this creed made religion seem unreal. Adams blamed Boston Unitarianism—the prototype of Nietzsche's "weightless" Christianity—for his lifelong spiritual plight. His religious instinct ("the most powerful emotion of man, next to the sexual") vanished, "and could not be revived, although one made in later life many efforts to recover it." The fault, in Adams's view, lay in nineteenth-century liberal culture—in the moderate men of Harvard College, in the anemic idealism spawned by the Concord transcendentalists, in the decorous morality of the respectable classes. Above all, the fault lay in the complacent belief in progress of the bourgeoisie. By 1870, Adams noted dryly, "evolution from lower to higher raged like an epidemic."[74]

Under the shadow of his father and his father's own culture, the "Henry Adams" *persona* of *The Education* emerged as a weak and faintly ridiculous figure, a nervous youth growing to overcivilized manhood. By his late twenties, his identity seemed to be only "a bundle of disconnected memories. . . ." Adams's difficulties were compounded by his continuing submissiveness toward his father. Remembering their relationship, Adams stressed his own passivity and lack of direction, his unfitness for the position of private secretary to the Minister, his inability even at twenty-six to earn "five dollars in any occupation." By exaggerating his own incompetence, Adams dramatized his failure to free himself from paternal expectations, as well as from the ideals of the dominant culture. A series of subordinations to the father's will culminated in the son's acceptance of a Harvard appointment. To please his father, Adams began "a new education, on lines he had not chosen, in subjects for which he cared less than nothing; in a place he did not love, and before a future which repelled." If this description distorted his outlook at the time, it accurately reflected the perspectives of his mature identity. Adams labelled the chapter on his move to Harvard "Failure." He had become a schoolmaster, "a man employed to tell lies to little boys." It was the path of accommodation to paternal values as well as to the wider culture. "Education, systematic or accidental, had done its worst. Henceforth, he went on, submissive."[75]

Yet even as a young man, Adams realized he had never altogether submitted to the dominant pattern of socialization. In his twenties, he began discovering cracks in the surface of the nineteenth-century world view. After noticing the flaws in Sir Charles Lyell's *Principles of Geology*, which postulated a theory of uniform progress through natural selection, Adams "was conscious that, in geology as in theology, he could prove only Evolution that did not evolve; Uniformity that was not uniform; and Selection that did not select." To Adams, Darwinism could only show change: "To other Darwinians—except Darwin—Natural Selection seemed a dogma to be put in the place of the Athanasian creed; it was a form of religious hope; a promise of ultimate perfection." Adams's distaste for a lawful universe made him suspicious of claims to certainty made by Darwinian positivists. Suppressing his doubts, he temporarily joined the positivist quest for Unity. But he remained drawn to the image of the *Pteraspis*—the ganoid fish unchanged since Silurian times, emblem to Adams of the flaws in Darwinian positivism. The *Pteraspis* did more than suggest "Evolution that did not evolve"; it also portended a radical turn of Adams's father-search, away from liberal faith in progress and toward the complexities of postpositivist science. The fish symbolized a kind of substitute parentage. "To an American in search of a father," said Adams, "it mattered little whether the father breathed through lungs, or walked on fins, or on feet."[76]

The *Pteraspis* was a provisional symbol of father-displacement. As *The Education* moved to Adams's later years, its protagonist's doubts multiplied. As he began a new antipositivist education, the *Pteraspis* gave way to the Dynamo: "for Adams's objects its value lay chiefly in its occult mechanism." In the "Prayer to the Virgin of Chartres," the Dynamo had symbolized masculine science; in *The Education* it played a more complex role, suggesting the confusion of the father-search amid new scientific discoveries. The experiments of Michael Faraday with electricity and those of Marie Curie and Wilhelm Konrad Roentgen with radiation suggested the existence of forces which could not be mechanically measured. To Adams, the new forces undermined the claims of scientists to certainty. X rays, in particular, "were little short of parricidal in their wicked spirit towards science." They killed the positivist father.[77]

Ultimately, Adams's revolt against positivism led him to issues at the heart of the late-nineteenth-century crisis of cultural authority: the problematic nature of causality, the fragmentation of the autonomous self, the blurring of moral and intellectual certainty. He was "staggered" by "evidence of growing complexity, and multiplicity, and even contradiction, in life." After reading Karl Pearson on the limits of scientific research and Henri Poincaré on the notion of hypothesis as convenience, Adams concluded: "Chaos was the law of nature; Order was the dream of man." Amid twentieth-century multiplicity, the attempt to form universal scientific laws —above all the law of progress—had become quixotic. Familiar ideas of autonomy and causality receded as "man depended more and more absolutely on forces other than his own, and on instruments which superseded his senses."[78] And if the new physics undermined the concept of a unified cosmos, the new psychology discredited the unified self.

> The new psychology . . . seemed convinced that it had actually split personality not only into dualism, but also into complex groups, like telephonic centres and systems, that might be isolated and called up at will, and whose physical action might be occult in the sense of strangeness to any known form of force. Dualism seemed to have become as common as binary stars. Alternating personalities turned up constantly, even among one's friends.[79]

More than any other antimodernist, Adams was attuned to the pervasiveness of late-Victorian ambivalence as well as to the growing fascination with unconscious mind and multiple personality. In his view, the modern personality "took at once the form of a bicycle-rider, mechanically balancing himself by inhibiting all his inferior personalities, and sure to fall into the sub-conscious chaos below, if one of his inferior personalities got on top. The only absolute truth was the subconscious chaos below, which every one could feel when he sought it." Normal waking consciousness was a precarious achievement, a product of "artificial balance." And the "perfect poise" of men like Adams's father was even more precarious. The apparently rational man "was an acrobat, with a dwarf on his back, crossing a chasm on a slack-rope, and commonly breaking his neck."[80]

Adams was fascinated by the "subconscious chaos," but he also feared it. This placed him in sharp opposition to the therapeutic drift within the wider culture—the tendency to sentimentalize the unconscious as a benign wellspring of liberation. Like William James (and Freud), Adams knew the unconscious contained impulses far less tractable than those invoked by mind cure. Adams admitted that, after studying his own mind, "he woke up with a shudder as though he had himself fallen off his bicycle."[81] His own unconscious sheltered fearful demons; for his own psychic survival, he avoided "letting go" and preserved his commitment to conscious control. Adams's attraction to the "feminine" realm of instinctual vitality could only be expressed in sublimated form; his mature identity remained an ambivalent fusion of "masculine" and "feminine" values.

For Adams, the problem became: with the decline of Protestant ardor, how could one generate sufficient energy to sustain ambivalence? Mere *bricolage* was insufficient; Adams could not live on the "free play" of contradictory ideas alone. His impulse toward dialectic was rooted in psychic necessity. He needed to join multiplicity and unity, a ferment of vitality with a larger framework of meaning.

At the beginning of *The Education,* he obliquely affirmed that need. Recalling his own resistance to school, Adams wrote: "From cradle to grave this problem of running order through chaos, direction through space, discipline through freedom, unity through multiplicity, has always been, and *must always be* the task of education, as it is the moral of religion, philosophy, science, art, politics, and economy; but a boy's will is his life, and he dies when it is broken, as the colt dies in harness, taking a new nature in becoming tame."[82] This was the conflict underlying Adams's work. Like other antimodern vitalists, Adams accepted the imposition of order on instinctual chaos as the necessary condition of maturity. Yearning for a regenerated adulthood, Adams sought to balance instinct and intellect in dialectical unity. Searching for a restoration of infinite meaning, he transcended the cult of experience and explored the larger realms of faith. Yet he remained a perpetual pilgrim, wandering between past and future, hoping to generate renewed belief even as his rationality destroyed it.

To maintain the balance of tensions in his character, to sustain a coherent sense of selfhood, Adams looked first toward the energy derived from the "subconscious chaos"—the source of the "absolute truth" residing in unmediated emotional experience. The leitmotif of vitalism ran through the early chapters of *The Education*. Adams's first steps in education were sensuous. At age three, he said, he learned the color yellow and the taste of a baked apple. Though his sensuous education remained subordinated to more conventional patterns of socialization, it advanced fitfully: in the Quincy summers, in "the passionate depravity of the Maryland May," in the "soft forms felt by lost senses" of Europe's medieval atmosphere. These "soft forms" were portents of the "feminine" values Adams exalted in the later chapters, alternatives to masculine diplomacy and politics. After six years in London and two in Washington, Adams found that " 'the vast maternity' of nature showed charms more voluptuous than the vast paternity of the United States Senate."[83] Escaping masculine ego ideals, he took to the woods as he had fled to the backroads of medieval Europe.

But these early vitalist impulses were insufficient for Adams's needs, partly because they lacked a dimension of meaning. Failing to suggest any larger unity, they created further moral confusion. In a crucial passage, Adams dismissed his youthful vitalism as part of an aimless cult of experience. Remembering his reaction to Antwerp, Adams wrote:

> The taste of the town was thick, rich, ripe, like a sweet wine; it was medieval, so that even Rubens seemed modern; it was one of the strongest and fullest flavors that ever touched the young man's palate; but he might as well have drunk out his excitement in old Malmsey, for all the education he got from it. Even in art, one can hardly begin with Antwerp Cathedral and the Descent from the Cross. He merely got drunk on his emotions, and had then to get sober as he best could. He was terribly sober when he saw Antwerp half a century afterwards. One lesson he did learn without suspecting that he must immediately lose it. He felt his middle ages and the sixteenth century alive. He was young enough, and the towns were dirty enough, to retain the sense of reality. As a taste or a smell, it was education, especially because it lasted barely ten years longer; but it was education only sensual. He never dreamed of trying to educate himself to the Descent from the Cross.[84]

Unlike many of his contemporaries, Adams recognized the shortcomings of a commitment to intense experience as an end in itself. He understood that, without a larger religious or ethical framework, antimodern vitalists only got drunk on their emotions. Though he yearned like the rest for a "sense of reality" dirty enough to be exciting, he sought to transcend "education only sensual."

Adams rejected unalloyed vitalism for another reason as well. To him, it sentimentalized uncontrolled instinctual life: it overlooked the arbitrary violence in nature and the murderous rage in the unconscious mind. Adams knew better. He had shuddered at his own unconscious impulses; he had looked on, horrified, while nature remained indifferent to his sister's deathbed agonies. Adams knew that what was natural was not altogether beneficent. This insight contained a key resource for resistance;

ultimately it helped to prevent Adams's antimodern dissent from being reassimilated into the sleeker, therapeutic version of modern culture that was emerging at the turn of the century.

Adams's account of his sister's death marked a critical point in his effort to transcend vitalism and attain larger meaning. According to him, Louisa had been the first woman he allowed to dominate him; now she was yielding to Nature, dying of tetanus in an Italian hotel room while Adams looked on.

> Death took features altogether new to him, in these rich and sensuous surroundings. Nature enjoyed it, played with it, the horror added to her charm, she liked the charm, and smothered her victim with caresses. Never had one seen her so winning. . . . For many thousands of years, on these hills and plains, Nature had gone on sabring men and women with the same air of sensual pleasure.[85]

Under these circumstances, the notion of a beneficient Nature became preposterous: she seemed "a phantasm, a nightmare, an insanity of force." The problem for Adams was how to live his life amid that insanity. The vitalist worship of force, though he was drawn to it, provided little solace. Pondering "the usual anodynes of social medicine," he decided: "Stoicism was perhaps the best; religion was the most human." But Louisa's death made the idea of a personal deity seem blasphemous. "God might be, as the [medieval] Church said, a substance, but He could not be a Person."[86] Rejecting the pieties of nineteenth-century Protestantism, Adams continued to seek an infinite dimension of meaning.

Louisa's death pointed Adams toward a religious quest; Marian's death accelerated it. The twenty-year gap in *The Education*'s narrative signified her centrality to Adams's life. Though he never mentioned her name, he admitted in the chapter "Twenty Years After" that "for reasons that had nothing to do with education, he was tired; his nervous energy ran low; and, like a horse that wears out, he quitted the race-course, left the stable, and sought pastures as far as possible from the old." Adams recalled his oceanic impulse "to sleep forever in the trade-winds under the southern stars, wandering over the dark purple ocean, with its purple sense of solitude and void." And he recorded his effort to embody Nirvana in the monument on his wife's grave in Rock Creek Cemetery. After Augustus Saint-Gaudens had completed the haunting, hooded figure, Adams spent many hours near it—usually lost in brooding thought, sometimes distracted by tourists' comments on the figure. To him, the reactions of the American visitors betokened their secular cast of mind: "none felt what would have been a nursery-instinct to a Hindu baby or a Japanese jinricksha-runner." Even the clergy had lost faith in eventual union with the Infinite; they saw only despair.[87]

Sharply attacking the flaccidity of urban Protestantism, Adams revealed his restless discontent in a secularizing culture. Mankind seemed to care for nothing beyond food and drink; they showed no more evidence of moral betterment than the *Pteraspis,* or shark. Hoping for signs of genuine progress, he studied the religious press: "Not an act, or an expression, or an image, showed depth of faith or hope." Adams's father-search seemed mired in an "aching consciousness of religious void."[88]

Then he found the road to Chartres. In 1895, Anna Cabot Mills Lodge persuaded him to accompany her family on their cathedral pilgrimage through Normandy. As Adams wrote with deliberate double meaning: "one found one's self for the first time at Caen, Coutances, and Mont-Saint-Michel in Normandy." Recounting his growing fascination with medieval culture, Adams unfolded his reeducation in irrational faith. "The mind resorts to reason for want of training, and Adams had never met a perfectly trained mind." There was no hope, in other words, of his transcending reason altogether; yet he groped for transcendence before the Virgin of Chartres. Unlike the anemic "monthly-magazine-made American female," the Virgin embodied the power of the Eternal Woman: Sex. Like Diana of the Ephesians or the Oriental mother-goddesses, the Virgin "was goddess because of her force; she was the animated Dynamo; she was reproduction—the greatest and most mysterious of all energies; all she needed was to be fecund."[89] The flight from male ego ideals ended in the mystery of maternity.

Rooted in his yearnings for generativity, Adams's apotheosis of the Virgin was part of his wider fascination with the thirteenth century as "the point of history when man held the highest idea of himself as a unit in a unified universe."[90] It was the opposite pole of twentieth-century multiplicity, posing a coherent self and universe against the fragmented sense of selfhood and splintering intellectual universe which bedevilled the late-Victorian bourgeoisie. The paradox was that, in Adams's view, medieval people attained this feeling of wholeness only by subordinating themselves to the capricious, irrational power of the Virgin. They did what Adams longed to do: they joined instinctual vitality with a supernatural framework of meaning. But the moment they abandoned instinctive faith in maternal unity and began trying to impose the masculine unity of rationality, the fragmenting father-search had begun. A unified framework of meaning was possible only if one abandoned logic and common sense, accepted the absurdity at the heart of existence, and chose to make an irrational leap of faith in the Infinite. This was the only lasting synthesis for the dialectic between Dynamo and Virgin.

In *The Education* as in *Chartres,* Adams could not achieve that synthesis. Though he felt the Virgin's force "to the last fibre of his being," it was as energy and not as faith. He could not embrace dependence, even on the Virgin. He was too imbued with ideals of autonomy, too modern; he had to keep on about the father's business—even though the Dynamo had transformed it. Despite Adams's earlier dismissal of politics, he still loved the corridors of power, and he described his consultation with Secretary of State John Hay as "probably . . . the moment of highest knowledge that a scholar could reach." And despite his fear of the Dynamo, he displayed a Faustian fascination for the power it embodied. He announced that the twentieth-century American, "—the child of incalculable coal-power, chemical power, electric power, and radiating energy, must be a sort of God compared with any former creation of nature."[91] Both *The Education* and the later speculative essays used rational analysis to discredit rationality; they abandoned nineteenth-century unity only to search for an equally chimerical twentieth-century version. To be sure, not the theories themselves but the process of theorizing attracted Adams; he presented no ironclad positivist laws. Yet even the process of theorizing signified a masculine impulse toward reasoning—the "stupid business" Adams claimed to despise. He became, in a sense, a twentieth-century Aquinas. His late work was a kind of *summa*—a synthesis of antimodernism as precarious in its dialectical unity and as dependent on faith, at bottom, as the Thomist synthesis had been. When faith failed, heaven was lost; the supernatural framework collapsed in a thousand dialectics, and Adams was doomed to wander.

In the end, Adams's ambivalence sustained his greatest strengths as a cultural critic. Recognizing insoluble conflict as part of the human condition, Adams protested the rationalization of both outer and inner life. Riven by tension between autonomy and dependence, doubt and faith, he rejected all efforts to banish irrationality and contradiction in the name of social or personal harmony. He attacked the "amiable doctrines of Kropotkin" as well as the platitudes of Unitarian Boston.[92] Collectivist or individualist, all were based on unfounded faith in human goodness; all pointed toward the therapeutic megastate Adams envisioned and abhorred. Transcending the provincialism of his Brahmin caste, he grasped the deepest dilemmas of his own time and ours.

The moral foundation for Adams's mature cultural criticism was his tragic sense of life. At first fleeing his painful ambivalence, he finally chose to embrace it, sustaining it with a moral commitment to stoicism and a religious desire for faith. Of all frameworks of meaning, he had written, "Stoicism was perhaps the best; religion was the most human. . . ." A vitalist cult of experience was not on the agenda. It was Adams's great insight to realize that the vitalist faith in unmediated "reality" lacked tragic depth, that it was entwined with the evasive banality of the optimistic national creed. "America has always taken tragedy lightly," he observed. "Too busy to stop the activity of their twenty-million-horse-power society, Americans ignore tragic motives that would have overshadowed the Middle Ages; and the world learns to regard assassination as a form of hysteria, and death as neurosis, to be treated by a rest-cure." One natural outgrowth of American optimism, Adams suggested, was a therapeutic world view epitomizing the secular search for harmony and well-being. The therapeutic flight from tragedy was ultimately a flight from death itself, a death which had been rendered meaningless by the decline of supernaturalism.[93]

Adams realized that the decision to endure ambivalence might have religious as well as moral significance. For him, as for Bigelow, stoical "manliness" was insufficient; he yearned for an infinite dimension of significance, though he repudiated all static theological systems. With his late work, Adams joined such skeptical believers as Unamuno and James in the twilight world between doubt and faith. Rooted in idiosyncratic psychic needs as well as wider cultural ferment, Adams's longings epitomized the pathos of the antimodern impulse. It is possible to imagine him still, as he described himself in *The Education,* "kneeling before the Virgin's window in the silent solitude of an empty faith, crying his culp, beating his breast, confessing his historical sins, weighed down by the rubbish of sixty-six years' education, and still desperately hoping to understand."[94]

Yet there was more than pathos in Henry Adams. Revaluating dependence, he attained a profounder autonomy. A product of psychic, class, and cultural circumstances, his work transcended them all to become a major critique of modern values in crisis. Provoked by the banality of Protestant theology and the sexless aridity of Victorian morality, he also recognized the shortcomings of the vitalist alternative. Delighted by the smashing of positivist certainties, he realized that postpositivist science demanded the impossible: "a new social mind" to control it. Our century of technocratic destructiveness has confirmed his pessimistic judgment. In his restless experimentation with contrariety and process, in his refusal to rest content with unity or stasis, in his acceptance of a fragmented self in a fragmented universe, Adams prefigured the "modern consciousness" celebrated by many avant-garde artists and intellectuals in the twentieth century.

But the notion of Adams as "modernist" must be qualified. Most modernist authors in the twentieth century have been hostile to the secular, urban, bourgeois culture of the modern West. In large measure, literary modernism arose as both religious and secular dissent from historical modernity. Such writers as Adams, Yeats, or Eliot acknowledged the fragmentation of self and universe but also yearned for a restored sacred center at the heart of modern spiritual chaos. Such writers as Jarry, Apollinaire, or Cummings, on the other hand, rejected supernatural meaning along with bourgeois banality; sometimes in search of wholeness, sometimes in celebration of chaos, they embraced cults of authenticity and self-fulfillment. Both religious and secular emphases led toward sharp critiques of modern culture. But the secular emphasis was more easily accommodated to newer, more permissive modes of capitalist cultural hegemony. Under a twentieth-century regime which multiplied wants and sanctioned total gratification, the avant-garde cult of self-fulfillment some-times only exaggerated the culture it set out to repudiate.

Adams resisted such accommodation. He clung to a wavering hope for an infinite framework of meaning, though it might seem incomprehensible to his own mind; he could never celebrate self-fulfillment, though it might seem preferable to Unitarian moralism. He preserved an enduring protest against America's emerging secular culture. He remained, to the end, an antimodern modernist.

# EPILOGUE

A CENTURY AGO, IN "THE LEGEND OF THE GRAND Inquisitor," Dostoevsky envisioned the coming triumph of modern bureaucratic authority. The Grand Inquisitor, anticipating his reign on earth, tells Christ:

> We shall give them the quiet humble happiness of weak creatures such as they are by nature. Oh, we shall persuade them at least not to be proud, for Thou didst lift them up and thereby taught them to be proud. We shall show that they are weak, that they are only pitiful children, but that child-like happiness is the sweetest of all. . . . They will marvel at us and will be awestricken before us, and will be proud at our being so powerful and clever. . . . Yes, we shall set them to work, but in their leisure hours we shall make their life like a child's game. . . . Oh, we shall allow them even to sin, they are weak and helpless. . . .
>
> And they will be glad to believe our answer, for it will save them from the great anxiety and terrible agony they endure at present in making a decision for themselves. And all will be happy, all the millions. . . .[1]

This was the vision which haunted the antimodern imagination: a docile mass society—glutted by sensate gratification, ordered by benevolent governors, populated by creatures who have exchanged spiritual freedom and moral responsibility for economic and psychic security. Though none imagined the alternatives as starkly as Dostoevsky, nearly all antimodernists sensed (however dimly or fleetingly) that they somehow had to choose between a life of authentic experience and the false comforts of modernity, between Christ and the Grand Inquisitor. But ironically the pursuit of authentic experience in a secular age often became circular and self-referential. In the West, particularly the United States, intensity of feeling—physical, emotional, even spiritual—became a product to be consumed like any other. Recoiling from the vision of the Grand Inquisitor, antimodern dissenters furthered its fulfillment.

But only in part. Even on its own narrowly utilitarian terms, the vision has failed. The Grand Inquisitor is no longer a withered churchman but a sleek corporate or government executive who rehabilitates the "antisocial," entertains the restless, and feeds the hungry—but only some of them, some of the time. The new and subtler rationalization of twentieth-century culture has not suppressed the continuing irrationalities of the business cycle. Even in the affluent West, economic security remains problematic except for the well-to-do minority. And (more important for my purposes), psychic fulfillment, though it has become an obsessive goal, seems equally elusive for all classes. The denial of sin, the abandonment of moral responsibility, the sacrifice of freedom—nothing has bought the happiness promised by prophets of modernity. Antimodern dissenters, despite their drift toward accommodation, nevertheless preserved a powerful insight—a feeling, sometimes clearly articulated and sometimes only dimly sensed, that the modern secular utopia was after all a fraud.

This is only another way of stating my major theme. In America as in Europe, antimodernism had a dual significance: it promoted accommodation to new modes of cultural hegemony while it preserved an eloquent edge of protest. On the European continent, antimodern cultural tendencies energized fascist and Nazi ideology; in Great Britain, they underlay an imperialist worship of force as well as a persistent nostalgic pastoralism among Tories and Socialists alike. In the United States, antimodernism revitalized familiar bourgeois values and paved the way for new ones: it eased the transition from classical to corporate liberalism, and from a Protestant to a therapeutic world view. At the same time, antimodern impulses reinvigorated traditions of Catholic corporatism in Europe and decentralist agrarianism in Great Britain and America; antimodernism also pervaded the transatlantic revolt against the deterministic positivism of the nineteenth century—a revolt which energized the emerging avant-garde in literature and art, and which deepened some varieties of philosophical and religious thought. The whole subject of antimodernism's long-range impact is enormous; in what follows, I can only suggest some of its broader implications.

In the United States, the social impact of antimodernism was wide-ranging and complex. Antimodern impulses helped WASP elites to become a unified and self-conscious ruling class.[2] Gothic architecture and medieval heraldry provided collective symbols—often with Anglophile overtones—for an emerging national bourgeoisie. Premodern emblems certified modern, upper-class institutions: the metropolitan men's club, the suburban country club, the prep school, the private university, even the "Arthurian" interiors of corporate boardrooms. Appropriated for modern ends, traditional symbols lost content. Ideals of craftsmanship and martial vigor melded with ideologies of efficiency, imperialism, and "tough-minded realism," which in turn helped rally the upper bourgeoisie to reassert its dominance. Joining republican tradition and romantic activism, cults of outer experience reinforced familiar virtues of discipline and productivity. In such forms as "Do-it-Yourself" craftsmanship and the "modern chivalry" of sport, antimodern activism spread throughout American society, reviving bourgeois values among the ordinary as well as the well-to-do. Applied to later forms of activism, the term "antimodern" loses meaning; activist quests became less dissents from modernity than agenda for bourgeois self-reformation. As part of a broad and complex movement toward class revitalization the antimodern impulse helped to sustain a resilient achievement ethos. The drive to perform, to make one's mark in the world, is still very much with us.

But something has changed: the performance often occurs in a moral void. The apparent revitalization of familiar values at the turn of the century also reinforced newer tendencies in American culture. By uprooting traditional symbols from time, place, and purpose, the *fin-de-siècle* bourgeoisie contributed to the symbolic impoverishment of Western culture and also, in a larger sense, to that pervasive sense of unreality which had provoked antimodernism in the first place. Among the middle and upper classes, as daily life often became reduced to the quiet desperation of bureaucratic routine, many were touched by longings for the bodily testing of work or even war. And if they lost sight of larger frameworks of meaning, the way was opened for activist cults of risk-taking and physical exertion —the "hard" side of the therapeutic quest for self-fulfillment. In all these cases, antimodern activists invoked tradition while they subtly (and often unintentionally) undermined it.

In the passive modes of antimodernism, the cults of inner experience, there were more apparent connections with new, therapeutic modes of capitalist cultural hegemony. The concern of aesthetes for the promotion of "good taste," as well as for the acquisition and enjoyment of premodern *objets d'art,* prefigured more general patterns of consumption. Vitalist fascination with spiritual ecstasy as an end in itself, rather than as a path of salvation, pointed toward the twentieth century's self-referential search for authenticity—as did the yearning for an "oceanic feeling" in mystical or aesthetic contemplation. As belief in the supernatural wavered, the loss of conscious selfhood might become simply another route to self-fulfillment. Seeking authentic experience in their own inner lives, many antimodernists joined devotees of mind cure in sentimentalizing unconscious impulse. Depriving instinct of its darker dimensions, they exacerbated the weightlessness they had set out to escape. Even as they rejected older forms of rationalization, they promoted a new and subtler rationalization of the inner life. And most important: they remained imprisoned in the problematic self. Lacking firm religious or ethical commitments, antimodern dissenters became immersed in endless self-absorption—the "morbid introspection" they had longed to transcend.

However circular, both active and passive quests for authenticity reinforced the dominance of bureaucratic corporate authority. By undermining larger spiritual or ethical frameworks, the preoccupation with intense experience often devalued political action and focused discontent on exclusively personal issues. In part a reaction against the threat to autonomy posed by emerging bureaucratic institutions, the quest for authenticity also accommodated Americans to the new bureaucratic regime.

Historians and social scientists have long realized that the years around the turn of the century marked the crucial period in the shift from entrepreneurial to managerial capitalism; more recently they have begun to explore the connections between private and public bureaucratization, and the impact of both on everyday life in America. In workplace, school, and home, managerial and professional elites were appropriating authority and decisionmaking power from ordinary citizens.[3] Untutored voters gave ground to "expert commissions," independent entrepreneurs to corporate hierarchies, skilled workers to "scientific" managers, parents to child-rearing specialists. Sanctified as a liberation by corporate liberal ideologues like Simon Nelson Patten and Walter Lippmann, the process was sharply accelerated by World War I and has since been repeatedly celebrated by the corporate liberals who have dominated the academic professions. Only recently have a few historians begun to view the triumph of the bureaucratic ethos in a more critical spirit. I hope I have contributed to that critical history by suggesting some previously unnoticed cultural and psychological dimensions of this turn-of-the-century transition.[4]

The triumph of the bureaucratic ethos was never complete, nor was it simply a matter of bureaucrats imposing their will on a helpless populace. Indeed, a wide cross-section of Americans shared the bureaucratic faith in human progress and collaborated in the bureaucratic transformation. This was especially true of the educated bourgeoisie, including many antimodernists.

Shaped by the institutions and values of the emerging corporate system, antimodernism paradoxically often looked forward rather than backward. Unable to transcend the outlook of their class, many antimodernists correctly perceived their interests to lie with the new bureaucratic ethos. But —and here is the point I want particularly to underscore—their accommodation was more than a matter of rational calculation; it also stemmed from underlying commitments to the nascent therapeutic vision. There was a crucial affinity between the therapeutic world view and the rise of bureaucratic authority. Both stressed becoming over being, the process of experience rather than its value or result. As Allen Tate put it in 1953: "We no longer ask: 'Is it right?' We ask: 'Will it work?' "[5] The same narrow "pragmatism" has often characterized both the bureaucratic policymaker and the seeker of self-realization who is unable to transcend his immediate experience.

Antimodern longings for authentic experience, by promoting the self-absorption of the therapeutic world view, provided fertile emotional ground for the growth of the twentieth-century corporate system. Weary of "overpressure" and "morbid introspection," antimodernists (like many of their contemporaries) were ready for a more permissive, more leisurely style of living. Unable to sustain larger frameworks of belief, they substituted medical for moral or religious standards of value. Anxious to recreate a disintegrating sense of selfhood, they embarked on self-absorbed quests for authenticity. In part, antimodernism was a reaction against the psychic effects of bureaucratization and secularization—the sense of impotence, the feeling of "weightless" unreality; but it also helped to reinforce those tendencies by accelerating the therapeutic search for well-being, which in turn accommodated the individual to the sources of his anxiety.

From its *fin-de-siècle* origins among the educated and affluent, therapeutic self-absorption has since spread widely, concentrating in the professional classes but reaching far beyond them. Now it pervades our dominant culture, touching people who have never been "analyzed" and who are only dimly aware of psychiatry. Contrary to Rieff and other critics, the therapeutic world view is not and never has been tied to formal regimens of psychotherapy; it is a constellation of concerns about self, energizing a continuous, anxious quest for well-being. From the therapeutic view, well-being is no longer a matter of morality but of physical and psychic health. And health is often defined in terms of spurious "normality," smooth adjustment, ceaseless "growth," and peace of mind. The insoluble conflicts in psyche and society fall away. Whether it assumes psychic scarcity or psychic abundance, the therapeutic world view is both a symptom and a source of the continuing evasive banality in modern culture.

Ever since the early twentieth century, the therapeutic orientation has been promoted by social engineers and apologists for welfare capitalism. They have devalued public life not only by insulating government from the electorate, but also by reducing political issues to psychological issues; they have sought to create a civilization in which, as the young Walter Lippman wrote, "Politics would be like education—an effort to develop, train, and nurture men's impulses."[6] Retailoring the revolt against positivism to corporate institutional life, the theorists of manipulative liberalism have urged the freeing of instinctual impulses in order to channel them into "constructive" purposes. The leaders of the burgeoning advertising industry have had similar ends in view. Recognizing the cash value of a therapeutic sensibility, they have manipulated needs and underwritten a notion of self-fulfillment through voracious acquisition. Yearnings for authenticity have been well suited to the class interests of managerial and professional elites.

Yet it is easy to overemphasize the role of elites in spreading a therapeutic world view. One must remember that twentieth-century cultural development has created a congenial atmosphere for therapeutic conceptions of reality. Since the pre–World War I era, the sense of unreality has gradually enveloped nearly all of American society. The growing requirements of a consumer-oriented economy have accelerated the market's ceaseless cycle of creation and destruction. Under capitalism, "all that is solid melts into air, all that is holy is profaned," Marx wrote. At the same time, industrialization per se has played a major role in spreading the sense of unreality. Agrarian patterns of living have virtually disappeared; Americans have exchanged the drudgery of the farm for the boredom of the factory and the bureaucracy. More dependent than ever on impersonal decisions made in distant cities, more insulated than ever from primary processes of life and death, many contemporary Americans—like their turn-of-the-century predecessors—feel vaguely impotent, cut off from "real life."[7] The sense of unreality afflicts the self as well as the external world: it reinforces the feeling of ego-disintegration common to many "normal" Americans as well as psychiatric patients. And it has been immeasurably strengthened by the continued softening of mainstream Christianity. The platitudinous creed of Henry Ward Beecher and Lyman Abbott has spread throughout much of American society. Accommodating itself to a secularizing culture, liberal Christianity has forgotten the stratum of hardness in the Christian tradition, evaded the tragic contradictions at the heart of life, and lost much of its ability to impart a sense of gravity and larger meaning to the human condition. It may be that the current reawakening of evangelicalism is now providing a genuine source of resistance to the secularizing drift. Certainly I do not presume to understand such a vast phenomenon; but I confess I am skeptical of any religious movement which offers conversion as a cure for anxiety and which promises that Christianity will somehow make life easier. My sense is that much (though not all) of the resurgent evangelicalism has joined liberal Christianity in surrendering to therapeutic ideals.

It is no wonder, then, that yearnings for the authentic, the natural, the real pervade contemporary American culture. Cults of outer and inner experience, which once focused on premodern character, now emerge in a bewildering variety of forms. The "hard" or active side of antimodernism resurfaces in the persistent desire to test oneself physically by confronting the reality of the natural world—whether on a homestead in Vermont or a hiking trail in Montana. The "soft" or passive side of antimodernism reappears most conspicuously in the continuing (and no longer necessary) assault on the modern superego by "cultural radicals," in the proliferation of popular therapies promising spontaneity and instinctual liberation, and in the efforts to escape a disintegrating sense of selfhood by attaining the "oceanic feeling" through drugs or Oriental mystical practices. The list could be extended indefinitely. Without question, many contemporary Americans have enthusiastically embraced the "fun morality" prefigured in *fin-de-siècle* cults of experience. Fun morality is still a "morality"; the implication is that one *ought* to be having fun. It is the perfect mode of acculturation for consumer capitalism. But behind the fun, there sometimes seems to be a note of urgency—the play is so frenetic, the pleasure-seeking so relentless. One suspects that, for Americans at least, the quest for authenticity conceals a desperate flight from a meaningless existence.[8]

Many of these flights have preserved an important dimension of social protest, but only if the seeker preserves some larger framework of meaning outside the self. To put it another way, the quest for authenticity was most successful as dissent when it was most genuinely antimodern. One thinks of the agrarian communards of the 1960s and the principled opposition to the bureaucratic "rationality" of the Vietnam War. It seems to me that when those movements were rooted in larger loyalties they presented their most effective protest, and that when they succumbed to the dominant ethos of individual fulfillment they lost moral force and faltered.

The lack of firm commitments to wider values has doomed much of the antimodern legacy to continued circularity and accommodation. Vitalist yearnings for intense experience have continually resurfaced during the twentieth century. As self-fulfillment and immediate gratification have become commodities on the mass market, calls for personal liberation have begun to ring hollow. The quest for alternative values gradually has become a casual choice among "alternative life styles." The avant-garde has lost its critical edge and has ended by caricaturing the culture it set out to criticize.

Yet each generation of cultural radicals seems doomed to repeat the mistakes of its predecessors. Throughout the twentieth century, Americans have heard the same attacks on "repression" as the central problem of their society, the same demands for "personal growth" as a remedy for all psychic and cultural ills. The Greenwich Village intellectuals of the pre–World War I era, the expatriate artists of the twenties, the therapeutic ideologues of the thirties and forties—none have realized the hidden affinities between their liberationist ideology and the dominant culture of consumer capitalism. The novelist Jack Kerouac, for example, unwittingly caricatured the proliferating, insatiable wants of consumer capitalism when he described walking "in the Denver colored section, wishing I were a Negro, feeling that the best the white world had offered was not enough ecstasy for me, not enough life, joys, kicks, darkness, music, not enough night." Kerouac's eagerness for "night" suggested an effort to transcend the banality of much vitalist thinking, but the tendency toward sentimentality was still apparent. Simple-minded vitalism has afflicted bohemian as well as bourgeois.[9] This failure of imagination occurred most recently among some of the cultural radicals of the 1960s, whose "revolution" was rapidly transformed into a consumer bonanza of stereos, designer jeans, and sex aids.

Like their antimodern precursors, contemporary seekers of authenticity often lack any but the vaguest ethical or religious commitments. Their obsession with "meaning" masks its absence from any frame of reference outside the self. Their preoccupation with will and choice underscores an inability to will or choose. What begins in discontent with a vapid modern culture ends as another quest for self-fulfillment—the dominant ideal of our sleeker, therapeutic modern culture. The effort to re-create a coherent sense of selfhood seems fated to frustration. Every failure inaugurates a new psychic quest, until the seeker is embroiled in an interminable series of self-explorations.[10] This continually frustrated search is the logical outcome of antimodernism in America: the vision of a self in endless development is perfectly attuned to an economy based on pointless growth and ceaseless destruction.

Modern secular liberalism (in either its nineteenth- or twentieth-century versions) has by now revealed the moral hollowness at its core. The crisis of cultural authority continues; our society is still pervaded by antimodern longings not only in private but in public life. Most obviously, there has been a resurgence of a pseudoconservative Right—"pseudoconservative" because it is led by apologists for capitalism demanding a return to such "traditional values" as unrestrained corporate expansion, and by militarists promising moral regeneration through imperialist violence. But however cynical or self-deceiving right-wing leaders may be and however thoroughly their ideology is entangled with liberal assumptions, the contemporary Right expresses some genuinely antimodern sentiments shared by many Americans and long epitomized in republican moralism and Protestant fundamentalism. The tributes to family solidarity, the invocations of the work ethic, the idealization of the local community, the distrust of giant bureaucracies, even the pervasive religiosity—all, despite their elements of cant and contradiction, reflect profound moral anxieties that liberal "pragmatists" ignore at their peril. Beneath official pieties, the Right embodies a wholly understandable yearning for an authentic, unchanging bedrock of moral values and beliefs that can withstand the disintegrative effects of modernization.

While American antimodernism still plays a role in the continuing transformation of capitalist cultural hegemony, European antimodernism has pointed in different directions. To be sure, there were significant parallels between the United States and Great Britain, where liberal traditions and parliamentary institutions were strongest, and where the reigning ideology of utilitarianism provided a powerful counterweight to antimodern sentiments. British antimodernism, too, was often absorbed in bourgeois militarism or athleticism—or diffused in the vague pastoralism of Tory radicals and middle-class socialists. But the British veneration for their "green and pleasant land" has sparked a more powerful communal tradition than that inspired by American antimodernism. At once organicist and decentralist, British antimodernists have sought to break up factories and bureaucracies in order to re-create possibilities for satisfying work and personal relations in small communities; their schemes have ranged from the distributism of Hilaire Belloc and G. K. Chesterton (which sanctioned private property) to the guild socialism of G. D. H. Cole (which envisioned a decentralized workers' state). In a society where class structure and class consciousness have remained strong, British antimodernism has drawn strength from aristocratic and working-class hostility toward bourgeois values; it has been a diffuse but influential cultural force. As a wellspring of anticapitalist sentiment, the antimodern legacy in Britain has reinforced skepticism toward material progress, serving as both a contributing cause and an *apolo-*

*gia* for Britain's relative economic decline in the twentieth century.[11]

On the European continent, antimodern quests for authenticity have animated an even wider variety of ideologies. As William McGrath has shown, many *fin-de-siècle* Viennese joined antimodern vitalism with populist political commitments. Yet throughout the Continent, antimodern sentiments also energized a strain of authoritarian decentralism stretching from Louis Gabriel de Bonald, the traditionalist Catholic opponent of the French Revolution, to Charles Maurras, the leader of the fascistic *Action Française*. Scorning the abstract authority of parliamentary bureaucracies, decentralist critics sought to restore local, personal forms of authority—the family, the parish, the community. Sometimes, as in Austrian Social Catholicism, decentralists aligned with trade unionists or other more egalitarian elements, with whom they shared a hostility toward the atomizing tendencies in industrial capitalism. Nearly always, the decentralist vision surrounded the individual with religious as well as secular frameworks of meaning.[12]

Theoretically, the decentralist critique blocked arbitrary state power by stressing the importance of mediating social groups between the individual and the state. But decentralism was rooted in a potentially totalitarian sentiment: a feeling that parliamentary institutions were not only impotent but inauthentic—the chief barrier, in many minds, to a politics of authenticity. That sentiment was reinforced by the developing crisis of cultural authority. The insulation from danger and discomfort, the loss of will in widespread neurasthenia, the fragmenting sense of selfhood, the growing uncertainty about ultimate meaning and purpose, all powered longings for a restoration of heroic possibilities in life. Eager for transcendence, many overcivilized Europeans turned to Fascism. It became a kind of pseudoreligion, exalting self-sacrifice and suffering in the service of the state, promising a false transcendence in the cult of the Leader.

The most successful pseudoreligion took root in Germany, where a crisis of cultural authority was especially severe. A long romantic tradition had provided ideological weapons for *fin-de-siècle* critics of overcivilization; their dire prophecies seemed fulfilled in the institutional breakdown following World War I. As J. P. Stern has observed, Hitler skillfully exploited bourgeois fears of impotence and unreality. It was no accident that Oswald Spengler, who envied "everyone who *lives*," also admired the achievements of Naziism (though he thought Hitler "a fool"). Unlike those who live vigorously, Spengler complained, "I have only brooded, and whenever I was really offered the possibility of living I drew back and let it pass, only to regret it bitterly as soon as it was too late." Hitler manipulated those who felt cut off from "real life"; he offered the regeneration of the will through heroic suffering.[13] Above all, he promised the re-creation of an authentic self. Stern writes: "To be authentic means not so much to be honest about one's self as to be all of a piece. But if the self is tattered and torn and full of fears? Then it must be made all one, even in the act of exhibiting its wounds. And the myth which makes it so will bear the signs of its origins." The Nazi myth labelled the Jew as the quintessentially modern man—urban, rootless, rational, immersed in the "inauthentic" realm of commercial exchange. In a sense, the war to exterminate the Jews marked the ultimate extension of one form of antimodernism.[14]

Yet even in its most extreme political manifestations, the antimodern quest for authenticity wore a Janus face. Rooted in reaction against modernizing tendencies, it also reinforced them. Mussolini and Hitler were fascinated with machines; more important, despite their visions of an agrarian utopia, they spearheaded the creation of giant mechanized economies and government bureaucracies. While their ideologies scorned bourgeois complacency, their regimes incarnated bourgeois virtues of order, efficiency, and productivity. Indeed, one could say that fascist activism caricatured the capitalist commitment to ceaseless "growth." Even fascist antimodernism remained committed to modernity.[15]

On both sides of the Atlantic, antimodernism reinforced the devaluation of parliamentary politics and the rise of new modes of cultural hegemony: consumer capitalism in America, fascism in Europe. But it also continued to reveal a philosophical and religious significance. Many heirs of antimodernism preserved a profounder tradition of dissent than that embodied in communalism or decentralism, a tradition animated by cults of inner experience but often seeking self-transcendence and hoping for infinite meaning.

That tradition of antimodern dissent has survived most conspicuously in avant-garde art and literature—the cultural "modernism" that has so often protested the effects of modernization. To be sure, the avant-garde quest for authenticity has often merged with twentieth-century hegemonic cultures, not only consumer capitalism in America but fascism in Europe: the Italian Futurist Filippo Marinetti became an enthusiastic Fascist, urging his followers to "sing the love of danger, the habit of energy and boldness."[16] But alongside the fascination with energy for its own sake, there has been an insistent desire to locate a transcendent Being in the midst of frenetic becoming.

The longing for transcendence helps to account for the mythic dimension in so much twentieth-century art and literature. "Only a horizon ringed about with myths can unify a culture," Nietzsche wrote in *The Birth of Tragedy* (1872).[17] In subsequent decades, more artists have sensed disunity in their cultures and themselves; like *fin-de-siècle* antimodernists, they have sought the healing wholeness of primitive myth. The appropriation of sacred symbols from Africa, the Americas, Polynesia, and the Orient has continued unabated since the late nineteenth century; the decline of interest in medieval symbols suggests a widening conviction among the avant-garde that European religious traditions are played out, exhausted.

Yet non-European religious traditions may not be far behind. The devaluation of symbols is a global process; it advances daily. Given the continuous destruction of tribal cultures by modernizing elites, it is not surprising that some avant-gardists have sought spiritual authenticity directly, without mediating symbols. The color-field painters among the Abstract Expressionists tried to create a mythic art detached from all symbolic associations. To express the sacred, the painter had to avoid all established images, ideas, and forms. "The familiar identity of things has to be pulverized in order to destroy the finite associations with which our society increasingly enshrouds every aspect of our environment." Mark Rothko wrote. Rothko, Clyfford Still, and Barnett Newman all used vast expanses of color to create a sense of infinite oceanic boundlessness.[18] Though they abandoned the antimodern quest for myth, the color-field painters were nevertheless motivated in part by one of the fundamental antimodern impulses: the drive to recover some sense of transcendent meaning in a desanctified universe.

For some twentieth-century artists and intellectuals, the drive toward transcendence seemed to require the embrace of persistent inner conflict. In minds troubled by tense ambivalence, the antimodern legacy survived and sustained some of the profoundest cultural criticism of the twentieth century. That criticism was both moral and religious. In Freud's later work, it involved a stoical acceptance of the price exacted by instinctual repression—a kind of secular doctrine of Original Sin. For Miguel de Unamuno, the problem of ambivalence had a larger significance. In *The Tragic Sense of Life in Men and Nations* (1912), Unamuno declared insoluble contradiction to be the fundamental principle of the spiritual life. Confronting in his Catholic creed the rationally absurd dogma of transubstantiation, he wavered between reason and desire. And beneath that struggle lay a deeper one: between the longing for personal immortality and the foreknowledge of death. Unamuno resolved to embrace a "faith based on uncertainty," filled with "passionate doubt." And he pledged himself to a quixotic battle against all forms of static certainty—whether scientific or theological—"in the interests of restoring a new and impossible Middle Ages, dualistic, contradictory, impassioned."[19]

Unamuno pointed to the most enduring importance of the antimodern quest for spiritual authenticity. By sustaining the ambivalent fusion of doubt and faith, religious antimodernism helped skeptical believers to recover the sense of tragic conflict at the heart of the Christian tradition —the conflict between the longing for transcendence and the fact of human finitude. To accept that conflict was to hope for a faith that survived its own death daily. It was an ancient hope, and it has animated religious thought from Pascal to Kierkegaard. In the twentieth century, it has often been most powerfully expressed in an antimodern idiom—not only by

Unamuno, but also by Henry Adams, and by Adams's spiritual descendant
T. S. Eliot.

Having wandered through the "Unreal City" created by modernizing
forces, Eliot abandoned the despair of "The Waste Land" (1922) and
emerged in 1930 to write "Ash Wednesday." The poem, like Adams's
"Prayer to the Virgin of Chartres," is a heterodox profession of faith. In
the first section, the speaker is self-conscious, secular, and superficially
complacent. He knows

> that time is always time
> And place is always and only place
> And what is actual is actual only for one time
> And only for one place
> I rejoice that things are as they are and
> I renounce the blessèd face
> And renounce the voice
> Because I cannot hope to turn again
> Consequently I rejoice, having to construct something
> Upon which to rejoice

The last three lines make clear that the speaker's complacency is only
superficial. He is surrounded by images of drought and suggestions of
psychic impotence ("these wings are no longer wings to fly/ But merely
vans to beat the air/ The air which is now thoroughly small and dry"). He
is moved to pray, but he does so clumsily, formally. He is Eliot's vision of
the consummate modern, recalling Adams praying hesitantly before the
Virgin of Chartres.

The remainder of the poem charts the speaker's halting pilgrimage
toward a revitalized (though still ambivalent) affirmation of belief. Eliot
first celebrates the extinction of selfhood in meditative contemplation.
Clinging to hopes of supernatural redemption, he does not associate meditative self-extinction with death, but rather with the boundlessness of
infinity.

> Under a juniper-tree the bones sang, scattered and shining
> We are glad to be scattered, we did little good to each other,
> Under a tree in the cool of the day, with the blessing of sand,
> Forgetting themselves and each other, united
> In the quiet of the desert. This is the land which ye
> Shall divide by lot. And neither division nor unity
> Matters. This is the land. We have our inheritance.

As the poem proceeds, the desert imagery begins to recede. The
speaker begins to catch regenerative glimpses of vitalist Nature, which
Eliot surrounds with floral and water imagery and links with the mysterious half-appearances of the Virgin. The speaker still cannot see her

"blessed face"; nor can he hear the "voice." Despite his mystical decomposition of selfhood, he still walks in darkness, with the growing awareness that there is

> No place of grace for those who avoid the face
> No time to rejoice for those who walk among noise and deny the voice

The speaker refuses any longer to deny the voice, even though he still cannot hear it. He has become a restless seeker. The revitalization of his will to believe, even in the continuing absence of firm belief, emerges in both the substance and the direction of his prayers. He no longer prays selfishly ("May the judgment not be heavy on us") but acknowledges "Our peace in His will"—even if His will is to withhold the Word and hide the blessed face. And the language of his concluding prayer is no longer formal, but personal. It is as deeply felt as Adams's "Prayer," but more powerful.

> Blessèd sister, holy mother, spirit of the fountain, spirit of the garden,
> Suffer us not to mock ourselves with falsehood
> Teach us to care and not to care
> Teach us to sit still
> Even among these rocks,
> Our peace in His will
> And even among these rocks
> Sister, mother
> And spirit of the river, spirit of the sea,
> Suffer me not to be separated
>
> And let my cry come unto Thee.[20]

"Ash Wednesday" represents antimodern ambivalence in its most finely distilled and sublimated form. The conflict between desire for autonomy and longing for maternal union has become the cosmic struggle between doubt and faith. Like Adams, Eliot has become an antimodern modernist —resolving to search for faith even while accepting the knowledge which erodes it, resigning himself to the insoluble contradictions in his own psyche. This attitude, in its aversion to static systems, is a thoroughly "modern" one. But in a more profound sense, it is as old as the Biblical cry: "Lord, I believe; help thou mine unbelief."

# Biographical
# Appendix

The list on the following pages includes nearly all my dramatis personae who expressed antimodern sentiments. It is intended to be comprehensive, not exhaustive. For lack of information, some entries are incomplete and some are absent altogether. What remains is a reasonably thorough social portrait of a complex cultural tendency. From this compilation, it ought to be clear that antimodernism was most prevalent among the better educated strata of the old-stock ruling class.

A note on the category "religious background and/or affiliation": An arrow indicates a change in religious affiliation; a comma indicates that the parents of the person in question had different religious affiliations, with the father's listed first.

| NAME | FATHER'S OCCUPATION | SPOUSE | CHIEF RESIDENCES |
|---|---|---|---|
| Adams, Brooks (1848–1927) | Lawyer Diplomat | Evelyn Davis | Boston Quincy, Massachusetts |
| Adams, Henry (1838–1918) | Lawyer Diplomat | Marian Hooper | Boston Washington, D.C. |
| Addams, Jane (1860–1935) | Miller | None | Cedarville, Illinois Chicago |
| Batchelder, Ernest (1876–?) | Unknown | None | Nashua, New Hampshire Minneapolis Pasadena, California |
| Balch, Emily Greene (1867–1961) | Lawyer | None | Boston Wellesley, Massachusetts |
| Baxter, Sylvester (1850–1927) | Unknown | Lucien Millet | Boston |
| Bigelow, William Sturgis (1850–1926) | Physician | None | Boston |
| Bourne, Randolph (1886–1918) | Clerk, Printer Stationer | None | Bloomfield, New Jersey New York City |
| Brooks, Van Wyck (1886–1963) | Stockbroker | Eleanor Stimson Gladys Billings | Plainfield, New Jersey New York City Bridgewater, Connecticut |
| Browne, Charles Francis (1859–1920) | Unknown | Turbie Taft | Natick, Massachusetts Paris Chicago |
| Cabell, James Branch (1879–1958) | Physician | Priscilla Shepard Margaret Waller | Richmond, Virginia |
| Carman, Bliss (1861–1929) | Lawyer | None | Fredericton, New Brunswick New York City New Canaan, Connecticut |
| Carus, Paul (1852–1919) | Clergyman | Mary Hegeler | Ilsenberg, Germany Dresden, Germany Chicago |

| CHIEF OCCUPATIONS | EDUCATION | RELIGIOUS BACKGROUND AND/OR AFFILIATION |
|---|---|---|
| Historian Lawyer | Harvard College Harvard Law | Unitarian→ Agnostic→ Congregational |
| Journalist Historian | Harvard College | Unitarian→ Agnostic |
| Settlement-house worker Social reformer | Rockford College (Rockford, Illinois) | Quaker |
| Designer Teacher | Massachusetts Normal Art School School of Arts and Crafts (Birmingham, England) | Unknown |
| Professor of economics Social reformer | Bryn Mawr College Paris, Berlin (graduate study) | Unitarian→ Quaker |
| Journalist | Leipzig Berlin | Unknown |
| Physician Orientalist | Harvard College Harvard Medical | Unitarian→ Buddhist |
| Essayist | Columbia University | Presbyterian→ Agnostic |
| Journalist Literary critic | Harvard College | Episcopalian |
| Designer Lithographer Painter | Boston Museum of Fine Arts École de Beaux Arts (Paris) | Swedenborgian |
| Novelist | College of William and Mary | Episcopalian |
| Journalist Poet | University of New Brunswick University of Edinburgh Harvard University | Episcopalian→ Unitrinian |
| Philosopher | University of Tubingen | Lutheran→ Monist |

| NAME | FATHER'S OCCUPATION | SPOUSE | CHIEF RESIDENCES |
|---|---|---|---|
| Clemens, Samuel (1835–1910) | Merchant Lawyer | Olivia Langdon | Hannibal, Missouri San Francisco Hartford, Connecticut New York City |
| Cram, Ralph Adams (1863–1942) | Clergyman | Elizabeth Carrington | Hampton Falls, New Hampshire Boston |
| Crawford, Francis M. (1854–1909) | Sculptor | Elizabeth Berdan | Bagni di Lucca, Italy New York City Sorrento, Italy |
| Crosby, Ernest (1856–1907) | Clergyman | Fannie Schieffelin | New York City |
| Dennett, Mary Ware (1872–1947) | Textile merchant | William Hartley Dennett (divorced) | Boston New York City |
| Dinsmore, Charles (1860–1941) | Physician | Annie L. Beattie | New York City New Haven, Connecticut |
| Dix, Morgan (1879–1915) | Army officer | Emily Woolsey | New York City Philadelphia |
| Forman, Justus Miles (1879–1915) | Unknown | None | Leroy, New York New York City |
| Freer, Charles Langdon (1856–1919) | Unknown | None | Detroit New York City |
| Frederic, Harold (1856–1908) | Chair finisher Freight conductor | Grace Williams | Utica, New York London |
| Guiney, Louise I. (1863–1920) | Army officer | None | Boston Oxford, England |
| Hall, G. Stanley (1844–1924) | Farmer | Cornelia Fisher Florence Smith | Ashfield, Massachusetts Boston Worcester, Massachusetts |
| Hazeltine, Mayo (1841–1909) | Unknown | None | New York City |
| Hearn, Lafcadio (1850–1904) | Army officer | Setsu Koizumi | Cincinnati New Orleans Yokohama, Japan Kobe, Japan Tokyo |

| CHIEF OCCUPATIONS | EDUCATION | RELIGIOUS BACKGROUND AND/OR AFFILIATION |
|---|---|---|
| Novelist | Public Schools | Methodist→ Agnostic |
| Architect Author | Public Schools | Unitarian→ Episcopalian |
| Novelist | University of Rome Harvard University Cambridge University | Episcopalian |
| Journalist Social reformer | New York University Columbia Law | Presbyterian→ Secular humanist |
| Leatherworker Social reformer | Boston Museum of Fine Arts | Unknown |
| Clergyman Professor of divinity | Dartmouth College Yale Divinity School | Congregationalist |
| Clergyman | Columbia College General Theological Seminary | Episcopalian |
| Author | Yale University | Unknown |
| Railroad executive Art collector | Public Schools | Unknown |
| Journalist Novelist | Public Schools | Methodist |
| Poet Critic | Elmhurst Academy (Providence, Rhode Island) | Roman Catholic |
| Psychologist University president | Williams College Union Theological Seminary Harvard University | Congregational→ Agnostic |
| Journalist | Harvard College | Unknown |
| Journalist | Seminary (Yvetot, France) | Episcopalian,→ Roman Catholic→ Buddhist |

| NAME | FATHER'S OCCUPATION | SPOUSE | CHIEF RESIDENCES |
|---|---|---|---|
| Hooker, Brian (1880–1946) | Unknown | Doris Cooper | New York City Farmington, Connecticut |
| Hovey, Richard (1864–1900) | Lawyer | Henrietta Russell | Boston Washington D.C. New York City |
| Hubbard, Elbert (1859–1915) | Physician | Bertha Crawford (div.) Alice Moore | Bloomington, Illinois East Aurora, New York |
| James, William (1842–1910) | Author | Alice H. Gibbens | New York City Cambridge, Massachusetts |
| Kennedy, William S. (1850–1929) | Clergyman | Adeline Lincoln | Cleveland Boston |
| Lodge, George Cabot (1873–1909) | U.S. Senator Historian | Elizabeth Davis | Washington, D.C. |
| Longfellow, Henry Wadsworth (1807–1882) | Lawyer | Mary Potter Frances Appleton | Portland, Maine Cambridge, Massachusetts |
| Lowell, James Russell (1819–1891) | Clergyman | Maria White Frances Dunlap | Cambridge, Massachusetts |
| Lowell, Percival (1855–1916) | Textile merchant | Constance Keith | Boston Flagstaff, Arizona |
| Mabie, Hamilton Wright (1846–1917) | Merchant | Jeannette Trivet | Cold Spring, New York New York City Summit, New Jersey |
| McIlvaine, James Hall (1846–1921) | Clergyman | Grace P. Biddle | Utica, New York Providence, Rhode Island New York City Pittsburgh |
| Major, Charles (1856–1913) | Lawyer | Alice Shaw | Indianapolis, Indiana Shelbyville, Indiana |
| Mann, Cameron (1851–1932) | Clergyman | Mary LeCain | Watkins, New York Kansas City, Missouri Fargo, North Dakota |

| CHIEF OCCUPATIONS | EDUCATION | RELIGIOUS BACKGROUND AND/OR AFFILIATION |
|---|---|---|
| Author<br>Translator | Yale University | Unknown |
| Poet | Dartmouth College | Congregationalist→<br>Episcopalian |
| Soap salesman<br>Author<br>Bookbinder | Public Schools<br>Harvard University | Baptist<br>Secular humanist |
| Psychologist<br>Philosopher | Lawrence Scientific School<br>Harvard Medical | Swedenborgian→<br>Christian existentialist |
| Author | Harvard College | Unknown |
| Poet | Harvard College | Episcopalian |
| Poet | Bowdoin College | Unitarian |
| Poet<br>Critic<br>Professor of literature | Harvard College<br>Harvard Law | Unitarian |
| Journalist<br>Astronomer | Harvard College | Unitarian |
| Editor<br>Author | Williams College | Episcopalian |
| Clergyman | Princeton University<br>Princeton Theological Seminary | Presbyterian |
| Author<br>Lawyer | Michigan State University | Unknown |
| Bishop | Hobart College<br>General Theological Seminary | Episcopalian |

| NAME | FATHER'S OCCUPATION | SPOUSE | CHIEF RESIDENCES |
|---|---|---|---|
| Matthews, Brander (1852–1929) | Merchant | Ada Smith | New Orleans New York City |
| Norris, Frank (1870–1902) | Jeweler | Jeannette Black | San Francisco |
| Norton, Charles Eliot (1827–1908) | Clergyman | Susan Sedgwick | Cambridge, Massachusetts Ashfield, Massachusetts |
| Pepper, George Wharton (1867–1949) | Physician | Charlotte R. Fisher | Philadelphia |
| Pennell, Elizabeth Robbins (1855–1936) | Stockbroker | Joseph Pennell | Philadelphia London |
| Pennell, Joseph (1860–1926) | Teacher Shipping clerk | Elizabeth Robbins | Philadelphia London |
| Perry, Thomas Sergeant (1845–1928) | Lawyer | Lilla Cabot | Newport, Rhode Island Boston |
| Pressey, Edward P. (1870–?) | Unknown | Unknown | Montague, Massachusetts |
| Pyle, Howard (1853–1911) | Leather manufacturer | Anne Poole | Wilmington, Delaware |
| Repplier, Agnes (1855–1950) | Merchant | None | Philadelphia Paris |
| Rollins, Carl P. (1880–1960) | Unknown | Margaret Dickey | West Newbury, Massachusetts Boston New Haven, Connecticut |
| Ross, Denman (1853–1935) | Unknown | None | Cincinnati Cambridge, Massachusetts |
| Sanborn, Alvan (1866–?) | Unknown | Marie Perrin | Boston Paris |

| CHIEF OCCUPATIONS | EDUCATION | RELIGIOUS BACKGROUND AND/OR AFFILIATION |
|---|---|---|
| Professor of dramatic literature Author | Columbia University Columbia Law | Episcopalian |
| Novelist | University of California | Presbyterian, Episcopalian |
| Editor Professor of fine arts | Harvard College Harvard College | Unitarian→ Agnostic |
| Professor of law Lawyer | University of Pennsylvania University of Pennsylvania Law | Episcopalian |
| Author | Sacred Heart Convent, Torresdale, Pennsylvania | Roman Catholic |
| Illustrator | Pennsylvania Acadamy of Fine Arts Pennsylvania School of Industrial Art | Quaker |
| Author Critic | Harvard College Harvard University | Quaker, Episcopalian→ Agnostic |
| Clergyman | Harvard College | Unitarian |
| Artist Author | Art Students League (New York City) | Quaker, Swedenborgian |
| Essayist | Sacred Heart Convent, Torresdale, Pennsylvania | Roman Catholic |
| Printer Professor of design | Harvard College | Unknown |
| Professor of design | Harvard College Harvard University (Ph.D.) | Unknown |
| Journalist | Amherst College | Unknown |

| NAME | FATHER'S OCCUPATION | SPOUSE | CHIEF RESIDENCES |
|---|---|---|---|
| Santayana George (1863–1952) | Civil servant | None | Cambridge, Massachusetts Paris Rome |
| Scudder, Vida (1861–1954) | Clergyman | None | Wellesley, Massachusetts |
| Simkhovitch, Mary K. (1867–1951) | Army officer | Vladimir G. Simkhovitch | Chestnut Hill, Massachusetts New York City |
| Starr, Ellen Gates (1859–1940) | Farmer Merchant | None | Laona, Illinois Chicago |
| Stickley, Gustav (1858–1942) | Cabinetmaker | Eda Simmons | Osceola, Wisconsin Syracuse, New York |
| Storrs, Richard (1821–1900) | Clergyman | Mary E. Jenks | Braintree, Massachusetts Brookline, Massachusetts Brooklyn, New York |
| Taylor, Henry Osborne (1856–1941) | Merchant | Julia Isham | New York City |
| Traubel, Horace (1858–1919) | Printer | Anne Montgomerie | Camden, New Jersey |
| Triggs, Oscar Lovell (1865–?) | Clergyman | Laura McAdoo | Greenwood, Illinois Minneapolis Chicago |
| Van Allen, William H. (1870–1931) | Educator | None | Cameron, New York New York City Boston |
| Volk, Douglas (1856–1935) | Sculptor | Marion B. Larrabee | Pittsfield, Massachusetts New York City |
| Warren, Herbert L. (1857–1917) | Unknown | Catharine C. Reed | Manchester, England Boston |
| Wharton, Edith (1862–1937) | *Rentier* | Edward Wharton | New York City Paris |

| CHIEF OCCUPATIONS | EDUCATION | RELIGIOUS BACKGROUND AND/OR AFFILIATION |
|---|---|---|
| Philosopher<br>Poet | Harvard<br>Harvard University | Agnostic,<br>Roman Catholic |
| Professor of English | Smith College<br>Oxford University | Congregationalist→<br>Episcopalian |
| Social reformer | Boston University<br>Radcliffe College<br>University of Berlin<br>Columbia University | Episcopalian |
| Social reformer<br>Bookbinder | Rockford College (Rockford,<br>    Illinois) | Unitarian→<br>Episcopalian→<br>Roman Catholic |
| Editor<br>Furniture manufacturer | Public schools | Presbyterian |
| Clergyman<br>Author<br>Orator | Amherst College<br>Andover Theological Seminary | Congregational |
| Historian | Harvard College<br>Columbia Law | Episcopalian |
| Editor | Public schools | Reform Judaism→<br>Secular humanism |
| Professor of literature<br>Author<br>Social reformer | Cornell College (Iowa)<br>University of Minnesota<br>Oxford University<br>University of Berlin<br>University of Chicago | Methodist |
| Clergyman | Syracuse University<br>Hobart College | Episcopalian |
| Artist | Tutors,<br>Chicago and Rome | Unknown |
| Architect<br>Professor of architecture | Owens College, Manchester,<br>    England<br>Massachusetts Institute of<br>    Technology | Unknown |
| Novelist | Private tutors at home | Episcopalian |

## 1. ROOTS OF ANTIMODERNISM: THE CRISIS OF CULTURAL AUTHORITY DURING THE LATE NINETEENTH CENTURY

1. Some of these issues are discussed in John Higham, "The Re-Orientation of American Culture in the 1890's" in his *Writing American History* (Bloomington, Ind., 1973), pp. 73–102 and in Christopher Lasch, "The Moral and Intellectual Rehabilitation of the Ruling Class" in his *The World of Nations* (New York, 1973), pp. 80–91. But Higham neglects the class dimension of his "reorientation" and Lasch is primarily concerned with political and economic rather than cultural developments. On the European side, three among many thoughtful explorations of *fin-de-siècle* cultural ferment are H. Stuart Hughes, *Consciousness and Society: the Re-Orientation of European Social Thought, 1890–1930* (New York, 1958); Fritz Stern, *The Politics of Cultural Despair* (Berkeley, 1961); and Carl Schorske, *Fin-de-Siècle Vienna: Politics and Culture* (New York, 1979).

2. Perry Miller, *The New England Mind: from Colony to Province* (Boston, 1961) and Sacvan Bercovitch, *The American Jeremiad* (New York, 1978) suggestively explore the hegemonic function of the jeremiad.

3. See Max Weber, *Economy and Society,* 3 vols., ed. and trans. Guenther Roth and Claus Wittick (Berkeley, 1968), especially vol 1, chaps. 1–4; 2, chaps. 7–8; 3, chaps. 10, 11, 14, for his fullest discussion of the concept of rationalization.

4. Henry Ward Beecher, "The Advance of a Century," *New York Tribune*, Extra no. 33, Independence Day Orations, 4 July 1876, pp. 37–44, reprinted in *Democratic Vistas, 1860–1880*, ed. Alan Trachtenberg (New York, 1970). The quotation is from p. 70.

5. Andrew Carnegie, *Triumphant Democracy* (New York, 1886), p. 1. Popular enthusiasm for material progress is amply documented in such anthologies as Henry Nash Smith, ed., *Popular Culture and Industrialism, 1865–1890* (New York, 1967).

6. For useful background on the second industrial revolution, see David S. Landes, *The Unbound Prometheus: Technological Change and Industrial Development in Western Europe from 1750 to the Present* (Cambridge, England, 1959); Douglas C. North, *Growth and Welfare in the American Past: a New Economic History*, 2nd ed. (Englewood Cliffs, N.J., 1966); and Robert Higgs, *The Transformation of the American Economy, 1865–1914* (New York, 1971). Quotations on the Corliss engine are taken from John F. Kasson, *Civilizing the Machine: Technology and Republican Values in America, 1776–1900* (New York: Penguin Books, 1977), p. 164. Storrs on the bridge is quoted in Alan Trachtenberg, *Brooklyn Bridge: Fact and Symbol* (New York, 1965), p. 125.

7. Some of the complex economic developments mentioned in this paragraph are ably explored in Fred Albert Shannon, *The Farmer's Last Frontier: Agriculture, 1860–1897* (New York, 1945); Alfred D. Chandler, *The Visible Hand: the Managerial Revolution in American Business* (Cambridge, Mass., 1977); David Noble, *America by Design: Science, Technology, and the Rise of Corporate Capitalism* (New York, 1977); and Thomas C. Cochran and William Miller, *The Age of Enterprise: a Social History of Industrial America,* (New York: Harper Torchbook, 1961).

8. The concept of hegemony can be pieced together from Antonio Gramsci, *Selections from the Prison Notebooks,* ed. and trans. Quentin Hoare and Geoffrey Nowell Smith (New York, 1971) and *The Modern Prince and Other Writings,* ed. and trans. Louis Marks (New York, 1967).

9. See especially Williams's "Base and Superstructure in Marxist Cultural Theory," *New*

*Left Review* 82 (November–December 1973): 3–16 and his *Marxism and Literature* (New York, 1976).

10. See Herbert Gutman, *Work, Culture, and Society in Industrializing America* (New York, 1977), especially the title essay; Daniel T. Rodgers, *The Work Ethic in Industrial America, 1850–1920* (Chicago, 1978), especially pp. 160–74; "Recording Time of Employees," *Scientific American* 69 (12 August 1893): 101. Daniel Rodgers, "Tradition, Modernity, and the American Industrial Worker," *Journal of Interdisciplinary History* 7 (1977): 655–81 rightly cautions against a rigid distinction between "traditional" and "modern" work habits. Both Rodgers and Gutman stress widespread and continuing resistance to modern work discipline.

11. Alexis de Tocqueville, *Democracy in America* [1835, 1840], 2 vols. (New York: Vintage Books, 1960), 2: 136–42; "Modern Science in Its Relations to Pain," *Century* 36 (August 1888): 632–34. For a perceptive discussion of the democratization of comfort (including Pullman cars, indoor plumbing, and central heating), see Daniel Boorstin, *The Americans: the Democratic Experience* (New York, 1973), pp. 332–36, 346–58. For the quotation from Mary Boykin Chesnut, I am indebted to Professor C. Vann Woodward, who is preparing an edition of her diary. On narcotics use in general among nineteenth-century Americans, see John S. Haller and Robin M. Haller, *The Physician and Sexuality in Victorian America* (New York, 1974), chap. 7, and David S. Musto, *The American Disease: Origins of Narcotics Control* (New Haven, 1973), pp. 1–13.

12. "The Moral Drift of Our Time," *Christian Union* 27 (31 May 1883): 428–29.

13. Max Weber, *The Protestant Ethic and the Spirit of Capitalism*, trans. Talcott Parsons (New York, 1958). The best restatement and defense of Weber's thesis is David Little, *Religion, Order, and Law* (New York, 1965). The historiography of the ethic of self-control is vast and growing. For particularly useful background, see D.W. Howe, "Victorian Culture in America" in Howe, ed., *Victorian America* (Philadelphia, 1976), pp. 3–28; Rodgers, *Work Ethic*, chaps. 1, 5–8; Haller, *Physician and Sexuality*, chaps. 2, 3, 5.

14. On the creation of a modern superego, see Norbert Elias, *The Civilizing Process: the History of Manners*, trans. Edmund Jephcott (New York, 1977), which masterfully synthesizes Freudian and Weberian concepts. On Kellogg, see his *Man, the Masterpiece, or Plain Truths Plainly Told, About Boyhood, Youth and Manhood* [1886] (Battle Creek, Mich., 1894), especially pp. 445–53, and the witty discussion of Kellogg in Joseph F. Kett, *Rites of Passage: Adolescence in America from 1790 to the Present* (New York, 1977), pp. 164–65.

15. Sudhir Kakar, *Frederick Winslow Taylor: a Study in Personality and Innovation* (Cambridge, Mass., 1970) adduces much information about the psychic sources of Taylor's drive toward efficiency. See also Taylor's classic *Principles of Scientific Management* (New York, 1911) and Harry Braverman's brilliant Marxian interpretation of Taylorism in *Labor and Monopoly Capital: the Degradation of Work in the Twentieth Century* (New York, 1974), pp. 85–138.

16. Those questions have been raised by Charles E. Rosenberg, "Sexuality, Class, and Role in 19th Century America," *American Quarterly* 25 (May 1973): 131–53; Morse Peckham, "Victorian Counterculture," *Victorian Studies* 18 (March 1975): 257–76; Carl Degler, "What Ought to Be and What Was: Women's Sexuality in Nineteenth Century America," *American Historical Review* 79 (December, 1974): 1467–90; and *At Odds: Women and the Family in America from the Revolution to the Present* (New York, 1980).

17. See, for example, Paul Faler, "Cultural Aspects of the Industrial Revolution," *Labor History* 15 (Summer, 1974): 367–94; Gutman, "Work, Culture, and Society"; and Daniel Scott Smith, "Family Limitation, Sexual Control, and Domestic Feminism in Victorian America" in *Clio's Consciousness Raised: New Perspectives on the History of Women* (New York, 1976), pp. 119–36.

18. My argument in this and the following paragraphs is based on: William E. Bridges, "Family Patterns and Social Values in America, 1825–1875," *American Quarterly* 17 (Spring, 1965): 3–11; Steven Mintz, "Studies in the Victorian Family," (Ph.D. diss., Yale University, 1979); Nancy F. Cott, *The Bonds of Womanhood: "Woman's Sphere" in New England, 1780–1835*

(New Haven, 1977); Carroll Smith-Rosenberg, "The Hysterical Woman: Sex Roles and Role Conflict in Nineteenth Century America," *Social Research* 39 (1972): 652–78; Carol Christ, "Victorian Masculinity and the Angel in the House," in Martha Vicinus, ed., *A Widening Sphere: Changing Roles of Victorian Women* (Bloomington, Ind., 1977), pp. 146–62; Kathryn Kish Sklar, *Catharine Beecher: a Study in Domesticity* (New Haven, 1973); and Smith, "Domestic Feminism."

19. Smith, "Domestic Feminism", p. 132. On the domestic ideal as a reflection of male longings and self-doubts, see Christ, "Victorian Masculinity," and Rodgers, *Work Ethic*, p. 208. Tocqueville's observation is in *Democracy in America*, 2: 219.

20. For a typically self-congratulatory example of this attitude, see Henry T. Finck, "The Scope of Modern Love," *Harper's Monthly* 103 (July 1901): 277–78.

21. W.D. Howells, *Criticism and Fiction* [1891] (New York, 1959), p. 62. Ann Douglas, *The Feminization of American Culture* (New York, 1977), perceptively discusses this theme.

22. Robert E. Spiller et al., *Literary History of the United States* (New York, 1963), embodies the conventional wisdom on this point.

23. See Irvin G. Wyllie, *The Self-Made Man in America* (New Brunswick, N.J., 1954) and John G. Cawelti, *Apostles of the Self-Made Man* (Chicago, 1965). The quotation is from Wyllie, p. 40.

24. Clark Kerr et al., *Industrialism and Industrial Man: the Problems of Labor and Management in Economic Growth* (Cambridge, Mass., 1960), p. 43. On nineteenth century inequality, see, for example, Lee Soltow, *Men and Wealth in the United States, 1850–1870* (New Haven, 1975).

25. Quoted in Paul F. Boller, Jr., *American Thought in Transition: the Impact of Evolutionary Naturalism, 1865–1900* (Chicago, 1969), p. 71.

26. See Boller, *American Thought*, pp. 70–77; also Joseph Dorfman, *The Economic Mind in American Civilization*, 4 vols. (New York, 1946–1951), vol. 3, pt. 1.

27. D.H. Meyer, *The Instructed Conscience: the Shaping of the American National Ethic* (Philadelphia, 1972), pp. 24, 47, 51. The quotation is from p. 102.

28. My interpretation of Spencer is based largely on J.D.Y. Peel, *Herbert Spencer: the Evolution of a Sociologist* (New York, 1971) and Robert C. Bannister, *Social Darwinism: Science and Myth in Anglo-American Social Thought* (Philadelphia, 1979). Both of these books avoid the error of Richard Hofstadter, *Social Darwinism in American Thought*, rev. ed. (Boston, 1955), which presents Spencer as a "Social Darwinist" and apologist for laissez-faire capitalism and which exaggerates the popularity of Darwinian notions of struggle among the American middle and upper classes.

29. Peel, *Spencer*, pp. 20, 214–15; Bannister, *Social Darwinism*, pp. 28–29, 55.

30. Bannister, *Social Darwinism*, especially chap. 2; Goldwin Smith, "Has Science Yet Found a New Basis for Morality?" *Contemporary Review* 45 (1882): 770.

31. Bannister, *Social Darwinism*, chap. 3.

32. William Evarts, quoted in E.L. Youmans, ed., *Spencer on the Americans* (New York, 1883), p. 28. Compare Hofstadter's account of the banquet in *Social Darwinism in American Thought*, pp. 48–49 with Bannister's in *Social Darwinism*, pp. 76–78.

33. John Fiske to his mother 13 November 1873, quoted in Milton Berman, *John Fiske: the Evolution of a Popularizer* (Cambridge, Mass., 1961), pp. 103–4.

34. Phillips Brooks, "The Essential in Religion," *The Christian Union* 21 (9 June 1880): 528–29. See also "The Moral Drift of Our Time."

35. Susan Coolidge, "Miracle," *Christian Union* 25 (16 February 1882): 159.

36. Elizabeth Stuart Phelps, *The Gates Ajar* [1868], 2nd ed. (Boston, 1871), pp. 124, 153, 166, 186–87. Ann Douglas perceptively discusses "the domestication of death" in *Feminization of American Culture*, chap. 6, as does James Farrell in "The Nature of a Natural Death" (Paper presented at the Organization of American Historians Annual Meeting, New Orleans, 12 April 1979).

37. Perry Miller, *The Life of the Mind in America* (New York, 1965), pp. 85–91; [Rollo Ogden], "Religious Statistics," *Nation* 43 (16 December 1886): 494–95. The best account of the entangling alliance between capitalism and urban Protestantism is Henry May, *Protestant*

*Churches and Industrial America* (New York: Harper Torchbooks, 1967). Herbert Gutman, "Protestantism and the American Labor Movement: the Christian Spirit in the Gilded Age," *American Historical Review* 72 (October 1966): 74–101, points out that where evangelical perfectionism persisted, it could generate revolt as well as complacency.

38. Phillips Brooks, "The Man With Two Talents," in *Twenty Sermons*, 4th ser. (New York, 1887): 194; Beecher, quoted in May, *Protestant Churches*, p. 94.

39. H.W. Beecher, "The Moral Uses of Luxury and Beauty," *Christian Union* 25 (16 March 1882): 257–58; [Beecher], "A Plea for Lent," *Christian Union* 21 (11 February 1880): 123; Rev. Charles Cuthbert Hale, "The Church. Is it a Social Club—or a Divine Foundation?" *Christian Union* 27 (10 May 1888): 370; [Ernest Howard], "The Decay of the New England Churches," *Nation* 43 (4 November 1886): 367–68.

40. For the standard critique of Gilded Age culture, see H. N. Smith, "Introduction" to *Popular Culture*, and Stow Persons, *The Decline of American Gentility* (New York, 1973).

41. Edmund S. Morgan, "The Puritan Ethic and the Coming of the American Revolution," in Jack P. Greene, ed., *The Re-Interpretation of the American Revolution* (New York, 1968), p. 238.

42. Morgan, "Puritan Ethic," p. 239; H. Trevor Colbourn, *The Lamp of Experience: Whig History and the Intellectual Origins of the American Revolution* (Chapel Hill, 1965). The two most exhaustive explorations of the republican mentality during the Revolutionary era are Bernard Bailyn, *The Ideological Origins of the American Revolution* (Cambridge, Mass., 1967), and Gordon Wood, *The Creation of the American Republic* (Chapel Hill, 1969).

43. Perry Miller, *Nature's Nation* (Cambridge, Mass., 1963), and "Nature and the National Ego," in *Errand into the Wilderness* (New York, 1964), pp. 204–16.

44. D.H. Meyer, *The Instructed Conscience: The Shaping of the American National Ethic* (Philadelphia, 1973); James McLachlan, "American Colleges and the Transmission of Culture: the Case of the Mugwumps," in Stanley Elkins and Eric McKitrick, eds., *The Hofstadter Aegis: a Memorial* (New York, 1974), pp. 184–206. On textbooks, see Ruth Miller Elson, *Guardians of Tradition: American Schoolbooks in the Nineteenth Century* (New York, 1964).

45. Charles Eliot Norton, *Notes of Travel and Study in Italy* (Boston, 1856), p. 300; Walt Whitman, *Democratic Vistas* (New York, 1871), p. 43.

46. Theodore Roosevelt, "What 'Americanism' Means," *Forum* 17 (April 1894): 196–206; Richard Burton, "The Healthful Tone for American Literature," *Forum* 19 (April 1895): 249–56; "Editor's Study," *Harper's Monthly* 90 (May 1895): 967–69; George Frederic Parsons, "The Growth of Materialism," *Atlantic Monthly* 60 (August 1887): 157–72.

47. Woods Hutchinson, "The Physical Basis of Brain-Work," *North American Review* 146 (May 1888): 522–31. For three among many examples of nostalgic pastoralism see [E.L. Godkin], "The Decline of New England," *Nation* 49 (5 December 1889): 445; "The Sadness of Rural Life," *Atlantic Monthly* 65 (May 1890): 713–15; and Maurice Thompson, "The Rustic Muse," *Chap-Book* 6 (1 January 1897): 145–52.

48. On the beginnings of a consumer economy, see Cochran and Miller, *Age of Enterprise*, p. 311; Boorstin, *Democratic Experience*, pp. 89–164; and Chandler, *Visible Hand*, pts. 3 and 4. Chandler discusses Duke on pp. 290–91.

49. Quoted in John Higham, *Strangers in the Land: Patterns of American Nativism, 1860–1925* (New York: Atheneum Books, 1973), pp. 42, 138. See also Richard Sennett, "Middle Class Families and Urban Violence: the Experience of a Chicago Community in the Nineteenth Century," in Stephan Thernstrom and Richard Sennett, eds., *Nineteenth Century Cities: Essays in the New Urban History* (New Haven, 1969), pp. 386–420.

50. See, for example: James Henry Hayne, "Socialistic and Other Assassinations," *Atlantic Monthly* 46 (October, 1880): 466; Alexander Winchell, "Communism in the United States," *North American Review* 136 (May 1883): 454, 466; Francis A. Walker, "What Shall We Tell the Working Classes?," *Scribner's* 2 (November 1899): 619–27; "The Political Menace of the Discontented," *Atlantic Monthly* 77 (October 1896): 447.

51. Stephan Thernstrom summarizes recent work in "The Boston Case and the American

Pattern," chapter 10 of *The Other Bostonians: Poverty and Progress in the American Metropolis, 1880–1970* (Cambridge, Mass., 1973).

52. C.S. Denny, "The Whipping Post for Tramps," *Century* 40 (March 1895): 794; Bram Stoker, "The American 'Tramp' Question and the Old English Vagrancy Laws," *North American Review* 190 (November 1909): 605–14.

53. "Changes in Drinking Habits," *Nation* 48 (16 May 1889): 399–400; Robert Grant, *Fourscore* (New York, 1895); William Blaikie, "Is American Stamina Declining?," *Harper's Monthly* 79 (July 1889): 241–44; "The Physical Character of Industrial Man," *Scribner's* 15 (June 1894): 791–92.

54. Francis A. Walker, "Immigration and Degradation," *Forum* 11 (August 1891): 634–44; Frederick L. Hoffmann, "The Decline in the Birth Rate," *North American Review* 189 (May 1909): 675; Henry Cabot Lodge, "The Restriction of Immigration," *North American Review* 152 (January 1891): 27–36; Judge J.A. Jameson, "Is Our Civilization Perishable?," *North American Review* 138 (March 1884): 205–15. On the general subject of upper-class nativism, see Higham, *Strangers*, pp. 94–105, 147–48, and Barbara Solomon, *Ancestors and Immigrants: a Changing New England Tradition* (Cambridge, Mass., 1956).

55. Geoffrey Champlin, "The Decline of New England," *North American Review* 146 (May 1888): 588–89; [George Harvey], "Cynicism and Decadence," *North American Review* 185 (7 June 1907): 350; James Weir, Jr., M.D., "The Methods of the Rioting Striker as Evidence of Degeneration," *Century* 48 (October 1894): 952–53.

56. Henry Childs Merwin, "On Being Civilized Too Much," *Atlantic Monthly* 79 (June 1897): 838–46; "Law and Order Leagues," *Century* 26 (October 1883): 948–49.

57. Letter, Charles Eliot Norton to James Russell Lowell, 14 May 1878, in Sara Norton and M.A. DeWolfe Howe, eds., *The Letters of Charles Eliot Norton*, 2 vols. (Boston, 1913), 2:81; Fitz John Porter, "How to Quell Mobs," *North American Review* 141 (September 1885): 351–60; Richard J. Henton, "Organizations of the Discontented," *Forum* 7 (July 1889): 540, 551; James C. Malin, *Confounded Rot about Napoleon: Reflections upon Science and Technology, Nationalism, World Depression of the Eighteen-Nineties, and Afterwards* (Lawrence, Kan., 1961), chap. 1; Henry Holt, "Fallacies Underlying Social Discontent," *Forum*, 18 (February 1895). On the prevalence of the volcano image, see Neil Harris, "Introduction" to his *The Land of Contrasts, 1880–1901* (New York, 1973), p. 17.

58. Charles Baudelaire, "Les Sept Vieillards," in *Les Fleurs du Mal* (1857), my translation; T.S. Eliot, "The Wasteland," (1922).

59. Siegfried Giedion, *Mechanization Takes Command* (New York: Norton Library, 1969), pp. 329–33. For the view of eclecticism as a sign of exuberance, see Howard Mumford Jones, *The Age of Energy: Varieties of American Experience, 1865–1915* (New York, 1971), especially chap. 3.

60. Edward A. Ross, "New Varieties of Sin," *Atlantic Monthly* 95 (May 1905): 594. Martha S. Bensley, "Is the Arts and Crafts Movement Degenerate?" *Independent* 58 (8 June 1905): 1305, discusses the impact of interdependence on work. Robert S. Wiebe, *The Search for Order, 1877–1920* (New York, 1967), is implicitly concerned with the impact of an interdependent market economy. Thomas Haskell, *The Emergence of Professional Social Science: the American Social Science Association and the Nineteenth Century Crisis of Authority* (Urbana, 1977), especially chap. 2, explores interdependence with great precision and theoretical sophistication. I am especially indebted to Haskell's analysis.

61. Ralph Waldo Emerson, "Fate," [1852] in his *Collected Works*, Century ed. (Boston, 1903), 6:9.

62. Gerald Stanley Lee, "The Dominance of the Crowd," *Atlantic Monthly* 76 (December 1900): 754–61; "The Conditions of Genius," *Scribner's* 41 (March 1907): 379; Louise Imogen Guiney, *Patrins* (Boston, 1897), p. 31; Letter, Charles Eliot Norton to S.G. Ward, 19 September 1900, in *Letters of Norton*, 2:300; Rudolph Eucken, "The Present Estimate of the Value of Human Life," *Forum* 34 (April 1903): 608–16.

63. David Riesman, with Nathan Glazer and Reuel Denney, *The Lonely Crowd: a Study of the Changing American Character,* 3rd ed. rev. (New Haven, 1969), pp. 21, 25, 127.

64. See Erving Goffman, *Relations in Public: Micro Studies of the Public Order* (New York, 1971); Riesman, *Lonely Crowd,* p. 157.

65. For an excellent discussion of Franklin's use of social masks, see Robert F. Sayre, *The Examined Self: Franklin, James, Adams* (Princeton, 1964), chap. 1. Harris's discussion is in *Humbug: The Art of P.T. Barnum* (New York, 1973), chaps. 2, 3. The phrase "simple, genuine self" is from Emerson's *Journals,* and is quoted in R.W.B. Lewis, *The American Adam* (Chicago, 1955), p. vi.

66. Henry James, *The Portrait of a Lady* [1881] (Cambridge, Mass.: Riverside, 1963), pp. 172-73.

67. Andrew Hedbrooke, "Individual Continuity," *Atlantic Monthly* 58 (August 1886): 263–67. For an effort to salvage a sense of selfhood from "the fragmentariness and multiplicity of life," see Ethel Dench Puffer, "The Loss of Personality," *Atlantic Monthly* 85 (February 1900): 195–204. The classic statement of the relation between selfhood and a cosmopolitan existence is Georg Simmel, "The Metropolis and Mental Life," in Kurt Wolff, trans., ed., *The Sociology of Georg Simmel* (London, 1950), pp. 409–26.

68. Riesman, *Lonely Crowd,* p. 149. On New Thought and mind cure, see A. Whitney Griswold, "The American Cult of Success," *American Journal of Sociology* 40 (1934): 309–18; Donald Meyer, *The Positive Thinkers: a Study of the American Search for Health, Wealth, and Personal Power from Mary Baker Eddy to Norman Vincent Peale* (New York, 1965); and Gail Parker, *Mind Cure in New England* (Hanover, N.H., 1973).

69. William James, *Principles of Psychology,* 2 vols. (New York, 1890), 1: 294; George Herbert Mead, *Mind, Self, and Society* (Chicago, 1934).

70. See works cited in n. 46, above, and Frank T. Presbrey, *The History and Development of Advertising* (New York, 1929).

71. L.L. Whyte, *The Unconscious Before Freud* (New York, 1960), p. 161; Henri Ellenberger, *The Discovery of the Unconscious* (New York, 1970), chaps. 3, 4, 5; Nathan G. Hale, *Freud and the Americans: the Beginnings of Psychoanalysis in the United States, 1876–1917* (New York, 1971), pp. 116–150; "The Felt Location of the 'I,' " *Atlantic Monthly* 59 (January 1887): 136–37; H.C. Wood, "A Study of Consciousness," *Century* 40 (May 1890): 72–76; H. Addington Bruce, "Insanity and the Nation," *North American Review* 187 (January 1908): 79.

72. Arthur E. Fink, *Causes of Crime: Biological Theories in the United States, 1800–1915* (Philadelphia, 1938), chap. 7; Mark H. Haller, *Eugenics: Hereditarian Attitudes in American Thought* (New Brunswick, N.J., 1963), pp. 3–57.

73. Daniel G. Brinton, M.D., "Popular Superstitions of Europe," *Century* 56 (September 1898): 649; Alexander Sutherland, "Necessity and Responsibility," *North American Review* 168 (March 1899): 269–75.

74. "Slave or Master?," *Century* 25 (April 1883): 953–54. See also "The Impersonal Element in Social Life," *Scribner's* 32 (September 1902): 379–80.

75. Charles E. Rosenberg, *The Trial of the Assassin Guiteau: Psychiatry and Law in the Gilded Age* (Chicago, 1968), chap. 2.

76. Ibid., pp. 142–50, 155–56, 189–97.

77. Ibid., pp. 191, 255.

78. In most states, the criterion for evaluating insanity remained the M'Naghten Rule, which emphasized impairment of intellect or understanding rather than will. Under M'Naghten, the appropriate question for Guiteau was: did he know the bullet would kill Garfield? See Abraham S. Goldstein, *The Insanity Defense* (New Haven, 1967), chaps. 4, 5.

79. J.J. Elwell, M.D., "The Moral Responsibility of the Insane," *North American Review* 134 (January 1882): 1–8; "Mob or Magistrate," *Century* 27 (April 1884): 944–45; I.C. Parker, "How to Arrest the Increase of Homicides in America," *North American Review* 162 (June 1896): 667–73; William A. Hammond, "A Problem for Sociologists," *North American Review*

135 (November 1882): 422–32; "Lesson of the Czolgosz Trial," *Nation* 72 (31 October 1901): 333. On the spread of parole and indeterminate sentence, see Blake McKelvey, *American Prisons. A Study in American Social History Prior to 1915* (Chicago, 1915), pp. 130–35, 161–62, 215–17 and David J. Rothman, *Conscience and Convenience: the Asylum and Its Alternatives in Progressive America* (New York, 1980).

80. Quoted in Meyer, *Instructed Conscience*, p. 93.

81. For two recent and in my judgment unsuccessful attacks on the concept of secularization, see David Martin, "Towards Eliminating the Concept of Secularization," in J. Gould, ed., *Penguin Survey of the Social Sciences* (London, 1965), and Andrew M. Greeley, *Unsecular Man: the Persistence of Religion* (New York, 1972).

82. Quoted in Karl Jaspers, *Nietzsche and Christianity*, trans. E.B. Ashton (Chicago, 1961), p. 14, from *Nachgelassen Werke, Nietzsches Werke*, ed. Elisabeth Forster-Nietzsche (Leipzig, 1903), 13: 316–17.

83. See the provocative essay by Marshall Berman, " 'All That is Solid Melts into Air': Marx, Modernism, and Modernization," *Dissent* 25 (Winter, 1978): 54–73, especially 66.

84. For three among many examples of this argument, see Goldwin Smith, "The Religious Situation," *North American Review* 187 (April 1908): 523; Christopher Stuart Patterson, "Christianity the Conservator of American Civilization," *Century* 36 (October 1888): 855–56; William Barry, "Signs of Impending Revolution," *Forum* 7 (April 1889): 165–74. For the radical-secular nexus in Europe, see Owen Chadwick, *The Secularization of the European Mind in the Nineteenth Century* (Cambridge, Eng., 1975).

85. Peter Berger, *The Sacred Canopy: Elements of a Sociological Theory of Religion* (New York, 1967) is the most concise statement of his view.

86. Froude is quoted in Walter Houghton, *The Victorian Frame of Mind, 1830–1870* (New Haven, 1957), p. 86. On this point in general, see Paul Carter, *The Spiritual Crisis of the Gilded Age* (DeKalb, Ill., 1971) and D.H. Meyer, "American Intellectuals and the Victorian Crisis of Faith," in Howe, *Victorian America*, pp. 59–77.

87. T.T. Munger, *The Appeal to Life* (Boston, 1887), pp. 33–34.

88. Quoted in Miller, *Colony to Province*, p. 179. On the persistence of witchcraft and diabolism, see Keith Thomas, *Religion and the Decline of Magic* (London, 1971), pp. 154–160, 571–77.

89. Jonathan Edwards, "The Eternity of Hell Torment," in *Works*, 4th ed., 4 vols. (New York, 1843), 4: 278.

90. Charles Grandison Finney, *Sermons on Important Subjects* (New York, 1836), p. 10; Maximilian Rudwin, *The Devil in Legend and Literature* (Chicago, 1931) pp. 270–99; "Mr. Beecher's Theology," *Christian Union* 26 (19 October 1882): 329; "The Scriptures and Future Punishment," *Christian Union* 26 (13 July 1882): 22–23. See also Ira V. Brown, *Lyman Abbott, Christian Evolutionist: a Study in Religious Liberalism* (Cambridge, Mass., 1963), pp. 130–45. On the decline of Satan and hell, see Edward Langton, *Satan, a Portrait* (London, 1947), and Geoffrey Rowell, *Hell and the Victorians* (Oxford, 1974).

91. Phillips Brooks, "The Safety and Helpfulness of Faith," *Christian Union* 23 (22 June 1881): 589; Gladstone, quoted in Rowell, *Hell*, p. 212.

92. Lydia Commander, *The American Idea* (New York, 1907), p. 156.

93. "Modern Science in Its Relation to Pain," p. 632.

94. William James, *The Varieties of Religious Experience* [1902] (New York: Collier Books, 1961), p. 239. See also Ross, "New Varieties of Sin," p. 595.

95. George Santayana, "The Poetry of Christian Dogma," in *Interpretations of Poetry and Religion* (New York, 1900), p. 103. For an example of evangelical alarm, see Rev. Edward H. Jewett, *Diabolology: the Person and Kingdom of Satan* (New York, 1890), p. 65. A more liberal but equally concerned view was expressed by Austin Bierbrower, "One Drift in the New Theology," *Christian Union* 27 (4 January 1883): 4.

96. George Wolfe Shinn, "What Has Become of Hell?," *North American Review* 170 (June

1900): 837–49; G.T. Knight, "The New Hell," *North American Review* 179 (July 1904): 135. On the parallel between liberalizing religion and liberalizing penology, see Eugene Smith, "The Old Penology and the New," *North American Review* 184 (4 January 1907): 80–86; Rowell, *Hell*, pp. 13, 14; McKelvey, *American Prisons*, pp. 24–29, 38–39.

97. "The Passing of the Devil," *Scribner's* 25 (April 1899): 508.

98. [Hammond Lamont], "The Open Mind," *Nation* 77 (24 September 1903): 243–44; [Rollo Ogden], "Some Blessings of Intolerance," *Nation* 52 (28 May 1891): 434–35; John H. Denison, "The White Death of the Soul," *Atlantic Monthly* 97 (June 1906): 754–63; "Concerning Convictions," *Atlantic Monthly* 60 (July 1887): 137–38. For examples of concern that toleration had lessened intensity of conviction, see J. Baldwin Brown, "The Roots of the Present Unbelief," *Christian Union* 24 (21 September 1881): 268; Frances P. Cobbe, "Secular Changes in Human Nature," *Forum* 9 (March 1890): 189–90; Vida D. Scudder, "Democracy and the Church," *Atlantic Monthly* 90 (October 1902), 521–27; "The Growth of Religious Tolerance," *Century* 67 (December 1903): 312–14; Ernest Cushing Richardson, "Our Superiority in Religion," *Century* 105 (March 1910): 382.

99. "The Melancholy of Modern Fiction," *Atlantic Monthly* 69 (May 1892): 716; Merwin, "On Being Civilized Too Much," 839.

100. Laurence Jerrold, "The Uses of Perversity," *Chap-Book* 5 (15 July 1896): 194–98; "The Decay of Personality," *Scribner's* 20 (September 1896): 387.

101. "Editor's Study," *Harper's Monthly* 79 (June 1889), 151–54; Lewis Morris, "The Disuse of Laughter," *Forum* 24 (November 1897): 319–24; Frederic Harrison, "The Decadence of Romance," *Forum* 15 (April 1893): 216–24; Henry C. Potter, "The Decadence of Enthusiasm," *Christian Union* 27 (15 February 1883): 137; "The Decay of Personality," 387; Agnes Repplier, "The Decay of Sentiment," *Atlantic Monthly* 60 (July 1887): 67–76.

102. Leon Edel, ed., *The Diary of Alice James* (New York, 1964), p. 149. Nathan G. Hale argues persuasively that by the turn of the century, sexual repression was exacting a serious emotional toll, and that the resulting crisis of "civilized" sexual morality helped create a favorable atmosphere for the reception of Freud's ideas. See Hale, *Freud and the Americans*, pp. 462–80. The evidence adduced by Carl Degler, "What Ought to be and What Was," qualifies but does not refute Hale's fundamental point. For a useful overview which notes the limitations of Degler's position see Sarah Stage, "Out of the Attic: Studies in Victorian Sexuality," *American Quarterly* 27 (October 1975): 480–85.

103. "Modern Self-Consciousness," *Atlantic Monthly* 86 (October 1900): 573–74; Hamilton Wright Mabie, *Essays in Literary Interpretation* (New York, 1892), pp. 1, 4, 42–43.

104. In general, American reviewers of Nordau admitted that he had a valid point—much of modern culture was "degenerate"—but they objected that he had destroyed his case by overstatement. See, for example, Charles L. Dana, "Are We Degenerating?," *Forum* 19 (June 1895): 458–65; Aline Gorren, "The New Criticism of Genius," *Atlantic Monthly* 74 (December 1894): 794–800, and "Nordau's Degeneration," *Nation* 60 (9 May 1895): 360. On "morbid introspection," see "A Cure for Self-Consciousness," *Nation* 40 (9 April 1885): 300; "The Spartan Virtue," *Scribner's* 8 (December 1890): 659–60; Gelett Burgess, "The Legend of St. Valentine," *Lark* 1 (February 1896); Van Wyck Brooks, *New England: Indian Summer, 1865–1915* (Boston, 1940), pp. 186, 200; Merwin, "On Being Civilized Too Much," 840; "Editor's Study," *Harper's Monthly* 69 (November 1884): 964.

105. C.E. Green, "The Lay of the Lost Hero," *Chap-Book* 4 (15 April 1896): 530–31; F. Marion Crawford, "False Taste in Art," *North American Review* 135 (July 1882): 89–98; Brooks, *Indian Summer*, pp. 100, 214. "The Oppressiveness of Modern Novels," *Atlantic Monthly* 85 (May 1900): 716–17; Arthur Symons, "The Decadent Movement in Literature," *Harper's Monthly* 87 (November 1893): 858–67; Royal Cortissoz, "Egotism in Contemporary Art," *Atlantic Monthly* 73 (May 1894): 644–52.

106. Anna C. Brackett, "The Technique of Rest," *Harper's Monthly* 83 (June 1891): 46–55.

107. George Miller Beard, *American Nervousness. Its Causes and Consequences* (New York,

1881), pp. 5, 7, 8. For an illuminating discussion of neurasthenia, see Barbara Sicherman, "The Paradox of Prudence: Mental Health in the Gilded Age," *Journal of American History* 62 (March 1976): 890–912. Sicherman avoids a common error: she does not discuss neurasthenia as exclusively a "woman's complaint."

108. Beard, *American Nervousness*, p. 1.

109. S. Weir Mitchell, *Wear and Tear, or Hints for the Over-Worked* (Philadelphia, 1887); Robert T. Edes, "The New England Invalid," *Boston Medical and Surgical Journal* 133 (11 July 1895): 53–57; Edward Cowles, *Neurasthenia and Its Mental Symptoms* (Boston, 1891); Kate Gannett Wells, "The Transitional American Woman," *Atlantic Monthly* 46 (December 1880): 818; Cyrus Edson, "Do We Live Too Fast?," *North American Review* 154 (February 1892): 281–86; "An Apology for the Irritable," *Scribner's* 62 (November 1907): 634.

110. T.B. Aldrich, "Insomnia," *Century* 45 (November 1892): 28.

111. H. Addington Bruce, "Insanity and the Nation," *North American Review* 187 (January 1908): 70–79.

112. "Insanity and Civilization," *Nation* 41 (29 October 1885): 356–57; C.Z. Bartol, "Civilization and Suicide," *Forum* 2 (September 1886): 40–48; William Mathews, "Civilization and Suicide," *North American Review* 161 (April 1891): 470–84; "A Blot on Modern Civilization," *Munsey's* 16 (October 1896): 128. On similar observations among Europeans, see Ellenberger, *Discovery of the Unconscious;* and Emile Durkheim, *Suicide: a Study in Sociology*, trans. John A. Spaulding and George Simpson (New York, 1951) [first pub. Paris, 1897].

113. Beard, *American Nervousness*, pp. 20, 96–97; Edes, "New England Invalid," 53; H.S. Williams, " 'Wages of Sin': General Paresis of the Insane," *North American Review* 155 (December 1892): 744–53; Bartol, "Civilization and Suicide," 41.

114. Edwin Lassiter Bynner, "Diary of a Nervous Invalid," *Atlantic Monthly* 71 (January 1893): 33–46; "Domesticated Nervousness," *Scribner's* 22 (February 1898): 251; M. Olivia Sage, "Responsibilities of Leisured Women," *North American Review* 181 (November 1905): 712–21.

115. Beard, *American Nervousness*, pp. 96–135; John H. Girdner, "Theology and Insanity," *North American Review* 168 (January 1899): 77–83; "The Effect of Christian Science and Mind Cure on 'the Regular Practice,' " *Century* 41 (April 1891): 950–51; "Noise in Modern Life," *Scribner's* 31 (April 1902): 506–7; Phillip G. Hubert, "For the Suppression of Noise," *North American Review* 151 (November 1894): 633–34.

116. Beard, *American Nervousness*, pp. 120–21; Edes, "New England Invalid," 56, 107. See also Sigmund Freud, " 'Civilized' Sexual Morality and Modern Nervous Illness" (1908), in James Strachey, ed., *Complete Works* (London, 1959), 9:177–204.

117. Mathews, "Civilization and Suicide," 483; "The Penalty of the Systematic Life," *Scribner's* 35 (February 1904): 249–50; Herbert Spencer, "The Gospel of Relaxation," *Popular Science Monthly* 22 (January 1883): 354–59.

118. [E.L. Godkin], "American Overwork," *Nation* 35 (16 November 1882): 417; "Genius and Insanity," *Nation* 39 (9 October 1884): 315–17; [G.S. Hall], "Overpressure in Schools," *Nation* 41 (22 October 1885): 338–39; G. Stanley Hall, Felix Adler, Thomas Hunter, and Mary Putnam Jacobi, "Educational Needs," *North American Review* 136 (March 1883): 284–304; Eliot Gregory, "A Nation in a Hurry," *Atlantic Monthly* 85 (May 1900): 609–13; Olive Schreiner, *Woman and Labor* (New York, 1911), pp. 44–45; "On Taking One's Dessert First," *Scribner's* 44 (October 1908): 506–7; "Editor's Study," *Harper's Monthly* 89 (October 1894): 799–801.

119. "Editor's Study," *Harper's Monthly* 89 (October 1894): 801; William James, "The Gospel of Relaxation," *Scribner's* 25 (April 1899): 499–507; William A. Hammond, "How to Rest," *North American Review* 153 (August 1891): 215–19; J.M. Buckley, "How to Safeguard One's Sanity," *Century* 60 (July 1900): 374–80; Brackett, "The Technique of Rest"; Hale, *Freud and the Americans*, pp. 60–63.

120. Sicherman, "Paradox of Prudence" provides an exhaustive discussion of this approach.

121. Charlotte Perkins Stetson [Gilman], "The Yellow Wallpaper," *New England Magazine*, n.s., 5 (January 1892): 647–56.

122. "A Help to Wholesome Living," *Century* 58 (November 1899): 321–22; Brackett, "The Technique of Rest," 55; Hale, *Freud and the Americans*, pp. 225–49; Meyer, *Positive Thinkers*, pp. 83–91, 307; Parker, *Mind Cure in New England*. For examples of similar longings for liberation embodied in popular fantasy see Dee Garrison, "Immoral Fiction in the Late Victorian Library," in Howe, *Victorian America*, pp. 141–57.

123. Simon Nelson Patten, *The New Basis of Civilization* [1907] (Cambridge, Mass.: John Harvard Library, 1968), pp. 143, 213, 215; J.P. Lichtenberger, "Is the Freer Granting of Divorce an Evil?" American Sociological Society *Papers and Proceedings*, 3 (1908): 171, quoted in David Kennedy, *Birth Control in America: the Career of Margaret Sanger* (New Haven, 1970), p. 68. Both Kennedy and Garrison (n. 120 above) see the shift toward self-fulfillment as somehow "revolutionary." But there are more insightful discussions by Warren Susman, " 'Personality' and the Making of Twentieth Century Culture," in John Higham, ed., *New Directions in American Intellectual History* (Baltimore, 1979), pp. 212–16; and by Christopher Lasch, *The New Radicalism in America, 1889–1963* (New York, 1965), especially chap. 5. On the new social engineering in general, see Robert Wiebe's perceptive discussion of an emerging "bureaucratic orientation" in *Search for Order*, chap. 5. See also Morton White, *Social Thought in America: the Revolt Against Formalism*, 2nd ed. rev. (Boston, 1957), the standard exposition of neoliberal thought which overlooks its manipulative dimension and acclaims its "antiformalism" as a liberation. For a more perceptive view of the social implications of neoliberalism, see James Weinstein, *The Corporate Ideal in the Liberal State, 1900–1918* (Boston, 1968).

124. Philip Rieff, *The Triumph of the Therapeutic: Uses of Faith after Freud* (New York, 1966), p. 13.

125. Ibid., especially pp. 1–107, 232–61; Christopher Lasch, *Haven in a Heartless World: the Family Besieged* (New York, 1977) and *The Culture of Narcissism: American Life in an Age of Diminishing Expectations* (New York, 1978).

126. Johann Wolfgang von Goethe, *Italian Journey 1786–1788*, entry for 27 May 1782, trans. W.H. Auden and E.B. Mayer (New York, 1962), p. 312, quoted by Rieff, p. 24; "Passing of the Devil," 508.


2. THE FIGURE OF THE ARTISAN:
ARTS AND CRAFTS IDEOLOGY

1. For the impact of rationalization and the division of labor on work, see (among many possible examples) Karl Marx, *Capital* [1867], trans. Samuel Moore and Edward Aveling, 3 vols. (New York, 1967), vol. 1 pt. 4; David Brody, *Steelworkers in America: the Non-Union Era*, (New York: Harper Torchbooks, 1960), especially chaps. 1 and 2; James Barrett, "Work and Community Among Chicago's Packing House Workers, 1894–1920" (Ph.D. diss., University of Pittsburgh, 1980). For the post-Taylor denouement, see Harry Braverman, *Labor and Monopoly Capital: the Degradation of Work in the Twentieth Century* (New York, 1974), which contains a cogent critique of Bell and other theorists of "postindustrial society" on pp. 293–374.

2. On working class resistance to rationalization, see David Montgomery, *Workers' Control in America* (New York, 1979) and Herbert Gutman, *Work, Culture, and Society in Industrializing America* (New York, 1977), particularly the title essay.

3. Clifford Geertz, "Ideology as a Cultural System" in David Apter, ed., *Ideology and Discontent* (New York, 1964), pp. 47–76 is a helpful start in defining ideology, but retains the functionalist insensitivity to class interests and divisions. David Brion Davis, *The Problem of Slavery in the Age of Revolution, 1770–1823* (Ithaca and London, 1975), pp. 14, 349 subtly adapts Geertz to a Gramscian framework.

4. John Ruskin, *The Stones of Venice*, vol. 2 [1853] in E. T. Cook and Alexander Wedder-

burn, eds., Ruskin's *Collected Works* (London, 1903), 10: 188–201; John D. Rosenberg, *The Darkening Glass: a Portrait of Ruskin's Genius* (New York, 1961), pp. 95–101, 131, 139, 188–89. For an early and short-lived effort to establish an American version of the Guild, see Charles H. Kegel, "Ruskin's St. George in America," *American Quarterly* 9 (Winter, 1957): 412–20.

5. William Morris, "How I Became a Socialist," in Holbrook Jackson, ed., *William Morris On Art and Socialism* (London, 1947), p. 276.

6. William Morris, "The Aims of Art," ibid., p. 89; Morris, "The Revival of Handicraft," ibid., p. 226; Norman and Jeanne Mackenzie, *The Fabians* (New York, 1977), p. 101.

7. A. R. Orage, "Politics for Craftsman," *Contemporary Review* 91 (June 1907): 787–88; "The Revival of Handicraft," p. 226; Martin Wiener, "The Myth of William Morris," *Albion* 8 (Spring, 1976): 67–82; Mackenzies, *Fabians*, pp. 180–81, 344.

8. Mackenzies, *Fabians*, pp. 101, 111, 250, 394.

9. Ibid., pp. 380–81; Raymond Williams, *Culture and Society, 1780–1950* (New York, 1958), pp. 148–58, 199–264; Rosenberg, *Darkening Glass*, pp. 144–45; David Marquand, *Ramsay MacDonald* (London, 1977), pp. 24–26, 403. On English pastoralism: Raymond Williams, *The Country and the City* (London, 1973), especially chap. 1.

10. Charles Eliot Norton, *Historical Studies of Church Building in the Middle Ages: Venice, Siena, Florence* (New York, 1880), pp. 44, 62–63, 90–91, 156–57, 164; Norton, "Some Aspects of Civilization in America," *Forum* 20 (January 1896): 642. For a biographical discussion of Norton, see chap. 6 below.

11. Norton to S. G. Ward, 14 April 1901, in Sara Norton and Mark A. DeWolfe Howe, ed., *Letters of Charles Eliot Norton*, 2 vols. (Boston, 1913) 2: 305; *Historical Studies*, pp. 28–29, 141–142.

12. Kermit Vanderbilt, *Charles Eliot Norton* (Cambridge, Mass., 1959), pp. 127–128; Allen H. Eaton, *The Handicrafts of New England* (Boston, 1949), pp. 281–291. Norton's presidential address is quoted in Eaton, p. 283.

13. Factual background on the leaders of the Chicago and Boston Societies is in Max West, "The Revival of Handicraft in America," U.S. Bureau of Labor, *Bulletin* 55 (1904): 1573–1622. Biographical information on Triggs is from *The National Cyclopedia of American Biography*, 68 vols. (New York, 1891– ), 12 (1904): 543.

14. David Karsner, *Horace Traubel* (New York, 1919), especially chap. 1; Franklin Wentworth, "Beautiful Rose Valley Where Art and Life are One," *Artsman* 3 (October 1905): 5–22. Rose Valley never numbered more than sixty resident craftsmen, all of whom were foreign-born. When the colony succumbed to financial woes in 1908, Traubel left to propagandize for Eugene Debs.

15. "New Clairvaux Plantation, Training School, Industries and Settlement," *Country Time and Tide* 3 (February 1903): 121–22. At its maximum, the colony numbered twenty-nine.

16. Frank Luther Mott, *A History of American Magazines, 1885–1905* (Cambridge, Mass., 1957), pp. 639–48. There are several breezy, misinformed biographies of Hubbard, none of which can compare to Mott's succinct account.

17. *Cyclopedia of American Biography*, 14:290; Gustav Stickley, "The Craftsman Movement: Its Origin and Growth," *Craftsman* 21 (October 1913): 17–26; John Crosby Freeman, *The Forgotten Rebel: Gustav Stickley and His Craftsman Mission Furniture* (Watkins Glen, N.Y., 1966), pp. 10–20.

18. Edward P. Pressey, "The Sin of Urbanity," *Country Time and Tide* 3 (December 1902): 45–54; Jenkin Lloyd Jones, "The Art of the Twentieth Century," *Brush and Pencil* 7 (March 1901): 379–80; "The Flood of Fiction," *Craftsman* 5 (November 1903): 195. See also "Is New York Civilized?", *Philistine* 26 (May 1908): 161.

19. "A Word About Joking," *Craftsman* 6 (July 1904): 391.

20. Ernest Crosby, "The Sheep and the Goats," *Craftsman* 7 (December 1904); 282–83; "Wise and Witty Saws of Calvin Mack," *Country Time and Tide* 1 (October 1902): 20; [Elbert Hubbard], "The City of Tagaste," *Philistine* 9 (June 1899): 5.

21. Gustav Stickley, "The Use and Abuse of Machinery, and Its Relation to the Arts and Crafts," *Craftsman* 11 (November 1906): 205.

22. Douglas Volk, "The Human Element in Arts and Crafts," *Brush and Pencil* 11 (March 1903): 443–44; Oscar Lovell Triggs, "The Arts and Crafts," *Brush and Pencil* 1 (December 1897): 47.

23. Jane Addams, *Twenty Years at Hull House* [1910] (New York: Signet Classics, 1960), p. 65.

24. "Als Ik Kan," *Craftsman* 16 (September 1909): 709; Triggs, quoted in "Recent Literature," *Artsman* 2 (September 1905): 403; Triggs, *Chapters in the History of the Arts and Crafts Movement* (Chicago, 1902), p. 10; editorial, *Country Time and Tide* 8 (June 1906): 33. See also Louise Heald, "Afraid of Life," *Artsman* 1 (September 1904): 471–72 and Triggs's announcement in his *The Changing Order* (Chicago, 1905), p. 45: "I do not want an art of scholars, but of men."

25. [Hubbard], "Tagaste," p. 5; Will Price, "Do We Attack the Machine?" *Artsman* 2 (February 1904): 173.

26. Irene Sargent, "John Ruskin," *Craftsman* 1 (November 1901): 9; "Chips from the Craftsman's Workshop," *Craftsman* 6 (July 1904): 410; "Als Ik Kan," *Craftsman* 13 (January 1902): 15; Bertha H. Smith "The Way of the Pushcart Man," *Craftsman* 9 (November 1905), 218–28.

27. My discussion of perfectionism follows John L. Thomas, "Romantic Reform in America, 1815–1865," *American Quarterly* 17 (Winter, 1965), 656–81.

28. [Theodore Dwight Weld], *The First Annual Report of the Society for Promoting Manual Labor in Literary Institutions* (New York, 1833).

29. Jean B. Quandt, "Religion and Social Thought: the Secularization of Postmillenialism," *American Quarterly* 25 (October 1973): 290–309.

30. Editorial, *Country Time and Tide* 1 (February 1902). On the connection between New Clairvaux and indigenous antebellum utopias, see Mary C. Crawford, "A Day of New Clairvaux," *Country Time and Tide* 2 (August–September 1902): 3, and Napoleon Hoagland, "Adin Ballou: The American Who Impressed Tolstoy," *Country Time and Tide* 2 (August–September 1902): 18–29.

31. "Building a Meeting House," *Country Time and Tide* 1 (March 1902): 92–94; J. P. Hylan, "The Science of Sabbath Observance," *Country Time and Tide* 1 (March 1902): 105–112; Horatio Dresser, "Higher Law Department," *Country Time and Tide* 3 (midwinter, 1903): 112–113.

32. Charles Wagner, "The Religion of the Home," *Craftsman* 7 (November 1904): 141; Oscar Lovell Triggs, "The New Doctrine of Work," *The Changing Order* (Chicago, 1905), pp. 195–98; Peter Burrowes, "The Sacrament of Common Things," *Artsman* 1 (February 1904): 165–68; Will Price, "The Rose Valley Fact and Spirit," *Artsman* 2 (January 1905): 129; Traubel, "Is Rose Valley Worthwhile?" Artsman 1 (October 1903): 5–11; Quandt, "Religion and Social Thought," pp. 308–309.

33. Edward Pearson Pressey and Carl Purington Rollins, *The Arts and Crafts and the Individual* (Montague, Mass., 1904), p. 18; Volk, "The Human Element in Arts and Crafts," p. 444; Mary Augusta Milliken, "Precious Things," *Handicraft* 2 (July 1903): 93–96; W., " 'The Divorce of Art from Life,' " *Handicraft* 5 (April 1912): 7–8.

34. Edward Pearson Pressey, "Village Industries: Home-Making," *Country Time and Tide* 1 (June 1902): 209; W. B. Truesdell, "Convenient Sanitary Dwellings," *Country Time and Tide* 7 (November 1904): 25; Bertha H. Smith, "The Gospel of Simplicity as Applied to Tenement Homes," *Craftsman* 9 (October 1905): 83; Irene Sargent, "A House and Home," *Craftsman* 2 (September 1902): 245; "Modern Nomads: The Tragedy of the Moving Van," *Craftsman* 22 (May 1912): 215; "Als Ik Kan," *Craftsman* 24 (August 1913): 549.

35. Editorial, "A Foundation for Craftsmanship," *Handicraft* 5 (August 1912): 78–79; Pressey and Rollins, *Arts and Crafts and Individual,* p. 10; Irene Sargent, "A Chapter from

Prince Kropotkin," *Craftsman* 4 (June 1903): 209–20; Sidney Morse, "The Disadvantages of Specialization," *Craftsman* 16 (April 1909): 24–31; Vivian Burnett, "The Boy of Today and Country Life," *Craftsman* 9 (January 1906): 489–94; Edward Pearson Pressey, "The Country Church Industrial," *Country Time and Tide* 1 (March 1902): 82–92, and "Country New England," *Country Time and Tide* 1 (April 1902): 129; Hettie Wright Graham, "The Fireside Industries of Kentucky," *Craftsman* 1 (January 1902): 45; Gustav Stickley, "Plans of the Craftsman for Next Year," *Craftsman* 15 (October 1908): 114–15.

36. Horace Traubel, "Rose Valley in General," *Artsman* 1 (October 1903): 23; Traubel, "Is Rose Valley Worthwhile?," pp. 5–11; R. Maulde de la Claviere, *The Art of Life*, quoted without publisher or page references in *Craftsman* 6 (April 1904): 53; Percival Wiksell, "The Peculiar Joys of Artsmanship," *Artsman* 2 (October 1905): 5; Rabbi Joseph Leiser, "Simplicity, a Law of Nature," *Craftsman:* 2 (August 1902): 226.

37. William Morris, "Useful Work vs. Useless Toil," in Jackson, *Art and Socialism*, pp. 175–87; untitled poem, *Country Time and Tide* 2 (July 1902): 22; editorial, *Country Time and Tide*, 2 (July 1902): 1 (October, 1902), 1; Percival Wiksell, "The Love of Work," *Artsman* 2 (July 1905): 322–23; editorial, *Artsman* 1 (April 1904): 267–68. See also Arthur Payne, "The Influence of the Arts and Crafts Movement on Manual Training," *Handicraft* 4 (October 1911): 243–48, and Stickley's reference to Ruskin as "apostle of the Doctrine of Work," *Craftsman* 2 (August 1902): iii. There were two faint attempts to keep Morris's distinction intact: *Artsman* I (July 1904): 403, which quoted one of his antidrudgery aphorisms, and a brief caveat in Pressey, "Sin of Urbanity," p. 47.

38. Irene Sargent, "The Gilds of the Middle Ages," *Craftsman* 1 (December 1901): 2–25; E. H. Crosby, "The Wealth of St. Francis: A Study in Transcendental Economics," *Craftsman* 3 (October 1902): 33–46; "From the Artsman Himself," *Artsman* 3 (October 1905): 23–24; "Bernard of Clairvaux, a medieval hero of simplicity," *Country Time and Tide* 9 (August 1907): 11; George N. Holcomb, "The Social Teaching of John Wycliffe," *Country Time and Tide* 6 (July–August 1904): 85–92.

39. Sargent, "Gilds," p. 25; "Chips from the Craftsman Workshops," *Craftsman* 7 (November 1904): 225; "1001 Nights Entertainment," *Country Time and Tide* 6 (August–September 1904): 93–96.

40. On changing views of aesthetics, see Neil Harris, *The Artist in American Society: the Formative Years, 1790–1860* (New York, 1966), and Roger Stein, *John Ruskin and Aesthetic Thought in America, 1840–1900* (Cambridge, Mass., 1967).

41. William Hagerman Graves, "Pottery: Its Limitations and Possibilities," *Handicraft* 2 (March 1904): 253–54.

42. Editorial, *Handicraft* 3 (April 1910): 33; editorial, *Handicraft*, 3 (September 1910): 229–30; editorial, *Handicraft* 3 (November 1910): 299; Jury Report, *Handicraft* 3 (March 1912): 429.

43. "Twelfth Night Revels," *Handicraft* 3 (February 1911): 425–27. For discussion of the problem of machine-made ornament, see Frederick Allen Whiting, "What the Arts and Crafts Movement Has Accomplished," *Handicraft* 3 (June 1910): 94. Veblen's criticism was in *The Theory of the Leisure Class* [1899] (New York, 1931), p. 162.

44. The most comprehensive treatment of post–Civil War educational reform is Lawrence Cremin, *The Transformation of the School, 1876–1957* (New York, 1961), but Joel F. Spring, *Education and the Rise of the Corporate State* (Boston, 1972), is more critical and perceptive. Sol Cohen, "The Industrial Education Movement, 1906–1917," *American Quarterly* 20 (Spring, 1968): 95–110, is illuminating, but my analysis of Craftsmen as education reformers is most indebted to the brilliant discussion by Christopher Lasch, *The New Radicalism in America: the Intellectual as a Social Type* (New York, 1965), especially pp. 158–165.

45. Ellen Gates Starr, "Art and Labor," in *Hull House Maps and Papers* (New York, 1895), pp. 165, 179, 167.

46. For Addams's reading of Ruskin, see *Twenty Years at Hull House* [1910] (New York,

1960), pp. 43–48. For her personal experience with the desperation of factory workers ibid., p. 178, and *The Spirit of Youth and the City Streets* (New York, 1909), pp. 122, 126, 135; Dewey's influence: *Twenty Years,* p. 172.

47. Marion Foster Washburne, "A Labor Museum," *Craftsman* 6 (September 1904): 570–80; Francis Tiffany, quoted in *Artsman* 1 (December 1903): 95; Triggs, "The Idealism of the Day"; Denman W. Ross, "The Arts and Crafts: A Discipline," *Handicraft* 1 (January 1903): 229–35; Parker H. Sercomb, "The Evils of American School Systems," *Craftsman* 16 (September 1909): 603–11.

48. "A Little Journey to Tuskegee," *Philistine* 19 (July 1904): 51; Irene Sargent, "Brain and Hand," *Craftsman* 1 (January 1902): 41–44; Oscar Lovell Triggs, *William Morris* (Chicago, n.d.), p. 38, and *Chapters in the History of the Arts and Crafts Movement* (Chicago, 1902), p. 123; Oscar Lovell Triggs, "The Workshop and the School," *Craftsman* 3 (October 1902): 30.

49. Clarence Osgood, "Raising the Standard of Efficiency in Work: Practical Training Given by the Manhattan Trade School for Girls," *Craftsman* 12 (September 1907): 634–40; Lockwood Deforest, "Suggestions of Industrial Education," *Handicraft* 4 (April 1910): 1–6; Arthur Dean, "The Relation of Manual Training in the Public Schools to Industrial Education and Efficiency," *Craftsman* 14 (April 1908): 74–81; "Als Ik Kan," *Craftsman* 14 (April 1908): 117, and 8 (May 1905): 171; Charles Richard Dodge, "Riches—and the Pursuit of Happiness," *Craftsman* 11 (November 1906): 232–33.

50. Daniel Coit Gilman, "Hand-Craft and Rede-Craft," in *The Launching of a University* (New York, 1906), p. 283, first published in *Century* (October 1886).

51. "Home Training in Cabinet Work," *Craftsman* 8 (April 1905): 86; "Als Ik Kan," *Craftsman* 8 (August 1905): 687; Raymond Riordan, "Interlaken, An Outdoor School Where Boys Through Their Own Efforts Learn How to Think and How to Work," *Craftsman* 22 (May 1912): 177; "New Clairvaux," *Country Time and Tide* 1 (January 1902): 18. Stickley identified Interlaken as the model for the Craftsman Farms School.

52. "A Day of New Clairvaux," *Country Time and Tide* 2 (August–September 1902): 13; editorial, *Artsman* 1 (June 1904): 342; "Als Ik Kan," *Craftsman* 13 (October 1907): 115; J. George Frederick, "The Play Confessions of a Busy Man," *Craftsman* 13 (February 1908): 565.

53. Quoted in *Craftsman* 7 (November 1904): 228–29, and in *Artsman* 2 (November 1904): 66.

54. Irene Sargent, "The Rise and Decadence of the Craftsman: an Historical Note," *Craftsman* 1 (November 1901): 14.

55. "Als Ik Kan," *Craftsman* 13 (March, 1908), 722–25; Gustav Stickley, "The National Spirit of Speculation," *Craftsman* 13 (December 1907): 313.

56. Walker, "The Museum and the School," p. 39; "Artsmanship as Viewed in Recent Literature," *Artsman* 2 (July 1905): 331; Triggs, "Workshop and School," pp. 30–32; Gustav Stickley, "The Guild Stamp and the Union Label," *Craftsman,* 13 (January 1908): 378–83.

57. "Als Ik Kan," *Craftsman* 11 (December 1906): 385; William Empson, *Some Versions of Pastoral* (London, 1935).

58. J. T. Coolidge, "A Few Considerations of Japanese Woodcarving," *Handicraft* 2 (June 1903): 53; Marguerite Glover, "Simple Life in Japan—Achieved by Contentment of Spirit and a True Knowledge of Art," *Craftsman* 10 (August 1906): 614.

59. "Als Ik Kan," *Craftsman* 12 (June 1907): 351; Horace Traubel, "The Problem of Cheap and Dear," *Artsman* 2 (October 1904): 17–22; editorial, *Artsman* 1 (July 1904): 377; editorial, *Philistine* 7 (December 1898): 22–23; Will Price, "What Do We Mean by Artsmanship?," *Artsman* 2 (October 1904): 13.

60. Arthur A. Carey, "The Past Year and Its Lessons," *Handicraft* 1 (April 1902): 4, 7–8, 23, 25.

61. H. Langford Warren, "The Qualities of Carving," *Handicraft* 1 (December 1902): 199; Mary Ware Dennett, "The Arts and Crafts, an Outlook," *Handicraft* 2 (April 1903): 16, and "Aesthetics and Ethics," *Handicraft* 1 (May 1902): 30–38, 39.

62. H. Langford Warren, "Our Work and Prospects," *Handicraft* 2 (December 1903): 183, 187.

63. Sylvester Baxter, "The Artist as Craftsman," *Handicraft* 1 (August 1902): 106.

64. Carl P. Rollins, "A Principle of Handicraft," *Handicraft* 4 (June 1911): 91–96.

65. Ibid., p. 96.

66. "Report of the Executive Committee Meeting of July 10, 1911," *Handicraft* 4 (August 1911): 195; Mary Ware Dennett, "The Arts and Crafts Problem and a Way Out," *Handicraft* 4 (August 1911): 209–20. Mira Edson, "A Way Out for Craftsmen," *Handicraft* 4 (November 1904): 280–84; Janet Payne Bowles, "A Situation in Craft Jewelry," *Handicraft* 3 (December 1910): 309; Letter from H. L. Warren to National League, *Handicraft* 3 (December 1910): 332, emphasis in original.

67. Will Price, "Answers for Charles Cantor," *Artsman* 2 (May 1905): 271; "The Commercial Value of Design," *Craftsman* 5 (March 1904): 546; W. M. Bangs, "The Revival of Handicraft," *Craftsman* 6 (May 1904): 188; Fra Elbertus, "Helpful Hints for Business Helpers," *Philistine* 26 (February, 1908), 81; editorial, *Country Time and Tide* 6 (July–August 1904): 142–44; "The Altrurian Army of Production," *Country Time and Tide* 6 (April 1902): 136–42.

68. E. H. Rogers, "Pilgrims and Profit Sharing," *Country Time and Tide* 6 (February 1902): 61–62; Mary Rankin Cranston, "The Social Secretary—an opportunity for employer and employee to understand each other," *Craftsman* 10 (July 1906): 489–93; Mable Tuke Priestman, "A Co-operative Village for Working People—Beautiful and Practical and a Four Percent Investment," *Craftsman* 10 (July 1906): 494–506; "Als Ik Kan," *Craftsman* 9 (March 1906): 870–72.

69. Mary K. Simkhovitch, "Handicrafts in the City," *Craftsman* 11 (December 1906): 365; Claude Bragdon, "The Sleeping Beauty," *Craftsman* 4 (August 1903): 344; Sargent, "Notes from the History of Textiles," p. 23; Samuel Howe, "The Plan's the Thing," *Craftsman* 3 (February 1903): 293; editor's note, *Craftsman* 4 (April 1904): 108. For two other explicit welcomes to mechanization, see Horace Traubel, "Degeneracy and the Artsman," *Artsman* 2 (June 1905): 289–300, and C. Howard Walker, "The Status of the Craftsman," *Handicraft* 5 (August 1912): 71–73.

70. Triggs, "The Arts and Crafts," pp. 47–48.

71. Oscar L. Triggs, "The New Industrialism," *Craftsman* 3 (November 1902): 185. For a strikingly similar passage, see George D. Herron, "Makers and Singers," *Artsman* 1 (January 1904): 119–20. Wright's manifesto, "The Art and Craft of the Machine," was reprinted in *Brush and Pencil* 8 (May 1901), 77–90.

72. Oscar L. Triggs, "A School of Industrial Art," *Craftsman* 3 (January 1903): 215–23.

73. Praise for Triggs: *Artsman* 1 (December 1903): 101, and *Handicraft* 1 (July 1902): 103; George Willis Cooke, "Green Acre Department," *Country Time and Tide* 3 (February 1903): 164; Gustav Stickley, "Waste: Our Heaviest National Liability," *Craftsman* 20 (July 1911): 344–48.

74. Alvan F. Sanborn, "The Scope and Drift of the American Arts and Crafts Movement," *Forum* 40 (September 1908): 254–64.

75. Sylvester Baxter, "Handicraft, and Its Extension, at Ipswich," *Handicraft* 1 (February 1903): 253.

76. William Sloane Kennedy, "A Craftsman's Lakeside Cottage," *Artsman* 1 (May 1904): 285–90; Bliss Carman, "A Quiet Day at the Ghost House," *Craftsman* 10 (June 1906): 282; "Als Ik Kan," *Craftsman* 10 (June 1906): 396–97; "A Craftsman House," *Craftsman* 5 (February 1904): 499; "Als Ik Kan," *Craftsman* 5 (November 1905): 278–79; "The Motor Car and Country Life," *Craftsman* 20 (May 1911): 227.

77. Horace Traubel, "Keeping in the Historic Line," *Artsman* 1 (April 1904): 247; [Stickley] "Chips from the Craftsman Workshop," *Craftsman* 5 (October 1903): 100–101.

78. Sanborn, "Scope and Drift," p. 256; Mott, *History of American Magazines, 1885–1905*, p. 643; Gustav Stickley, "The Craftsman Movement: Its Origin and Growth," *Craftsman* 25

(October 1913): 17–26, and biographical information in *National Cyclopedia of American Biography*, 14: 290; Hawley McClanahan, "Rose Valley in Particular," *Artsman* 1 (October 1903): 13; Horace Traubel, "Where Is Your William Morris?," *Artsman* 1 (October 1903): 121–32; "New Clairvaux Plantation," *Country Time and Tide* 3 (February 1903): 129; advertisement, *Country Time and Tide* 1 (January 1902), back cover.

79. The quotations are from Triggs, "The Idealism of the Day," p. 80, and *Chapters*, p. 151.

80. Addams, *Twenty Years*, p. 92.

81. Ross, "A Diagnosis," 229–31; editor's note, *Craftsman* 7 (January 1905): 489–90; Ernest Batchelder, "Arts and Crafts in America: Work or Play?," *Craftsman* 16 (August 1909): 544–49. See also Triggs, *The Changing Order*, p. 29: "The daring, strength, titanic energy, intelligence, and majesty evidenced in many of the modern business temples indicate precisely one, and perhaps the dominant, feature of American character." Cofounder of the People's Industrial College was Parker H. Sercomb, a retired Chicago banker.

82. See the thoughtful discussion by Albert Roland, "Do-It-Yourself: a Walden for the Millions?" in Hennig Cohen, ed., *The American Culture: Approaches to the Study of the United States* (Boston, 1968), pp. 272–82.

83. "National Education," *Country Time and Tide* 1 (May 1902): 172.

3. THE DESTRUCTIVE ELEMENT:
MODERN COMMERCIAL SOCIETY AND
THE MARTIAL IDEAL

1. J. G. A. Pocock, *Politics, Language, and Time: Essays on Political Thought and History* (New York, 1971), chaps. 3, 4.

2. On the martial ideal in the South, see: Samuel L. Clemens, *Life on the Mississippi* (New York, 1882), pp. 332–34, 374–76; Rollin G. Osterweis, *Romanticism and Nationalism in the Old South* (New Haven, 1949); William R. Taylor, *Cavalier and Yankee: the Old South and American National Character* (New York, 1961).

3. Taylor, *Cavalier*, chap. 3; George Fredrickson, *The Inner Civil War: Northern Intellectuals and the Crisis of the Union* (New York, 1967).

4. The most recent and exhaustive analysis of "feminization" is Ann Douglas, *The Feminization of American Culture* (New York, 1977). On the obsolescence of Scott's attitudes, see George Pellew, "The New Battle of the Books," *Forum* 5 (July 1888): 570.

5. On the proliferation of three-stage models, see Robert H. Wiebe, *The Search for Order, 1877–1920* (New York, 1967), pp. 140–42, and David Noble, *The Paradox of Progressive Thought* (New York, 1958). The phrase "more elaborate moral organization" is from Henry T. Finck, "The Scope of Modern Love," *Harper's Monthly* 103 (July 1901): 277–78.

6. Review of *The Castellated and Domestic Architecture of Scotland, Nation* 50 (27 February 1890): 187; Thomas A. Janvier, "The Chateau Galliard," *Harper's Monthly* 109 (August 1904): 338; E. H. Blashfield and E. W. Blashfield, "The Man at Arms," *Scribner's* 3 (January 1888): 3. The notion of the Middle Ages as an intrinsically violent period pervades such latter-day whig historiography as Henry Charles Lea, *A History of the Inquisition of the Middle Ages*, 3 vols. (New York, 1887), and his collection of essays, *Superstition and Force* (New York, 1866).

7. On the influence of the "magazine revolution," see Frank Luther Mott, *A History of American Magazines, 1885–1905* (Cambridge, Mass., 1905), and James D. Hart, *The Popular Book: a History of America's Literary Taste* (New York, 1950), chap. 11.

8. Edwin H. Cady, *William Dean Howells: the Realist at War* (Syracuse, 1958), p. 53. For another example of this view, see Robert E. Spiller et al., *Literary History of the United States* (New York, 1963), chap. 50.

9. Van Wyck Brooks, *New England: Indian Summer* (New York, 1940), pp. 100, 214; H. H.

Boyesen, "Why We Have No Great Novelists," *Forum* 2 (February 1887): 497; Ernest Earnest, *Silas Weir Mitchell, Novelist and Physician* (Philadelphia, 1950), p. 174.

10. John La Farge, "The American Academy at Rome," *Scribner's* 28 (August 1900): 256; H. H. Boyesen, "The Hero in Fiction," *North American Review* 168 (May 1889): 594–601; Charles Dudley Warner, "Modern Fiction," *Atlantic Monthly* 51 (April 1883): 464–74; "The Oppressiveness of Modern Novels," *Atlantic Monthly*, 85 (May 1900): 716–17.

11. Lee Wilson Dodd, "Frail Singers of Today," *Century* 70 (September 1905): 746; Edward W. Barnard, "Ballade of Chivalry," *Munsey's* 11 (September 1894): 555. " 'Criticism' vs. 'Escape,' " *Scribner's*, 44 (September 1908): 377–78; Agnes Repplier, "Old Wine and New," *Atlantic Monthly* 77 (May 1896): 688–96; [Emma N. Ireland], "Recent Fiction," *Nation* 51 (4 September 1890): 195.

12. G. Stanley Hall, "The Ideal School as Based on Child Study," *Forum* 32 (September 1901): 24–39; Dorothy Ross, *G. Stanley Hall: the Psychologist as Prophet* (Chicago, 1972), pp. 315, 323; "Culture of the Young Imagination," *Atlantic Monthly* 49 (April 1882): 569–70. Review of Sidney Lanier, *The Boys' King Arthur, Scribner's Monthly* 22 (December 1880): 322; [F. A. March], "The Morte D'Arthur," *Nation* 50 (2 January 1890): 15–16; "The Age of Scott's Heroines," *Atlantic Monthly*, 69 (January 1892): 139–42.

13. T. S. Perry, "Sir Walter Scott," *Atlantic Monthly* 46 (September 1880): 313–19.

14. R., "Sir Walter Scott," *Century* 58 (December 1899): 367.

15. Agnes Repplier, "The Praises of War," *Atlantic Monthly* 68 (December 1891): 798; George Holme, "Scott's Life Scenes and Life Works," *Munsey's* 11 (September 1894): 628; [Goldwin Smith], "New Editions of Walter Scott," *Nation* 56 (18 May 1893): 370; Charles Eliot Norton, "Introduction" to *The Complete Poetical Works of Sir Walter Scott* (New York 1894): iv; Andrew Dickson White, "Introduction" to E. H. Woodruff, "Walter Scott at Work," *Scribner's*, 5 (February 1889): 131–32.

16. Henry Osborne Taylor, *The Medieval Mind*, 2 vols. (Boston, 1911), 1: 163n; Walter Houghton, *The Victorian Frame of Mind, 1830–1870* (New Haven, 1957), pp. 325–40.

17. "Changes of Taste in Fiction," *Century* 60 (July 1900): 476; William Dean Howells, "The New Historical Romances," *North American Review* 171 (December 1900): 935–36.

18. Andrew Lang, "Some Tendencies in Fiction," *North American Review* 161 (July 1895): 153; Bliss Carman, "Mr. Gilbert Parker," *Chap Book* 1 (1 November 1894): 339–43; Frank Norris, "The 'Nature' Revival in Literature," in *The Responsibilities of the Novelist* (New York, 1902), p. 141.

19. Abram S. Isaacs, "Gentler Living," *North American Review* 192 (July 1910): 101–6.

20. Levin Schücking, *The Sociology of Literary Taste* (Chicago, 1966), p. 89.

21. "War as a Moral Medicine," *Atlantic Monthly* 86 (December 1900): 735–38; Charles F. Thwing, "The Ethical Functions of Foot-ball," *North American Review* 173 (November 1901): 627–31; John Corbin, "The Modern Chivalry," *Atlantic Monthly* 89 (May 1902): 601–11; John Higham, "The Re-Orientation of American Culture in the 1890's," in *Writing American History: Essays on Modern Scholarship* (Bloomington, Ind., 1973), pp. 86, 89.

22. Joseph Hamblen Sears, "Football: Sport and Training," *North American Review* 153 (December 1891): 750–53; "Editor's Study," *Harper's Monthly* 87 (November 1893): 960–61; Frederic L. Paxon, "The Rise of Sport," *Mississippi Valley Historical Review* 4 (September 1917): 144–68.

23. Mark Sullivan, *Our Times: the United States, 1900–1925*, 5 vols. (New York, 1926), 1: 236; Thomas F. Gossett, *Race: the History of an Idea in America* (Dallas, 1963), pp. 54–369.

24. Leonard W. Bacon and Charles A. Northrop, *Young People's Societies* (New York, 1900), pp. 35–40; Joseph F. Kett, *Rites of Passage: Adolescence in America, 1790 to the Present* (New York, 1977), p. 304n.

25. Kett, *Rites of Passage*, pp. 197–98.

26. Amos R. Wells, "The Christian Endeavour Movement: II. A New Religious Force," *New England Magazine*, n.s. 6 (June 1892): 524; Kett, *Rites of Passage*, pp. 195–98.

27. E. P. Evans, "Medieval and Modern Punishment," *Atlantic Monthly* 54 (September 1884): 302–8; "Law and Order Leagues," *Century* 26 (October 1883): 948–49; "The Lash for Wife-Beaters," *Munsey's*, 14 (November 1895): 243; C. S. Denny, "The Whipping Post for Tramps," *Century* 49 (March 1895): 794; Elbridge Gerry, "Must We Have the Cat-o-Nine Tails?," *North American Review* 160 (March 1895): 318–24.

28. "Lynch Law as an Argument for Law Reform," *Century* 37 (February 1889): 633–34.

29. Judge J. A. Jameson, "Shall Our Civilization Be Preserved?," *North American Review* 138 (April 1884): 336–48.

30. Raymond T. Bye, *Capital Punishment in the United States* (Philadelphia, 1919), pp. 5–9.

31. Mayo W. Hazeltine, "Nordau's Theory of Degeneration," *North American Review* 160 (July 1895): 735–52.

32. Richard Hofstadter, "Cuba, the Philippines, and Manifest Destiny," in Armin Rappaport, ed., *Essays in American Diplomacy* (Berkeley, 1967), pp. 149–70.

33. Sarah Grand, "The Man of the Moment," *North American Review* 158 (May 1894): 626; Brooks, *Indian Summer*, p. 179; "The Nobler Side of War," *Century* 56 (September 1898): 794.

34. George Fredrickson, *The Inner Civil War: Northern Intellectuals and the Crisis of the Union* (New York, 1966), chaps. 11, 14; James C. Malin, *Confounded Rot About Napoleon: Reflections Upon Science and Technology, Nationalism, World Depression of the Eighteen-Nineties, and Afterwards* (Lawrence, Kan., 1961), chaps. 3, 4, 6; Higham, "Re-Orientation," p. 83; [W. E. Griffis], "Japanese Physical Training," *Nation* 78 (18 February 1904): 135–36; [F. J. Mather], "The Real Issues of the War," *Nation* 78 (18 February 1904): 122; Oscar King Davis, "Japanese Devotion and Courage," *Century* 69 (November 1904): 139–51; Joaquin Miller, "The Fisher of Nippon," *Century* 68 (June 1904): 318; Homer Lea, *The Valor of Ignorance* (New York, 1909).

35. Edwin Caskoden [Charles Major], *When Knighthood Was In Flower*, 2nd ed. (Indianapolis, 1898), pp. 16, 31; F. Marion Crawford, *Via Crucis, a Romance of the Second Crusade* (New York, 1899), p. 57; [S. L. Clemens], *The Personal Recollections of Joan of Arc* (New York, 1896); Mary Hartwell Catherwood, *The Days of Jeanne D'Arc* (New York, 1897); Percy MacKaye, *Jeanne D'Arc* (New York, 1906); Francis C. Lowell, *Joan of Arc* (Cambridge, Mass., 1896).

36. Justus Miles Forman, "The Maid of Landevennec," *Harper's Monthly* 109 (September 1904): 497–505. See also Brian Hooker, "Ysobel de Corveaux," *Harper's Monthly* 121 (August 1910): 327–39.

37. Repplier, "Praises of War," pp. 800, 804.

38. Crawford, *Via Crucis*, p. 116. For one of many examples of fictional racism, see Cyrus Townsend Brady, "Barbarossa," *Century* 63 (November 1901–February 1902).

39. Helen Leah Reed, "The Manxman," *Chap-Book* 2 (15 December 1894): 116; [W. F. Allen], "Freeman's American Lectures," *Nation* 36 (11 January 1883): 40–41; Richard Burton, "The Renascence of English," *Forum* 20 (October 1895): 181–92; "The Historical Value of the Vinland Sagas," *Atlantic Monthly*, 60 (December 1887): 856; Louis Dyer, "The 'Millenary' of Alfred at Winchester," *Century* 62 (July 1901): 396–98; Brander Matthews, "The English Language: Its Debt to King Alfred," *Harper's Monthly* 103 (June 1901): 141–45.

40. Richard Hovey, "Comrades," in *Songs from Vagabondia* (Boston, 1894), p. 54; *The Marriage of Guenevere* (New York, 1891), act 4, sc. 1; "The Call of the Bugles," quoted in Allan Houston MacDonald, *Richard Hovey: Man and Craftsman* (Durham, N.C., 1957), pp. 203–204.

41. Theodore Roosevelt, *The Strenuous Life* (New York, 1900), pp. 1, 4.

42. Theodore Roosevelt, quoted in *Works*, 28 vols. (New York, 1906), 18: 66–67; Richard Hofstadter, *The American Political Tradition* (New York, 1949), p. 205; Elting Morrison, ed., *The Letters of Theodore Roosevelt*, 1: 535; Crawford, *Via Crucis*, p. 115.

43. John P. Mallan, "The Warrior Critique of the Business Civilization," *American Quarterly* 8 (Fall, 1956): 216–30; Roosevelt, *Strenuous Life*, p. 9; Benjamin Harrison, "Military Instruction in Schools and Colleges," *Century* 47 (January 1894): 468–69; *Rand-McNally Guide to the World's Fair* (Chicago, 1894), n.p.

44. Walter La Feber, *The New Empire* (Ithaca, 1963); "Imperialism and Industrialism," *Scribner's* 24 (November 1898): 635–36.

45. Richard Slotkin, *Regeneration Through Violence: the Mythology of the American Frontier, 1600–1860* (Middletown, Conn., 1973) has brilliantly explored this theme.

46. Alexis de Tocqueville, *Democracy in America* [1835, 1840], 2 vols. (New York: Vintage Books, 1960), 2: 136–42; D. H. Meyer, *The Instructed Conscience: the Shaping of the American National Ethic* (Philadelphia, 1972), p. 46; Thomas Haskell, *The Emergence of Professional Social Science: the American Social Science Association and the Nineteenth Century Crisis of Authority* (Urbana, Ill., 1977), p. 109n.

47. Oliver Wendell Holmes, Jr., quoted in Fredrickson, *Inner Civil War*, p. 219; Repplier, "Praises of War," p. 804; Stephen French Whitman, "The Noble Family of Beaupertys," *Harper's Monthly* 115 (July 1907): 195–203; Nora Hopper, "Little John's Song," *Chap-Book* 5 (15 October 1896): 433; Clinton Scollard, "Taillefer the Trouvère," *Atlantic Monthly* 70 (October 1892): 464.

48. Carman and Hovey, *Songs from Vagabondia*, pp. 4, 54.

49. [Thomas Wentworth Higginson], "Recent American Poetry," *Nation* 59 (20 December 1894): 468–69.

50. Hovey, "Call of the Bugles," quoted in MacDonald, *Hovey*, p. 207.

51. Repplier, "Praises of War," p. 804.

52. Eugene White, "A Song of Good Fighting," *Chap-Book* 6 (1 March 1897): 317–18; Bryan Hooker, "Swanhild," *Harper's Monthly* 120 (January 1910): 197–206.

53. H. W. Mabie, "How Thor Fought the Giant Hrungner," *Christian Union* 23 (8 June 1881): 753–54; Crawford, *Via Crucis*, p. 131.

54. [Major], *Knighthood*, p. 9.

55. Neil Harris, "The Culture of Catastrophe," (paper delivered at National Humanities Institute, New Haven, Conn., 17 November 1975); Crawford, *Via Crucis*, p. 178.

56. Rev. Cameron Mann, "The 'Thousand and One Nights' and the 'Morte D'Arthure,'" *North American Review* 183 (18 January 1907): 153, 154, 156.

57. Mildred I. McNeal, "Storm Song of the Norsemen," *Century* 61 (December 1900): 342–44; Arthur Colton, "The Shepherd and the Knight," *Atlantic Monthly* 117 (March 1906): 384–85; Margaret Sherwood, "Pan and the Crusader," *Atlantic Monthly* 106 (August 1910): 164; Crawford, *Via Crucis*, p. 266; Major, *Knighthood*, p. 107.

58. Margaret Steele Anderson, "Pain," *Century* 74 (May 1907): 117.

59. Crawford, *Via Crucis*, p. 273.

60. L. H. Hammond, "Knights Errant," *Century* 56 (August 1898): 583.

61. Besant, "London—Saxon and Norman," p. 289; Repplier, "Praises of War," p. 803.

62. Carman and Hovey, *Songs from Vagabondia*, p. 36.

63. William James, "The Moral Equivalent of War" [1910], in John J. McDermott, ed., *The Writings of William James* (New York, 1968), pp. 666–67.

64. Oliver Wendell Holmes, Jr., "Memorial Day" [1884], in *Speeches* (Boston, 1913), p. 62; Holmes, "The Soldier's Faith" [1895], ibid., p. 59.

65. Higham, "Re-Orientation," pp. 82–83.

66. Repplier, "Praises of War"; Agnes Repplier, "Ennui," *Atlantic Monthly* 71 (June 1893): 738–84; Elizabeth Bisland, "The Abdication of Man," *North American Review* 167 (August 1898): 190–99, and "The Time-Spirit of the Twentieth Century," *Atlantic Monthly* 87 (January 1901): 15–22; [Clemens], *Personal Recollections*, especially bk. 2; Mary Hartwell Catherwood, *Days of Jeanne d'Arc* (New York, 1897); Crawford, *Via Crucis*, p. 90.

67. Mercedes M. Randall, *Improper Bostonian: Emily Greene Balch* (New York, 1964), p. 69.

68. Louise Imogen Guiney, *Goose-Quill Papers* (Boston, 1885), p. 118; LIG to her father, (n.d.) Autumn, 1872, in Grace Guiney, ed., *The Letters of Louise Imogen Guiney*, 2 vols. (New York and London, 1926), 1: 8; LIG to her father, ibid. (n.d.), Autumn, 1876; LIG to H. E. Clarke, ibid., 8 January 1895, 1:61. Henry G. Fairbanks, *Louise Imogen Guiney* (New York, 1973), is a competent, informative biography. Nicholas John Loprete, "The Knight Errant: a Study of Heroism in the Works of Louise Imogen Guiney" (M.A. thesis, Columbia Univer-

sity, 1956), places a heavy-handed but suggestive Freudian stress on Guiney's "father fixation."

69. Fairbanks, *Guiney,* chap. 1.

70. Ibid., chap. 6; LIG to Dora Sigerson, (n.d.), Autumn, 1899, *Letters,* 2: 7; LIG to Rev. G. Bliss, S.J., n.d. [1918], ibid., 240.

71. LIG, "The Kings," in *Happy Ending: The Collected Lyrics of Louise Imogen Guiney* (Boston, 1909) pp. 3–4.

72. LIG, "Of the Golden Age," ibid., pp. 41–42; LIG to W. H. Van Allen, 13 January 1898, in *Letters,* 1: 226.

73. LIG To H. E. Clarke, 15 August 1895, in *Letters* 1: 72; Christopher Lasch, *The New Radicalism in America, 1889–1963: the Intellectual as a Social Type* (New York, 1965), p. 68; LIG, "Memoir," in *Carmen by Prosper Mérimée,* trans. Edmund H. Garrett (Boston, 1896), pp. xii–xiii.

74. LIG to Charlotte E. Maxwell, 13 August 1903, in *Letters,* 2: 90.

75. Carroll Smith-Rosenberg, "The Female World of Love and Ritual: Relations Between Women in Nineteenth-Century America," *Signs* 1 (Autumn, 1975): 1–29.

76. Franklin Walker, *Frank Norris, a Biography* (New York, 1932), chap. 1; William B. Dillingham, *Frank Norris: Instinct and Art* (Lincoln, Neb., 1969), chap. 1.

77. Frank Norris, "Introduction" to *Yvernelle,* Argonaut Edition of Norris's *Works* (New York: 1928), 6: 250–51.

78. Frank Norris, "Grettir at Drangey," *Everybody's Magazine* 6 (March 1902): 257–65. On Norris's fascination with Icelandic sagas, see Dillingham, *Instinct and Art,* p. 55.

79. Frank Norris, *Moran of the Lady Letty* (Garden City, N.Y., 1928), p. 214; Frank Norris, "A Plea for Romantic Fiction," in *Responsibilities of the Novelist,* p. 218; Frank Norris, *The Octopus* (Garden City, N.Y., 1928), p. 41. On Norris's Anglo-Saxon racism, see Dillingham, *Instinct and Art,* p. 78.

80. Norris, "Salt and Sincerity," in *Responsibilities,* pp. 264–65, and "Novelists of the Future," ibid., pp. 208–9.

81. Dillingham, *Instinct and Art,* p. 90; Norris, "Novelists of the Future," p. 209.

82. Frank Norris, "Lauth," *Overland Monthly,* 2nd series, 21 (March 1893): 244.

83. Norris, "The Frontier Gone at Last," in *Responsibilities,* pp. 73–75. On Norris's admiration for big business, see Dillingham, *Instinct and Art,* p. 94. There is a suggestive discussion of Norris and the inability of other turn of the century novelists to escape commercial definitions of success in David Brion Davis, "Stress-seeking and the Self-Made Man in American Literature, 1894–1914," in S. Klausner, ed., *Why Man Takes Chances* (Garden City, N.Y., 1968), pp. 105–131.

84. Arthur Beringause, *Brooks Adams: a Biography* (New York, 1955), pp. 20–30, 36–37.

85. BA to Charles Francis Adams, April 1868, quoted in Beringause, *Adams* pp. 44–45. Emphasis mine.

86. Henry Adams to BA, January 1881, Adams Collection, Houghton Library, Harvard University, Cambridge, Mass. Emphasis in original.

87. BA to Henry Adams, 25 November 1893, Houghton Library.

88. BA, quoted in Charles Hirschfeld, "Brooks Adams and American Nationalism," *American Historical Review* 69 (January 1964): 385.

89. Brooks Adams, *The Law of Civilization and Decay,* 2nd ed. (New York, 1896), pp. 78, 81.

90. Ibid., pp. 83, 84.

91. Ibid., pp. 129, 145, 148.

92. Ibid., pp. 164, 187–189, 211–12.

93. Ibid., p. 383.

94. Beringause, *Adams,* pp. 164, 208–9. Roosevelt's review of the *Law* appeared in *Forum* 22 (December 1896): 575–79.

95. Brooks Adams, "War and Economic Competition," *Scribner's* 31 (March 1902): 344–52; Beringause, *Adams,* p. 219.

96. BA to Henry Adams, 1 May 1903, Houghton Library.

97. Brooks Adams, "Unity in Modern Education," *Boston University School of Law Bulletin* (1908): 9–11; BA to Robert Grant, 20 July 1909, quoted in Beringause, *Adams*, p. 323; BA, quoted in Beringause, *Adams*, p. 363.

98. BA to Henry Adams, 13 October 1895, Houghton Library.

99. Beringause, *Adams*, pp. 303, 321, 387.

100. Daniel G. Brinton, M.D., "Popular Superstitions of Europe," *Century* 56 (September 1898): 643–44. The phrase "primal, dark veracity" is from D. H. Lawrence's *Studies in Classic American Literature* [1923] (New York, 1972), p. 29.

101. See "A Farewell to Arms," *New York Review of Books* 24 (23 June 1977): 3–6, Styron's revealing review of Caputo's *A Rumor of War,* and Richard Sennett, "Surrender of the Will," *New York Review of Books* 21 (18 April 1974): 30.

102. Lionel Trilling, "The Fate of Pleasure," in *Beyond Culture* (New York, 1965), pp. 57–87. Trilling extends this argument obliquely but suggestively in *Sincerity and Authenticity* (New York, 1973).

103. H. W. Mabie, "A Comment on Some Recent Books," *Chap-Book* 2 (15 May 1895): 368–69.

104. Joseph Conrad, *Lord Jim* (Cambridge, Mass., Riverside Press, 1958), p. 153.

## 4. THE MORNING OF BELIEF: MEDIEVAL MENTALITIES IN A MODERN WORLD

1. On the growth of dissatisfaction with positivism, see H. Stuart Hughes, *Consciousness and Society: the Reorientation of European Social Thought, 1890–1930* (New York, 1958), especially chap. 2, and Owen Chadwick, *The Secularization of the European Mind in the Nineteenth Century* (London, 1975), pp. 239–50. For the influence of Carpenter on the American Arts and Crafts movement, see chapter 2 above.

2. Norbert Elias, *The Civilizing Process: the History of Manners,* trans. Edmund Jephcott (New York, 1977), pp. 140–43, 175. Similar developments are traced by Philippe Ariès in his classic *Centuries of Childhood: a Social History of Family Life* (London, 1962).

3. Elias, *Civilizing Process*, pp. 127–29, 152. The book as a whole is a masterful synthesis of Freudian concepts with historical sociology.

4. J. H. Plumb, "The New World of Children in Eighteenth Century England," *Past and Present* 67 (May 1975): 64–93.

5. Peter Coveney, *The Image of Childhood: the Individual and Society. A Study of the Theme in English Literature,* 2nd ed. rev. (Baltimore, 1967), chap. 1. See also George Boas, *The Cult of Childhood* (London, 1966).

6. William Wadsworth, "Intimations of Immortality from recollections of Early Childhood," 11. 66–76.

7. Social sources of the ideology of domesticity are discussed in Christopher Lasch, *Haven in a Heartless World: the Family Besieged* (New York, 1977), pp. 166–68; Joseph F. Kett, *Rites of Passage: Adolescence in America, 1770 to the Present* (New York, 1977), pp. 114–15; Nancy F. Cott, *The Bonds of Womanhood: "Woman's Sphere" in New England, 1780–1835* (New Haven, 1977), chap. 2; and Ann Douglas, *The Feminization of American Culture* (New York, 1977), chap. 2.

8. Review of *The Child and Childhood in Folk-Thought, Nation* 62 (13 February 1896): 139. For a typical discussion of the "child type" in primitive cultures, see Alexander F. Chamberlain, "The 'Child-Type,' " *Pedagogical Seminary* 6 (December 1899): 471–84. On the growth of "scientific" nostalgia for childhood, see Bernard Mergen, "The Discovery of Children's Play," *American Quarterly* 27 (October 1975): 399–420.

9. The development of Hall's theories is perceptively discussed in Dorothy Ross, *G. Stanley Hall: the Psychologist as Prophet* (Chicago, 1972), and expertly summarized in Kett, *Rites of Passage,* pp. 216–21. For an inquiry into the personal tensions energizing his public role, see chapter 6, below.

10. For the European background of the recapitulation theory, and its American applica-

tion, see Charles Everett Strickland, "The Child and the Race: the Doctrines of Recapitulation and Culture Epochs in the Rise of the Child Centered Ideal in American Educational Thought, 1875–1900" (Ph.D. diss., University of Wisconsin, 1963).

11. The phrase "progress from Rome toward reason" appears in G. Stanley Hall, *Adolescence: Its Psychology and Its Relations to Physiology, Anthropology, Sociology, Sex, Crime Religion and Education*, 2 vols. (New York, 1904), 2: 318. Hall's commitment to discipline and productivity is evident throughout the work. See also Bernard Wishy, *The Child and the Republic: the Dawn of Modern American Child Nurture*, (Philadelphia, 1967). Mergen, "Discovery of Children's Play," also discusses the recognition of play as an agent of socialization.

12. Hall, *Adolescence*, 2: 747; G. Stanley Hall, "Notes on Early Memories," *Pedagogical Seminary* 6 (December 1899): 496–97.

13. G. Stanley Hall, "The Ideal School as Based on Child Study," *Forum* 32 (September 1901): 24–39; Hall, *Adolescence*, 2: 649.

14. John Ashmead, "The Idea of Japan, 1853–1895, Japan as Described by American and Other Travellers from the West," (Ph.D. diss., Harvard University, 1951), pp. 518–25, 535; George Trumbull Ladd, "Mental Characteristics of the Japanese," *Scribner's* 17 (January 1895): 82; Lafcadio Hearn, *Glimpses of Unfamiliar Japan*, 2 vols. (Boston and New York, 1894), 1: 130, 2: 389, 666, and *Gleanings in Buddha-Fields* (Boston and New York, 1897), p. 32; Mabel Loomis Todd, "With the Eclipse Expedition to Japan," *Nation* 49 (1 September 1889): 169; Theodore Worls, "An American Artist in Japan," *Century* 38 (September 1889): 670–86; Mary Gay Humphreys, "Trade-Unions in Japan," *Century* 61 (April 1901): 892–97; A. B. deGuerville, "Japan's Fair Daughters," *Munsey's* 14 (December 1895): 341–50; [W. E. Griffis], Review of J. A. B. Scherer, *Japan To-day, Nation* 78 (12 May 1904): 377–78; "Recent Books on Japan," *Atlantic Monthly* 75 (June 1895): 830–41. The decline of romantic attitudes toward Japan is foreshadowed in Rev. Henry C. Potter, "Impressions of Japan," *Century* 61 (March 1901): 663–70, and fully shown in H. W. Mabie, *Japan To-Day and Tomorrow* (New York, 1914).

15. Review of H. W. Mabie, ed., *Norse Stories Retold from the Eddas, Nation* 71 (27 December 1900): 509; Henry Blake Fuller, "Westminster Abbey," *Century* 45 (March 1893): 704; Review of *The Chronicle of Froissart*, trans. Sir John Boucheer, Lord Berners, *Nation* 57 (5 April 1894): 255–56; David Coit, "The Poetic Element in the Medieval Drama," *Atlantic Monthly* 56 (September 1885): 407.

16. Joseph Pennell, "The Feast of the Two Marys," *Century* 43 (April 1892): 884–88; H. H., "The Village of Oberammergau," *Century* 25 (March 1883): 663–70. See also [G. Stanley Hall], "The Passion Play," *Nation* 31 (12 August 1880): 110–11; Hans Deorient, "The Passion Play at Oberammergau," *Forum* 29 (July 1900): 545–54; Rev. John Jay Lewis, "The Peasants and the Passion Play," *Munsey's* 23 (September 1900): 792–98.

17. Edith Wharton, "Chartres," *Scribner's* 14 (September 1893): 287.

18. Randolph Bourne, "An Hour in Chartres," *Atlantic Monthly* 114 (August 1914): 217.

19. M. Mansfield, trans., *The Legend of the Holy Fina, Virgin of San Giminiano* (New York, 1908), p. xv; James Branch Cabell, *Chivalry* (New York, 1909), p. 3.

20. Mansfield, *Holy Fina*, pp. i–xvi; Coveney, *Image of Childhood*, pp. 240–45; Chadwick, *Secularization of the European Mind*, pp. 250–51, mentions the overlap between a "cult of childishness" and interest in medieval saints. Justin Kaplan, *Mr. Clemens and Mark Twain* (New York, 1966), p. 315n., reports the traditional belief (accepted by Twain) that Joan had never menstruated.

21. Henry Charles Lea, *A History of the Inquisition of the Middle Ages*, 3 vols. (New York, 1887), 1: 260–61; Rev. J. H. McIlvaine, *St. Francis of Assisi: Six Addresses in Lent* (New York, 1902), p. 88; Henry Osborne Taylor, *The Medieval Mind*, 2 vols. (Boston, 1911), 1: 415; Henry Neville Maugham, *The Husband of Poverty* (Boston, 1897), pp. 31–32. On the growth of Protestant admiration for Francis, see Wallace K. Ferguson, *The Renaissance in Historical Thought* (Cambridge, Mass., 1948), pp. 296–304.

22. Maurice Egan, *Everybody's St. Francis* (New York, 1912), p. 101; Gabriel Monod, *Les*

*maîtres de l'histoire, Renan, Taine, Michelet* (Paris, 1895), p. 43, quoted in Ferguson, *Renaissance*, p. 296.

23. George Bernard Shaw, "Preface" to *St. Joan* (Baltimore: Penguin Books, 1952), p. 25; [S. L. Clemens], *Personal Recollections of Joan of Arc* (New York, 1896), pp. 235, 461. See also Percy MacKaye, *Jeanne D'Arc* (New York, 1906), in which Joan announces (p. 119): "If your luck be lame, rub it with elbow grease."

24. Maugham, *Husband of Poverty*, pp. 9–10; McIlvaine, *St. Francis*, pp. 83, 91.

25. For two other examples of medieval saints as embodiments of moral will *contra* modern flaccidity, see Vida D. Scudder, *St. Catherine of Siena as Seen in Her Letters* (New York, 1905), p. 5, and Arthur T. Pierson, *St. Catherine of Siena, an Ancient Lay Preacher, a Study of Sanctified Womanhood and Power in Prayer* (New York, 1898). Scudder taught English at Wellesley (see chap. 5, below); Pierson edited the evangelical *Missionary Review of the World.*

26. Richard S. Storrs, *St. Bernard of Clairvaux* (New York, 1893), especially pp. 157, 399, 392, 445, 449.

27. Ibid., pp. 184, 169, 6, 580.

28. Ernest Batchelder, "How the Medieval Craftsman Created Beauty by Meeting the Constructive Problems of Gothic Architecture," *Craftsman* 16 (April 1909): 47–48; M. Irwin MacDonald, "Canterbury Cathedral: A History in Stone of Gothic Architecture and the Life From Which It Sprang," *Craftsman* 17 (December 1909): 367; Bourne, "An Hour in Chartres," p. 217.

29. Harriet Monroe, "A Bit of Old France," *Atlantic Monthly* 86 (July 1900): 58–62; Lowell, *The Cathedral*, p. 46.

30. H. W. Brewer, "Lights and Shadows of a Bygone Day," *Scientific American Supplement* 49 (3 February 1900): 20144. For similar laments, see Mansfield, *Holy Fina*, pp. xlii–xlv, and [J. T. Clarke], review of C. E. Norton, *Historical Studies of Church Building in the Middle Ages*, *Nation* 31 (11 November 1880): 345.

31. Brewer, "Lights and Shadows," 20144.

32. Angelina La Piana, *Dante's American Pilgrimage: a Historical Survey of Dante Studies in the United States, 1800–1944* (New Haven, 1948), is a useful guide to the growing nineteenth-century interest in Dante, with particular reference to Longfellow, Lowell, Norton, and the Dante Society.

33. Van Wyck Brooks, *An Autobiography* (New York, 1963), p. 120, in a sardonic description of a Dante evening at Norton's, gives this partial and misleading impression.

34. T. W. Parsons, "On a Bust of Dante" (1841), in his *Poems* (Boston, 1893), pp. 1–4. For other examples of earlier views, see "Dante," *The Philadelphia Album and Ladies Literary Portfolio* 5 (16 April 1831): 123–24, and James Haskins, "To Dante" in his *Poetical Works* (Hartford, 1848).

35. Eugene Benson, "Dante and Shakespeare," *Appleton's Journal* 7 (27 April 1872): 468–69.

36. Frances B. Sanborn, "Dante," *Unitarian Review* 17 (March 1882): 223–24.

37. Charles B. Dinsmore, *The Teachings of Dante* (Boston, 1901), p. 43; Oscar Kuhns, "Dante as a Tonic for To-Day," *Dial* 23 (September 1897): 110.

38. George Santayana, *Three Philosophical Poets* (Cambridge, Mass., 1910), p. 123. On the superiority of Dante's certitude to Spencer's Unknowable, see Dinsmore, *Teachings*, pp. 215ff.

39. Susan Blow, *A Study of Dante* (New York, 1886), pp. 1, 3. A more typical Hegelian approach to Dante was W. T. Harris, *The Spiritual Sense of the Divine Commedia* (New York, 1889), which presented Dante as a nineteenth-century German metaphysician. Dinsmore, *Teachings*, p. 89, also praised Dante's stress on the enormity of sin, as did Augustus Hopkins Strong, "Dante and the Divine Comedy," in his *Philosophy and Religion* (Rochester, 1888), pp. 513–14.

40. Vida D. Scudder, *The Life of the Spirit in the Modern English Poets* (Boston, 1895), pp. 143–45; Santayana, *Three Philosophical Poets*, pp. 205–6. Emphasis in original.

41. Charles B. Dinsmore, "Dante's Message," *Atlantic Monthly* 85 (June 1900): 825–34.

42. Santayana, *Three Philosophical Poets*, p. 208; Dinsmore, "Message," 832; Blow, *Study*, p. 7.

43. Kuhns, "Dante as a Tonic for To-Day"; Dinsmore, *Teachings*, p. 41.

44. Ibid., pp. 4–5.

45. Dinsmore, "Message," 826; A. B. Carr, "Nel Mezzo del Cammin," *Scribner's* 17 (February 1895): 227; J. E. C. Sawyer, "The Spiritual Significance of the Divine Comedy," *Methodist Review* 83 (March 1901): 236. The stress on character and will could also contain fears of popular indiscipline, as Dinsmore showed in *Teachings*, p. 157: "Dante teaches us that liberty is a more comprehensive and significant word than democracy has dreamed. . . . It is no easy thing granted by a legislature, but must be attained by infinite toil and suffering."

46. William James, *The Varieties of Religious Experience* [1902] (New York: Collier Books, 1961), p. 280; [J. M. Hart], "Recent Celtic Literature," *Nation* 53 (8 October 1891): 279. For more on medieval extremism, see Alvan F. Sanborn, "English Medieval Life," *Lippincott's* 56 (July 1895): 793–802; Taylor, *Medieval Mind*, 1: 335; Dinsmore, *Teachings*, p. 111; Brewer, "Lights and Shadows"; Margaret Field, "The Legend of King Arthur," *Munsey's* 12 (October 1894): 66, 70.

47. James, *Varieties*, pp. 53, 214, 216; Louise Imogen Guiney, "English Lyrics Under the First Charles," *Harper's Monthly* 53 (May 1890): 946; Vida D. Scudder, *Le morte Darthur of Sir Thomas Malory and Its Sources* (New York, 1917), p. 64.

48. Henry Osborne Taylor, *The Classical Heritage of the Middle Ages* (New York, 1901), p. 18. See also Storrs, *St. Bernard*, pp. 271–72, 344–45, and John Corbin, "A Middle English Nativity," *Harper's Monthly* 94 (December 1896): 6.

49. Corbin, "Nativity," 4; Emily James Putnam, "The Lady of the Castle," *Atlantic Monthly* 106 (September 1910): 355; William Emory Smyser, "Romanticism in Tennyson," *North American Review* 192 (October 1910): 510–11; Fuller, "Westminster Abbey," 717. Two other examples: Thomas Hastings, "The Evolution of Style in Modern Architecture," *North American Review* 191 (February 1910): 205, referred to the "feverish and morbid aspiration of medieval times," and Eleanora Kennicut, "The Saints," *Scribner's* 46 (December 1909): 714, discussed the Augustinian "trait of mystic longing" in medieval piety. For a psychoanalytic explication of erotic elements in medieval piety, see Herbert Moller, "Affective Mysticism in the West," *Psychoanalytic Review* 52 (Summer, 1965): 259–74. Joe Lee Davis, "Mystical vs. Enthusiastic Sensibility," *Journal of the History of Ideas* 4 (June 1943): 303–19, points to distinctions which suggest that, from a rigorous theological standpoint, late Victorians confused medieval religiosity with nineteenth-century enthusiasm.

50. I draw these distinctions from Denis de Rougement, *Love in the Western World*, trans. Montgomery Belgion, (New York: Anchor Books, 1957), pp. 170–74.

51. Egan, *Everybody's St. Francis*, p. 11; Lea, *Inquisition*, 1: 234. See also Theodore Child, "A Christmas Mystery in the Fifteenth Century," *Harper's Monthly* 78 (December 1888): 59–77; Dinsmore, *Teachings*, p. 111; Taylor, *Mind*, 1: 345, 2: 89; H. W. Mabie, "Some Modern Readings from Dante," in *Essays in Literary Interpretation* (New York, 1892), pp. 200–204.

52. Elizabeth Robins, "Mischief in the Middle Ages," *Atlantic Monthly* 48 (July 1881): 2. For childish emotionalism within a moral framework, see Storrs, *St. Bernard*, p. 414.

53. Ibid., p. 8.

54. Ibid., p. 1.

55. Richard Hovey, *Launcelot and Guenevere*, 5 vols. (New York, 1907), presented Guenevere as a prophetic New Woman and Arthur as the custodian of a static past; Louis K. Anspacher's play *Tristan and Isolde* (New York, 1904) offered a platitudinous version of the legend, in which the lovers' passion is consummated only in death; Edith Wharton, "Ogrin the Hermit," *Atlantic Monthly* 104 (December 1909): 844–48, reinterprets the hermit's mes-

sage to Tristan and Isolde as a benediction on their "heathen innocence." The reference to "children gamboling" is in Mansfield, *Holy Fina,* pp. xv–xvi. For other examples of youthful vitality attached to medieval culture, see Coit, "Poetic Element in the Medieval Drama"; "An Arthurian Journey," *Atlantic Monthly* 65 (June 1890): 829; Olivia Howard Dunbar, "Peire Vidal—Troubadour," *Harper's Monthly* 108 (December 1903): 4; "Teaching American Children to Play: Significance of the Revival of Folk Dances, Games, and Festivals by the Playground Association," *Craftsman* 15 (December 1908): 197; Marjorie Bowen, "An Initial Letter," *Harper's Monthly* 120 (April 1910): 663–67.

56. On the growing model of a "youth culture," see John Higham, "The Re-Orientation of American Culture in the 1890's," in his *Writing American History: Essays on Modern Scholarship* (Bloomington, Ind., 1973), pp. 77–88.

57. Howard Pyle, "American Art," *Handicraft* 1 (September 1902): 137–38.

58. Kaplan, *Mr. Clemens and Mark Twain,* chap. 14; Henry Nash Smith, *Mark Twain: the Development of a Writer* (Cambridge, Mass., 1962), chap. 7, and *Mark Twain's Fable of Progress* (Berkeley, 1964).

59. Mark Twain, *A Connecticut Yankee in King Arthur's Court* [1889] (New York: Signet Classic, 1963), pp. 21, 25, 32, 73. Kaplan, *Mr. Clemens and Mark Twain,* pp. 294–95, explicitly links the Yankee's England with Twain's Hannibal.

60. Twain, *Connecticut Yankee,* pp. 318–20.

61. Ibid., pp. 67–73, 90–97; James, *Varieties,* p. 384.

62. Scudder, *Morte Darthur,* pp. 183, 400–401.

63. [Ephraim Emerton], "Lea's History of the Inquisition," *Nation* 38 (20 March 1884): 259–60; H. W. Mabie, "Some Modern Readings from Dante," pp. 200–204, and "Personality in Literary Work," in *Essays in Literary Interpretation,* pp. 42–43.

64. Boris Sidis, "A Study of Mental Epidemics," *Century* 52 (October 1896): 849–53. Emphasis in original.

65. "Dreams and the Subconscious," *Scribner's* 46 (September 1909): 380.

66. John Fiske, review of Jeremiah Curtin, *Myths and Folklore of Ireland, Atlantic Monthly* 66 (October 1890): 568–72. For early notice of the folklore vogue, see, for example, [T. F. Crane], "Recent Folk-Lore Publications," *Nation* 50 (12 June 1890): 475.

67. John Ruskin, "Fairy Stories," in E. T. Cook and Alexander Wedderburn, eds., *The Works of John Ruskin,* 39 vols. (London, 1903–1912), 19: 233–39; Frank Luther Mott, *A History of American Magazines,* 5 vols. (Cambridge, Mass., 1938–1957), 3: 503, 4: 151; Wishy, *Child and the Republic,* chap. 15.

68. Coveney, *Image of Childhood,* p. 250; Louise Imogen Guiney, *Brownies and Bogles* (Boston, 1888); Vanderbilt, *Norton,* p. 178.

69. W. B. Yeats, *The Celtic Twilight* (London, 1893), p. 19; Richard Gutman, *Wagner: the Man, His Mind and His Music* (New York, 1968), chap. 13. See also [T. F. Crane], "An Oriental Story-Book," *Nation* 44 (14 April 1887): 324, which comments on the literary fashion of "popular tales."

70. [Hammond Lamont], "Fondness for Old Follies," *Nation* 81 (14 September 1905): 215–16; Coveney, *Image of Childhood,* pp. 240–250. See also Strickland, "Child and the Race," p. 187, for W. T. Harris's critique of fairy tales as promoters of arrested development.

71. Ross, *Hall,* p. 271; Bryan Hooker, "Fairy Tales," *Forum* 40 (October 1908): 375–76; Bruno Bettelheim, *The Uses of Enchantment: the Meaning and Importance of Fairy Tales* (New York, 1976).

72. Ernest Rhys, "Broceliande," *Harper's Monthly* 112 (January 1906): 265. See also Ethel A. Murphy, "Sanctuary," *Harper's Monthly* 112 (March 1906): 512, in which the author flings herself into Night as a refuge from "the set faces straining toward the crown" and "the imperious race for place and name."

73. Carl Schorske, "The Quest for the Grail: Wagner and Morris," in Kurt Wolff and

Barrington Moore, eds., *The Critical Spirit: Essays in Honor of Herbert Marcuse* (Boston, 1967), pp. 228–31.

74. Ella Wheeler Wilcox, "The Prelude to 'Tristan and Isolde,' " *Munsey's* 12 (December 1894): 288.

75. Joseph Sohn, "The Mission of Richard Wagner," *North American Review* 192 (November 1910): 657–70, offers a devotee's complaint.

76. Lang, quoted in Lamont, "Fondness," 215.

77. Sigmund Freud, "The Uncanny," in *Collected Papers*, 5 vols. (London, 1956), 5: 368–407. Freud, with his positivistic outlook, preferred to say that the animistic world view had been "surmounted," but "repressed" seems truer to the historical framework supplied by Elias as well as to Freud's overall purpose in the essay.

78. Ibid., p. 396.

79. Elizabeth Robins Pennell, "The Relation of Fairies to Religion," *Atlantic Monthly* 53 (October 1884): 457–67; Scudder, *Morte Darthur,* p. 17.

80. Agnes Repplier, "On the Benefits of Superstition," *Atlantic Monthly* 58 (August 1886): 177–86.

81. Blanche Willis Howard, "After the Passion Play," *Christian Union* 21 (30 June 1880): 592–93.

82. James, *Varieties,* p. 299. For other examples of this quality of "spectatorship," see pp. 101, 163, 188, 260.

83. In addition to works already cited, see, for example: Abby Langdon Alger, trans., *The Little Flowers of St. Francis of Assisi* (Boston, 1887); Edmund Gardner, ed., *The Cell of Self-Knowledge: Seven Early English Mystical Treatises* (New York, 1910); Eveline Warner Brainerd, comp., *Great Hymns of the Middle Ages* (New York, 1909); and the literature cited in the review essay "Medieval Reprints," *North American Review* 191 (January 1910): 140–42.

84. Moncure D. Conway, "Contemporary Supernaturalism," *Forum* 1 (May 1886): 284–93; Frances Albert Doughty, "A Southern Woman's Study of Boston," *Forum* 18 (October 1894): 238–49; C. S., "Buddhism for the Masses," *Book Buyer* 20 (July 1900): 478.

85. Elizabeth Stuart Phelps, "The Psychical Wave," *Forum* 1 (June 1886): 377.

86. James, *Varieties,* p. 221; Sigmund Freud, *Civilization and Its Discontents* (London, 1957), pp. 8–11; Paul Carus, trans. *Angelus Silesius* (Chicago, 1909), pp. xxiv–xxv.

87. Paul Carus, "The Dawn of a New Religious Era," *Forum* 16 (November 1893): 388–96; Hearn, *Gleanings,* p. 212. Annie Besant, "What Theosophy Is," *Outlook* 48 (14 October 1893): 665–66, assimilated theosophy to evolutionary optimism. The horror of missionaries and tourists at the concept of Nirvana is noted in Ashmead, "Idea of Japan," p. 371, but Protestants could recommend meditative passivity as an antidote to thoughtless busyness. See "Another Lost Art," *Christian Union* 31 (23 April 1885): 4.

88. Bourne, "An Hour in Chartres," 217.

89. Taylor, *Medieval Mind,* 1: 13. For other examples of the stress on medieval otherworldliness and contempt for bodily comfort, see 2: 32, 280, 358; Claude Phillips, "The Quality of Emotion in Modern Art," *North American Review* 174 (March 1902): 348–49; Storrs, *St. Bernard,* pp. 193, 221–22, 230–31.

90. Rougement, *Love,* p. 46. For an extreme example of the medieval *askesis,* see Mansfield, *Holy Fina,* pp. 10–11. [Marie S. Stillman], "Assisi and St. Francis," *Nation* 55 (27 October 1892): 317–18, referred to "that great scheme of self-abusement and self-sacrifice" as a key to Franciscan asceticisms.

91. I am indebted for this information to Professor David Huntington of the University of Michigan Department of the History of Art.

92. James, *Varieties,* p. 292. The reference to "oysters, ice cream, and fun" is quoted by James on p. 289n.

93. Max Scheler, *Von Umsturz der Werte* (Bern, 1955), p. 114, quoted in Philip Rieff, *The Triumph of the Therapeutic* (New York, 1966), p. 18.

94. Taylor, *Classical Heritage,* pp. 5, 14–15. See also the description of monastic personality on p. 182.

95. James, *Varieties,* pp. 292, 216.

96. The phrase is the title of James's chap. 3 in *Varieties.*

97. Chadwick, *Secularization,* pp. 240–50; Eugen Weber, "The Secret World of Jean Barois: Notes on the Portrait of an Age," in John Weiss, ed., *The Origins of Modern Consciousness* (Detroit, 1965), pp. 79–109; George Mosse, *The Crisis of German Ideology: Intellectual Origins of the Third Reich* (New York, 1964). These, of course, are only a few of many inquiries into the political dimensions of European antimodernism—a subject I shall explore at greater length in the epilogue of this study.

98. Roger Shattuck, *The Banquet Years: the Origins of the Avant-Garde in France, 1885 to World War I,* rev. ed. (Freeport, N.Y., 1972), pp. 24–25, 38–39.

## 5. THE RELIGION OF BEAUTY: CATHOLIC FORMS AND AMERICAN CONSCIOUSNESS

1. By sacramentalism, I mean the conviction that the sacraments of the Church (at most seven: Baptism, Penance, Holy Communion, Confirmation, Matrimony, Holy Orders, and Extreme Unction) are necessary agencies of Divine grace—that they are the outward and visible signs of God's presence on earth.

2. See, for example: George B. DeMille, *The Catholic Movement in the American Episcopal Church,* 2nd ed. (New York, 1950); René Brimo, *L'Évolution du Gout aux États-Unis d'après L'Histoire Des Collections* (Paris, 1938); Aline Saarinen, *The Proud Possessors* (New York, 1958); Walter C. Kidney, *The Architecture of Choice: Eclecticism in America, 1880–1930* (New York, 1974).

3. Charles William Eliot to T. W. Higginson, 31 March 1896, Eliot Papers, Houghton Library, Harvard University, Cambridge, Mass.; Thorstein Veblen, *The Theory of the Leisure Class* (New York, 1899). For more recent examples of these preoccupations, see Stow Persons, *The Decline of American Gentility* (New York, 1973); Martin Green, *The Problem of Boston* (New York, 1966); and Van Wyck Brooks, *New England: Indian Summer* (New York, 1940).

4. Henry Wadsworth Longfellow, *Outremer* [1833], in his *Collected Prose Works,* 2 vols. (New York, 1861) 1: 26; Neil Harris, *The Artist in American Society: the Formative Years, 1790–1860* (New York, 1966), p. 148; Washington Irving, *Sketchbook,* in his *Collected Works,* 19 (New York, 1865), 17.

5. Nathaniel Hawthorne, quoted in Harris, *Artist in American Society,* p. 148. *Appleton's,* cited in Roger Stein, *John Ruskin and Aesthetic Thought in America, 1840–1900* (Cambridge, Mass.; 1967), p. 227; Elizabeth Robins Pennell, "Beauvais: the Magnificent Fragment," *Century* 77 (May 1909): 45, later published in her *French Cathedrals* (New York, 1909). On the revaluation of aesthetic experience, see Harris, *Artist,* chaps. 5 and 6, and Stein, *Ruskin* chaps. 3, 10.

6. Brimo, *L'Évolution,* bk. 2. See also *The Collection of George Grey Barnard* (New York, 1941), "Introduction," n.p., and Walter Muir Whitehill, *Museum of Fine Arts Boston: a Centennial History* (Cambridge, Mass., 1970), chap. 4.

7. Brimo, *L'Évolution,* pp. 127–50.

8. The most perceptive study of the movement to establish authority is Thomas Haskell, *The Emergence of Professional Social Science: the American Social Science Association and the Nineteenth Century Crisis of Authority* (Urbana, Ill., 1977).

9. Neil Harris, "The Gilded Age Revisited: Boston and the Museum Movement," *American Quarterly* 14 (Winter, 1962): 545–66; Whitehill, *Museum of Fine Arts Boston,* chap. 6.

10. Both E. Digby Baltzell, *The Protestant Establishment: Aristocracy and Caste in America* (New York, 1964), pp. 113–35, and Dixon Wecter, *The Saga of American Society, 1607–1937* (New York, 1937), pp. 387–97, chronicle the creation of premodern emblems of upper-class authority, but neither understands the social significance of the phenomenon, as a movement toward elite stability in an era of uncertainty.

11. James McLachlan, *The American Boarding School: an Historical Study* (New York, 1970). McLachlan is so intent on discrediting the idea that boarding schools promoted "aristocratic" ideals that he fails to note their role in creating a new national upper class.

12. John Higham, *History: the Development of Historical Studies in the United States* (Englewood Cliffs, N.J., 1965), pp. 8–9.

13. Brimo, *L'Évolution,* p. 150. My translation.

14. Francis Steegmuller, *The Two Lives of James Jackson Jarves* (New Haven, 1951), chaps. 10–16; Saarinen, *Proud Possessors,* pp. 93–101. For the coexistence of primitivism and refinement, see Mrs. Schuyler Van Renssalaer, "Durham Cathedral," *Century* 35 (December 1887): 230.

15. Brimo, *L'Évolution,* p. 145; Mrs. Hearst, cited in Saarinen, *Proud Possessors,* p. 76. On the aesthete's public role, see Stein, *Ruskin,* chap. 10.

16. Bigelow's neurasthenia will be discussed at length in chap. 6, below; on Gardner, see Louise Hall Tharp, *Mrs. Jack* (Boston, 1965), pp. 36–37; on Freer, see Saarinen, *Proud Possessors,* p. 141.

17. Akiko Murakata, ed., "Selected Letters of Dr. William Sturgis Bigelow" (Ph.D. diss., George Washington University, Washington, D.C., 1971), pp. 2–5; Morris Carter, *Isabel Stewart Gardner and Fenway Court* (Boston, 1925), p. 89; Saarinen, *Proud Possessors,* p. 141.

18. Stein, *John Ruskin,* chaps. 9, 10; Matisse, translated and excerpted in Robert Goldwater and Marco Treves, eds., *Artists on Art* (New York, 1972), p. 413.

19. Letters, Ida A. Higginson to Isabel Stewart Gardner, 15 April 1909, and (undated) 1918, cited in Carter, *Fenway Court,* pp. 232–33; Letter, William James to Isabel Stewart Gardner, 1 January 1903, cited in Carter, *Fenway Court,* p. 201.

20. George Santayana, "At Noon," *Scribner's* 11 (January 1892): 76; Van Wyck Brooks, *An Autobiography* (New York, 1965), p. 124.

21. Henry Adams, *Esther, a Novel* [1884] (New York, 1947), p. 12.

22. Lyman Abbott, *Impressions of a Careless Traveller* (New York, 1909), p. 57; William B. Chisholm, "Christmas and Modern Ritual," *Century* 47 (December 1893): 313–14; John P. Hyland, *Public Worship: a Study in the Psychology of Religion* (Chicago, 1901), p. 7. Stein, *Ruskin,* chap. 3, and James T. Early, *Romanticism and American Architecture* (New York, 1965), chap. 4, describe early Protestant adaptation of Gothic.

23. Niebuhr's classic, Turnerian statement of the church-sect typology is in *The Social Sources of Denominationalism* [1929], 2nd ed. (Hamden, Conn., 1954), pp. 17–19. More recent statements are David Moberg, *The Church as a Social Institution* (Englewood Cliffs, N.J., 1962), chap. 4, and Bryan R. Wilson, *Religion in Secular Society* (London, 1966), chap. 7, especially pp. 107–109. For one republican moralist's alarm, see Washington Gladden, "Christianity and Aestheticism," *Andover Review* 1 (January 1884): 13–24.

24. Richard Sennett, *The Fall of Public Man* (New York, 1976), p. 37; Chisholm, "Modern Ritualism," 314.

25. Rev. Francis Tiffany, *In Memory of Loammi Goodenow Ware* (Burlington, Vt., 1892), p. 52.

26. Katherine Coolidge, "In the Cathedral," *Atlantic Monthly* 84 (November 1899): 711. Three of many examples of Protestant admiration for the effects of Catholic ritual: Henry Codman Potter, "The Significance of the American Cathedral," *Forum* 13 (May 1892): 351–59; "Editor's Easy Chair," *Harper's Monthly* 75 (August 1887): 472; and [G. Stanley Hall], "The Passion Play," *Nation* 31 (12 August 1880), 110–11.

27. Stein, *John Ruskin,* chap. 10; W. J. Stillman, "The Decay of Art," *New Princeton Review* 2 (July 1886): 21.

28. See, for example, Alice Brown, "The Artisan," *Harper's Monthly* 107 (November 1903): 261.

29. "A Ritual of Life," *Scribner's,* 37 (February 1905): 251–52. A similar point was made by Louis Pope Gratacap, *Apologia Pro Ritu: Philosophy of Ritual* (New York, 1887).

30. Anthropologists and students of comparative religion were stressing the "childlike" mentalities which responded to ritual. Some ritualists like Huysmans (in *La Cathédrale*) turned that notion on its head. See chapt. 4, above. For a more recent attempt at a similar reversal,

extolling the primitivist appeal of ritual, see Robert Bocock, *Ritual in Modern Industrial Society: a Sociological Analysis of Ritual in Modern England* (London, 1973).

31. "Some Recent Fiction," *Atlantic Monthly* 83 (March 1899): 523.

32. Harold Frederic, *The Damnation of Theron Ware* [1896] (New York: Rinehart, 1961), pp. 43–44.

33. Ibid., pp. 72–73, 242.

34. Ibid., p. 259.

35. DeMille, *Catholic Movement*, chaps. 2, 4, pp. 79–83; E. Digby Baltzell, *Philadelphia Gentlemen: the Making of a National Upper Class* (Glencoe, Ill., 1958), p. 249, and chap. 10. On the English background, see Owen Chadwick, ed., *The Mind of the Oxford Movement* (London, 1963) and James F. White, *The Cambridge Movement* (New York, 1962).

36. Baltzell, *Philadelphia Gentlemen* p. 248. Baltzell implies this view, as does Van Wyck Brooks in *New England: Indian Summer, 1865–1915* (New York, 1940).

37. Claude Gilkyson, *St. Mark's: One Hundred Years on Locust Street* (Philadelphia, 1948), p. 45.

38. Brooks, *Indian Summer*, p. 114.

39. Morgan Dix, in *Sermons Preached at the Church of the Advent, Boston, On the Day of Its Consecration, and the Sunday Following, 1894* (Boston, 1894), p. 33. C. A. Briggs, "The Alienation of Church and People," *Forum* 16 (November 1893): 371.

40. Max Weber, *The Protestant Ethic and the Spirit of Capitalism* [1904], trans. Talcott Parsons (New York, 1958), pp. 116–17.

41. George Wharton Pepper, *Philadelphia Lawyer* (New York, 1944), p. 312. To cite only two of many influential studies on the legitimating role of religion: Emile Durkheim, *The Elementary Forms of the Religious Life* [1915], trans. Joseph Ward Swain (New York, 1968), and Mary Douglas, *Natural Symbols: Explorations in Cosmology* (London, 1966).

42. Henry May, *Protestant Churches and Industrial America* (New York: Harper Torchbook, 1967), p. 186; Potter, "American Cathedral," 358.

43. DeMille, *Catholic Movement*, pp. 133–49; Robert Cheney Smith, S.S.J.E., *The Cowley Fathers in America: the Early Years* (Boston, 1965), pp. 1–28.

44. Smith, *Cowley Fathers*, pp. 32–37, 61; George L. Richardson, *Arthur C. A. Hall* (Cambridge, Mass., 1932), chaps. 5, 16.

45. Vida Dutton Scudder, *Father Huntington* (New York, 1949); DeMille, *Catholic Movement*, pp. 141–44.

46. DeMille, *Catholic Movement*, pp. 175–77; Dix, in *Sermons Preached at the Church of the Advent*, p. 38.

47. Ferdinand Ewer, *Catholicity, Protestantism, and Romanism* (New York, 1879), p. 296; Dix, in *Sermons Preached at the Church of the Advent*, p. 33; Grafton, ibid., pp. 17–18.

48. There has been a revival of sympathetic interest in Cram recently, most of it due to renewed appreciation for pre–International Style eclecticism. Discussions of Cram's thought, such as Robert Muccigrosso, "Ralph Adams Cram: the Architect as Communitarian," *Prospects* 1 (1975), and Douglas Tucci, *Ralph Adams Cram: American Medievalist* (Boston, 1975), are marred by their isolation of Cram from wider social and cultural developments. Albert Bush-Brown, "Cram and Gropius: Traditionalism and Progressivism," *New England Quarterly* 21 (March 1952): 3–22, is interesting but flawed by its failure to recognize the possible uses of Cram's "traditionalism" by modern elites, as well as by its equation of architectural "progressivism" with egalitarianism.

49. Ralph Adams Cram, *My Life in Architecture* (Boston, 1936), p. 23.

50. Ibid., pp. 6–7, 19, 92–93. See also Ralph Adams Cram, *The Decadent, Being the Gospel of Inaction* (Boston, 1893).

51. Cram, *My Life*, pp. 46–57.

52. Ibid., p. 57.

53. Ibid., p. 85.

54. Ralph Adams Cram, "On the Restoration of Idealism," in *The Gothic Quest,* 2nd ed. (New York, 1915), pp. 17–30, reprinted from *The Knight Errant* 1 (1893).

55. Ralph Adams Cram, *Impressions of Japanese Architecture and the Allied Arts* (New York, 1905), p. 208.

56. Ralph Adams Cram, *The Substance of Gothic: Six Lectures on the Development of Architecture from Charlemagne to Henry VIII* (Boston, 1917), p. 132.

57. Ralph Adams Cram, *The Ministry of Art* (Boston, 1914); *My Life,* p. 52; and *Gothic Quest,* p. 49.

58. Ralph Adams Cram, *The Significance of Gothic Architecture* (Boston, 1918), pp. 23, 24; *Gothic Quest,* p. 101; and *Ministry of Art,* p. 52.

59. Cram, *Ministry of Art,* pp. 220–21; *Gothic Quest,* p. 57; *Significance of Gothic,* pp. 8–9; and *My Life,* p. 182.

60. Cram, *Ministry of Art,* pp. 56–57; *Gothic Quest,* pp. 85, 330; and *Substance of Gothic,* p. 199.

61. Cram, *Ministry of Art,* p. 231, and *Significance of Gothic,* pp. 10–15. Robert Nisbet has emphasized the emerging emphasis on mediating structures in *The Sociological Tradition* (New York, 1966), chaps. 3, 4, 5.

62. Ralph Adams Cram, *Walled Towns* (Boston, 1919), pp. 37–43, 90, 97.

63. Cram, *My Life,* pp. 289–98. Cram's later polemics are collected in *Convictions and Controversies* (Boston, 1937).

64. Cram, "Restoration," 24, and *Walled Towns,* p. 27. Fears of enervation underlay his critique of mechanization: "Strength comes from the earth, weakness from the machine," he wrote in *My Life,* p. 231.

65. Cram, *Substance of Gothic,* p. 34. The obsession of post–World War II sociologists with community is well documented in E. Digby Baltzell, ed., *The Search for Community in Modern America* (New York, 1968), and in two works by Robert Nisbet, both of which look toward medieval Europe as a model of decentralized communalism: *The Quest for Community* (New York, 1953) and *Twilight of Authority* (New York, 1975). Tocquevillians like Nisbet share Cram's elitist myopia; they are equally insensitive to the role of capitalism, as distinguished from "individualism."

66. Siegfried Giedion, *Mechanization Takes Command* (New York: Norton Library, 1969), pp. 329–33; Cram, *Significance of Gothic,* pp. 30–31. After the Bolshevik revolution, Cram said Russia had been "ruined because she lost her symbols." On Jung's approach to symbols and its limitations, see Philip Rieff, *The Triumph of the Therapeutic* (New York, 1966), especially chaps. 2, 5.

67. Cram, *My Life,* p. 233; Ada Louise Huxtable, "The Troubling Legacy of Ralph Adams Cram," *New York Times,* 23 November 1976, p. 51. For Cram's account of his disagreement with the Princeton trustees (over the use of High Church liturgy in the Princeton chapel), see *My Life,* p. 123.

68. Vida Dutton Scudder, *On Journey* (New York, 1937), pp. 15, 72–74. Most historians have overlooked Scudder. The most comprehensive treatment is chap. 4 of Peter J. Frederick, *Knights of the Golden Rule: the Intellectual as Christian Social Reformer in the 1890's* (Lexington, Ky., 1976), a descriptive summary which concentrates mainly on her political beliefs and controversies.

69. Scudder, *On Journey,* pp. 72–73.

70. Ibid., pp. 78, 84.

71. Ibid., pp. 93–94.

72. Ibid., pp. 49–53.

73. Ibid.

74. Ibid., pp. 113–14.

75. Ibid., p. 139.

76. Vida Dutton Scudder, *Social Ideals in English Letters* (Boston, 1898), p. 227, and *On Journey*, p. 172.

77. Scudder, *On Journey*, pp. 98. 177–80.

78. Vida Dutton Scudder, "Democracy and the Church," *Atlantic Monthly* 90 (October 1902): 521–27, and *The Letters of St. Catherine of Siena* (New York, 1905), p. vii.

79. Scudder, *On Journey*, p. 90; Vida Dutton Scudder, *Le Morte Darthur of Sir Malory, Its Sources* (New York, 1917), pp. 171, 371.

80. Scudder, *Social Ideals*, p. 83; Vida Dutton Scudder, *The Disciple of a Saint* (New York, 1909), p. 359.

81. Scudder, *On Journey*, pp. 53, 231–32.

82. Scudder, *Letters of Catherine*, p. vi.

83. Vida Dutton Scudder, *Father Huntington* (New York, 1940), p. 113, and *Socialism and Character*, pp. 94, 108.

84. Scudder, *Socialism and Character*, pp. 146–47, 186.

85. Scudder, *Discipline of a Saint*, p. xiii; *Social Ideals*, chap. 1.

86. Scudder, *Socialism and Character*, p. 291, and *On Journey*, pp. 280, 281, 131.

87. Vida Dutton Scudder, *The Witness of Denial* (New York, 1895), p. 68, and *On Journey*, pp. 363–67.

88. Abraham Myerson, M.D., and Rosalie D. Boyle, "The Incidence of Manic-Depressive Psychosis in Certain Socially Important Families," *American Journal of Psychiatry* 98 (July 1941): 11–21.

## 6. FROM PATRIARCHY TO NIRVANA: PATTERNS OF AMBIVALENCE

1. This is not to say that Freud's "discovery" of ambivalence was unaffected by the late-nineteenth-century fascination with dual personalities, multiple selves, etc. The concept of ambivalence, like so many Freudian insights, was a product of a specific cultural milieu. On this point, see Cushing Strout, "The Uses and Abuses of Psychology in American History," *American Quarterly* 28 (Summer, 1976): 326. Strout makes another point worth quoting here, as a caveat for this chapter's use of psychological explanations: "Finding hidden reasons . . . is not like finding hidden causes; it is rather like redescribing what somebody is doing so as to make clearer what the point of a seemingly inappropriate action is. Explaining action is at least taking account of the belief system within which an agent acts and seeing the action as an expression of beliefs, intuitions, intentions, and choices. This type of explaining may be supplemented by lawlike generalizations about correlated conditions and consequences, but they are different modes" (325). I should also add that I use "masculine" and "feminine" throughout this chapter in their Victorian senses, not in any effort to ascribe universal traits.

2. Arthur Christy, *The Orient in American Transcendentalism* (New York, 1932), pp. 113–14; Leo Marx, *The Machine in the Garden: Technology and the Pastoral Ideal in America* (New York, 1964), pp. 279–81.

3. Marx, *Machine in the Garden*, especially p. 281.

4. William E. Bridges, "Family Patterns and Social Values in America, 1825–1875," *American Quarterly* 17 (Spring, 1965): 3–11; Steven Mintz, "Studies in the Victorian Family" (Ph.D. diss., Yale University, New Haven, Conn., 1980), chap. 2; Nancy F. Cott, *The Bonds of Womanhood: "Woman's Sphere" in New England, 1780–1835* (New Haven, 1977), p. 98. Of course, one can overemphasize the contradictions in the dominant pattern of socialization. In many cases, apparent contradictions may have complemented each other.

5. Mintz illuminates these conflicts in his discussion of Robert Louis Stevenson's relationship with his father. See "Victorian Family," chap. 2.

6. This argument is based on the works cited in chapter 1, footnotes 18 and 19.

7. Such "official" Victorian values as male chastity may have been embraced only by a

relatively narrow segment of the population. See Charles S. Rosenberg, "Sexuality, Class, and Role in 19th-Century America," *American Quarterly* 25 (May 1973): 131–53; Morse Peckham, "Victorian Counterculture," *Victorian Studies* 18 (March 1975): 257–76.

8. M. E. Braddon, *Lady Audley's Secret*, 2 vols. (Leipzig, 1862), 2: 9: 164, quoted in Walter E. Houghton, *The Victorian Frame of Mind, 1830–1870* (New Haven, 1975), p. 243. Houghton's entire book brilliantly explores the oscillations of the Victorian self. Sklar explicitly notes the point in *Catharine Beecher*, p. 246. On invalidism and suffering, see the suggestive remarks by Mintz, "Victorian Family," chap. 2.

9. On the moral problems raised by the disintegrating sense of selfhood, see chap. 1, above.

10. See chap. 3, above, and Houghton, *Victorian Frame of Mind*, pp. 251–62.

11. Edith Wharton, *A Backward Glance* (New York, 1934), p. 151; Mrs. Winthrop Chanler [Margaret Terry Chanler], *Autumn in the Valley* (Boston, 1936), pp. 24–25.

12. *Dictionary of American Biography*, s.v. "Jacob Bigelow" and "Henry Jacob Bigelow."

13. [William Sturgis Bigelow], *Henry Jacob Bigelow: a Memoir* (Boston, 1894), pp. 13, 24–37. Susan Sturgis Bigelow was the daughter of the wealthy China trader William Sturgis, and the sister of Ellen Sturgis Hooper, whose daughter Marian married Henry Adams. So WSB and Marian Adams were first cousins.

14. Ibid., pp. 144–45, 179.

15. Henry Cabot Lodge, *Early Memories* (New York, 1913), pp. 37–38, 86.

16. Akiko Murakata, ed., "Selected Letters of Dr. William Sturgis Bigelow" (Ph.D. diss., George Washington University, Washington, D.C., 1971), pp. 2–5; WSB to Henry Cabot Lodge, 6 April 1875, Lodge Papers, Massachusetts Historical Society, Boston, Mass.

17. John F. Fulton, *Harvey Cushing: a Biography* (Springfield, Ill., 1946), p. 495; WSB to Dr. William F. Whitney, 12 April 1913, in Murakata, "Bigelow," p. 359.

18. Fulton, *Cushing*, p. 495; Murakata, "Bigelow," pp. 2–5; *DAB*, s.v., "William Sturgis Bigelow."

19. Marian Adams to William Hooper, 21 December 1879, in Ward Thoron, ed., *The Letters of Mrs. Henry Adams* (Boston, 1936), p. 222; *DAB*, "Bigelow"; Murakata, "Bigelow," p. 5.

20. Erik H. Erikson, *Young Man Luther: a Study in Psychoanalysis and History* (New York, 1958), p. 65. Emphasis in original.

21. My understanding of depression draws on the papers in Willard Gaylin, ed., *The Meaning of Despair: Psychoanalytic Approaches to Depression* (New York, 1968), which range from Freud's classic "Mourning and Melancholia" to the more recent perspectives of ego psychology.

22. WSB to E. S. Morse, 15 November 1917, in Murakata, "Bigelow," p. 434.

23. Ernest Fenollosa to HCL, 23 July 1884, Lodge Papers.

24. WSB to HCL, 30 September 1883, Lodge Papers.

25. Chanler, *Autumn*, p. 24; Marian Adams to William Hooper, 29 January 1883, in Murakata, "Bigelow," p. 6.

26. Murakata, "Bigelow," pp. 6–7, 120n; WSB to Kanryo Naobayashi, 12 August 1914, ibid., p. 381.

27. Sadajiro Yamanaka, "An Introduction to the Catalogue [of WSB's Collection]," Tokyo Art Club (n.p., 1935).

28. Henry Adams to John Hay, 28 June 1887, in Worthington C. Ford, ed., *The Letters of Henry Adams, 1858–1891* (Cambridge, Mass., 1930), p. 384; WSB to Phillips Brooks, 19 August 1889, in Murakata, "Bigelow," p. 83.

29. WSB to HC, 8 November 1890, Lodge Papers.

30. Murakata, "Bigelow," p. 184; WSB to HCL, 16 January 1889, Lodge Papers.

31. Murakata, "Bigelow," pp. 13–14. During 1897–1903, Bigelow also tried to transcend self-absorption through his pathetic courtship of the Wagnerian soprano, Milka Ternina. He recognized it was a doomed "obsession." (WSB to HCL, 12 September 1899, Lodge Papers.)

32. WSB to KN, 16 July 1895, 20 March 1899, and 22 August 1902, in Murakata "Bigelow" pp. 122, 173, 205; George Cabot Lodge to Anna Cabot Mills Lodge, 22 May 1902, Lodge Papers; WSB to KN, 7 October 1902, in Murakata, "Bigelow," p. 208; WSB to HCL, 24 February 1903, Lodge Papers.

33. WSB to Phillips Brooks, 19 August 1889, in Murakata, "Bigelow," p. 83.

34. William Sturgis Bigelow, *Buddhism and Immortality* (Boston and New York, 1908), pp. 39–40.

35. Ibid., pp. 60–61, 66, 75–76.

36. Lawrence W. Chisolm, *Fenollosa: the Far East and American Culture* (New Haven and London, 1963), chap. 10, especially p. 108; Bigelow, *Buddhism and Immortality*, p. 74. Chisolm illuminates the distinctions between Fenollosa and Bigelow; he also sensitively (if briefly) analyzes Percival Lowell and George Cabot Lodge.

37. Murakata, "Bigelow," pp. 16–17; WSB to HCL, 14 October 1909, and to Anna Cabot Mills Lodge, 1 September 1911, Lodge Papers; Henry Adams to HCL, 5 September 1909 [incorrectly dated], in Harold Dean Cater, ed., *Henry Adams and His Friends* (Cambridge, Mass., 1947), p. 663; Dr. Frederick C. Shattuck to Theodore Roosevelt, 7 May 1912, quoted in Murakata, "Bigelow," pp. 18–19. Henry Adams said of WSB that "he seems to find bed a happy resource. At all events he is not in Boston." HA to Mable Hooper LaFarge, 10 July 1909, Adams Collection, Houghton Library, Harvard University, Cambridge, Mass.

38. Fulton, *Cushing*, p. 479.

39. WSB to Keien Ajari, 10 June 1921, in Murakata, "Bigelow," pp. 495–96.

40. Bigelow, *Buddhism and Immortality*, p. 57.

41. Percival Lowell, "Augustus Lowell," *Proceedings of the American Academy of Arts and Sciences* 37 (August 1902): 653; S. Foster Damon, *Amy Lowell: a Chronicle with Extracts from Her Correspondence* (Boston and New York, 1935), pp. 14–33; Horace Gregory, *Amy Lowell: Portrait of the Poet in Her Time* (New York, 1958), p. 5; Abbott Lawrence Lowell, *Biography of Percival Lowell* (New York, 1935), p. 5, 7.; PL to Barrett Wendell, 21 October 1878, Wendell Papers, Houghton Library, Harvard University, Cambridge, Mass.

42. PL to Wendell, 13 April 1884 and 23 June 1884, Wendell Papers; Lowell, *Biography*, p. 17.

43. PL, quoted Lowell, *Biography*, p. 31; Percival Lowell, *The Soul of the Far East* (Boston, 1888), p. 24; Percival Lowell, *Occult Japan or the Way of the Gods* (Boston, 1894), p. 283.

44. Lowell, *Occult Japan*, p. 367.

45. Lowell, *Biography*, pp. 98–101.

46. Louise Leonard, *Percival Lowell: an Afterglow* (Boston, 1921), p. 41.

47. Alexis de Tocqueville, *Democracy in America*, 2 vols. [1835, 1840], (New York: Vintage Books, 1960), 2: 202–25. The quoted phrase is on p. 219. Mintz, "Victorian Family," chap. 3, perceptively discusses the effect of domestic ideals on patriarchy.

48. Wharton, *Backward Glance*, pp. 150–51. John Crowley, *George Cabot Lodge* (New York, 1976), is an informative biography. [Henry Adams], *The Life of George Cabot Lodge* (Boston, 1911), reprints some revealing letters.

49. George Cabot Lodge to Anna Cabot Mills Lodge, 7 March 1892 and 17 December 1892, Lodge Papers; John Garraty, *Henry Cabot Lodge: a Biography* (New York, 1953), pp. 191, 193; HCL to HA, 22 March 1891, reel 9, Henry Adams Papers, Microfilm Edition, MHS. For Bay's early relations with his parents, see GCL to ACML, 10 October 1885, Lodge Papers. All subsequent citations of letters, unless otherwise noted, are in Lodge Papers.

50. GCL to ACML, 21 March 1893; Crowley, *Lodge*, p. 27.

51. GCL to ACML, 20 February 1893; June 1894; 25 September 1893; 12 December 1893; 20 March 1895.

52. Crowley, *Lodge*, pp. 28–31; WSB to KN, April 1895, in Murakata, "Bigelow," p. 119.

53. GCL to ACML, December 1895; 6 January 1896; 16 January 1896.

54. GCL to ACML, 20 March 1896.

55. *Poems and Dramas of George Cabot Lodge,* 2 vols. (Boston and New York, 1911), 1: 81. For Lodge's explication of the poem, see GCL to WSB, 10 December 1897, in [Adams], *Lodge,* pp. 68–71. On his recurring desire for "will-lessness," see GCL to ACML, 22 March 1897, February 1897.

56. [Adams], *Lodge,* pp. 72–82.

57. GCL to ACML, July 1899, March 1901, May 1901; GCL to HCL, September 1900, June 1901; GCL to ACML, August 1901; Crowley, *Lodge,* pp. 63–64; *Poems and Dramas,* 1: 227. See also GCL to ACML, September 1899, in which he fears lowering "Pa's opinion of me which is low enough for all practical purposes now."

58. GCL to ACML, March 1901, June 1904; Garraty, *Henry Cabot Lodge,* p. 271.

59. Spring-Rice, quoted in [Adams], *Lodge,* p. 148; F. C. Shattuck, "William Sturgis Bigelow," *Proceedings of the Massachusetts Historical Society* 60 (October 1926): 17.

60. For the impact of domestic ideology on liberal Protestantism, see Barbara Welter, "The Feminization of American Religion, 1800–1860," in Mary Hartman and Lois Banner, eds., *Clio's Consciousness Raised: New Perspectives on the History of Women* (New York, 1975), pp. 137–57; Ann Douglas, *The Feminization of American Culture* (New York, 1977), p. 110; "The Womanly in God," *Christian Union* 23 (9 March 1881): 226–27. Ministers carefully dissociated their views from Mariolatry, but the potential for movement toward Catholicism stemmed from their analogies between Mother-love and God-love—particularly after the domestic ideal had been infused with vitalist imagery deifying maternity. Further, as Douglas points out, it was a common view that ritualized religions appealed especially to women's emotionalism and love for beauty. The links between Catholicism and the domestic ideal were implicit but pervasive. For a suggestive discussion of male efforts to escape paternal domination by embracing "feminine" values of spontaneity and creativity, see Howard R. Wolf, "British Fathers and Sons: From Filial Submissiveness to Creativity," *Psychoanalytic Review* 52 (Summer, 1965): 197–214.

61. Kermit Vanderbilt, *Charles Eliot Norton: Apostle of Culture in a Democracy* (Cambridge, Mass., 1959), pp. 1, 23. This biography is informative but neglects the complexity of Norton's inner life.

62. Andrews Norton to Charles Eliot Norton, 27 January, 15 February, 14 March 1843, Norton Papers, Houghton Library, Harvard University, Cambridge, Mass. Unless otherwise noted, all subsequent letters cited are from this collection.

63. AN to CEN, 5 May 1843; CEN to George Woodberry, 11 October 1877, Woodberry Papers, Houghton Library.

64. CEN to his family, 26 September, 20 October 1850.

65. Vanderbilt, *Norton,* pp. 55–60. On the oppressiveness of family relations, see for example CEN to (his sister) Grace Norton, 15 June 1853: ". . . I should hardly write now were it not that I desire to avoid Mother's insinuations about my never writing when I am away."

66. Charles Eliot Norton, *Notes of Travel and Study in Italy* (Boston, 1859), pp. 1–2.

67. Vanderbilt, *Norton,* p. 60.

68. CEN to Howells, August 1868, ibid., p. 104.

69. Vanderbilt *Norton,* pp. 108–110; CEN to Sir John Simon, 22 May 1870.

70. Erik H. Erikson, "Identity and the Life Cycle," *Psychological Issues* 1 (1959), 97. Historians have usually traced Norton's disillusionment to his failures in the public arena. He was, the argument goes, a "displaced patrician" no longer able to influence a vigorous democracy. This view is partial, misleading, and wholly insensitive to psychological issues. For a typical example, see John G. Sproat, *"The Best Men": Liberal Reformers in the Gilded Age* (New York, 1968).

71. CEN to Simon, 31 July 1874; CEN to Howells, 28 July 1895 in Sara Norton and Mark A. DeWolfe Howe, eds., *Letters of Charles Eliot Norton,* 2 vols. (Boston, 1913), 2: 230; CEN to Simon, 6 February 1882; CEN to Sir Leslie Stephen, 8 July 1899, *Letters* 2: 284.

72. CEN to Simon, 18 March 1878; CEN to Woodberry, Christmas, 1881, *Letters,* 2,

128; CEN to Goldwin Smith, 14 June 1897; CEN to Woodberry, 11 October 1877.

73. CEN to the Rev. J. B. Harrison, 14 October 1880, *Letters*, 2, 114; CEN to Ruskin, 3 April 1883; CEN to Simon, 23 August 1879; CEN to Sara Norton, 22 November 1891, in *Letters*, 2: 209.

74. Dorothy Ross, *G. Stanley Hall: the Psychologist as Prophet* (Chicago and London, 1972), pp. 1–76. On Hall's friendship with Norton, see G. Stanley Hall, *Life and Confessions of a Psychologist* (New York, 1923), pp. 170–72.

75. Ross, *Hall*, pp. 253–56.

76. G. Stanley Hall, "How Johnnie's Vision Came True" [1902], in *Recreations of a Psychologist* (New York, 1920), pp. 128–46. Quotations from pp. 133–35.

77. Ross, *Hall*, pp. 256–58; G. Stanley Hall, *Adolescence: Its Psychology and Its Relations to Physiology, Anthropology, Sociology, Sex, Crime, Religion, and Education*, 2 vols. (New York, 1904), 2: 627, 646.

78. Hall, *Adolescence*, 1: xvii, 66–68; 2, 264, 338–39.

79. Hall, *Life and Confessions*, pp. 571–78.

80. Van Wyck Brooks, *An Autobiography* (New York, 1965), p. 124.

81. James Hoopes, *Van Wyck Brooks: in Search of American Culture* (Amherst, Mass., 1977), pp. 8–22. This biography contains valuable information from manuscripts but it is reticent on psychological issues, and it does not connect Brooks's inner tensions to comparable ones in the wider culture.

82. Brooks, *Autobiography* p. 70; Hoopes, *Brooks*, p. 21.

83. Hoopes, *Brooks*, pp. 19–20.

84. Brooks, *Autobiography*, pp. 243, 244.

85. Conversation with Professor David Brion Davis, Department of History, Yale University, New Haven, Conn. 22 September 1978.

86. Van Wyck Brooks, "Diary," Brooks Papers, University of Pennsylvania Library, Philadelphia, Pa., quoted in Hoopes, *Brooks*, p. 20.

87. Brooks, *Autobiography*, pp. 87–120; Brooks to Eleanor Stimson, 10 September 1905, quoted in Hoopes, *Brooks*, pp. 45–46.

88. Brooks, *Autobiography*, p. 100.

89. Van Wyck Brooks, "The Wine of the Puritans" [1908], in Claire Sprague, ed., *Van Wyck Brooks: the Early Years: a Selection from His Works, 1908–1921* (New York, 1968), pp. 2–3.

90. Ibid., pp. 37, 43, 55, 56, 59.

91. Hoopes, *Brooks*, pp. 1, 70, 85.

92. Van Wyck Brooks, *The Soul: an Essay Toward a Point of View* (San Francisco, 1910), pp. 10, 15.

93. Ibid., pp. 16, 19, 30.

94. Ibid., pp. 23–29, 32.

95. Ibid., p. 40. The quotation is from *The Imitation of Christ*, 3: 14: "O greatness immeasurable! O sea that none can cross! Now I recognize myself as wholly and only nothing! Where now can pride lurk unseen? Where now is my Confidence in my former virtue?" (trans. Leo Sherley-Price).

96. Van Wyck Brooks, "America's Coming-of-Age," in Sprague, ed., *The Early Years*, p. 127.

97. Brooks, *Autobiography*, p. 255; Hoopes, *Brooks*, pp. 129–35; Randolph Bourne and Van Wyck Brooks, "The Retort Courteous," *Poetry* 12 (September 1918): 341–44; Van Wyck Brooks, "The Literary Life," in Harold Stearns, ed., *Civilization in the United States* (New York, 1922), p. 182.

98. Brooks, *Autobiography*, p. 439.

99. Ibid. Hoopes, *Brooks*, chap. 7, provides the most comprehensive information on Brooks's breakdown.

100. Van Wyck Brooks, *The Opinions of Oliver Allston* (New York, 1941), p. 229, 205.

## 7. FROM FILIAL LOYALTY TO RELIGIOUS PROTEST: HENRY ADAMS

1. The classic statements of the "displaced patrician" view are Van Wyck Brooks, *New England: Indian Summer* (New York, 1940), pp. 250–75, 354–72, 474–90, and Richard Hofstadter, *The Age of Reform: from Bryan to F. D. R.* (New York, 1955), pp. 91–93. More recent statements include Morton and Lucia White, *The Intellectual Versus the City* (Cambridge, Mass., 1962), pp. 58–74; Frederick C. Jaher, *Doubters and Dissenters: Cataclysmic Thought in America, 1885–1918* (New York, 1964); and Stow Persons, *The Decline of American Gentility* (New York, 1973), pp. 204–17. Martin Green, *The Problem of Boston* (New York, 1966), chap. 7, an idiosyncratic version of Adams as a displaced patrician, is often more insightful than the preceding treatments. Recent formalist literary criticism of Adams includes Vern Wagner, *The Suspension of Henry Adams* (Detroit, 1969); Melvin Lyon, *Symbol and Idea in Henry Adams* (Lincoln, Neb., 1970); and Robert Mane, *Henry Adams on the Road to Chartres* (Cambridge, Mass., 1971), pt. 2. John C. Rowe, *Henry Adams and Henry James: the Emergence of a Modern Consciousness* (Ithaca and London, 1976), is the most elegant and persuasive formalist critique; it labels Adams a *bricoleur* on p. 122. The most important exceptions to my criticism of Adams scholarship are R. P. Blackmur's essays, recently collected in *Henry Adams*, ed. Veronica Makowsky (New York, 1980), and Ernest Samuels's brilliant 3-vol. biography (see below), to which I am especially indebted.

2. Henry Adams to Henry Cabot Lodge, 31 July 1876, in Worthington C. Ford, ed., *Letters of Henry Adams*, 2 vols. (Boston, 1930–1938), 1: 294; Ernest Samuels, *The Young Henry Adams* (Cambridge, Mass., 1948), p. 7; Martin Duberman, *Charles Francis Adams, 1807–1886* (Boston, 1960), pp. 30–39.

3. Charles Francis Adams, Jr., to HA, 9 October 1858, Adams Family Papers, microfilm edition, reel 545; HA to CFA, Jr., 13 March 1859, in Ford, *Letters*, 1: 24; HA to his mother 1 July 1860, ibid., 1: 61; Samuels, *Young Henry Adams*, pp. 42, 46, 57, 66, 69, 75.

4. Samuels, *Young Henry Adams*, pp. 98, 144–45; HA to CFA, Jr., 15 March 1862, in Worthington C. Ford, ed., *A Cycle of Adams Letters, 1861–1865*, 2 vols. (Boston, 1920), 1: 119; HA to CFA, Jr., 14 February 1862, ibid., 1, 112–13.

5. Quoted in Samuels, *Young Henry Adams*, p. 160.

6. HA to CFA, Jr., 21 May 1869, in Ford, *Letters* 1: 160.

7. HA to Charles Milnes Gaskell, 8 February 1872, in Ford, *Letters* 1: 222; HA to CMG, 14 June 1876, ibid., I, 288.

8. CFA, Sr., Diary, 17 October 1877, Adams Family Papers, reel 87.

9. HA to Sir Robert Cunliffe, 29 May 1882, Adams Family Papers, reel 597; HA to CMG, 24 September 1882, in Ford, *Letters* 1: 339; HA to Hay, 8 April 1883, ibid., 1: 350.

10. HA to CFA, Jr., 30 October 1863, in Ford, *Cycle*, 2: 96; HA to Samuel J. Tilden, 24 January 1883, in Harold Dean Cater, *Henry Adams and His Friends* (Boston, 1947), p. 120.

11. Robert F. Sayre, *The Examined Self: Franklin, Adams, James* (Princeton, 1964), typifies the literary formalist's inattention to this stage in Adams's psychic career. Sayre argues (pp. 118–19) that Adams omitted the 1870s and 1880s from *The Education* because his identity was relatively stable during those years. In actuality, they marked the crucial period in the redefinition of his identity.

12. HA to HCL, 13 May 1880, in Ford, *Letters* 1: 323.

13. CFA, Sr., Diary, 2 March 1872, and HA to CMG, 25 November 1877, Adams Family Papers, reels 84 and 595.

14. Duberman, *Charles Francis Adams*, p. 397; Ernest Samuels, *Henry Adams: the Middle Years* (Cambridge, Mass., 1958), pp. 28–29, 160, 274, 430 n.24.

15. HA to Hay, 8 October 1882, in Ford, *Letters* 1, 341; HA to HCL, 29 October 1881, ibid., 1: 330.

16. HA to Hay, 29 May 1883, Adams Family Papers, reel 598.

17. Samuels, *Middle Years*, p. 23.

18. HA to Hay, 8 December 1885, Adams Family Papers, reel 599; Henry Adams, *The Education of Henry Adams* [1907] (New York, 1931), p. 317.

19. HA to Cunliffe, 10 November 1889, Adams Family Papers, reel 600; HA to CMG, 24 November 1889, in Ford, *Letters* 1, 402; HA to Cunliffe, 17 January 1887, Adams Family Papers, reel 599; Samuels, *Middle Years*, pp. 280–81.

20. Sigmund Freud, "Mourning and Melancholia," trans. Joan Riviere, in *Collected Papers*, 4 vols. (London, 1956), 4: 159.

21. For brief but illuminating discussions of these issues, see Edward N. Saveth, "The Heroines of Henry Adams," *American Quarterly* 8 (Fall, 1956): 231–42, and Samuels, *Middle Years*, pp. 280–81.

22. Frances Snow Compton [Henry Adams], *Esther: a Novel* (New York, 1884), p. 97.

23. Ibid., pp. 173, 302.

24. Ibid., pp. 104, 290, 208.

25. Ibid., p. 296.

26. Ibid., pp. 259–72, 273–74.

27. Samuels, *Middle Years*, pp. 245–46, 293–94.

28. On this point, see the suggestive discussion by David S. Barber, "Henry Adams' *Esther:* the Nature of Individuality and Immortality," *New England Quarterly* 45 (June 1972): 227–40.

29. [Adams], *Esther*, pp. 133, 129, 97.

30. HA to Hay, 9 July 1886, in Ford, *Letters* 1: 369; HA to Anna Cabot Mills Lodge, 25 November 1891, ibid., 1: 532.

31. Henry Adams, "Buddha and Brahma," *Yale Review*, n.s., 5 (October 1915): 82–89.

32. HA to ACML, 18 June 1889, in Ford, *Letters* 1: 399.

33. Samuels, *Middle Years*, pp. 322, 170 n 37; Brooks Adams, "The Heritage of Henry Adams," p. 102 in *The Degradation of the Democratic Dogma* [1919], (New York: Harper Torchbook, 1968); HA to Elizabeth Cameron, undated notes, Adams Family Papers, reel 600.

34. Sonnet enclosed with HA to EC, 3 January 1888, Adams Family Papers, reel 600; Samuels, *Middle Years*, pp. 326–33, 416–18.

35. HA to Lucy Baxter, 15 August 1890, Henry Adams Papers, Houghton Library, Harvard University, Cambridge, Mass.

36. HA to EC, 31 August 1890, in Ford, *Letters* 1: 407; HA to EC, 27 September 1890, Henry Adams Papers, Massachusetts Historical Society, Boston, Mass.

37. HA to Hay, 16 October and 17 November 1890, in Cater, *Adams*, pp. 200, 217; HA to Lucy Baxter, 26 November 1890, Adams Papers, Houghton Library, Harvard, Cambridge, Mass.

38. HA to EC, 27 June 1889, in Ford, *Letters* 1: 400; HA to ACML, 21 October 1890, ibid., 1: 429; Henry Adams, *Tahiti* [1891], ed. Robert Spiller (New York, 1946).

39. The phrase is from HA to Royal Cortissoz, 20 September 1911, in Ford, *Letters* 2: 571–72; HA's references to his own and others' neurasthenia pervaded his correspondence.

40. HA to Cecil Spring Rice, 12 February 1897, ibid., 2: 123; HA to CMG, 26 November 1893, ibid., 2: 35.

41. HA to Brooks Adams, 3 November 1901, Adams Papers, Houghton Library.

42. HA to EC, 3 August 1896, in Ford, *Letters* 2: 113; HA to Mabel Hooper LaFarge, 12 January 1897, in Henry Adams, *Letters to a Niece and Prayer to the Virgin of Chartres* (Boston and New York, 1920), p. 90; HA to EC, 19 October 1900, in Ford, *Letters* 2, 298; HA to MHL, 23 September 1895, in *Letters to a Niece*, p. 87.

43. HA to MHL, 6 October 1894, ibid., pp. 75–76.

44. HA to Hay, 7 September 1895, in Carter, *Adams*, pp. 346–47.

45. HA to EC, 16 April 1900, in Ford, *Letters* 2: 285. The critique of Unitarianism is in the *History* 9: 239–40.

46. HA to BA, 4 March 1900, in Cater, *Adams*, p. 487; HA to EC, 26 February 1900, in Ford, *Letters*, 2: 271.

47. On the dissemination of matriarchal anthropology, see Joseph Campbell, "Introduction" to *Myth, Religion and Mother Right: Selected Writings of J. J. Bachofen*, trans. Ralph Manheim (Princeton, 1967), pp. xxv–lvii, and Lisa Appignanesi, *Femininity and the Creative Imagination* (London, 1971), chap. 1. The seminal source was J. J. Bachofen, *Das Mutterecht* (Stuttgart, 1861).

48. Henry Adams, "The Primitive Rights of Women," in his *Historical Essays* (New York, 1891), p. 38. Max Baym, *The French Education of Henry Adams* (New York, 1951), pp. 29, 157, documents Adams's reading of Baudelaire, whose "La Géante" ( in *Les Fleurs du Mal)* expressed longings for dependence on a mountainous Great Mother.

49. The poem is reprinted in Adams, *Letters to a Niece*, pp. 125–34.

50. Henry Adams, *Mont-Saint-Michel and Chartres* [1904], (New York: Anchor Books, 1959), pp. 2, 9, 59, 11, 35.

51. Ibid., pp. 94, 151–53.

52. Ibid., p. 369.

53. Ibid., p. 109.

54. Ibid., pp. 212–13.

55. Ibid., p. 140.

56. Ibid., p. 290.

57. Ibid., p. 307.

58. Ibid., pp. 383, 361.

59. Ibid., pp. 379, 402, 420. Michael Colacurcio, "The Dynamo and Angelic Doctor: the Bias of Henry Adams' Medievalism," *American Quarterly* 17 (December 1965): 696–712, acutely analyzes Adams's critique of Aquinas as "modern scientist," but fails to add that Adams actually presented Aquinas as a protopositivist.

60. Adams, *Chartres*, pp. 415, 416.

61. Ibid., p. 422.

62. Ibid., pp. 215, 287, 291, 300.

63. Ibid., pp. 384, 359.

64. Ibid., p. 213.

65. Adams, *Education*, p. 345; Edward N. Saveth, "Henry Adams and the Waning of America's Patriciate," *Commentary* 24 (October 1967): 302–9.

66. Adams, *Education*, p. xvi.

67. On the link between the manikin and the Confidence Man, see Rowe, *Henry Adams and Henry James*, p. 30.

68. Adams, *Education*, p. 3.

69. Ibid., pp. 9, 39. The allusion recalled St. Augustine's *Confessions* and also the "childlike" Francis of *Chartres* (p. 384) who loved nature "as intensely as a child loves the taste and smell of a peach."

70. Adams, *Education*, p. 37.

71. Ibid., pp. 48, 26–27.

72. Ibid., pp. 28, 81.

73. Ibid., p. 74.

74. Ibid., pp. 33–34, 55, 63, 92, 101, 284.

75. Ibid., pp. 209, 110–11, 117, 194, 294, 313.

76. Ibid., pp. 231–32, 229.

77. Ibid., pp. 380–81.

78. Ibid., pp. 451, 485.

79. Ibid., p. 433.

80. Ibid., p. 434.

81. Ibid.

82. Ibid., p. 12. Emphasis mine.
83. Ibid., pp. 5, 44–46, 246, 268, 90, 282.
84. Ibid., p. 74.
85. Ibid., p. 288.
86. Ibid., pp. 288–89.
87. Ibid., pp. 316–29.
88. Ibid., p. 352.
89. Ibid., pp. 354, 370, 384.
90. Ibid., pp. 434–35.
91. Ibid., pp. 469, 424, 496.
92. Ibid., p. 407.
93. Ibid., p. 416.
94. Ibid., p. 471.

EPILOGUE

1. Fyodor Dostoevsky, *The Brothers Karamazov* [1880] trans. Constance Garnett, (New York: Signet Classics, 1957), p. 239.
2. On the persistence of old wealth and power, see Gabriel Kolko, "Brahmins and Business, 1870–1914: A Hypothesis on the Social Basis of Success in American History," in Kurt H. Wolff and Barrington Moore, eds., *The Critical Spirit: Essays in Honor of Herbert Marcuse* (Boston, 1967), pp. 343–63; Frederic Cople Jaher, "The Boston Brahmins in the Age of Industrial Capitalism," in Jaher, ed., *The Age of Industrialism in America* (New York, 1968); Frederic Cople Jaher, "Nineteenth Century Elites in Boston and New York," *Journal of Social History* 5 (1972): 32–77; John Ingham, "Robber Barons and the Old Elites: a Case Study in Social Stratification," *Mid-America* 52 (1970): 190–204; and Stephan Thernstrom, *The Other Bostonians: Poverty and Progress in the American Metropolis, 1880–1970* (Cambridge, Mass., 1973). On the revitalization of bourgeois values, see Christopher Lasch, "The Moral and Intellectual Rehabilitation of the Ruling Class" in his *The World of Nations* (New York, 1973), pp. 80–99.
3. David M. Kennedy, "Overview: the Progressive Era," *Historian* 37 (May 1975): 453–68. Kennedy offers a useful guide to the recent literature on the rise of managerial elitism in the "progressive" era.
4. For the beginnings of a critical view, see James Weinstein, *The Corporate Ideal in the Liberal State* (Boston, 1968) and Christopher Lasch, *Haven in a Heartless World: the Family Besieged* (New York, 1977), though the latter book in particular is marred by overstatement.
5. Allen Tate, "The Man of Letters in the Modern World," in *The Forlorn Demon* (Chicago, 1953), p. 10.
6. Walter Lippmann, *A Preface to Politics* [1913] (Ann Arbor, 1962), p. 65.
7. Thomas Haskell, *The Emergence of Professional Social Science: the American Social Science Association and the Nineteenth Century Crisis of Authority* (Urbana, Ill., 1977), astutely identifies one source of disorientation which helped to create a demand for "expert" knowledge—the decline of the conviction that one could easily assign causes to events.
8. Christopher Lasch, *The Culture of Narcissism: American Life in an Age of Diminishing Expectations* (New York, 1978) presents a thoughtful analysis of contemporary quests for authenticity but tends to neglect the role played by secularization.
9. Jack Kerouac, quoted in César Graña, *Modernity and Its Discontents: French Society and the French Man of Letters in the Nineteenth Century* (New York: Harper Torchbooks, 1967), p. 180. Graña provides an illuminating discussion of avant-garde vitalism as a response to rationalization, but he does not see the fatal dialectic in the rationalization process: the creation of abundance which undermines commitments to work discipline, eases the shift from an ethos of production to one of consumption, and often transforms avant-garde vitalism from a critique to a caricature of the dominant culture. Marshall Berman, " 'All That is Solid Melts

Into Air': Marx, Modernism and Modernization," *Dissent* 25 (Winter, 1978): 54–73, and Carl E. Schorske, "Politics and the Psyche in *Fin-de-Siècle Vienna:* Schnitzler and Hofmannstal," *American Historical Review* 66 (July 1961), 930–46, provide correctives to Graña.

10. See the interesting (though ahistorical) discussion by Robert Jay Lifton, "Protean Man," *Partisan Review* 35 (Winter, 1968): 13–27.

11. Raymond Williams, *Culture and Society, 1780–1850* (New York, 1958); Martin Wiener, "England is the Country: Modernization and the National Self-Image," *Albion* 1 (1971): 198–211.

12. William McGrath, *Dionysian Art and Populist Politics in Austria* (New Haven, 1974); Robert Nisbet, *The Quest for Community* (New York, 1953), and *The Sociological Tradition* (New York, 1966).

13. J. P. Stern, *Hitler: the Führer and the People* (London, 1975), especially chap. 2; Oswald Spengler, quoted in Alastair Hamilton, *The Appeal of Fascism: a Study of Intellectuals and Fascism, 1919–1945* (London, 1971), p. 112. See also Fritz Stern, *The Politics of Cultural Despair* (Berkeley, 1961).

14. Stern, *Hitler,* p. 27.

15. For illuminating discussions of the voluminous literature on the relationship between fascism and modernizing tendencies, see Henry Ashby Turner, "Fascism and Modernization," *World Politics* 24 (July 1972): 547–64, and A. James Gregor, "Fascism and Modernization: Some Addenda," *World Politics* 26 (April 1974): 370–84.

16. Marinetti, quoted in Hamilton, *The Appeal of Fascism,* p. 3.

17. Frederich Nietzsche, *The Birth of Tragedy and the Genealogy of Morals,* trans. Francis Golffing (New York: Anchor Books, 1956), p. 136.

18. Irving Sandler, *The Triumph of American Painting: a History of Abstract Expressionism* (New York, 1970), p. 150; John Fischer, "Mark Rothko: Portrait of the Artist as an Angry Man," *Harper's Magazine* 241 (July 1970): 23.

19. Miguel de Unamuno, *The Tragic Sense of Life in Men and Nations* [1912] (Princeton, 1972), pp. 133, 120, 353, 354.

20. T. S. Eliot, "Ash Wednesday," in his *Collected Poems 1909–1962* (New York, 1970), pp. 85–95.

# Index

ABOUT THE AUTHOR

T. J. Jackson Lears, who has taught at Yale and the University of Missouri, and been a Fellow at the Woodrow Wilson International Center for Scholars, is currently professor of history at Rutgers University. He is a contributor to the *New Republic,* the *Nation,* and *Wilson Quarterly,* and coeditor (with Richard Wightman Fox) of *The Culture of Consumption* (1983) and *The Power of Culture* (1993). *No Place of Grace,* his first book, was nominated for a National Book Critics Circle Award.